a treasury of
jewish humor

Other books by the same author:

A TREASURY OF JEWISH FOLKLORE
SUPERMAN: THE LIFE OF FREDERICK THE GREAT

a treasury of
Jewish humor

• edited by •
nathan ausubel

M. EVANS AND COMPANY   NEW YORK

Library of Congress Cataloging-in-Publication Data

A Treasury of Jewish humor.

Reprint. Originally published: Garden City,
N.Y.: Doubleday, 1951.
1. Jewish wit and humor.   I. Ausubel, Nathan,
1899–
PN6231.J5T74   1988   808.87'935203924   88-7022

ISBN 0-87131-546-7 (pbk.)

First paperback edition

Gym-Na-Si-A, from *Tevye's Daughters*, by Sholom Aleichem; © 1949 by the children of Sholom Aleichem and Crown Publishers.   *The Jack of All Trades, The Story of the Cantor, A Jewish Cat*, from *The Bridal Canopy*, by S. J. Agnon; translated by I. M. Lask; © 1937 by Doubleday & Company, Inc.   *The Awakening*, from *Benya Krik and Other Stories*, by Isaak Babel; edited by Avrahm Yarmolinsky; © 1948 by Schocken Books, Inc.; *In Odessa*, from *Benya Krik and Other Stories*, by Isaak Babel; translated by Avrahm Yarmolinsky; reprinted by permission of Schocken Books, Inc.   The extract from *Bondy, Jr.*, by Ludwig Hatvany-Deutsch; © 1931 by Alfred A. Knopf, Inc.   *Sam Kravitz, That Thief*, and *Mushrooms in Bronx Park*, from *Jews Without Money*, by Michael Gold; © 1930; published by Liveright Publishing Corporation.   *The Gift of the Emperor* and *The Technical Expert*, by Leo Katz; © 1937 by Leo Katz; reprinted by permission of *Commentary* and the author.   *One Way of Getting a Hundred Pounds*, from *Night and the City*; © 1946 by Gerald Kersh; *Aunt Esther's Galoshes* and *Mrs. Rivkin Grapples with the Drama*, from *Go Fight City Hall*, by Ethel Rosenberg; © 1949 by Ethel Rosenberg; reprinted by permission of Simon and Schuster, Inc.   *A Letter from the Bronx*, © 1937 by Arthur Kober, originally published in *The New Yorker;* reprinted by permission of the author.   *Nationalism* and *Retrospect*, by Karl Kraus; translated by Albert Bloch; © 1930 by the Four Seas Co.; reprinted by permission of Bruce Humphries, Inc.   *The Hussar Who Loved Three Jews*, from *The Captain of Saint Margaret's*, by Ferenc Molnar; © 1945 by Ferenc Molnar; reprinted by permission of Duell, Sloan and Pearce, Inc., and Cassell & Company, Ltd.

Waiting for Santy, by S. J. Perelman; © 1936 by S. J. Perelman; originally published in *The New Yorker;* reprinted by permission of Random House, Inc.   *Uncle Julius and the BMT*, © 1946 by Ethel Rosenberg, from *Commentary*.   *With the Aid of the One Above* and *Saved by the Sale*, from *With One Foot in America;* © 1947, 1948, 1949, 1950 by Yuri Suhl; reprinted by permission of The Macmillan Company and Brandt & Brandt.   *Einstein*, from *Collected Parodies*, by Louis Untermeyer; © 1926 by Harcourt, Brace and Company, Inc.   *Résumé*, from *The Portable Dorothy Parker;* © 1926, 1944 by Dorothy Parker; and ~~*The Modern Intellectual,* from~~ *The Pure in Heart*, by Franz Werfel, translated by Geoffrey Dunlop; © 1931 by The Viking Press, Inc.; reprinted by permission of The Viking Press.

M. Evans and Company, Inc.
216 East 49 Street
New York, New York 10017

Manufactured in the United States of America

9 8 7 6 5 4 3 2 1

IN MEMORY OF
TWO JESTING
PHILOSOPHERS
  MORRIS AND ANDREW OLDER
FATHER AND SON

An Appreciation

I wish to make grateful acknowledgment to all those individuals and institutions of learning that have so generously helped me in the preparation of this work.

Thanks are especially due the following members of Doubleday & Company, Inc.: to Mel Evans, whose initial enthusiasm for the project and grasp of the special problems it posed helped give it direction and scope; to my editor, Pauline Rush Fadiman, for her discriminating taste and sound judgment in the preparation of the manuscript; to Christine Pollard, for her helpfulness in obtaining reprint permissions from the copyright owners of materials included in this anthology; to Lawrence Sherman for his kind helpfulness; to Alma Cardi and Sabra Mallett of the Art Department in appreciation of their fine taste; to Rose Pesin Wishengrad, posthumously, whose sensitive understanding of Jewish cultural values has left its imprint on these pages.

I especially wish to acknowledge my great indebtedness to Rabbi I. Edward Kiev, Librarian of the Hebrew Union College—Jewish Institute of Religion in New York, for enriching me with his learning and understanding of Jewish life and culture, and for making available to me literary materials in the library's collection.

I extend my thanks to Menashe Vaxer, Jewish scholar, bibliophile, and bookdealer, for generously supplying me with judicious advice and hard-to-obtain books.

Thanks are also due the following for information, books, and other assistance so generously supplied:

Dr. Alfred Berlstein and A. Mill of the Slavonic Division of the New York Public Library; Philip Shan; Bernard Ziffer; Robert Warshow, managing editor of *Commentary;* the Jewish Division of the New York Public Library; its chief, Dr. Joshua Bloch; his assistant, Abraham Berger; and staff librarians Marie Coralnik, Dora Steinglass, and Fanny Spivack; Mendel Elkin and the Library of the Yiddish Scientific Institute; Isaac Goldberg and the Hebrew Union College Library in Cincinnati; and not least Rabbi Philip Goodman and the Jewish Book Council of America.

Finally, just a word of appreciation for Marynn Older Ausubel—my wife, *nebbech,* who is my best friend and my most unflinching critic. It was her constant preoccupation with my work as it progressed, editorially and technically, that rendered a backbreaking and eyestraining task relatively easy.

N.A.

Acknowledgments

The author has made every effort to trace the ownership of all copyrighted material. In the event of any question arising as to the use of any selections the author, while expressing regret for any error he may have made, will be pleased to make the necessary correction in future editions of this book.

Thanks are due to the following authors, publishers, publications, and representatives for permission to use the selections indicated:

Philip Adler, for "Mendel Marantz—Genius," by David Freedman, from *Mendel Marantz;* copyright, 1925, Langdon Publishing Co.

Jacob Adler, for "Bluff," "My Pinya," and "Yente Telebende," by B. Kovner.

American Jewish Historical Society, for "The Heavy Loser," from *Letters of a California Pioneer;* contributed by Albert M. Friedenberg.

Estate of Sholom Aleichem, for excerpts from *Menachem-Mendel, Fortune-Hunter; Mottel-Paysee dem Chazzen's Yingel; Rabchik;* and from *Sholom Aleichem Buch.*

Sholem Asch, for his story "The Academy," translated by Nathan Ausubel.

Helen Black, for "The Squash," by Dovid Bergelson; "Package Tsoress," by M. Vulfarts; "Statistics," "Two Pleasures," and "The Gramophone," by Z. Wendroff.

James Clarke & Co., Ltd., for "The Immortal Orange," by Z. Schneour; translated by Hannah Berman, from *Yisroel.*

Citadel Press, for "Foods," from *Meet the Folks,* by Sammy Levenson.

Abraham Cronbach, for "A Jewish Beggar's Complaint," from *Religion and Its Social Setting,* 1933.

E. Bloomgarden Dworkin, for "A Share of Paradise," by Yehoash.

Irving Fineman, for his story "An Interview with Ahashuerus," from *The Menorah Journal,* August 1925.

Louis Golding, for "Angels in Chayder," from his novel *Forward from Babylon.*

H. Gutman, for "The Real Customers" and "No Enemy of His."

Hebrew Publishing Co., for "The Last Kopeck," by S. Frug.

Jewish Frontier, for "The Balance Sheet of My Life," by Lion Feucht-wanger.

The Jewish Publication Society of America, for "The Flea Song," by Yehudah Al-Charizi; "The Mirror," by Yehuda Halevi, from *Jewish Literature and Other Essays,* by Gustav Karpeles; "Zoology," by Yehoash, from *The Feet of the Messenger;* "The Luftmensch" and "The Sabbath Question in Sudminster," from *Ghetto Comedies,* by Israel Zangwill; "The Neo-Hebrew Poet," from *Children of the Ghetto,* by Israel Zangwill; "The Short Friday," by Chaim Nachman Bialik, from *Aftergrowth;* and "One Two Three," by Chaim Nachman Bialik; translated from the Yiddish by Joseph Leftwich in *The Golden Peacock,* edited by Joseph Leftwich.

Pauline Kobrin, for "The Temptation of Reb Mottel," "The Milchiger Synagogue and the Blind Preacher," and "The Soul That Mice Nibbled Up," by Leon Kobrin.

Joseph Leftwich, for "The Theater," by Jacob Gropper; translated from the Yiddish by Joseph Leftwich in *The Golden Peacock.*

Ludwig Lewisohn for "Two Views of Jews," from his book *The Island Within.*

Solomon Libin, for his story "Schlemihlov's Works."

Menorah Journal, for "An Interview with Ahashuerus," by Irving Fineman; "The Lady of Zion," by Israel Zangwill; "Marginal Annotations," by an Elder of Zion, "Heresy of the Water-Taps," by Jean-Richard Bloch; translated by Clifton Fadiman.

Ghenya Nadir, for "Ruined by Success," "Nuttose and Protose," and "My First Deposit," by Moishe Nadir.

Esther Ogus, for "The Shofar-Blower of Lapinishok," and "The Essrig," by Aaron D. Ogus.

Samuel Ornitz, for his story "Yom Kippur Fressers," from *Haunch, Paunch, and Jowl.*

Routledge and Kegan Paul, Ltd., for "The Departed Physician," and "Wise People," by Benjacob, "A Husband's Complaint," by M. Mandelkern, and "The First Gray Hair," by Yehudah Halevi, in

Hebrew Satire, by Joseph Chotzner; "An Epitaph," by Benjacob, in *Hebrew Humour,* by Joseph Chotzner.

Abraham Reisen for his stories "The Last Hope," "The Loan," and "Avrom the Cobbler."

Salman Schneour, for his story "The New Police Chief," from *Song of the Dnieper.*

Donald J. Walsh, for his translation of "Going to the Library," by César Tiempo, from *Commentary.*

Ann Wolfe, for "Hilaire Belloc," from *Lampoons,* by Humbert Wolfe.

Sophia Zevin, for "A Nogid's Luck," "A Pack of Troubles for One Cent," by Israel Zevin.

Why Jews Laugh

My grandfather was a sage, full of Talmud-learning and the synagogue-stove wisdom of plain people. Way back, when I was a child, I often used to hear him say with a twinkle in his eye: "A worm in a jar of horseradish thinks its life is the sweetest in all the world."

And as the years went by and my grandfather—fragrant be his memory—passed on, I found out that there were quite a few people who thought exactly like the worm in his proverb. For them, their little jar of local horseradish served as the entire universe. Not a shadow of doubt ever darkened their conviction that their national life and culture were far sweeter than any other, and superior too.

There is a tongue-in-cheek story that the folk sages like to tell on a cold winter evening as they sit huddled around the stove in the synagogue.

Once a disciple of the Rabbi of Sanz went on a visit to another town. Naturally, on the Sabbath he went to hear the local rabbi preach in the synagogue. Now this rabbi was celebrated for his wit. He crackled so with jolly quips and parables that the entire congregation rocked with laughter. Only our disciple from Sanz sat through all the merriment with a stolid, unsmiling face. The man sitting next to him was filled with wonder.

"What's the matter, Uncle?" he asked. "Why aren't you laughing? Are you sick or something?"

"Sick? God forbid!" replied the loyal disciple from Sanz. "You see . . . I'm a stranger in this town."

I, for one, should understand this attitude very well, for I was once a confirmed horseradisher myself. Fortunately, I managed to crawl my way out of the jar rather early in life. And I found it was quite a world and full of surprises.

For instance, one discovery I made was that each people had its own distinctive genius for gaiety. Nor was there anything either peculiar or alien in it for the rest of mankind. Quite the contrary, I found that there was one tongue everybody in the world could understand—the language of laughter.

But regardless whether you happen to be a laugh-patriot of Sanz, of Addis-Ababa or Ho-Hokus, there is one thing you will recognize: although all good humor is universal in its appeal, nevertheless *there are differences* produced by special conditions of life and patterns of culture. And it is precisely these differences that add so much flavor, relish, and variety to the laughter of mankind. Now you may be a Swede with smörgåsbord as your favorite dish, or an Englishman with roast beef as your national pride, but why—may I ask—should that prevent you from enjoying a nice slice of *gefillte fish* swimming in its own delicious sauce? A bit of horseradish—without the worm, of course—goes fine with it!

Consider the character of Jewish humor. It is usually no mere ha-ha-ha and ho-ho-ho. In the beginning, perhaps, you find it all quite puzzling. First you laugh at a Jewish joke or quip. Then, against your will, you suddenly fall silent and thoughtful. And that is because Jews are so frequently jesting philosophers. A hard life has made them realists, realists without illusions.

What do you suppose makes Jews joke so much about adversity? It is the instinct for self-preservation. By laughing at the absurdities and cruelties of life they draw much of the sting from them. True, more likely than not, the laughter is rueful ·and ironic, but that is exactly why it hits the nail on the head, lays bare the simple truth. The jester's bells make an honest tinkle, and his comic capers conceal his inner gravity. His satire and irony have one virtue: you never for a moment suspect that his barbs are directed at you. And so you laugh boisterously, feeling not a little superior to the poor *shmiggege,* while all the time it is you who are the target!

In Jewish humor comedy and tragedy are joined together like Siamese twins. "Laughter through tears" is what the Jewish folk philosopher chooses to call it. You laugh in order to give yourself courage not to grieve, and you shed a tear or two because the human comedy is often no mere laughing matter. When it is distilled with pathos, laughter achieves a certain balance of sanity. It gives one perspective and a view out of chaos. That's what makes the Yiddish wag wink at you in his sly manner as he says comfortingly: "Now don't you worry! While you can't live from pleasure you positively won't die from trouble!"

Jewish humor in the role of comforter! It's a very old practice. When you're hungry, sing; when you're hurt, laugh, the synagogue-stove sage seems to counsel. And in the history of human misery few peoples have been hungrier than the Jews or hurt more. That's why the Jews have done a mighty lot of singing, especially in a minor key, and have done a heap of laughing, even if sometimes it's done with a *krechtz.*

What! You mean to say you don't know what a krechtz is? In Yiddish a krechtz means a groan. When a Jew gives a krechtz he puts his whole heart and soul into it: *"Oy, vay is meer!"* (That means, translated into English melodrama: "Oh, woe is me!") What makes it Jewish is not the groan, nor the Yiddish exclamation, but the overtones of world weariness. When a Jew gives such a groan you can well believe him that the world is coming to an end. And it usually does. But, fortunately, the world has more lives than a cat, and after each disaster it invariably starts all over again, giving the Jew another chance for a hearty krechtz. Why, it has even gotten so that when a Yiddish-speaking Jew—and he belongs to the majority of Jews in the world—has passed through some highly enjoyable experience he gives a mighty krechtz and mutters appreciatively: *"Oy, vay is meer!"*

So we see that among Jews laughter and tears, comedy and tragedy, the groan and the chuckle—the *oy vay!* and the *ha-ha*—are tangled up like a ball of thread after a playful kitten gets through with it. And that also explains why Jewish humor has so many faces. One moment it ripples joyously only to be suddenly muted by a wistfulness which is the mark of the jester turned philosopher.

The question then is: What makes the Jew such an irrepressible jester? What gives so much of Jewish humor its ruefulness?

And the answer is: The Jews are a very ancient people, and they have navigated all the seven seas of misery since they became Pharaoh's bondsmen in Egypt.

Take, for instance, my patriarchal grandfather in the old country. Like most Jewish grandfathers there, he had a flowing gray beard, but his troubles were even more patriarchal, more flowing and gray. He possessed an unrelenting logical mind and, like all harassed Jews, he was a realist who looked at life with a wry detachment. I recall him as a gnome-like little man with a gentleness about him that came partly from old age and as much from the mellowness of wisdom. Perhaps my love for my grandfather makes me romanticize his image somewhat, but as I recall it, his face had that simple dignity with which Rembrandt endowed the portraits of his Amsterdam rabbis. Nonetheless, despite his dignity and his gravity, whenever my grandfather would come face to face with the foibles of people a quizzical smile danced in his eyes and he rocked with laughter. Sometimes his laughter was ironical, sometimes bitter, but never do I remember it as cruel or malicious; it was always warm and kind, a generous overflow of the old tired heart.

It took me many years to discover the reason for that. When Jewish humor turns harsh and cruel, as unfortunately it sometimes does, it is out of line with the folk tradition of laughter among Jews.

That tradition grew out of Jewish ethical values which direct the individual to laugh *with* people rather than *at* them.

The Jewish jester is not cynical because he is a philosopher. The foolish and sometimes mean antics of people merely fill him with a brittle, indulgent laughter. And if you happen to have a sensitive ear you will also discern in it overtones of regret.

"A *meshuggeneh*, a crazy world—believe me!" seems to be the wry conclusion of all his quips and capers.

Perhaps you've heard this lively duel fought with logical rapiers between the anti-Semite and the Jew.

All our troubles come from the Jews!

Absolutely! From the Jews—and the bicycle riders.

Bicycle riders! Why the bicycle riders?

Why the Jews?

For some two thousand years the Jews have been sharpening their wit as well as their wits on the logical grindstone of the Talmud. This may explain why so much of Jewish humor has an intellectual character. Now take the humor of other peoples. While, of course, it shares many of the significant characteristics of Jewish humor, much of this laughter is tickled forth by comic situations, by punning, or by repartee. Humor thus becomes an end in itself—to arouse both laughter and admiration for nimbleness of wit. But Jews, since the days of the Talmud, have been indestructible moralists and teachers. They have turned the joke, the quip, and the humorous characterization into pedagogic aids with which to illustrate, to illuminate, and to improve. That is why the humorists among Jews are psychological imps engaged in minute dissection of character, in exposing human vagaries and the topsy-turvy ways of "this meshuggeneh world."

Don't be surprised if you find in this compilation a large amount of self-criticism disguised as irony, satire, and caricature. Know one thing: the Jewish wit is often a wolf in sheep's clothing. Ostensibly he is merely trying to amuse his fellow Jews with his drolleries, but actually the sly fellow is aiming at making them think. And once they start laughing they fall right into his trap.

The Jewish humorist is deft with his analytical scalpel. He cuts deep into your hide and makes you think that he is only tickling you under the armpit. As if they were only the hidden petticoats of an onion, he lays bare layer after layer of his fellow Jew's psychic tissue. Now you must guard yourself against going all the way with those psychologists who say that because of this trait Jewish humor is masochistic or exhibitionistic. Likely as not this surgical introspection is a calculated method for ridiculing out of existence the foibles and incongruities in Jewish character.

Moreover, one must not make the mistake in thinking that the self-depreciation of Jewish character you find in Jewish humor is an admission of moral inferiority to other peoples. Other peoples, argues Dr. Freud, are perhaps less ready to admit their shortcomings. . . .

In almost every section of this book will be found characterizations bearing striking resemblance to one another, and this notwithstanding the fact that they were written in different languages, countries, and times. This is due to the fact that wherever Jews have lived they have had common traditions to draw from and almost the same historic experiences. Similar circumstances give rise to similar psychologic types, defying some of the laws of time and geography.

Humor is mainly concerned with negative aspects of life. It is a form of criticism. Consequently, by the very nature of its materials a book such as this is bound to be, in the main, a gallery of human folly. Could it be otherwise? While people can laugh easily at the absurd, the pretentious, even the mean, they are hardly likely to be sent into gales of laughter by the sincere, the upright, the noble. Virtue is no laughing matter.

Jewish humorous characterization, as you will discover in this book, has its own merry laws. It parades before you a diverting, as well as exasperating, company of bores, eccentrics, half-baked geniuses, sly skeptics, Talmudic hair-splitters, learned numbskulls, compulsive no-sayers, *schlemihls, schlimazls, schnorrers,* and *schacher-machers,* pipe-dreamers and star-gazers. In short, it is a human comedy, the *Jewish Human Comedy.* And the picture of people, of life, and truth that it delineates so gaily with smiles, chuckles, guffaws, chortles, and belly laughs—washed down with occasional sighs, groans, moans, gulps, and tears—now isn't that its own justification? *Nu,* what do you say, dear reader?

N.A.

Contents

LOVE!, 99

LOVE-SHMOVE, 100

CURDLED LOVE, 127

LOVE WITH GELT, 129

LOOSE-FOOTED AND DEFT-HANDED, 149

SCHACHER-MACHERS AND FINAGLERS, 150

I'M TELLING YOU—ARE YOU WRONG!, 247

A-AH! PLEASURE!, 285

PLEASURES OF THE POOR, 310

JEWISH FOOD, 355

WHAT'S THERE TO LAUGH AT?, 379

SHMENDRIKS AND SHMIGGEGES • FOOLS AND SIMPLETONS, 380

GEVALT! IT'S NOT SO GOOD!, 417

SCHLIMAZLS: THE LUCKLESS, 418

GENIUSES AND OTHER MESHUGGENEH PEOPLE, 641

CONTRIBUTORS, 725

GLOSSARY, 729

I TURN THIS WAY
—I TURN THAT WAY

Luftmenschen · MEN-OF-AIR

Many trades—few blessings

Do you know what a luftmensch *is?*
You don't? Well, let me tell you.
*Perhaps you've heard the story of the poor ghetto Jew with
the worried look who was being questioned by the anti-Semitic police
inspector in a Polish town.*

"What's your trade, Jew?"
"Who has a trade?"
"What's your regular business then?"
"Who has a regular business?"
"But you do something, don't you?"
"Yes and no, Your Excellency! That is—I do and I don't."
*"Psiakrew! What do you mean, you do and you don't? How the
devil do you earn a living?"*
*"A living you call it yet! May my worst enemy make a better one!
Well, you see it's like this, Your Excellency. . . . First I give myself
a turn this way . . . then I give myself a turn that way . . . and in
between,* nu, *I make a living!"*
That's a luftmensch!

*It's quite possible you've known the luftmensch under another
name—as a jack-of-all-trades. But when you get right down to it a
jack-of-all-trades is a lot different. He is merely an unstable fellow, a
psychological misfit who is incapable of putting his heart into any
steady occupation. For that reason he tinkers with many. He lacks
the interest and the staying-power for sustained effort and never
achieves any measure of competence in anything.*

*But now take a luftmensch. First of all he had to be a Jew. Being
a luftmensch was a Jew's special monopoly because he was a product
of the economic rootlessness of ghetto life. Furthermore, the luftmensch could be charged with all kinds of failings, but certainly not
with laziness. If anything, his most marked characteristic was his
strenuous exertions trying to make a living. He ran himself ragged in
search of his daily bread. And if he appears to have been flighty, a
will-o'-the-wisp darting after fortune that was always just around the
corner and yet always eluding him, it was only because the highly
competitive life of the ghetto, in which there were more tailors than*

gabardines and more shopkeepers than cash customers, never allowed him to be anything more than an improviser, and a feverish one at that.

The literal meaning in both German and Yiddish of the word "luftmensch" is "air-man," a human plant so to speak, whose roots do not reach down into the life-giving earth but only into the empty air. And from the thin air, it would seem, the ghetto Jew had to draw his meager nourishment like a magician. Because he could not make a living from one trade or business, he got a perverse kind of comfort from not making it from a dozen callings. At least this served him as a convenient alibi. It was an ironclad reassurance to him that if he was a failure in life it wasn't, God forbid, because he hadn't tried hard enough! Now tell the truth—was it his fault if he had knocked his head against the stone wall on Dead End Street? It was the meshuggeneh world, that's what it was.

The luftmensch was a restless creature, always philandering with his mazl, his luck. The life-urge to survive was powerful in him, you can be sure of that. He was an optimist who never wavered, with a pipe full of dreams which no shower of adversity could ever quench. He was always planning and hoping, in a plaintive sort of way. Who knows? Could be! He'd prosper in his new venture if only his Jewish luck would relent a bit! And if it turned out in the end, as it usually did, that his dream of fortune had begun to wither on the vine he'd turn out his hopefulness to graze in greener pastures.

A poet, a lyric poet at that, was the luftmensch, and quite a bit of an adventurer besides. But being an Old Testament Jew who had tasted the bitter herbs of failure so often, he was also somewhat of a philosopher, and most frequently an honest man.

So many character types in Jewish humorous literature stem from frustration. Life for the Jew was always uncertain and insecure. Opportunity to earn even a marginal livelihood was limited and all his practical activities were virtually smothered by legal restrictions, social custom, and religious bigotry. This explains why there were so many misfits and eccentrics in Jewish life, going under the comical names of luftmenschen, schlemihls and schlimazls, schacher-machers and trombeniks, shmendriks, lemeshkes, shmiggeges, and the like.

Not that it hadn't always been hard for the Jew! There is, for instance, the ancient Talmudic quip: "The provisions are so scanty and the road is so long!" Well, with the passing of the centuries the provisions became a lot scantier and the road of wandering a great deal longer.

When you get right down to it, until quite recent times there were few trades and callings Jews were allowed to practice. For the most part it was peddling, pawnbroking, moneylending, and the old clo' business, and these only because Christians would not engage in them, considering them too mean. For example, after the Reformation the German princes in a burst of generosity allowed "their Jews" to engage "in coarse trades" and in "the unprofitable occupations."

Since early Christian times Jews were old clo' and junk dealers. We have it on the authority of the chronicler Paulus Diaconus that when the Colossus of Rhodes, one of the Seven Wonders of the World, fell in 653 A.D., a Jewish merchant from Emessa bought the debris as junk and caravaned it off on the backs of nine hundred camels. Today the junk and old clo' business, still harboring many a misfit luftmensch, although less so than in former days, is reckoned as a Jewish business, thus demonstrating the power of a tradition to continue even under altered circumstances.

Although today, with the breakdown of the ghetto and with the increase of opportunity, the luftmensch has largely disappeared, it was in the overcrowded East European ghettos of the nineteenth century that the luftmensch and pipe dreamer really came into his own. He luxuriated in numbers as well as in the high degree of his desperation. Practically every Jew and his neighbor was a luftmensch And you can well imagine what happened when luftmensch collided with luftmensch! The fine arts of improvisation and enterprise had to be focused, so to speak, on the head of a pin. The Yiddish folksaying, "He tried to scratch his way up the wall with his bare fingers," must have originated then. To be sure, there were a great many artisans and factory workers among Jews, but work was scarce and wages were low and so they always lived next door to pauperism.

The prospects weren't much gayer for the Jewish tradesman, since commerce is conducted on the basis of credit. Ghetto Jews found it almost impossible to obtain credit, for to any prospective creditor with eyes in his head it was plain that most of their ventures were foredoomed to failure. Because of this, Jewish tradesmen went into the odds and ends of commerce. With a capital of only a few rubles they were able to open up hole-in-the-wall shops and street stalls and stock them with a small supply of cheap wares in common demand. In an economic survey as recent as 1900, it was found that the average Jewish "merchant" in Czarist Russia, where most Jews of the world lived, could earn about twenty kopecks (about ten cents) a day.

Luckiest, of course, were the dealers in foodstuffs; if things got really bad they could at least eat up their business.

The luftmensch may have been poor in worldly chattels, but oh was he rich in children—"a famillionaire," as Heine would say.

It was perfectly clear that to keep the home fires burning a Jewish "famillionaire" had to be on guard against putting all his eggs in one basket. And so to tinker with a number of trades or businesses was the prudent thing. You know how it is: here a bit, there a bit—God willing, he'd patch together some sort of a living out of all of them!

A classic example of the luftmensch was Leone da Modena, the gifted Jewish humanist of sixteenth century Venice. He himself listed twenty-six callings that he followed, starving on all of them. He was rabbi, cantor, preacher, rabbinical judge, teacher of Hebrew Studies to both Jews and Gentiles, Italian playwright, Hebrew poet, theatrical producer, ghost writer, music teacher, commercial agent, shadchan, translator, printer, proofreader, writer of legal documents, composer of epitaphs for Jewish tombstones, seller of charms and talismans, secretary of charitable and other Jewish societies, etc., etc. Then there were two additional professions he neglected to list, out of delicacy no doubt. One was card playing, but the wheel of fortune never turned round for him; he was always on the verge of winning large sums of money, but missed by a hair's breadth. A second profession was alchemy. So feverish was this Renaissance prototype of Menachem-Mendel, Sholom Aleichem's Yiddish-ghetto version of a pipe dreamer and fortune hunter, in his desire to get rich that he almost killed himself trying to transmute base metals into gold. Needless to say, he died a pauper.

Now do you know what a luftmensch is?

N.A.

THE LUFTMENSCH

BY ISRAEL ZANGWILL

Leopold Barstein, the sculptor, was sitting in his lonesome studio, brooding blackly over his dead illusions, when the postman brought him a letter in a large, straggling, unknown hand. It began "Angel of God!"

He laughed bitterly. "Just when I am at my most diabolical!" He did not at first read the letter, divining in it one of the many begging letters which were the aftermath of his East-End Zionist period. But he turned over the page to see the name of the Orientally effusive scribe. It was "Nehemiah Silvermann, Dentist and Restaurateur." His laughter changed to a more genial note; his sense of humour was still saving. The figure of the restaurateur-dentist sprang to his imagination in marble on a pedestal. In one hand the figure held a cornucopia, in the other a pair of pincers. He read the letter.

3A, The Minories, E.

Angel of God,
I have the honour now to ask Your very kind humane merciful cordial nobility to assist me by Your clement philanthropical liberal relief in my very hard troublesome sorrows and worries, on which I suffer violently. I lost all my fortune, and I am ruined by Russia. I am here at present without means and dental practice, and my restaurant is impeded with lack of a few frivolous pounds. I do not know really what to do in my actual very disgraceful mischief. I heard the people saying Your propitious magnanimous beneficent charities are everywhere exceedingly well renowned and considerably gracious. Thus I solicit and supplicate Your good very kind genteel clement humanity by my very humble quite instant request to support me by Your merciful aid, and please to respond me as soon as possible according to Your generous very philanthropy in my urgent extreme immense difficulty.
Your obedient Servant respectfully,
Nehemiah Silvermann,
Dentist and Restaurateur

Such a flood of language carried away the last remnants of Barstein's melancholia; he saw his imagined statue showering adjectives from its cornucopia. "It is the cry of a dictionary in distress!" he murmured, re-reading the letter with unction.

It pleased his humour to reply in the baldest language. He asked for details of Silvermann's circumstances and sorrows. Had he applied to the Russo-Jewish Fund, which existed to help such refugees from persecution? Did he know Jacobs, the dentist of the neighbouring Mansel Place?

Jacobs had been one of Barstein's fellow-councillors in Zionism, a pragmatic inexhaustible debater in the small back room, and the voluble little man now loomed suddenly large as a possible authority upon his brother-dentist.

By return of post a second eruption descended upon the studio from the "dictionary in distress."

3A, The Minories, E.

Most Honourable and Angelical Mr. Leopold Barstein,

I have the honour now to thank You for Your kind answer of my letter. I did not succeed here by my vital experience in the last of ten years. I got my livelihood a certain time by my dental practice so long there was not a hard violent competition, then I had never any efficacious relief, protection, then I have no relation, then we and the time are changeable too, then without money is impossible to perform any matter, if I had at present in my grieved desperate position £4 for my restaurant, then I were rescued, I do not earn anything, and I must despond at last, I perish here, in Russia I was ruined, please to aid me in Your merciful humanity by something, if I had £15 I could start off from here to go somewhere to look for my daily bread, and if I had £30 so I shall go to Jerusalem because I am convinced by my bitter and sour troubles and shocking tribulations here is nothing to do any more for me. I have not been in the Russo-Jewish fund and do not know it where it is, and if it is in the Jewish shelter of Leman Street so I have no protection, no introduction, no recommendation for it. Poverty has very seldom a few clement humane good people and little friends. The people say Jacobs the dentist of Mansel Place is not a good man, and so it is I tried it for he makes the impossible competition. I ask Your good genteel cordial nobility according to the universal good reputation of Your gracious goodness to reply me quick by some help now.

Your obedient Servant respectfully,
Nehemiah Silvermann,
Dentist and Restaurateur

This letter threw a new but not reassuring light upon the situation. Instead of being a victim of the Russian troubles, a recent refugee from massacre and robbery, Nehemiah had already existed in London for ten years, and although he might originally have been ruined by Russia, he had survived his ruin by a decade. His ideas of his future seemed as hazy as his past. Four pounds would be a very present help; he could continue his London career. With fifteen pounds he was ready to start off anywhither. With thirty pounds he would end all his troubles in Jerusalem. Such nebulousness appeared to necessitate a personal visit, and the next day, finding himself in bad form, Barstein angrily bashed in a clay visage, clapped on his hat, and repaired to the Minories. But he looked in vain for either a dentist or a restaurant at No. 3A. It appeared a humble corner residence, trying to edge itself into the important street. At last, after wandering uncertainly up and down, he knocked at the shabby door. A frowsy woman with long earrings opened it staring, and said that the Silvermanns occupied two rooms on her second floor.

"What!" cried Barstein. "Is he married?"

"I should hope so," replied the landlady severely. "He has eleven children at least."

Barstein mounted the narrow carpetless stairs, and was received by Mrs. Silvermann and her brood with much consternation and ceremony. The family filled the whole front room and overflowed into the back, which appeared to be a sort of kitchen, for Mrs. Silvermann had rushed thence with tucked-up sleeves, and sounds of frying still proceeded from it. But Mr. Silvermann was not at home, the small, faded, bewigged creature told him apologetically. Barstein looked curiously round the room, half expecting indications of dentistry or dining. But he saw only a minimum of broken-down furniture, bottomless cane chairs, a wooden table and a cracked mirror, a hanging shelf heaped with ragged books, and a standing cupboard which obviously turned into a bedstead at night for half the family. But of a dentist's chair there was not even the ruins. His eyes wandered over the broken-backed books—some were indeed "dictionaries in distress." He noted a Russo-German and a German-English. Then the sounds of frying penetrated more keenly to his brain.

"You are the cook of the restaurant?" he inquired.

"Restaurant!" echoed the woman resentfully. "Have I not enough cooking to do for my own family? And where shall I find money to keep a restaurant?"

"Your husband said——" murmured Barstein, as in guilty confusion.

A squalling from the overflow offspring in the kitchen drew off the mother for a moment, leaving him surrounded by an open-eyed juvenile mob. From the rear he heard smacks, loud whispers and whimperings. Then the poor woman reappeared, bearing what seemed a scrubbing-board. She placed it over one of the caneless chairs, and begged his Excellency to be seated. It was a half holiday at the school, she complained, otherwise her family would be less numerous.

"Where does your husband do his dentistry?" Barstein inquired, seating himself cautiously upon the board.

"Do I know?" said his wife. "He goes out, he comes in." At this moment, to Barstein's great satisfaction, he did come in.

"Holy angel!" he cried, rushing at the hem of Barstein's coat, and kissing it reverently. He was a gaunt, melancholy figure, elongated to over six feet, and still further exaggerated by a rusty top-hat of the tallest possible chimneypot, and a threadbare frockcoat of the longest possible tails. At his advent his wife, vastly relieved, shepherded her flock into the kitchen and closed the door, leaving Barstein alone with the long man, who seemed, as he stood gazing at his visitor, positively soaring heavenwards with rapture.

But Barstein inquired brutally: "Where do you do your dentistry?"

"Never mind me," replied Nehemiah ecstatically. "Let me look on you!" And a more passionate worship came into his tranced gaze.

But Barstein, feeling duped, replied sternly: "Where do you do your dentistry?"

The question seemed to take some moments penetrating through Nehemiah's rapt brain, but at last he replied pathetically: "And where shall I find achers? In Russia I had my living of it. Here I have no friends."

The homeliness of his vocabulary amused Barstein. Evidently the dictionary *was* his fount of inspiration. Without it Niagara was reduced to a trickle. He seemed indeed quite shy of speech, preferring to gaze with large liquid eyes.

"But you *have* managed to live here for ten years," Barstein pointed out.

"You see how merciful God is!" Nehemiah rejoined eagerly. "Never once has He deserted me and my children."

"But what have you done?" inquired Barstein.

The first shade of reproach came into Nehemiah's eyes.

"Ask sooner what the Almighty has done," he said.

Barstein felt rebuked. One does not like to lose one's character as a holy angel. "But your restaurant?" he said. "Where is that?"

"That is here."

"Here!" echoed Barstein, staring round again.

"Where else? Here is a wide opening for a *kosher* restaurant. There are hundreds and hundreds of Greeners lodging all around— poor young men with only a bed or a corner of a room to sleep on. They know not where to go to eat, and my wife, God be thanked, is a knowing cook."

"Oh, then, your restaurant is only an idea."

"Naturally—a counsel that I have given myself."

"But have you enough plates and dishes and tablecloths? Can you afford to buy the food, and to risk its not being eaten?"

Nehemiah raised his hands to heaven.

"Not being eaten! With a family like mine!"

Barstein laughed in spite of himself. And he was softened by noting how sensitive and artistic were Nehemiah's outspread hands—they might well have wielded the forceps. "Yes, I dare say that is what will happen," he said. "How can you keep a restaurant up two pairs of stairs where no passer-by will ever see it?"

As he spoke, however, he remembered staying in an hotel in Sicily which consisted entirely of one upper room. Perhaps in the ghetto Sicilian fashions were paralleled.

"I do not fly so high as a restaurant in once," Nehemiah explained. "But here is this great empty room. What am I to do with it? At night of course most of us sleep on it, but by daylight it is a waste. Also I receive several Hebrew and Yiddish papers a week from my friends in Russia and America, and one of which I even buy here. When I have read them these likewise are a waste. Therefore have I given myself a counsel, if I would make here a reading-room they should come in the evenings, many young men who have only a bed or a room-corner to go to, and when once they have learnt to come here it will then be easy to make them to eat and drink. First I will give to them only coffee and cigarettes, but afterwards shall my wife cook them all the *Delicatessen* of Poland. When our custom will become too large we shall take over Bergman's great fashionable restaurant in the Whitechapel Road. He has already given me the option thereof; it is only two hundred pounds. And if your gentility——"

"But I cannot afford two hundred pounds," interrupted Barstein, alarmed.

"No, no, it is the Almighty who will afford that," said Nehemiah reassuringly. "From you I ask nothing."

"In that case," replied Barstein drily, "I must say I consider it an excellent plan. Your idea of building up from small foundations is most sensible—some of the young men may even have toothache—but I do not see where you need me—unless to supply a few papers."

"Did I not say you were from heaven?" Nehemiah's eyes shone again. "But I do not require the papers. It is enough for me that your holy feet have stood in my homestead. I thought you might send money. But to come with your own feet! Now I shall be able to tell I have spoken with him face to face."

Barstein was touched. "I think you will need a larger table for the reading-room," he said.

The tall figure shook its tall hat. "It is only gas that I need for my operations."

"Gas!" repeated Barstein, astonished. "Then you propose to continue your dentistry too."

"It is for the restaurant I need the gas," elucidated Nehemiah. "Unless there shall be a cheerful shining here the young men will not come. But the penny gas is all I need."

"Well, if it costs only a penny——" began Barstein.

"A penny in the slot," corrected Nehemiah. "But then there is the meter and the cost of the burners." He calculated that four pounds would convert the room into a salon of light that would attract all the homeless moths of the neighbourhood.

So this was the four-pound solution, Barstein reflected with his first sense of solid foothold. After all, Nehemiah had sustained his surprise visit fairly well—he was obviously no Crœsus—and if four pounds would not only save this swarming family but radiate cheer to the whole neighbourhood—

He sprung open the sovereign-purse that hung on his watch-chain. It contained only three pounds ten. He rummaged his pockets for silver, finding only eight shillings.

"I'm afraid I haven't quite got it!" he murmured.

"As if I couldn't trust you!" cried Nehemiah reproachfully, and as he lifted his long coat-tails to trouser-pocket the money, Barstein saw that he had no waistcoat.

II

About six months later, when Barstein had utterly forgotten the episode, he received another letter whose phraseology instantly recalled everything.

To the most Honourable Competent Authentical Illustrious Authority and Universal Celebrious Dignity of the very Famous Sculptor.

3A, The Minories, E.

Dear Sir,

I have the honour and pleasure now to render the real and sincere gratitude of my very much obliged thanks for Your grand gracious clement sympathical propitious merciful liberal compassionable cordial nobility of your real humane generous benevolent genuine very kind magnanimous philanthropy, which afforded to me a great redemption of my very lamentable desperate necessitous need, wherein I am at present very poor indeed in my total ruination by the cruel cynical Russia, therein is every day a daily tyrannous massacre and assassinate, here is nothing to do any more for me previously, I shall rather go to Bursia than to Russia. I received from Your dear kind amiable amicable goodness recently £4 the same was for me a momental recreateing aid in my actual very indigent paltry miserable calamitous situation wherein I gain now nothing and I only perish here. Even I cannot earn here my daily bread by my perfect scientifick Knowledge of diverse languages, I know the philological neology and archaiology, the best way is for me to go to another country to wit, to Bursia or Turkey. Thus, I solicit and supplicate Your charitable generosity by my very humble and instant request to make me go away from here as soon as possible according to Your humane kind merciful clemency.

Your obedient Servant respectfully,
Nehemiah Silvermann,
Dentist and Professor of Languages

So an Academy of Languages had evolved from the gas, not a restaurant. Anyhow the dictionary was in distress again. Emigration appeared now the only salvation.

But where in the world was Bursia? Possibly Persia was meant. But why Persia? Wherein lay the attraction of that exotic land, and whatever would Mrs. Silvermann and her overflowing progeny do in Persia? Nehemiah's original suggestion of Jerusalem had been much more intelligible. Perhaps it persisted still under the head of Turkey. Not least characteristic Barstein found Nehemiah's tenacious gloating over his ancient ruin at the hands of Russia.

For some days the sculptor went about weighed down by Nehemiah's misfortunes, and the necessity of finding time to journey to the Minories. But he had an absorbing piece of work, and before he could tear himself away from it a still more urgent shower of words fell upon him.

3A, The Minories, E.

I have the honour now, [the new letter ran] to inquire about my decided and expecting departure. I must sue by my quite humble and very instant entreaty Your noble genteel cordial humanity in my very hard troublous and bitter and sour vexations and tribulations to effect for my poor position at least a private anonymous prompt collection as soon as possible according to Your clement magnanimous charitable mercy of £15 if not £25 among Your very estimable and respectfully good friends, in good order to go in another country even Bursia to get my livelihood by my dental practice or by my other scientifick and philological knowledge. The great competition is here in anything very vigorous. I have here no dental employment, no dental practice, no relations, no relief, no gain, no earning, no introduction, no protection, no recommendation, no money, no good friends, no good connecting acquaintance, in Russia I am ruined and I perish here, I am already

*desperate and despond entirely. I do not know what to do and what
shall I do, do now in my actual urgent, extreme immense need. I
am told by good many people, that the board of guardians is very
seldom to rescue by aid the people, but very often is to find only
faults, and vices and to make them guilty. I have nothing to do there,
and in the russian jewish fund I found once Sir Asher Aaronsberg
and he is not to me sympathical. I supply and solicit considerably
Your kind humane clement mercy to answer me as soon as possible
quick according to Your very gracious mercy.*

Your obedient Servant respectfully,
Nehemiah Silvermann,
Dentist and Professor of Languages

As soon as the light failed in his studio, Barstein summoned a
hansom and sped to the Minories.

III

Nehemiah's voice bade him walk in, and turning the door-handle
he saw the top-hatted figure sprawled in solitary gloom along a caneless chair, reading a newspaper by the twinkle of a rushlight. Nehemiah sprang up with a bark of joy, making his gigantic shadow bow
to the visitor. From chimneypot to coat-tail he stretched unchanged,
and the same celestial rapture illumined his gaunt visage.

But Barstein drew back his own coat tail from the attempted
kiss.

"Where is the gas?" he asked drily.

"Alas, the company removed the meter."

"But the gas-brackets?"

"What else had we to eat?" said Nehemiah simply.

Barstein in sudden suspicion raised his eyes to the ceiling. But
a fragment of gaspipe certainly came through it. He could not, however, recall whether the pipe had been there before or not.

"So the young men would not come?" he said.

"Oh yes, they came, and they read, and they ate. Only they did
not pay."

"You should have made it a rule—cash down."

Again a fine shade of rebuke and astonishment crossed his lean
and melancholy visage.

"And could I oppress a brother-in-Israel? Where had those
young men to turn but to me?"

Again Barstein felt his angelic reputation imperilled. He hastened
to change the conversation.

"And why do you want to go to Bursia?" he said.

"Why shall I want to go to Bursia?" Nehemiah replied.

"You said so." Barstein showed him the letter.

"Ah, I said I shall sooner go to Bursia than to Russia. Always Sir Asher Aaronsberg speaks of sending us back to Russia."

"He would," said Barstein grimly. "But where is Bursia?"

Nehemiah shrugged his shoulders. "Shall I know? My little Rebeccah was drawing a map thereof; she won a prize of five pounds with which we lived two months. A genial child is my Rebeccah."

"Ah, then, the Almighty did send you something."

"And do I not trust Him?" said Nehemiah fervently. "Otherwise, burdened down as I am with a multitude of children——"

"You made your own burden," Barstein could not help pointing out.

Again that look of pain, as if Nehemiah had caught sight of feet of clay beneath Barstein's shining boots.

" 'Be fruitful and multiply and fill the earth,' " Nehemiah quoted in Hebrew. "Is not that the very first commandment in the Bible?"

"Well, then, you want to go to Turkey," said the sculptor evasively. "I suppose you mean Palestine?"

"No, Turkey. It is to Turkey we Zionists should ought to go, there to work for Palestine. Are not many of the Sultan's own officials Jews? If we can make of *them* hot-hearted Zionists——"

It was an arresting conception, and Barstein found himself sitting on the table to discuss it. The reverence with which Nehemiah listened to his views was touching and disconcerting. Barstein felt humbled by the celestial figure he cut in Nehemiah's mental mirror. Yet he could not suspect the man of a glozing tongue, for of the leaders of Zionism Nehemiah spoke with, if possible, greater veneration, with an awe trembling on tears. His elongated figure grew even gaunter, his lean visage unearthlier, as he unfolded his plan for the conquest of Palestine, and Barstein's original impression of his simple sincerity was repeated and re-enforced.

Presently, however, it occurred to Barstein that Nehemiah himself would have scant opportunity of influential contact with Ottoman officials, and that the real question at issue was, how Nehemiah, his wife, and his "at least eleven children" were to be supported in Turkey. He mentioned the point.

Nehemiah waved it away. "And cannot the Almighty support us in Turkey as well as in England?" he asked. "Yes, even in Bursia itself the Guardian of Israel is not sleepy."

It was then that the word "Luftmensch" flew into Barstein's mind. Nehemiah was not an earth-man in gross contact with solidities. He was an air-man, floating on facile wings through the æther. True, he spoke of troublesome tribulations, but these were mainly dictionary distresses, felt most keenly in the rhapsody of literary composition. At worst they were mere clouds on the blue. They had nothing in common with the fogs which frequently veiled heaven from his own vision. Never for a moment had Nehemiah failed to remember the blue, never had he lost his radiant outlook. His very pessimism was merely optimism in disguise, since it was only a personal pessimism to be remedied by "a few frivolous pounds," by a new crumb from the hand of Providence, not that impersonal despair of the scheme of things which gave the thinker such black moments. How had Nehemiah lived during those first ten years in England? Who should say? But he had had the wild daring to uproot himself from his childhood's home and adventure himself upon an unknown shore, and there, by hook or crook, for better or for worse, through vicissitudes innumerable and crises beyond calculation, ever on the perilous verge of nothingness, he had scraped through the days and the weeks and the years, fearlessly contributing perhaps more important items to posterity than the dead stones, which were all he, the sculptor, bade fair to leave behind him. Welcoming each new child with feasting and psalmody, never for a moment had Nehemiah lost his robustious faith in life, his belief in God, man, or himself.

Yes, even deeper than his own self-respect was his respect for others. An impenetrable idealist, he lived surrounded by a radiant humanity, by men become as Gods. With no conscious hyperbole did he address one as "Angel." Intellect and goodness were his pole-stars. And what airy courage in his mundane affairs, what invincible resilience! He had once been a dentist, and he still considered himself one. Before he owned a tablecloth he deemed himself the proprietor of a restaurant. He enjoyed alike the pleasures of anticipation and of memory, and having nothing, glided ever buoyantly between two gilded horizons. The superficial might call him shiftless, but, more profoundly envisaged, was he not rather an education in the art of living? Did he not incarnate the great Jewish gospel of the improvident lilies?

"You shall not go to Bursia," said Barstein in a burst of artistic fervour. "Thirteen people cannot possibly get there for fifteen pounds or even twenty-five pounds, and for such a sum you could start a small business here."

Nehemiah stared at him. "God's messenger!" was all he could gasp. Then the tall melancholy man raised his eyes to heaven and uttered a Hebrew voluntary in which references to the ram whose horns were caught in the thicket to save Isaac's life were distinctly audible.

Barstein waited patiently till the pious lips were at rest.

"But what business do you think you——?" he began.

"Shall I presume dictation to the angel?" asked Nehemiah with wet shining eyes.

"I am thinking that perhaps we might find something in which your children could help you. How old is the eldest?"

"I will ask my wife. Salome!" he cried. The dismal creature trotted in.

"How old is Moshelé?" he asked.

"And don't you remember he was twelve last Tabernacles?"

Nehemiah threw up his long arms. "Merciful Heaven! He must soon begin to learn his *Parshah* (confirmation portion). What will it be? Where is my *Chumash* (Pentateuch)?" Mrs. Silvermann drew it down from the row of ragged books, and Nehemiah, fluttering the pages and bending over the rushlight, became lost to the problem of his future.

Barstein addressed himself to the wife. "What business do you think your husband could set up here?"

"Is he not a dentist?" she inquired in reply.

Barstein turned to the busy peering flutterer.

"Would you like to be a dentist again?"

"Ah, but how shall I find achers?"

"You put up a sign," said Barstein. "One of those cases of teeth. I daresay the landlady will permit you to put it up by the front door, especially if you take an extra room. I will buy you the instruments, furnish the room attractively. You will put in your newspapers—why, people will be glad to come as to a reading-room!" he added smiling.

Nehemiah addressed his wife. "Did I not say he was a genteel archangel?" he cried ecstatically.

IV

Barstein was sitting outside a café in Rome sipping vermouth with Rozenoffski, the Russo-Jewish pianist, and Schneemann, the Galician-Jewish painter, when he next heard from Nehemiah.

He was anxiously expecting an important letter, which he had instructed his studio-assistant to bring to him instantly. So when the man appeared, he seized with avidity upon the envelope in his hand. But the scrawling superscription at once dispelled his hope, and recalled the forgotten *Luftmensch*. He threw the letter impatiently on the table.

"Oh, you may read it," his friends protested, misunderstanding.

"I can guess what it is," he said grumpily. Here, in this classical atmosphere, in this southern sunshine, he felt out of sympathy with the gaunt godly Nehemiah, who had doubtless lapsed again into his truly troublesome tribulations. Not a penny more for the ne'er-do-well! Let his Providence look after him!

"Is she beautiful?" quizzed Schneemann.

Barstein roared with laughter. His irate mood was broken up. Nehemiah as a petticoated romance was too tickling.

"You shall read the letter," he said.

Schneemann protested comically. "No, no, that would be un-gentlemanly—you read to us what the angel says."

"It is I that am the angel," Barstein laughed, as he tore open the letter. He read it aloud, breaking down in almost hysterical laughter at each eruption of adjectives from "the dictionary in distress." Rozen-offski and Schneemann rolled in similar spasms of mirth, and the Italians at the neighbouring tables, though entirely ignorant of the motive of the merriment, caught the contagion, and rocked and shrieked with the mad foreigners.

3A, The Minories, E.

Right Honourable Angelical Mr. Leopold Barstein

I have now the honour to again solicit Your genteel genuine sympathical humane philanthropic kind cordial nobility to oblige me at present by Your merciful loan of gracious second and propitious favourable aidance in my actually poor indigent position in which I have no earn by my dental practice likewise no help, also no protection, no recommendation, no employment, and then the competition is here very violent. I was ruined by Russia, and I have nothing for the celebration of our Jewish new year. Consequentially upon your merciful archangelical donative I was able to make my livelihood by my dental practice even very difficult, but still I had my vital subsistence by it till up now, but not further for the little while, in consequence of it my circumstances are now in the urgent extreme immense need. Thus I implore Your competent, well famous good-hearted liberal magnanimous benevolent generosity to respond me in Your beneficent relief as soon as possible, according to Your kind grand clemence of Your good ingenuous genteel humanity. I wish You a happy new year.

Your obedient servant respectfully,
Nehemiah Silvermann,
Dentist and Professor of Languages

But when the reading was finished, Schneemann's comment was unexpected.

"*Rosh Hashanah* so near?" he said.

A rush of ghetto memories swamped the three artists as they tried to work out the date of the Jewish New Year, that solemn period of earthly trumpets and celestial judgments.

"Why, it must be to-day!" cried Rozenoffski suddenly. The trio looked at one another with rueful humour. Why, ghetto could not even realize such indifference to the heavenly tribunals so busily decreeing their life-or-death sentences!

Barstein raised his glass. "Here's a happy new year, anyhow," he said.

The three men clinked glasses.

Rozenoffski drew out a hundred-lire note.

"Send that to the poor devil," he said.

"Oho!" laughed Schneemann. "You still believe 'Charity delivers from death!' Well, I must be saved too!" And he threw down another hundred-lire note.

To the acutely analytical Barstein it seemed as if an old superstitious thrill lay behind Schneemann's laughter as behind Rozenoffski's donation.

"You will only make the *Luftmensch* believe still more obstinately in his Providence," he said, as he gathered up the new year gifts. "Again will he declare that he has been accorded a good writing and a good sealing by the Heavenly Tribunal!"

"Well, hasn't he?" laughed Schneemann.

"Perhaps he has," said Rozenoffski musingly. *"Qui sa?"*

THE JACK-OF-ALL-TRADES

BY S. J. AGNON
TRANSLATED FROM THE HEBREW BY I. M. LASK

There's a story told of a teacher of little children, a very poor fellow indeed, may the Merciful One preserve us from his fix, who made up his mind to sell snuff tobacco. So when he'd be sitting teaching children at the table his finger would be keeping the place for them while his foot would be pounding the leaves; yet it didn't give him what to eat. Then thinking it over he began teaching girls how to read, cypher, and add up; and he'd write them charms to be attractive; and for women in the family he wrote slips for guarding the newborn baby and keeping the not-good ones[1] at a distance. Besides which he used to recite Torah for pay, and blow the shofar, and take his place before the Holy Ark to pray for the congregation; and he would whisper away warts and bake the extra matzoth for Passover. And still he didn't have what to eat.

So he decided to become a beadle. He hired himself out to the Court[2] and became its beadle and signed as witness on bills of divorcements. And still he didn't have enough to eat.

Then he said to himself, See here, I meet the girls and I'm the beadle of the Court, and if any man divorces his wife I'm the first to know about it; let's go and become a matchmaker. So he went and began to spend his time making matches, and even then he didn't have what to eat. Well, said he, since I have to sign all fit and proper on bills of divorcement I'm becoming well versed in the art of writing; and he decided to become an engraver of inscriptions upon tombstones; but even then he didn't have what to eat.

So he stood and prayed and wept before Him, may He be blest, and he said, Lord of the Universe, so many of the kinds of crafts to be found in your world do I know, and yet must I die of starvation?

At this His Blessed Name signed to Dikarnusa, the angel appointed over sustenance, to give a living to that teacher of little children. Off went Dikarnusa. When he returned the Holy and Blest One said to him, Have you given him sustenance, Dikarnusa? All through the town I went, said Dikarnusa, without finding any teacher of little children, only there was a maker of snuff tobacco. Said the Holy and Blest One to Dikarnusa, by your life, Dikarnusa, I didn't mean anybody else except that fellow.

So Dikarnusa went off. When he came back the Holy and Blest One asked, Well, have you made him a living? All through the town I went, said the angel, without finding either a maker of snuff tobacco or a teacher of little children; but maybe you were thinking of the fellow who sits teaching the girls and writing their mothers slips for the safety of their newborn babies? By your life, said the Holy and Blest One, he's the one I have in mind.

So Dikarnusa departed. Upon his return He asked, Well, have you given him a living? By Your Great Name I swear, said the angel, that it's all through the town I've been and visited all the girls without finding him. Said the Holy and Blest One, Maybe he's standing at prayer or

¹*Evil spirits and demons* ED. ²*Rabbinical court* ED

reciting the Torah or blowing the shofar or wishing away warts or choosing wheat for the extraspecial Passover matzoth. Go and see.

When he returned he said, it is known full well before Your Glory Seat that I've been everywhere you said without finding him. Your Holy Torah says I haven't seen him, the ears of wheat say none of us know of him, the warts say we have not heard as much as a whisper, the angels created by the blowing of the shofar say he has not brought them to being. Maybe he's been busy at the Court and delayed there, said God.

So Dikarnusa went off. Did you find him? God asked on his return. No, said the angel. Then he must be standing pairing matches, said He. Dash off to him before he has a chance of perishing of hunger. So off rushed the angel and back he flew. Dikarnusa, said the Holy and Blest One, he's still wailing about his living. Quick, be off to the graveyard where he may be hammering inscriptions.

Dikarnusa spread his wings and set off with a bar of gold, to find him in the graveyard, perished of hunger and already cold.

A JEW KNOWS ALL TRADES

> on *Purim* he delivers *shalach-monehs*—
> on *Pesach* he bakes *matzoths*—
> on *Shabuoth* he is a gardener—
> on *Tishah b' Ab* he is a soldier—
> on *Sukkoth* he is a builder—
> on *Hanukkah* he pours lead *draydlach*—
> and on *Rosh Hashana* he blows the *shofar*.

FROM WHAT A LITVAK MAKES A LIVING

BY DER TUNKELER (JOSEPH TUNKEL)
TRANSLATED FROM THE YIDDISH BY NATHAN AUSUBEL

He sat opposite me at a nearby table in the Café Le Bourbon on the Boulevard Saint-Michel, and fixed me with a determined look.

He had the face of an old, battered valise that had been knocked about through every country in the world. The scars on his face looked like the many colored labels that are pasted on a traveler's luggage at the borders and customs stations. Every fiber of him, every movement spoke of utter homelessness.

He was the pure wanderer type; it was difficult to tell his nationality.

"Pardon, monsieur! Aren't you Der Tunkeler?" he asked me in an outlandish Yiddish, a Yiddish of many blends he must have acquired from a great deal of roaming through all the Jewish settlements and ghettos in the world.

"Yes, I am Der Tunkeler," I answered. "And who are you?"

"Oh, you won't recognize me, but I recognized you right away. We're from the same town. My mother was Dvoira the Blintze Baker. I'm a Litvak, monsieur!"

"In that case you must be Bentze," I said. "What a mischievous boy you were with such fiery eyes! You mimicked everybody and everything. What wonderful imitations you could give of a cat, a dog, or a pig!"

"Oui, oui, monsieur, that's me, your humble servant, s'il vous plaît!"

"What are you doing in Paris? Are you a native, or are you just here for a while?"

"Oh, mon Dieu! If I could only begin to tell you the experiences this Litvak here has gone through in his life, one thousand and one nights wouldn't be enough for it. I'd like you to know, mister, that I've traveled all over the world. I was *na konye ee pod konyom, tshort poberi!*[1] You would like, monsieur, I should tell you about them, nicht wahr? Garçon, une bock, s'il vous plaît!"

The waiter brought him his bock, and he seated himself at my table and began to talk. His Yiddish was well peppered with words and idioms culled from many languages—Russian, Polish, Italian, French, German, Spanish, and English. And he also used words whose language origin I could not determine.

"Voilà! No doubt you remember, monsieur, that I suddenly disappeared from our town in Lithuania when I was a youth. That was after I had mimicked our town *maggid* one Sabbath afternoon. I delivered a sermon in the synagogue, how do you call it, a *drosha*? I wrapped my face in my *tallis* and everyone imagined that I was the maggid. But right in the middle of my sermon, who should come in but the maggid himself! Believe me, there was hell to pay. They whacked into me so that I lost count of the blows. The following morning I took the train to St. Petersburg.

"I arrived in the capital without a shilling in my pocket and no residence permit. So I became a Tartar and sold oriental caftans.

[1] *Russian for "on the horse and under the horse, the devil take it!"*

After a while the police caught up with me and, since I was unable to produce a residence permit, they sent me out of the city. From there I went to Rostov-on-the-Don and became a Chinese; I sold Chinese silk kimonos made in Lodz. But the police caught me again, still without a residence permit, and they sent me to Siberia. But, disguising myself as a girl, I escaped over the border. C'est ça, monsieur!

"Alors, I arrived in Vienna without a peso in my pocket and knocked about the streets like a tramp. At last I cornered a job: I was to impersonate a lion in a menagerie on the Prater. You surely must have heard the story about the lion that called out 'Hear, O Israel,' and of the tiger that answered him: 'The Lord our God, the Lord is One.' Well, the lion was I, monsieur.

"One fine day my bluff was discovered. The audience tore my lion's skin off me, beat me without mercy and wanted to tear me limb from limb. It was a narrow escape I had that time, sacramento!

"C'est ça! After that, alors, I went to the Tyrol and found myself a new job. In the small mountain village I was engaged as 'echo-man.' The place was a well-know spa and so the local hotel proprietors employed me to make echoes. That is, I hid in the mountains and whenever one of the guests let out a yell I let out the echo, and not once either but seven times in succession like the 'To the Chief Musician' of the Book of Psalms. Yak boga kocham![1] I awoke echoes that were comme il faut! Très chic!

"It goes without saying that the guests caught me 'at work' and belabored me so that I yelled with genuine echoes. Donnerwetter, once more!

"Alors, I had to run away from there, too, and went to Switzerland. I found a job in a small village near Zurich as a 'waterfall-man.' That is, I hid in a hill and poured down water. This waterfall bore the name of 'William Tell Waterfall.' It was well known in the neighborhood among all the tourists and summer guests. I showed great talent and temperament in the way I poured the water. As soon as the tram arrived with guests I'd spill down such a cataract that the tourists stood overawed, watching this wonderful phenomenon of nature. My employer would stand below giving a brief lecture on the fall and selling picture postcards of the scene.

"To make a long story short, here, too, they caught me 'with the goods.' It seems that some tourists were curious to find out the source of the waterfall, so they went in search of it and they found it, all right; they found me on the hill pouring down barrels of water. They got so

[1]*Polish for "as I love God!"*

angry they poured the barrels of water over me, so that I began to look like a waterfall myself.

"Do you have a cigarette, monsieur? S'il vous plaît, merci!

"For a short time I suffered from an inflammation of the lungs, and, when I got better, I went to Berlin. I immediately found employment there in Luna Park. I became a fakir and took on the name of Zara Zitra of Calcutta. The man who engaged me dressed me up like a maharajah and taught me all kinds of hocus-pocuses and tricks. What they really were I haven't the faintest idea. At a certain time I had to crawl into a box and again at a certain time I had to crawl out of the box. I crawled in and I crawled out, crawled in and crawled out, and muttered Hindu proverbs in a mysterious voice.

"To my misfortune I crawled out of the box one day at the wrong minute and hell let loose in the audience. People yelled, 'Give us back our money!' and they tore down the tent. My employer let his rage out on me, threw me out, and didn't even pay me a centime. All he gave me were some wounds on my face; you can still see the scars, *psiakrew!*

"Does a Litvak ever get lost? Mais non! Jamais! I bought passage to New York and went to work in Coney Island in a Little Russian company as a Haidamak Cossack chieftain by the name of Haidochropenko and, oy, did I dance a *hopak!* From there I went to Rio de Janeiro where I became a gypsy and sang gypsy songs in a Russian restaurant. After a while I went to Buenos Aires. There I became a Turk; I wore a red *yarmulka* and sold Turkish nuts.

"In the meantime, new dances like the shimmy and the fox trot became the rage. I went to Paris and became a teacher of the new dances. Temperament I had plenty, a Litvak I am, so I became a Western cowboy and taught the tango, the shimmy, the Boston and Java. I myself composed the most beautiful dances, such as the Congo, the Texas, the Honolulu, and the Chile. The most fashionable people studied dancing with me. Garçon! Une absinthe, s'il vous plaît!"

He took a sip of his drink and continued.

"Yes, I earned money but competition became too keen and the dancing business went to the dogs. All Litvaks had gone into the dancing business. One became a Filipino, another a Moroccan, another a Sicilian. A black year on them all! They all became exotic dancers. What was I to do but look for a new job.

"I did not have to look long, monsieur, Paris is quite a village, you know, and a Litvak never gets lost. I found employment as an apache in a beer den on Montparnasse. I put on an apache cap, tied a red handkerchief around my neck and grunted. In short, I made a living, monsieur! C'est ça!

"Recently, chèr monsieur, I opened my own business. Why did I have to work for others all my life? So I opened an Apache Cellar, a hole-in-the-ground in a Montmartre alley. In this cellar they used to sell sauerkraut and pickles, so I cleaned it all out and called the place the Sans Culotte. On the walls I painted all kinds of freaks and nightmares, and I engaged several apaches to sit around every evening and look murderous. Needless to say, the tourists came flocking.

"C'est ça, mon chèr! As you see me, this Litvak, Bentze the son of Dvoira the Blintze Baker of your home town, has already been everything in the book: a Turk, a Tartar, a Gypsy, an echo-man, a waterfall spiller, a Moroccan, a Little Russian Cossack chieftain, a Chinese, an apache, and now I am myself a proprietor of an apache den.

"Come around some evening, monsieur, to my place! You don't have to be afraid. My apaches are nice people just like you and I. One of them is a Hebrew teacher from Vitebsk, another is a pocketbook maker from Warsaw, and the others are former cap makers from the "Pletzel"—you know, that's what we Yiddish-speaking Jews call the Place de Rivoli. Well, I must get along now; I have to see what my 'sans culottes' are doing. Garçon, l'addition! Adieu, monsieur, good-by, auf wiedersehen, au revoir, a rivederci, seit gesund!"

There are more would-be slaughterers than chickens.

Pipe Dreamers and Fortune Hunters Kreplach *that you see in a dream are no* kreplach

MENACHEM-MENDEL, FORTUNE HUNTER
AN EXCERPT FROM THE EPISTOLARY NOVEL, *Menachem-Mendel*

Menachem-Mendel is no hero out of a novel and, moreover, he is no imaginary person. He is nebbech, *a Jew "of the whole year round." The author is personally and intimately acquainted with him. Together he and I have traveled a stretch of life of almost twenty years. I got to know him in the year 1892 on "The Small Exchange" in Odessa. Afterwards, the two of us, side by side, went through all the seven purgatories of Gihenom in the city of Yehupetz on the Exchange. We then went together to St. Petersburg and to Warsaw, we struggled together through all kinds of crises, and knocked about from one business into another. And, oy vay! we found no luck anywhere! . . . . For everything that is built on air and wind has got to collapse in the long run.—Sholom Aleichem*

BY SHOLOM ALEICHEM
TRANSLATED FROM THE YIDDISH BY NATHAN AUSUBEL

(*Menachem-Mendel in Yehupetz writes to his wife Sheine- Sheindel in Kasrilevke.*)

To my dear wife, the wise, the virtuous, the pious Sheine-Sheindel, long life to her!

First of all, I'd like to inform you that, God be praised, I'm well and am enjoying life and peace. And may the blessed God arrange matters so that we should always hear from each other only good news and of happy experiences. Amen!

Secondly, I wish to inform you that all week long I've been lying sick in Boiberik, that is, God forbid, not dangerously sick—I've been suffering merely from a nasty illness. What happened was that I fell on my back, so that now I'm unable to turn from one side to the other. By this time I already feel a little better, although all week long I thought I was going out of my mind. Believe me, it was no small matter to be kept away from the Stock Exchange for eight long days and not to know the quotations! All that time I was imagining that such terrific things were going on there that the world was simply turning over! God willing, maybe today or the day after, I shall most certainly go to the city. In the meantime, I'm writing you this letter; I so want to have a talk with you and, while I'm at it, give you a correct accounting of my affairs, so that you shouldn't think that I'm out of my head, that I am, God forbid, crazy, or that I have been duped.

At this moment there lie in my portfolio, all told, 150 shares of Putivil, 100 shares of Transport, 5 of Maltzever, 5 of Lileputlech, 5 Vegelech, and some Premies. As for Putivil and Transport, I'm holding them on margin (I planked down a deposit of three rubles). When the time will come for me to sell them—and sell them I surely will—I'll have left, after deducting all expenses, a clear profit of four or five thousand rubles. Besides that I'm "long" on some twenty or thirty shares of Putivil and Maltzever. From them I reckon to make a profit of seventeen or eighteen hundred rubles. So there you already have a total of seven thousand rubles. The five Maltzever that I bought for cash I figure cheaply at four thousand rubles, because it will be a disgrace and a shame if in a short time they wouldn't be worth at least two thousand rubles apiece, although for the last few days they've gone down a bit. But that decline is nothing more than a manipulation on the part of the St. Petersburg speculators so that they should be able to "uncover." But the real stuff still remains, and by that I mean the Lileputlech and the Vegelech! Here you have my figures clear as gold: until *ultimo* we have eighteen days, and, since the Lileputlech are advancing a hundred rubles a day, we have the sum of eighteen hundred times five and that amounts exactly to nine thousand rubles.

Now what about the Vegelech? They're advancing at the rate of one hundred and fifty rubles a day, so there you have eighteen, times one hundred and fifty, times five. Doesn't this amount to thirteen thousand five hundred rubles? And then where is *epis Volga* in my calculation? And *Dnieper*? And *Don*?

In short, I'm not sewing for myself a big purse by any means, but I figure that all in all, making allowances for all expenses, such as *cartage* and *stealage*, all in all I'll make close to forty-fifty thousand! May the Blessed God help that ultimo should pass smoothly! Then, God willing, I'll realize on all my "little papers" and I'll be able "to turn over on the other side." That means that I'll be "bearish" and start playing the market *à la baisse*. I'll trade in everything and I'll coin money even on the "left side."

And after that I'll become "bullish" and play *à la hausse*, and once again I'll earn a nice fat pile. If the God above only wills it the fifty thousand can grow into a hundred thousand and the hundred thousand into two hundred thousand and the two hundred thousand into four hundred thousand, and so on and so forth until it will swell into a million. How else, *narrele*, do you think one can become a *millionchik*, a Brodsky? And who do you suppose a Brodsky is anyway? Just a man of flesh and blood who eats and drinks and sleeps exactly like you and me! May I see everything that's good in this world if I didn't clap my own eyes on him once! That's how I know.

In short, you needn't aggravate yourself on account of it. I've made a close study of this speculation business and am considered such an expert on the Exchange that, believe it or not, they even come to me for advice. With God's help I've gotten quite a hang of the game!

Now as to what you say that you have no faith in all this and urge me to quit it—that doesn't surprise me in the least. Now you take Chinkis! There's a certain speculator whose name is Chinkis. He's a very passionate speculator and an incurable card player. By day he plays the market and by night he plays cards. Only the other week he had the following experience: he dreamed at night that he was at a card game and that he got a bad hand. That he took as a sign that he should be "bearish" and play the market à la baisse. So he went to St. Petersburg and Warsaw and, in the course of only one day, unloaded his entire portfolio of stocks. Needless to say, he's now tearing his hair for this piece of foolishness.

Serves him right! Let him not believe in dreams!

I'm eagerly looking forward to tomorrow when I'll find out the quotations. I've decided that, as soon as I get to the city, I'll call on the jeweler and get you a brooch and a pair of diamond earrings and, if I'll have time enough, I'll run over to Padol Street and buy you some underwear, tablecloths, towels, yard goods for the children's shirts, and epis other household furnishings. Now don't you go and say that, God forbid, I've forgotten all about you!

And because I'm rushed for time I'm going to cut short this letter. In my next letter, God willing, I'll write you everything in detail. For the present may God keep us both in health and prosperity. Kiss the children for me and give my hearty regards, to each one separately: to your father and mother, and to everybody else. Also tell Berel-Benyomin in my name that he shouldn't take it so to heart: a wife is a gift of God. The Lord gives and the Lord takes—blessed be the Name of the Lord!

Your husband,
Menachem-Mendel

P.S. Good that I've reminded myself! What you wrote concerning Wassilkov shows me that you did not get my meaning at all. Because I lack a residence permit I've no legal right to live in the city. Therefore, I wish to become a merchant. But this I cannot do until I've been at least for half a year a registered resident of Wassilkov. And just as soon as I can get permission to live here I'll rent, God willing, a house on Padol Street and settle you and the children there in a good hour.

Why really are you so angry at Yehupetz? I think it's because you're not acquainted with it and its inhabitants. The city itself, it goes without saying, is a *tzatzkele!* And as for its inhabitants, they're as precious as gold and silver! They're all so gentle, so genial, men as well as women. They've only one little weakness—they're passionate card players. As soon as night falls they plunge into card games and they sit there without budging until the crack of dawn. And they keep on calling out "Pass!" all the time. The grown-ups play a game called Preference, while the little ones play Stukelka, Oka and even Tertel-Mertel.

The above-mentioned

II

(*Sheine-Sheindel in Kasrilevke writes to her husband Menachem-Mendel in Yehupetz.*)

To my worthy dear husband, the rich, the famous, the wise, the learned Menachem-Mendel, may his light never grow dim!

First of all I wish to inform you that, God be praised, we are all in the best of health. God grant that you are the same and may we further hear of no worse.

Secondly, I'm writing you, dear husband, that, God forbid, you shouldn't take it amiss—a *mazl-tov* is coming to you! That precious brother of yours, your Berel-Benyomen, has remarried again in a good and lucky hour! What do you say to him? He couldn't even wait two full months after his wife's funeral! So he rode off to Berditchev, from where the whole world imports its stepmothers, and he brought home for his children a mama. And of all things she had to be a girl of nineteen! The devil take all men—what sort of conduct is that? What does my mother, long life to her, say? "Better that we should remain widows after you men than that you should make orphans of our children!"

I imagine I can see you crying, Mendel, were you, for instance, God forbid, to outlive me. May the Yehupetzer ladies never live to see that day! They'd buzz around you like bees and, before even the thirty days of mourning would be over, one of them would be sure to sting you. You'd then become, as my mother would say, "A kosher spoon in a kosher pot!" You'd remain a Yehupetzer for the rest of your days.

You say you're a cock-of-the-walk there, Mendel. Nu, go ahead, show off, flutter around, jump into the fire for all I care! One thing I can tell you, I'm not coming out to you, even if I should know that you were lying on your deathbed. Nor am I impressed very much with your fifty thousand rubles. First of all, you belong to me with the fifty thousand or without the fifty thousand. And secondly, your fifty thousand have the value of a pinch of snuff to me. What does my mother say: "So long as money is on paper it's still paper!"

I'll tell you the whole truth, dear husband; if you are able to count in your hand a few rubles and you want to wait until it will become fifty thousand, either you are a *meshuggener* or you're just a bandit and a wicked man! When you do that you just show no pity for your children or your wife, may she live to be a hundred and twenty!

Now how do you like the way he nourishes me with tomorrows? *Tomorrow* he's going to the jeweler's . . . *tomorrow* he's going to get me underwear . . . everything *tomorrow!* You big fool! Let God worry about tomorrow! *You* better buy me today what you promise. Grab what you've got, snatch it up—it'll be as good as found! My mother, life and health to her, expresses it very wisely. She says, "What earthly use do you have, daughter, of jewelry, tablecloths, and towels? Better let him send you money," says she. "The Angel of Death," says she, "doesn't ask the corpse whether he's got a shroud on."

I'm going to wait a couple of weeks more until I'll feel all well. Then I'll get me into a cart, God willing, and I'll come over to see you. And when I do come, I'll give you such a time of it that no one will envy you! I warn you—I'll dog your footsteps, I'll follow you wherever you'll go! I guarantee you that you'll run from Yehupetz in the middle of the night, as devoutly expects out of the depths of her heart

Your truly devoted wife,
Sheine-Sheindel

III

(*Menachem-Mendel in Yehupetz writes to his wife Sheine-Sheindel in Kasrilevke.*)

To my dear wife, the virtuous, the wise, the pious, Sheine-Sheindel, long life to her!

First of all, I'd like to inform you that, God be praised, I am well and am enjoying life and peace. And may the blessed God arrange matters so that we should always hear from each other only good news and of happy experiences! Amen!

Secondly, I wish to inform you that matters have taken a bad turn here, namely: the prices that are now being quoted in St. Petersburg have made everything grow dark before my eyes. It struck us here in Yehupetz like a thunderbolt, like an exploding bomb! All the stockbrokers' offices are in a state of deep gloom, just as if an earthquake had shaken the town. And right after the bad news from St. Petersburg the Warsaw Exchange also marked a heavy decline in prices.

Oh what a mad dashing hither and thither there took place! What a din, what terror, what panic! All the speculators ran for cover, dried up, so to speak, and I among them.

The Exchange was closed! The offices remained deserted, the brokers walked about downcast and worried.

Just try and picture it, dear wife; the Maltzever, which I had figured to sell very cheaply at 2000 rubles, "thought it over" and collapsed to 950! Now take, for example, Putivil. Who could have thought that from 180 they'd shrink to 67? About Transport it's no use talking even. Transport really got it in the neck—no one even wants to hold it in the hand! The same can be said for Volga and Dnieper and Don, and all the other stocks.

But all this is as gold compared to what's happening in Warsaw. A catastrophe has struck Warsaw! Ever since the world began such a slaughter has not been seen as in Warsaw! What do you think Warsaw did? She too "thought it over" and flung Lileputlech from 2450 rubles down to 620! And then Vegelech! They already were up so fine, so high! We thought: *ut ut!* any day now they're going to reach 3000 rubles. And how high, let me ask you, do they stand today? You wouldn't even guess! Four hundred stinking rubles!

Nu, how do you like such stock quotations? It's the end of the world, I'm telling you! And *ach* and *vay* to Warsaw! First she acts real nice, drives and drives the prices up all the time, and suddenly, right smack in the middle, *na!*—there you have a lively wedding! What the cause for this somersault was no one knows. One person says one thing, one person says another. It all comes from money, I mean it comes from not having any money. In German they call it *Geldmangel*, a scarcity of money, and in our language we call it very simply: "We haven't got a kopeck."

No doubt you'll ask: "Why, goodness me, wasn't it only yesterday that money was rolling in all the gutters?" *Takkeh,* that's a question! What actually happened was that the speculators got a good cooking, and I among them.

To tell you the truth, I'm a lot angrier at Warsaw than I'm at St. Petersburg. Nu, all right St. Petersburg—so what? It moves slowly over there. Every day there's a steady drop of twenty-thirty rubles and that's enough. That's at least in a businesslike way. But Warsaw! May every decent Jew be spared from ever knowing it! That's *epis* a kind of Sodom, the Compassionate One protect us from it! There isn't a day when Warsaw doesn't slump down with a hundred and fifty, with two hundred, and even with three hundred rubles at a time. It's just one slap down after another, so that we're all stunned. We haven't even time enough to look around us.

Oh that Warsaw! Millions it's costing us, I'm telling you—millions! *Gevalt!* Where were our wits?

Ah, if I had only followed your advice, dear wife! I would now be in a position of thumbing my nose at the world three times over. Even Brodsky wouldn't be my equal. But plainly it must be the will of God. Quite likely the right hour hasn't struck yet for me. It's my luck that my broker, long life to him, doesn't ask me for the few rubles that I owe him on my account. On the contrary, he's sorry for me. He told me that when times will get better he may be able to throw some good tips my way so that I should be able to earn a ruble or two.

In the meantime, there's nothing I can do. Today it's corpses and not speculators that are walking around the Exchange. The brokers are all idle, it's dark and bitter everywhere you turn. Speculation, they say, is all but dead, and won't be able to get up again, not even on the Day of the Resurrection! There's simply nothing to turn to. If I had just a little cash I'd be able to get by one way or another, and I'd wait until the bad times are over. For how do they say? "The sky hasn't fallen down on the earth yet."

How foolish to give up hope! My heart tells me that before long there'll be plenty to do, because God lives and Yehupetz is a city. If not this, it'll be that! But my one worry is: where will I get some jinglers? How does your mama say? "If you've got no fingers you can't thumb your nose!"

I've asked several people about a small loan for a short time but they swore to me that there is hardly any cash in the city now. Even the richest are tight in money. People simply stretch out on all fours begging for a groschen.

Oh, if the blessed God would *epis* perform a miracle with me! Robbers should fall on me and kill me or I should die, just so, while walking on the street, because dear wife, I can no longer bear it all! Funny, isn't it! My financial position was already so secure, I had, as they say, "a full cap," and suddenly—there you have it!

Because I feel very downhearted I'm cutting short my letter. God willing, in my next letter I'll write you everything in detail. For the present, may God keep us in health and prosperity. Write me what the children, long life to them, are doing and how your health is. Give my hearty regards to each one separately: to your father and mother and to everybody else.

Your husband,
Menachem-Mendel

P.S. Good that I have reminded myself! The world has a saying that after a fire one gets rich. What I mean to say is that after the disaster we've gone through one should be able to do golden business. You can pick up everything for almost next to nothing, you can buy the finest stocks for practically no money. I can predict that anybody who will now go to St. Petersburg or Warsaw to buy *epis* he can make a fortune! When all is said and done, I think I have a right to boast that I understand this game through and through. To be able to speculate on the Exchange you've got to have three things: brains, luck, and money. As for brains, blessed be the Lord, I have as much as all the other speculators here have. Luck, of course, is for God to distribute. And money? Money is in the pocket of Brodsky!

The above-mentioned

IV

(Sheine-Sheindel in Kasrilevke writes to her husband Menachem-Mendel in Yehupetz.)

To my worthy dear husband, the rich, the famous, the wise, the learned Menachem-Mendel, may his light never grow dim!

First of all, I wish to inform you that, God be praised, we are all in the best of health. God grant that you are the same, and may we further hear of no worse.

Secondly, I'm writing you, dear husband, that although I really should be writing a lot to you I have nothing to say. What is there to say? What would I get out of it if I were to tell you what's in my heart and thus bury you alive, God forbid? Would it help me any? You know very well I'm not *Blumeh-Zlateh* who is a husband-eater. Don't be afraid, I'm not going to eat you up! I'm not going to say one cross word, not even clack my tongue. But one thing I do want to ask you, may apoplexy strike my enemies' bones! Go ahead and tell me if I didn't warn you beforehand that this was just the way it would end? You say if I didn't write you all the time: "I'm telling you, Mendel, run away from Yehupetz as from a fire!" Of what good are rags and paper shares to you, I ask you? As mama says, "Stay at home so you won't wear out your boots!"

So did you listen to me? So you got stuck like a nail in Yehupetz! Why, he's ready to break his neck for those fine creatures over there! Oh, may they break their necks for you and for me and for all of us and for all Israel! Believe me, I wouldn't be the one to go on all fours before them for a loan, better let God give them easy sickness with May fever for a whole year! How does my mother, long life to her, say? "Better beg of God than of the most generous person."

Really, you surprise me very much, Mendel! You know better than I what the holy books say: "He who lives by violence shall die by violence!" So why do you write such foolishness? Don't you know that everything comes from God? You yourself see how the Master of Creation is carrying on with you in order to teach you a lesson not to lust after easy songbirds in Yehupetz! A Jew has got to work hard, has got to live by the sweat of his brow, and has got to earn bread for his wife!

Just take a look at Nechemiah! He is a decent young fellow and knows what's written in the holy books, too, may I have such a good year! And just the same, see how he knocks himself out running around to all the fairs! He goes everywhere on foot and slaves away like a horse. Maybe he too would prefer to do what you are doing, walk all over Yehupetz swinging his cane? Maybe he too would rather not put his hand into cold water, would prefer to trade in papers, go sleigh-riding to Boiberik, and, just like you, watch the Yehupetzer ladies play that fine game, Ferdel-Merdel? But too bad—he can't do that! He's got a wife at home and her name is Blumeh-Zlateh. And whenever Blumeh-Zlateh throws a look at Nechemiah he loses his tongue. He knows already what she means. Nu, so just let him try to return home from Yarmelinetz and not bring her a little coat, a little hat, a little parasol (oy, may she not enjoy all those things, oy, may she have *tzoress* and get apoplexy in her heart, that slut!).

So what am I trying to bring out? That I have to be satisfied with words, just words! You keep on writing me: you're buying me this, you're buying me that—it's all wind and an empty attic, I'm telling you!

Maybe you think I'm just dying for your gifts? I need them like I need a hole in the head—your brooches and your diamonds! I'll settle for them with that I should live to see you in good health. It's hard for me to believe that you're still among the living. Last night Grandma Tzeitel, peace to her memory, appeared to me in a dream. She looked exactly the same as when she was alive, not a bit changed.

That I take as a bad omen, it frightens me! Therefore, I'd like to see you get home and in good health as soon as possible, which is the dearest wish today and always of

Your truly devoted wife,
Sheine-Sheindel

—God'll help!
—Oy, if only He'll help me until He'll help me!

He owes God for his soul
and the butcher for the meat.

HER RICH AMERICAN COUSIN

BY ZYGMUNT SCHORR
TRANSLATED FROM THE YIDDISH BY NATHAN AUSUBEL

Kreindl owns a little store with all sorts of odds and ends. In Kreindl's store you can buy what you can't find anywhere else in town: an odd button, a clothes hanger, a dresshook, a ribbon, a heavy needle, a this and a that and other trifles. All her "merchandise" is contained in a few large and small boxes. Nonetheless she draws her livelihood from it. She dresses decently, goes to the cinema on Saturdays and holy days, and pays an occasional visit to the Yiddish theater, where she gets her money's worth of laughter and tears. She lives modestly and even manages to put by a little something for her daughter against the right day when the right young man will appear.

But what is man? A creature prey to envy!

It so happened that Kreindl's neighbor received one hundred dollars from a relative in America. When Kreindl heard the great news she almost jumped out of her skin. Everybody had a relative in America, everybody received sum after sum of money from over there, got "set up," so to speak, overnight. Only Kreindl's cousin was not heard from.

It was at least twenty years since her cousin went off to America. Very likely, she piled up for herself a nice little fortune, might even have become a princess in the Golden Land! But believe you me, success turns people into pigs. Ashamed of poor relations, no doubt.

Kreindl knew what she was going to do, she'd write her cousin such a tart letter that she would see Constantinople before her eyes! It certainly was lucky that she found out her address.

So Kreindl seated herself at the table, rolled up her sleeves, reflectively rubbed her forehead and wrote the following *megillah* to her cousin in America.

> *My dear Hasheh-léb!*
>
> *I wish to inform you that the entire family is well and happy and I wish to hear the same from you. We searched for a trace of you all these twenty years, especially I, your Aunt Kreindl. I, your Aunt Kreindl, am now old and gray and have gotten a weak head and a sick heart out of longing and looking for your address. And having found you at last after twenty years, I beg you to write me immediately or, if you wish, to cable me. I am anxious to know if you are alive, whether you are married (I hope so, Almighty God!), whether you have any children (I certainly hope to God it's so!), and what you've done in America all these twenty years? Also do let me know when you plan to pray at the graves of your ancestors.*
>
> *Much has happened to us in the meantime. I, your Aunt Kreindl, have become (may you never be proven so!) a widow and my little daughter an orphan. May no Evil Eye fall on her, but she is a gifted child! Do send her a trifle for her birthday.*
>
> *I also wish to inform you that Aunt Lifsheh died and her daughter, that is your cousin, has risen high in the world. Her husband is an official in an insurance company and he is making out. (May it not happen any worse to all Jews!)*
>
> *Your Uncle Mottel is on his feet at last and is a dealer in sunflower seeds. (May I have what he loses in bad debts alone!)*
>
> *Zlateh, you know Zlateh who went from house to house selling kerosene, well she's now making her own kerosene. People say she's got naphtha tanks in Borislav and one tank, so the wags say, she wears on her hat. (May no worse happen to all Jewish daughters!)*
>
> *Bernard, whom you knew when he was just a little drip-nose, is an engineer and will soon graduate from Polyclinic.*
>
> *Only Genendl's daughter—pardon me for mentioning it—is a loose woman and lies in every gutter. She, as well as her family, is doing well and should you hear to the contrary, don't you believe it!*
>
> *I greet and kiss you, also my little daughter greets and kisses you. Do send her a trifle for her birthday!!!*
>
> *Your devoted Aunt Kreindl*

Weeks and even months went by, yet Kreindl's cousin wasn't heard from. Kreindl wrote one letter after another. She registered them to make sure they were being received. In every one of them she begged Hasheh-*léb* to send her orphaned daughter a trifle for her birthday, just to show her that she had her in mind. She could send her anything she pleased—something for her trousseau, or a contribution to her dowry—it did not matter what. Also, let no one tell her that things were going badly with her and her orphan. God be praised, she was doing very well indeed and she mustn't believe contrary reports.

After fifteen months a postcard arrived. Aunt Kreindl became confused with joy. She burst into tears, embraced and kissed her daughter, and thanked Almighty God that he had at last sent redemption to her and hers. She put on her spectacles and went to the window to read the postcard from America. It read:

> *Dear Aunt Kreindl!*
>
> *This is to inform you that I have received all of your ninety-five letters and postcards, and also twenty-six cablegrams. You must forgive me for not answering you. My poor head was turned with troubles, and even now I'm burdened with them. Since I see from your letters and telegrams (which must have cost you a fortune!) that you're well off, I therefore implore you, dear Aunt Kreindl, to have God in your heart and help me. Things go very badly with me here in America and I'm going out like a candle. Have pity on me, I beg you, send me whatever you can and as much as you are able. The rest you can collect from among the other relatives who, as you have informed me so often, are well off, God be praised!*
>
> *I'll always cherish your memory for this lovingkindness and may God reward you for your good heart!*
>
> *I greet you, dear Aunt Kreindl, and I greet your gifted daughter, my cousin, and congratulate her on her birthday from the bottom of my heart.*
>
> *Your poor Hasheh*

When she reached the end of the postcard Aunt Kreindl fell in a dead faint.

RUINED BY SUCCESS

BY MOISHE NADIR (ISAAC REISS)
TRANSLATED FROM THE YIDDISH BY NATHAN AUSUBEL

Veveh Ribel, a man of—how should I know? Let's say he was forty-five years old. Well, he opened a delicatessen store. The store was tiny, shabby, almost like Veveh himself. There was only one difference. Veveh himself looked much more delicate than his delicatessen, and a lot younger besides.

From all this we have said here one can easily understand that Veveh Ribel was not a fictional character but a living person. If he had been invented, how would we have known that his name was Veveh? And how would we have known that he was short and anemic-looking?

When Veveh Ribel opened his delicatessen for business, with all its fine summer flies, sharpened knives, dill pickles, and the large pot of mustard, he emerged from behind the counter in his white apron that looked like ironed innocence although a bit wrinkled. He took a good look around him at his new business, his wonderful business! And since Veveh Ribel, besides having a business with mustard, dill pickles, and delicatessen, also had a wife, he said to her:

" 'T sparkles!"

Having made this approving remark he moved several steps backwards, the better to take in the whole store with the happy future it promised for him. And as he looked he became lost in thought.

"What are you thinking about, Veveh?" asked his wife.

"I'm thinking that something is still missing to make the store look perfect."

"F'r instance what, Veveh?"

"We should put in the window a *husha*[1] flowers and wish ourselves luck in our new business."

"You mean with the word 'Success' on it?"

"Sure, with 'Success'!"

"With blue ribbons?"

"With blue ribbons."

"And how much should it cost, Veveh?"

"About fifteen dollars."

"Do you think we've got to have it, Veveh?"

"Of course we've got to have it!" snapped Veveh, a little angrily because his wife didn't understand what was needed for a business, especially for a delicatessen store.

The following morning the boy from the florist's came dragging in a huge wreath for fourteen dollars. It was in the form of a horseshoe. In the center, spelled out in the language of cotton roses, was the word SUCCESS!

---

[1]*Husha is a New York Yiddish corruption of "horseshoe."*

"So we already got good-luck wishes, too!" said Veveh gleefully to his Vevehche. "And the store—'t sparkles! You can see yourself in it like a mirror. Now all we need is a lot of customers and 't'll be all right."

"That's what I think too, Veveh," said his wife. "Shall I put the mustard in another place?"

"Leave the mustard alone! Let it stand where it stands. Don't touch it, and don't start up with it!"

"All right! Stop yelling so, Veveh."

"Who's yelling? I'm just telling you not to monkey with the mustard. We put it down, so let it stand!"

"Who is moving the mustard?"

"Of course you're not moving the mustard, but didn't you just say you wanted to? 'T looks as if you can't stand that the mustard should be in one spot."

Veveh didn't speak to his wife directly, but to the mirror, just like a barber when he talks to a customer. At the same time he saw in the mirror the reflection of the wreath which stood in the window with the word SUCCESS on it.

"A beautiful wreath, I should live so! Good as gold!" thought Veveh into the mirror. He caressed the folds of his apron and thought that he looked like a regular delicatessen man that had already been in the delicatessen business for God knows how many years! And the word SUCCESS was very good for the business too! A delicatessen business likes it very much if you wish it SUCCESS.

One day passed, then two and three, and still Veveh didn't earn anything. Everything was good and fine and marvelous, but earn any money he didn't. That was because there was no one from whom to earn. No customers entered the store, although the word SUCCESS shrieked from the window with a scarlet scream.

On the fifth day, Veveh looked into the mirror and saw that he was wearing an apron that looked like a legend of once-upon-a-time whiteness. His eyes looked so sad, clouded over.

"Bitter!" he muttered to the reflection of his wife who was standing on guard over the pot of mustard. "Bitter! You can't even see a living customer!"

" 'T's not good!" agreed his wife from the depth of the mirror.

"I see SUCCESS is already dried up!" commented Veveh. "The letters are already good and dusty and faded from the sun," said he, "and we've got to get a new SUCCESS. 'T's not nice for the customers to let stand such an old SUCCESS in the window!"

"Nu, so let's buy a new SUCCESS," agreed his despondent wife, her sleepy face looking dejectedly at him through the mirror.

"I *takkeh* have got to go out right away and buy a new SUCCESS!" said Veveh, and he gave a deep, deep groan.

A few hours later there stood in Veveh Ribel's delicatessen show window a new flower husha with the magic word SUCCESS in bright cotton roses.

Just the same no customers came to eat in Veveh's delicatessen. And the weeks paraded by, one after another, like soldiers in a row.

Still Veveh did not earn any money. How could he earn any when there was no one from whom to earn? No one entered his store because the neighborhood was a strictly anti-delicatessen neighborhood, and because Veveh was altogether a bad businessman. The little money that they still had went away on hushas. Almost every week they put out a new one wishing themselves SUCCESS.

"What's to be done?" asked Veveh of his wife's reflection. (Looking in the mirror had already become a fixed habit with him. His wife existed for him only in her mirrored reflection.)

" 'T's bad!" agreed his wife.

"Bad? That's putting it too mildly," sighed Veveh. " 'T's bitter as gall!"

"You know the collector will soon come for the rent."

"And the lox man should be here any day."

"And how about the man from the pickles?"

"And from the mustard?"

"And from the pastrami?"

In this manner Veveh and his Vevehche went over their entire list of debts. And Veveh, the big delicatessen man, who kept on wishing himself SUCCESS all the time, took a quick look at his newest husha flowers that stood in the window and glowed into the street with a flaming SUCCESS. And he murmured with a sigh that was already several weeks old:

"Ah, that SUCCESS—it's murdered me! If not for the money I spent on it, I'd have been able to hold on to the business a while longer. Could be it would have begun to pay. But this big SUCCESS has cut my throat! I've already spent my last penny on it and now I'm ruined for good, for good!"

And as he said these words he bent over his fourteen-dollar husha flowers that stood in the window, and his tears fell thick and fast and bedewed the roses that mocked at him with their derisive cottony laughter.

THE LAST HOPE

BY ABRAHAM REISEN

TRANSLATED FROM THE YIDDISH BY NATHAN AUSUBEL

"If I only wanted to I could go to Chaim Schwartzman; he'd positively lend me a few rubles. He's a good friend of mine; he'd surely, surely, lend them to me. Oh, he's a fine man!"

Layzer would always talk that way whenever things got really bad, whenever the cold winter would suddenly descend on his household and there was no firewood for the hearth, or whenever Pesach would come and there were no matzos, or even whenever a child of his would fall sick and there was no money for the doctor.

When he'd boast about his friend Schwartzman, Layzer couldn't look into the faces of his wife and children. He talked gravely into his beard, as if he were holding counsel with it.

Hasheh, Layzer's wife, would clutch at his words like a drowning person holding onto a straw, and each time he'd talk about it she'd rebuke him bitterly:

"All you can do is talk, but you never do anything about it! Once and for all, why don't you go to see Schwartzman? Put on your Sabbath kapote and pay your friend a visit."

"Ach! Of course he'd lend me, he'd positively lend me!" insisted Layzer. "Weren't we friends once? I'm sure he'd recognize me. What a question! Of course he'd recognize me!"

Then he started a new tune: "You ask how long we haven't met? Well, let's see now, altogether it'll be. . . ."

"Don't keep putting it off, Layzer, but go and see him," his wife would cut in sharply on his reminiscing. "Go! We're dying for a groschen!"

"I'm positive he'd lend us some money," replied Layzer. But, as usual, instead of addressing Hasheh, he muttered the words into his beard.

The mere thought that his friend Schwartzman would "positively" lend him the money if he only asked him for it was dearer to him than the money itself. Why fritter away a fine hope like that for a few measly rubles?

"Let me have a hope in reserve," he'd say to himself comfortingly.

"Nu, so what? Are you going or not?" his wife would nag at him.

"Lend me, he positively would," Layzer kept on repeating his old tune, "but I won't go! Now is not the time. Maybe we'll get along this time without him. Somehow—God will help!"

"Talk, talk! But when it comes to doing anything—!" and Hasheh would sadly shake her head, her wrinkled face would become even more wrinkled, and the hopeless look in her eyes would grow deeper.

But it didn't seem to bother Layzer any. "She's only a woman, that's what she is! Can she understand how important a hope can be to a person?"

What would he accomplish anyway if he'd go and borrow a few rubles from his friend? They'd melt away in no time and again he'd remain without any money, and worse yet, without a single hope. And should a really critical time come, what would he do then? He'd be left high and dry without even a hope! Why, one could go crazy that way!

"I haven't the slightest doubt that he'd lend me some money!" he'd confidently assure Hasheh.

As this point Hasheh wouldn't answer him; she'd no longer be on speaking terms with him.

"A foolish woman!" he'd mock at her in his thoughts. "What does she understand anyway? She understands nothing, simply nothing!"

Many years passed, and in those many years there were many cold winters, winters without wood to heat the house, without warm clothes, and without whole shoes. In those many years there were also many Passovers that clamored for matzos. There were also many times when the children fell sick and needed the doctor. But how could they send for him when they hadn't even a kopeck? Three children died this way, and there was no money even to find a grave for them, because graves for children also cost money. All this and more happened, yet Layzer remained stubborn and wouldn't call on his rich friend of long ago. He'd persist in his old tune: "Of course he'd lend me, but I won't go to see him. He'll come useful some other time, never fear!"

Later on, times grew much worse for Layzer, and he was even more helpless than before. The cold winter moved relentlessly in on him, a child fell critically sick, the clay oven caved in, a bed got broken, his boots no longer would support any patches, the knob on the door fell off and disappeared and so the door remained open while the cold blasts of the wind roared through the house. Dire need clutched at his throat with its cold bony fingers. He struggled to loosen its grip and, in his despair, he again thought of his rich friend.

"Hasheh, now at last I'm going over to Chaim Schwartzman to ask him for a loan of a few rubles," he muttered distractedly.

But in his voice could no longer be heard that tone of certainty that Schwartzman would positively lend him the money. He felt as if something had just fluttered out irrevocably through the open door. It was his hope—his last remaining hope. . . .

I hope to have no other hope
than the hope never to hope.—Moritz G. Saphir

SAM KRAVITZ, THAT THIEF

BY MICHAEL GOLD

"Why did I choose to come to America?" asked my father of himself gravely, as he twisted and untwisted his mustache in the darkness. "I will tell you why: it was because of envy of my dirty thief of a cousin, that Sam Kravitz, may his nose be eaten by the pox.

"All this time, while I was disgracing my family, Sam had gone to America, and was making his fortune. Letters came from him, and were read throughout our village. Sam, in two short years, already owned his own factory for making suspenders. He sent us his picture. It was marveled at by every one. Our Sam no longer wore a fur cap, a long Jewish coat, and peasant boots. No. He wore a fine gentleman's suit, a white collar like a doctor, store shoes, and a beautiful round fun-hat called a derby.

"He suddenly looked so fat and rich, this beggarly cobbler's son! I tell you, my liver burned with envy when I heard my father and mother praise my cousin Sam. I knew I was better than him in every way, and it hurt me. I said to my father, 'Give me money. Let me go at once to America to redeem myself. I will make more money than Sam, I am smarter than he is. You will see!'

"My mother did not want me to go. But my father was weary of my many misfortunes, and he gave me the money for the trip. So I came to America. It was the greatest mistake in my life.

"One should not do things through envy. There is a story in the Talmud that illustrates this. Once there was a man who owned a beautiful little dog and a big ugly jackass. Every night while eating his supper the man would take the dog on his lap and feed it and stroke its head affectionately. The dog would kiss him and lick his face. The jackass watched this for a time, and became envious.

"So one night at supper he entered the house and sat himself on the man's lap, too. He licked the man's face with his rough tongue, and embraced him affectionately with his legs.

"But the man did not stroke the jackass's head in return, or feed him choice food. No, the man was very angry. He took a stick and beat the surprised jackass and chased him out of the house. The moral of this is, do not envy other people's good luck.

II

"I am not discouraged, children. I will make a great deal of money some day. I am a serious married man now and no greenhorn. But then I was still a foolish boy, and though I left Rumania with great plans in my head, in my heart a foolish voice was saying: 'America is a land of fun.'

"How full I was of all the *Baba* stories that were told in my village about America! In America, we believed, people dug under the streets and found gold anywhere. In America, the poorest ragpicker lived better than a Rumanian millionaire. In America, people did little work, but had fun all day.

"I had seen two pictures of America. They were shown in the window of a store that sold Singer Sewing Machines in our village. One picture had in it the tallest building I had ever seen. It was called a skyscraper. At the bottom of it walked the proud Americans. The men wore derby hats and had fine mustaches and gold watch chains. The women wore silks and satins, and had proud faces like queens. Not a single poor man or woman was there; every one was rich.

"The other picture was of Niagara Falls. You have seen the picture on postcards; with Indians and cowboys on horses, who look at a rainbow shining over the water.

"I tell you, I wanted to get to America as fast as I could, so that I might look at the skyscrapers and at the Niagara Falls rainbow, and wear a derby hat.

"In my family were about seventy-five relatives. All came to see me leave Rumania. There was much crying. But I was happy, because I thought I was going to a land of fun.

"The last thing my mother did was to give me my cousin's address in New York, and say: 'Go to Sam. He will help you in the strange land.'

"But I made up my mind I would die first rather than ask Sam for help.

III

"Well, for eleven days our boat rocked on the ocean. I was sick, but I wrote out a play called 'The Robbers' of Schiller and dreamed of America.

"They gave us dry herring and potatoes to eat. The food was like dung and the boat stank like a big water closet. But I was happy.

"I joked all the way. One night all of us young immigrants held a singing party. One young Rumanian had an accordion. We became good friends, because both of us were the happiest people on the boat.

"He was coming to a rich uncle, a cigarmaker who owned a big business, he said. When he learned I had no relatives in America, he asked me to live at his uncle's with him. I agreed, because I liked this boy.

"*Nu,* how shall I tell how glad we were when after eleven days on the empty ocean we saw the buildings of New York?

"It looked so nice and happy, this city standing on end like a child's toys and blocks. It looked like a land of fun, a game waiting for me to play.

"And in Ellis Island, where they kept us overnight, I slept on a spring bed that had no mattress, pillow, or blankets. I was such a greenhorn that I had never seen a spring before. I thought it was wonderful, and bounced up and down on it for fun.

"Someone there taught me my first American words. All night my friend Yossel and I bounced up and down on the springs and repeated the new funny words to each other.

"Potato! he would yell at me. Tomato! I would answer, and laugh. Match! he would say. All right! I would answer. Match! all right! go to hell! potato! until every one was angry at us, the way we kept them awake with our laughing and yelling.

"In the morning his uncle came for us and took us home in a horsecar.

"I tell you my eyes were busy on that ride through the streets. I was looking for the American fun.

IV

"Nu, I will not mention how bad I felt when I saw the cigarmaker uncle's home. It was just a big dirty dark room in the back of the cigar store where he made and sold cigars. He, his wife, and four children lived in that one room.

"He was not glad to have me there, but he spread newspapers on the floor, and Yossel and I slept on them.

"What does it matter, I thought, this is not America. Tomorrow morning I will go out in the streets, and see the real American fun.

V

"The next morning Yossel and I took a long walk. That we might not be lost, we fixed in our minds the big gold tooth of a dentist that hung near the cigar shop.

"We walked and walked. I will not tell you what we saw, because you see it every day. We saw the East Side. To me it was a strange sight. I could not help wondering, where are all the people running? What is happening? And why are they so serious? When does the fun start?

"We came to Allen Street, under the elevated. To show you what a greenhorn I was, I fell in love with the elevated train. I had never seen anything like it in Rumania.

"I was such a greenhorn I believed the elevated train traveled all over America, to Niagara Falls and other places. We rode up and down on it all day. I paid the fare.

"I had some money left. I also bought two fine derby hats from a pushcart; one for Yossel, and one for me. They were a little big, but how proud we felt in these American fun-hats.

"No one wears such hats in Rumania. Both of us had pictures taken in the American fun-hats to send to our parents.

VI

"This foolishness went on for two weeks. Then all my money was gone. So the cigarmaker told me I should find a job and move out from his home. So I found a job for seven dollars a month in a grocery store. I lived over the store, I rose at five o'clock, and went to bed at twelve in the night. My feet became large and red with standing all day. The grocerman, may the worms find him, gave me nothing to eat but dry bread, old cheese, pickles, and other stale groceries. I soon became sick and left that job.

"For a week I sat in Hester Park without a bite of food. And I looked around me, but was not unhappy. Because I tell you, I was

such a greenhorn, that I still thought fun would start and I was wait‑
ing for it.

"One night, after sleeping on the bench, I was very hungry in
the morning and decided to look up my rich cousin, Sam Kravitz. I
hated to do this, but was weak with fasting. So I came into my cousin's
shop. To hide my shame I laughed out loud.

" 'Look, Sam, I am here,' I laughed. 'I just come off the boat, and
am ready to make my fortune.'

"So my cousin Sam gave me a job in his factory. He paid me
twenty-five cents a day.

"He had three other men working for him. He worked himself
He looked sick and sharp and poor and not at all like the picture of
him in the fun-hat he had sent to Rumania.

VII

"Nu, so your father worked. I got over my greenhorn idea that
there was nothing but fun in America. I learned to work like everyone
else. I grew thin as my cousin.

"Soon I came to understand it was not a land of fun. It was a
Land of Hurry-Up. There was no gold to be dug in the streets here.
Derbies were not fun-hats for holidays. They were work-hats. Nu, so
I worked! With my hands, my liver, and sides! I worked!

VIII

"My cousin Sam had fallen into a good trade. With his machines
he manufactured the cotton ends of suspenders. These ends are made
of cotton, and are very important to a suspender. It is these ends that
fasten to the buttons, and hold up the pants. This is important to the
pants, as you know.

"Yes, it was a good trade, and a necessary one. There was much
money to be made, I saw that at once.

"But my cousin Sam was not a good businessman. He had no
head for figures and his face was like vinegar. None of his customers
liked him.

"Gradually, he let me go out and find business for him. I was
very good for this. Most of the big suspender shops were owned by
Rumanians who had known my father. They greeted me like a relative. I drank wine with them, and passed jokes. So they gave me their
orders for suspender ends.

"So one day, seeing how I built up the business, Sam said: 'You shall be my partner. We are making a great deal of money. Leave the machine, Herman. I will take care of the inside shop work. You go out every day, and joke with our customers and bring in the orders.'

"So I was partners with my cousin Sam. So I was very happy. I earned as much as thirty dollars a week; I was at last a success.

"So a matchmaker came, and said I ought to marry. So he brought me to your momma and I saw at once that she was a kind and hard-working woman. So I decided to marry her and have children.

"So this was done.

IX

"It was then I made the greatest mistake of my life.

"Always I had wanted to see that big water with the rainbow and Indians called Niagara Falls.

"So I took your momma there when we married. I spent a month's wages on the trip. I showed America to your momma. We enjoyed ourselves.

"In a week we came back. I went to the shop the next morning to work again. I could not find the shop. It had vanished. I could not find Sam. He had stolen the shop.

"I searched and searched for Sam and the shop. My heart was swollen like a sponge with hate. I was ready to kill my cousin Sam.

"So one day I found him and the shop. I shouted at him, 'Thief, what have you done?' He laughed. He showed me a paper from a lawyer proving that the shop was his. All my work had been for nothing. It had only made Sam rich.

"What could I do? So in my hate I hit him with my fist, and made his nose bleed. He ran into the street yelling for a policeman. I ran after him with a stick, and beat him some more. But what good could it do? The shop was really his, and I was left a pauper.

X

"So now I work as a house painter. I work for another man, I am not my own master now. I am a man in a trap.

"But I am not defeated. I am a man with a strong will. I will yet have another shop. All I need is three hundred dollars; and I will find this three hundred dollars somehow.

"Yes! yes! I will show my cousin yet! I will show the world how I can run a suspender ends shop!

"I will have no partners this time. I will work alone. I will show your mother how a man makes his fortune in America! Look at Nathan Straus! Look at Otto Kahn! They peddled shoelaces when they first came here! I have had a better start, and should go farther than they!

"I am certain to be rich! I will make a schoolteacher out of you, Esther! You will dress in a fine waist and a pompadour and be a teacher. Isn't that wonderful, Esther?"

"Yes, poppa."

"And you, Mikey, will be a doctor! You will be what I would have been had I kissed a priest's hand. It is a great thing to be a doctor. It is better to have wisdom than to have money. I will earn the money, Mikey, and make you a doctor! How do you like that? Will you do it?"

"Yes, poppa," I said sleepily.

Hope may give a man strength,
but not sense.

It's a bargain to buy an ox for a groschen
—but what if you have no groschen?

—What is the heaviest thing in the world?
—An empty pocket.

The poor cowherd dreams
that if he were rich
he'd drive the cattle to pasture
riding on a horse.—Heinrich Heine

I'm going crazy from so much hope!

A DASH OF VINEGAR

Ironic Tales

*When the heroes go off the stage
the clowns come on.—Heinrich Heine*

There are many ways of being peppery, vinegary, and acidulous. For instance, when a Frenchman is ironic he is gay, full of subtlety and charming malice. He is *très gentil* as he wounds. But when a Jew is ironic, likely as not he stings, gadfly fashion. His wit has real bite. He puts no sugar into his bitter chocolate. Perhaps the Frenchman's gay irony springs from his robust pleasure in life, and the Jew's cosmic irony from his collision with the incongruities of life. Naturally, his laughter cannot be entirely hearty. It does not gurgle up from the belly. If you wish, you might even call it "head-laughter."

I've known Jews who are ironic in the same way others are asthmatic. It's endemic with them. We might suppose that the circumstances of their lives made them that way. Jews are compulsive satirists and they ironize at the mere flutter of an eyelash. Heinrich Heine, the greatest ironist in literature, was such a one. The Yiddish poet-wit, Moishe Nadir, was another.

Irony is probably the most civilized form of humor. At any rate, it's the most trenchant expression of criticism. When one wishes to be humorously critical of another he is ironic. And should he happen to be a bit of a self-torturer he is likely to turn this weapon of razor-sharpness on his own weaknesses.

I think the following true anecdote aptly combines Jewish defensive self-irony with criticism of others.

Some years before Chaim Nachman Bialik, the great Hebrew poet, died, there was a great deal of talk in the newspapers that he was to be awarded the Nobel Prize for literature. However, in the end someone else got it.

With great indignation an acquaintance of the poet's came to condole with him. Bialik merely smiled and tried to brush off the matter.

"In case you'd like to know," he said, "I'm really glad I didn't get the prize. Now everybody's my friend and feels sorry for me. My, my, how angry they are in my behalf! 'Now isn't that a scandal!' they say. 'Imagine such a thing—Bialik, the great poet Bialik, doesn't get the Nobel Prize! And—tsk! tsk!—just look whom they gave it to! To

*X, that so-and-so! Why he can't even hold a candle to Bialik!' On the
other hand, my friend, what if I had been awarded the Nobel Prize?
Then, I'm sure, some of the very same people who are now so indignant on my account would have said: 'Nu, nu, so what's so wonderful
about getting the Nobel Prize? Why even that poet Bialik got one!' "*

N.A.

BALANCE SHEET OF MY LIFE

BY LION FEUCHTWANGER

TRANSLATED FROM THE GERMAN BY ANITA GRANNIS

The writer L. F. was born in the 1880's in a Bavarian city called
Munich, which at that time had 437,112 inhabitants.

He received instruction from a total of 98 teachers in 211 subjects, including Hebrew, applied psychology, the history of the upper-
Bavarian princes, Sanskrit, Gothic gymnastics and methods of figuring compound interest, but not including the English language, political
economy, or American history. It took the writer L. F. 19 years to
wipe out 178 of these 211 subjects completely from his consciousness.

During his studies, the name of Plato was mentioned 14,203
times, that of Frederick the Great, 22,614 times, and that of Karl
Marx, no times.

In his doctorate examination, L. F. failed in Old High German
grammar and literature because he was not sufficiently conversant with
the fine points involved in unhorsing your opponent in a tournament.
On the other hand, he was highly successful in the anthropology examination, when, in reply to the question, "Into what great groups are
human characteristics divided?", he answered, as was expected of him,
"Into physical and spiritual."

Berlin, the capital of Germany, had 4,872,394 inhabitants when
L. F. was a student in its university. Among these were 1,443 actors,
167 generals, 1,107 writers and journalists, 412 fishermen, 1 Kaiser,
9,213 students, 112,327 landladies, and one genius.

The writer L. F. spent 14 years in the schools and univer-
sities of Berlin and Munich, 5½ months in the army, 17 days as a
prisoner of war, and then later 11 years in Munich. The rest of
his life he lived in comparative freedom.

On 3,013 days he had insufficient means, and on 294 days he
had no means at all. He signed 382 contracts, had 412 conversations
on religious. 718 on social. 2,764 on literary, and 248 on financial

matters, as well as 19,549 conversations on everyday affairs, principally laundry, shaving, and heating.

The writer L. F., in the flower of his manhood, was 5 feet 4 inches tall, and weighed 134½ pounds. At that time he had 29 of his own teeth, with buckteeth in front, and 3 gold teeth besides. He had heavy dirty-blond hair and wore spectacles. He was a good swimmer and a poor dancer. He liked all kinds of seafood, did not care for puddings, enjoyed hot baths, hated dogs and tobacco. He was fond of good wine but not of strong liquor and coffee. He was sympathetic toward vegetarianism and had high praise for the dietary of the Hindus, but in practice was a heavy meat-eater.

There is little doubt that if he had restrained his love of the flesh, he would have reached a considerably riper old age. But in his best years he ate meat from 8,237 cattle, 1,712 game-birds and 1,432 fowls. He consumed 6,014 sea-fish, 2,738 river and fresh water fish, not including oysters, mussels and the like—and all with the greatest of pleasure, though he was often impressed when he considered how much life had to perish in order that his might be sustained.

Germany, when the writer L. F. flourished there, numbered 63,284,617 so-called souls; 667,884 of these were employed in the postal service and on the railroads. There were 40,103 doctors, 856 critics, 8,287 writers, and 15,043 midwives. Of officially registered idiots and cretins there were in Germany 36,461. The writer L. F. had the misfortune to have to do with a great number of them. Three of them are today high officials of the Reich.

In the city of Munich, where the writer L. F. spent the longest period of his life, there were in his last year in that city 137 talented persons, 1,012 above the average, 9,002 normal, 537,284 subnormal, and 122,962 complete anti-Semites. Of the 537,284 subnormal, 8,318 are now employed in high governmental offices or in intellectual callings; of the 9,002 normal, 112 are so employed; of the 1,012 above the average, 17; and of the 137 talented, one. It is a testimony to the unusual vitality of the writer L. F. that he could draw 407,265 breaths in the air of this city without noticeable injury to his intellectual health.

The writer L. F. committed 22,257 venial sins, resulting mostly from indolence and a somewhat phlegmatic search for pleasure. He also committed two real sins. He did 10,069 good works, mostly out of comfortable good nature, and two really good deeds, of which he himself is really rather proud.

The writer L. F. once possessed one house, which was once confiscated. Six times he had considerable property, which 4½ times ebbed away through inflation and once was confiscated; and one citizenship, which he was deprived of. He possessed, when the National Socialists came into power, 28 manuscripts, 10,248 books, 1 auto, 1 cat, 2 turtles, 9 flowerbeds and 4,212 other objects which were either destroyed, killed, lost, or otherwise removed when the National Socialists ransacked the house. The police declared three times that this had taken place at the order of the Prussian Minister of the Interior, and four times that it was done by communists dressed up as National Socialist officers.

The writer L. F. was once married. He saved one girl from drowning, two youths from becoming actors, and six not untalented young persons from the profession of letters. In 106 cases of this sort, he flatly refused his counsel.

The writer L. F. wrote eleven plays, among them three good ones which have never been produced, one very ordinary one which was produced 2,346 times, and one really bad one which, because he did not give permission for its production, was presented without his permission 876 times. In the ordinary, much-played drama, he let a typographical error slip through which completely destroyed the sense of 41 verses. These verses were spoken by 197 actors in 2,346 performances without being noticed by a single one of them, or by a director, or by anyone in the audiences of nearly 1,500,000.

Of the four romances written by L. F., 527,000 copies were printed in Germany. Since L. F. had declared that among the 164,000 words contained in Hitler's book, "My Battle," there were 164,000 offenses against German grammar or style, his own books were proscribed and twenty copies were burned; 943 very bad and 3,248 bad slanders against him were circulated, and in 1,584 officially inspired newspaper articles and 327 radio speeches his books were characterized as poison to the German people.

With the impoverisation of the government, the rest of this poison was widely sold in German editions abroad, in order to bring in foreign money. In this way the officially subventioned German Reichsbank acquired more than $13,000; the writer L. F., $0. The $13,000 did not include L. F.'s bank balances, which were also seized. The bank then further demanded of him that since his house and property had been confiscated he should pay 63,214 marks on account of any future literary activity outside of Germany; and since no further taxes could be levied on property which had been confiscated, it was recommended that he be severely punished for—of all things—"exportation of capital."

The writer L. F. could type as many as seven pages in an hour; he could write as many as thirty lines of prose and four of poetry. In an hour of poetry writing, he lost almost 11½ ounces.

The world made many demands upon the writer L. F. He received 8,784 manuscripts for examination and comment from young writers who were insulted if he took longer than two days to read their works. Eighty-four of these manuscripts were destroyed, together with L. F.'s, when the National Socialists plundered his house.

Seventeen thousand one hundred and sixty-nine persons sought his autograph, and 826 ladies applied for a position as his secretary. He had 202 relatives, 3,124 acquaintances, and one friend. Of his 52 close acquaintances, 22 fell in the four years of the war, and 19 were done in in two years of the National Socialists' ascendancy. Eleven are alive today.

Two thousand forty-eight persons wanted an opinion from the writer L. F. as to whether Christ, Shakespeare, Bismarck, Lenin, Theodor Herzl, or Hitler was the greatest man who ever lived. Five hundred and fifteen persons wished information on how to write; 714 telephone calls came to him from anonymous persons who called him a pig of a Jew; 2,084 questionnaires he declined to answer.

Despite the danger involved for the writers, L. F. received 5,344 letters from Germany by underground means, in which his activity was commended.

L. F. was perfectly happy 19 times in his life, and abysmally miserable 14 times. Five hundred eighty-four times the inexpressible folly of the world pained and confused him to the point of stupefaction. Then he became inured to it.

He knows full well that achievement is not necessarily synonymous with success, and that even if it were, man is not prone to achievement. Hence, if anyone should ask him, "Are you satisfied with your life up to the present time?" he would answer, "Yes. If I had to, I'd live it all over again."

When we know just a few faults of someone else we say:
> *"How well I know him!"*
But when we know many of his virtues we say:
> *"Why, I hardly know him!"*

—How are you making out?
—Like a saint in this world.

THE IMPRACTICAL SCHOLAR

A poor but learned Talmudist worked on his Bible commentary with great zeal.

"How impractical!" remarked the rich man of the town. "Why don't you stop writing—it'll get you nowhere!"

"And if I stopped writing—would it get me anywhere?" asked the scholar.

WITH THE AID OF THE ONE ABOVE

BY YURI SUHL

In the eyes of his *landsleit* my father was a big success in America. "Imagine!" they would say, with the kind of pride that only a landsman takes in the achievements of a fellow landsman. "Imagine! He comes here a poor widower from Pedayetz. A regular greenhorn. Only a year and a half in the country. So he marries a widow with a business and he's in business already! *Nu?* What do you say to that, ah?"

The fact that the entire business consisted of a pushcart on Seigel Street, with a few rolls of faded piece goods, neither dampened the enthusiasm of the landsleit nor restrained their imagination. My father, too, did not want to disillusion them. Outwardly, at least, he even appeared to be happy. "Pinch your cheeks and keep the color rosy," he would say. "Why should other people know what's going on in your heart? It's bad enough that you have to know."

But from close friends and members of the family he did not hide his unhappiness. "Business! Everything in America is business!" he would say with scorn. "Rockenfeller is in business and I am in business. But there seems to be a slight difference. He has the millions and I have the rags. Every day I look all over Seigel Street for Mr. Rockenfeller's pushcart and I can't find it. But mine, thank God, I find every day."

My father could not see how spending the precious days of one's life trying to attract a customer to a pushcart could be considered a "success in America." To him this was a degrading occupation. One's days should be filled with learning and not with watching a pushcart. One's mind should be filled with the lofty thoughts of the ancient rabbis, not with dollars and cents.

"So you hustle away your whole life," he would say, with a thoughtful nod of the head, "and all you have to show for it is a bank book. So when you are six feet underground, can you tell the worms: 'Easy there. Don't eat me so fast. I'm not just anybody around here. I got money in the bank.' Or, a hundred and twenty years from now you can knock on the door of Paradise and say: 'Let me in. I belong here. I have a bank book.' Oh, no. You can't fool the One Above. So that's America. You hustle away this world, and you don't prepare for the next."

For such views my father found very few sympathetic ears. His fellow peddlers on Seigel Street considered them outmoded and even deserving of ridicule.

"He's talking like a greenhorn," they would say.

"A fine state of affairs if Pedayetz is finding fault with America!"

"America," my father would say, bitterly. "Right away they threaten you with America. What would it hurt America if it didn't mutilate your soul so much?"

"Who is bothering your soul? Do with it whatever you want."

"That's the trouble. Nobody bothers with it. In Pedayetz I was poor and my soul was rich. Here I am poor and my soul is poor."

My father soon realized that it was no use trying to convince them of the truth of his words. Nobody even cared to listen. He decided that the least he could do was to keep an eye on his own soul; not to let it become impoverished; not to let the giant jaw of America gobble it up. He took with him a holy book wherever he went; on the subway, on the trolley. Even if only for a brief moment, even if there was just enough time to open it, look at it, and close it again, it was worth it. Just holding it in his hand was worth it.

But when he took the holy book with him to the pushcart, he was carrying it a bit too far, my stepmother thought.

He had already served his period of apprenticeship, when they both were at the cart. She had patiently taught him how to measure a yard of goods, how to rip off evenly the bought portion from the rest of the piece, how to make a reluctant customer interested and an interested one more so; in general, how to get the "feel" of the market, the "spirit" of the business. Although she admitted that his head was more in the clouds than on the pushcart, she finally felt that the time had come for him to be on his own, at least during part of the day while she was busy shopping for the house and preparing the meals.

But she had miscalculated. No sooner had she left him alone at the pushcart than he opened the book and lost himself in it. This had a catastrophic effect on sales. In the beginning she consoled herself out loud: "That's how it is with business. You never know. One day you're so busy you need at least three pairs of hands to attend to your customers; and the next day you sit with your hands folded, you stare your eyes out, the customer looks straight at you and doesn't see you.

After a while she began to complain mildly at the supper table. "Tell me, Chaim, dear," she would say, when the meal was fairly under way, "tell me, how do you manage to keep the customers away from you so thoroughly? I can understand business is bad one day, so it is better the next. I can understand a day of only bad customers. They bargain with you, they eat your heart out, they nag you to death. But you, my dear, manage to keep away from the pushcart the good ones and the bad ones every day of the week. How do you do it, tell me?"

My father had but one explanation, of which he never tired. "If the One Above had willed it I would have had not one sale but ten. And if I didn't have any, then the One Above willed it so."

Against the One Above there was no arguing. He giveth and He taketh. Even my stepmother knew that, although from a woman not much learning was expected. But why the One Above should so consistently pick on so pious a Jew as my father was enough to arouse her suspicion, and one day she set out to investigate the matter.

She took a stroll on Seigel Street and placed herself in a doorway opposite the pushcart. Seigel Street was teeming with shoppers and bargain hunters, peddlers were lustily hawking their wares and waving pieces of merchandise in the air to attract customers to their pushcarts, but my father was totally oblivious of it all. His pushcart was merely a prop for the Talmud over which he kept swaying back and forth, as though he were in a corner of the synagogue or in his own kitchen. If a customer did stop long enough at his cart to examine the material, he would either not see her at all, or raise his eyes for a brief indifferent look, as if to say: "You want to buy, buy. You don't want to, don't buy."

My stepmother walked over to the pushcart and, making believe she was a customer, fingered a piece of goods and waited for my father to acknowledge her presence. "How much is a yard of this?" she said, growing impatient.

My father raised his eyes and his face colored slightly. "So you are spying on me," he said, somewhat embarrassed.

"Not on you," she said. "On the One Above."

Just to show him that it was he and not the Almighty who was to blame for the lack of sales, she stepped behind the pushcart, rolled up her sleeves, picked up a piece of merchandise, and, waving it back and forth, called out to the passers-by: "Bahgens, *veibelech* [women], bahgens!" When this failed to attract any customers, she stepped out from behind the pushcart, raised her voice even louder, and thrust the goods into the hands of the shoppers. "Just examine it, please! You don't have to buy it. I wouldn't charge you for examining. Just touch it with your own hands! If you can find a better bahgen elsewhere, I'll give it to you for nothing. Just feel it with your own hands!"

This tactic brought results and after the third sale she turned to my father and said: "Nu, what did I tell you? If the world says, 'God helps those who help themselves,' the world is not crazy. Customers don't fall down from heaven. You have to drag them over. This is what you call common sense. And a man who is wise enough to learn the Talmud and other holy books should be wise enough to have a little common sense."

My father did not reply in words, but the expression on his face was unmistakably articulate to anyone who knew him. In one hand he held the book and with the other he fingered a piece of material. Suddenly he turned and walked away. Obviously he was not meant for business. The One Above had willed it so. The One Above had even put it into my stepmother's head to go to Seigel Street that afternoon to check up on him and see for herself.

No, my stepmother was no match for the One Above. My father never returned to the pushcart.

*Man's attitude towards great qualities in others
is often the same as towards high mountains—
he admires them but he prefers to walk around them.—Moritz Saphir*

*People do not kill time—
time kills them.—Moritz Saphir*

THE SHORT FRIDAY

BY CHAIM NACHMAN BIALIK
TRANSLATED FROM THE HEBREW BY I. M. LASK

If those who are up and doing betimes on ordinary Fridays deserve praise, those who are up and doing betimes on the Short Friday deserve it far more. There is no excuse for laziness on the Short Friday at the turn of the year! Any sign of laziness whatsoever, and you may end up by desecrating the Sabbath, God forbid. Satan is always sure to be up to his nefarious tricks just when the danger is greatest.

So it is in no way remarkable that the rabbi, Reb Lippe, long life to him, who was a gentle sort of Jew and timorous by nature, began to take steps against the Short Friday long before daylight. He treated himself with the greatest strictness, for he feared and trembled exceedingly lest, God forbid, he might be even a little bit late; for then the entire order of his day would be spoilt.

Nor is there anything to scoff at in the order of Reb Lippe's day. Figure it out for yourself, and scrutinize the items closely. To begin with, there was the *Tikkun Hazot,* or Midnight Prayers for Zion, consisting of both *Tikkun Rahel* and *Tikkun Leah.* (It would take a long time to explain both of these in full, but very briefly, Rahel here represents the *Shechinah* or Divine Presence in Exile, according to the words of the prophet Jeremiah who wrote, "A voice is heard in Ramah, lamentation and bitter weeping, Rahel weeping for her children, refusing to be comforted for her children who are not." Leah, on the other hand, represents the *Shechinah* or Divine Presence which unties itself with each son of Israel through the study of the Torah. Clearly no trifle these; certainly not for Reb Lippe.)

Then came the Psalms arranged according to the days of the week; things to say and hors d'oeuvres before and after the prayers proper; the prayers proper; a few chapters of the Mishna; a lesson in *Gemara;* two or three paragraphs of the *Shulhan 'Aruch,* which gives all the laws for the daily life of the Jew; and last but not least two readings of the actual text, and one of the Aramaic translation, of the Portion of the Week. All this was for the sake of the Lord. And now, how about himself? Food, that is to say. What was he to do, being, after all, flesh and blood! You have to eat, in spite of yourself some times. . . .

A fresh series of tasks began after the noon hour. First the bath; then his nails had to be pared; then he prepared snuff for Sabbath; and the like. To which must be added his decisions, as called for, on questions of Jewish law and life, and on occasion a *Din Torah* or case to be heard and decided according to Jewish law. It is a known fact that quarrels are peculiarly frequent on Sabbath Eves. . . . And what with one thing and another, your day has gone! Before you turn this way and that, the sun's already setting.

So it is in no way surprising, as has been said, that Rabbi Lippe, rising valiant as a lion on the morning of the Short Friday, together with the morning star, hastened to wash his hands and set about his duties at once. Would that he might enter the day and come forth therefrom in peace! He trembled for fear lest a moment run to waste. From time to time his eyes rested on a venerable ancient, laden with limbs and years—the old grandfather clock which hung on the wall in front of him. He very much feared and dreaded, did Reb Lippe, that he might, God forbid, miss one of his daily duties, in which case he would begin his Sabbath without an easy mind, God forbid.

Yet the sages have long since said that all things depend on luck. And neither wisdom nor understanding nor nimbleness are of avail, be it known, against luck. . . .

Give ear therefore and hearken to this tale of woe.

II

Reb Lippe had finished all preliminaries of the early morning, as described above, and was just about to concentrate on the prayers proper, when suddenly his door creaked, and a pillar of vapor, bearing a gentile in its midst, entered the house.

"Why should this fellow be at my door so early?" the rabbi wondered somewhat uneasily, shivering slightly and cowering at the wave of cold which had entered the house.

The gentile stood his whip against the doorpost, took off his gloves, thrust his hand into his bosom, groped about, and finally withdrew from thence and handed to the rabbi a folded missive, crumpled and dirty all over. The rabbi read the missive through and shrugged his shoulders.

One of the devil's tricks! His heart had warned him! The wealthy Reb Getzi, the rich farmer of the neighboring village, was inviting him to be present at a *Berit* (circumcision ceremony). Whereas, ran the missive, whereas he, namely Reb Getzi, was on this day introducing his first grandson, the firstborn child of his firstborn daughter, into the Covenant of our Father Abraham, therefore, on account of the said reason, he honored him, namely the rabbi, long life to him, with the high office of *Sandak* or Godfather. It was therefore incumbent upon him, namely the rabbi, to give himself the trouble of coming down to the village; and to do so immediately. The wintersleigh stood waiting. . . .

The worthy farmer Reb Getzi, begging his pardon, was no great scribe, and no reader could course headlong through his letters. This time, however, he had taken wise precautions and had added three sufficient interpretations.

The first was a new currency note worth three rubles all nicely wrapped up; a "living and talking" bill which passed there and then from hand to hand; from the hand of the peasant to that of the rabbi, pardon the proximity.

The second was a sack of huge potatoes and beside it, trussed, a protesting goose, well fattened. The servant-girl had removed this luscious brace from the sleigh, and they lay in the kitchen.

The third was even plainer and simpler. It was a fine, warm, broad, fur overcoat with felt overshoes which Reb Getzi had sent him at the hands of that gentile, and which came from the winter store of garments of Reb Getzi's own worthy and honorable self, in order that the rabbi, long life to him, might wrap himself up well and keep properly warm.

These three plain interpretations promptly cleared the eyes, as they say, of the rabbi, and his luminous intellect immediately compassed the entire affair.

"Tut tut, what's to be done," he sighed. "Doubtless this is the will of the Holy and Blest One; the Covenant of Circumcision, an injunction of that magnitude! . . . But all the same it's advisable to take counsel with the *rebbetzin*."

Reb Lippe entered the next room where the rebbetzin was, did whatever he had to do, stayed as long as he needed to stay, and came out clad in a white shirt and his Sabbath *zhupitza* (long coat), all ready to take the road. In the first room he now put on, over the zhupitza, the overcoat that had been sent him, tugged the yellow overshoes on to his feet above his black boots, covered the skullcap on his head with his round furskin Sabbath *shtreimel*, girded his loins with the red belt of Ivan the emissary; and so, magnificently arrayed in these garments with their commingling of sacred and profane, Reb Lippe stopped and kissed the *mezuzah* on the doorpost. Then he departed from the house.

The wintersleigh which stood in front of the house was roomy and well bedded with hay and straw. Reb Lippe climbed in and settled himself comfortably, as though he were quite at home. The gentile covered the rabbi's feet with straw and chaff and also got in. He whistled once, and the sleigh slid off across the snow.

III

The road was good and smooth and the mare was lively. Verily a contraction of the road, as described in legend. . . .

Within an hour, and before day dawned, the rabbi had reached the village and the house of the celebrants.

The guests had already assembled. After drinking something warm they stood up and prayed with the quorum of ten according to all requirements of the law. It turned out that a certain butcher, who had happened to come to the village to buy calves, had a pleasant voice and acted as the Emissary of the Congregation. His Hebrew, to be sure, was a trifle out of sorts. He could not quite make up his mind whether he wanted the winds to blow and rain to fall as in winter, or the dew to drop as in summer; but that was not serious. Finally they spat out as is fitting and seemly with the last prayer *'Alenu,* in sign of dismissal of the emptiness and vanity worshiped by the peoples of the lands and the families of the earth. Satisfactorily done with prayer, the order of the Circumcision commenced at an auspicious hour.

The baby in his diapers and swaddling clothes was brought in and passed from hand to hand. The uncle passed him to the father's uncle; the father's uncle to the brother's son; the brother's son to the father's father; the father's father to the mother's father; and so on and so forth till he finished up on the lap of the *Sandak,* where that was done which had to be done. . . . After it was over the passage began in reverse order. They lifted the tiny pink body, tied hand and foot, and wailing and shaking and quivering all over, and sent him back the way he had come: from the lap of the Sandak to the arms of the father; from the arms of the father to the arms of the mother's father; from the arms of the mother's father to the arms of the father's father; and so on and so forth until the tiny mite was returned to the source of his being behind the walls, where he became a little quieter.

And now came the vital issue—namely the feast.

Reb Getzi the farmer is a hospitable Jew, blessed by nature with a friendly eye and a big heart even at ordinary times; and now that the Holy and Blest One had permitted him to live to see a little grandson, firstborn son of his firstborn daughter, he was more hospitable than ever. So it stands to reason that the feast was worthy of a king. There was fish that brought to mind the Bible verse about the great whales. For meat they had a whole calf, a dozen geese and three fattened swans, to say nothing of hors d'oeuvres such as stuffed crop, smooth, velvety stomachs, and breast and tongues and fried craws and other such trifles. And now for the pudding, the far-famed pudding with all its raisins!

Dismissing victuals, let us proceed to liquor. Reb Getzi, be it known, was an ordinary Jew without any particular pretensions and fancies; if he says brandy, it means brandy; that is brandy plain and simple, meaning not less than ninety-five per cent spirit, and right old stuff at that! Meaning? Meaning brandy stored in his cellar for years and years and put away at the very beginning—at the very beginning, mark you—for the first grandson whenever he might see fit to arrive. By all means let the rabbi drink just one glass more, this tiny glass—and Getzi stuffed into the rabbi's hand a fair-sized glass. "Please just this! Please drink, Rabbi! There's nothing to be afraid of! Why, is this brandy? No, it's no brandy at all, it's purest, smoothest olive oil, running smooth into the glass without the slightest splash or sound. Real olive oil! As sure as his name was Getzi! Please, Rabbi, long life to you, long life!"

Getzi the farmer became tipsy. His fleshy, hairy face began to flush and shone like a polished samovar, while his eyes seemed to roll in fat. . . . From time to time he thrust a finger towards his heart, prodded himself and murmured: "Getzi, do you know what? You're an old man from now on. . . . You're a grandpa! Do you hear? Hee hee hee, you're a grandpa. And what's happened to your old woman? Why, she's a g-g-g-granny! . . . Where are you, g-g-g-granny? Come along! Grandpa wants to drink to your very g-good health! Come here, come here, don't be ashamed, the rabbi will say amen. . . . Won't you, R-r-rabbi!"

And at this point Reb Getzi took the rabbi by the shoulder, gripped him with all his strength and shook him like a sack of potatoes; then suddenly fell on his neck and began kissing him heartily. Joyful and happy, he wept and laughed at the same time because of the honor, hee hee hee, the honor which Reb Lippe, the rabbi long life to him, had shown to him, namely to Getzi, by his life and head, the honor. And but for him, the rabbi, long life to him—hm, hm, hm. . . .

"Well, well, that will do! Long life to you," Reb Lippe soothed the weeping Getzi, swallowing a sip very carefully from the glass.

"Long life to you! But why are you crying? There's no need to cry, no need at all. . . ."

Reb Getzi took heart of comfort and wiped the tears away with his sleeve. "You've put it well, Rabbi, as sure as my name's Getzi! There's no need to cry. No need. But long life, and again long life! And long life above all things! That means—real life! A l-l-life with a decent living. . . . Oh, oh, Rabbi," and here Reb Getzi began weeping once more with redoubled fervor, "oh, oh, oh, how to manage to make a li-v-i-ing!"

And Reb Lippe, who was gentle and softhearted by nature, could not bear to watch the sorrow of the master of the house, and did him the last true kindness of drinking another little drop with him, and another little drop, and another little. . . .

Meanwhile the day, the Short Friday of all days, began to decline. Reb Lippe, who had himself grown slightly fuddled, roused himself once and again, and tried to rise on his shaky feet in front of the table. "Ah, ah, ah," he complained, shaking his head, spreading out his hands and stammering. "It's Sabbath Eve! The short day. . . ." But Reb Getzi would have none of this and would not listen; Reb Getzi grabbed both his hands and would not let go.

Meanwhile Ivan the coachman was sitting at ease in the kitchen, likewise doing his heart good with feasting. He felt particularly pleased that they had inducted the little one into the faith, and in his joy he tossed glass after glass down his throat: one, once and again, twice and again, thrice and again, and again and again. . . .

In the middle of this the clock struck three. Reb Lippe started up from his seat in great haste, but his legs were not in any such hurry. After he had risen and put on his two overcoats and more, namely his bearskin and sheepskin, had buckled on his red leather belt and had thrust his legs into those two barrels, namely the heavy overshoes, his legs refused to pay the slightest attention to him. Instead of moving forward, Reb Lippe suddenly found his bulging self sitting down on a bench in the middle of the house. He tried to shift himself. "Eh-eh-eh," he panted. But it was no use. He did not move.

The "oil" that had entered Reb Lippe's bones apparently had done its work. But Reb Lippe did not regret this in the least. On the contrary, he felt very cheerful and good-humored, and while his body, with outspread hands and working fingers, was trying to shift itself willynilly from its place, his voice came chirruping from his throat like a bird, chirruping and cackling!

"Hee, hee, hee, Reb Getzi, my legs. . . ."

"Hee, hee, hee!" laughed all the guests in turn. "The rabbi!"

At length, with the aid of Him who giveth the weary strength, and a little extra aid from the guests, the bulging, bulky body began to move, and the two fine creatures, namely the rabbi, Reb Lippe long life to him, and Ivan the coachman his companion, pardon the proximity, departed from the house in an auspicious and favorable hour; and aiding one another and leaning each on the other's shoulder, they climbed into the winter sleigh in perfect order.

So once again our rabbi sat at ease in the sleigh, his body wrapped up and his legs covered. And once again Ivan sat on the driver's seat. One long and cheerful whistle and the mare lifted up her legs. . . .

And here we reach the main part of the story.

IV

No sooner had the sleigh started and our rabbi wriggled deep into his covers, than he suddenly felt a pleasant warmth, sweet as honey, spreading throughout his limbs. The lids of his eyes were taken captive in the toils of slumber and his head began to nod. "Hee, hee, hee, the oil!" the rabbi silently laughed to himself, feeling, as it were, grains of sand in his eyes, "pure olive oil!" And the moment the sleigh had crossed the little bridge beyond the village, there fell upon the rabbi a divine slumber—and he slept.

At the same time Ivan the gentile was sitting on his seat having a little chat with his mare, just a friendly chat out of the goodness of his heart, promising her, when the time should be ripe, all sorts of fine things for the future, provided, that is, that she would pick her way and not depart from the straight path. While yet he held converse with her thus, behold the whip and reins slipped from his hands, his head under its round sheepskin hat sank into the bosom of his overcoat, and within a moment, there he was, snoring for all the world like any swine.

As for the mare, the moment she sensed herself at liberty, she straightway forgot all the wise counsel of her owner and his promises of delights to come; and when she reached the crossroads she stopped and hesitated for a moment as though considering whether to take this way or that. Then she suddenly tugged at the sleigh with all her strength and by way of compromise turned neither here nor there but straight between and out into open country.

Meanwhile clouds gathered, and day began to turn to darkness while the mare was on her way. Snow fell plentifully; it was coarse and moist, mixing up the whole world and hiding the traces of the roads. Presently the mare, it would appear, began to doubt whether she had done wisely, and even began to consider the advisability of a penitent return in her tracks. But since she, with her mere animal eyes, could see no way of correcting the matter, she placed herself in the hands of Heaven and continued to plod ahead through the gloom, downcast in spirit and lop-eared, plodding silently, as though her eyes were closed, across countless little piles of snow and briar-roots, plodding on and dragging the sleigh behind her together with all that was therein. . . . And who knows where the mare might not have finally arrived had she not suddenly met with some obstacle. But the obstacle once met with, the sleigh overturned. Our two startled travelers woke up suddenly in a heap of snow, and found themselves surrounded by darkness and gloom.

"What's this?" gasped the rabbi in astonishment, struggling to get out of the snow. Suddenly he remembered all that had happened, and felt as though he had been struck over the head with a heavy hammer.

Was it possible, on the Sabbath!

The rabbi wished to cry a great and exceedingly bitter cry; he could not. The whole of his being cowered and congealed in the dread thought of that single word, Sabbath! Yet, when at length the power of spech returned to him, a roar, like to a lion's, burst from his throat:

"Ivan, Ai Vai!"

Within this roar, which burst from the depths of his heart and which comprised the only three words of the language of the gentiles that were known unto our rabbi, there could be found all this: a bitter outcry and a beseeching for mercy, the fear of God and an acceptance of the evil decree, remorse and complaint, and all sorts of other feelings that words are too poor to express. . . .

Meanwhile Ivan stood cursing and attending to the overturned sleigh and tangled reins. From time to time he kicked at the belly of his mare, reproaching her with the transgressions of her equine forefathers and foremothers for a thousand generations back. When his repairs were completed, he invited the "Rabbin" to seat himself again. Reb Lippe raised his eyes to the night; whence was his aid to come? But aid there was none.

For a moment he thought that he would not budge hence. Here in the field let him stay, and here in the field let him celebrate the Sabbath. Let him be slain rather than transgress! Were there then so few tales of pious men and men of righteous deeds who had hallowed the seventh day in forests and deserts? Why, for example, there was the tale of Ariel the lion-angel! Hadn't the Holy and Blest One sent yonder pious one a lion in the desert to guard him until the *Habdalah* ceremony, and for riding upon after the *Habdalah?* . . . Yet when Reb Lippe looked round him at the darkness once again, his courage died away. Towards the left his eye could distinguish a real kind of forest, a forest dark and dire with dread, filled with noise and the howlings of the tempest; and we know by tradition that even an ordinary forest must be regarded as potentially perilous, containing robbers and wild beasts. . . . And to the right—why, there was bare, desolate, open country, all shrouded in white. Out of the snow rose and thrust themselves all kinds of half-shapes and lumps in which black and white were mingled and which looked like tombstones in the graveyard. His Blessed Name alone knew what those queer things might be: devils, wild beasts, dead men—or just plain briars and brambles. . . . From every side through the darkness there massed to leap upon him whole legions of ounces and pards and basilisks. . . .

"Nay indeed!" Reb Lippe changed his mind. "A matter of life sets the Sabbath aside! 'And live according to them,' it is written; we are not required to die for them; and miracles are not to be counted on. Anyway, who knows whether I am worthy of having a miracle done for my sake. . . ."

And now Reb Lippe could clearly recognize a huge ounce or pard, huge and exceedingly dreadful, which stood facing him, sending sparks flying toward him out of its phosphorescent eyes, and gnashing cruel, crooked fangs at him. Reb Lippe's flesh began to creep, and his eyes all but bulged from their sockets. . . .

"Nay indeed and nay again!" Reb Lippe decided the question once for all in very fear of death as he clambered back into the sleigh. "In all full truth, according to the deepest intention of the law, I am in no way called upon to sacrifice my life for this thing. Rather the reverse! Travel on the Sabbath is not prohibited in the Five Books of the Torah; it is one of 'their' later supplements. Refraining from labor—and, as to that. . . ."

By this time Reb Lippe found himself sitting right within the sleigh. But still he tried, sighing and moaning and groaning, to seat himself there uncomfortably, in an unnatural sort of way to prove the urgency of the case. The sleigh made its smooth way through the darkness, while Reb Lippe began whispering to himself the service for the Inauguration of the Sabbath, and his heart felt broken and degraded.

May it ne'er befall you, all ye who use the roads! That winter's night was as long and uneventful for Reb Lippe as any jubilee of years. The poor mare was already weary and walked on without any more strength within her. The sleigh bumped on the uneven surface of the ground and set the shaken body of Reb Lippe dancing. His bones were all but shaken out of him along the road. The trees of the forest, grave old ancients, with broad snow-burdened branches, passed before his eyes in silent reproach and great wrath. Thickets of dwarf oaks, the little folk of the forest, stared gaping with their pointed heads under their snow-caps and wondered in astonishment who and what this Reb Lippe might be, this Rabbi of the Town and Master of the City, whose heart had led him to travel on the Sabbath day. Thorns and briars bowed their faces to the ground in shame, and the wind in the weeping willows sorrowed and wailed and howled: oh and woe for the profanation of the Name, and oh and woe for the shaming of the Torah!

V

At about midnight the sleigh finally reached an inn standing lonely by the wayside, sunk up to its windows in the snow. The mare was covered with lather and white frost, weary to death, while the travelers were all but falling to pieces. The beard, earlocks, moustache, and overcoat-top of the rabbi had become one solid piece of glass. There could be no question of traveling beyond this point. The hostler of the inn, an old gentile, came out to them. The rabbi entered the inn and the sleigh disappeared into the courtyard.

The room which the rabbi entered was inhabited by a desolate chill and the mournful gleam of a sooty lantern. From the neighboring room came the snoring of the family. On the table stood two brass candlesticks in which the candles had burnt out, and on the thick homewoven linen tablecloth were scattered crumbs, dishes, and bones, the relics of a Sabbath meal. Reb Lippe turned his head away so as not to look at them. Frozen almost into one lump and burdened with his heavy clothes, he flung himself down, while yet there was life in him, on a hard, bare bench next to the wall, and buried his head in the bosom of his overcoat.

Yes, that's how it was. He, the rabbi, had profaned the Sabbath. . . . How great and mighty the profanation of the Holy Name! How would he look people in the face on the morrow? And what would he say on the Day of Judgment? Alas and alack for the shame and reproach!

And he wept. His thawing beard and earlocks and moustache wept with him. His head and limbs felt as heavy as lumps of lead. He wanted to move but could not. Has the hour of death arrived, he thought, and trembled with the fear of death. Yes indeed, this must be the hour of death; it was time to confess.

The rabbi's lips, of themselves, began to repeat the words of the Confession. "Oh, oh, merciful and gracious God, long suffering and mighty in lovingkindness and truth. . . . Prithee do it not, have mercy! Lord of the Universe, forgive and have pity, we being flesh and blood, and very worms. . . . The habitudes of a man! In sooth I have sinned, I have gone astray, I have transgressed. . . . Yet these sheep, my wife and my children, wherein have they sinned?"

For a long, long time he suffered from sleeplessness. All his body was washed in cold sweat, yet it seemed as though fire were flaming in his bones. Through his fever he dimly whispered all kinds of strange verses. He combined extracts from the Mishna with verses from the Five Books of Moses, sayings of our sages of blessed memory with prayers and entreaties. Heavenly thoughts regarding such matters as reward and punishment, Hell and Paradise, the beating in the grave and the Angel of Death whirled in his disordered mind in confusion together with domestic affairs; his wife a widow, his children orphans, a daughter ripe for wedding, the rabbinical dues, the communal impost on yeast. . . .

The poor rabbi struggled with all these unhappy thoughts, and moaned and groaned until dawn. Only then did he pass into a hard and uneasy sleep, a slumber born of and bearing with it suffering, bringing with it short, uneven breathing. And so he slept.

VI

Reb Lippe lay in the inn on the bench, wrapped up in his overcoat, sweating and dripping from his thawing beard and earlocks, and sleeping through unhappy dreams. Meanwhile the Holy and Blest One up in His Heaven was engaged in His work, setting the cocks crowing at the dawn, and rolling the darkness away before the light. And once the cock crew, and through the little frost-covered windows there broke into the room the stern, pale, chill light of a winter's dawn, Feivka the innkeeper sneezed, belched, said "Pah!" and woke up. At a single bound he was off his bed, put on his heavy kneeboots, set his short coat round his shoulders and went out into the big room to see who had arrived at his inn during the night. He entered and looked, then stood gazing stupefied. In front of him on the bench, rolled up in his overcoat at length, lay the rabbi, Reb Lippe!

At first Feivka thought this must be illusion and some devil's hocus-pocus. He bent down and gazed again, staring long and thoroughly. He gazed, above, below and from the side. "By my life, it's the rabbi! Himself! Here's that trumpet of a nose and his wizened face."

It seemed to Feivka that he must be crazy. "What's this?" says he to himself. "Sabbath—*and* the rabbi? Am I drunk or mad? . . ." Suddenly he smote himself on the forehead with his fist. "Oho Feivka, ignoramus and son of an ignoramus that you are! There must be a mistake here, and a nasty mistake at that. Fancy getting mixed up as to the days of the week, Feivka! Yes, yes, Feivka, you've fallen in properly, and all the worse for you and your life. You've been living around with Esau, and by reason of your many sins you've confused the proper order of the days. Oho, a nice affair, a fine business, as I'm a Jew. Tomorrow the whole village will know about it. Pah!"

The moment Feivka realized what had happened, he dashed off to remove all the signs of Sabbath from the house before the rabbi woke up and caught him. To begin with, he put away the brass candlesticks, the remains of the Sabbath meal, and the white tablecloth. Then he rushed into the bedroom and brought his startled wife and daughter out of bed.

"Get to work quick, you lazy carcasses, you carrion! Come on, come on, may the plague take you!" he ordered.

"What's the matter, who's here?" his wife started, awake.

"To hell with you, may the earth swallow you up, you big cow; don't raise your voice! Get up at once and take the food out of the stove, quick. . . ."

For a while she could not understand what her husband was talking about. But when a heavy blow of his fist had made the matter quite clear, she jumped up and dressed and hurried to the stove.

"Out with it, out with everything, may the plague take you," said her husband impatiently. "Porridge and pudding and all. Into the waste-barrel with it, empty it all out. Don't keep as much as a sign of it!"

And straightway the whole appearance of the house was transformed. Sabbath departed and weekday arrived. Fire burned, crackling in the wide-mouthed stove. The pot-bellied samovar was stoked up with fuel and began humming. Hammer and axe were heard. Yuchim the hostler was chopping wood and fixing things and knocking in nails where they were needed, and also where they were not needed. Feivka himself had condescended to take up his stand at the trough, kneading dough for all he was worth. His daughter, a tall fat-cheeked girl with a dirty face, who stood confused in the middle of the house unable to understand what was going on, received a couple of boxes on the ear and one pinch from her father's dough-covered hands, and promptly began to peel potatoes into a big pot. "Peel, peel away, the plague take you both!" Feivka urged his womenfolk, while he himself kneaded the dough with all his might. . . . He was expecting the rabbi to wake up any moment, was Feivka; but when he finished his kneading and the rabbi still slept, he hurriedly put on his old, crushed and shapeless round fur hat from the rents of which hung bits of thread, bared his arm, and began to wind his *tefillin* strap round his arm as befits a weekday, and to repeat the morning prayers to their ordinary weekday tune.

Meanwhile the door turned ceaselessly on its hinges and peasants in their overcoats, holding their whips, began tramping in and out. The room filled up with steaming breath and chill of snow and *machorka* smoke, and the smell of the coats and stamping feet and tongues awagging.

While praying, Feivka took particular care to walk up and down in front of the spot where the honored rabbi slept, singing his *halleluyas* in their weekday tune at the top of his voice. He kept an observant corner of his eye on the rabbi while doing so, as if to say, "Sleep, Rabbi, sleep, and may you enjoy it. Now I'm not afraid of you any more. Now you have the right to get up even."

And sure enough, the rabbi chose just that moment to shift his weary body somewhat. "Good luck to you, Feivka," said the innkeeper to himself. "Just look, but don't spoil things."

And at once Feivka vanished amid the *machorka* smoke and the multitudes of overcoats. And from his newfound spot he continued to keep a watchful eye on the rabbi and to sing at the top of his voice, and in the weekday tune, "Halleluyah, halleluyah!"

VII

Now when our rabbi woke up, all his pains and aches woke up with him. "Oh, oh, oh! My whole head is sick and my bones feel as though they had been torn apart!" He raised half his body with great difficulty and opened his eyes. What was this? Where was he? At the bathhouse? No, in an inn. And where was the Sabbath? There was no sign or memory of the Sabbath! Peasants, a weekday crowd. And a samovar was boiling just over there.

"In that case," came a dreadful thought that set all the rabbi's bones trembling and made his purple face even more purple, "in that case I went on sleeping all through the Sabbath and the night of the departure of the Sabbath as well. Here on the bench, in the presence of Feivka and in sight of the gentiles, I lay and slept through a full twenty-four hours. And without hallowing the Sabbath, and without Sabbath prayers, and without celebrating the end of the Sabbath and beginning of the week. Lord of the Universe, what have you done to Lippe?"

Black dread fell on the rabbi and despair took his heart by storm. He all but fainted. God had made things exceedingly bitter for him, too bitter. . . . "And why?" the heart within him cried out. "Lord of the Universe, tell me why?"

Through the cloud of machorka smoke came the gentile Ivan, whip in hand:

"Time to start, Rabbi. The sleigh's ready."

The rabbi rose groaning and turned to the door. He reeled like a drunkard and forced his way between the peasants with difficulty. At the door the broad horny hand of Feivka gripped his own.

"Peace be with you, R-r-rabbi!"

"Peace, peace," the rabbi evaded him and hurried out. "I've no time."

"Peace, peace," responded Feivka after him. "Go in peace, R-r-rabbi, and the Lord prosper your way."

Both sides preferred things so at the moment and neither detained the other. Feivka hastened to bang the door to after the fleeing rabbi, as much as to say, "Bless you!" while the rabbi set his heart upon climbing into the sleigh.

"Haya, Ivan, Ivan," he began to urge the driver.

But what was the hurry? To flee? Whither? The rabbi himself had no idea what to answer to these questions. But just at the moment Reb Lippe was not asking many questions or cogitating deeply. Whatever he was doing seemed to be done automatically, without his knowledge or attention. There was one sole and solitary thing for which his soul ceaselessly prayed: "Lord of the Universe, bring about a miracle and turn the road into a vast length and distance of thousands upon thousands of leagues. Let years and decades pass and jubilees be gone, and meanwhile let me journey and journey and journey. . . . If I am not worthy of a miracle, then I pray Thee take my soul, Lord of the Universe, I am willing to forego everything—but take my soul. . . ."

But the prayer of Reb Lippe went unanswered. The sleigh bore him as though with the wings of eagles, and the polished, smooth road seemed to bound below them. The cloudy night was followed by a wintry sun and the white countryside was bright and cheerful. The ravens picking along the road made way for the hasting sleigh, and welcomed it with their hoarse cries of "Kraa, kraa!"

Reb Lippe was ashamed in the presence of the ravens and in the presence of the shining sun and the white snow. He bowed his head and hid it within the collar of his coat, and once again reverted to his despairing thoughts. And from that point he neither saw nor heard nor felt anything more. He placed his spirit in the hands of the God of Spirits, and left his weary body in the speeding sleigh:

"Let be whatever must be. . . ."

VIII

And at the noon hour, when the congregation left the synagogue and, in all the glory of the Sabbath, was returning home at the sides of the road and in the midst thereof, and when everybody was wishing everybody else a good Sabbath, in that selfsame moment there sped toward them from the outskirts a speedy sleigh. And in that selfsame sleigh—woe unto the eyes that did the like behold!—sat the rabbi, Reb Lippe!

> *It is easier to fight for one's principles than to live up to them.—Alfred Adler*

THE LITTLE HANUKKAH LAMP

BY I. L. PERETZ
TRANSLATED FROM THE YIDDISH BY NATHAN AUSUBEL

After all, it's *Hanukkah!* Therefore, I'm going to tell you how a Jew by the name of Shloime-Zalmen, who had once been rich and lost everything (may you not meet with a like fate!), pulled himself up again with the aid of a little Hanukkah lamp. . . .

And don't make the mistake of thinking that this little Hanukkah lamp was made of gold! Not even of silver! It was actually made of brass, and it was quite broken at that. It was just an old hand-me-down from generation to generation . . . twisted out of shape too, and one of its eight candleholders was broken.

Suddenly Shloime-Zalmen became prosperous again.

How so? This has nothing to do with the subject. Nevertheless, since you insist I'm going to tell you.

They say that once, when he came across a soldier on the street carrying some iron bars, he bought them from him cheap. On coming home, when he tried to file the iron, what do you think he found? Gold! Stolen from the bank, you know.

However, when a Jew suddenly gets rich he turns everything upside-down. First of all, our Jew changed his clothes. He became a "Deitsch"[1] and his wife a regular "Frenchie." She promptly threw away her *sheitel*. Two sons they had, so they took them out of the Jewish *cheder* and placed them in the *goyisher gymnasium*. Then they began to change the appearance of their home. There was, for instance, the bookcase full of sacred works. Who needs sacred works? So they sent them to the House of Study as a gift. The case itself, an old one, they chopped up into kindling for the oven. In its place his wife placed a full-length mirror: all of a sudden she felt like seeing herself from top to bottom! So they called in the junkman and they sold him the old furniture for next to nothing. In place of it they bought Louis XIV antiques, small, charming, gilded, and upholstered, but with twisted little legs on wheels. A pleasure! People were afraid to sit down on them.

Then they had some old silver: little *esrog* boxes and spice holders, which they sold for a fraction of their value or gave away as wedding gifts to their relations. Then they bought fine glassware and crystal, fancy flowerpots and vases, in keeping with the fashion of the world, "modern" so to speak.

And since the world is a revolving planet, before long everything began going upside down for Shloime-Zalmen—with the buttered side down. He could no longer send any money to his sons abroad, was barely able to postpone payment on his notes to his creditors, and nowhere was there the possibility of getting a loan.

Matters got worse and worse. He rummaged about; there wasn't even anything left to pawn. Louis XIV had fallen apart, the fine glassware and crystal was shattered, a few broken pots remained, held together with plaster.

[1]*One who dresses in the western style like a* Deitsch, *i.e., a German, in contrast to the traditional ghetto dress of long* kapote, yarmulke, *and* shtrymel. ED.

So they lived, in dire need.

And when you live in dire need you begin to think a bit about your Jewishness.

Shloime-Zalmen's wife borrowed a *Teitsch-Chumesh*[1] from a neighbor and she'd read it. Now *Pan* Solomon, erstwhile known as Shloime-Zalmen, reverted back again to plain Shloime-Zalmen. Once in a while he'd put on his tallis and tefillin and recite his prayers.

Once, when Hanukkah came around, he had a strong desire to kindle the Hanukkah lights and to pronounce the benedictions over them. Little candles they managed to get. They then went into the kitchen for a slab of wood on which to fix the candles, but they found none, not even a splinter of kindling.

Suddenly, Shloime-Zalmen recalled that long, long ago he had found once an old Hanukkah lamp and had thrown it up on top of the oven.

"Shloime-Zalmen," begged his wife, "do climb up and take it down."

So, risking life and limb, they placed a chair on the table which they shoved alongside the oven. Shloime-Zalmen climbed on top of the heap. The chair wobbled and squeaked, indeed Louis XIV was groaning. But at last the Hanukkah lamp was brought safely down.

It was so thickly covered with dust that they managed to wipe it off only after much effort. Then Shloime-Zalmen began to recite the blessings over the lights.

And this he did every day until the eighth day. However, that last night they'd have to go to bed without supper. That wasn't so jolly! And Shloime-Zalmen sat on one side of the table and his wife sat on the other, and they both fell into deep painful thought. It looked very much as if they'd have to die of hunger.

Suddenly there was a ring at the door. So they opened. In came a young man, an acquaintance of theirs who was an agent for all sorts of things.

"What is it you want?" they asked him.

The agent could barely keep back his laughter. He told them that a crazy Englishman had just come to Warsaw. He was clean shaven, or perhaps it was just a woman in disguise . . . bought up all kinds of broken things . . . in fact, at the very moment he was waiting in the vestibule.

"Let him come in!" said Shloime-Zalmen. "We'll surely find something. After all, I've been a householder for such a long time."

[1] *A Yiddish version of the Pentateuch.*

Shloime-Zalmen and his wife exchanged looks. What sort of old things did they have, they wondered? In the meantime, the Englishman had come in, couldn't wait long enough to be asked in, and then, too, the door stood invitingly open. He took off his fur coat, and when he caught sight of the little Hanukkah lamp he grabbed it up like a hot pancake. He held it in his trembling hands. His eyes sparkled peculiarly.

"Didn't I tell you *meshuggeh!*" whispered the agent.

"Wie viel, wie viel!" chanted the Englishman in German.

In short, they sold the Hanukkah lamp, relying entirely on the crazy Englishman's sense of fairness. They took whatever he offered.

After the Englishman and the agent had left and the couple were alone, Shloime-Zalmen exclaimed:

"Really meshuggeh!"

"And maybe perhaps it was Elijah the Prophet?" added his wife. "He might, you know, have paid us a visit on account of the merit we earned with our lighting of the Hanukkah lamp."

None the less, they had enough for supper that night, and for breakfast the next morning, and also something to go to market with.

The money they got proved really lucky. The wheel of fortune began to turn backwards and up again.

And once more Shloime-Zalmen started calling himself *Pan* Solomon.

When things go well, everything goes well. Shloime-Zalmen and his wife received from their children abroad letters full of *naches.* The son in London had become an engineer, had risen in the world, had got married. He invited his father and mother to come to London and get acquainted with their daughter-in-law.

So they went.

After rejoicing with their son and his wife at home they set out to view the sights of London, first public buildings and factories, then theaters, concert halls, and exhibitions.

One day, they were taken to an art museum. Just try to imagine how stunned the old couple were when in one of the exhibition halls in a glass case they came face to face with their little old Hanukkah lamp! They recognized the laughing lions, the little trees with the birds on them, one of the crooked legs, and one of the half-broken candleholders.

"So he wasn't at all meshuggeh!" concluded *Mister* (now in England) Solomon.

"And it wasn't Elijah the Prophet, either," added *Mrs.* (now in England) Solomon.

To talk loudly, in fact to ask questions, in the presence of their young English daughter-in-law didn't seem quite proper.

So they began to think about it. . . .

Nu, maybe you, too, would like to think about it? . . . .

I never think of the future;
it comes soon enough.—Albert Einstein

EINSTEIN

A PARODY IN THE MANNER OF EDW-N MARKH-M
BY LOUIS UNTERMEYER

> *We drew our circle that shut him out,*
> *This man of Science who dared our doubt.*
> *But ah, with a fourth-dimensional grin*
> *He squared a circle that took us in.*

When some Gentiles talk about
a wealthy man of my people
they call him an Israelite;
but if he is poor
they call him a Jew. . . .—Heinrich Heine

> *Money is a metal shoe elevator for small people*
> *to make them look as tall as others.—Moritz Saphir*

> > *Why the people of Israel*
> > *adhered to their God*
> > *all the more devotedly*
> > *the worse they were treated by Him,*
> > *that is a question*
> > *we must leave open.*
> > *—Sigmund Freud*

> *Any stigma will do to beat a dogma.—Philip Guedalla*

RÉSUMÉ

BY DOROTHY PARKER

Razors pain you;
Rivers are damp;
Acids stain you;
And drugs cause cramp.
Guns aren't lawful;
Nooses give;
Gas smells awful;
You might as well live.

KOSHER CHRISTMAS

A Jewish family had settled in the small New England town, and, as the years went by, they became thoroughly assimilated. In most ways they could hardly be told apart from their Christian neighbors. At yuletide they always had a Christmas tree for their little boy, Irving, who was as delighted with it as any other child in town.

One Christmas, when the boy was six, he was invited to a party given by a gentile playmate. When he got home from the party he was full of breathless curiosity.

"Tell me, Daddy," he asked, "do Gentiles, too, believe in Christmas?"

THE JEW IN HIM

A Jew once became a convert to Christianity. A clergyman began to instruct him in the tenets of his new faith. After several months of close application to his religious studies, his tutor asked him:

"Now, my son, that you already know the doctrines of your church, please tell me whether you have completely rooted out of yourself the last vestiges of your Jewishness."

The convert hung his head guiltily and replied:

"I must confess that I simply can't rid myself of three Jewish traits, no matter how hard I try. I still love bagel with lox, chopped liver with radish, and *oy!* am I still afraid of dogs!"

NATIONALISM

BY KARL KRAUS

> *This is what I so indignantly chide:*
> *You are not the son of my mother.*
> *It remains each nation's particular pride*
> *Not to belong to the other.*

Vanity of Vanities

> *The heart of man may be compared to a wurst;*
> *no one can tell exactly what's inside.*

THE SEVEN AGES OF MAN

FROM THE *Midrash*

Seven times in one verse (said Rabbi Simon, the son of Eliezer), did the author of Ecclesiastes make use of the word "vanity" in allusion to the seven stages of human life.

The first commences in the first year of human existence, when the *infant* lies like a king on a soft couch, with numerous attendants clustered about, all ready to serve him and eager to testify their love and attachment by kisses and embraces.

The second commences about the age of two or three years when the darling *child* is permitted to crawl on the ground; and like an unclean animal, delights in dirt and filth.

Then, at the age of ten, the thoughtless *boy*, without reflecting on the past, or caring for the future, jumps and skips about like a young kid on the green, contented to enjoy the present moment.

The fourth stage begins about the age of twenty, when the *young man*, full of vanity and pride, begins to set off his person by dress. Like a young unbroken horse he prances and gallops about in search of a wife.

Then comes the matrimonial state, when the poor *man*, like the patient ass, is obliged, however reluctantly, to toil and labor for a living.

Behold him now in the *parental state*, when, surrounded by helpless children craving his support and looking to him for bread, he is as bold, as vigilant—and as fawning too—as the faithful dog, guarding his little flock and snatching at everything that comes in his way, in order to provide for his offspring.

At last comes the final stage, when the decrepit *old man*, like the unwieldy though sagacious elephant, becomes grave, sedate, and distrustful. He then also begins to hang his head down towards the ground, as if surveying the place where all his vast schemes must terminate, and where ambition and vanity are finally humbled to the dust.

THE FIRST GRAY HAIR

BY YEHUDAH HALEVI [TWELFTH CENTURY]

> *One day I saw a gray hair in my head;*
> *I plucked it out when thus to me it said:*
> *"Think, if thou wilt, that thou art rid of me,*
> *I've twenty friends who soon will mock at thee."*

LINES ON THE DEATH OF MOISHE NADIR

COMPOSED BY HIS VERY SELF
TRANSLATED FROM THE YIDDISH BY JOSEPH KLING

> *To the memory of Moishe Nadir—*
> *Once among the living*
> *And neatly combed—*

Who did spend two or three hours daily
On the perfect knotting of his cravat,
And who loved his every finger nail;
Loved, and esteemed, and protected
His precious self
From approaching locomotives
And chilling draughts. . . .
Now he lies cold,
And uncombed,
And without a cravat. . . .
And I,
With a smile,
And a bow of reverence,
Place here at his feet
This wreath of verse. . . .

LINES ON MOISHE NADIR—REDIVIVUS

COMPOSED BY HIS VERY SELF

Halleluja!
I sing to you my beloved friend,
Moishe Nadir. . . .

So sad it was,
So very sad,
The thought that you are dead,
Without a soul,
And a cravat,
And all sinful desires. . . .

And now,
Oh, how I rejoice
That you are thoroughly alive again,
And blithe,
And youthful,
And popular with the ladies,
And a brilliant after-dinner speaker. . . .

And how sweet it was
Of your handsome father
And charming mother
To marry each other
That they might bear you,
Their adored son,
Their prodigy. . . .
Halleluja!

Self-complacency is pleasure accompanied by the idea
of oneself as cause.—Baruch Spinoza (Ethics)

Vitriolic Tales

Better an honest smack in the face
than a false kiss.

THE SHOFAR BLOWER OF LAPINISHOK

BY AARON D. OGUS
TRANSLATED FROM THE YIDDISH BY NATHAN AUSUBEL

This happened in the days when the Polish nobility was all powerful, when each played the role of kinglet over his own town and village.

Count Jarszhevski, the *Poretz* of Lapinishok, was an eccentric fellow, capricious and quite mad besides, like all other wealthy landowners of the time. If he suddenly got an idea about something, it had to take place right away. As soon as he uttered something with his *tréfeneh* lips nothing in the world could change it. Many of the townspeople suffered greatly from his crazy caprices, although, to give the devil his due, there were not a few who did very well by him.

He would, for instance, on a whim order Berel the watercarrier to dance a *kazatske* right in the middle of the street and for the amusement that it gave him he'd throw him a ruble. Mendel the bagel-baker often used to leave the palace courtyard with a fine fat coin and all because he had come to entertain the Count, wearing a garland of bagel around his neck and singing *Ma Japhet* from the Sabbath liturgy. If anybody dared oppose the count's will he'd drive him out of his house or order him whipped. Such a *meshuggener* goy that was!

Take, for instance, Moishe-Yossel the *melamed*. He was one pious, upright Jew! In fact, one might even say a pure-hearted, unworldly *tzaddik*. He was also an *uriman*, a pauper whose poverty had no limit. He had three grown-up wenches to provide dowries for and half a *minyan* of smaller fry to feed, but his earnings were never enough for that. So he lived in great want all his days and never could make ends meet. His luck was that he, Moishe-Yossel himself, and his wife used to fast every Monday and Thursday. If not for that they wouldn't have had a crust of dry bread for the children.

It was this Moishe-Yossel who on all the holy days used to sing the entire *Shachris* prayers before the congregation in the Great Synagogue. He also blew the shofar. He had held sole right to this honor for many years.

Moishe-Yossel was already past sixty at the time, but his singing of the prayers and his blowing on the shofar were still as good as in his best days. Especially celebrated was he for his performance on the shofar. His intonation of the prayer *Lamnatzeach*, his *Borchu*, his *Shechionu* were exquisite, but his shofar blowing was really something to hear! He never faltered or broke in the middle of a note, never made an error by substituting one tone cluster in the triad for another. The notes from his shofar issued so clearly, so smoothly that it was a pleasure to hear. And when finally he sounded the long, deep blast, the walls of the synagogue literally shook.

True enough, it often happened that he blew into the shofar so hard that, when he was through, he'd start spitting blood. But a Jew like Moishe-Yossel couldn't be bothered with such trifles. Nu, so what if he bled a little! Have you any idea how much blood a person has?

And although everybody was delighted with his singing and with his shofar blowing, it never occurred to the communal authorities to provide Moishe-Yossel with the necessary expenses for the holy days. They didn't even make him a gift of a bottle of wine or brandy, with which to recite the benediction. People in Lapinishok did not bother themselves with such things, nor was Moishe-Yossel the kind of person to make demands on the community.

This was nothing unusual. The rabbi, the rabbinical judge, and the *chazan*, whom the community was definitely obligated to support, were themselves three-story paupers. Take the rabbi: he wore a *kapote* with threadbare sleeves; the rabbinical judge never owned a sound pair of boots; and as for the chazan, he didn't make enough to buy himself a *yarmulka*.

This neglect by the community was a favorite peeve of Moishe-Yossel.

"There's no lot as wretched as that of us synagogue officials," he used to complain. "Now take the *goyim*. Among them the priests and the choir singers live like princes. They dwell in fine houses, eat well, and ride around in handsome carriages drawn by first-class horses. But just take a look at our rabbi, our rabbinical judge, and our chazan! They can't even make ends meet. Furthermore, goyim feel reverence for their religious officials. But Jews take them in a matter-of-fact way. It's all so dull, so work-a-day!" And he often used to say jokingly: "If you have to take a religious post, by all means choose it among the goyim."

Once—it happened to be the first day of Rosh Hashanah—Count Jarszhevski suddenly got a crazy idea to visit the Great Synagogue and watch Jews at their prayers. He entered just before shofar-blowing time, when Moishe-Yossel began intoning Lamnatzeach. The Poretz went forward to the east wall and stood next to the rabbi.

It happened that at this time Moishe-Yossel's heart was full of woe. The season had been a bad one, and most of his pupils in his *cheder* hadn't paid their fees. Also a child of his was ailing, and on top of that his goat had gone and died. That's why, when he intoned Lamnatzeach, it was with such deep emotion that he could have melted a stone. The Poretz himself was so moved by it that he stood motionless, holding his breath.

Finally, when the time came for Moishe-Yossel to blow the shofar, a holy silence fell on all, on the Count as well as on the worshipers.

Moishe-Yossel took his place in the pulpit. He was dressed awesomely in his white kittel, the pious man's shroud, and his tallis was wrapped around his head. And, when he pronounced the benediction, *Lishmo Kol Shofar,* the candelabra on the ceiling literally trembled.

Then he began to blow the shofar, winding up every brief declamatory statement with a piercing blast, so that it sounded as though the Heavenly Hosts were singing "Hosanna."

The Poretz was enchanted by this Jewish ceremony. He stood with mouth agape until after the last tone, which Moishe-Yossel produced so flawlessly and sustained so long that the Count was simply amazed. He ran up to the pulpit and said to Moishe-Yossel:

"Moshke, tomorrow at noon I want you to come to my palace, in the same clothes you're wearing now and with your shofar! I want you to perform this ceremony, exactly as you did it just now, for my family and the guests."

Everybody was thunderstruck by the Count's command. Moishe-Yossel stood stunned, unable to move a limb. All the worshipers in the synagogue were pale and trembling and looked mutely at Moishe-Yossel. Such an outrageous blasphemy hadn't been heard of since the Destruction of the Temple in Jerusalem by Titus—to use the Heavenly Mysteries for the entertainment of drunken goyim, and on Rosh Hashanah too!

The Poretz left the synagogue, entered his carriage, and rode off. Immediately a wild tumult broke out in the synagogue. But the rabbi rose up sternly and ordered that the recitation of the *Mussaf* prayers be begun. After the service they'd hold a meeting and then decide what to do about it.

During the Mussaf prayers, Moishe-Yossel was dissolved in tears, imploring Heaven for aid. He was so spent and broken at the end that they had to half-carry him home.

The services over, all the dignitaries went to confer with the rabbi at his house. But they couldn't find any means by which to make the Count withdraw his decree: everybody knew that he never changed his mind in such matters. And, inasmuch as they were certain that were Moishe-Yossel to fail to make his appearance at the palace the Count would order him to be whipped and he might, God forbid, die yet, therefore the rabbi gave Moishe-Yossel rabbinical sanction to blow the shofar for the Poretz, everything being permitted when life itself is endangered.

Before noon the following morning on the second day of Rosh Hashanah, Moishe-Yossel started out for the Count's palace dressed in his kittel and tallis with the shofar under his arm. Before he left, the rabbi blessed him in the synagogue.

"Reb Moishe-Yossel," he said, "you are now like one of the Ten Martyrs whom they led before the Roman tyrant. Go, and may God be with you!"

The sound of lamentation arose in the synagogue, and the cries of Moishe-Yossel himself pierced the Seventh Heaven.

Almost the entire town accompanied Moishe-Yossel to the gates of the palace and stood there waiting for him to come out again. Most of the pious were afraid that, because of his fright and grief, Moishe-Yossel wouldn't be able to blow the shofar properly, and God forbid, that dog of dogs, the Poretz, might have him whipped. So they stood in a nearby field, intoned the Psalms, and prayed to God for Moishe-Yossel's protection.

The poor melamed was led into the great hall where the Poretz, his family, and his invited guests, were assembled. Then the Poretz ordered him to sing the prayers and blow the shofar exactly the way he did it the day before in the synagogue.

With a broken heart, crushed and meek, Moishe-Yossel intoned Lamnatzeach. He fervently uttered the blessing recited before blowing the shofar, and because he felt certain that he was treading the martyr way to "Glorify His Name," he blew upon the shofar as he had never blown before—in one breath, so to speak.

When he had finished, the Count and all the assembled cried, "Bravo!" and applauded him.

When Moishe-Yossel left the palace, his fellow townsmen saw him come out weeping. His wife and children ran towards him with outcries of joy just as if he were coming back from the other world.

"Moishe-Yossel! . . . *Tattele!*" they cried and threw themselves on his neck.

Moishe-Yossel drew his wife to his breast and sobbed like a child.

"What are you crying for?" asked his wife. *"Narrele,* better thank Him who endures forever that you came through that ordeal unhurt."

"Narrele yourself! It's for joy I'm crying. I thank and praise the Almighty for it."

And thus saying, he put his hand into his pocket and took out a bag of money.

"Look at this, wife!" said he tearfully. "For forty years I led the prayers and blew the shofar for Jews, and what did I get out of it? Nothing! And here, just once, for a few minutes I blew shofar for a goy, and what does he do but gives me three hundred rubles! Enough for the dowries for our three daughters! What did I always tell you? If you've got to blow the shofar blow it for the goyim!"

There are tears of grief and tears of joy,
but I've yet to see someone
whose eyes have grown red
from tears of joy.—Moritz G. Saphir

WHY THE RICH GIVE ALMS

The Preacher of Dubno was once asked why it was that a rich man would sooner give alms to a blind man or to a cripple than to a needy scholar.

"If the rich man prefers to aid a cripple or a blind man," explained the Preacher, "it is because of selfishness. Seeing them, he is frightened at the thought that he himself might someday become a cripple or blind. So he gives them alms, but actually he gives it to himself. On the other hand, why should he give aid to a poor scholar? He knows very well that not even when the dead will rise again can he ever hope to become one himself!"

THE PIOUS CAT

BY I. L. PERETZ

TRANSLATED FROM THE YIDDISH BY NATHAN AUSUBEL

One after another they bought three canaries, and all three of them, one by one, the cat ate up.

This was no ordinary cat, to be sure, but a really pious soul! That is why she wore the traditional Jewish white jacket and had limpid eyes in which the sky was mirrored.

So pious was the cat that she'd wash herself ten times a day. And when she ate she ate quietly, out of everybody's way, in a corner.

All day long she'd eat only what was *milchig*. Only when night fell would she eat meat, kosher mouse meat, naturally.

She never hurried at her meals like some coarse creature. She didn't grab and gulp up the mouse she caught like a *fresser,* but took her time, even played with it. Why shouldn't the mouse live another second? Let it dance around a bit, tremble a little more, have a chance to recite the Confession before death. Surely everybody knows that a pious cat never grabs.

When they first brought a canary into the room she took great pity on it, felt a tugging at the heartstrings.

"Ach! Such a pretty little thing!" she sighed. "Such a little one too! To think that this delightful creature isn't going to have a share in the World to Come!"

That the canary was not going to inherit any of the Life Hereafter, of that the cat was certain. First of all, when it bathed itself, it was just like a freethinking *Deitch*—plunging its whole body into the little bowl of water. Secondly, once it was put in the cage, it was already a dangerous beast, even though a sweet young singing bird. My-my! Such immoral singing! The way it whistled and the way it stared into the sky without the slightest respect! Ach, how it struggled to get out of the cage, to join the rest of the sinful world, to breathe the free air, to escape through the open window!

Nu, say yourself, was there ever a time that a cat sat in a cage? Have you ever heard a pious cat whistle with such insolent abandonment?

"Ach, what a pity!" lamented the pious cat in her pious heart. "After all, a canary, too, is a living thing, has a precious soul, a spark from on high!"

And the eyes of the cat brimmed over with tears.

"It's quite clear: the whole trouble lies in that the creature's sinful body is so beautiful! That's why its life on earth is so merry, the evil spirit so strong inside of it. Nu, say yourself, how can such a small, sweet bird stand up against the terrifying spirit of evil? And the longer it lives, the more it sins and the greater will be its final punishment. Ha!"

And a holy fire was ablaze in the cat, the fire of Pinchas ben Elezar, the Priest. She leaped upon the table where the cage with the canary stood, and the feathers began to fly. . . .

Oh, how they beat the cat! She took the blows as though they were coming to her, groaned piously and meowed, caterwauling: "I have sinned, O Lord!"

So help her God, she was never going to commit such a sin again!

The wise cat understood well enough why they beat her. From now on she was going to watch her step, not do anything to bring blows down on her.

It was clear enough, thought the cat: they beat her because she had messed up the room with the feathers, because she had left blood stains on the white embroidered tablecloth. An act like that one must carry through neatly, quietly, and piously, so that not even a single feather should fly, not a drop of blood should fall.

And so it came about that when they bought another canary and left it alone in the room, she strangled it in a quiet, refined manner and swallowed it feathers and all.

Oh, how they beat the cat!

Now she first understood that her punishment had nothing to do with feathers, nor with bloodstains on the tablecloth. The real reason for the beating she got was that she had broken the Commandment, "Thou shalt not kill." One must love one's fellows and forgive them their trespasses, and not with "the four kinds of death of the tribunal" can one improve this sinful world. One's got to lead sinners back onto the path of the righteous, one's got to preach to them, touch their hearts. Why, a canary that's a penitent might achieve spiritual heights to which even the most pious cat could not aspire!

And as she thought these thoughts, the cat began to feel that her heart was bursting with joy. She was through forever with the wicked cruel old times! She'd spill blood no more!

Pity, pity, and once again pity!

And thus it was that she approached the third canary with pity.

"Don't be afraid!" she murmured in the softest voice that ever came out of a cat's mouth. "To be sure, you're a sinner, but I'm not going to do you any harm, because I have pity on you. In fact, I'll not even try to open the cage. Why I won't even touch you! . . . Ah, you say nothing! Very good! It's better to say nothing than to sing immoral songs. . . . What, you're quaking! That's still better! Quake, my child, quake, but not for me! Tremble before the Creator of the Universe, before His dear Name! . . . How much better for you it would be that you'd remain so, silent, pure, and quaking. . . . I'll tell you what I'm going to do for you. I'll help you quake. Out of my pious soul I'll breathe into you submission, sweetness, and piety. With my own breath I'll suffuse faith into your body, fear of God into your little bones, penitence and contrition into your little heart!"

Now the cat first began to realize how good it was to be forgiving, what a joy it was to breathe into someone piety and righteousness.

And the pious heart in the pious white cat grew bigger and bigger. But the canary could not endure the stench of the cat's righteous breath—so it suffocated!

> *If you're going to dwell too much*
> *on how right you are,*
> *you'll wind up by being wrong.*

THE DOCTOR DOESN'T WORRY

The doctor was checking up on the health of his patient.

"Fine, fine! Mr. Cohen! You're doing much better," he consoled him after completing his examination. "Your general condition is improved. There is only one thing that doesn't look so good—your floating kidney. But that doesn't worry me a bit!"

"And if you had a floating kidney, do you think I'd worry about it?" snapped back Mr. Cohen.

QUALIFICATIONS OF AN EXPERT

"Do tell me, Rabbi," once asked the president of a congregation, "why it is that a godly man like you is always talking about business matters? Now take me, I'm a businessman, but once I leave my office I do nothing but talk about spiritual matters."

"This follows a very sound principle!" answered the rabbi.

"What principle is that, Rabbi?"

"Oh, the principle that people usually like to discuss things they know nothing about."

THE LAST KOPECK

BY S. FRUG
TRANSLATED FROM THE YIDDISH BY NATHAN AUSUBEL

In a little town named Shmoinevke there once lived Reb Leibele Peltzel, blessed be his memory! And from his time on to this day, not a single year passes but that there shouldn't be born in this little town at least a half dozen pair of twins. And concerning this celebrated little town a certain story is told that's well worth telling.

Once, on a beautiful sunny morning, word got around that in the entire town there wasn't even a single kopeck to be found. On the surface, such a statement might sound like a crazy exaggeration, for how could it be that among an entire townful of Jews there shouldn't be even one kopeck left?

True enough, it happened quite frequently that half the Jews of the town didn't have a single kopeck to lay their hands on, not even a broken groschen, didn't have any flour for *challeh,* nor straw to make a fire with, nor a whole shirt to cover their backs. At the same time, *takkeh,* the tax-collector, ate roast *kishkes,* the Crown Rabbi crunched *crabs* every day and had rusks with his coffee too. And then, how do you think it was, please tell me, with a doctor who ran a *tréfeneh* kitchen, an apothecary with a smooth-shaven chin, a tavernkeeper who played cards on *Shabbes,* and a moneylender who could tell you exactly how many feather beds, pillows, and candlesticks there were in the town? These were the dignitaries, so to speak, without whom apparently even the smallest Jewish town in the world does not seem to be able to get along.

But the way matters stand nowadays, certain things take place in the world which really run counter to all the laws of nature. That is why I'm going to tell you how it happened that if you were to look in all Shmoinevke from today until tomorrow, you wouldn't find one Jew (may such a thing never happen to you!) who had even a single kopeck left in his pocket. It wouldn't do you any good even if you offered a whole ruble for a kopeck!

When the rabbi heard this astonishing bit of news, he first of all washed his hands and pronounced the benediction which is recited on beholding a new thing. Then he summoned the leading householders of the town to an emergency meeting.

The *shammes* dashed frenziedly around the town, like one who had just swallowed poison, calling the people to the meeting. And right after the *Ma'ariv* service, after the first star appeared in the sky, they assembled at the house of the rabbi.

The rabbi first took a long pinch of snuff. Then he coughed, cleared his throat, and said:

"My masters! We can't have any complaints against the Creator of the Universe. Of course, He's always right, and His judgment is always right, and a Jew is duty-bound to accept everything that happens with resignation. Certainly, on account of our many sins we aren't worthy of even a thousandth part of the mercy and grace that He shows us. Therefore, we must recognize that whatever good God, blessed be He, works for us it is only on account of the merit of our ancestors. Especially, my masters, does this hold true with regard to the coming of the Messiah for which Jews have been praying and waiting these thousands of years. Do tell me please: do you think that in the face of our good deeds and our piety and our Jewishness, we should go ahead and sacrifice the Redemption by proceeding to question God's will? One must never question any of God's acts. The Gemara says:

" 'The son of David will not come as long as there is one man in the world who possesses a single *perutah!'*

"Oh, my fellow Jews, offer praise to His dear Name, because in all Shmoinevke today there isn't left one single kopeck! That's a sign that the Messianic Era has arrived at last! Therefore, Jews, get ready for his coming! . . ."

For a little while the townsmen of Shmoinevke sat in stunned silence. What? The Messiah was coming! "Get ready, Jews, for his coming!" That, to be sure, was no small order. True enough, what Jew is there who doesn't expect that at any time he'll hear the call of the Messiah's shofar, the long blast that will resound from one end of the world to the other? What Jew is there who doesn't expect that on the Mount of Olives will then appear the Righteous Redeemer astride his white steed? But for the rabbi to go ahead and say just like that, "Get ready, Messiah's coming! . . ."

"Rebbe," finally stammered one of the householders, "does this mean then that Palestine and the 'Lovers of Zion' and all the agricultural colonies, and—"

At this point Menashe-Mendel, the building contractor, pulled out of his breast pocket a thick wad of papers that was tied up with blue woolen thread. Bringing the palm of his hand down on the table with a bang he cried: "My masters, hold on a while! This very day I've made up the account for the bathhouse. In fact, I even had the intention of asking the rabbi, long life to him, to call a special meeting in order to—"

"Ha? . . . What did he say?" voices asked eagerly on every side. "Account? . . . What account? . . . Whose account? . . . Why is he dragging his accounts into this?"

"Sha, my masters, *sha!"* the rabbi pleaded. "There's something Reb Menashe-Mendel wants to tell us!"

A hushed silence fell on all.

"Tell us, Reb Menashe-Mendel," said the rabbi, turning to the contractor, "tell us what you wanted to say."

"I wanted to say that with regard to my calculation, there's a balance. . . . I mean with regard to my account of the bathhouse, there's some communal money left over!"

"A balance! How much? How much?"

"A kopeck!"

Fumbling among his papers, Menashe-Mendel drew forth a rolled up piece of paper, unfolded it, and laid on the table a kopeck.

Deep silence reigned throughout the room. Those who sat near the table gaped in bewilderment at the kopeck. The young men who sat in the rear eagerly craned their necks to get a glimpse of it, just as if they had never seen a kopeck in their lives.

Finally, the rabbi said to the contractor: "A balance, you say, Reb Menashe-Mendel? Of course you're right: a balance is a balance! But isn't it possible that you've made an error, Reb Menashe-Mendel? You can understand that sometimes one makes an error in a calculation."

"An error! An error! Of course there's an error!" voices cried out on every side. "What do you say to that! Right in the middle of everything he has to drag in his account, his contractor's account!"

"This is really a joke!" cried Menashe-Mendel angrily. "Simply a joke, as I'm a Jew! After I made up my account last year and I reported to you a deficit for the bathhouse, everybody began to yell, 'It's a fraud, it's a fraud! According to his own account we figure that there must be a balance of at least a hundred and fifty rubles!' What? Now isn't that the truth? Yet here when I'm telling you that there is a balance left and slap it down on the table in hard cash before your very eyes, you say again that it can't be!"

Here the rabbi interrupted. "Reb Menashe-Mendel," said he, "I beg of you a thousand pardons! Please don't take to heart what those young fellows are saying. They're fools, they don't know what they're talking about! Et, don't let them worry you! What's important, after all, is not the calculation—the main thing is the kopeck!"

And turning to the assembled, the rabbi said. "My masters, it appears that on account of our many sins we Jews may not yet be redeemed. The Messiah cannot come yet because all the signs which are to precede his coming and which are so exactly described in the Gemara have not yet been fulfilled. As you see, we still have some communal money left."

"Rebbe!" called out Reb Kalman, one of the householders. He was one sage of a Jew! In former years he had served as the foremost adviser in all of the town's communal affairs. "Rebbe," said he, "if what you say is the case, then we've got to consider the matter carefully from every angle and try to find a solution for it."

"Why not?" replied the rabbi. "Say yourself, Reb Kalman, what is to be done?"

Reb Kalman sat lost in thought for a moment, then he spoke:

"Rabbi, it's my opinion that the kopeck should be thrown into the river."

"Into the river!" the young men exclaimed in excitement. "Did you hear that? He says we should throw it into the river!"

"Sha, sha!" rebuked the rabbi. "Keep silent, young fellows! Give us older men a chance to say something! . . . M-m-m. . . . And what do you think about this, Reb Shloime, and you, Reb Avrum-Ber, and you, Reb Mordchi?"

Reb Shloime, a *lamdan,* stroked his beard reflectively, coughed, and then said:

"Into the river? No, not into the river! First of all, it would violate the rabbinic injunction against destroying something unnecessarily. Second of all, what sort of a plan is it anyway to throw a good coin into the river? It's even possible that a pike in the water might swallow it, and it's also not out of the range of possibility that one of us might accidentally catch or buy it. And so again *takkeh,* in this way we'd get back our own kopeck! Of course, you might argue that we're no fishermen and that we certainly won't buy any fish, because where do we have the money? True enough! But we all know that for God there is nothing that is impossible. Therefore, this is my advice: Since we have to get rid of the kopeck, in order to hasten the Redemption, then the sin of destroying something is not so great, and since to throw the kopeck into the river would make, as Reb Shloime has pointed out, no sense at all, better let us throw it into the *mikveh!* You know how it is, there are no fish in the mikveh and no one goes fishing in there. Besides, at the bottom lies such a deep, thick mud that the kopeck will sink right into it and be lost sight of forever."

"Yes, yes! That's *takkeh* a good plan!" many voices chimed in enthusiastically.

"No, dear Jews, no! This is no plan at all!" called out Reb Mordchi Yannever, an "enlightened" Jew, who had for the past fifteen years served as the head of the Talmud-Torah. "That's no plan at all—to take communal funds and throw it into the mud! Let me propose something better. For the last ten years, the roof of the Talmud-Torah has been leaking. Wouldn't it be more just to appropriate the kopeck for repairs? What do you think, Herr Gluzman?"

Reb Shloime Gluzman, the treasurer of the great synagogue in Shmoinevke, caressed his little grey beard and said:

"Of course, you're right, Reb Mordchi. The Talmud-Torah *takkeh* stands in need of repairs, and it would *takkeh* be a just thing . . . but not now! It stands to reason that if the Messiah will come we'll no longer have any need of Talmud-Torahs. True, we won't need any houses of study or synagogues either, but there's a great difference between a Talmud-Torah and a house of study, you know. What's a Talmud-Torah after all? It's no more than a Jewish elementary school, but a synagogue or a house of study, that's a *holy place!* You say that the roof leaks in the Talmud-Torah. Nu, and you think that in the synagogue it doesn't leak? In your roof you have three holes—our synagogue has thirteen! And you can be sure that when the Messiah will come we'll not be able to take along with us either the Talmud-Torah or the synagogue! But to leave behind us a synagogue, a holy place, that's full of holes, that's absolutely a desecration of God's Name! My advice is, therefore, that the kopeck should be appropriated for repairs on the synagogue."

"Did you say 'desecration of God's name'?" shrilly cried Reb Gershon Tchvok, the treasurer of the Burial Society. "No, Reb Shloime, better let me talk! A synagogue is definitely a holy place and is any time of greater importance than a Talmud-Torah! Nu, and what about a cemetery? Ha? The rabbi says that the Messiah is going to come. Very good! Suppose we take out of the synagogue all the Torah scrolls, the *menorah* before the Ark, the hanging candelabra, the Ark curtains and the laver, even all the loose prayer-book leaves that are stored under the reader's desk. So what remains? Just four walls and a ceiling! But take the cemetery with all its graves and tombstones— they'll remain! Now tell me if I'm wrong, my masters, when I say that for the last twenty years the cemetery has been without a fence, and the pigs, cattle, and horses go grazing there and mess up the graves. Now isn't that a desecration of God's Name, and wouldn't it be more just to spend the kopeck on a cemetery fence? I maintain: the cemetery should have priority over the synagogue! Then again, doesn't our synagogue get more income than the cemetery?"

"Income! Did you say 'income'?" Reb Shloime Gluzman asked, starting up. "What do you mean? Don't I give an account of every kopeck the synagogue takes in?"

"And do you report expenses for repairs, too?" a young scalawag asked mockingly.

"Ha? What did you say? For repairs?" shrieked the synagogue treasurer. "And what about the Burial Society and its members— those drunkards, those guzzlers! Do you ever ask an accounting from them?"

"Herr Gluzman, I beg you to put a rein on your tongue!" shrieked Reb Gershon Tchvok. "You'd better not start up, or else—!"

"My masters, my masters!" cried the rabbi. "I beg of you! . . .
Gevalt! . . . Householders! . . . Jews!"

II

That same evening, at the very same time that the meeting was
taking place at the home of the Shmoinevke rabbi, an angelic messenger came flying to the Messiah and informed him so and so, and
of such and such: that in a certain little town by the name of Shmoinevke, all the Jews were left without a single kopeck. True enough, a
communal kopeck did remain. However, what they were going to do
with it was being considered at the rabbi's house that very moment.
You know how it is: Jews (long life to them!) can spend hundreds
and even thousands of communal rubles without even blinking an eyelash, so would they go and create difficulties on account of a single
kopeck! After all, what the Gemara says about the coming of the
Messiah had to be fulfilled!

"What? Not a single kopeck!" exclaimed the Messiah in amazement. "How can such a thing be? How could it happen that Jews
shouldn't have one kopeck left? So the question remains: how did it
happen that an entire community has become so impoverished? And,
inasmuch as for the Creator of the Universe nothing is impossible, and
inasmuch as what the Gemara says must be fulfilled, therefore I've got
to go down and see for myself what's going on in Shmoinevke."

The Messiah then ordered that the white ass be taken out of the
heavenly stable and that the shofar of the Redemption be readied.

The ass, which had been confined in its stall for hundreds of years,
was so covered with dirt and dust that it took a great deal of angelic
effort to wash and currycomb it. The shofar was also so dusty that
for a whole hour they had to soak it in vinegar. Most naturally, having seen and heard everything that went on among Jews during several
thousand years, the Messiah had no idea that he would so soon have to
go down and redeem the Children of Israel. He would never have
thought it possible that Jews could remain without a single kopeck!
No more money, no more Jewish rich, no more Jewish philanthropists!

III

Swift as an eagle sped the Righteous Redeemer on the beautiful
white ass. Through field and forest stretched the long road to Shmoin-

evke. And sweet as the voice of a violin sang the Messiah with the words of the Psalmist:

"When the Lord brought back those that returned to Zion. . . ."

The voice of the Messiah floated over mountain and valley, over field and forest, over river and abyss. The farther he rode, the more radiant shone his face. At last he arrived in Shmoinevke.

As he entered the town, the meeting in the rabbi's house had just come to an end. And it ended *takkeh* just as you might have expected. The conferees were tearing into one another's beard and *payes*, exchanging fiery blows and sizzling slaps, and throwing fragrant curses about like chick-peas.

One was yelling: "For the Talmud-Torah!"

A second: "For the synagogue!"

A third: "For the cemetery!"

The fourth and the fifth and the sixth naturally came to the assistance of the first, the second, and the third. But above all the shouting rose the screeching of women and the weeping of children. Pandemonium reigned in Shmoinevke that day, and the earth trembled!

"I see I've come too early!" murmured the Messiah in confusion.

And so saying, he turned the white ass around and trotted back to Heaven.

VERY FINE PEOPLE

BY PETER ALTENBERG

Fruit merchant: We also have fruit for very fine people!
Peter Altenberg: What do you mean by *very fine people?*
Fruit merchant: Very fine people are those who buy very fine fruit.

HILAIRE BELLOC

BY HUMBERT WOLFE

> *Here lies Hilaire Belloc, who*
> *Preferred the Devil to a Jew.*
> *Now he has his chance to choose*
> *Between the Devil and the Jews.*

You have deprived the Jews of air; they have thus been preserved from rottenness. You have strewn the salt of hatred in their hearts; their hearts have thus been kept fresh. You have imprisoned them for the whole long winter in a cellar [ghetto], and stopped up the cellar door with dung; while you, exposed to the frost, were half frozen to death.—Ludwig Börne.

LOVE!

Love-Shmove

*Love is a sweet dream
and marriage is the alarm clock.*

It is a universal pastime to laugh at love, the institution of marriage, and mothers-in-law. In this pleasurable sport Jews are no exception. If anything, their ironic bent lends itself ideally to spoofing at these sacred values. This is helped along no end by the farcical situations in which Jews sometimes find themselves in relation to the opposite sex, on account of social customs which have survived from the patriarchal family life of former times.

Come to think of it, love, in its modern sense, is of only quite recent origin. Because most Jews were allowed to become latter-day Europeans only two or three generations ago, they discovered a little tardily the romantic passion sighed over by poets. Some dyspeptic authorities on love seem to think they didn't miss very much. Most Jews have only given de facto recognition to romantic love thus far. If they gave it de jure acceptance hundreds of matrimonial agents now profitably occupied would be forced into selling life insurance exclusively.

It seems as though it were only the other day when all Jewish marriages were made in Heaven. On earth below, their agent, the shadchan, acted as intermediary, charging for so much bliss only a paltry one or two per cent commission. He was Cupid, but Cupid who spoke volubly in Yiddish, who wore a beard and a gabardine, carried a little black memorandum book in his vest pocket and, instead of a bow and arrow, a huge umbrella which he wielded like a mace of office.

What do you suppose the young folks in the past had to say in the matter of marriage? Probably only a meek "yes, papa." The Fifth Commandment has always appealed to the filial piety of Jews. As soon as any pair of future fathers-in-law took a liking to each other, to each other's family tree, and to each other's style of chess playing or Talmudic disputation, the marriage canopy was dusted off and the musicians were hired without loss of time. Then they'd sit down leisurely over a good glass of brandy and before the proper witnesses they'd draw up the marriage contract.

Nothing whatsoever was left to fate or to the imagination. With

meticulous precision, this in order to avoid vulgar squabbles and mis-
understandings later on, they'd note down exactly how much dowry
the bride would bring her husband. They'd render an itemized account
of her trousseau down to her last underskirt and bustle, making plain
of what materials this and that garment was to be made, whether of
batiste, velvet, or satin. They'd make it perfectly clear whether the
groom could expect a heavy gold watch and chain, or just a silver one
without a chain, as a wedding gift from his future father-in-law. Black
on white the bride's father would inscribe as an everlasting memorial
his agreement to provide the young couple with bed and board for the
first few years of wedded life, and to furnish the son-in-law with
pocket money so much per month or annum. Also the groom's gifts to
the bride were carefully recorded so that later on there'd be no cause
for cavil or complaint. Now to the naked untrained eye all this might
seem as only the mercenary transaction of small shopkeepers. But to
those concerned the sentiment of the heart wasn't in the least bit com-
promised by calling a spade a spade and then getting a good grip on
the spade in the end.

"Love is a fine thing," says the Yiddish wag, "but love with
noodles is even tastier."

N.A.

STATISTICS

TOLD BY YOINA THE SHADCHAN

BY Z. WENDROFF
TRANSLATED FROM THE YIDDISH BY NATHAN AUSUBEL

Would you like to know? In all the world you can't find a worse
trade than marriage brokerage!

First of all, it's the kind of thing into which every busybody sticks
his nose. Is a *melamed* on the lookout for an extra ruble, he becomes
a *shadchan* on the side! And take my word for it, even a merchant
who deals in flax or in dried mushrooms is not beneath acting as
go-between if it comes his way. How many young married women
are there who get so sick and tired of doing nothing that, in order to
distract themselves, they turn to matchmaking?

Who today isn't a shadchan? A preacher is a shadchan, a
shammes is a shadchan, a *chazan* is a shadchan, and every other

Yankel and Shloime is a shadchan! If I come to you to propose a match for your son or your daughter and you go to the proper party to make inquiries about it, your consultant right away insists on becoming a partner to the deal.

Second of all, there is the business of love! Ever since this disease became a contagion among Jews my profession is all washed out! What are you going to do about it when they don't need any shadchan, when they don't want any shadchan? And truth to say, they can find a mate without my assistance, no? Can you imagine, nowadays boys and girls go walking together as free as birds, and wherever you go you hear nothing from them but "shu-shu-shu" and again "shu-shu-shu"! They do whatever they please, do you understand what I mean or don't you? So what the devil do they need Yoina the shadchan for? Believe me, to all these troubles I've already gotten used. All right! Grab, tear, butt in, snatch a share of my broker's fee, even love-shmove, there are still enough decent Jews left in the world who won't choose mates for their children without the aid of a shadchan! But this is the first time it has happened to me that the science of mathematics should enter my brokerage business and rob me of my livelihood!

Let me tell you how it happened. You know Malchiel Ginspriger, the wealthy exporter. He had a son, Tzalieh they called him, a gifted boy, all right, accomplished in his studies, wrote a fine hand, played chess well, even fiddled a bit, had a smattering of Hebrew and an aptitude for business as well. But all that was as nothing compared to his talent for reckoning with figures—one in the world! If you'd ask me, he was a little too much absorbed in those calculations of his. One might say it was a sort of obsession of his. No matter when or where you'd meet him or what you should talk about with him, he'd invariably lead you to the science of mathematics. He maintained that no other science could compare with it, that the total knowledge of mankind was as nothing, compared to mathematics.

"What do I care about your astronomy—shmastronomy!" he'd argue, that fellow Tzalieh. "They teach you, for instance, that on the planet Mars there are mountains and valleys and lakes, that on the sun there are spots, that on the moon there are mountains and valleys and the devil knows what else. Now, tell me, am I obliged to believe all that? And what if they were to tell me that there is a country-fair in the sky every Thursday—must I believe that too?

"Take geography, for instance. Here, they say is Europe and there America, here Africa and there Asia, here the North Pole and there the Equator. This country here has so many square miles, that country there so many; this ocean is that wide, that mountain is that high. Nu, I ask you, how do they know all that? Did they measure them?

"Do you want another example? Let us take the science of medicine. One doctor says: 'What you need is cupping.' You go to another doctor and he prescribes leeches. You go to a third and he throws his hands up in horror. 'Leeches!' he cries, 'why that's dangerous! They'll suck your blood!' In short, if one says 'day' the other says 'night.' So I ask you, how can we believe the doctors?"

Let me tell you that Tzalieh didn't have a too high opinion of the other branches of knowledge either. He said that zoology was nothing but a joke. He'd ask me: "Does it make any difference to you, Reb Yoina, whether the bedbug, I beg your pardon, has forty-eight or eighty-four legs? And granted that you knew how long an elephant lived can you make a whole *Shabbes* from it? Believe me, to find out how much milk your own cow gives is a lot more valuable to you than to know how bears and snakes and adders live."

In this respect, you see, he's right. No matter what branch of knowledge he'd talk about he'd make ashes and mud out of it. Chemistry, that was black magic! History, he said, was all lies from beginning to end. For proof, all the historians told different stories, each in his own way, and just as he damn pleased.

What lesson was to be learned from all this? That there was no valid branch of knowledge except mathematics!

That, said Tzalieh, was something you could rely on at all times. Add, subtract, divide, multiply—you're on solid ground here, you understand? Thank heavens, you can't suck arithmetic from your fingers: two times two is always four. You can twist about like a snake until next year and present a thousand brilliant arguments, but you can't make three times three equal ten! Two times six is always twelve and no philosopher can do any hairsplitting about it. You can even be the biggest freethinker, even not believe in the Messiah, but you can't find fault with the rules of arithmetic. Do you need any more proof that it is the supreme science of all? Tell me then, can you do without calculations? Whether you erect a house, or construct a bridge, or build a railroad—you've always got to calculate what and how much!

Tzalieh already showed symptoms of this obsession to calculate when he was little. Barely had he begun going to *cheder* when he discovered that he got great pleasure in counting the number of steps he took from his home to the cheder and then back again. He had an irresistible desire to count the houses on the way and the number of palings in the fences. He calculated how many strokes from the *melamed's* rod a pupil got each semester, counting ten strokes to each flogging and not less than two floggings per diem.

For a long time he tortured his brain with the following calculation: how many bagel did he eat in a year, figuring six bagel per day? What confused him a little was the week of Passover when only matzos are allowed and the other holy days when only *challeh* twists are eaten.

When Tzalieh got older and his father took him into his business, he'd sit all the time and calculate the possible profits on merchandise that had not yet been bought. If business was slow a certain week he'd hand his father a detailed analysis of how much he'd lose. He found no greater pleasure than to figure out how much income all the houses of the city would bring him if they belonged to him, how much it cost the Czar to maintain his army, figuring twenty-seven kopecks a day for each soldier, also how many matches were used up each day in the town. In short, he involved himself in all kinds of fantastic silliness with his statistical computations. And, God forbid, should you only try to belittle statistics he'd overwhelm you with his arguments. Was there a single country in the world that could exist without statistics? Everybody would remain ignorant of everybody else, the whole world would go to rack and ruin without statistics.

Tell me, please, have you ever heard of such an obsession before?

Whenever I proposed a match for him, whether with this girl or that one, I had my hands full. As soon as I presented the proposition to him he'd make a dash for pencil and paper and tried to figure out how much net dowry he'd get, how much a housewife could save per week with extra economies, how many children a woman could bear until she was forty-eight, how much each child cost its parents from the day it was born until the day it married, also how much money it costs to marry off a daughter. In short, he calculated that a fellow like himself could not consider a girl with a dowry one kopeck less than five thousand rubles!

If you think that bothered me a lot you're mistaken. All right, he wanted five thousand, let it be five thousand! I've got all kinds of matches. So I wrote away to my partner in Pinsk. He had just the right girl for him: good family and good money, although truth to tell, the girl herself was not such an *ai-ai-ai!* But what do you want—a girl blessed with every attraction?

It looked as if we had already come to an agreement with him;

he had checked up on his calculations and found everything was in order. Then what the devil do you think should happen?

One day he caught sight of Chatzkel the melamed's daughter, you know the little milliner who came down from Warsaw and opened a shop of gewgaws and strings of beads. Well, as soon as he saw her he got all on fire.

So you'll ask, what happened to all his fine calculations, to his statistics? Let me tell you, he forgot all about that—forgot that he ever was a merchant and the son of a merchant, forgot that the girl was only a poor melamed's daughter. Apparently, he must also have forgotten that he had once calculated that he couldn't possibly afford to accept a dowry a kopeck less than five thousand rubles; he had forgotten to calculate how much his wife's poor relations would cost him.

In short, he melted away for love of her like butter in a frying pan.

At first I had no inkling of his infatuation. But when next I went to see him about the girl in Pinsk, I grew somewhat uneasy when I saw that the fellow acted coldly to the whole business. Seeing how it was, I spoke plainly to him: when could I count on him to go with me to Pinsk? Instead of answering my question, he drew me aside and whispered to me:

"Do you know what I'm going to tell you, Reb Yoina? Let's forget about the girl in Pinsk; nothing can come out of that. But don't you fear, Reb Yoina! If you'll show the real stuff you're made of, you'll get the shadchan's fee anyway. In fact, I'm going to give you a ready-made *kaleh* for the plucking. All you have to do is to go and talk to her. That's all!"

"Good enough," I replied, "let's hear! Maybe you've discovered something better."

"Indeed, I have," he confided to me with shining eyes.

"Who is she?"

"The daughter of Chatzkel the melamed, you know the milliner from Warsaw."

I looked at him as if he had gone crazy. Was the fellow out of his mind or just a nitwit? Malchiel Ginspriger and Chatzkel the melamed—a fine combination! An accomplished middle-class young man like Tzalieh, a merchant, and Chienke the milliner! Just right for each other, no doubt about it! Tzalieh apparently read my glance for he said to me slowly:

"Why do you look at me so, Reb Yoina? The girl is a beauty, a big-city girl with a business which in time will bring in more than five thousand smackers, believe me! There's no one like her in the whole town and—"

"And what, may I ask, will your father say to that?"

"That should be no concern of yours, Reb Yoina. All you have to do is to pop the question for me to the girl, and, if she'll only agree, I'll settle the dowry matter myself with her father. As for your broker's fee, don't you worry, Reb Yoina. I'll compute it on the basis of a five thousand ruble dowry."

In all my born days I never saw anybody fall as flat as a Hanukkah *latke* for a girl as did Tzalieh!

Then I thought it over. So what, why should I worry about it? Do you want Chienke the milliner, let it be Chienke the milliner! You're crazy—all right, so be! What do I care, as long as my broker's fee is secure! I was afraid only of one thing. Should Malchiel find out about it, he'd stand the world on its ear. However, one thing I didn't forsee: that Chatzkel's daughter would say *no*. Well, she did!

"What! I marry that crazy mathematician?" she laughed scornfully. "Why, he'll count every barley grain in my soup!"

You'd think my young man would be discouraged wouldn't you? Not at all. He sent me to her again and again. He was ready to renounce every expectation of a dowry. On the contrary, he proposed to fit her out at his own expense in silks and satins. Even more, he'd pay her father a handsome sum in addition. But do you think it helped any? It helped like cupping helps a corpse! Her father, though, had no objection at all to the match. Why not? Worse, you know, could happen than to become Malchiel Ginspriger's relative! But Chienke didn't want to hear of it. And Tzalieh remained deaf to every other marriage proposal I brought him.

"It's no use, your efforts, Reb Yoina," he told me. "It's either Chatzkel's daughter or nothing!"

Hearing these words I decided to give him up. He was a bad risk for my business. I knew from sad experience in the past that when a boy sets his heart on a girl it's all over with him. Maybe later, in time, he'd come to his senses. But at the moment I thought it wiser not to bother him.

What happened after that? Well, the young fellow did not rest. The more stubborn she showed herself in turning him down, the more determined he was to get her.

Then a bright idea struck him: why shouldn't he have a talk with her personally? It would be a shame not to.

But this was easier said than done. He waited for an opportune time when there was nobody in her shop. Then he went in on the pretext that he needed change for a three-ruble note. Having completed his transaction, he didn't know what to do from there on. Lamely, he remarked what a fine life a good wife could have with him, a merchant with a fine income. And then, as if by the way, he cunningly remarked that he was an only son and that after one hundred and twenty years he would inher—.

The more he spoke the more set became Chienke's mouth and the harder she stared at the wall.

It may be interesting for you to know that Tzalieh was a bashful fellow. When he saw how coldly she behaved toward him, he lost all power of speech and simply didn't know what to do with his hands.

Suddenly he got an idea: "I'll show her that I'm just as intelligent as those numbskull Warsaw fashion plates whom she prefers to me, no doubt."

And then he opened up on her full blast all about the science of mathematics and statistics.

Know one thing: when Tzalieh starts talking about mathematics and statistics he becomes another person altogether. No more bashful, he stops stuttering, becomes a regular professor!

"What you've just said about arithmetic," he sailed in just as if they'd not talked about anything else for the past three hours, "tell me now, what in your opinion is as useful as arithmetic? Whether you buy a pound of sugar or build a ship—can you do without calculation? Of course not!

"Now take, for instance, statistics—that means the knowledge of the number of everything—surely you don't mean to tell me that there's anything more important than that! Say that you are planning to get married. In that case it's good to know everything you can about the subject. Today, for instance, we have six million Jews in Russia, of which 1,300,039 are marriageable young men and 2,275,000 are girls. In that case we have one and three-fourths girls to every boy, no? Or take the statistical fact that there are 600,111 marriages every year. Now what does that mean? It means that every year 957,047 girls don't get married. Let us compute how many old maids there accumulate in a decade . . . if in one year—."

Tzalieh stopped dead in his tracks. He looked at Chienke and his jaw dropped. She sat deathly pale and wide-eyed. She wanted to say something, but she needed air and couldn't come out with it.

"Eh-eh? How many girls do you think remain old maids each year?" Tzalieh continued pressing his advantage. "Nine hundred and fifty seven thousand and forty-seven!" he spat the last words out at her in a voice of doom. Seeing how he had struck home he continued with greater emphasis. "And not one of these girls has the slightest hope of ever getting married!"

"Never?" asked the milliner trembling.

"Never!" replied Tzalieh with finality. "I ask you—whom will they marry? Who's left, if each and every year 957,047 girls become old maids? It's frightful, really! Take my advice while there's still time and marry me. I'll make you a good husband."

Seeing that the situation didn't look so bright, what do you think the Warsaw minx did? She lowered her eyes and murmured:

"Well and good—I'll marry you! But be a good husband to me."

Nu, what is there for me to add? The two were engaged. So I went to see the fellow.

"Tzalieh, where is my broker's fee?" I asked him.

All he did was laugh.

"Broker's fee?" he asked in pretended amazement. "What broker's fee? Did you negotiate the match?"

"Er, no!" I stammered, "but—"

"Were you my shadchan?" he asked mockingly.

"Well, who *was* the shadchan?"

"Statistics!"

Nu, what do you say to that? A new kind of shadchan—statistics! Feh!

Women are most adorable when they are afraid; that's why they frighten so easily.—Ludwig Börne

But there is this much of good in Platonic love: it does not prevent a man from dreaming by day and sleeping at night, and anyway, it's so inexpensive. . . .—Heinrich Heine

Many women look like angels until you see them
crunching bread and herring.

THE TEMPTATION OF REB MOTTEL

BY LEON KOBRIN
TRANSLATED FROM THE YIDDISH BY NATHAN AUSUBEL

"Come in!"

My door creaked, someone opened it carefully and, before entering, shoved in a basket covered with black oilcloth. Behind it, shuffling
in a very discreet manner, came a man with a pointed little beard. He
had a pallid complexion, small troubled eyes and wore an old hat
pulled well over his ears.

In short, behind the basket covered with the black oilcloth there
stood before me my *landsman* Mottel—you know, the husband of
Chana-Beileh. There he stood, all of his gawky self: long bony body,
narrow angular shoulders, and ungainly hands and feet.

"Good morning to you!" he greeted me in a hoarse voice. And
placing his basket on one chair, he seated himself on another.

"A visitor!" I welcomed him. "What are you doing these days,
Reb Mottel?"

"What can I do? I'm a peddler. Sometimes I earn a few pennies
and sometimes a hole in the head from some little loafer."

He took out of his pocket a cigarette butt and a match which he
rubbed against the sleeve of his old coat. His bit of cigarette lit, he
drew on it passionately, letting the smoke out through the nostrils of
his long "cherry" nose. He stroked his little beard nervously with his
emaciated fingers, regarded me closely with his troubled eyes, and said
nothing.

"And how's your old woman, Chana-Beileh?" I inquired.

"Chana-Beileh?" he echoed my question without answering it.
He then lowered his eyes and again fell silent.

"Is she well?" I asked, out of politeness.

"*Et!*" he exclaimed noncommittally. He got up from his chair
and began pacing up and down my room, gesticulating with his long
hands and muttering something incomprehensible into his beard.

From this I gathered that his wife, Chana-Beileh, was probably sick and that was why he was so distraught.

"Is she sick?" I asked.

He sat down again and opened up on me all in one breath with great excitement:

"Sick-schmick! And if she were sick a hundred years, so what? She'll outlive me, never mind! As long as I can remember she was always a thin, washed-out lump of misery, a blessing that had turned sour—*et!*" And he made a despairing gesture.

I looked at him in surprise. What was he talking about, anyway?

"I've come to you about an important matter," he began suddenly.

Again he got up from his chair in excitement but immediately sat down.

"What is it?"

"I'm going to tell you."

But he couldn't still his excitement. Again he leaped up, paced the room up and down. "Oy, oy, oy!" he groaned, and he hunched together his bony shoulders as though he were in pain.

I could see that what my Reb Mottel was in a dither to talk to me about must be really important.

"Why are you so upset, Reb Mottel?" I asked him.

He turned his troubled face to me and replied:

"Listen carefully. You're my landsman. I remember you when you were only a little fellow. I was acquainted with your father, and before him with your grandfather, may we be blessed with as many years as he was! That's why I want you to do me a favor."

"What sort of a favor?"

"I want you to give me your advice. You're a writer, so you'll understand the matter that troubles me," he murmured piteously.

"Reb Mottel, what do you mean?"

"I mean. . . . I have a trouble on my hands; it's driving me crazy!"

It took him a while to calm himself. Then he began:

"Who would have thought that it could ever happen to me? I've been married for twenty years. *Takkeh,* Chana-Beileh is no great beauty. She's been ailing for the last twenty years, may you be spared such misery! Here she has a headache, there she has a pain around her heart. If not, she gets a cramp in the side, a pain in her back! Her face —it's all skin and bones, a fright to look at! But a Jew is a Jew, and merely because his wife is not good-looking is no reason why he should find himself a better-looking one, a sweetheart, for instance. Such ugly ideas never occurred to me, believe me! I knew she was my wife and nothing else mattered. I lived like any other decent Jew; had eight children with her, five sons and three daughters. They all left home; three married sons live in London and an unmarried son and two girls live in Argentina. Then my youngest son and youngest daughter are in Johannesburg in South Africa. And as for Chana-Beileh and me —well, you know that yourself, we've been in New York for the past five years. I could make a living from peddling if I didn't have to pay so much money for my three-room flat, fifteen dollars I pay my landlord every month! It's not so easy, I assure you, to scrape together such a fortune! To make ends meet we have to keep two boarders.

"One day, about six months ago, there moved into my flat a fellow and a girl. The fellow looked like a nice young man; he was good-looking and he dressed like a man with plenty of money. The girl was a *tzatzke*, beautiful like a doll, I'm telling you! She was tall, nice and plump, with cheeks like red apples, and eyes that sparked fire.

"They said, so they said, that they were engaged. Who was I to doubt them? All I cared about was that they should pay their rent —that's all!

"In short, the girl worked in a shop and the fellow—well, one day he worked and ten he didn't. The girl, Kady was her name, she just fainted away for him; she kept her eyes pasted to his all the time. She fed him with the most expensive and best food: with *sardine-kelach*, with roasted *herringlach*, with cheese and butter, and what the devil else you can think of! Suppers they ate together in a restaurant, went to theater together, to balls . . . in short, she almost croaked for him!

"Would you believe it, I got to hate her for her *tréfeneh* gullet. For instance, whenever she sat down to drink tea she'd make a ruin of my sugar. She had strong teeth, so she stuffed her mouth full of my sugar and *chromshk, chromshk, chromshk!* I'm telling you, my gall bladder almost burst, and Chana-Beileh's too!"

"Have you any idea what a peddler must do before he can earn a penny? And there sits a fat, healthy wench with her fellow, and with your own eyes you watch them gobble up at least five cents' worth of sugar at a time. So naturally I got to hate Kady like the plague. To me, as I already told you, they were tréf, tréf like pork! I just couldn't look at them!

"One day I fell on a plan. I said to Chana-Beileh, 'I'll tell you what you do: you put aside enough lumps of sugar for four glasses of tea, two glasses for him and two glasses for her. Give them three lumps for each glass. Then take out the rest of the sugar from the bowl, as if to say, "Here are your lumps of sugar, and may you choke on them!" '

"So what do you suppose our Kady did? As the saying goes, 'She heard us ten times like the cat.' She wasn't at all lazy but went down into the grocery store and bought a paper sugar on my account, and again she went on making chromshk, chromshk with her fellow.

"So, naturally, they got to be even more tréf to me, and my dearest wish was that they should only croak. Just the same, I kept quiet. What could I do—say something? They'd only get angry and move out! So I shut my mouth, and from aggravation Chana-Beileh's aches and pains got even worse.

"Month after month passed by this way. All of a sudden, Kady lost her job in her shop! She didn't work one week, she didn't work another. Her fellow still went about lazying around the house and didn't even want to go out and look for a job. Naturally, what would you expect, Kady's heart grew bitter against him. 'This and that,' said she to her fellow, 'so long as I worked, it didn't bother me that you didn't work, but now you've got to help me out until I'll get another job.'

"It all ended up by their quarreling, and the fellow went away, walked out, disappeared as if the ground had swallowed him up!

"Nu, did Kady carry on! She looked for him here, she looked for him there, among the *landsleit*, among her acquaintances—no use! So she came home, locked herself up in her room, and cried and cried. No more did she drink tea, no more did she chromshk my sugar. And when I saw how she let my sugar alone I stopped being angry at her. I even felt a little sorry for her. How does the saying go? 'When a Jewish daughter is made unhappy, Jewish blood is being spilled.' My Chana-Beileh, who by nature has also a good heart, cursed the fellow for all he was worth: 'May he collapse like an old house, the *mamzer!* May my toothache gnaw his heart!' In short, if you want to get a couple of nice curses all you have to do is start up with Chana-Beileh.

"In this way, Monday passed, Tuesday and Wednesday too. On Thursday when I came home from my peddling, Chana-Beileh ran towards me looking scared. 'Quick, Mottel! Kady's passed out, she's fainted!'

"Of course I ran into the girl's room together with Chana-Beileh. I saw her tossing on her bed, with her face fiery red and her hair all mussed up. She was laughing and crying at the same time and couldn't draw her breath.

" 'She has *nebbech* convulsions,' said Chana-Beileh. 'We've got to rub vinegar over her heart. If not, she might die yet, God forbid!'

"My wife then ordered me to unbutton Kady's blouse. Nu, what would you have done? Naturally, I remained standing like a clay *goilem*. What do you mean, I should go crawling up to a girl and unbutton her blouse? Chana-Beileh understood only too well what was bothering me, so she said: 'It's nothing to get worried about, you're an old man already. When life is in danger it's allowed. Raise her up from the pillow, I've no strength for it.' And Chana-Beileh ran out to fetch the bottle of vinegar from the closet.

"In the meantime, I was thinking to myself: 'Chana-Beileh's right. It's allowed when life is in danger!'

"I swear to you, may God help both you and me, that I had absolutely no sinful thought in mind, only to help a Jewish daughter *nebbech* in danger of her life. With my own ears I heard her cry and laugh and gasp for breath! With my own eyes I saw her almost suffocate. Nu, tell me, could I stand and not help her?

"In short, I began to unbutton her blouse. My hands shook and my knees knocked together. What would you expect? This was the first time in my life I had ever done such a thing. And as I unbuttoned her blouse she laughed and cried still louder. I tried to calm her, I patted her cheek, '*Sha, sha,* Kady,' I said, '*Sha, sha!*'

"Having undone her blouse, I shut my eyes and turned my face away just as if I had been scalded with boiling water. At that moment Chana-Beileh came dashing in with the vinegar.

'Take off her corset too, Mottel,' she yelled. 'We've got to rub her all over!'

"I did what Chana-Beileh asked me, and I must confess that I had thought about that too, even before she told me.

"And suddenly, *mamele,* my heart! All the seven suns began to shine and dazzle my eyes! I grew hot and cold, cold and hot, I'm telling you! I had never seen such a doll in all my life. Her skin was white as milk, like fresh-fallen snow."

Reb Mottel fell silent. He took off his hat and scratched his head with a despairing gesture. "Oy, oy!" he moaned. "Since then she's simply driven me out of my mind. I go around without a head!"

"So what happened after that, Reb Mottel?" I asked him.

"What should have happened? From that day on I couldn't look at Chana-Beileh; she disgusted me. From that time on I was no longer her Mottel. I'm telling you, I'm a *meshuggener* now, a low-down bum! When I'm at home I only want to look at Kady. When she looks at me, I feel as if her eyes were burning into my heart, burning large holes in it. Now, whenever she drinks tea, I want her to use up all the sugar, may it be for her health! And when I hear her chromshk the sugar, as she did before, I get a warm feeling all over, just as if I were listening to a good musician play a *dobri dzhen*[1] at a wedding. And when she's not home I can't rest. I find my home ugly without her, gloomy and cold, when she's not there.

"I heap reproaches on myself. 'A fire on your head, Mottel! What's all this for? Think for a moment, you low life, you who bring shame on all Israel! Why, you're already standing with one foot in the grave!'

"But what's the use? Argue with Mottel today, argue with Mottel tomorrow, when Mottel is no longer Mottel, woe to him! Since Mottel has a heart, her eyes burn holes through him. Since Mottel has a brain, her lovely face dazzles him. Since Mottel has ears, her sweet voice bewitches him. Since Mottel has eyes, they don't want to see anyone else but her. Wherever Mottel goes, stands, and sits, he only sees her, that doll who is more beautiful than all the seven suns, whose skin gleams whiter than milk, than freshly fallen snow. No, I can't run away from her! Woe is me, but I really can't!

"You can see now why I've come to you. Give me advice, what shall I do? To ask Kady to move out of my house—I haven't got the strength for that. Sometimes I think maybe it would be better if I went to live with one of my children overseas. Where do you thing I ought to go? To London? Argentina? South Africa? And do you think that even in Argentina or South Africa I'll no longer see her face or that she'll leave me alone? Will I ever be able to forget her? I can't believe it. I always see her before my eyes. She mixes up my thoughts even when I don't see her. *Oy vay!* What a misfortune!"

> *A man fell in love with a woman who resided*
> *in the street of the tanners.*
> *If she had not lived there,*
> *he would never have entered this evil-smelling section;*
> *but since she dwelt there, the street seemed to him*
> *like the street of the perfumers.—The Zohar*

The cleverest woman finds a need for foolish admirers.

[1] *Polish for "good day."*

GOING TO THE LIBRARY

BY CÉSAR TIEMPO (ISRAEL ZEITLIN)
TRANSLATED FROM THE SPANISH BY DONALD WALSH

Ma, can I wash my hair with kerosene and put on my sky-blue dress to go to the Library?

All right, darling, and see if you can get yourself a young man, like the rest of the girls: it's about time.

TRUE DEVOTION

The old Philadelphia couple were talking. All their children had been married off and they were left alone.

"How long can we live?" said the old man to his wife, heaving a deep sigh. "We haven't many years left. Death strikes without warning, you know, and it's no use making any plans. But let me tell you, should one of us die suddenly, believe me I'm not going to sit down and mourn—I'll take a trip to Israel!"

Like a great poet, Nature is capable of producing the most stunning effects with the smallest means. Nature possesses only the sun, trees, flowers, water, and love. But for him who feels no love in his heart, none of these things has any poetic value. To such an individual the sun has a diameter of a certain number of miles, the trees are good for making a fire, the flowers are divided into varieties, and water is wet.—Heinrich Heine

ONE TWO THREE

BY CHAIM NACHMAN BIALIK
TRANSLATED FROM THE YIDDISH BY JOSEPH LEFTWICH

One two three four five six seven eight.
Marry your girl before it's too late.

Do not reflect, do not delay,
Or someone else will snatch her away.
Once I had honey, but did not eat,
And another came and found it sweet.
There were two sisters—one was fair,
The second was dark, and dark her hair.
They were both lovely and good to see,
And I loved them both equally.
I pondered and pondered with aching head.
I couldn't decide which to wed.
Months passed and still I could not see
Which I should ask my wife to be.
Till, alas, two devils came one day,
And carried both of them away.
Now I am old and sick and worn,
Brokenhearted and forlorn.
And I say to all who will listen to me,
Don't let your lives like my life be.
One two three four five six seven eight,
Marry your girl before it's too late.
Do not reflect, do not delay,
Don't let another snatch her away.

A CONQUEST

BY MORITZ G. SAPHIR
TRANSLATED FROM THE GERMAN BY NATHAN AUSUBEL

It was in Nuremberg in the year 184–. I arrived in the morning and went to sleep right away. One cannot too strongly recommend to travelers that when they arrive at a strange place they go promptly to bed. This gives the police a sort of prima facie guarantee that the traveler is quite a harmless person and so long as he is asleep he definitely cannot cause anybody any anxiety.

After I awoke from a sound sleep, the landlord of the Bavarian Hof, Herr Auerheimer, presented himself to extend his welcome to such a distinguished guest and to inquire of me which of the Nuremberger curiosities I wanted to see first. Without hesitation I chose a beefsteak and a pint of red wine with which to drink it down.

I was acquainted with Nuremberg and its curiosities from before, and I came there only at the invitation of my friend Count . . . . n in order to spend with him several days at his countryseat near Nuremberg.

When I learned that the Summer Ball on the Dutzendteich, an amusement place in Nuremberg where the local beau monde liked to gather, was to take place that very evening, I decided to go there right away. Why not add another sample to their collection of fashionables? My God, so much went under the designation of "Beautiful World" that never made the world any more beautiful, that without going through any conscience-struggle I could hardly wait until evening for "The Beautiful World, Saphir & Co." to assemble.

I spent the rest of the morning in Furth, which is the Bavarian Jerusalem. It chanced to be on the Sabbath and I visited the synagogue where I heard a sermon on "The Chapter About the Cow," the red cow that Moses ordered to be burned. The rabbi spoke about this red cow as if he had stayed in the same boarding house with her. He knew how many hairs she had in her tail and what sort of upbringing she got, and he tried for a full hour on the clock to clear up the mystery why the red cow had to be burned. And I would gladly have called out to him, "The cow was red, hence a radical cow, therefore she was burned." But the preacher rambled on for a while longer about this red cow that had to be "without a blemish," a demand that I thought was a little too unfairly exacting of earthly cows. I was expecting that any moment the rabbi would begin discussing the scientific question whether the red cow ought to give white milk. But luckily he didn't.

In the afternoon I returned to Nuremberg. When evening came, I went by equipage to the Dutzendteich, I mean I went in a carriage furnished by the Bavarian Hof. Before leaving, I had carefully made my toilette and took questioning counsel of my mirror as to how I looked, but the mirror was like every other counselor—it was in complete agreement with me. Has it ever happened yet that anyone should feel displeased with the judgment of his mirror? I, for one, was delighted with the reflection of myself in the mirror. I was fairly certain that the way I looked I was bound to make at least one conquest at the ball, and so with this pleasant anticipation I rode off to the Dutzendteich. The Dutzendteich was a delightful little place, with an open-air summer dance pavilion and a salon. It had a great many tiny lakes scattered among the green copses and there were shady woodland paths for wandering.

The "Beautiful World" was mostly gathered when I arrived, and with my coming it was complete. The fashionable Nuremberger ladies, you must know, never take anyone to their hearts until they first get a firm grip on him. But they certainly are lovely and lovable, and I thought to myself, "Good! They can have *him!*"—meaning the humorist Saphir, naturally.

I explored every lake, went through all the rooms, walked through all the alleys and copses. The sensuous music, the cool of the evening, the balsamlike fragrance of the pine trees, the surging throng, the garland of young beautiful women—all these cast a spell on me and brought me into a mood for love. I had been love-starved for such a long time that I was quite eager to let a pair of beautiful dark eyes bring the light into my own.

I let my eyes wander about and suddenly became aware of a young woman looking fixedly at me with inquiring eyes. "Ha! This one here is in love with me!" I jubilated. "I've captured her heart and fancy without even trying!"

Everybody knows that love is the work of a single instant! Where does love come from and whereto does it go? It comes just like a cinder that flies into the eye! It was the cinder that flew into this girl's eye, and from her eye right into her heart!

From that moment on I felt blissful. *I was loved!* I wandered about the grove where the girl was sitting like a restless spirit. I saw that she was staring at me again and again! I felt decently sorry now that I knew myself so lovable. The poor dear! I went out into a side alley in order to think over the whole matter and try to find ways and means by which I could save her from despair.

It was in this side alley that I eavesdropped on the following conversation between various voices talking inside of me.

I heard Self-Love, a vigorous, muscular individual with a penetrating voice, say, "It's quite natural, this sudden love-catch! You are a devilishly handsome fellow! You know, a good figure is everything in a man, besides his money of course! You have a face that is most attractive and full of intelligence. In short, you possess a *je ne sais quoi* that makes love conquests easy for you."

A charming person, this Self-Love fellow! I could go on listening to him for hours. But suddenly a deep bass voice interrupted. That was Understanding. He was an absurd fellow who had never known love. I heard him rumble, "But surely this Saphir is not so stupid as to consider himself so dangerous that all a girl has to do to fall in love with him is to look at him! My God! Hasn't he ever seen himself in a mirror?"

I could have killed that coarse fellow then and there!

Self-Love fell silent for a while and then replied:

"Na, why not? Although his nose isn't exactly what you'd call Roman, nevertheless it does look a bit Italian, for it has a flat bridge. But you must admit he does have a mouth that speaks for itself: it's lovable and *gemütlich* and yet has such a piquant curl in the corners! Hasn't he a bold arching forehead and a noble carriage?"

I heartily agreed with this person. "That one's a very clever fellow!" I thought with rapture.

But then suddenly I heard a croaking voice like that of an old lady. It was Experience. She had to add her mustard to the conversation.

"But you don't mean to tell us that you've never been deceived by appearances?" she rasped in a nasal drawl. "Aren't you ever going to learn anything from past experience?"

I was angry enough to burst and thought, "The old chatterbox! She can't bear others to talk about love, out of sheer envy!"

At this point I heard the almost whispered tones of a flutelike voice, the most charming voice imaginable. It belonged to Vanity, and I heard her say, "Don't allow yourself to be bullied like that! Haven't you achieved one success after another in your life? Isn't it reasonably possible, then, that this girl has heard of you? After all, you are a celebrity! And you know that women are as passionately fond of celebrities as they are of Brussels lace! She is in love with you because you are a famous man!"

"Oh!" I exclaimed gratefully when I heard this. "I can see that there are still thoughtful and truth-loving souls in the world! This one has certainly struck the nail on the head!"

I now heard a gentle lisping voice; it belonged to Foresight. She said, "Now look here, don't go and make yourself ridiculous! Take good care that you don't become the butt of a joke for somebody!"

"Just see what this simpering creature has dug up to disturb the peace!" I muttered to myself.

In the next instant a loud merry voice broke in. It was Humor.

"So what?" asked he. "The passing hour is simply begging that you take it by the wing as it speeds by. Why all this philosophizing when all it's going to be is a gay adventure? And if all's well you might even find two instead of one amusing hour. Isn't that enough?"

"This Humor is certainly a murderous fellow." I muttered. "An old practitioner!"

To make a long story short, Humor, Self-Love, and Vanity came out triumphant in the argument.

At this very instant, the lovely girl was taken in hand by a friend. She gave the other a gentle poke in order to draw me to her attention. I noticed that and became more convinced than ever that she was head-over-heels in love with me. I followed the two girls at a discreet distance as they made their way to the refreshment hall.

On the way I collided with my friend H., the editor of the *N.K.* I hung on his arm. "Friend," I confided to him, "I've just made a conquest; I want you to help me."

"What! Where? How did it happen?"

"Come, I'll show her to you. I wouldn't be at all surprised if you knew her—such a beauty! In that case, you'll have to introduce me!"

We entered the refreshment hall as I was telling him everything. After a little search we found the pretty charmer at a table with her friend and an elderly lady. As soon as she saw me she whispered something into the old lady's ear, and thereupon the old lady began to regard me with great interest.

"Now, do you see?" I said triumphantly to my friend H. "She has just talked to the old lady about me! It's just as I told you!"

Dr. H. looked at the three women and said to me, "Hm! Fortunately, I know her. Why that's the beautiful Julie, the daughter of the wealthy merchant N.N.! I'm very well acquainted with the family; the old woman is her grandmother, and I'll be glad to introduce you."

I was overjoyed! We approached their table. I could now see Julie quite close. Hers was one of the most charming faces I had ever seen—fresh, lovable, and rosy. She had lively dark eyes, lips like apple blossoms and teeth like the flocks of King Solomon. Thick, black locks fell on dazzling white shoulders that would have done honor to a sculptor working in marble.

When we got to the table, finally, H. and I bowed slightly and then we drew up two chairs. My glances fell on Julie like flaming bombs. I immediately started a conversation with her, with these very witty words: "It's a lot cooler here than it is outside."

Then Dr. H. said, "I wish to introduce to you my friend, Herr Saphir. You surely know his name well."

Julie looked at me and said, "No, I don't think I've had the honor of ever hearing of him."

"There you are!" I heard *Understanding* mutter to *Vanity* inside of me. "Didn't I hear you say before that she has fallen in love with him because he is a celebrity?"

But Self-Love sailed in quickly at this opening with the rejoinder:

"Why this way it's even more flattering! She is in love solely with his personality!"

I took Julie away from the others for a while and went for a stroll with her. I said to her all the many foolish and clever idiocies that philosophers and madly-in-love coxcombs are in the habit of saying. And I could see for myself how she became ever less constrained and more trustful toward me from minute to minute.

At last I told her, while my friend H. was entertaining the other two ladies, that she had been drawing my attention all evening and that for my part I had felt myself irresistibly drawn to her.

She smiled and replied, "Yes, I too noticed you right away and kept on staring at you all the time."

I began to babble for sheer joy. I drew still closer to her and asked her, shamefaced, "Do tell me, dear Fräulein, and to what do I owe the honor of your flattering interest?"

She regarded me for an instant without embarrassment and then she answered innocently, "Oh! How strongly you resemble my dear grandfather who has just died!"

I now looked at the girl more closely. Such mistakes one makes! Why, she was positively hideous!

THE BROOCH

BY PETER ALTENBERG

She had a friend find out how much I had paid for the amethyst brooch I gave her as a gift.

"Fifteen lire," she said to me afterwards. "I know what that means to you!"

"To me it means—love!"

"Would you have bought me the brooch if it had cost twenty-five lire?"

"Yes."

"And forty, too?"

"No."

"Why?"

"Because that is more than my circumstances would allow."

"But that's exactly where true love first begins!"

"Not with me! With me it comes to an end there!"

A man is young if a lady can make him happy or unhappy.
He enters middle age if a lady can make him happy
but can no longer make him unhappy.
He is old and gone if a lady can make him
neither happy nor unhappy.—Moritz Rosenthal

A LETTER FROM THE BRONX

BY ARTHUR KOBER

Bella Gross riffled the pages of the dictionary, paused at a leaf headed "dike," ran her finger down a column of words and, when she came to "dilatory," wrote "tardy and inactive" on a slip of paper. She thumbed the book again, hunted for "epistle," and snagged it after a little difficulty owing to her uncertainty over its spelling. She made the notation, "a formal letter."

Fortified by these two items, Bella was ready to plunge into the writing of the grave and important letter she had long planned. Whenever she engaged in such elaborate preliminaries—unearthing the coverless dictionary and bringing it into the dining room, placing pen, ink, and paper on the oilcloth table cover, using her "good" stationery, bought at a sale at Macy's—it was an indication that she was going to compose something of momentous importance.

And this letter to Monroe Rosenblatt, written in her mind time and time again, was of importance. Bella was finally going to do what she had so very often told her friends Jennie and Sarah she would do: "Give Monroe back to the Indians." It was one thing to make fine promises under a romantic summer moon at Kamp Kill Kare. It was another thing, she thought with burning indignation, to fulfill those pretty promises under the harsh and prosaic moon over the Bronx.

Bella reached for a sheet of her good stationery, so impressively monogrammed with the letter "G." No, she thought, no use wasting the paper. This letter needed careful construction. It would be better to make a rough draft first and then rewrite it. She disappeared into her bedroom for a moment and returned with several sheets of business stationery which she had filched from her office.

She dipped her pen in the ink, corrugated her forehead in deep reflection, and then, under several printed lines which read "Solomon

Silk Mills, Harry I. Solomon, Pres., Silks, Acetates—Plain and Novelty, 'A Satisfied Customer Is Our Best Recommendation,' " she wrote, "Dear Monroe."

She studied this a moment. "Dear Monroe." No, that sounded too warm, too inviting, too intimate. That was hardly her present attitude toward him. Dear Monroe, indeed! She suddenly had it! All that was necessary was to add "Rosenblatt" to the salutation. "Dear Monroe Rosenblatt." That was it—formal, severe, cold, implacable. "I should have written"—she stopped to consult her notes, and then went on, slowly and painstakingly, employing an almost childish chirography—"this epistle before the present inst. but the reason"— again there was a visual consultation with the notes—"I was so dilatory was because I wanted to carefully weigh what was on my chest. Now that I have weighed same I am going to get it off my chest irregardless of whom it affects even though it be—" There was only a moment's pause to consider grammar, and then she wrote, "I."

"First of all," she went on, "I don't want to throw up anything to your face but I feel this matter must be thrown up. Namely you might of forgotten about the fact that when I left 'Kamp Kill Kare' you declared yourself with all sorts of promises galore. I took you at your word in connection with the matter and gave up some 'contacts' which to me I didn't want to give up, at the same time I thought inasmuch as you declared yourself the fair and square thing to do was not to go 'galvinating' around, not that I am the 'galvinating' type girl inasmuch as I wouldn't stoop to be that common. But still in all I wanted to be fair and square with you. In fact one 'contact' I had was very serious inasmuch as the certain party was 'matrimonyally-inclined' along the lines of marriage, only I thought he should have his two feet on the ground first because too many marriages end up on the rocks due to circumstances over which the girl in the matter has no controll. He's a professional person with a college degree."

Bella allowed her mind to dwell on Max Fine for a moment. Poor Mac! A fine fellow—intelligent, well educated—a Certified Public Accountant. If only he had a substantial income. Well, what's done is done. It's silly to regret. Still in all, Mac's a fine boy, she thought, one whose friendship was certainly well worth keeping. Perhaps she ought to attend the regular meetings of the Excelsior Social Club. She had avoided these because of the embarrassment that would follow upon seeing and talking with Mac, the club's president. Oh, well. She sighed deeply, picked up the pen, and continued writing.

"For some time now we've been going out regularly with each

other like clock-work. In fact, so regularly have we been going out with each other that one of my girl friend's (Jennie) commented on same and said, 'We're beginning to look like two peas in a pot' and everybody was taking matters for granted. To be crudly blunt about the matter, I too thought that the issue was understood. I hope you won't think me 'mercinarilly-inclined' if I mention the fact that I didn't bring up the matter of a ring but the matter was brought up by you, yourself. Well all you did was to bring up the matter without bringing up the ring. We been seeing each other regularly like clock-work and not once did you lift a little finger to get same but all you did was to talk 'a poor mouth' about how business was bad and the responsibilities you got and gee whiz, people are not buying merchandise like they used to and this, that and the other thing.

"In other words, Monroe, I suddenly came to the realization that I had no protection whatsoever in giving up my 'contacts' for what? So that you can keep me on tender hooks. So that you can come to my house for supper again and again, compliment my Mother on saying the food is very lucious, and then suddenly we wake up and find we got a boarder with us, only boarders at least pay the rent.

"Well I think that in view of this attitude on your part, in view of the fact that all the time you are saying that business conditions are bad so that we got to assume it don't warrant any serious step on your part, not even to the extent of a ring, in view of the fact that I am giving up chances which to me may prove valuable as I am not growing any younger each day and opportunities don't hang on trees, all a girl has to do is to go out and pick it off the tree just like if it was an apple or some piece fruit, in view of all this, Monroe, suppose we better call it just 'quits.'

"Now please don't get the idea I am calling you 'A Cheap Skate' just because I haven't got a ring to show on my finger. I am not placing you in that catagory whatsoever inasmuch as you have on several occasions shown me a very good time. Still in all if you had merely said to me 'O.K. Billie. String along with me for another couple months till business conditions gets on its feet and then everything will be O.K.' I would of been only too pleased and happy to have strung along with you. But you didn't even have this common courtesy to the girl to who you apparently seemed so crazy about at camp last summer when you swore to me that this here was no typical summer romance you write down on ice it's quickly forgotten, but would culminate to a mutual union. Oh, no, not you! After all promises are cheap and cost nothing. What have you got to loose? Say, it's a wonder to me I'm openning my eyes now. God knows they were closed long enough before.

"So you see, Monroe, why it's better for me to get this matter off my chest once and for all rather than I should waste my time brooding about it because I just can't dismiss things with a snap of the fingers. Perhaps if I was the type girl who could dismiss things with a snap of the finger I would be better off today, believe me. So, Monroe, leave us call it 'quits' and just say it all comes under the heading of 'Experience.' I'm afraid that even if you should dig up a ring, and judgeing from the way your business is at the moment I can just imagine what type ring you would dig up, I'm afraid I'd still have to say 'I'm sorry, I'm not interested.' You had your chances and too bad, you didn't make the most of them. Better luck with some other girl next time. As for me, don't worry. I got along very nicely without you a long time before I met you, and I'll still get along without you inasmuch as I have some very worth-while 'contacts,' friends who don't talk a 'poor mouth' whenever they have to dig in their pockets, be it a ticket for a movie or just a chocolate ice-cream Sunday.

"This letter means 'finis' so please don't reply nor communicate with me via the phone inasmuch as I will be out. I am not 'soreheaded' the least bit about the matter but I merely want to drop it once and for all.

"Assuring you of my sincerest feelings about the matter, and trusting that you meet a girl who appreciates you a little more than I do in view of the whole situation, I am—"

Bella wondered if "Very truly yours" wasn't just a bit too businesslike and formal. But that was exactly what she wanted to be. She wrote, "Very truly yours, Bella Gross." There! Signing "Bella" instead of "Billie" would make him realize that their relationship was completely over.

She picked up the scribbled pages and read them carefully. Once or twice she stopped to make a correction and to consult the dictionary about spelling. When she had finished reading what she had written, she added, "P.S. Please excuse the handwriting." She then reached for a sheet of her good paper, inked her pen, glanced at the rough draft, and started to write, "Dear Monroe Rosenblatt."

Love makes of the wisest man a fool,
and of the most foolish woman—a sage.—Moritz G. Saphir

DRAMATIC CRITICISM

Rosie did not know how to break the news to her father. But one day she gathered the necessary courage to say to him:

"Papa, I'm engaged!"

For a moment her father remained speechless, as if lightning had struck him.

"Who is he?" he finally asked.

"He's an actor on Broadway, papa."

Her father turned pale.

"An actor! On Broadway?" he gasped. "You've gone crazy— you don't know what you're doing! Why, have you any idea what an actor is? He's a playboy, a loose, immoral fellow! As long as I live you're not going to marry an actor!"

"But I love him, papa!" cried Rosie with shining eyes.

"Love-shmove! What's that got to do with it?" rasped her outraged father. "An actor is a bum, that's all!"

But Rosie was determined and, little by little, she broke down her father's resistance and to such an extent that he consented to go and see her sweetheart perform on Broadway.

Throughout the play the father sat intently watching the young man in his role. When the final curtain fell and the lights went on he turned to his daughter and said:

"Rosie, darling, you can have my permission now—you can marry him! He looks like a fine boy. He's handsome, he's got personality, and he's convinced me that he's no actor—thank God!"

ON THE TWIN HORNS OF A DILEMMA

BY SHOLOM ALEICHEM

I was struggling with the dilemma: Should I marry an old woman? *That* I absolutely didn't want. Should I marry then a young woman? That sort I positively wanted. So I married her!

Curdled Love

A sweetheart—is milk, a bride—is butter,
and a wife—is cheese.—Ludwig Börne

We live together very happily,
that is, I don't have a moment's peace by day or night.
—Heinrich Heine

A beautiful and at the same time a true wife
is as great a rarity as a good translation of a poem.
Such a translation is usually not beautiful when it is true,
and not true when it is beautiful.—Moritz G. Saphir

WHY HUSBANDS RUN AWAY

A woman ran to the rabbi's house and tearfully appealed to his secretary: "Please ask the rabbi to help find my husband—he's run away!"

The secretary wrote down her request and brought it to the rabbi in his study. A moment later he came out again and said to the woman, "The rabbi wishes to assure you that your husband will return to you shortly."

"May God repay the rabbi ten thousand times for his kindness!" cried the woman overjoyed. And she went away.

After she had gone the rabbi's secretary said to some bystanders, "Oy vay—the poor woman! Her husband will never return to her!"

"Don't you believe in what the rabbi says?" someone asked in surprise.

"What a question to ask? Of course I do!" answered the secretary. "But you see, the rabbi only saw her petition—I saw her face!"

Every woman should marry—
and no man.—Benjamin Disraeli

*In how many lives does Love really play a dominant part?
The average taxpayer is no more capable of a "grand passion"
than of a grand opera.—Israel Zangwill*

*Music played at weddings
always reminds me of the music played for soldiers
before they go off to battle.—Heinrich Heine*

*When you fall in love
you lose your wits,
but you only become aware of it
after you're married.—Moritz G. Saphir*

*Ach! what things people are capable of doing
for love—of themselves!*

THE MIRROR

BY YEHUDAH HALEVI

*Into my eyes he lovingly looked,
    My arms about his neck were twined,
And in the mirror of my eyes,
    What but his image did he find?*

*Upon my dark-hued eyes he pressed
    His lips with breath of passion rare.
The rogue! 'Twas not my eyes he kissed;
    He kissed his picture mirrored there.*

*The mirror is the conscience of women;
they never do a thing without first consulting it.—Moritz G. Saphir*

SELF-LOVE

BY SOLOMON MAIMON

On another occasion I defended Helvetius' system of self-love. He [a friend] brought against it the objection that we surely love other persons as well as ourselves. "For instance," said he, "I love my wife." And to confirm this he gave his wife a kiss. "That doesn't disprove anything I've said," I replied. "Really, why do you kiss your wife? You kiss her because you find pleasure doing so."

Love With Gelt

Love is sweet—
but it's tastier with bread.

THE APPRAISAL

BY ZYGMUNT SCHORR
TRANSLATED FROM THE YIDDISH BY NATHAN AUSUBEL

At a table in a corner of the café sat Mama and Papa and Daughter. The old folks were dressed in their Sabbath best, their daughter was gotten up with middle-class elegance.

Mama was reading an illustrated journal, Papa the *Press*, and Daughter was reading the *Chivilla*.

It was ten minutes past eight.

Papa, nervous, smoked one cigarette after another; Mama paged through her journal but her mind was elsewhere. Daughter was all absorbed in her reading. She pretended not to know what it was all about. She didn't want to know.

When the hands of the clock pointed to a quarter to nine, two men came up to their table: an elderly individual and a young man with him. Mama made a joyous gesture, while red spots broke out on the face of Daughter, who was pretending to be absorbed in an advertisement.

"What a coincidence!" exclaimed with simulated innocence the elderly man, a well-known *shadchan*. "What are you folks doing here? On a visit to Lemberg? Tsk, tsk—imagine the unexpected places where you can meet people! Why, I haven't see you for ages! What's news with you?"

"Oh, one keeps alive!" mumbled Papa disparagingly.

"Now what do you say to the weather, eh?"

"M-m-nieh! Just like business."

"And business?"

"Just like the weather!"

Both laughed.

"And I suppose this is your little daughter," gushed the shadchan. "May no Evil Eye fall on her! A regular Fräulein! I'm very glad to meet you, Fräulein! It's a pleasure, Fräulein! Why I knew you when you were a little girl! Tsk, tsk, how she's shot up—like a birch tree! Heh, heh, heh, what a beauty! Just like Mama was when she was a girl!"

At the compliment Mama smiled like a bedbug.

The elderly individual, half good friend and half shadchan, led the conversation. But soon Papa brushed him aside. He began to probe experimentally, to take the young man's pulse, so to speak. He questioned him; how long had he been a merchant? . . . What did he sell? . . . How much profit did he make a year? . . . And did he by any chance know the firm of Holitzer and Politzer in Biala? . . . And by the way, what was today's stock quotation for copper? . . . And did he know whether conserve containers were a good risk?

"Young man, tell me, please, how far did you get with your studies?" gurgled Mama. "Of course you'll finish them! It would be a pity to drop them after so much effort, wouldn't it? You know, the title 'Doktor' is nothing to be sneezed at. 'Herr Doktor! Herr Doktor!' Hasn't it got a superior ring, and besides, isn't it sometimes armor against need?"

Daughter finally took over the conversation. She had read a lot and she talked only about literature. Why, only a few days ago, she had finished *Colas Breugnon*, the newest work by Romain Rolland!

Tolstoy, Dostoievsky, Rolland! She glowed over the three monarchs of literature. Her only pleasure was a good book or fine music, she said delicately. Richard Strauss she idolized, but as for Schoenberg—m-m-m!

Then the young people got all tangled up with each other in a discussion about music and art. But their elders persisted in getting to the point.

The half good-friend and half shadchan asked Papa and Mama on the quiet whether they were serious about the dowry. Was Papa really in a position to give what he said he would give, and could he guarantee it? Was the house for the young folks burdened down with any mortgages? What about the trousseau, and the furnishings?

Then falling into his role as shadchan, he went into ecstasies.

"Have you any idea what a treasure that young man is? He doesn't smoke, he doesn't play cards, he doesn't drink, he's a small eater. He's so thrifty, he wears a suit of clothes four years. Then he has it altered and wears it another few years. Do you know how he wears his cuffs? On both sides! That I'm telling you in confidence. Believe me, he's a clever, intelligent young fellow with a fine mind and he belongs to a well-to-do family. True, he hasn't the title 'Doktor,' but please keep in mind that he's attended law school for sixteen months."

"Take my daughter," interrupted Mama vaingloriously. "Have you any conception what sort of a jewel she is? Happy and blessed is he who'll get her for a wife! There isn't a thing she can't do. She presses and she cooks, she washes and she bakes, she weaves and she embroiders, she sews and she paints. And above else, she is a respectable girl! She never is out of her mother's sight. I ask you, where can you find such a girl nowadays?"

So they talked and traded and bargained. The merchandise was thoroughly examined. The match was at last consummated, and the buyer was satisfied with the price.

For the last time Daughter has a rendezvous with her true love. She swears to him that he's the only one she has ever loved. But what is she to do? She cannot, God forbid, carry on an everlasting struggle against her dear parents! She cannot bring ruin on her family and drive her darling Papa into an early grave! Therefore, she implores him to forget her. Time heals all wounds!

And the young man has his last tryst with his lady love. He swears that she is the only one he has ever loved, but in this world what can you do without money? Without money both of them would be unhappy, now wouldn't they? And above all he wanted her to be happy, *very, very* happy!

The deposit on the dowry is paid, engagement gifts are bought, both parties investigate each other's financial standing, announcements are printed, notices are sent out to the newspapers (let their enemies get apoplexy from it!). Then they argue over the broker's commission with their half friend half shadchan. He argues earnestly but vaguely that because there's a river between Lemberg and Janow he's entitled to three percent for his brokerage fee. In the end they settle for two and a half.

Mazl tov! Mazl tov!

The piece of business is settled. Cause for celebration! A young pair betrothed—out of love, of course! It was pure love at first sight!

THE WEDDING

The darling daughter was stubborn; she insisted on wearing a travel costume to the rabbi's house for the marriage ceremony, instead of a wedding gown. She said that immediately after the ceremony they would go on their honeymoon to Semmering.

Mama hated eccentric and intellectual ways. "What sort of business is this, leap in a travel costume under the *chupeh* at the rabbi's house and then away! What's all the leaping for? What's all this hurry about? God knows but that you might give people ideas that something very peculiar was taking place. What would be really decent respectable, and fitting for people of wealth like us is a wedding at the Temple, a dinner at a fashionable restaurant for all the nearest of kin and for a few good friends who certainly would send gifts of silver!"

Under no circumstances would Papa give in to his daughter's caprice, nor would he consider Mama's suggestion for a Temple ceremony.

"What's really decent, respectable, Jewish, and fitting for people of wealth like us—and above all it's cheaper—is a wedding at home, just as God has commanded, without any fancy frills." Did he marry Mama in a Temple? No! Did Grandma marry in a travel costume and did she rush off to Semmering for her honeymoon? Definitely not! Some people might even get the idea that his child had no father to look after her properly, if she got married at the rabbi's, or to follow Mama's crazy notion, to have a catered dinner in a restaurant. Was he Papa or was he not? He knew his duty well enough. Under no circumstances would he allow the marriage ceremony to take place anywhere but at home.

Daughter now let loose torrents of tears. She protested: what was the idea of gathering together all kinds of strange demons to stuff them like geese and then allow herself to be stared at and to be gossiped about by them? Furthermore, she wanted no bridal veil, no banal ceremonies, and no long sermons! She knew well enough what the moral principles of marriage were. Lastly, who was it that was getting married—herself or Papa and Mama?

Mama bit her lips, drew in her eyebrows, and let fall a tear. She murmured resentfully: "Small children, small enemies; big children, big enemies. But just wait! Soon the big enemies will give birth to little enemies and you'll get a taste of the same joys that I'm tasting now. As for you, Papa, you don't know what you're talking about! It's easily said, 'the wedding is going to take place at home!' How could you think of such a thing? Who's got the strength to slave away for weeks on end making all the preparations and then to serve a whole mob of hungry people? And after it's all over, everyone no doubt will turn his nose up and draw up an inventory of grievances: 'There was not enough meat, but they did make up for that lack with plenty of horseradish. . . . And what do you say to that—in the whole almond strudel there wasn't one single almond! . . . . Some compote —you'd think they'd use sugar! Well you're wrong, it was cooked with saccharine.' Take my advice, it's best to have a catered dinner; each will get his own portion and everyone alike."

Hearing Mama say this, Papa got all wrought up. Pounding on the table, he cried, "A fine arrangement indeed! Let me warn you! Uncle Reb Chaiml will surely not come to the wedding!"

Papa had his way; the wedding took place at home.

Papa and Mama, together with bride and groom, sat huddled together as the groom wrote down the names of those to be invited to the wedding. In the end they forgot to include this one and that one, naturally every one of them "dear and cherished friends." But no one was really disappointed. Some of the uninvited sighed with relief, "The smallest trifle you could buy for a wedding gift costs a fortune today." Of course, there were some who were offended, and Papa apologized hypocritically: "Believe me, I had you in mind. (May God have me in mind as well for health and fortune!) But you're a good friend, aren't you? Does a friend wait for invitations, I ask you? He comes himself, no? Whether with or without an invitation."

The bride stood at last under the marriage canopy, dazzling in her bridal charm. "A bride's charm," loudly exclaimed an aunt of hers. "Just look at the groom!" called out the groom's aunt. "He shines like the sun!" And the bride's little heart beat ever faster and louder, and the groom's heart almost stopped beating altogether. All around them stood aunts and cousins wiping their eyes and blowing their noses. One aunt was so dissolved in tears that all the onlookers were deeply moved. Weeping thus, she inched towards the door into the room where the sweet table stood.

In a high hat and frock coat the rabbi stood holding forth in German. In his wedding sermon he recalled dear grandma "rejoicing in her share of the joys of Paradise." Alas! having been dead twenty years, it was too bad she could not be present at the wedding of her darling granddaughter. He talked and talked about grandma for so long that all the old women began to sob, turning the wedding into a funeral.

And when the great question was put to the bride, she answered, "Yes," in a weak voice. And the groom answered firmly, "Yes," in the meantime fixing his mother-in-law with a significant look, as if he were saying, "You and I will get along well with each other from a distance."

Then the rabbi said, "Amen, selah." Thereupon, there broke out an enthusiastic embracing and kissing and smacking, and while they were so engaged, the more practical guests made a dash for the sweet table.

On the grand piano were laid out opened and unopened wedding gifts: a coffee grinder and a plaster figurine, and a demitasse service and another demitasse service, and still another demitasse service. Then a sardine platter and another sardine platter, and still another sardine platter. Then a flower pot, then a saltcellar and another saltcellar, and still another saltcellar. A picture, a *nature-morte* which was a still life more dead than still, a pair of lump-sugar tongs, a set of dessert dishes and another set of dessert dishes. Only gifts of practical use! And for these presents the wedding guests gorged themselves and guzzled to their heart's content. Dear God, may none of the food disagree with them!

THE SWEET TABLE

The rabbi had come at last to the end of his sermon:
"And you, dear bride, will find in your groom a dear companion in your new life before you. Hand in hand and step by step, you'll

walk together. You will share with him sorrow and joy, love and devotion. It is love and devotion that constitute the firm foundation of
Jewish family life and which distinguish the Jewish woman. You, wife,
must follow your husband, that is you must walk together with him
hand in hand and step by step. Amen! And now—

" 'May the Lord bless you and guard you. . . .' "

Slowly the wedding guests began to make their way to the door.

" 'May He cause His countenance to shine upon you. . . .' "

With their children at home in mind, the guests got ready their
handkerchiefs, kerchiefs, napkins, and little silk and velvet bags which
they had brought along for this very purpose. Mamas again and again
instructed their children how to behave properly at the sweet table.

" '. . . . and bring you peace!' Amen!" concluded the rabbi.

"Mazl tov! Mazl tov!" was the general rejoicing. "Let it be
with great mazl, and may you live to have further joy and peace!
. . . . With God's will may you marry off your other children! . . . .
May they get to be wealthy and great and may they plant a garden! . . . . With health and with life!" ". . . and with satisfaction!" cried out an old aunt. "And may they make a living, oy-vay!
Yes, a living!" a poor relation murmured fervently. ". . . and may
He bring a cure for all the sick in Israel!" groaned an old woman
thinking of her gallstones.

More embraces, more hugs, kisses, and good wishes, and the
thunder of loud smacks.

Soon the dining-room doors were thrown open, and the guests
fell upon the sweet table like starving locusts.

With both hands a fat woman was shoveling tortes into her kerchief. She hastily gave it to her daughter to tuck away safely in the big
pocket of her coat hanging in the vestibule. "Get a move on you!"
she cried to her husband with irritation. "Why are you standing there
with folded hands like a clay *goilem?* Take out your handkerchief and
grab some strudel or something? Don't you know tomorrow is little
Esther's birthday? Do you want us to have nothing to celebrate with?"

In a corner sat a cousin of the groom, and she ate up her share
for the present she had brought, a genuine tin coffee grinder. She
stowed away one piece of honey cake after another. She ate without
taking breath, with both cheeks packed. "I suffer from headache," she
later explained apologetically, "and for headache, you know, it's good
to exercise your jaws." She wiped the perspiration from her forehead
after her exertions, and sighed with contentment.

Almost in an instant the sweet table was emptied.

The festivity came at last to an end. Each one said good-by to the bride's mother, smothered her with good wishes, and, with by-the-way casualness, asked her for just a little package of honey cake for the children and for the neighbors. "At least one little piece, and from each kind of torte."

And so each one, taking a little package of sweets, returned home with bulging pockets. For a whole week after the wedding, guests had tortes and cake with their tea.

One always brings a good appetite
—to someone else's feast.

A rich man's daughter is always a beauty.

When the bride and groom kiss
the shadchan *can go home.*

BONDY, JR.

BY LAJOS HATVANY-DEUTSCH
TRANSLATED FROM THE GERMAN BY HANNAH WALLER

Hermann did not wish to embark upon matrimony until the business was in so flourishing a condition as to enable him to marry into one of the best firms in Pest. This was not so easy as he had imagined. The rich firms in the capital with marriageable daughters would have nothing to do with the provincial Hermann Bondy. "Why, yes," said the haughty fathers and still haughtier bejewelled mothers contemptuously, "he is handsome, he is capable, he has money, he is hardworking, he is clever, he will certainly go far, but—he comes from Miskolcz."

In vain did Hermann change his Miskolcz mascot into a "Virgin of Ofen"; the established magnates reproached him for having a shop at all. "I cannot give my daughter to a general stores dealer," declared

Gustav Blau, a respected banker and the president of the Council. Neither could Hermann break the ban put on him by these aristocratic Jews by claiming that the detached office behind the shop, which he now, in the language of great cities, called his counting-house, should give him a standing as, practically, a banker in good society, owing to the extensive grain- and wool-broking carried on there. No, in spite of the counting-house, Bondy of Miskolcz remained a *nouveau riche,* an upstart tradesman from nowhere.

But the parvenu had his revenge on this snobbish old-established society, and not in business matters only. In awe-struck whispers the Jews of Pest passed round the report that the upstart took his mistresses where he pleased from among the wives of their leading men. It was even said that the pretty, willowy daughter of powerful Gustav Blau still cherished a secret passion for the Miskolczer after her pride had led her to marry Artur Wottitz.

But there is an end to everything, to youth and folly and to the age of adventure too; and once this is definitively ended, the gayest of young sparks wearies of sinful love. After the disturbances of the Revolution, Hermann, now nearly thirty-five, resolved to seek the aid of his provincial connexions in looking for a wife with a view to establishing the solidarity and credit of his firm and setting his personal position on a sound basis. Out of the many offers received, he was most drawn towards the daughter of a business friend in the Batchka, a certain Salomon Fischer. The girl, Regine, was said to be rich and not without domestic virtues. Her reputation was of the best and she was considered pretty into the bargain. Bent on acting in opposition to his grandfather's and father's principles on this point also —that is, on obtaining a pretty wife if possible and not merely a rich and honourable one—Hermann therefore chose Salomon Fischer's daughter out of all the suitable parties recommended to him. Moreover the firm of Bondy had up till then had very little to do with the Batchka, and its prudent head now set himself to make contacts there, so that if the marriage fell through, he would at least have covered his travelling expenses. After mature consideration, then, Hermann mounted the diligence, determined that his visit to the Batchka should combine pleasure with business, the personal affair of the marriage with the outside connexions of the firm.

Regine was a slender maiden, passably pretty though anaemic, with pale-edged lips and an olive-brown complexion from which a pair of gentle deer's eyes looked out. In her short insignificant life there had been only two events worth naming. The one had taken place on that occasion when the pupils of the then famous Israelite school for girls in Pest were sent out to help the trench-diggers when the Austrian army was approaching. Regine was not equal to the hard work, and after she had dug a spadeful or two, she fainted.

The other event also caused her nearly to lose her senses. It was when the Russians had marched into the city, and the pupils at the school scattered like sparrows on a tree at the firing of a gun. Little Regine was sent to relations in Pest at the yellow-painted rambling Marokkaner Hof until her widowed father should be able to make his way through the troops to fetch his daughter home. The view from this house was over a wide, empty square on which Cossacks were camping in tents round the booth of the German theatre. Regine was watching the excited mob of Russians from the window when she felt herself seized from behind and passionately kissed. It was a *Honvéd,* a hero covered with dust, who, after the hot kisses, began to stammer:

"I beg your pardon . . . I thought it was . . . I really thought. . . ."

What he really thought, the handsome captain, was that his fiancée, Kornelie von Palikovics, was still living there. She had in fact been there the year before, when her fiancé had gone to fight for freedom and fatherland. But she had gone away. Where was she now? Who knew?

The young officer, who was almost a boy and bore no trace of the bloody struggle on his fresh young face, stood there looking at Regine. The light from his clear shining eyes shone straight into the young girl's brown stars.

"Kornelie is like you, madam. She is a brunette too. And slender." After which the *Honvéd* was silent, for a convulsive choking came into his throat. Tears burst from his eyes and he struck his hand to his heart so violently that a cloud of dust rose from the red-braided brown tunic.

"Will you have a glass of water?" asked the girl shyly, her own eyes dim with tears.

"Thank you," he replied. "Yes, please."

Whereupon Regine took the jug from the sideboard (or "credence," as it was called in those parts) and fetched fresh water from the kitchen. A glass was found in one side of the credence, and this she filled with a shaking hand and gave to the captain.

After thanking her the young man asked: "Perhaps your parents will know where my fiancée has gone?"

"I am staying with relations," she replied.

"Then might I speak to them?"

"I am sorry, they have gone out. There is no one at home."

"I must beg your pardon once more, madam," he stammered in embarrassment, while Regine, who was again standing close to her strange visitor, felt a pleasing languor steal over her.

The captain's arms twitched as if he were preparing for a second embrace, but the timid desire was not strong enough to translate itself into action. Nevertheless Regine backed towards the credence, feeling, no doubt, in her subconsciousness the bold masculine intention. She pulled out a drawer and took a cloth with which to wipe the glass before putting it back.

The officer looked about him distractedly. Then a groan burst from him: "Ah, Kornelie, where are you?" And without looking back he dashed out of the room.

After this, Regine spent some very disturbed nights of shame-faced recollection, while her windows shook with the wild songs of the Russians outside. Then her father came to fetch her back to the remote village in the Batchka. In packing she hid among her clothes the precious glass from which the *Honvéd* had drunk.

She had hardly been at home a month, with the memory of her passionate hero only a little less vivid, when her father surprised her one night as she was going to bed, with the announcement: "Tomorrow the fiancé is coming." Papa Salomon was always taciturn and he wasted no more words on this occasion than on any other. There was no trace whatever of jesting in his broad greasy face, yet the girl thought he could hardly be entirely serious.

But there was no denying the seriousness next morning when her father gave her his orders: "Your fiancé is here. Give us a good dinner. Make yourself smart."

Under the three pendulous folds of his chin the old Jew showed a wrinkled neck, and under that a chest so round and barrel-like that it was like a hump on the front instead of the back. Lower still came the protruding belly. An enormous black ebony snuff-box bulged in his waistcoat, and that this was no mere ornament could be seen from the smudges on either side of his long coat and even on the low-cut waistcoat and the shirt. His short bristly moustache was also thick with snuff. There he stood, the apoplectic old man, on his elephantine legs, with a gold ring dangling from the lobe of his ear to cure his persistent headache. And his slim little daughter, who stood facing him, looked into the grey eyes lying between rolls of fat and saw from his expression that Salomon had exercised his paternal authority to decide his child's fate. Irrevocably! And as she had been brought up to think, and really believed, that daughters are married by their fathers, she proceeded obediently to the kitchen to make sure of a good dinner. Then she put on her best dress, of greeny-brown plaid silk, with the many frills, and the fichu she had inherited from her mother. The sight of herself in the mirror as she dressed brought back to her mind for the last time the young officer's kiss. From the lowest shelf of the linen-cupboard she took the glass, filled it with water and drank from it, then flung it far out over the garden hedge on to the road. And with the harsh shiver of the breaking glass peace was again restored to this fluttered virgin soul.

Salomon Fischer had done a little Latin in his day, and his greeting to his guest was a loud: *"Quomodo vales!"* He then held out the open snuff-box without ceremony to his future son-in-law with the fine Moses head. Taking a vigorous pinch, Hermann sneezed repeatedly, then opened the discussion in his best High German. Above all, the question of the dowry had to be settled quite satisfactorily. After that he had to reassure the old man as to his own firm and fortune. With much polite handing of snuff, nose-blowing, sneezing, and prolonged and obstinate bargaining, the dowry was at last fixed at seventy-five thousand gulden to the satisfaction of both parties, and Salomon—known locally as the "Terror of the Batchka"—was able to conduct his son-in-law from the office to the whitewashed dining-room.

Although Regine hardly dared to lift her eyes, she seemed nevertheless to be pleasantly surprised to find her fiancé so handsome and imposing a figure. It was only his long beard that she found alarming. Hermann too was pleased. "She's very pretty," he whispered to his father-in-law. "Image of her mother," replied Salomon laconically, "God be with her."

He then washed his hands according to the prescribed rite, put on his hat, and sat down to table. While cutting the bread he murmured a low blessing. And Hermann had to follow his pious host's example despite the ironical scepticism he had acquired from Börne and Heine. Next came the discreet lapping of soup and after that the pike prepared with nuts, a supremely critical dish, demanding silence on account of the many bones. After this fish, cooked in its own juice, had been devoured, rice was served; a white mountain this, with soft masses of goose-liver protruding from its steaming sides and here and there brown rivulets escaping from the rich meat. The appetizing odour from this course had hardly set their nostrils quivering before the diners' tongues were loosed.

"And all this was cooked by my daughter," boasted Salomon as the guest plunged his spoon appreciatively into the rice. With a smile behind his bushy beard and a slight bow to Regine, Hermann expressed his profound appreciation of her cookery. The girl did not dare to look up, but kept her brown eyes fixed on her plate, with the long lashes concealing them. Then she ventured a tentative glance from her own plate to Hermann's. Was the visitor merely being polite or was he really enjoying his dinner? The glance wandered up the napkin tucked into Hermann's chin, along the dark beard thrown in relief by the white damask, and still upward as far as the chewing jaws. It was at once a reassuring and a pleasing sight. Hermann was in the act of swallowing the rice, the kernels of which stuck to his beard and moustache. Greatly encouraged, the gentle daughter of the house of Fischer raised her glance all at once to the hat-brim, so oddly set in motion by the vigorous movement of the jaws. Finally she ventured to look into Hermann's eyes, which at the moment flashed a dark glowing glance at her own brown ones. On this the chaste curtain of eyelids was drawn once more and Hermann likewise turned away in embarrassment. But old Salomon had caught the young people's looks and he smacked his lips happily over the liver and rice. "Seems to me quite perfect. They like each other."

The maid then brought in the braised beef with horse-radish and vinegar sauce and sugar and ground almonds. Herr Salomon began to abuse the Revolution. He always had his Latin tags in readiness and he now gave his views of the corruption of the people with great complacency. *"Mundus vult decipi, ergo decipiatur."* The people, he insisted, needed no liberty; on the contrary, they should be held in check and made to work. That was the chief thing. The Austrians were right in keeping men at their work by means of the bayonet.

Now, however much Hermann in his soul craved for peace and order, he knew only too well that when it was a case of doing good business with Hungarian landowners, it was necessary to abuse the Germans—which in those regions meant the Austrians. Therefore he did not venture, even within the four walls of the Fischer homestead, to praise the Austrian Government. He would go so far as to admit that the Austrians, once they had restored order, even though it were by force, would certainly keep their promise and bestir themselves for the good of poor defeated Hungary. They would build roads and railways, and in a few years it would be worth while to do business with such a state.

"Well, and what more does one want?" challenged his senior.

"I admit that business is beginning to thrive again," said Hermann, with his eyes on Regine (since it was possible, having rounded the dangerous corner, to risk enthusiasm for the now harmless ideals), "but the people are oppressed, there is no liberty."

"Have you not had enough of liberty yet, young man?" asked the "Terror of the Batchka" ironically.

But at this point Hermann Bondy recalled the iambics which the Marquis of Posa flung at the tyrant Philip II of Spain: "Sire, give us back . . ." These he declaimed with such appreciation of their fulminating splendour that Regine now definitely succumbed to the fascinations of her cavalier. The effect of the half-understood verses—or, rather, perhaps, of the voluptuous rich baritone—was visible in her rapt look. Old Salomon's thick lip curled in derision. He merely waved his hand, but with such contempt that the verses froze on Hermann's lips.

"One mistake Austria has made," said Salomon, smiling, "about which your Schiller has written no poems. They leave us no peace with their taxes. They exact them, without consideration, to the last farthing."

It was now Hermann's turn to stand up for the Austrians. "I have no objection to taxation," he said, "now that I know that, when one of us has to pay, the nobility have to pay too."

In his enthusiasm his face had flushed so red as to make his beard even blacker by contrast. It was obvious that he was genuinely uplifted by his consciousness that one thing was salvaged from the wreck of Liberty, Equality, and Fraternity—an equality that existed, at least in the mind of the tax-gatherer, between magnate and bourgeois, the removal of the humiliating difference between the cavalier and the common taxpayer. True, Hermann himself paid no taxes, or hardly any, for he knew how to elude the most ferret-like Austrian officials. But the sensibilities of this corn-broker and disciple of Heine and Börne were so elastic that he managed to speak as he felt and act as his interest dictated. Quite forgetting his misleading statements of income and the false oath sworn before the court, he repeated that he would willingly pay his taxes as long as Prince Esterházy paid his. But Salomon's interpretation of the revolutionary principle: Equal burdens for all citizens of the State, was that Esterházy should indeed pay—that was right enough—but it did not in the least follow that he, Salomon Fischer, should have to pay too.

"But are we not tiring the young lady with such talk?" inquired Hermann politely of Reginchen, who had retired into herself. She now picked up a dumpling on the end of her fork and was about to reply, when Salomon forestalled her.

"My daughter is a sensible little girl and likes to listen when sensible people talk of sensible things." He then turned the conversation to the Pest Exchange, complained that the high rate and this stupid playing at revolutions had taken away the value of paper money and depressed the rate of the best annuities.

"That is true, no denying it," agreed Hermann. "But people with ready money ought to buy annuities now at the present low rate. Rothschild is doing it. Then as soon as things improve externally, the rates must necessarily rise too."

"My dear Herr Bondy, you are still young. For, else, how should you say *must?* What is there that is certain on Change? Nothing! Something may always turn up: a revolution, a war—any old thing—and down comes the crash, and where's your annuity then? I tell you I mean to stick to my ready money."

Hermann for his part was interested in the landowners of the Batchka, with whom he hoped to do business, and he forgot Regine so completely over this thrilling conversation that the old man was obliged to draw his guest's attention to her.

"How's this for coffee? No one in the Batchka can make it except my Regine."

"Upon my word, it is first-rate, excellent. May I have another cup?"

Regine filled it, and Hermann, who was both a clever fellow and a ladies' man, now gave her his flattering attention.

"Are you fond of a good joke, Fräulein Regine?"

"Oh yes," she murmured.

"Well, let's have one," grunted Salomon.

"Do you know the one about the rich Jew who would send his son to Germany, cost what it might, to a German village, so that the boy could learn pure German?"

"Do I know it, indeed!" interrupted Salomon. But then, adhering to the principle that the young people must get to know each other, he rapped the table with his snuff-box, offered the prospective bridegroom a pinch, and got up to leave the two alone, the man with the ringing voice, and the shy whispering girl.

"I have not heard the joke before," said Regine in a soft agitated voice, politely anxious to steer herself and her guest through the embarrassing moment.

By way of prelude Hermann leaned his elbow on the table,

moving his lower arm rhythmically for a while, curved thumb and first finger into a circle, and continued to dangle his hand to and fro when at last he embarked afresh on the anecdote, his serious eyes dancing for once with amusement. The story worked up very gradually to the moment when the point of the jest became visible, looming ahead like a mountain peak in the fog. The Jewish lad, instead of learning German, taught his own dialect to the whole village. This was the point, but Hermann never reached it. The joke was lost in laughter, fits of which shook the narrator ever more and more violently as he neared his goal. "Ha ha!" he laughed and "Hi-hi!" came the giggling girlish echo from between Regine's little squirrel's teeth.

The alternation of ha ha and hi-hi had a decisive effect on both parties. Once the crust of embarrassment had melted, they made friends rapidly, as those about to marry should, and their laughter rang out heartily.

Regine related the story of the barricades, when digging had so upset her that she fainted. She talked of the Russians, too, and how recklessly they threw themselves into their wild dances, just as the Magyars did into their *csárdás*. And their singing, like that of the Magyars, ended in shouting. But Russians had such tiny, tiny eyes, and their cheek-bones stood out. No one could call them handsome. Of the *Honvéd* she said nothing, although he was a handsome Hungarian if ever there was one.

Hermann, anxious, for his part, to show himself in the most favourable light, dwelt upon the advantages of his social position. He was in constant business communication with the leading families, Blau and Wottitz. Indeed (smiling complacently), he might say that he was on a friendly footing with them. In Vienna he was made free of the Rosenthals' house, and the Rosenthals had been ennobled by the Emperor Francis. Rosenthal von Poselitz was the full style, he added. And his eyes brightened as he ran through the names of all the aristocratic Jewish families in turn, aiming no doubt at showing the advantages and possibilities of such a good match. Everything was open to a Jew today, as he further informed her. "Very different from a hundred years ago, isn't it?"

But Regine seemed not to know how things were a hundred years ago. She knew neither the old world nor the new and had no vanity. Only half her attention was given to Hermann's many wise sayings. Occasionally her eyelids fluttered, that was all. Her handsome fiancé's skilfully knotted cravat absorbed her far more than his words. And Hermann, seeing that human vanity struck no response in Regine, tried to wring words from her on the question of material interests. "As I had the honour of telling your father, my business has shown a tendency to increase day by day since the unrest of the Revolution," he informed her, meaning that she who became Hermann Bondy's wife might consider herself a lucky woman. Then, as this opening likewise failed, he tried to move Reginchen with the story of the unfortunate Jakob. For better effect he squeezed out a tear, and at once a tear glistened in Regine's eye. They had now talked together, laughed together, and in the end cried together, and Hermann's glance at the table, with Regine's hand resting on it, suggested the next step. He bent over the little hand, roughened by housework, with the short red podgy fingers and dull rounded nails, and was about to press a rapturous kiss on it, but the girl pulled it away and laid it on her knee. She sat up straight and pale on her chair and was so frightened that she forgot to lower her eyes. It was undoubtedly the picture of Hermann and his black beard which was reflected in the young girl's startled eyes, but the picture she saw was that of the blond *Honvéd* whom she had seen but once and in whose arms she had lain—for a space of seconds.

An embarrassed silence set in. Two hearts beat to the clock's ticking. To break the spell Hermann began to recite Heine in that famous baritone which he had found so invaluable in its effect on women's tender hearts. After repeating: "Thou'rt like a lovely flower," he made Regine a formal offer, and she, yielding to her own maidenly feelings and the paternal command, said yes, uncertainly, and held out her hand with the feeling that now it was permitted. He was the first to hold this small moist member, which had never been pressed by a man's hand. He would have to wait until after supper to give his fiancée the kiss on her forehead, in the presence of her father, which would be the kiss of betrothal and at the same time the kiss of farewell. For early the next day Hermann was leaving to visit the great market centres and villages of the wheat-growing Batchka—Baja, Neusatz, Maria-Theresiopel—where he was awaited by his new business acquaintances.

"So soon?" stammered Regine, with a lump in her throat.

"Why, yes, business is business, you know," was the matter-of-fact reply. Then, remembering his rôle, Hermann pressed his folded hands to his breast and began to sing: "Brother, little brother mine," but broke off to make the prosaic correction: "That is, in this case it should be 'Sister, little sister mine.' " And half in fun, half in earnest, as if to tease her, he put on a theatrical voice to roll out the lines:

> *"Sister, little sister mine,*
> *Part we must, so why repine?"*

"It's his work that matters," grunted Salomon, in full approba-
tion of this obedience to the call of business and duty.

At this first shock to her young love, Regine felt like a child
caught in mischief as she stood there with these brutal business men.
Of course work came first. Duty before everything. Fischers and
Bondys had no time for loving. Regine could see that, but it was none
the easier for her. She gulped down her emotion gallantly, then waved
a mute farewell to her fiancé. Good night, Hermann, good night,
happiness, love, bliss!

In the spare room on the bedside table lay Regine's album, open.
It was evidently intended that the fiancé should leave his inscription
there like all those guests before him who had scribbled words of
wisdom under pressed or painted violets or forget-me-nots, as the
case might be. "Be modest like this violet," read one, and: "What says
this forget-me-not? Ah, fair maid, forget me not!" Hermann pondered
long over a suitable contribution. At last he thought of: "Past are the
pleasant days spent at Aranjuez." But, as no poetical licence could
justify the conversion of the one pleasant day spent with Regine into
the plural, he preferred, as an accurate man of business, to adapt his
favourite lines to the circumstances. He therefore wrote, in picturesque
lettering: "Past is the pleasant day spent at Aranjuez." Then he went
to bed. But he was soon disturbed by the reflection that this was not,
after all, the right motto for a lover, still less a fiancé. It was too sad.
Resigned, rather than cheerful. He would have liked to add something
cheerful that was at the same time witty and amorous, say: "They're
still to come, those pleasant days down at Aranjuez." Luckily there
was still room between the original inscription and the signature, and
the additional line, conveying a lover's pleasurable anticipation, wittily
expressed, was duly entered in the album in the same florid style.

In the morning, Hermann breakfasted with his father-in-law.
Regine presided over the tray. On this occasion, as on the day when
she handed the young officer his glass of water, her hands shook with
excitement, and she spilt a few drops from the coffee-pot.

"Take care, or you'll get it from me," roared Salomon.

"Oh, but she's now my betrothed. From today on she is responsible to me and me only, and what she 'gets' she will get from me.
And just to show you, my dear father-in-law, how I respect your

wishes, I am going to punish Regine for her clumsiness—like this."
And Hermann got up and planted a smacking kiss through his beard
on his betrothed's lips.

It must be admitted that Hermann was not only rich, not only
well educated—anyone can be rich if he works and has luck, or well
educated if he spends money on books and has the patience to read
them—but, and this is only to be had by the grace of God and cannot
be bought for any money, he was a fine, really fine, man, and intelligent, really extremely intelligent. He was full of nice feelings and had
a beautiful mind. He was well brought up, quite a cavalier, and—
what was all-important—he placed the firm, his clients, and his work
before everything. A very lucky girl indeed was Regine.

After breakfast, Salomon took his son-in-law aside and bowed
him into his counting-house again. He offered him a cigarette, cleared
his throat, looked at him in a rather embarrassed way, and finally
began to talk.

"I am happy. I say it as a father. You will make a fine couple.
God made you for each other. I can see that my daughter pleases you
and I do not need to tell you how much she likes you. In a word, as
regards the dowry. . . ."

In a word, that is, as Papa Salomon thought he could detect the
love-germ in the satisfaction displayed by both parties, he had set
himself to work on the young man's feelings to the extent of reducing
the dowry proposed on the previous day by about fifteen thousand
gulden. But Hermann would not relinquish a single kreuzer.

"But what about the love in it? Is that nothing?" demanded Salomon indignantly, as he made his next offer, of sixty-five thousand.

"That has nothing to do with it. It is a thing by itself. Do not let
us confuse the issues. Now that I know your charming daughter, I
shall still, though with a heavy heart, give her up rather than the full
sum of seventy-five thousand agreed upon at our meeting yesterday."

Startled by the vigorous resistance put up by Hermann, Salomon
forced his fat face to smile.

"Ha ha, ha ha!" he laughed, clapping Hermann on the back
and shoulders, "that's what I like. That I call well spoken. If you had
said, now, that you would relinquish part of the dowry, I should have
told you that the whole marriage was off. For I am not going to give
my daughter to any lovesick booby who cannot protect his own interests. I will give my daughter, my one daughter, to a sober man only,
to you only. For to you, my dear son, I can safely confide her, ha ha,
ha ha!"

But from the windows the coach could now be seen waiting for its passenger under the acacias in front of the church. The "children" hurried out, with just five minutes of happiness to spare, and Salomon trotted behind them. Then came the parting, and the threads which bound their hearts broke like late autumn gossamer. There stood the horses, neighing and stamping at the crack of the whip, and there sat the coachman, with thick hair hanging out under the shady hat-brim and a bronze shimmer of well-oiled skin between the wide pantaloons and the shirt reaching to his belt. His navel shone like the grinning disk of a heraldic sun. Around the coach stood Jewish women with false partings and Jewish girls in long pigtails. They were waiting. For Hermann. Waiting to see the fiancé. "And a very fine man was he!" they sang.

This chorus of approval helped to assuage Regine's grief as she blushingly kissed her betrothed for the last time. Then she waved her handkerchief until the coach was swallowed up in the clouds of dust.

Quickly as the engagement had come about, it was, as was right and proper, a long time before the marriage took place. In the meantime Hermann sent his bride every day—as was also right and proper —an elegant letter on long, broad sheets of paper with the heading of the Bondy firm. The pages were covered with his fine even characters. "He writes beautifully," commented Salomon with great satisfaction. "What beautiful things he writes!" carolled Regine, and the letters, strewn with quotations from Heine, were exhibited proudly to the Jewish girls in the village. Once, though, the writer wrote something offensive which made Reginchen blush: "For breakfast at the kiosk I get rolls that are as tiny as the corns on your tiny feet." It surprised Regine very much that anyone should dare to write such things to her. She could feel her feet naked and white and cold under her shoes and stockings. After this she showed her fiancé's letters to nobody.

Love to a man, as to a magnet, has the greatest attraction only when it is combined with a certain metal.—Moritz G. Saphir

When a scholar goes out in search of a bride he should take an ignoramus along with him as expert.—The Talmud

LOOSE-FOOTED
AND DEFT-HANDED

Schacher-Machers
and Finaglers

*Shloime—why don't you keep moving around
so people'll think you're doing big business?*

The average Jew has little patience with the finagler and the
schacher-macher, *the manipulator and the skuldugger, the nasty fellow and the petty swindler. He is shocked into incredulity by their
bluff and sleight-of-hand cunning, by their greed and* chutzpah, *which
is the Hebrew for unmitigated nerve. The Jewish folk have a saying:
"He's such a* schacher-macher *that he can talk it into you that your
lung and liver are located in your nose."*

*Mean and low characters are no novelty among any people. "But
you know how it is," jokes the Yiddish folk wag, "it's a lot easier for
a hunchback to see the hump on someone else." It also looks a lot
funnier on the other fellow. This is apropos of the jaundiced way
some Gentiles regard the shortcomings they say they discover in Jews,
generalizing the faults of some Jews into faults of all Jews.*

*Concerning this talent of the anti-Semite to see the beam in the
Jew's eye and to ignore the mote in his own, the following Jewish
story is a parable to inscribe, as Scripture says, on the tablets of the
heart.*

Mrs. Karger and Mrs. Borgenicht, landsleit *from the same town
in the old country, met again after a separation of some years at a
wedding in the Bronx. And so they sat cosily reminiscing about by-
gone times.*

*"Oy! How ugly! That boy over there!" suddenly exclaimed Mrs.
Karger, pointing with a slight shudder at a youth standing nearby.
"Just look at all the pimples on his face! Excuse me for the words,
Mrs. Borgenicht, but it's enough for a person to throw up!"*

*"You should shame yourself in your far neck, Mrs. Karger!"
bristled Mrs. Borgenicht. "How dare you say such a thing about
my Sammy!"*

"What? Did you say your Sammy!" *murmured Mrs. Karger
aghast. Then quickly recovering, she beamed: "It's all right, Mrs.
Borgenicht! Don't you worry! On Sammy they're so becoming!"*

The reader will find that the selections in this and other sections of this anthology pay ample attention to the pimples on Sammy's face, and if they are not exactly becoming they are hardly intended to be so. The genuine humorist or wit is always devoted to truth and, if his barbs hurt, it is only because he has struck home.

"No one judges Jewish sins more sternly than Jews themselves; no flock expels black sheep more implacably than the Jewish," wrote Max Nordau.

In Jewish life, where mutual aid and uprightness were primary necessities for survival, unscrupulous, antisocial characters were despised more than elsewhere. But at all times there was the intellectual curiosity present to understand why they behaved the way they did, and in that understanding their antics stood out in absurd comic relief.

N.A.

BLUFF A STORY OF THE DEPRESSION

BY B. KOVNER (JACOB ADLER)
TRANSLATED FROM THE YIDDISH BY NATHAN AUSUBEL

"How are you making out Beril? And what's the news about *parnosseh*, eh? Are you working?"

"What work? Who works? Where's there work? I can no longer remember the time when I was working."

"So what are you doing? One has got to live, no? You've got to eat, clothes you must wear, a home you've got to have."

"Nu, there's always a way. One doesn't live, one doesn't eat, one is dressed in tatters, and one doesn't pay any rent."

"Are you trying to tell me, Beril, that you haven't got a cent to your name?"

"Not a groschen!"

"You can tell me the truth, Beril, because I'm not going to borrow any money from you. I have, thank God, provided for myself so that I don't have to depend on others."

At this, Beril became lost in thought. Finally he said, with a forced smile:

"Since you're well provided, I'll tell you the whole truth: I too am well off! My heart told me long ago that a depression would come and that I'd be out of work, so I saved a bit of cash in the good days. No, I didn't trade on Wall Street, neither did I deposit my few dollars in the Bank of the United States which went flop. Believe me, I didn't throw my money around. That's why I'm getting along now."

"So why didn't you tell me right away that you had a few dollars put by?"

"I'll tell you the truth. I was afraid that you might be in trouble and so you'd want to borrow money from me. And who is willing to lend money nowadays, who can and who dares? These days, if you lend somebody a few dollars, you can forget about them. But since you tell me that you're well off, I'm telling you the truth that I too don't need anybody's help."

"Since you've been so frank with me, Beril, I'll be just as frank with you. The truth is that I'm *takkeh* in great trouble. I don't have a red cent, neither money nor work. Sometimes my wife and I go to bed without eating supper. To pay rent is out of the question. I'm already behind four months in my rent, and my landlord rips the hide off me. He threatens to put me out on the street. If I could only pay him for one month, he'd be willing to wait. If you could only lend me at least fifty! And since, as you say you have *takkeh* provided for yourself in the good days, you'd do me a great favor, Beril, if you'd lend me that fifty. When I start working I'll pay you back."

As Beril listened he turned pale, his lips began to tremble and he stammered in a strange voice:

"Well . . . since you've been good enough to tell me the whole truth I'll do the same. Believe me, that even if you should want to cut my throat I wouldn't be able to show you a penny. I've already borrowed from everyone I could. I've already pawned everything that has any value. There's no work. My children also don't work, and whenever I lay my hands on a borrowed dollar I give half to the children and half I keep for myself. My wife doesn't even own a pair of whole stockings. So help me, that's the honest truth!"

"I don't understand you at all, Beril! Before, you told me that you're so well off, that you provided for yourself during good times, that you didn't gamble on Wall Street, didn't deposit your money in the Bank of the United States, and that, thank God, you needed nobody's help. And now you go ahead and tell me that you are dead broke! What do you mean? As I see it, you're merely bluffing."

"Well . . . I told you all that because you told me that things aren't so bad with you and that you don't need anybody's help. Since you're already provided for I've nothing to fear. But later, when you told me that you're in trouble and that you asked me to lend you fifty . . . well, you understand! So I'm telling you the truth—the honest truth—if I could, I'd borrow a fifty myself somewhere. But where do you find fifties rolling around today? Nobody has anything. Take Chaim-Hersh, his tongue already is hanging out; Usher-Menashe stands in the breadline; Shachne-Lemmel goes around begging; Mechel-Moishe goes out like a candle. Nu, so I ask you, from whom can I borrow fifty? From whom?"

"Listen Beril, my friend, you don't have to complain to me; I don't want to borrow any money from you. Just out of curiosity I wanted to feel your pulse, to see whether it's possible to get a loan of a few dollars from you in time of need. But it hasn't come to that point yet, Beril! Since you've just told me the *truthful* truth, I too will tell *you* the truthful truth. I really don't need anybody's help. I had enough sense in my head to provide for a rainy day. Yes, Beril, thank God I'm provided for! And even if I had nothing I'd never come to ask you for a loan. I know you and I know your character too. I know that you don't like to do anybody a favor. Even if you were a millionaire I wouldn't come to ask you for a loan. I'd rather go to bed without supper than depend on you."

"That's just a lot of talk! You'd change your mind."

"I swear I wouldn't!"

"I don't believe you."

"Beril, I swear by my children that it's so!"

"Well . . . if you really mean it, I'll tell you now the truth, the whole truth. I'm as well off as you are. Maybe even better! And I too don't need anybody's help. If I complained, it was only because I was afraid that you were going to ask me for a loan. Everybody is watching out for his own hide. So we bluff and lie and feel the other fellow's pulse, and the other fellow does exactly the same thing."

> *You can't force anyone to love you or to lend you money.*

CHEAPER BY FAR

When the bank refused to lend Feitelman ten thousand dollars on a risky real-estate venture, he went to call on his lodge brother, the big cloak-and-suiter Hyamson, as a last resort.

"Hyamson, my friend," he said, "I've come to ask you to lend me ten thousand dollars."

Hyamson nodded politely, reflectively puffed on his cigar, but didn't answer.

Thinking he hadn't heard him correctly the first time, Feitelman repeated his request. Still Hyamson didn't answer.

Finally, exasperated Feitelman burst out, "Why don't you say something, Hyamson? You owe me an answer at least."

Slowly Hyamson took the cigar out of his mouth. Looking intently at Feitelman he said, "Sure, Feitelman, I owe you an answer. But better I should owe you an answer that that you should owe me ten thousand dollars!"

TO TIDE HIM OVER

A disciple sought the advice of his rabbi.

"I'm poor, Rabbi. My wife is sick and my children are hungry."

"Go home. God will help you," advised the rabbi.

"Thank you, thank you, Rabbi!" gushed the poor man gratefully. "I'm sure God will help me! But until He does, won't you be good enough to lend me five rubles?"

BASIS FOR FRIENDSHIP

Goldstein, Cohen, and Wishnick, three dress manufacturers, were walking in New York's garment center when Karp, the well-known dress jobber, passed by.

"Good morning!" said he with a friendly wave of his hand.

"Good morning!" they all chorused with flattering warmth.

"He said 'good morning' to me, not to you two," remarked Goldstein.

"What makes you so sure?" asked the other two.

"Because just last week I lent him ten thousand dollars."

"Smarty!" snorted Cohen. "I'll bet my bottom dollar it was me he greeted!"

"Sez you!" sneered the other two.

"Sure!" said Cohen, grinning. "It couldn't be anyone but me, because for the last two years I have owed him five thousand dollars and he'd like to see them back, I'm sure."

Wishnick laughed.

"Don't kid yourselves, both of you!" he mocked. "After what you've just said, I'm sure it must have been me that Karp greeted. You see, I don't owe him any money and he doesn't owe me any. So why shouldn't he give me a 'good morning'?"

BUSINESS!

BY SHOLOM ALEICHEM

1. *Bad!* "He earns and I lose."
2. *Fair!* "Both of us earn."
3. *Good!* "I earn and he loses."

ONE WAY OF GETTING A HUNDRED POUNDS

BY GERALD KERSH

Fabian telephoned Figler at one o'clock.

Figler changed his address several times a year, but was usually to be found somewhere in the residential area between Southampton Row and the Gray's Inn Road—that somber, comfortless jungle of smoky apartment houses, inhabited by a shifting population of men without property who arrive in a hurry and frequently leave by night; where tradesmen give no credit, and rent is payable strictly in advance. Figler was a bachelor, and occupied a single room on the ground floor of a house in Tavistock Place. Why Tavistock Place? It sounded good. Why the ground floor? He found it comforting to be within leaping distance of the street.

When Fabian rang, he was poring over a sixpenny scrapbook bulging with mysterious newspaper cuttings. He closed it, and put a heavy vase on top of it, before going to the phone. When he spoke:

"Hello?"

"Figler?"

"I don't know if he's in. Who's speaking?"

"Harry Fabian."

"Oh, hello, Harry. What is it?"

"Listen, Figler; about that hundred quid. . . ."

"Yes?"

"I got it."

"You what?" exclaimed Figler, with something like consternation.

"Sure. Now we're ready to start."

"Oh, sure, Harry. But listen——"

"When can I meet you?"

"Uh. . . . Almost any time. But I'm a bit rushed at the moment. Better make it tonight."

"Tonight? Where, up at Anna's?

"Yes."

"Say, listen. Got the money?"

"Who, *me?* I can write out a check——"

"No checks, Figler; cash."

"What? You don't trust me?"

"Sure, sure I trust you. But anybody could write out a check. Would you pool in a hundred pounds cash on *my* check?"

Figler could find no reply to this; he simply said: "What, have you got cash?"

"Listen!" Fabian rustled a newspaper in the mouthpiece of his telephone. "One hundred in notes. D'you hear 'em? Ain't that music? If you got money in the bank, you can easy draw it out, can't you?"

"Ha-ha-ha-ha-ha! Can I draw it out! . . . But all the same, you ought to trust my check."

"Would you trust mine?"

"Between friends——"

"There ain't no friendship in business. You said so yourself; *i* say so too. I got my half. Now let's see yours, and get going. Let's do real business for a change—we're in on the heavy sugar. No funny stuff——"

"Don't adopt that attitude just because you got a hundred quid in your pocket for the first time in your life, Harry! I'm willing to come in on a straight fifty-fifty basis, but if you think you can order me about——"

"Now, don't be silly, Figler."

"All right. Meet me at half-past ten in Anna's."

"Half-past ten in Anna's, okey-doke."

"Good-by."

"So long."

Ping went the receiver as Figler rang off. He went back to his room, seething with anger. *Damn him!* he thought. *How the devil did he manage to get hold of a hundred quid so quick? And how the devil am I supposed to get a hundred by tonight?* He took out his bankbook, and found that he had exactly thirty-one pounds and ninepence to his credit. *A hundred pounds he gets! Since when has he been a businessman? The little rat!*

Figler paced the room. Then he took out a fat, old-fashioned notebook with glossy black covers. This was Figler's Bible: it contained his gospel, and the rules in accordance with which he ordered his life. It was packed with names and addresses of wholesalers, covering every imaginable line in merchandise. Figler had compiled it gradually, during a lifetime of tortuous research in the snake-haunted hinterland of questionable commerce. It was a kind of cabala of buying and selling. If you approached Figler with a consignment of spoiled birdseed, perished elastic garters, rusty umbrella ribs, warped butter patters, out-of-date calendars, or shaving papers left over from the nineties, he would run a finger up and down the pages, smoke a cigarette, look up, choke, recover, and say: "Uh . . . I can dispose of this stuff on a fifty-fifty basis. . . ." Buyers attached to film companies had offered him considerable sums for his notebook; but that was the one thing in the world which Figler would not sell. It was more than his living—it was his life.

He sat down with it, and smoked a cigarette.

Smoke bubbled through his congested bronchial tubes, as through a hookah. *"Uh!"* exclaimed Figler. He threw away his cigarette end, and put on his hat; locked up the book, tapped himself on the bosom with a clothes brush, and went out.

First of all, Figler went to Mortimer Street, to a ground-floor office with a plate which said: RETAILERS' SUPPLIES LTD., P. PINKUS. He walked in. A secretary stopped him.

"Pinkus?" said Figler.

"Aoh, Mr. Pinkus is awfully busy; he can't see anybody today."

"Ah. In that case, I'll go right in," said Figler. Looking straight in front of him, with a calm, preoccupied expression on his face, he brushed past the secretary, and went into an inner office. This was a small, plywood room, not much larger than the average bathroom, and ankle-deep in papers. The wastepaper basket overflowed with catalogues; incalculable accumulations of bills, chits, receipts, and proforma invoices, impaled on old wire files like skewers of cats' meat, hung in festoons around the walls, and curled up in the warm, damp air. On the desk an electric heater, in the form of a copper bowl, breathed waves of stifling heat into the face of Mr. Pinkus. He was a short, heavy, excitable man, with a cigarette in his mouth. The smoke rose in a straight blue bar, until the heat waves caught it and spun it out into nothingness.

He looked up as Figler came in.

"What is it? What is it? What is it, Joe? Busy, busy. What is it?"

"Listen," said Figler, "tell me; how are you fixed for bentwood chairs?"

"Bentwood chairs!" shouted Pinkus. "A fire on bentwood chairs! All I get, all day long, is bentwood chairs and bentwood chairs! I've been sitting here on pins and needles with bentwood chairs—and now *he's* here with bentwood chairs!"

"Ssh! All this excitement. You can't get them, eh?"

"Of course I can't get 'em. If I want to buy off Lipsky, I can get a million of 'em. But who's going to buy bentwood chairs off Lipsky, that twicer!"

"Listen. The sort of bentwood chairs you want is the little round chairs with curly backs, eh?"

"Curly backs! You can't get a bentwood with a curly back——"

"Lipsky bought 'em all up."

"So he's telling me! I've been spitting blood over it, and he's telling *me!*"

"All right. I can get hold of some."

"How many?"

"Twenty gross."

"Twenty gross? How much?"

"Lipsky's charging seventy bob a dozen. I'm cutting his price."

"How much by?"

"Eleven bob a dozen."

"Go on! Fifty-nine bob a dozen you're asking?"

"Fifty-nine bob per dozen."

"I can use twelve gross."

"Yes, I dare say you can. But you are having no more than three gross."

"Now why should you *be* like that? I can clear you out the whole stock without nonsense——"

"Listen," said Figler patiently, "and don't talk so silly. You know as well as I do that Lipsky's got every small round bentwood chair on the market. Is that so?"

"Well?"

"Give me a straight answer, yes or no."

"All right, well?"

"All right. I got a few gross. So if I got 'em to dispose of at a cut price, you got to consider, Pinkus, I also got two-three friends in the business apart from yourself who I want to do a good turn to."

"Well?"

"So if you want three gross at fifty-nine bob a dozen, say yes or no, and I can deliver this afternoon on receipt of check. If not, all right. Well?"

"All right, I'll take the three gross. You said fifty-five bob a dozen?"

"Fifty-nine!"

"Ah, come on! Don't be silly! You can knock me off fourpence on a chair."

"Pinkus, don't make a fool of yourself. Here am I, cutting the price down"—Figler clicked the nails of his thumb and forefinger, as one who kills an invisible louse—"like *that*, and you argue! Listen; don't let's have no argument, because I got no time. I can't cut another farthing. Ain't I got to live? Now you know me; I'm straight. I got a reputation to lose. The three gross; fifty-nine bob a dozen. If you said, 'Fifty-eight and elevenpence three farthings,' I'd say, 'No! Definitely no!' A hundred and six pound four shillings for three gross. Yes, or no."

"A hundred and six pounds."

"A hundred and six pound four."

"Forget the four shillings!"

"A hundred and six pound four!"

"All right, I'll take 'em."

"Seven-and-sixpenny chairs I offer him for fifty-nine bob a dozen, so he's doing me a favor by taking 'em! I'll deliver this afternoon to your warehouse. I want your check the minute the goods arrive."

"All right. You'll wait a week."

"Listen, Pinkus; you know me. I don't give no credit. I can't. Ask yourself. How am I going to give hundred pounds of credit. Cash are the terms. Otherwise, no deal."

"Well, I can do with the stuff. As a matter of fact, I got an urgent delivery to make——"

"I know. To Wilson."

"Who told you about Wilson?"

"Never mind. I know. When have you got to deliver?"

"At once, if not sooner. I should have delivered yesterday."

"Yes, I heard. All right, I'll let you have the stuff today, as soon as I get your check."

"Figler, we've been doing business for years, and I trust you like my own brother. If you say the stuff's all right, I know it's all right. When can I see it?"

"Four o'clock."

"I can't get away. Say six."

"All right, six."

"I'll make a note of the amount. I'll give you the check right away. A hundred pounds. . . ."

"A hundred and six pound four."

"Four! Four! A hundred and six pound!"

"—Four shillings."

"All right. See you later."

Figler went out.

Now Fabian, in Figler's place, would certainly have taken a taxi; but Figler, who was a connoisseur of traffic congestion and relative speeds, ambled into the Underground. Twenty minutes later, he was sniffing and coughing in the offices of Lipsky and Company, in Bishopsgate. Lipsky junior was a young, sharp man, expert in the ways of buyers, wise to the habits of salesmen; calm; detached; a Darwin of the restaurant supply business, who might have undertaken a scientific classification of the vague flora and elusive fauna of the catering world.

Figler said to him:

"I would like some of those little round bentwood chairs—number seventy-two X."

"Seventy-two X? Certainly! As many as you like! Very nice line. Can't get them anywhere else, you know. Seventy shillings a dozen to you."

"Well, it's like this, Mr. Lipsky. I'm getting these chairs for a fellow who's opening a new place up North."

"Oh, up North, eh? What kind of place?"

"A sort of lecture hall, or something."

"Might I ask where?"

Without hesitation, Figler replied: "A town near Blackburn, some place called Darwen."

"Darwen. . . . Yes?"

"Well, business is business. I want to make a few bob out of it, so you'll drop a few bob on a dozen——"

"Can't be done, I'm afraid."

"Ah, yes it can! You know me. We've done business together for years. *You* won't be down! I'm buying these chairs on my own responsibility, myself. So be a good fellow and let me have them for sixty-five."

"Well, I'll tell you what I'll do. You can have three gross at sixty-seven and six."

"I think you might be a little more generous with me, considering we've been doing business together for so many years——"

"That's just it. Business is business. Apart from business, I'll be as generous as you like. If you're on the floor, come to me and you're always sure of a ten-pound note. But business is business."

"Come on!" wheezed Figler, in a coaxing voice. "Sixty-six bob. That's five-and-six a chair."

"Yes, and you couldn't get that chair anywhere for seven shillings."

"Well, look here. Give me three months to pay."

"I can't do it."

"You trust me?"

"I trust you. I've never heard of you letting anybody down. All the same, you're an individual, not a firm, and I can't do it. But look here. I'll tell you what I'll do. I'll meet you halfway. Pay me half down, and I'll take your check for the other half, postdated twenty-eight days."

"At sixty-six bob?"

"I'll make it sixty-seven shillings a dozen, and not a farthing less. That's rock bottom."

"Look here: make it a third down——"

"No, I've told you the best I can do, and I wouldn't do that for anybody else."

"Well . . . could I have the stuff at once?"

"Day after tomorrow?"

"Say I wanted it now?"

"Can't be done. All the vans are out."

"Oh, that's all right. I've got a van."

"Since when?"

"Oh, I been doing business on a bigger scale just lately. I hired one. Well, all right, get the invoice out, and I'll let you have my check."

"All right, Mr. Figler. It'll be sixty pounds six shillings."

"Call it sixty pounds."

"And six shillings."

Figler wrote a check for sixty pounds, and pushed it across the desk. Lipsky took it very calmly, thanked Figler, and said: "In that case make out your second check for sixty pounds twelve shillings."

"Sixty pounds."

"—Twelve," said Lipsky.

Figler wrote the second check for sixty pounds ten shillings.

Lipsky laughed. "All right, you old devil. You can give me a cigar for the other two shillings."

"Pleasure!" said Figler. He took out a large Bolivar which somebody else had given him a month or two before, and which he had brought out with him in anticipation of some such friendly gesture.

The men shook hands. Figler went out.

As soon as he reached the street, Figler began to hurry. He found himself, now, in one of those fantastically precarious positions in which the fiddler not infrequently finds himself. He had given Lipsky a check for £60, when there was no more than £30 to his credit in the bank. He knew that that check would be paid in by three o'clock. If it were not met, his credit would be killed: he would be ruined. Curious as it may seem, Figler was able to exist almost entirely on account of his unspoiled reputation as a man whom it was safe to trust; and this reputation now hung in the balance. He changed a shilling into pennies, and went into a telephone booth. Then he rang the Magniloquencia Cigar Co.

"Hello! I want to speak to Mr. Cohen. . . . Figler. . . . Hello, Cohen? Listen. I want a thousand of your Coronas, at once. . . . Yes. . . . No, I couldn't pay before the middle of next month. . . . All right. . . . Of course! You know me, don't you? . . . Thanks very much, Cohen. . . . Yes, a little better, thank you; only a bit stuffy in the head. You quite well? The family? . . . Good, good! Good-by!"

As quick as lightning, Figler's fat fingers twirled the dial again.

"Hello! Figler speaking! Is that Mr. Gold? Here, listen, Gold; could you do with a thousand Magniloquencia Coronas? You can have 'em for thirty-two pounds, cash. . . . What? . . . *What?* . . . Stocked up with 'em? What d'you mean? Eh? . . . Don't be silly, of course you could sell them! . . . Is that definite? You got ten thousand in stock? *Ten thousand!* Oi! . . . All right. Good-by."

Figler broke out into a cold sweat. He rang Havana Cigar Distributors, but the proprietor was not in. Cheapside Tobacco (1937), Ltd., had more Magniloquencias than they knew what to do with. At this point, Fabian would have said: "Bloody hell!" but Figler never swore. He changed his tactics, and rang the Liquid Gold Egg Company.

"Hello!" said Figler. "Get me Mr. Shiptzel. . . . Figler. . . .

Hello, Shiptzel, this is Figler. . . . Figler, not Tiddler! . . . How are you? . . . I'm lovely. . . . A little stuffy in the head. Listen, is my credit good for a few tins of frozen eggs? . . . Oh, not more than forty pounds' worth. . . . Sure, middle of next month is all right, isn't it? Well, thanks. . . . Yes, I've tried syringing my nose, but it does no good. . . . Well, good-by."

Without hesitation, Figler rang the Appleton Bakeries. "Appleton? . . . Figler here. Listen: what are you paying for eggs? . . . *Eggs!* Not legs! . . . You are, eh? well, I can let you have Liquid Gold three farthings a pound cheaper. . . . It's a fact! I got hold of a few that Bobzer was storing before the price went up. . . . Yes, I can deliver now if you like, but I got to have cash. . . . Of course they're genuine! You know me, don't you? . . . Yes. . . . Yes. . . . Yes. . . . Cash on delivery, then. Very good. Good-by."

Figler breathed again. He dialed the Bullet Transport Company. "Hello! Bullet? Figler here. . . . Hello, Isaac! How's Betty? . . . Oh, a little stuffy in the head. . . . Listen, I want a van—a one-ton van. . . . Twenty hundredweights, one-ton; are you deaf, or what? . . . Only for the day. . . . Shut up, do you take me for a millionaire? . . . Make it a quid. . . . Oh, all right, twenty-five bob. Have it ready at once. I'm coming right over."

Figler rang off, and then got another number. "Hello! Cleartype Signs? Figler speaking. . . . Hello, Yossel! How *are* you? . . . Oh, a little stuffy in the head. . . . Listen. I want you to put your quickest man on to a streamer, about five feet by eighteen inches. . . . Ordinary paper—I just want to stick it on the side of a van. . . . Here are the words: FIGLER MERCHANDISE CO. Got it? Plain black letters on yellow. I got to have it within an hour. . . . Don't kid me, I don't pay a penny more than three-and-six. Good-by."

He came out of the telephone booth, mopping his forehead, and rode on a bus to the Bullet Transport Company. Squeezed beside the driver, he went in a one-ton van to Cleartype Signs, where the conspicuous black-and-yellow streamer: FIGLER MERCHANDISE CO., was pasted where all the City might read it; sped, with a roaring of exhausts, to Stepney, where he picked up the eggs; delivered them at the Appleton Bakeries, where he received a check for thirty-five pounds two shillings and sixpence.

"Lipsky's, Bishopsgate," said Figler to the driver.

As the chairs were being loaded, he took a taxi to his bank, and paid in Appleton's check. Then he rang Pinkus.

"Listen, Pinkus, I got the chairs in the van. Should I deliver them straight to your warehouse, or where? Say quick; I'm in a hurry. . . . All right, meet me at the warehouse with the check, in half an hour. Good-by."

They met at the warehouse. Pinkus looked at the chairs with approval, which he expressed in the following words:

"Well. . . . You haven't altogether swindled me."

"Swindle you? You ought to go down on your bended knees and thank me!" said Figler.

"Here's the check," said Pinkus, "a hundred and six quid."

"A hundred and six pound *four!*"

"Ah! A business for four lousy shillings! Here, here's a cigar, and shake hands on it!" And putting a hand into his breast pocket Pinkus pulled out a scabrous and battered Romeo y Julieta, which Figler recognized, by the cracks, as one which he had given to Pinkus nearly four months previously.

Figler dragged himself to a teashop, sat down heavily, and made notes in a penny notebook.

He had bought three gross of chairs for £120, and sold them for £106. He had bought a load of liquid eggs for £40 and sold it for £35. This made a dead loss of £19. £19, plus cost of hiring van; streamers, telephone calls, taxi, et cetera—say £21.

Then what had Figler done that was clever?

He had simply started another circle of credit. He had a hundred pounds in hand. With this capital, he intended to become a wrestling promoter. He owed Lipsky £60, and Liquid Gold £40. When these bills had to be met, he would buy, on credit, say half a dozen grand pianos, with the proceeds of which he would punctually settle the two debts. Then, his credit being still more firmly established, and his reputation being further strengthened, he could always rely on a consignment of goods from Lipsky or Liquid Gold, with which he could pay the piano manufacturer. By this time, Mr. Gold would have got rid of his stock of Magniloquencia Cigars, with the manufacturers of which Figler's credit still held good—and so Figler could go on and on, always owing somebody something, always robbing Peter to pay Paul, always digging one pit to fill another, always managing to keep a little bank balance and a good name; all by means of words and paper.

Innumerable tradesmen of good repute contrive to keep their heads above water in much the same way.

"Pot of tea," said Figler to the waitress, "two poached eggs on toast, and a sugar bun; and if ever a man worked hard for his bit of grub, my dear, that man is before you!"

EVERYONE IS SATISFIED

A customer who did not like to haggle over price went into a Canal Street clothing store.

"I don't like to bargain," he said. "That's why I've come here. I've heard this is a one-price store."

"We're strictly a one-price outfit," the proprietor assured him, and proceeded to fit a suit to him.

Having chosen a suit the customer asked, "How much is this?"

"I like a man of your type because you don't bargain," replied the clothier. "On my part, I don't like to ask dear and sell cheap. Therefore my friend, I'm not going to ask you thirty dollars for the suit, nor am I going to ask you twenty-five dollars for the suit, nor am I even going to ask you twenty dollars and forty-nine cents. All I'm going to ask you is twenty dollars—and not a cent more nor less!"

"I always like a one-price clothier like you," beamed the customer. "I'm not going to offer you twenty dollars for the suit, I'm not even going to offer you fifteen dollars for the suit. All I'll offer you is ten dollars."

"Sam," cried the clothier to his errand boy, "pack up this gentleman's suit!" And to the satisfied customer: "Wear this suit in good health, wear it long, and tear it quick and call again."

DEFERRED JUDGMENT

Once a Jewish "merchant," who kept a stall in a village marketplace in Poland bought a sack of prunes from another "merchant." When he examined the prunes, however, he found them full of worms. Without loss of time he hailed the seller before the communal elder.

Now the elder was a very old man and he had a sweet tooth. So he took out his spectacles, put them on his nose, and began examining the prunes. First he tasted one prune judiciously, then another and another. Still not satisfied, he continued to taste them with a speculative air.

This went on for about fifteen minutes. Then, completely sated, the elder pushed the prunes away from him with disgust.

"Why do you waste my time?" he cried. "What am I, a prune expert?"

A SURE WAY TO SUCCEED

FROM THE *Midrash*

A youth grew up in a certain king's household and the king came to feel a deep affection for him. One day he said to him:

"Ask whatever you wish and I'll give it to you."

The youth thought and thought:

What shall I ask him for? Shall I ask for precious gems, for gold and silver? He'll surely give them to me. Shall I ask for expensive clothes? These too he'll gladly give to me. What among them should I choose? Why not ask for his daughter? As his son-in-law I can then have everything.

THE INGENIOUS IGNORAMUS

Into a small Russian village once came a rabbi to apply for the rabbinical post that was vacant there. He was a good and wise man, was the rabbi, but with all that a terrible preacher and a worse scholar.

On the Sabbath day, right after the morning service, he mounted the pulpit ready to deliver a sample sermon. But go ahead and speak when there is just nothing to say!

But how does the saying go? "Where there is Torah there is also *chochma.*"

"My masters," began the rabbi resolutely. "Do you know what *sedra* we read today and about what I'm going to preach to you?"

"No," answered the congregation with one voice.

"If you don't know, then you aren't worthy enough to have it explained to you!" cried the rabbi indignantly. And he left the pulpit.

Downcast with shame, the members of the congregation left the synagogue.

The following Sabbath morning the synagogue was again filled with worshipers, and once more the rabbi mounted the pulpit.

"My dear Jews," began the preacher, "do you know what sedra we read today and what passage of Torah I'm going to expound?"

Intimidated by its experience of the previous Sabbath, the congregation cried out like one man, "Yes, we know!"

"You do, do you? In that case, why do you need *me* to explain?" cried the rabbi impatiently. And he left the pulpit.

And the third Sabbath, when the congregation gathered again, the rabbi once more mounted the pulpit.

"My masters," he asked, "do you know what sedra we have this week and what it is that I'm going to preach about today?"

Now the members of the congregation were very canny and they had decided to profit from their past experience. So some cried out: "We know!" and some cried out, "We don't know!"

The rabbi was taken aback. For a moment he stood undecided. Then he sternly began to rebuke the congregation:

"For the life of me I can't see why you need me to explain it to you! My advice is: Let those of you who know tell those who don't know!"

And with these words he descended from the pulpit.

GOD'S IMPATIENCE

A stingy man once came upon a most tempting walnut tree. He suddenly felt a strong desire to eat the nuts. So he took his coat off and began to climb the tree. As he started he prayed:

"Dear God, if You'll make it easy for me to climb to the top of ane tree, I promise to put ten rubles into the charity box in the synagogue."

Halfway up the tree, he reconsidered the whole matter:

"Ten rubles is really too much—just for a few nuts! I'll give three."

Finally, he reached the top branch. Arrogant now, he said, "Why should I give my good hard cash to some miserable beggars?"

No sooner had he said this than the branch on which he rested broke, and he fell with a thud to the ground on his rear end.

His face twisted with pain, he turned reproachfully to heaven.

"What's the matter, God, anyway?" he asked. "Right away You've got to hit! Maybe, if You hadn't been in such a hurry, I'd have given something!"

THE SABBATH QUESTION IN SUDMINSTER

BY ISRAEL ZANGWILL

There was a storm in Sudminster, not on the waters which washed its leading Jews their living, but in the breasts of these same marine storekeepers. For a competitor had appeared in their hive of industry —an alien immigrant, without roots or even relatives at Sudminster. And Simeon Samuels was equipped not only with capital and enterprise—the snowy plate-glass front of his shop revealed an enticing miscellany—but with blasphemy and bravado. For he did not close on Friday eve, and he opened on Saturday morning as usual.

The rumour did not get round all Sudminster the first Friday night, but by the Sabbath morning the synagogue hummed with it. It set a clammy horror in the breasts of the congregants, distracted their prayers, gave an unreal tone to the cantor's roulades, brought a tremor of insecurity into the very foundations of their universe. For nearly three generations a congregation had been established in Sudminster— like every Jewish congregation, a camp in not friendly country— struggling at every sacrifice to keep the Holy Day despite the supplementary burden of Sunday closing, and the God of their fathers had not left unperformed His part of the contract. For "the harvests" of profit were abundant, and if "the latter and the former rain" of their unchanging supplication were mere dried metaphors to a people divorced from Palestine and the soil for eighteen centuries, the wine and the oil came in casks, and the corn in cakes. The poor were few and well provided for; even the mortgage on the synagogue was paid off. And now this Epicurean was come to trouble the snug security, to break the long chain of Sabbath observance which stretched from Sinai. What wonder if some of the worshipers, especially such as had passed his blatant shop-window on their return from synagogue on Friday evening, were literally surprised that the earth had not opened beneath him as it had opened beneath Korah.

"Even the man who gathered sticks on the Sabbath was stoned to death," whispered the squat Solomon Barzinsky, to the lanky Ephraim Mendel, marine-dealers both.

"Alas! that would not be permitted in this heathen country," sighed Ephraim Mendel, hitching his praying-shawl more over his left shoulder. "But at least his windows should be stoned."

Solomon Barzinsky smiled, with a gleeful imagining of the shattering of the shameless plate-glass. "Yes, and that wax-dummy of a sailor should be hung as an atonement for his—Holy, holy, holy is the Lord of Hosts; the whole earth is full of His glory." The last phrase Solomon suddenly shouted in Hebrew, in antiphonal response to the cantor, and he rose three times on his toes, bowing his head piously. "No wonder he can offer gold lace for the price of silver," he concluded bitterly.

"He sells shoddy new reach-me-downs as pawned old clo," complained Lazarus Levy, who had taken over S. Cohn's business, together with his daughter Deborah, "and he charges the Sudminster donkey-heads more than the price we ask for 'em as new."

Talk of the devil——! At this point Simeon Samuels stalked into the synagogue, late but serene.

Had the real horned Asmodeus walked in, the agitation could not have been greater. The first appearance in synagogue of a new settler was an event in itself; but that this Sabbath-breaker should appear at all was startling to a primitive community. Escorted by the obsequious and unruffled beadle to the seat he seemed already to have engaged—that high-priced seat facing the presidential pew that had remained vacant since the death of Tevele the pawnbroker—Simeon Samuels wrapped himself reverently in his praying-shawl, and became absorbed in the service. His glossy high hat bespoke an immaculate orthodoxy, his long black beard had a rabbinic religiousness, his devotion was a rebuke to his gossiping neighbours.

A wave of uneasiness passed over the synagogue. Had he been the victim of a jealous libel? Even those whose own eyes had seen him behind his counter when he should have been consecrating the Sabbath-wine at his supper-table wondered if they had been the dupe of some hallucination.

When, in accordance with hospitable etiquette, the new-comer was summoned canorously to the reading of the Law— "Shall stand Simeon, the son of Nehemiah"—and he arose and solemnly mounted the central platform, his familiarity with the due obeisances and osculations and benedictions seemed a withering reply to the libel. When he descended, and the *Parnass* proffered his presidential hand in pious congratulation upon the holy privilege, all the congregants who found themselves upon his line of return shot forth their arms with remorseful eagerness, and thus was Simeon Samuels switched on to the brotherhood of Sudminsterian Israel. Yet as his now trusting co-religionists passed his shop on their homeward walk—and many a pair of legs went considerably out of its way to do so—their eyes became again saucers of horror and amaze. The broad plate-glass glittered nakedly, unveiled by a single shutter; the waxen dummy of the sailor hitched devil-may-care breeches; the gold lace, ticketed with layers of erased figures, boasted brazenly of its cheapness; the procession of customers came and went, and the pavement, splashed with sunshine, remained imperturbably, perturbingly acquiescent.

II

On the Sunday night Solomon Barzinsky and Ephraim Mendel in pious black velvet caps, and their stout spouses in gold chains and diamond earrings, found themselves playing solo whist in the Parnass's parlour, and their religious grievance weighed upon the game. The Parnass, though at heart as outraged as they by the new departure, felt it always incumbent upon him to display his presidential impartiality and his dry humour. His authority, mainly based on his being the only retired shopkeeper in the community, was greatly strengthened by his slow manner of taking snuff at a crisis. "My dear Mendel," observed the wizened senior, flicking away the spilth with a blue handkerchief, "Simeon Samuels has already paid his annual subscription— and you haven't!"

"My money is good," Mendel replied, reddening.

"No wonder he can pay so quickly!" said Solomon Barzinsky, shuffling the cards savagely.

"How he makes his money is not the question," said the Parnass weightily. "He has paid it, and therefore if I were to expel him, as you suggest, he might go to Law."

"Law!" retorted Solomon. "Can't we prove he has broken the Law of Moses?"

"And suppose?" said the Parnass, picking up his cards placidly. "Do you want to wash our dirty *Talysim* [praying-shawls] in public?"

"He is right, Solomon," said Mrs. Barzinsky. "We should become a laughing-stock among the heathen."

"I don't believe he'd drag us to the Christian courts," the little man persisted. "I pass."

The rubber continued cheerlessly. "A man who keeps his shop open on Sabbath is capable of anything," said the lanky Mendel, gloomily sweeping in his winnings.

The Parnass took snuff judicially. "Besides, he may have a Christian partner who keeps all the Saturday profits," he suggested.

"That would be just as forbidden," said Barzinsky, as he dealt the cards.

"But your cousin David," his wife reminded him, "sells his groceries to a Christian at Passover."

"That is permitted. It would not be reasonable to destroy hundreds of pounds of leaven. But Sabbath partnerships are not permitted."

"Perhaps the question has never been raised," said the Parnass.

"I am enough of a *Lamdan* [pundit] to answer it," retorted Barzinsky.

"I prefer going to a specialist," rejoined the Parnass.

Barzinsky threw down his cards. "You can go to the devil!" he cried.

"For shame, Solomon!" said his wife. "Don't disturb the game."

"To Gehenna with the game! The shame is on a Parnass to talk like an *Epikouros* [Epicurean]."

The Parnass blew his nose elaborately. "It stands in the Talmud: 'For vain swearing noxious beasts came into the world,' and if——"

"It stands in the Psalmist," Barzinsky interrupted: " 'The Law of Thy mouth is better to me than thousands of gold and silver.' "

"It stands in the Perek," the Parnass rejoined severely, "that the wise man does not break in upon the speech of his fellow."

"It stands in the Shulchan Aruch," Barzinsky shrieked, "that for the sanctification of the Sabbath——"

"It stands in the Talmud," interposed Mendel, with unwonted animation in his long figure, "that one must not even offer a nut to allure customers. From light to heavy, therefore, it may be deduced that——"

A still small voice broke in upon the storm. "But Simeon Samuels hasn't a Christian partner," said Mrs. Mendel.

There was an embarrassed pause.

"He has only his wife to help him," she went on. "I know, because I went to the shop Friday morning on pretense of asking for a cuckoo-clock."

"But a marine-dealer doesn't sell clocks," put in the Parnass's wife, timidly. It was her first contribution to the conversation, for she was overpowered by her husband's greatness.

"Don't be silly, Hannah," said the Parnass. "That was just why Mrs. Mendel asked for it."

"Yes, but unfortunately Simeon Samuels did have one," Mrs. Mendel confessed, "and I couldn't get out of buying it."

There was a general laugh.

"Cut-throat competition, I call it," snarled Solomon Barzinsky, recovering from his merriment.

"But *you* don't sell clocks," said the Parnass.

"That's just it; he gets hold of our customers on pretense of selling them something else. The Talmudical prohibition cited by Mendel applies to that, too."

"So it wasn't so silly," put in the Parnass's wife, feeling vaguely vindicated.

"Well, you saw his wife," said the Parnass to Mendel's wife, disregarding his own. "More than I've done, for she wasn't in the synagogue. Perhaps *she* is the Christian partner." His suggestion brought a new and holier horror over the card-table.

"No, no," replied Mrs. Mendel, reassuringly. "I caught sight of her frying fish in the kitchen."

This proof of her Jewishness passed unquestioned, and the newborn horror subsided.

"But in spite of the fish," said Mr. Mendel, "she served in the shop while he was at synagogue."

"Yes," hissed Barzinsky; "and in spite of the synagogue *he* served in the shop. A greater mockery was never known!"

"Not at all, not at all," said the Parnass, judicially. "If a man breaks one commandment, that's no reason he should break two."

"But he does break two," Solomon thundered, smiting the green cloth with his fist; "for he steals my custom by opening when I'm closed."

"Take care—you will break my plates," said the Parnass. "Take a sandwich."

"Thank you—you've taken away my appetite."

"I'm sorry—but the sandwiches would have done the same. I really can't expel a respectable seatholder before I know that he is truly a sinner in Israel. As it is written, 'Thou shalt inquire and make search and ask diligently.' He may have only opened this once by way of a send-off. Every dog is allowed one bite."

"At that rate, it would be permitted to eat a ham-sandwich—just for once," said Solomon, scathingly.

"Don't say *I* called you a dog," the Parnass laughed.

"A mezaire!" announced the hostess, hurriedly. "After all, it's the Almighty's business, not ours."

"No, it's our business," Solomon insisted.

"Yes," agreed the Parnass drily; "it *is* your business."

III

The week went by, with no lull in the storm, though the plate-glass window was unshaken by the gusts. It maintained its flaunting seductiveness, assisted, people observed, by Simeon Samuels' habit of lounging at his shop-door and sucking in the hesitating speculator. And it did not shutter itself on the Sabbath that succeeded.

The horror was tinged with consternation. The strange apathy of the pavement and the sky, the remissness of the volcanic fires and the celestial thunderbolts in face of this staring profanity, lent the cosmos an air almost of accessory after the fact. Never had the congregation seen Heaven so openly defied, and the consequences did not at all correspond with their deep if undefined forebodings. It is true a horse and carriage dashed into Peleg the pawnbroker's window down the street, frightened, Peleg maintained, by the oilskins fluttering outside Simeon Samuels' shop; but as the suffering was entirely limited to the nerves of Mrs. Peleg, who was pious, and to the innocent nose of the horse, this catastrophe was not quite what was expected. Solomon Barzinsky made himself the spokesman of the general dissatisfaction, and his remarks to the minister after the Sabbath service almost insinuated that the reverend gentleman had connived at a breach of contract.

The Rev. Elkan Gabriel quoted Scripture. "The Lord is merciful and long-suffering, and will not at once awaken all His wrath."

"But meantime the sinner makes a pretty penny!" quoth Solomon, unappeased. "Saturday is pay-day, and the heathen haven't patience to wait till the three stars are out and our shops can open. It is your duty, Mr. Gabriel, to put a stop to this profanation."

The minister hummed and ha'd. He was middle-aged, and shabby, with a German diploma and accent and a large family. It was the first time in his five years of office that one of his congregants had suggested such authoritativeness on his part. Elected by their vote, he was treated as their servant, his duties rigidly prescribed, his religious ideas curbed and corrected by theirs. What wonder if he could not suddenly rise to dictatorship? Even at home Mrs. Gabriel was a congregation in herself. But as the week went by he found Barzinsky was not the only man to egg him on to prophetic denunciation; the congregation at large treated him as responsible for the scandal, and if the seven marine-dealers were the bitterest, the pawnbrokers and the linen-drapers were none the less outraged.

"It is a profanation of the Name," they said unanimously, "and such a bad example to our poor!"

"He would not listen to me," the poor minister would protest. "You had much better talk to him yourself."

"Me!" the button-holer would ejaculate. "I would not lower myself. He'd think I was jealous of his success."

Simeon Samuels seemed, indeed, a formidable person to tackle. Bland and aloof, he pursued his own affairs, meeting the congregation only in synagogue, and then more bland and aloof than ever.

At last the minister received a presidential command to preach upon the subject forthwith.

"But there's no text suitable just yet," he pleaded. "We are still in Genesis."

"Bah!" replied the Parnass, impatiently, "any text can be twisted to point any moral. You must preach next Sabbath."

"But we are reading the *Sedrah* [weekly portion] about Joseph. How are you going to work Sabbath-keeping into that?"

"It is not my profession. I am a mere man-of-the-earth. But what's the use of a preacher if he can't make any text mean something else?"

"Well, of course, every text usually does," said the preacher, defensively. "There is the hidden meaning and the plain meaning. But Joseph is merely historical narrative. The Sabbath, although mentioned in Genesis, chapter two, wasn't even formally ordained yet."

"And what about Potiphar's wife?"

"That's the Seventh Commandment, not the Fourth."

"Thank you for the information. Do you mean to say you can't jump from one Commandment to another?"

"Oh, well——" the minister meditated.

IV

"And Joseph was a goodly person, and well favoured. And it came to pass that his master's wife cast her eyes upon Joseph. . . ."

The congregation looked startled. Really this was not a text which they wished their pastor to enlarge upon. There were things in the Bible that should be left in the obscurity of the Hebrew, especially when one's womenkind were within earshot. Uneasily their eyes lifted towards the bonnets behind the balcony-grating.

"But Joseph refused."

Solomon Barzinsky coughed. Peleg the pawnbroker blew his nose like a protesting trumpet. The congregation's eyes returned from the balcony and converged upon the Parnass. He was taking snuff as usual.

"My brethren," began the preacher, impressively, "temptation comes to us all——"

A sniff of indignant repudiation proceeded from many nostrils. A blush overspread many cheeks.

"But not always in the shape it came to Joseph. In this congregation, where, by the blessing of the Almighty, we are free from almost every form of wrongdoing, there is yet one temptation which has power to touch us—the temptation of unholy profit, the seduction of Sabbath-breaking."

A great sigh of dual relief went up to the balcony, and Simeon Samuels became now the focus of every eye. His face was turned towards the preacher, wearing its wonted synagogue expression of reverential dignity.

"Oh, my brethren, that it could always be said of us: 'And Joseph refused'!"

A genial warmth came back to every breast. Ah, now the cosmos was righting itself: Heaven was speaking through the mouth of its minister.

The Rev. Elkan Gabriel expanded under this warmth which radiated back to him. His stature grew, his eloquence poured forth, polysyllabic. As he ended, the congregation burst into a heartfelt "*Yosher Koach!* [May thy strength increase!]."

The minister descended the Ark-steps, and stalked back solemnly to his seat. As he passed Simeon Samuels, that gentleman whipped out his hand and grasped the man of God's, and his neighbours testified that there was a look of contrite exaltation upon his goodly features.

v

The Sabbath came round again, but alas! it brought no balm to the congregation; rather, was it a day of unrest. The plate-glass window still flashed in iniquitous effrontery; still the ungodly proprietor allured the stream of custom.

"He does not even refuse to take money," Solomon Barzinsky exclaimed to Peleg the pawnbroker, as they passed the blasphemous window on their way from the Friday-evening service.

"Why, what would be the good of keeping open if you didn't take money?" naively inquired Peleg.

"*Behemah* [animal]!" replied Solomon, impatiently. "Don't you know it's forbidden to touch money on the Sabbath?"

"Of course, I know that. But if you open your shop——!"

"All the same, you might compromise. You might give the customers the things they need, as it is written, 'Open thy hand to the needy!' but they could pay on Saturday night."

"And if they didn't pay? If they drank their money away?" said the pawnbroker.

"True, but why couldn't they pay in advance?"

"How in advance?"

"They could deposit a sum of money with you, and draw against it."

"Not with me!" Peleg made a grimace. "All very well for your line, but in mine I should have to deposit a sum of money with *them.* I don't suppose they'd bring their pledges on Friday night, and wait till Saturday night for the money. Besides, how could one remember? One would have to profane the Sabbath by writing!"

"Write! Heaven forbid!" ejaculated Solomon Barzinsky. "But you could have a system of marking the amounts against their names in your register. A pin could be stuck in to represent a pound, or a stamp stuck on to indicate a crown. There are lots of ways. One could always give one's self a device," he concluded in Yiddish.

"But it is written in Job, 'He disappointeth the devices of the crafty, so that their hands cannot perform their enterprise.' Have a little of Job's patience, and trust the Lord to confound the sinner. We shall yet see Simeon Samuels in the Bankruptcy Court."

"I hope not, the rogue! I'd like to see him ruined!"

"That's what I mean. Leave him to the Lord."

"The Lord is too long-suffering," said Solomon. "Ah, our Parnass has caught us up. Good *Shabbos* [Sabbath], Parnass. This is a fine scandal for a God-fearing congregation. I congratulate you."

"Is he open again?" gasped the Parnass, hurled from his judicial calm.

"Is my eye open?" witheringly retorted Barzinsky. "A fat lot of good your preacher does."

"It was you who would elect him instead of Rochinsky," the Parnass reminded him. Barzinsky was taken aback.

"Well, we don't want foreigners, do we?" he murmured.

"And you caught an Englishman in Simeon Samuels," chuckled the Parnass, in whose breast the defeat of his candidate had never ceased to rankle.

"Not he. An Englishman plays fair," retorted Barzinsky. He seriously considered himself a Briton, regarding his naturalization papers as restrospective. "We are just passing the Reverend Gabriel's house," he went on. "Let us wait a moment; he'll come along, and we'll give him a piece of our minds."

"I can't keep my family waiting for *Kiddush* [home service]," said Peleg.

"Come home, father; I'm hungry," put in Peleg junior, who with various Barzinsky boys had been trailing in the parental wake.

"Silence, impudent face!" snapped Barzinsky. "If I was your father—— Ah, here comes the minister. Good *Shabbos* [Sabbath], Mr. Gabriel. I congratulate you on the effect of your last sermon."

An exultant light leapt into the minister's eye. "Is he shut?"

"Is your mouth shut?" Solomon replied scathingly. "I doubt if he'll even come to *Shool* [synagogue], tomorrow."

The ministerial mouth remained open in a fishy gasp, but no words came from it.

"I'm afraid you'll have to use stronger language, Mr. Gabriel," said the Parnass, soothingly.

"But if he is not there to hear it."

"Oh, don't listen to Barzinsky. He'll be there right enough. Just give it to him hot!"

"Your sermon was too general," added Peleg, who had lingered, though his son had not. "You might have meant any of us."

"But we must not shame our brother in public," urged the minister. "It is written in the Talmud that he who does so has no share in the world to come."

"Well, you shamed us all," retorted Barzinsky. "A stranger would imagine we were a congregation of Sabbath-breakers."

"But there wasn't any stranger," said the minister.

"There was Simeon Samuels," the Parnass reminded him. "Perhaps your sermon against Sabbath-breaking made him fancy he was just one of a crowd, and that you have therefore only hardened him——"

"But you told me to preach against Sabbath-breaking," said the poor minister.

"Against the Sabbath-breaker," corrected the Parnass.

"You didn't single him out," added Barzinsky; "you didn't even make it clear that Joseph wasn't myself."

"I said Joseph was a goodly person and well-favoured," retorted the goaded minister.

The Parnass took snuff, and his sneeze sounded like a guffaw.

"Well, well," he said more kindly, "you must try again tomorrow."

"I didn't undertake to preach every Saturday," grumbled the minister, growing bolder.

"As long as Simeon Samuels keeps open, you can't shut," said Solomon, angrily.

"It's a duel between you," added Peleg.

"And Simeon actually comes into to-morrow's *Sedrah* [portion]," Barzinsky remembered exultantly. " 'And took from them Simeon, and bound him before their eyes.' There's your very text. You'll pick out Simeon from among us, and bind him to keep the Sabbath."

"Or you can say Satan has taken Simeon and bound him," added the Parnass. "You have a choice—yourself or Satan."

"Perhaps you had better preach yourself, then," said the minister, sullenly. "I still can't see what that text has to do with Sabbath-breaking."

"It has as much to do with Sabbath-breaking as Potiphar's wife," shrieked Solomon Barzinsky.

VI

" 'And Jacob their father said unto them, Me have ye bereaved. Joseph is not, and Simeon is not, and ye will take Benjamin.' "

As the word "Simeon" came hissing from the preacher's lips, a veritable thrill passed through the synagogue. Even Simeon Samuels seemed shaken, for he readjusted his praying-shawl with a nervous movement.

"My brethren, these words of Israel, the great forefather of our tribes, are still ringing in our ears. To-day more than ever is Israel crying. Joseph is not—our Holy Land is lost. Simeon is not—our Holy Temple is razed to the ground. One thing only is left us—one blessing with which the almighty father has blessed us—our Holy Sabbath. And ye will take Benjamin." The pathos of his accents melted every heart. Tears rolled down many a feminine cheek. Simeon Samuels was seen to blow his nose softly.

Thus successfully launched, the Rev. Elkan Gabriel proceeded to draw a tender picture of the love between Israel and his Benjamin, Sabbath—the one consolation of his exile, and he skilfully worked in the subsequent verse: "If mischief befall him by the way on which ye go, then shall ye bring down my grey hairs with sorrow to the grave." Yes, it would be the destruction of Israel, he urged, if the Sabbath decayed. Woe to those sons of Israel who dared to endanger Benjamin. "From Reuben and *Simeon* down to Gad and Asher, his life shall be required at their hands." Oh, it was a red-hot-cannon-ball-firing sermon, and Solomon Barzinsky could not resist leaning across and whispering to the Parnass: "Wasn't I right in refusing to vote for Rochinsky?" This reminder of his candidate's defeat was wormwood to the Parnass, spoiling all his satisfaction in the sermon. He rebuked the talker with a noisy *"Shaa'* [silence]."

The congregation shrank delicately from looking at the sinner; it would be too painful to watch his wriggles. His neighbours stared pointedly every other way. Thus, the only record of his deportment under fire came from Yankele, the poor glazier's boy, who said that he kept looking from face to face, as if to mark the effect on the congregation, stroking his beard placidly the while. But as to his behaviour after the guns were still, there was no dubiety, for everybody saw him approach the Parnass in the exodus from synagogue, and many heard him say in hearty accents: "I really must congratulate you, Mr. President, on your selection of your minister."

VII

"You touched his heart so," shrieked Solomon Barzinksy an hour later to the Reverend Elkan Gabriel, "that he went straight from *Shool* to his shop." Solomon had rushed out the first thing after breakfast, risking the digestion of his Sabbath fish, to call upon the unsuccessful minister.

"That is not my fault," said the preacher, crestfallen.

"Yes, it is—if you had only stuck to *my* text. But no! You must set yourself up over all our heads."

"You told me to get in Simeon, and I obeyed."

"Yes, you got him in. But what did you call him? The Holy Temple! A fine thing, upon my soul!"

"It was only an—an—analogy," stammered the poor minister.

"An apology! Oh, so you apologized to him, too! Better and better!"

"No, no, I mean a comparison."

"A comparison! You never compared me to the Holy Temple. And I'm Solomon—Solomon who built it."

"Solomon was wise," murmured the minister.

"Oh, and I'm silly. If I were you, Mr. Gabriel, I'd remember my place and who I owed it to. But for me, Rochinsky would have stood in your shoes——"

"Rochinsky is lucky."

"Oh, indeed! So this is your gratitude. Very well. Either Simeon

Samuels shuts up shop or you do. That's final. Don't forget you were only elected for three years." And the little man flung out.

The Parnass, meeting his minister later in the street, took a similar view.

"You really must preach again next Sabbath," he said. "The congregation is terribly wrought up. There may even be a riot. If Simeon Samuels keeps open next Sabbath, I can't answer that they won't go and break his windows."

"Then *they* will break the Sabbath."

"Oh, they may wait till the Sabbath is out."

"They'll be too busy opening their own shops."

"Don't argue. You *must* preach his shop shut."

"Very well," said the Reverend Gabriel, sullenly.

"That's right. A man with a family must rise to great occasions. Do you think I'd be where I am now if I hadn't had the courage to buy a bankrupt stock that I didn't see my way to paying for? It's a fight between you and Simeon Samuels."

"May his name be blotted out!" impatiently cried the minister in the Hebrew imprecation.

"No, no," replied the Parnass, smiling. "His name must not be blotted out—it must be mentioned, and—unmistakably."

"It is against the Talmud. To shame a man is equivalent to murder," the minister persisted.

"Yet it is written in Leviticus: 'Thou shalt in any wise rebuke thy neighbour, and not suffer sin upon him.'" And the Parnass took a triumphant pinch.

VIII

"*Simeon* and Levi are brethren . . . into their assembly be not thou united: in their self-will they digged down a wall."

The Parnass applauded mentally. The text, from Jacob's blessing, was ingeniously expurgated to meet the case. The wall, he perceived at once, was the Sabbath—the Jews' one last protection against the outer world, the one last dyke against the waves of heathendom. Nor did his complacency diminish when his intuition proved correct, and the preacher thundered against the self-will—ay, and the self-seeking—that undermined Israel's last fortification. What did they seek under the wall? Did they think their delving spades would come upon a hidden store of gold, upon an ancient treasure-chest? Nay, it was a coffin they would strike—a coffin of dead bones and living serpents.

A cold wave of horror traversed the synagogue; a little shriek came from the gallery.

"I don't think I ever enjoyed a sermon so much," said the pawnbroker to the Parnass.

"Oh, he's improving," said the Parnass, still swollen with satisfaction.

But as that worthy elder emerged from the synagogue, placidly snuffing himself, he found an excited gentleman waiting him in the lobby. It was Lazarus Levy, whom his wife Deborah, daughter of S. Cohn (now of Highbury), was vainly endeavouring to pacify.

"Either that Reverend Gabriel goes, Mr. Parnass, or I resign my membership."

"What is it, Mr. Levy—what is the matter?"

"Everybody knows I've been a good Jew all my life, and though Saturday is so good for the clothing business, I've striven with all my might to do my duty by the Almighty."

"Of course, of course; everybody knows that."

"And yet to-day I'm pointed out as a sinner in Israel; I'm coupled with that Simeon Samuels. Simeon and Levy are brothers in their iniquity—with their assembly be not united. A pretty libel, indeed!"

The Parnass's complacency collapsed like an air-ball at a pin-prick. "Oh, nonsense, everybody knows he couldn't mean you."

"I don't know so much. There are always people ready to think one has just been discovered keeping a back-door open or something. I shouldn't be at all surprised to get a letter from my father-in-law in London—you know how pious old Cohn is! As for Simeon, he kept looking at me as if I *was* his long-lost brother. Ah, there comes our precious minister. . . . Look here, Mr. Gabriel, I'll have the law on you. Simeon's no brother of mine——"

The sudden appearance of Simeon through the other swing-door cut the speaker short. "Good Shabbos," said the shameless sinner. "Ah, Mr. Gabriel, that was a very fine sermon." He stroked his beard. "I quite agree with you. To dig down a public wall is indefensible. Nobody has the right to make more than a private hole in it, where it blocks out his own prospect. So please do not bracket me with Mr. Levy again. Good Shabbos!" And, waving his hand pleasantly, he left them to their consternation.

IX

"What an impudent face!" said the *Gabbai* [treasurer], who witnessed the episode.

"And our minister says I'm that man's brother!" exclaimed Mr. Levy.

"Hush! Enough!" said the Parnass, with a tactful inspiration. "You shall read the *Haphtorah* [prophetic section] next Shabbos."

"And Mr. Gabriel must explain he didn't mean me," he stipulated, mollified by the magnificent *Mitzvah* [pious privilege].

"You always try to drive a hard bargain," grumbled the Parnass. "That's a question for Mr. Gabriel."

The Reverend Gabriel had a happy thought. "Wait till we come to the text: 'Wherefore Levi hath no part nor inheritance with his brethren.' "

"You're a gentleman, Mr. Gabriel," ejaculated S. Cohn's son-in-law, clutching at his hand.

"And if he doesn't close to-day after your splendid sermon," added the Gabbai, "you must call and talk to him face to face."

The minister made a wry face. "But that's not in my duties."

"Pardon me, Mr. Gabriel," put in the Parnass, "you have to call upon the afflicted and the bereaved. And Simeon Samuels is spiritually afflicted, and has lost his Sabbath."

"But he doesn't want comforting."

"Well, Solomon Barzinsky does," said the Parnass. "Go to him instead, then, for I'm past soothing him. Choose!"

"I'll go to Simeon Samuels," said the preacher, gloomily.

x

"It is most kind of you to call," said Simeon Samuels as he wheeled the parlour armchair towards his reverend guest. "My wife will be so sorry to have missed you. We have both been looking forward so much to your visit."

"You knew I was coming?" said the minister, a whit startled.

"I naturally expected a pastoral visit sooner or later."

"I'm afraid it is later," murmured the minister, subsiding into the chair.

"Better late than never," cried Simeon Samuels heartily, as he produced a bottle from the sideboard. "Do you take it with hot water?"

"Thank you—not at all. I am only staying a moment."

"Ah!" He stroked his beard. "You are busy?"

"Terribly busy," said the Rev. Elkan Gabriel.

"Even on Sunday?"

"Rather! It's my day for secretarial work, as there's no school."

"Poor Mr. Gabriel. I at least have Sunday to myself. But you have to work Saturday and Sunday too. It's really too bad."

"Eh," said the minister blankly.

"Oh, of course I know you *must* work on the Sabbath."

"*I* work on—on Shabbos!" The minister flushed to the temples.

"Oh, I'm not blaming you. One must live. In an ideal world of course you'd preach and pray and sing and recite the Law for nothing so that Heaven might perhaps overlook your hard labour, but as things are you must take your wages."

The minister had risen agitatedly. "I earn my wages for the rest of my work—the Sabbath work I throw in," he said hotly.

"Oh come, Mr. Gabriel, that quibble is not worthy of you. But far be it from me to judge a fellow-man."

"Far be it indeed!" The attempted turning of his sabre-point gave him vigour for the lunge. "You—you whose shop stands brazenly open every Saturday!"

"My dear Mr. Gabriel, I couldn't break the Fourth Commandment."

"What!"

"Would you have me break the Fourth Commandment?"

"I do not understand."

"And yet you hold a Rabbinic diploma, I am told. Does not the Fourth Commandment run: 'Six days shalt thou labour and do all thy work'? If I were to close on Saturday I should only be working five days a week, since in this heathen country Sunday closing is compulsory."

"But you don't keep the other half of the Commandment," said the bewildered minister. " 'And on the seventh is the Sabbath.' "

"Yes, I do—after my six days the seventh is my Sabbath. I only sinned once, if you will have it so, the first time I shifted the Sabbath to Sunday, since when my Sabbath has arrived regularly on Sundays."

"But you did sin once!" said the minister, catching at that straw.

"Granted, but as to get right again would now make a second sin, it seems more pious to let things be. Not that I really admit the first sin, for let me ask you, sir, which is nearer to the spirit of the Commandment—to work six days and keep a day of rest—merely changing the day once in one's whole lifetime—or to work five days and keep two days of rest?"

The minister, taken aback, knew not how to meet this novel defence. He had come heavily armed against all the usual arguments as to the necessity of earning one's bread. He was prepared to prove that even from a material point of view you really gained more in the long run, as it is written in the Conclusion-of-Sabbath Service: "Blessed shalt thou be in the city, and blessed shalt thou be in the field."

Simeon Samuels pursued his advantage.

"My co-religionists in Sudminster seem to have put all the stress upon the resting half of the Commandment, forgetting the working half of it. I do my best to meet their views—as you say, one should not dig down a wall—by attending their Sabbath service on a day most inconvenient to me. But no sacrifice is too great to achieve prayerful communion with one's brethren."

"But if your views were to prevail there would be an end of Judaism!" the minister burst forth.

"Then Heaven forbid they should prevail!" said Simeon Samuels fervently. "It is your duty to put the opposition doctrine as strongly as possible from the pulpit." Then, as the minister rose in angry obfuscation, "You are sure you won't have some whisky?" he added.

"No, I will take nothing from a house of sin. And if you show yourself next Sabbath I will preach at you again."

"So that is your idea of religion—to drive me from the synagogue. You are more likely to drive away the rest of the congregation, sick of always hearing the same sermon. As for me, you forget how I enjoy your eloquence, devoted though it is to the destruction of Judaism."

"Me!" The minister became ungrammatical in his indignation.

"Yes, you. To mix up religion with the almanac. People who find that your Sabbath wall shuts them out of all public life and all professions, just go outside it altogether, and think themselves outside the gates of Judaism. If my father—peace be upon him—hadn't had your narrow notions, I should have gone to the Bar instead of being condemned to shopkeeping."

"You are a very good devil's advocate now," retorted the minister.

Simeon Samuels stroked his beard. "Thank you. And I congratulate *your* client."

"You are an *Epikouros,* and I am wasting my time."

"And mine too."

The minister strode into the shop. At the street-door he turned. "Then you persist in setting a bad example?"

"A bad example! To whom? To your godly congregation? Considering every other shop in the town is open on Shabbos, one more or less can't upset them."

"When it is the only Jewish shop! Are you aware, sir, that every other Jew in Sudminster closes rigorously on the Sabbath?"

"I ascertained that before I settled here," said Simeon Samuels quietly.

XI

The report of the pastor's collapse produced an emergency meeting of the leading sheep. The mid-day dinner-hour was chosen as the slackest. A babble of suggestions filled the Parnass's parlour. Solomon Barzinsky kept sternly repeating his *Delenda est Carthago:* "He must be expelled from the congregation."

"He should be expelled from the town altogether," said Mendel. "As it is written: 'And remove Satan from before and behind us.'"

"Since when have we owned Sudminster?" sneered the Parnass. "You might as well talk of expelling the Mayor and the Corporation."

"I didn't mean by Act of Parliament," said Mendel. "We could make his life a torture."

"And meantime he makes yours a torture. No, no, the only way is to appeal to his soul——"

"May it be an atonement for us all!" interrupted Peleg the pawnbroker.

"We must beg him not to destroy religion," repeated the Parnass.

"I thought Mr. Gabriel had done that," said the Gabbai.

"He is only a minister. He has no worldly tact."

"Then, why don't *you* go?" said Solomon Barzinsky.

"I have too much worldly tact. The President's visit might seem like an appeal to authority. It would set up his bristles. Besides, there wouldn't be me left to appeal to. The congregation must keep some trump up its sleeve. No, a mere plain member must go, a simple brother in Israel, to talk to him, heart to heart. You, Barzinsky, are the very man."

"No, no, I'm not such a simple brother as all that. I'm in the same line, and he might take it for trade jealousy."

"Then Peleg must go."

"No, no, I'm not worthy to be the *Sheliach Tzibbur!*" [envoy of the congregation].

The Parnass reassured him as to his merits. "The congregation could not have a worthier envoy."

"But I can't leave my business."

"You, with your fine grown-up daughters!" cried Barzinsky.

"Don't beshrew them—I will go at once."

"And these gentlemen must await you here," said the President, tapping his snuffbox incongruously at the "here," "in order to continue the sitting if you fail."

"I can't wait more than a quarter of an hour," grumbled various voices in various keys.

Peleg departed nervously, upborne by the congregational esteem. He returned without even his own. Instead he carried a bulky barometer.

"You must buy this for the synagogue, gentlemen," he said. "It will do to hang in the lobby."

The Parnass was the only one left in command of his breath.

"Buy a barometer!" he gasped.

"Well, it isn't any good to *me*," retorted Peleg angrily.

"Then why did you buy it?" cried the Gabbai.

"It was the cheapest article I could get off with."

"But you didn't go to buy," said the Parnass.

"I know that—but you come into the shop—naturally he takes you for a customer—he looks so dignified; he strokes his beard—you can't look a fool, you must——"

"Be one," snapped the Parnass. "And then you come to us to share the expenses!"

"Well, what do I want with a barometer?"

"It'll do to tell you there's a storm when the chimneypots are blowing down," suggested the Parnass crushingly.

"Put it in your window—you'll make a profit out of it," said Mendel.

"Not while Simeon Samuels is selling them cheaper, as with his Sabbath profits he can well afford to do!"

"Oh, he said he'd stick to his Sabbath profit, did he?" inquired the Parnass.

"We never touched on that," said Peleg miserably. "I couldn't manage to work the Sabbath into the conversation."

"This is terrible." Barzinsky's fist smote the table. "I'll go—let him suspect my motives or not. The Almighty knows they are pure."

"Bravo! Well spoken!" There was a burst of applause. Several marine-dealers shot out their hands and grasped Barzinsky's in admiration.

"Do not await me, gentlemen," he said importantly. "Go in peace."

XII

"Good afternoon, Mr. Samuels," said Solomon Barzinksy.

"Good afternoon, sir. What can I do for you?"

"You—you don't know me? I am a fellow-Jew."

"That's as plain as the nose on your face."

"You don't remember me from Shool? Mr. Barzinksy! I had the rolling up of the Scroll the time you had the elevation of it."

"Ah, indeed. At these solemn moments I scarcely notice people. But I am very glad to find you patronizing my humble establishment."

"I don't want a barometer," said Solomon hurriedly.

"That is fortunate, as I have just sold my last. But in the way of waterproofs, we have a new pattern very seasonable."

"No, no; I didn't come for a waterproof."

"These oilskins——"

"I didn't come to buy anything."

"Ah, you wish to sell me something."

"Not that either. The fact is, I've come to beg of you, as one Jew to another——"

"A *Schnorrer!*" interrupted Simeon Samuels. "Oh, Lord, I ought to have recognised you by that synagogue beginning."

"Me, a *Schnorrer!*" The little man swelled skywards. "Me, Solomon Barzinsky, whose shop stood in Sudminster twenty years before you poked your nose in——"

"I beg your pardon. There! you see I'm a beggar, too." And Simeon Samuels laughed mirthlessly. "Well, you've come to beg of me." And his fingers caressed his patriarchal beard.

"I don't come on my own account only," Barzinsky stammered.

"I understand. You want a contribution to the Passover Cake Fund. My time is precious, so is yours. What is the Parnass giving?"

"I'm not begging for money. I represent the congregation."

"Dear me, why didn't you come to the point quicker? The congregation wishes to beg my acceptance of office. Well, it's very good of you all, especially as I'm such a recent addition. But I really feel a diffidence. You see, my views of the Sabbath clash with those of the congregation."

"They do!" cried Barzinsky, leaping at his opportunity.

"Yes, I am for a much stricter observance than appears general here. Scarcely one of you carries his handkerchief tied round his loins like my poor old father, peace be upon him! You all carry the burden of it impiously in a pocket."

"I never noticed *your* handkerchief round your waist!" cried the bewildered Barzinsky.

"Perhaps not; I never had a cold; it remained furled."

Simeon Samuels' superb insolence twitched Barzinksy's mouth agape. "But you keep your shop open!" he cried at last.

"That would be still another point of clashing," admitted Simeon Samuels blandly. "Altogether, you will see the inadvisability of my accepting office."

"Office!" echoed Barzinsky, meeting the other's ironic fence with crude thwacks. "Do you think a God-fearing congregation would offer office to a Sabbath-breaker?"

"Ah, so that was at the back of it. I suspected something underhand in your offer. I was to be given office, was I, on condition of closing my shop on Saturday? No, Mr. Barzinsky. Go back and tell those who sent you that Simeon Samuels scorns stipulations, and that when you offer to make him Parnass unconditionally he may consider your offer, but not till then. Good-bye. You must jog along with your present apology for a Parnass."

"You—you Elisha ben Abuyai!" And, consoled only by the aptness of his reference to the atheist of the Talmud, Barzinsky rushed off to tell the Parnass how Simeon Samuels had insulted them both.

XIII

The Parnass, however, was not to be drawn yet. He must keep himself in reserve, he still insisted. But perhaps, he admitted, Simeon Samuels resented mere private members or committeemen. Let the Gabbai go.

Accordingly the pompous treasurer of the synagogue strode into the notorious shop on the Sabbath itself, catching Simeon Samuels red-handed.

But nothing could be suaver than that gentleman's "Good Shabbos. What can I do for you?"

"You can shut up your shop," said the Gabbai brusquely.

"And how shall I pay your bill, then?"

"I'd rather give you a seat and all the honours for nothing than see this desecration."

"You must have a goodly surplus, then."

"We have enough."

"That's strange. You're the first Gabbai I ever knew who was satisfied with his balance-sheet. Is it your excellent management, I wonder, or have you endowments?"

"That's not for me to say. I mean we have five or six hundred pounds in legacies."

"Indeed! Soundly invested, I hope?"

"First-class. English Railway Debentures."

"I see. Trustee stock." Simeon Samuels stroked his beard. "And so your whole congregation works on the Sabbath. A pretty confession!"

"What do you mean?"

"Runs railway-trains, lights engine-fires, keeps porters and signalmen toiling, and pockets the profits!"

"Who does?"

"You, sir, in particular, as the financial representative of the congregation. How can any Jew hold industrial shares in a heathen country without being a partner in a Sabbath business—ay, and opening on the Day of Atonement itself? And it is you who have the audacity to complain of me! I, at least, do my own dirty work, not hide myself behind stocks and shares. Good Shabbos to you, Mr. Gabbai, and kindly mind your business in future—your locomotives and your sidings and your stinking tunnels."

XIV

The Parnass could no longer delay the diplomatic encounter. 'Twas vain to accuse the others of tactlessness, and shirk the exhibition of his own tact. He exhibited it most convincingly by not informing the others that he was about to put it to a trial.

Hence he refrained from improving a synagogue opportunity, but sneaked one week-day towards the shop. He lingered without, waiting to be invited within. Thus all appearance of his coming to rebuke would be removed. His mission should pop up from a casual conversation.

He peeped into the window, passed and repassed.

Simeon Samuels, aware of a fly hovering on the purlieus of his web, issued from its centre, as the Parnass turned his back on the shop and gazed musingly at the sky.

"Looks threatening for rain, sir," observed Simeon Samuels, addressing the back. "Our waterproofs—bless my soul, but it surely isn't our Parnass!"

"Yes, I'm just strolling about. I seem to have stumbled on your establishment."

"Lucky for me."

"And a pleasure for me. I never knew you had such a nice display."

"Won't you come inside, and see the stock?"

"Thank you, I must really get back home. And besides, as you say, it is threatening for rain."

"I'll lend you a waterproof, or even sell you one cheap. Come in, sir—come in. Pray honour me."

Congratulating himself on catching the spider, the fly followed nim within.

A quarter of an hour passed, in which he must buzz about the stock. It seemed vastly difficult to veer round to the Sabbath through the web of conversation the spider wove round him. Simeon Samuels' conception of a marine-dealer's stock startled him by its comprehensiveness, and when he was asked to admire an Indian shawl, he couldn't help inquiring what it was doing there.

"Well," explained Simeon Samuels, "occasionally a captain or first mate will come back to England, home, and beauty, and will have neglected to buy foreign presents for his womenkind. I then remind him of the weakness of womenkind for such trophies of their menfolks' travel."

"Excellent. I won't tell your competitors."

"Oh, those cattle!" Simeon snapped his fingers. "If they stole my idea, they'd not be able to carry it out. It's not easy to cajole a captain."

"No, you're indeed a honeyed rascal," thought the Parnass.

"I also do a brisk business in chutney," went on Simeon. "It's a thing women are especially fond of having brought back to them from India. And yet it's the last thing their menkind think of till I remind them of it on their return."

"I certainly brought back none," said the Parnass, smiling in spite of himself.

"You have been in India?"

"I have," replied the Parnass, with a happy inspiration, "and I brought back to my wife something more stimulating than chutney."

"Indeed?"

"Yes, the story of the Beni-Israel, the black Jews, who, surrounded by all those millions of Hindoos, still keep their Sabbath."

"Ah, poor blacks! Then you've been half round the world."

"All round the world, for I went there and back by different routes. And it was most touching, wherever I went, to find everywhere a colony of Jews, and everywhere the Holy Sabbath kept sacred."

"But on different days, of course," said Simeon Samuels.

"Eh? Not at all! On the same day."

"On the same day! How could that be? The day changes with every move east or west. When it's day here, it's night in Australia."

Darkness began to cloud the presidential brow.

"Don't you try to make black white!" he said angrily.

"It's you that are trying to make white black," retorted Simeon Samuels. "Perhaps you don't know that I hail from Australia, and that by working on Saturday I escape profaning my native Australian Sabbath, while you, who have been all round the world, and have either lost or gained a day, according as you travelled east or west, are desecrating your original Sabbath either by working on Friday or smoking on Sunday."

The Parnass felt his head going round—he didn't know whether east or west. He tried to clear it by a pinch of snuff, which he in vain strove to make judicial.

"Oh, and so, and so—atchew!—and so you're the saint and I'm the sinner!" he cried sarcastically.

"No, I don't profess to be a saint," replied Simeon Samuels somewhat unexpectedly. "But I do think the Saturday was meant for Palestine, not for the lands of the Exile, where another day of rest rules. When you were in India you probably noted that the Mohammedans keep Friday. A poor Jew in the bazaar is robbed of his Hindoo customers on Friday, of his Jews on Saturday, and his Christians on Sunday."

"The Fourth Commandment is eternal!" said the Parnass with obstinate sublimity.

"But the Fifth says, 'that thy days may be long in the land which the Lord thy God giveth thee.' I believe this reward belongs to all the first five Commandments—not only to the Fifth—else an orphan would have no chance of long life. Keep the Sabbath in the land that the Lord giveth thee; not in England, which isn't thine."

"Oho!" retorted the Parnass. "Then at that rate in England you needn't honour your father and mother."

"Not if you haven't got them!" rejoined Simeon Samuels. "And if you haven't got a land, you can't keep its Sabbath. Perhaps you think we can keep the Jubilee also without a country."

"The Sabbath is eternal," repeated the Parnass doggedly. "It has nothing to do with countries. Before we got to the Promised Land we kept the Sabbath in the wilderness."

"Yes, and God sent a double dose of manna on the Friday. Do you mean to say He sends us here a double dose of profit?"

"He doesn't let us starve. We prospered well enough before you brought your wretched example——"

"Then my wretched example cannot lead the congregation away. I am glad of it. You do them much more harm by your way of Sabbath-breaking."

"My way!"

"Yes, my dear old father—Peace be upon him!—would have been scandalized to see the burden you carry on the Sabbath."

"What burden do I carry?"

"Your snuff-box!"

The Parnass almost dropped it. "That little thing!"

"I call it a cumbrous, not to say tasteless, thing. But before the Almighty there is no great and no small. One who stands in such a high place in the synagogue must be especially mindful, and every unnecessary burden——"

"But snuff is necessary for me—I can't do without it."

"Other presidents have done without it. As it is written in Jeremiah: 'And the wild asses did stand in the high places; they snuffed up the wind.'"

The Parnass flushed like a beetroot. "I'll teach you to know *your* place, sir." He turned his back on the scoffer, and strode towards the door.

"But if you'd care for a smaller snuff-box," said Simeon Samuels, "I have an artistic assortment."

XV

At the next meeting of the Synagogue Council a notice of motion stood upon the agenda in the name of the Parnass himself:

"That this Council views with the greatest reprobation the breach of the Fourth Commandment committed weekly by a member of the congregation, and calls upon him either to resign his seat, with the burial and other rights appertaining thereto, or to close his business on the Sabbath."

When the resolution came up Mr. Solomon Barzinsky moved as an amendment that weekly be altered into "twice a week," since the member kept open on Friday night as well as Saturday.

The Parnass refused to accept the amendment. There was only one Sabbath a week, though it had two periods. "And the evening and the morning were one day."

Mr. Peleg supported the amendment. They must not leave Mr.

Simeon Samuels a loophole of escape. It was also, he said, the duty of the Council to buy a barometer the rogue had foisted upon him.

After an animated discussion, mainly about the barometer, the president accepted the amendment, but produced a great impression by altering "twice a week" into "bi-weekly."

A Mr. John Straumann, however, who prided himself on his style, and had even changed his name to John because Jacob grated on his delicate ear, refused to be impressed.

Committed *bi*-weekly *by* a member sounded almost jocose, he argued. "Buy! buy!" it sounded like a butcher's cry.

Mr. Enoch, the kosher butcher, rose amid excitement, and asked if he had come there to be insulted!

"Sit down! sit down!" said the Parnass roughly. "It's no matter how the resolution sounds. It will be in writing."

"Then why not add," sarcastically persisted the stylist, " 'Committed *bi*-weekly *by* a member *by buying* and selling.' "

"Order, order!" said the Parnass angrily. "Those who are in favour of the resolution! Carried."

"*By* a majority," sneered the stylist, subsiding.

"Mr. Secretary"—the President turned to the poor Reverend-of-all-work—"you need not record this verbal discussion in the minutes."

"*By* request," said the stylist, reviving.

"But what's the use of the resolution if you don't mention the member's name?" suddenly inquired Ephraim Mendel, stretching his long lanky limbs.

"But there's only one Sabbath-breaker," replied the Parnass.

"To-day, yes, but to-morrow there might be two."

"It could hardly be to-morrow," said the stylist, "for that happens to be a Monday."

Barzinsky bashed the table. "Mr. President, are we here for business or are we not?"

"You may be here for business—I am here for religion," retorted Straumann the stylist.

"You—you snub-nosed monkey, what do you mean?"

"Order, order, gentlemen," said the Parnass.

"I will not order," said Solomon Barzinsky excited. "I did not come here to be insulted."

"Insulted!" quoth Straumann. "It's you that must apologize, you illiterate ichthyosaurus! I appeal to the President."

"You have both insulted *me*," was that worthy's ruling. "I give the word to Mr. Mendel."

"But——" from both the combatants simultaneously.

"Order, order!" from a dozen throats.

"I said Simeon Samuels' name must be put in," Mendel repeated.

"You should have said so before—the resolution is carried now," said the President.

"And a fat lot of good it will do," said Peleg. "Gentlemen, if you knew him as well as I, if you had my barometer to read him by, you'd see that the only remedy is to put him in *Cherem* [excommunication]."

"If he can't get buried it *is* a kind of *Cherem*," said the Gabbai.

"Assuredly," added the Parnass. "He will be frightened to think that if he dies suddenly——"

"And he is sure to take a sudden death," put in Barzinsky with unction.

"He will not be buried among Jews," wound up the Parnass.

"Hear, hear!" A murmur of satisfaction ran round the table. All felt that Simeon Samuels was cornered at last. It was resolved that the resolution be sent to him.

XVI

"Mr. Simeon Samuels requests me to say that he presents his compliments to the secretary of the Sudminster Hebrew Congregation, and begs to acknowledge the receipt of the Council's resolution. In reply I am to state that Mr. Samuels regrets that his views on the Sabbath question should differ from those of his fellow-worshipers, but he has not attempted to impress his views on the majority, and he regrets that in a free country like England they should have imported the tyranny of the lands of persecution from which they came. Fortunately such procedure is illegal. By the act of Charles I, the Sabbath is defined as the Sunday, and as a British subject Mr. Samuels takes his stand upon the British Constitution. Mr. Samuels has done his best to compromise with the congregation by attending the Sabbath service on the day most convenient to the majority. In regard to the veiled threat of the refusal of burial rights, Mr. Samuels desires me to say that he has no intention of dying in Sudminster, but merely of getting his living there. In any case, under his will, his body is to be deported to Jerusalem, where he has already acquired a burying-place."

"Next year in Jerusalem!" cried Barzinsky fervently when this was read to the next meeting.

"Order, order," said the Parnass. "I don't believe in his Jerusalem grave. They won't admit his dead body."

"He relies on smuggling in alive," said Barzinsky gloomily, "as soon as he has made his pile."

"That won't be very long at this rate," added Ephraim Mendel.

"The sooner the better," said the Gabbai impatiently. "Let him go to Jericho."

There was a burst of laughter, to the Gabbai's great astonishment.

"Order, order, gentlemen," said the Parnass. "Don't you see from this insolent letter how right I was? The rascal threatens to drag us to the Christian Courts, that's clear. All that about Jerusalem is only dust thrown into our eyes."

"Grave-dust," murmured Straumann.

"Order! He is a dangerous customer."

"Shopkeeper," corrected Straumann.

The Parnass glared, but took snuff silently.

"I don't wonder he laughed at us," said Straumann, encouraged. *"Bi*-weekly *by* a member. Ha! ha! ha!"

"Mr. President!" Barzinsky screamed. "Will you throw that laughing hyena out, or shall I?"

Straumann froze to a statue of dignity. "Let any animalcule try it on," said he.

"Shut up, you children, I'll chuck you both out," said Ephraim Mendel in conciliatory tones. "The point is—what's to be done now, Mr. President?"

"Nothing—till the end of the year. When he offers his new subscription we refuse to take it. That can't be illegal."

"We ought all to go to him in a friendly deputation," said Straumann. "These formal resolutions, 'Buy! buy!' put his back up. We'll go to him as brothers—all Israel are brethren, and blood is thicker than water."

"Chutney is thicker than blood," put in the Parnass mysteriously. "He'll simply try to palm off his stock on the deputation."

Ephraim Mendel and Solomon Barzinsky jumped up simultaneously. "What a good idea," said Ephraim. "There you have hit it!" said Solomon. Their simultaneous popping-up had an air of finality —like the long and the short of it!

"You mean?" said the Parnass, befogged in his turn.

"I mean," said Barzinsky, "we could buy up his stock, me and the other marine-dealers between us, and he could clear out!"

"If he sold it reasonably," added Mendel.

"Even unreasonably you must make a sacrifice for the Sabbath," said the Parnass. "Besides, divided among the lot of you, the loss would be little."

"And you can buy in my barometer with the rest," added Peleg.

"We could call a meeting of marine-dealers," said Barzinsky, disregarding him. "We could say to them we must sacrifice ourselves for our religion."

"Tell that to the marine-dealers!" murmured Straumann.

"And that we must buy out the Sabbath-breaker at any cost."

"Buy! buy!" said Straumann. "If you'd only thought of that sort of 'Buy! buy!' at the first!"

"Order, order!" said the Parnass.

"It would be more in order," said Straumann, "to appoint an executive sub-committee to deal with the question. I'm sick of it. And surely we as a Synagogue Council can't be in order in ordering some of our members to buy out another."

"Hear, hear!" His suggestion found general approval. It took a long discussion, however, before the synagogue decided to wash its hands of responsibility, and give over to a sub-committee of three the task of ridding Sudminster of its plague-spot by any means that commended itself to them.

Solomon Barzinsky, Ephraim Mendel, and Peleg the pawnbroker were elected to constitute this Council of Three.

XVII

The glad news spread through the Sudminster Congregation that Simeon Samuels had at last been bought out—at a terrible loss to the martyred marine-dealers who had had to load themselves with chutney and other unheard-of and unsaleable stock. But they would get back their losses, it was felt, by the removal of his rivalry. Carts were drawn up before the dismantled plate-glass window carrying off its criminal contents, and Simeon Samuels stood stroking his beard amid the ruins.

Then the shop closed; the shutters that should have honoured the Sabbath now depressed the Tuesday. Simeon Samuels was seen to get into the London train. The demon that troubled their sanctity had been exorcised. A great peace reigned in every heart, almost like the Sabbath peace coming into the middle of the week.

"If they had only taken my advice earlier," said Solomon Barzinsky to his wife, as he rolled his forkful of beef in the chutney.

"You can write to your father, Deborah," said Lazarus Levy, "that we no longer need the superior reach-me-downs."

On the Wednesday strange new rumours began to circulate, and those who hastened to confirm them stood dumfounded before great posters on all the shutters:

CLOSED FOR RE-STOCKING

The Old-fashioned Stock of This Business
Having Been Sold off to the Trade,
SIMEON SAMUELS
Is Taking the Opportunity
To Lay in the Best and Most Up-to-date
LONDON AND CONTINENTAL GOODS
For His Customers.
BARGAINS AND NOVELTIES IN EVERY DEPARTMENT

RE-OPEN SATURDAY NEXT

XVIII

A hurried emergency meeting of the Executive Sub-Committee was called.

"He has swindled us," said Solomon Barzinsky. "This paper signed by him merely undertakes to shut up his shop. And he will plead he meant for a day or two."

"And he agreed to leave the town," wailed Peleg, "but he meant to buy goods."

"Well, we can have the law of him," said Mendel. "We paid him compensation for disturbance."

"And can't he claim he *was* disturbed?" shrieked Barzinsky. "His whole stock turned upside down!"

"Let him claim!" said Mendel. "There is such a thing as obtaining money under false pretences."

"And such a thing as becoming the laughing-stock of the heathen," said Peleg. "We must grin and bear it ourselves."

"It's all very well for you to grin," said Solomon tartly. *"We've* got to bear it. You didn't take over any of his old rubbish."

"Didn't I, indeed? What about the barometer?"

"Confound your barometer!" cried Ephraim Mendel. "I'll have the law of him; I've made up my mind."

"Well, you'll have to bear the cost, then," said Peleg. "It's none of my business."

"Yes, it is," shouted Mendel. "As a member of the Sub-Committee you can't dissociate yourselves from us."

"A nice idea that—I'm to be dragged into your law-suits!"

"Hush, leave off these squabbles!" said Solomon Barzinsky. "The law is slow, and not even sure. The time has come for desperate measures. We must root out the plague-spot with our own hands."

"Hear, hear," said the rest of the Sub-Committee.

XIX

On the succeeding Sabbath Simeon Samuels was not the only figure in the synagogue absorbed in devotion. Solomon Barzinsky, Ephraim Mendel, and Peleg the pawnbroker were all rapt in equal piety, while the rest of the congregation was shaken with dreadful gossip about them. Their shops were open, too, it would seem.

Immediately after the service the Parnass arrested Solomon Barzinsky's exit, and asked him if the rumour were true.

"Perfectly true," replied Solomon placidly. "The Executive Sub-Committee passed the resolution to——"

"To break the Sabbath!" interrupted the Parnass.

"We had already sacrificed our money; there was nothing left but to sacrifice our deepest feelings——"

"But what for?"

"Why, to destroy his advantage, of course. Five-sixths of his Sabbath profits depend on the marine-dealers closing, and when he sees he's breaking the Sabbath in vain——"

"Rubbish! You are asked to stop a congregational infection, and you——"

"Vaccinate ourselves with the same stuff, to make sure the attack shall be light."

"It's a hair of the dog that bit us," said Mendel, who, with Peleg, had lingered to back up Barzinsky.

"Of the mad dog!" exclaimed the Parnass. "And you're all raging mad."

"It's the only sane way," urged Peleg. "When he sees his rivals open——"

"You!" The President turned on him. "You are not even a marine-dealer. Why are you open?"

"How could I dissociate myself from the rest of the Sub-Committee?" inquired Peleg with righteous indignation.

"You are a set of sinners in Israel!" cried the Parnass, forgetting even to take snuff. "This will split up the congregation."

"The congregation through its Council gave the Committee full power to deal with the matter," said Barzinsky with dignity.

"But then the other marine-dealers will open as well as the Committee!"

"I trust not," replied Barzinsky fervently. "Two of us are enough to cut down his takings."

"But the whole lot of you would be still more efficacious. Oh, this is the destruction of our congregation, the death of our religion!"

"No, no, no," said Solomon soothingly. "You are mistaken. We are most careful not to touch money. We are going to trust our customers, and keep our accounts without pen or ink. We have invented a most ingenious system, which gives us far more work than writing, but we have determined to spare ourselves no trouble to keep the Sabbath from unnecessary desecration."

"And once the customers don't pay up, your system will break down. No, no; I shall write to the Chief Rabbi."

"We will explain our motives," said Mendel.

"Your motives need no explanation. This scandal must cease."

"And who are you to give orders?" shrieked Solomon Barzinsky. "You're not speaking to a *Schnorrer*, mind you. My banking account is every bit as big as yours. For two pins I start an opposition Shool."

"A Sunday Shool!" said the Parnass sarcastically.

"And why not? It would be better than sitting playing solo on Sundays. We are not in Palestine now."

"Oh, Simeon Samuels has been talking to you, has he?"

"I don't need Simeon Samuels' wisdom. I'm an Englishman myself."

XX

The desperate measures of the Sub-Committee were successful. The other marine-dealers hastened to associate themselves with the plan of campaign, and Simeon Samuels soon departed in search of a more pious seaport.

But, alas! homœopathy was only half-vindicated. For the remedy proved worse than the disease, and the cutting-out of the original plague-spot left the other marine-stores still infected. The epidemic spread from them till it had overtaken half the shops of the congregation. Some had it in a mild form—only one shutter open, or a back door not closed—but in many it came out over the whole shop-window.

The one bright spot in the story of the Sudminster Sabbath is that the congregation of which the present esteemed Parnass is Solomon Barzinsky, Esq., J.P., managed to avert the threatened split, and that while in so many other orthodox synagogues the poor minister preaches on the Sabbath to empty benches, the Sudminster congregation still remains at the happy point of compromise acutely discovered by Simeon Samuels: of listening reverentially every Saturday morning to the unchanging principles of its minister-elect, the while its shops are engaged in supplying the wants of Christendom.

> *Business is a combination*
> *of war and sport.*—*André Maurois*

Think of Disraeli [Lord Beaconsfield], for whom any Jewish
community would have been too confining
since the British Empire was hardly big enough for him.—*Max Nordau*

THE ROPEWALKER

A poor Jew once came to a certain town and looked about for some means of livelihood. But finding none, he fell upon a stratagem. He posted notices all over the place that on the following Thursday he would walk on a rope stretched across the entire width of the lake. The price of admission would be five kopecks.

On the appointed day all the inhabitants of the town gathered at the lakeside to watch the performance. A rope had been strung across the lake and the "artist" made ready to begin. However, he took such a long time getting started that the crowd became impatient. Suddenly, the performer turned to the people and said:

"I want you to know that I am a fraud! I am no ropewalker at all. Should I attempt to do what I promised, I will most certainly fall into the lake, and since I can't swim, I will most likely drown. Now, my friends, if you think it right that on account of your five measly kopecks a man who is both a husband and a father should drown, then I am ready to begin the performance!"

ONE OF TWO THINGS

BY SHOLOM ALEICHEM

Good morning! "Blessed be thy coming!" A Jew! Reb Yankel, how are you? How's your wife, and your father-in-law, and your mother-in-law, and how's *gesheft?* You've probably come to give me back my money! It's really *takkeh* a long time already! What, no? Not time yet? What do you want of me anyway? Am I, God forbid. asking you for the money? Say yourself—am I pressing you for it? I'm only going to ask you just one plain question: What have you got against me, you robber? You *mamzer!* One of two things—give me back my money!

CREDIT VS. CASH

Said one innkeeper to the other:

"I rarely sell a man whisky on credit, but when I do I charge him double."

"I, on the other hand," said the second innkeeper, "charge less on credit than for cash."

"What's the logic in it?"

"Very simple: If a man doesn't pay on credit it makes my loss that much less."

THE BENEFIT OF DEBTS

BY MAX NORDAU

Only the very wealthy, against whose millions no one can insinuate a doubt, have the right to be modest in their way of living, but these have no cause to apply to my school of success. The poorer you are, the more necessary it is for you to make an imposing appearance. Dress well, have your surroundings elegant, live as if you were the heir to Golconda. This costs money? Very true, and lots of it too. But what if one doesn't happen to have any? Then go into debt. Debt? Certainly, my boy, certainly! There are few ladders that enable one to climb so rapidly and securely to the highest goals.

It is revolting when we reflect how debts have been traduced by pedants, and brought into disrepute. The cruelest wrong has been done to them. Much extravagance and license will be forgiven to the genius of Heine, but never his line: "Man, pay your debts!" What folly, what immorality! If you follow Heine's advice, you are lost! Just consider for a moment: Who is going to notice you, if you pay your way as you go along in petty narrow honesty? No one will turn to look after you. Join some threadbare company, live in an attic, eat dry bread, and never run into debt—you will soon feel the results. The dogs will bark at you, the watchmen will look you over with distrust, respectable people will double-lock their doors in your face. And the grocer whose customer you are will cease to take the slightest interest in you from the moment you have paid him the amount of his bill. If you are stricken down in front of his door his only thought will be how to remove the obstruction from his threshold.

Then, on the contrary, get everything on credit, pump where you can, and your condition will be transformed as if by magic. In the first place, all the enjoyments of life will be accessible to you that the poor beggar has to deny himself. Then your general appearance will arouse on all sides the most favorable impression. At last you will have a whole bodyguard or retinue of zealous, even fanatical, co-workers for your success. For each creditor is a friend, a well-wisher, an active agent for your protection. He will not allow anything to befall you. No father will exert himself to such an extent in your behalf as a creditor. The more you owe him, the greater his interest in seeing you prosper. He watches over you that not a hair of your head be rumpled, for your life is his money. He trembles when any peril threatens you, for your ruin is the grave of his claim.

Have heaps of creditors, young man, and your success is assured from the start! They will secure for you a rich wife, an exalted position, and a fine reputation. The most lucky investment is to apply the money of others to an ornamental design for your own existence.

You often hear it said: that a certain someone
became impoverished because he accumulated many debts.
That, of course, isn't correct.
If he became impoverished it was only because
he paid off his debts.—Moritz G. Saphir

CHEAPER AND BETTER

Mr. Geller was a generous but highly nervous man. He simply couldn't endure noise. Ever since the new tenant, Mr. Yachnetchek, moved into the upstairs apartment he had felt undone. All day long, and far into the night as well, he was obliged to listen to the furious running overhead in the long hallway of the Yachnetchek boy, little Irving. Up and down, up and down the hallway the precious boy pounded away until Mr. Geller felt the ceiling coming down over his ears.

Unable to endure the racket any longer, Mr. Geller went up to talk turkey to his tenant. After all, who was the owner of the house, who?

"Mr. Yachnetchek," he began in a landlord's plaintive voice, "this noise's got to stop! You must tell your boy to stop this noise!"

"What do you want me to do with him—chain him up like a bear?" retorted Mr. Yachnetchek. "After all, Irving is only five and a child's got to move around, you know!"

"All right! So he's got to move around! Who's asking you to tie him up? But at least you could buy a carpet for the hallway. That would stop the noise a little."

"Huh! And who'll pay for it? Do you think money grows on trees? If you don't like the noise he makes, go ahead and pay for the carpet yourself!"

"All right, I will!" impulsively agreed Mr. Geller, ready to do anything to escape the noise overhead.

In no time at all Mr. Yachnetchek presented a bill for fifty dollars to Mr. Geller who paid it gladly.

Wonderful to relate, the noise upstairs ceased entirely. Mr. Geller was overjoyed! Now he could relax again, and he felt that he had gotten off cheaply at that.

One day he said to Mrs. Geller: "That must be one fine thick runner I bought the Yachnetcheks. I'm curious to see what it looks like."

So Mr. Geller went upstairs to call on his tenant. But to his astonishment he saw no sign of any carpet in the hallway.

"Where's the runner?" asked the puzzled landlord. "I paid you fifty dollars for a runner—where's the runner?"

"If milk is cheap do I have to buy a cow?" parried Mr. Yach-netchek.

"I'll take no jokes from you, Yachnetchek! Where's the runner?"

"There is no runner—do you think I'm a fool? Why should I throw out fifty dollars for a runner? I bought my Irving a pair of thick felt slippers for $1.39. Isn't that just as good?"

Paskudniks and No-Goodniks

*I rub him with honey
and still he stinks from birch tar.*

IN ODESSA

BY ISAAK BABEL

TRANSLATED FROM THE RUSSIAN BY AVRAHM YARMOLINSKY

I was the one to open the conversation.

"Reb Arye Leyb," I said to the old man, "let us talk about Benya Krik.[1] Let us talk about his meteoric beginnings and his terrible end. Three black shadows block the paths of my imagination. Here is one-eyed Froim Grach. The rusty steel of his deeds—can you compare it to the dazzling strength of the King? And here is Kolka Pakovsky. This man's simple-minded ferocity had in it all that is needed for domination. And is it possible that Haim Drong couldn't recognize the brilliance of the new star? How is it, then, that Benya Krik alone reached the top of the rope ladder, while all the others were left hanging below on the limp rungs?"

Reb Arye Leyb, sitting on the cemetery wall, kept still. Before us stretched the green peace of the graves. A man who thirsts for knowledge must be patient. A man who possesses knowledge should be dignified. That is why Arye Leyb remained silent, perched on the cemetery wall. At last he said:

[1]*This character was allegedly modeled on Misha Yaponchik, a notorious Odessa gangster. It is said that at one time he headed the Jewish self-defense organization in Odessa, that he fought with the Reds against the White troops and was executed by a firing squad.—Avrahm Yarmolinsky*

"Why he, why not they, you want to know. Well, forget for a while that you've got spectacles on your nose and autumn in your soul. Stop raising hell at your desk and stammering in public. Imagine for a moment that you're a fellow who raises hell in public squares and stammers on paper. You're a tiger, a lion, a wildcat. You can spend the night with a Russian woman, and the Russian woman will be satisfied by you. You are twenty-five. If sky and earth had rings fastened to them, you would grab these rings and draw the sky down to the earth. And your papa is Mendel Krik, the teamster. What does such a father think about? He thinks about drinking a good glass of vodka, about socking someone on the jaw, about his horses—and about nothing else. You want to live, and he makes you die twenty times a day. What would you have done if you'd been in Benya Krik's boots? You'd have done nothing. But he did something. That's why he's King, while you fig with your fist in your pocket.

"Benya, he went to Froim Grach, who then already looked at the world with one eye and was what he is today. He said to Froim: 'Take me on, Froim. I want to be cast upon your shore. The shore I'm cast upon will gain by it.'

"Grach asked him: 'Who are you? Where are you coming from? And what do you live by?'

" 'Try me, Froim,' answered Benya, 'and let's stop chewing the rag.'

" 'Let's,' said Grach. 'I'll try you!'

"And the gangsters held a session to put their minds to the subject of Benya Krik. I wasn't at that session. But it is said that they did hold it. The late Lyovka Byk was elder then.

" 'What's going on under this Benchik's hat?' asked the late Lyovka Byk.

"One-eyed Grach gave his opinion: 'Benya doesn't talk much, but there's a flavor to his words. He says little, and you wish he'd say more.'

" 'If that's so,' exclaimed the late Lyovka, 'then let's try him on Tartakovsky.'

" 'Let's try him on Tartakovsky,' the council decided, and all those who housed a conscience blushed when they heard this decision. Why did they blush? You'll find out if you go where I'll lead you.

"Among us, Tartakovsky had the nicknames Yid-and-a-Half or Nine Holdups. He was called Yid-and-a-Half, because no one Jew could contain so much insolence and so much money as Tartakovsky. He was taller than the tallest policeman in Odessa and he weighed more than the fattest Jewess. And he was nicknamed Nine Holdups because the firm of Lyovka Byk and Company had held up his place not ten or eight times, but exactly nine. It now fell to Benya's lot to hold up Yid-and-a-Half for the tenth time. When Froim passed this information on to him, Benya said 'Yes' and walked out, slamming the door. Why did he slam the door? You'll find out if you go where I'll lead you.

"Tartakovsky has the soul of a murderer, but he's one of ours. He came from among us. He is our own flesh and blood, as if one mother brought us into the world. Half Odessa was employed in his stores. And it was his own Moldavanka people who made trouble for him. Twice they kidnaped him for ransom, and once during a program they staged his funeral, with a choir too. That was when the thugs from the Sloboda section were beating up the Jews on Bolshaya Arnautskaya Street. Tartakovsky ran away from them and came across a funeral procession with a choir.

" 'Who are they burying with a choir?' he asked.

"The passers-by told him it was Tartakovsky's funeral. The procession reached the Sloboda cemetery. Then our people took a machine-gun out of the coffin and made it hot for the Sloboda thugs. But Yid-and-a-Half hadn't expected that. Yid-and-a-Half was scared to death. And who in his position wouldn't have been scared?

"The tenth holdup of a man who had been buried once already— that was really uncivil. Benya, who wasn't King then yet, understood it better than anyone else. But he had said 'Yes' to Grach, and the same day he wrote Tartakovsky a letter like all letters of that kind:

> *"Highly Esteemed Ruvin Ossipovich!*
>
> *"Be so kind as to place under the rain-water barrel next Saturday. . . . Should you take it upon yourself to refuse, as you have recently done on several occasions, a grave disappointment in your family life awaits you.*
>
> *Respectfully, one whom you know,*
> *Benzion Krik*

"Tartakovsky, no dawdler, wrote his answer without delay:

> *"Benya!*
>
> *"If you were an idiot, I would have written to you as to an idiot. But I know that you are not, and God forbid that I should have to change my opinion. It looks as if you're making believe you're a child. Don't you know that there has been a bumper crop in Argentina and that we sit here and don't find one customer for*

our wheat? And upon my word, I'm tired of eating such bitter bread in my old age and having such a disagreeable time of it, after slaving all my life like the lowest teamster, and what do I have after a lifetime of hard labor? Ulcers, sores, aggravation, sleeplessness. Give up them fool ideas, Benya.

Your friend, much more than you imagine,

Ruvin Tartakovsky

"Yid-and-a-Half did his part. He wrote the letter. But the post-office didn't deliver it. When he got no answer, Benya got mad. The next day he showed up in Tartakovsky's office with four friends. Four masked young men carrying revolvers barged into the room.

" 'Stick 'em up!' they said and began brandishing their guns.

" 'Calm down, Solomon,' Benya remarked to one who shouted louder than the others, 'don't get into this habit of being nervous when you're on the job,' and turning to the clerk, who was white as death and yellow as clay, he asked him: 'Is Yid-and-a-Half at the plant?'

" 'The proprietor is not at the plant,' answered the clerk, whose name was Josif Muginstein and who was the bachelor son of Aunt Pessya—she sold chickens on Seredinsky Square.

" 'Who is in charge here, then?' they asked the unhappy Muginstein.

" 'I am in charge here,' answered the clerk, as green as green grass.

" 'Then with God's help, open the cashbox for us!' Benya ordered him, and so began an opera in three acts!

"Solomon, the nervous one, packed cash, securities, watches, and jewelry into a suitcase; the late Josif stood facing him with lifted hands; in the meantime Benya was telling stories from the life of the Jewish people.

" 'If he makes believe he's a Rothschild,' Benya was saying, referring to Tartakovsky, 'then let him burn on a slow fire. Explain it to me, Muginstein, as to a friend: he gets a business letter from me; why couldn't he get into a trolley for five kopecks then, and ride up to my place and have a glass vodka with the family and a snack, taking potluck? What kept him from having a heart-to-heart talk with me? "Benya," he could have told me, "thus and thus, here is my bank balance, wait a couple of days, let me get my breath, give me a chance to turn around. . . ." What would I have answered? Hog don't meet hog, but man meets man. Muginstein, do you get me?'

" 'I do,' answered Muginstein and told a lie, because it wasn't at all clear to him why Yid-and-a-Half, a respectable, substantial man, one of the leading citizens, should take a trolley to have a bite with the family of Mendel Krik, the teamster.

"Meanwhile misfortune was prowling around the house like a beggar at dawn. Misfortune burst into the office with a bang. And although this time it took the shape of a Jew by the name of Savka Butzis, it was as drunk as a water carrier.

" 'Haw-haw-haw!' shouted the Jew Savka. 'Beg your pardon, Benchik, I'm late,' and he stamped his feet and waved his arms. Then he fired a shot, and the bullet struck Muginstein in the stomach.

"Are words needed here? There was a man, the man is no more. There lived an innocent bachelor, like a bird on a bough, and now he has perished, stupidly. Came a Jew who looked like a sailor and fired a shot, not at some bottle with a surprise in it, but at a living man. Are words needed here?

" 'Clear out!' shouted Benya, and was the last to go. But as he was running off, he took time to say to Butzis: 'I swear by my mother's grave, Savka, you'll lie beside him. . . .'

"Now tell me, young gentleman, you who cut coupons off other people's bonds, what would you have done if you'd been in Benya Krik's boots? You don't know how you would have acted. But he knew what to do. That's why he is King, while we two sit on the wall of the Second Jewish Cemetery and shade our faces from the sun with our palms.

"Aunt Pessya's unfortunate son did not die at once. An hour after he was brought to the hospital Benya appeared there. He summoned the doctor-in-charge and the nurse and, without taking his hands out of the pockets of his cream-colored pants, he said to them: 'I want to see the patient Josif Muginstein get well. Just in case, let me introduce myself: I'm Benzion Krik. Spare no expense. Camphor, air cushions, a private room—you must give him everything. If you don't, remember that no doctor, not even a doctor of philosophy, needs more than six feet of earth. . . .'

"Nevertheless Muginstein died the same night. And it was only then that Yid-and-a-Half let himself be heard all over Odessa.

" 'Where does the police begin,' he bellowed, 'and where does Benya end?'

" 'The police ends where Benya begins,' sensible people answered, but Tartakovsky wouldn't calm down and in the end this is what happened: a red automobile with a music box in it played the first march from the opera *Laugh, Pagliacci* in Seredinsky Square. In broad daylight the automobile raced up to the little house where Aunt Pessya lived.

"The automobile thundered, spat smoke, glittered brassily, spread a stench of gasoline, and played arias on its horn. A man leaped out of it and walked into the kitchen, where little Aunt Pessya was writhing on the earthen floor. Yid-and-a-Half sat on a chair, waving his arms.

" 'You gorilla!' he shouted when he caught sight of the visitor, 'you bandit, you, may the earth spit out your corpse! Nice fashion you've started, killing living men. . . .'

" 'Mosoo Tartakovsky,' Benya Krik said to him in a quiet voice, 'it's the second day now that I been mourning for the deceased as for my own brother. But I know that you don't give a damn for my young tears. And where, Mosoo Tartakovsky, in what strong box did you lock up shame? You had the gall to send the mother of our late Josif a miserable hundred bucks. My brain, let alone my hair, stood on end when I heard the news. . . .'

"Here Benya paused. He had on a chocolate jacket, cream-colored pants and raspberry boots.

" 'Ten grand, in a lump sum,' he roared, 'and a pension for the rest of her life, may she live a hundred and twenty years. If not, then let's leave this room, Mosoo Tartakovsky, and get into my car.'

"There was a row between the two. Yid-and-a-Half and Benya had words. I wasn't there when the argument took place. But those who were remember it. The two agreed on five thousand outright and a monthly payment of fifty rubles.

" 'Aunt Pessya,' Benya said then to the disheveled little woman who lay on the floor, 'if you need my life, you can have it, but everybody makes mistakes, even God. A terrible mistake has been made, Aunt Pessya. But wasn't it a mistake on God's part to settle the Jews in Russia, where they've had to suffer the tortures of hell? Would it be bad if the Jews lived in Switzerland, where they'd be surrounded by first-class lakes, mountain air, and nothing but Frenchmen? Everybody makes mistakes, even God. Open your ears to what I'm saying, Aunt Pessya. You have five thousand in hand and fifty rubles a month till you die, may you live a hundred and twenty years. Josif will have a first-class funeral: six horses like six lions, two carriages for the wreaths, the choir from the Brody Synagogue, Minkovsky himself will sing at your late son's funeral.'

"The funeral took place the next morning. About this funeral ask the beggars who hang around the cemeteries. Ask the synagogue beadles about it, the kosher poultry men, or the old women from the Second Poorhouse. Odessa never saw such a funeral, and the world will never see another like it. That day policemen put on cotton gloves. The synagogues were wide open, they were decorated with greenery and blazed with electric lights. Black plumes swayed above the heads of the white horses that drew the hearse. Sixty choir boys walked in front of the procession. Boys they were, but they sang with the voices of women. Elders of the synagogue of the kosher poultry dealers led Aunt Pessya, one at either elbow. Behind them marched members of the Society of Jewish Salesmen, then came attorneys-at-law, physicians, and trained midwifes. On one side of Aunt Pessya were poultry-women from the Old Market, on the other the milk-maids from the Bugayovka district, wrapped in orange shawls. They stamped their feet like gendarmes on a holiday parade, and their wide hips gave off the odor of the sea and of milk. The employees of Ruvin Tartakovsky brought up the rear. There were a hundred of them, or two hundred, or two thousand. They wore black jackets with silk lapels and new boots that squeaked like suckling-pigs in a sack.

"And now I shall speak as the Lord did on Mount Sinai out of the burning bush. Fill your ears with my words. It was with my own eyes that I beheld all I beheld, sitting here on the wall of the Second Jewish Cemetery, alongside of lisping Moiseyka and Shimshon, from the cemetery office. It was I who saw it, I, Arye Leyb, the proud Jew who is neighbor to the dead.

"The hearse drove up to the cemetery chapel. The coffin was placed on the steps. Aunt Pessya trembled like a little bird. The cantor climbed out of his carriage and started the funeral service. Sixty choir boys echoed him. At that moment a red motor car shot out from behind a bend on the road. It played *Laugh, Pagliacci,* and came to a halt. The people were as quiet as the dead. The trees were silent, and the choir boys, and the beggars. Four men climbed out from under the red roof and, walking slowly, carried to the hearse a wreath of roses the like of which was never seen before. And when the service was over, four men placed their steel shoulders under the coffin and, with eyes blazing and chests thrust forward, marched in the ranks of the Society of Jewish Salesmen.

"In front walked Benya Krik, who had not yet been called King by anyone. He was the first to approach the grave. He stepped on the mound of earth and stretched out his arm.

"Kofman, of the burial brotherhood, ran up to him.

" 'What do you want to do, young man?' Kofman asked Benya.

" 'I want to make a speech,' answered Benya Krik.

"And he made a speech. It was heard by all who wanted to hear. It was heard by me, Arye Leyb, and by lisping Moiseyka, who was perched on the wall beside me.

" 'Gentlemen and ladies,' said Benya Krik, 'gentlemen and ladies,' he said, and the sun stood above his head like a sentry with a rifle. 'You have come here to pay your last respects to an honest toiler who perished for two cents. In my own name and in the name of all those who aren't present here, I thank you. Gentlemen and ladies, what did our dear Josif get out of life? A couple trifles. What was his occupation? He counted other people's money. What did he perish for? He perished for the whole working class. There are people already doomed to death, and there are people who haven't begun to live. And it just happened that a bullet that was flying at a doomed breast pierced that of Josif, who did not get anything out of life but a couple trifles. There are people who know how to drink vodka, and there are those who don't know how to drink it, but drink all the same. The result is that the first get pleasure from both joy and grief, while the second suffer for all those who drink vodka without knowing how. That is why, gentlemen and ladies, after we have said a prayer for our poor Josif, I will ask you to accompany to his grave Savely Butzis, unknown to you, but already deceased. . . .'

"After he made this speech, Benya Krik stepped down from the mound. The people, the trees, the cemetery beggars were all silent. Two grave-diggers carried an unpainted coffin to a near-by grave. The cantor, stammering, finished the prayers. Benya threw the first shovelful of earth into Josif's grave and walked over to Savka's. All the lawyers and the ladies with brooches followed him like sheep. He made the cantor chant the complete service over Savka, and the sixty choir boys joined in. Savka had never dreamed of such a service— believe the word of Arye Leyb, an old oldster.

"They say that on that day Yid-and-a-Half decided to retire from business. I wasn't there when he made that decision. But that neither the cantor nor the choir nor the burial brotherhood asked to be paid— that I saw with Arye Leyb's eyes. Arye Leyb is my name. And I could see nothing more, because the people, after walking slowly away from Savka's grave, began to run as from a house on fire. They rushed away in carriages, in carts, and on foot. And only the four who had come in the red car drove off in it. The music box played its march; the car shook and was off.

" 'A King,' said lisping Moiseyka, looking after the automobile, the same Moiseyka who edges me off the best seat on the wall.

"Now you know everything. You know who was the first to utter the word, 'King!' It was Moiseyka. You know why he didn't apply that name either to one-eyed Grach or to ferocious Kolka. You know everything. But what good does it do you, if you still have spectacles on your nose and autumn in your soul? . . ."

What the eyes can't see, the hands won't take.

A stony heart can be opened only with a golden hammer.

Some people grow tall by standing on the shoulders of others.

THREE TESTS

When a ne'er-do-well goes to buy a hatchet he tests it in three different ways.

He tries to cut a straw. If it cuts it, well enough. If it doesn't cut it —so what?

He strikes it against a hard stone. If sparks fly, well and good. If not—so what?

He conceals it under his coat. If the shopkeeper doesn't notice it, well and good. If he does—so what? He puts it back!

What is the test of good manners?
Being able to bear patiently with bad ones.—Solomon ibn Gabirol

THE LONG AND THE SHORT OF IT

A thief was loitering among the stalls in the market place. When the fish dealer wasn't looking, he picked up a big carp and hid it under his coat. As he was walking off, the fish vendor called after him:

"Listen uncle, next time you steal a fish be sure that either your coat is longer or the fish is shorter!"

THE PROPER PLACE

Once Chaim, the village sluggard, arrived home late at night from a lively celebration in town.

He knocked on the door.

"Open the door!" he cried.

"Go away! The Devil take you, you sot!" answered his wife bitterly.

"Open the door, quick!" pleaded Chaim. "See what I've brought you: some roast goose and a bottle of wine to drink it down."

When his wife heard this she opened the door.

"Where is the roast goose and the bottle of wine?" she asked eagerly.

"Right here!" replied Chaim, patting his round belly.

THE STORY OF THE CANTOR

BY S. J. AGNON
TRANSLATED FROM THE HEBREW BY I. M. LASK

My father-in-law will, I hope, pardon me for describing him as a very gross person, if you will excuse my saying so; but nevertheless his heart yearns toward the Torah like a horse for its stall. If a new preacher comes to deliver a sermon, my father-in-law goes off to town. Every Sabbath Eve he used to do what was requisite, seeing that he lived beyond an ordinary Sabbath day's journey, in order that if a sage came to town he could go and visit him. You cannot imagine what an attentive pair of ears look like if you have not seen him standing listening to the sage's sermon. His mouth was open, his two ears were pricked up, his face bright, and his heart was glad. Not that he could understand the greater part of the sermon, for he had never studied Bible or Talmud, and ever since he had come to man's estate had had to do with nothing but horses and carts. When he was young what was he but a wagoner, and when he grew old what did he do but let horses for hire. Nevertheless, half of the sermon he would manage to make out, even if he did make it out all topsy-turvy.

But there is one thing that even the most perfect and entire ignoramus can understand, and that is cantorship. My father-in-law's voice, he will doubtless forgive my saying, is like the creaking of a wheel that has not been greased for years on end; but his sense of hearing is very good, and his pair of ears are always open to songs and singing. If you ever saw a cantor and his choir, you could be sure that he was hanging around them; and he would bring them home and give them food and drink and give them a curricle and not ask for pay. Why, for a good tune he would have been prepared to pawn his very soul, so highly did he esteem it. But the thing for which he would have been prepared to give up his soul finally brought him to grief. And it happened like this.

Once a fine handsome young man with a pair of flashing eyes came along and asked, Have you a cart here that is leaving for such and such a place? And if there's no cart, said my father-in-law to him, wouldn't you be able to trudge the road afoot? Because if you can't, what use are your legs to a young fellow-me-lad like you? But I'm in a hurry, he answered, because I've made a contract with the cantor there. Are you a choir boy? he asks. And the young fellow answers, Yes, I'm a choir boy. Well, and if that's the case, said my father-in-law, why didn't you say so until now? D'you think you'll have a chance of getting away from us without doing the honors of your throat? Before I begin doing the honors of my throat, said he, first go and do my throat the honors. I can see that you're no fool, approved the old man, and ordered food and drink to be set before him at once.

And the young man ate and drank for a dozen cantors—and they're no bad trenchermen, as you know. My father-in-law watching him said, I can be certain that this young fellow will one day be a cantor in Israel; as the saying goes, As their eating is their service. And when at last he had finished he said to the young man, Now you've eaten and drunk, let's see what else you can do with your mouth.

Thereupon he began singing the special festival and penitential prayers. The whole air at once filled with song, as though it were a June night with the nightingale giving of its best. How can I speak about it or describe it to you? Our feet remained in my father-in-law's house, while our souls went wandering wide through the Halls of Music. And my father-in-law might well be compared to a hunter who has caught the wings of song. He there and then began praising himself and saying, You see, didn't I tell you he was the very wings of song themselves? From the cut of his face I saw that he was the very wings of song.

Listen, my lad, said the old man to him, do you want to go along?

Most certainly, said he. And I tell you that you won't leave this place, said my father-in-law. And why not? he asked. Now what is it you want to go along for, said my father-in-law, other than to be a cantor's assistant? By your life I'll turn you into a cantor yourself. Isn't it more worth while, I ask you, to be a cantor yourself than a cantor's assistant?

Now he was unwedded, and therefore couldn't rightly be a cantor; only my father-in-law had a daughter named Teibele, and it had just struck him that he could marry them to one another. And meanwhile the young man agreed to stay with them, and my mother-in-law used to see him in food and drink. And my wife and her sister used to bring him all manner of dainties in their aprons. And no more than a few days went by until the Engagement Contract was written between the praiseworthy virgin, Mistress Teibele, long life to her, daughter of the worthy Dov Ber known as Bertshi, may his Rock and Redeemer guard him, and between the bridegroom youth, his honor Master Ephraim, long life to him; the virgin Mistress Teibele, long life to her, desireth the bridegroom youth, his honor Master Ephraim, long life to him; and the father-in-law-to-be, Reb Bertshi, undertakes to maintain the bridegroom youth, his honor Master Ephraim, long life to him, in all matters appertaining to victuals, likewise to clothe him and shoe him as is seemly and fitting. The worthy Dov Ber, known as Bertshi, likewise promises to call upon the wardens, may their Rock safeguard them, to appoint him, namely and to wit, the bridegroom youth, his honor Master Ephraim, long life to him, as First Cantor of the Congregation in the Large Synagogue after his marriage; and should the bridegroom youth, his honor Master Ephraim, desire to accept a group, for service as choir, of those known as singers, he has the right to do so, and it is incumbent upon the aforesaid Reb Bertshi, the father-in-law-to-be, to assist and aid him to this end. This has been agreed upon by the two parties, namely and to wit, the honorable Dov Ber known as Bertshi on behalf of the betrothed Mistress Teibele, and the betrothed youth, his honor Master Ephraim, on behalf of himself. In witness whereof cometh the sign manual of so-and-so, a witness, and of somebody else, another witness.

And thus Ephraim came to live in my father-in-law's house and ate for his life. We soon had opportunities of learning from his habits that he was not particularly God-fearing, and, indeed, if you wish to say so, interpreted the law very leniently for his own requirements; but we winked the eye at his transgressions. If he was caught doing something wrong we held him blameless. Great is the esteem and affection in which a man is held, for it makes even the beam in his eye seem no more than a mote; and such is particularly the case with a bridegroom in the house of his betrothed, when his parents-in-law-to-be are fond of him and he is good-looking and has a fine voice.

Within a little while we heard that he had done this and that wrong action in such and such a place at such and such a time. Now what sort of answer did Bertshi have for the man who told him that he had seen his future son-in-law, Ephraim, doing this and that wrong thing in such a place on such a day? My father-in-law screeched at him, Mister whoever-you-are and whatever your father's name may have been, let me advise you to gouge out your eyes and stuff them into your mouth and don't go looking at things you don't deserve to see, and don't come atelling me of things I don't want to hear about. And before ever he finished he would have slapped the other man round the jaw.

All the while my father-in-law was journeying to town and back, spending his time on all kinds of wardens. At last he succeeded, by actual cash bribery, to have his prospective son-in-law, Ephraim, appointed as Cantor of the Congregation in the Large Synagogue on condition that he first married a wife. If that's the only objection, said Bertshi to the wardens, it needn't bother you at all, for he has a wife all ready waiting to wed him. And at once they began preparing for the wedding. Before the last month of the year was out they had come under the Bridal Canopy. It was then that my father-in-law said to me, Jacob Samson, pack up your traps and empty your quarters so as the young folk can come in.

But that's a chapter all to itself. Meanwhile, Ephraim married, and on the first night of the Penitential Prayers before the New Year he arrayed himself as Cantor of the Congregation and took his place before the Holy Ark in the Large Synagogue in town. Well, what is there to tell you? If I tell you that his voice was fine I've already said as much; and all the same, I can tell you that when he sang, "For Thine is the body and Thy work is the soul, therefore have pity upon Thy toil," it seemed to me that my soul was bound and united with the Creator of the Universe, and the Creator must assuredly do all He could to deliver His portion. Unless you saw my father-in-law in all his glory and pride when he watched his son-in-law before the Ark in the Large Synagogue with a silver edging to his tallith, you cannot imagine the joy that is possible to a father-in-law. For even though my father-in-law was reckoned a wealthy man he did not wear a silver crown to his tallith for fear the fine folk of the town would rebuke him.

So then my father-in-law began coddling him even more. He himself would go off to the chickens and fetch him all the newly laid eggs to soothe his throat, since a newly laid egg swallowed raw is good for the voice. I ask of you, Reb Yudel, please not to be annoyed with me for taking so long a time in telling these details, for they should be explained in Bertshi's defense when telling how he came to put me out of doors in order to make room for that wastrel. In the end you will see how our Holy Torah took her revenge of him for thrusting me out of hearth and home and keeping me at arm's length from study.

But for the present let us return to our first concern. And so Ephraim stood before the Holy Ark on the first night of the Penitential Prayers. Those who were in the synagogue held very highly of him, while those who had not been in the synagogue dismissed him for a song. But when the New Year came round, on which occasion almost all the town goes to pray in the Large Synagogue, there was nobody left to whistle him down. When he went down before the Holy Ark and began the Reader's Prayer, "Behold I, that am poor in deeds and quaking and terrified by the fear of Him Who dwelleth amid the praises of Israel, do come to stand before Thee and entreat for Thy people Israel who have sent me," a tremor of penitence passed through all hearts. I myself forgot all that had befallen me on his account, and I emptied my heart of all its secular thoughts and determined to repent my ways; and so I went on from strength to strength all through the prayer.

Of old the ancient ones complained, and indeed it is mentioned in the Holy Zohar, that on the New Year and the Day of Atonement, when we ought to consider the shaming of the Holy and Blest One and His Name which is profaned amid the gentiles, everybody bays like a dog, Give us children, give us grub, give us life, give us forgiveness and atonement. And not a man thinks to meditate on the shaming of the Holy and Blest One and upon His Name which is profaned amid the gentiles. But when Ephraim took his place and began, every man disregarded his own needs and requirements; and during his prayer everybody cleaved to Him, may He be blest. It was plain to be seen that Ephraim's prayers made their impression upon the hearts of all except Ephraim. For while he was praying one young man pulled aside the edge of Ephraim's tallith which covered his head, thinking to find him swimming in tears; and Ephraim poked out his tongue at him. Mind you, I don't say that it really was so, but I tell you what I heard.

During the Ten Days of Penitence between New Year and Atonement everybody in town was humming, "My dear son Ephraim," or else "Behold I that am poor," to the tune sung by Ephraim. And folk came crowding round the house to try and catch a note of his. But Ephraim remained silent. He was too busy eating and drinking to his satisfaction, pleasing his body and not depriving his soul even on the Fast of Gedaliah, when he did not fast because of a weak heart. On the Eve of Atonement he ate a great deal, as is enjoined, and drank far more than is enjoined. The plum harvest had been plentiful that year and plums were very cheap; so my father-in-law had made a liqueur like they do in Hungary, and Ephraim dived and drank without a stop. No matter how much I warned him to stop, he would persist in drinking. I'm not afraid, said he to us. It is a tradition I have received from my rabbi, may he rest in peace, who received it in turn from his rabbi, may he rest in peace, and his rabbi again from his rabbi, may he rest in peace, all the way back to the Holy Baal Shem Tov, may his merits protect us, to whom evildoers gave wine a hundred years old which was too strong to be drunk; what you have to do in such a case is to eat an apple and your drunkenness will depart; and this the Baal Shem did and did not grow drunk. And Bertshi, may he pardon me, sat there nodding his head in approval at every glass, and making nothing of me in his heart.

Atonement Eve came to an end and we rose from the table. I took off my boots and went across to my father-in-law to entreat his forgiveness and give him an opportunity of entreating mine. Think of all he had done toward me and all he ought to have asked my pardon about. But I was in no way cruelly inclined at that hour, and was entirely prepared to forgive him. He, however, paid no attention to me; he was too busy with Ephraim. We are but creatures of earth and dust, and I certainly regretted that my father-in-law disregarded me on account of that wastrel; nor was I free of jealousy at the time. But when we entered the synagogue and I saw how many people had come to hear Ephraim at prayer, my grief went, my pain vanished, and what was more, I began to feel proud of myself because Ephraim was my brother-in-law.

In brief, the sun began to sink and the Large Synagogue was full. As soon as Ephraim took up his stand and opened his mouth everybody burst out crying. I feel certain that even if a person had been present that had transgressed against the entire Torah, but heard

Ephraim praying that night, he would assuredly have repented. I wondered whether Satan himself could have avoided repentance.

After the prayer we left the prayer shawl and shroud in the synagogue and went out in order to rest a while. I spent that night in the same room as Ephraim. During the night I woke up and saw him standing beside the water barrel. I thought to myself that he wished to smell the water in order to reduce his thirst, turned myself over in bed and fell asleep again. When we woke up in the morning and prepared to go off to pray in the synagogue we could find no signs of Ephraim. So we thought he had gone on ahead of us; after all he was the Cantor of the Congregation and doubtless prepared his heart to find favor before Him, may He be blest. When we entered the synagogue we saw his clothes spread by the reader's desk just as he had left them the night before; but he himself was not there.

The initial reader began reciting, "Lord of the world Who 'gan to reign ere the first being was created"; the reader of the Morning Service began "O King seated upon a lofty and exalted throne"; but Ephraim had not yet arrived. All the congregation devoted their hearts to our Father in Heaven, while Bertshi and I kept watch at the door. When the time came for the Additional Service they began growing excited and fuming and storming and yelling, Where's the Cantor? Whereabouts is the Additional Prayer-sayer? Some of the congregation began joking, saying that he had gone to immerse himself before the Additional Prayers. Others began shouting that they should take another cantor and pray the Additional Service before midnight. From the women's gallery they called down that the cantor's wife had fainted. By the time they had roused her, her mother had fainted in turn.

Meanwhile I didn't know whether to go to the women's section to help my mother-in-law and sister-in-law out, or stay and look after Bertshi for fear he should fall down in a fit. For his face had turned black as a pot and his knees were shaking and his eyes had begun to run, and his whole body had shrunk to less than half, while his lips quivered, oh, the evil eye must have gained sway over us.

When midday came, the noise and shouting grew still greater. Some of the congregation stood banging on their seats and yelling, It's time to pray the Additional Prayers; and others shouted back at them, No, now we have to say the Afternoon Prayers first. And one cried to another, Where is the Cantor? Where is Ephraim? one answered the other. Either the angels had grown jealous of his prayers or else the demons had snatched him away, the Merciful One guard us. And it was right of the former Cantor, whom the wardens had displaced for the sake of Ephraim, to go rebuking them, You thankless lot that you are, it serves you right for forgetting the Prayer-sayer who offered up prayer for you and your households year after year till the reader's desk began to rot with his weeping, and for replacing him by this worthless youngster whom you didn't know in the beginning and whose end nobody ought to try and guess.

In brief, Ephraim did not take his stand at the reader's desk, but somebody else had to replace him. After the Day of Atonement was at an end, Bertshi summoned all his men and sent them everywhere in search of my brother-in-law. Reb Yudel, by your life I would have preferred to make a happy ending of it, but The Blessed Name desired to finish matters otherwise. The following day we heard that in a neighboring town they had found a Jew drunk and snoring in a wagon on the very Day of Atonement. Although nobody mentioned his name we knew that that sinner could be nobody but Ephraim.

And what was the story? Well, it was like this. On the Eve of Atonement he felt exceedingly thirsty; so he rose and drank water, but that didn't slake his thirst. So he went to a gentile woman who gave him wine to drink; and he drank and became so drunk that he could not tell the difference between the Day of Atonement and Purim, the Day of Enjoyment. When he left her place he saw a wagon standing and mounted upon it. He didn't notice the wagon moving and the wagon driver didn't notice him. In the morning they came to the other town, and Ephraim lay there on the floor of the wagon snoring like a swine; and just then the whole congregation was on its way to prayers.

When they saw a Jew lying drunk on Atonement Day they all were startled and cried out and woke him up; he began rubbing his eyes and said, Good morrow, Jews, for he still couldn't distinguish between his right hand and his left. Off came the slippers they were all wearing to clout him over the face; nor did they leave a whole bone in his body. And when they had done with him they hauled him to the synagogue and haled him before the rabbi.

And where may you have been last night? The rabbi asked Ephraim. And just then he became possessed by a spirit of foolishness which chattered out of his mouth for to anger the Creator and His creatures. I was, he gravely responded, at the house of such and such a gentile woman. Worthless lout that you are, cried the rabbi, what were you doing on so holy a night at the house of a gentile woman! Well, Rabbi, said Ephraim, it was like this. I was very thirsty and I wanted to drink, and I had too much decency to go into a Jew's house in order to ask for a drink of wine on Atonement Eve; so instead I went to a gentile woman.

Well, what more is there for me to tell you; we thought he was easygoing and found he was an evildoer. When a butcher offers forbidden meat for sale the All-Merciful preserves us, we break the utensils in which the meat was cooked; but what's to be done with a cantor who goes wrong? Can we take it out of the prayer books and Orders of Festival Prayers?

And what did Bertshi do? Seized himself by the hair of his head and tugged out his beard in handfuls and wailed, Woe's me for having given my daughter to such a transgressor in Israel. And this was what he said to Ephraim, Listen here, you scoundrel and evildoer and cause of misery to Jewry, I said I was going to do you the honor of giving you my daughter, Teibele, to wife, and I prepared a fine room for you, and on your account I turned out-o'-doors my son-in-law, Jacob Samson, whose shoes you don't deserve to lick; and I kept you on the best that was to be had and bought you a prayer shawl with a silver edging and made a cantor of you in the Large Synagogue. I don't have to tell you that it wasn't for your sake or because of your drunken forefathers that the wardens agreed to let you take a stand before the reader's desk on the Days of Awe, but because of the thirty-two good gulden I wasted for your sake in straight cash bribery. And then you have to pay it all back by putting this shame on me. Now let me swear to you as I'm a Jew that I shan't rest until I see myself revenged and you going from door to door to beg a piece of bread—and nobody will have pity on you and give it. Then maybe you'll feel remorse for your sins and you'll wail, Woe's me, what have I been up to, and you'll beat your breast in penitence so that your right hand will stick to your ribs. And if you think you'll have a chance of going back to your wife and getting out of it that way, let me tell you that if you try it, by your life I won't leave a whole bone in your body. You don't know what I'm like in a real rage; you'd better go and bury yourself alive before you come to me and get me into a rage! Listen to my warning and remember what I've told you, and now clear off!

Thereupon Ephraim found himself a place in the inns and gin palaces along with all the other outcasts; and he would drink brandy and beer with them and sing them our sacred songs; and it would happen that the gentiles would come there with their womenfolk and dance to the music of his prayer and song. And gradually he sank to the very bottom. But my father-in-law, may he pardon me, never waited until all his words had been fulfilled; instead he brought him back into his home, for he was afraid he would run away to Wallachia and leave his wife, Teibele, a deserted wife. He tried to persuade the scapegrace to give his wife a divorce, but what was his answer? I love my wife, and I shan't give her a divorce. And in that matter she too stood firm; he was light-minded and the mind of women is proverbially flighty; and so he suits her and she suits him. And so he still remains dwelling in my father-in-law's house, eating and drinking and lacking for nothing except penitence and good deeds. What is more, I have already heard the womenfolk whispering that we may soon hope to enjoy the celebration of the Covenant of Circumcision. Well, to which nothing can be added except the hope that the fruit may be better than the tree.

TRUE PIETY

It was on Yom Kippur. As dusk was falling and the prayers were drawing to an end in the synagogue, a man ran up to the rabbi looking deathly pale.

"Save me, Rabbi!" he cried.

"What—what is the matter?" gasped the rabbi, frightened.

"Not a drop of water has passed my lips since yesterday at sundown," the man explained. "I'm dying of thirst, Rabbi! Give me your permission to take a few drops of water!"

"Pull yourself together, my son. Don't you know it's a terrible sin to drink water on Yom Kippur? So don't be a weakling—fight back at the Spirit of Evil who's making you thirsty only to lure you into sin."

"It's no use, Rabbi. I can't hold out any longer. I'm dying of thirst!"

The rabbi heaved a deep sigh. What could one do?

"Shammes!" he called out. "Give this man a teaspoonful of water."

The shammes gave the man a teaspoonful of water. He gulped it down with a desperate expression; then, having tasted the water, his thirst became even more overpowering.

"Rabbi!" he groaned hoarsely. "Take pity and let me have a real drink of water. I'm just dying of thirst!"

The rabbi, who was a softhearted man, shrugged his shoulders and said:

"Very well, since you say your life is in danger, you may drink!"

With trembling hand, the man raised a glass of water to his lips and drank it down in one gulp.

"Thank you, thank you, Rabbi!" he gasped. "Believe me, next Yom Kippur I won't be so foolish as to eat any schmaltz herring in the morning!"

THE CANTOR'S ENDURANCE

A young cantor in a New England town was constantly at loggerheads with the trustees of the synagogue, and decided to leave his post. When the trustees heard of this they were filled with dismay.

"What are we going to do now?" they asked. "It's only one week before the High Holidays, and where will we get a new cantor to sing the service?"

So they sent a committee of three trustees to try to dissuade the cantor from leaving.

The cantor listened to their persuasive arguments and nodded his head appreciatively.

"What a pity!" he finally said. "If there were only five men like you in the congregation—would I be leaving now?"

The trustees felt flattered.

"You're honoring us too much, Cantor," they replied. "After all, you won't find it hard to find two more like us in the congregation."

"I'd settle for five like you any time," answered the cantor with a cold stare. "Unfortunately, there are more than two hundred like you in the congregation. And that's more than I can stand!"

WHEN PRAYER IS NO HELP

A saint and a sinner were once fellow passengers on an ocean voyage. Suddenly a storm broke. The ship seemed in danger of sinking. Thereupon all the crew and the passengers began to pray.

"Save us, O Lord!" cried the sinner.

"Sh-sh!" warned the saint. "Don't let God know you are here, or it will be the end of all of us!"

GENEROUS

The great Talmud scholar was at the point of death. The doctors had already given up all hope for him. So the rabbi of the town ordered all Jews to recite from the Book of Psalms. But even this did not help. As a last resort, the rabbi gathered all the Jews in the synagogue.

"I want each one of you," he said, "to donate before God a portion of the life allotted to you to add to the life of this dying man."

One man after another arose and donated from his life a year, a month, a week, and even a day, in order to help save the dying saint.

Suddenly, a man got up and in a loud voice cried out, "I donate twenty years——"

"Are you crazy?" gasped his neighbor, interrupting him. "Why so much?"

"——of my mother-in-law's life," continued the philanthropist.

THE DEPARTED PHYSICIAN

BY BENJACOB

Our doctor is dead; ah well, dry your tears;
Death's sad, but what use to resent it?
For, if he had lived for another few years,
There'd be none of us here to lament it.

THE MILCHIGER SYNAGOGUE
AND THE BLIND PREACHER

BY LEON KOBRIN
TRANSLATED FROM THE YIDDISH BY NATHAN AUSUBEL

The Milchiger Synagogue has a great reputation in the town of N. It stands in the neighborhood where all the petty thieves live.[1] It

[1]*As is the case with all non-Jewish groups eking out a sub-marginal existence in congested places, the larger ghettos also could boast of a slum area which spawned social rejects. These resided in a special neighborhood for themselves, in a ghetto within a ghetto, where they engaged in their shady activities, much to the distaste and resentment of the Jewish community. [The Editor]*

was their money that built the synagogue in the first place, and by their contributions and prayers it is sustained. It is there that they gather to discuss their "business affairs," to buy and sell their stolen goods, and talk about prospective "jobs." There they dream up new thieveries, and implore God's forgiveness for their old crimes.

Just a plain respectable Jew, "a *dope,* not a member of the trade," as the Milchigers put it, has no place in the congregation. It is even told that right after the Milchiger Synagogue was built, several curious "dopes" came to sample the services but all they got for their trouble was the "special treatment." Before they could even start their prayers —their prayer shawls and phylacteries vanished into thin air. And when one of them had the temerity to threaten that unless the missing articles were produced right away he would see to it that the authorities would close the Milchiger Synagogue, he was immediately surrounded by several robust fellows who "escorted" him out of the synagogue in such a "ceremonious" fashion that immediately after he ran to another synagogue to offer prayers of thanksgiving for having escaped with life and limb.

Why was the synagogue called the "Milchiger"? There are a variety of opinions about that. Some wags say that it is simply because all the members of its congregation drank "free" milk from the cows they have stolen. Still others maintain that this name was derived quite accidentally. At first they called their house of worship "The New Synagogue," but no sooner was the structure completed, than, as if by the design of the devil, the following incident took place:

One hot summer day, a Jewish farmer was driving his milk wagon past the New Synagogue. It was daybreak and the farmer was dozing in his driver's seat while his horse jogged slowly at its own sweet will over the familiar road to the market place. When the farmer awoke, the sun was already rising. He gave a great start—no milk cans and no milk! He rubbed his eyes, looked here and looked there in the wagon—it was empty! Good God! No cans and no milk! he wanted to stop his wagon. To his dismay he discovered that the horse was gone too! Naturally, he raised a great hullabaloo and a crowd of people soon gathered. When he told them of his misfortune they merely laughed. Finally, they took pity on him and told him that if he would contribute several rubles to the new synagogue, besides earning a heavenly reward thereby, he would also get back his horse and his milk cans. He readily agreed and made his contribution. The crowd then led him through the courtyard right into the synagogue. There, to his amazement, behind the lectern he saw his milk cans!

As he left the synagogue and recrossed the courtyard he suddenly heard behind him the soft whinnying of a horse. Turning round quickly —mama dear! what was he seeing? His own horse!

Now how the devil did the horse get there? Was he also hidden in the synagogue, wondered the farmer incredulously.

When he became too inquisitive, they advised him not to ask too many questions. If not, they assured him, he'd get such an answer that he'd see his dead grandmother!

When he got to the market place the farmer babbled of his strange adventure to everyone who cared to listen. Soon the whole town knew about it. From that time on the New Synagogue was nicknamed "The Milchiger Synagogue."

Whenever anyone in town had been robbed and wanted to get his goods back he had to apply to the Milchiger Synagogue. But it was clearly understood that he could come neither in anger nor with the police. Etiquette required that he have a conference with one of the elders of the congregation. Of course, where a minor theft was concerned he could negotiate about it directly with the *shammes*. However, he'd have to keep in mind that he couldn't behave like an unmannered *chutzpanik*, nor would it be wise for him to put on the grand air of an honest man talking down to a thief. In short, he'd have to conduct himself with affability, like one merchant doing business with another, or like one who comes to ask a favor.

From all this, one can see that the members of the congregation of the Milchiger Synagogue had instituted their own odd customs, constitution, and by-laws. Very definitely, they were jealous of their honor and their dignity, and they permitted no one to treat them slightingly with impunity.

They took the view that "everything is yours so long as I haven't stolen it; once I have stolen it, it has become mine. Therefore, if you want something back which was formerly yours and which now is mine, you must buy it from me. It's clearly understood that payment must be made in advance of delivery. Once that is done you can rest easy that the goods will be returned to you."

Everybody knows that the Milchigers always keep their word. They are people with their own brand of ethics and sense of justice.

One can, of course, make all kinds of arrangements with them. It happens occasionally that a violent quarrel breaks out between two solid citizens. It's easily understood that a "respectable dope" will not be champing at the bit for a fight, especially when he knows that his opponent is physically the stronger and might break every bone in his body. That is precisely where the worthies of the Milchiger Synagogue come in. For a few rubles they are ready to rent out their muscles to you. And you can rest assured that they'll always do a good job. There are not a few citizens in town who, begging your pardon, have gotten a good drubbing from a Milchiger, and ever since they have been ready to testify that not even Esau the Wicked had such handy fists!

Yes, the Milchigers are ready for every and all eventualities. Nothing frightens them. In fact, they feel as cozy in jail as in their own synagogue. For the police the Milchiger Synagogue represents a sort of bank. Whenever they feel like it they pay it a visit to make a cash withdrawal against their accounts.

However, in every other respect the members of the Milchiger Synagogue try to behave in the traditional Jewish fashion. They too bid against one another energetically for the honor of reading choice parts of the weekly Scriptural portion before the congregation, where everybody can see and hear them. And on the Festival of *Simchas Torah* they, too, compete with one another for leading places in the procession, eager to carry the Scrolls of the Law clasped in their arms.

However, one thing the Milchigers love above all—to hear a good cantor sing! And one thing they hate like poison—to listen to a *maggid* preach!

The story is told how once, soon after the Milchiger Synagogue had been completed, a wandering maggid somehow had strayed into its sacred precincts. He made his way to the reading desk, wrapped himself in his *tallis,* and began to preach. He took as his subject, "Man's Duty to Keep the Ten Commandments." When he finally came to "Thou shalt not steal," he gave a great start! Heaven preserve him! His tallis had disappeared from off his very shoulders! Alarmed, he tried to grab his hat and make a quick getaway. But the devil take it! Would you believe it, his hat too was gone! He put his hand to his head. Sure enough, his *yarmulka* wasn't there either!

For a moment he stood petrified with fear. Then he fell upon a stratagem. He raised his voice in a shout, "Now we come to the commandment, 'Thou *shalt* steal!' " He felt certain that with this revised version of the Eighth Commandment he would find favor in the eyes of the Milchigers and in this way would be able to rescue his tallis, hat, and yarmulka. But, barely had he uttered these words, when a hubbub arose in the synagogue. One of the Milchigers yelled, "Let's beat up the maggid!"

No sooner said than done! A dozen hands reached out for him and dragged him from the pulpit.

"Jews, Sons of the Compassionate! Why do you do this to me?" shrieked the bewildered maggid.

He got the following answer from Oreh the Stork who was the leader of the Milchiger Synagogue: "Uncle, when you said, 'Thou shalt not steal,' you merely blundered into the wrong pulpit. But, devil take you, when you went ahead and said, 'Thou *shalt* steal,' you shot your arrow over the mark. Isn't it bad enough that we are thieves! Now you come along and want to encourage us to be even bigger and better thieves by justifying our trade! And you pose as a holy maggid, you faker! Rub it into him, boys!"

From that day on there wasn't a single preacher to be found who dared even cross the threshold of the Milchiger Synagogue.

II

The *gabbai* of the Milchiger Synagogue was Shloime the Smack. He was a stout, muscular man of fifty with a ruddy face and a broad red beard. Ten years before, he had given up the "trade" and thereafter occupied himself solely with buying "merchandise" from the others. In this manner, he acquired considerable wealth and was the proud owner of several properties and three buxom daughters. The eldest daughter left the faith and married a Gentile butcher. The second daughter he married off to Bentze Pcheh, a *melamed's* son, a weak, pallid young fellow with a sparse black beard at which he was constantly tugging with long bony fingers.

"Pcheh," the Milchigers had nicknamed him because it was his most distinguishing physical characteristic. As their *baal-tefila* he would lead them in their prayers, and every time he had to intone a prayer or read from the Torah he would first clear his throat elaborately and let out between his teeth unearthly noises that sounded very much like "pcheh-pcheh!" In fact he was the only respectable "dope" tolerated in the Milchiger Synagogue. His father-in-law, Shloime the Smack, was very proud of him and showed off with him at every opportunity. The third daughter was still unwed, though she was receptive to marriage proposals. However, her father was strongly set against any match except with a refined young man, someone like Bentze Pcheh, for instance.

As has already been noted, the leader of the Milchiger Synagogue was Oreh the Stork. He was a horse dealer of long standing. For ten out of a twenty-year prison sentence he had been the recognized boss of the convicts in the jail where he had been confined; he was thoroughly at home there.

Oreh was a tall, bony man with narrow shoulders. He had a long pock-marked face and small piercing eyes and sported a pointed grey beard. More than once he'd come to the synagogue on the Sabbath as drunk as Lot. He would stagger about the House of Prayer and, with arms outstretched to the worshipers, he would cry out imploringly, "Pray, you thieves, pray I tell you! The Devil blast your hearts!"

And when he'd get very, very drunk, he'd wax sentimental, he'd embrace Shloime the Smack and try to kiss him. Or he would sob at the top of his voice, would beat his breast with all his might:

"Now who said that? Who said I'm not a respectable man, ha? I would like you to know that I am Oreh the Stork! I never steal anything myself, I only deal in low-priced horses. Am I to be blamed for that? Then why the hell do you say I'm not a respectable man, ha-a-a?"

Everybody began to laugh. This only excited Oreh the more. "What are you laughing at?" he screamed at them. "Do you think you're nicer people than I? Pray, you thieves! I'm telling you, pray, and the devil blast your hearts!"

The treasurer in the Milchiger Synagogue was Yisrolke the Rooster. He was a swarthy fellow with an immense black beard, large bulging eyes, and a curving little belly that was set up on short thick legs. He was a taciturn man who rarely opened his mouth to say anything, but sat quietly perched against the East Wall next to the Holy Ark, flanked on either side by the dignitaries Shloime the Smack and Oreh the Stork. He sat there benignly stroking his beard with a graceful gesture. Everybody agreed that he set the tone for everything in the Milchiger Synagogue. If a cantor was to be auditioned for the High Holy Days, it was Yisrolke the Rooster that he had to please first. And if he pleased Yisrolke he damn well pleased all Milchigers! Yisrolke was also the one who apportioned the honors for the reading of the Scriptural portion, and what he decreed was holy law for the entire congregation.

He was admired and even revered by the Milchigers for one very special distinction. All his life he had been trading in stolen horses and yet he had been clapped in prison only three times! An enviable record indeed.

The *shammes* of the Milchiger Synagogue was Getzel the Rabbit, a scrawny, agile little man of sixty. He was blind in one eye and displayed a long scar on his right cheek. Where once sat a human nose there was now exposed a reddish little bone with two slits. Winter as well as summer Getzel the Rabbit went about in a short, cotton-quilted caftan under which peered out the yellowed fringes of the small tallis which every pious Jew wears under his shirt.

This fellow Getzel was considered one of the most distinguished men in the congregation. No one had such varied experiences in life. Sometimes, when he was in a good mood, in wintertime after the evening service when the congregation would sit down to refresh itself with a keg of "half-stuff" and some roast goose, he would take his place at the hot glowing stove. The young scalawags would then gather around him, and he would regale them with accounts of his experiences.

"All of you consider yourselves masters in the trade, don't you?" he'd begin in a low mysterious voice. "Well, let me tell you: everyone of you, in my opinion, is nothing but a snot-nose! Why, the cholera take you, all of you piled in one heap aren't worth ten damns put together!" As he said this he'd give a cunning wink with his one good eye and click his tongue derisively. "You dopes, when I was eighteen years old I was already jumping into the kind of fires that would have singed all your chicken feathers off your back! For instance, you big shot there with the torn-off ear, or you great big Samson with the blackened eyes, I'm sure that each of you considers himself a master thief, a regular God-damn-it! Now you go ahead and tell me, which one of you would have dared break into the police inspector's own stable, eheh? The devil you would! But I, Getzel the Rabbit, did. I carried off an eagle I'm telling you, four years old! Rode it right out of the stable! And as for you, Master Inspector, I whistle at your father and at your father's father! *Nu, nu,* just you try and catch Getzel! *Haida!* Go ahead and catch the wind in the pasture! Ha, ha, ha!"

Getzel lashed into an enthusiasm about himself that proved contagious. All listened to him with great admiration, scratched the backs of their heads and nodded respectfully. The young man with the torn-off ear, Burechke Mamzer, a powerful, broad-boned fellow with carroty hair and with the face of a raven, leaped to his feet in enthusiasm, and gave Getzel such a thumping whack across the shoulders that he doubled up. "Once there were regular guys, ach!" cried Burechke in a hoarse voice.

And in order to emphasize the more his deep reverence for the "regular guys" of long ago, Burechke drank a toast to them in a thundering Russian.

Everybody laughed. Another keg of "half-stuff" was sent for. Now thoroughly tipsy, Getzel went on telling them more about his experiences, but with greater fire than before and with more details. He especially delighted his companions with the story which he never tired of telling, how he once robbed a gypsy. Rob a gypsy! Huh!

That sounded easier in telling than in the doing! For that, one either had to be a magician or a demon!

Getzel's reminiscing would subside only when the company reached the fourth keg of "half-stuff." Then he no longer sat but stood up, swaying on his legs and muttering to himself. He'd curse the gabbai, the president, the treasurer, and all the other members of the congregation. He'd wind up by shoving both his fists into his mouth. He'd bite them with a desperate wail, stamp his feet, and shriek:

"Where is justice? I ask. Once I was young and strong. So I lost an eye at my trade, then I lost my nose and had my cheek gashed up. By rights it is I who should have been gabbai in the synagogue! And now, what am I? Only a shammes! And who the hell is gabbai? Shloime the Smack! And who is president? Oreh the Stork! And who gets the blessings, the juiciest portions of Scripture to read in the synagogue? Again Shloime the Smack! And who do you think gets all the curses to read? Naturally, I, Getzel the Rabbit! Who else, I ask you? So there you have your justice! Shloime the Smack has a lot of property and honor. Is it because he is a holy rabbi? No—hell! He's only my pupil in thieving, the devil burn his soul! By rights shouldn't he have been shammes and I gabbai? Shouldn't I have his houses and he should sleep in the synagogue in my place? So where is justice, a plague on you all! Where is justice, where?" he thundered his question.

At such a time he was ready to do either one of two things—fight everybody or embrace everybody. If he but suspected that he was being made sport of he'd grab up a big slab of wood or anything else clublike that came to hand, and he would fling himself upon the rest with the outcry: "Get out, get out, you thieves! There's nothing here for you to steal! Get out!"

But whenever everyone agreed with him that only he was entitled to be gabbai in the Milchiger Synagogue, then he'd become as gentle as a lamb. He'd try to kiss everybody and would say, shedding bitter tears, "Just look at me! I've lost an eye, a nose, and half a cheek at my work, and in the end who is gabbai? The devil take it, only a shammes, a sh-sh-am-m-es!"

However, at all other times, when he was not drunk, he would bow supinely before the leaders of the Milchiger Synagogue. He was full of flattery for them and was ready to go through fire and water for them if they only hinted at it.

Thus, under the leadership of Shloime the Smack, Oreh the Stork, Yisrolke the Rooster, and Getzel the Rabbit, the affairs of the Milchiger Synagogue were conducted for years without any incident, until one fateful Sabbath.

III

On that Sabbath an extraordinary occurrence took place at the Milchiger Synagogue. Had the entire police force of the town of N. swooped down on them in a sudden raid, it would not have created such wild disorder, would not have so frightened to death the Milchigers.

Actually what happened was a very trifling incident. A maggid had preached in the Milchiger Synagogue! It was the celebrated Blind Maggid, a famed preacher whose fiery sermons had shaken up all of N. From all parts of the town Jews had gathered to hear his blazing exhortations—everybody, men, women, and children, the old and the young, and even the freethinkers.

The elders of the Milchiger Synagogue envied the other synagogues their luck. They decided that, come what may, they too must have that jewel of a maggid to preach to them. "Since he boils and bubbles he must be one handsome pot!" they agreed. "And since he is such a handsome pot, most definitely his place is in the Milchiger Synagogue! Where else?"

And when the Milchigers decided to do something they usually did it. So Shloime the Smack and Yisrolke the Rooster invited the Blind Maggid in the name of all Milchigers. That was on a Sabbath, only a few weeks before the High Holy Days.

After the reading of the Torah that Sabbath morning the shammes, Getzel the Rabbit, pounded on the reading desk for attention:

"*Sha!* Not so loud! The gabbai has asked me to announce that after the noonday meal at three o'clock this afternoon a holy maggid will hold forth in the synagogue. The congregation is therefore requested to behave like human beings during the sermon and not to engage in any antics. Because, says the gabbai: 'Feh! it's not nice!' I must also warn you not to dare try to steal the tallis from off the maggid's back, and similar doggish tricks."

Someone rolled up a towel into a hard ball at this juncture and flung it at Getzel with all his might, striking him smack in the face. This put an abrupt end to his speech. As he sprang aside in confusion, the congregation rocked with laughter and raised an awful din. Getzel came to at last and started shouting, "Thieves! Throw towels at me, eh? May the convulsions throw you around!"

The congregation subsided only when the idol of the Milchigers, Yisrolke the Rooster, appeared on the *Bima*. He gave a graceful stroke on his broad black beard and, fixing everyone with his bulging oxlike eyes, he boomed in his hoarse voice:

"Listen snot-noses! Today you've got to act like human beings! We're going to hear a maggid, a maggid, you understand, whom one can call a maggid, not just a dope! Quite likely, members from other congregations will come to hear him, so my advice to you is: behave like human beings! Let other people know that we have nothing to be ashamed of and can stand comparison with them."

After he had spoken, the Milchigers, with one voice, agreed that they'd engage in no "cur's tricks" during the Blind Maggid's sermon.

IV

The Milchiger Synagogue was packed to suffocation. People even stood on tables and benches. From the women's gallery through the little open lattice windows the female worshipers, some wearing caps and others wigs covered with silk kerchiefs, stuck their heads out. The maggid had not yet arrived, and, in the meantime, the audience scurried to find seats as near the Bima as possible.

Yisrolke the Rooster was the only official who had arrived thus far. He sat in his customary seat against the East Wall. His head was thrown back, his eyes were glazed with sleep, and his mouth was half opened as he dozed pleasantly. The gentle murmur of the trees in the orchard behind him, the cooling breeze that refreshingly blew through the open window on his neck, the buzz of conversation among the audience in the synagogue, and, on top of that, his stomach stuffed with Sabbath *cholent,* had made him feel very drowsy. How he longed for his bed at home! Now he regretted the whole silly business. Why the devil did they have to engage that maggid? What could a maggid do for them anyway? Did they expect to become saints right after his sermon? Ach! he could have been at home now sleeping so sweetly! A stupid mistake, he thought, dozing fitfully.

He tried very hard not to fall asleep; after all, it wouldn't look nice. What would people say? By sheer violence of will he forced open his bulging eyes, scratched his bearded chin sleepily and yawned out loud.

Suddenly he became aware of the disagreeable fatty taste of cholent in his mouth. "Ach! if I only had a little glass of tea here! The Devil take the maggid!" he thought resentfully. He had a bright notion: he'd call his wife home and later, after he'd had his tea, he'd come back to hear the maggid.

He had already begun to make his way to the door when, lo and behold, who should appear as if by the workings of the devil but Oreh the Stork, furiously elbowing his way through the crowd to his seat of honor at the East Wall. Quite drunk, Oreh grasped at Yisrolke by the lapel of his coat and shouted:

"They're bringing him! Shloime the Smack and his son-in-law Bentze Pcheh, and the shammes! Remember, you louts! behave like human beings!" he shouted at the congregation, fixing it threateningly with his little piercing eyes.

And he sat down, pushing Yisrolke into his seat next to him, still clutching his lapel.

Firmly Yisrolke pushed his hand away and observed with injured dignity that it wasn't nice to grab someone by the lapel. There were strangers from other synagogues present, and it was Oreh's duty to behave with dignity.

"I laugh at them all!" jeered Oreh. "Who's boss here anyway? If I wish I can send everybody to where red pepper grows, the very last dope of them! Just one word from them, and. . . . No so? I am Oreh and I dare you try do something to me!"

"Don't yell so!" Yisrolke tried to quiet him. "I'm simply ashamed to sit next to you. I'm going home."

He got up to go, but Oreh grabbed hold of his arm.

"Sit down!" he shouted, tugging at him. "So you're ashamed to sit next to me, eh? The nerve of you! Everybody knows you are Yisrolke the Rooster, an old horse thief, the Devil blast your heart!" And he gripped Yisrolke's arm and wouldn't let go of him.

Yisrolke became confused. He looked around to see if anyone had overheard what Oreh had said to him. Then, fixing his eyes wrathfully on Oreh, he muttered between his teeth:

"You jailbird! To whom do you think you're talking? Would you like to say good-by to your life for good, ha? Let go of my sleeve, I'm telling you!"

Oreh released him and gave him a drunken laugh. He cupped his face in his hands, leaned them on his bony knees, and swayed his long body to and fro. Then laughing in a mollifying way, he said:

"Oy, Rooster! You don't understand a joke, the Devil blast your heart! People take you for a wise one, but you're such an ass! Yisrolke *tatinka,* the Devil take your *batinka!* Aha, just look at him—he's offended! Are you really angry, Rooster? Ha, ha, ha!"

Yisrolke wanted to answer him sharply but he noticed that a number of strangers, attracted by Oreh's laughter, had fixed their eyes on them with curiosity. Yisrolke turned his back on the strangers with his face to the open window. Gracefully he stroked his beard, and for the special benefit of the strangers he piously began to intone something incomprehensible to the melody of the Psalms of David.

When Oreh became aware of the strangers' attention he stopped laughing. Stabbing at them with his piercing little eyes and gesticulating excitedly with his hands he shouted at them, "What are you butting in here for? Where do you think you are anyway? This is the Milchiger Synagogue! Our rule is: either you recite Psalms or you mind your own business, the Devil blast your hearts!"

Under his blazing eyes the strangers began to wilt and trembled with fear. Not standing on their dignity, they retreated in alarm, anxious to put as much space as possible between them and him. In their flight they collided with a group of young fellows, obviously among the very best the Milchigers could boast. They were dashing fellows, all right, their hats perched rakishly on the sides of their heads, their jackets flung loosely over their shoulders in gay-blade fashion, and wearing high boots. They had overheard what their leader Oreh had said to the dopes, and so without any invitation, they began to whack them lustily over their heads.

The strangers were perfectly bewildered. If they turned west they got a crack from the east, if they turned south they got a clout from the north. They held on desperately to their hats with both hands and after each bombardment tried to move back in another direction, but they could not escape the blows that were rained on them from every side.

What were they to do—take off their hats? First of all, they were in a holy place; does one take one's hat off in a house of God? Secondly, their hats provided some protective armor for their heads. But a Jew always finds a way out of danger, so the strangers drew the hems of their gabardines over their heads and energetically began to push their way to the door. At least get out alive!

This was all that the Milchigers needed. A roar of laughter shook the synagogue. The young bloods rolled up their sleeves and began to belabor the strangers on the buttocks with all their might. They thwacked away at them in a manner that was known among the Milchigers as "the butter-cakes." The wretched strangers did not dare look around them and patiently accepted the ordeal.

Praise be to God! They had already reached the door and were getting ready to leap through it when suddenly Getzel the Rabbit dashed into the synagogue with the cry: "Sha! Everybody keep quiet! He's coming! Make way!"

V

Led by Shloime the Smack and his son-in-law, Bentze Pcheh, the Blind Maggid entered the Milchiger Synagogue. A murmur rippled through the audience, but was stilled when Oreh the Stork brought his hand heavily down on the reading desk, crying, "Sha, you dopes!"

And then it grew as still as in a graveyard.

The Blind Maggid was tall and heavy-set with a long beard white as snow that reached down to the girdle of his satin *kapote*. As he walked he carried his head high and kept his sightless eyes fixed at one point in the air right over the heads of the congregation. With a solemn air Shloime the Smack helped make way for him to the Bima. Respectfully, the audience made way for the Blind Maggid. They tugged at each other's sleeves, smacked their lips, and tried to see how he looked.

When the maggid had mounted the Bima, the crush around it grew even greater. Every neck was craned in order to get a better view of him, and many strained on tiptoe for a glimpse. Yisrolke the Rooster and Oreh the Stork took their customary places at the East Wall, shutting out the daylight from the windows near them with their broad backs, and looked the maggid over with curiosity.

The blind preacher sat down and rested a moment from his exertions, his head bowed on his breast; it looked to many as if he was dozing. Near him on the Bima sat Shloime the Smack and his son-in-law Bentze, both with grave, pious faces bathed in perspiration. Also the shammes, Getzel the Rabbit, was there, standing to one side and squinting hard at the audience with his good eye. Pointing at the maggid, he whispered ecstatically and loud enough for everyone to hear, "A precious vessel, that man! You'll gush like a fountain when you'll hear him!"

It grew half dark in the synagogue, as if a cloud had descended upon the heads of the audience. The closely packed throng shut out the radiant summer daylight. It grew as stifling hot as a steam bath. The audience perspired heavily and kept on wiping their faces and necks, some with their sleeves, others with the hems of their kapotes, and some even with their bare fingers. There was a coughing and a sneezing and a gasping for breath all around.

Suddenly the maggid arose. Shloime and his son-in-law sprang eagerly forward to assist him. "A tallis," he asked softly, staring fixedly into the air with his sightless eyes. Getzel the Rabbit heard him and, agile as a cat, he leaped forward to the reading desk on the Bima and pulled a new tallis out of a drawer. He gave it to the maggid, saying, "There you have a tallis, Rabbi. It has hardly been used."

The old maggid turned his sightless eyes in Getzel's direction. On his emaciated, wrinkled face that looked like shrunken parchment appeared a smile that soon vanished. He shook his head bitterly and groaned. "Oy oy! Nu, what can I do?" And he extended his hand.

Shloime and Bentze led him to the reading desk. He felt the tallis with his hand, took off his *shtrymel,* the fur hat trimmed with fox-tail ends, and remained standing in his yarmulka. Then he put the tallis over his head. He continued to stare at one point without seeing, as if he were trying hard to listen to the breathing of the throng that came to hear him preach. Those who looked on his face could not surpress a feeling of uneasiness, even fear. With the tallis over his head, with his sightless eyes and snow-white beard and parchmentlike skin, he looked like a corpse that had just risen fro.n the grave.

Shloime and Bentze sat down near him; Getzel stood close to him. In order to hint to the audience what to expect from the maggid, he began in pantomime to wipe his eyes with the hem of his cotton-padded caftan. He twisted his face with grief. He sweated a lot, significantly nodded his head at the audience, and heaved a heart-rending sigh. His sighs were echoed by several strangers, obviously dopes. Like a contagion, ill-surpressed groans were heard on every side. Drunken Oreh the Stork also shook his head and moaned. Yisrolke the Rooster, who sat near him, was beside himself with annoyance. He perspired a lot, and the more he perspired the more annoyed he became with the maggid. He whispered to Oreh, "For God's sake, don't shake so, Oreh, and don't groan like that! Even without it we already have *Gihenom* here!" And he mopped his thick neck with a handkerchief, thinking glumly how much better it would have been if he were home now drinking a glass of tea.

"A *Gihenom* you call this, ha?" said Oreh, shaking his head. "You can picture yourself then how things are in the real *Gihenom?* Oh, brother, will they bang away at us there for all the thefts we have committed! I'm telling you, they'll fry us, they'll roast us! We'll simmer in caldrons of pitch and sulphur, never you fear!"

Yisrolke glared at Oreh angrily with his oxlike eyes. He wanted to retort crushingly to him, but in that very instant the old maggid brought his hand down on the reading desk with such suddenness that many jumped. His parchmentlike face became alive now and a ruddy flush suffused itself on his cheeks. He turned his unseeing eyes first in one direction and then in the other, as if he were trying to size up his audience, and then he began to preach.

He spoke gently, like a father about to tell his beloved children a story with a moral.

"Children!" he began. "Someone told me just before that the tallis I've been given to wear has hardly been used. Oy! Woe is me, and woe to you—you fools!

"This reminds me of a story which I'm going to tell you now. Pay attention, children, and store it up well in your minds," he cried out suddenly with anger.

Then, after a short pause, he continued:

"I once came to an inn and saw lying on the table a little tallis. Would you believe it, the tallis was laughing just like a human being! 'Little tallis,' I asked it, 'why do you laugh?' But the little tallis didn't answer and continued laughing. A second time I asked it, 'Dear little tallis, tell me, why do you laugh?' And again the tallis did not answer but went on laughing. For the third time I asked, 'Dear little tallis, do answer me! Why are you laughing?' And the little tallis answered at last, 'Know that the man to whom I belong has gone away, taking his *tefillin* along but, alas, he has left me behind. However, I know for certain that a time will come when he'll have to come back for me, and then, woe to him, he'll be forced to leave his tefillin behind.'

"Oy, children!" cried the maggid sorrowfully. "Pay heed to what that wise little tallis said to me! And the one that I am now wearing is also saying to me, 'Whether my owner has used me much or whether he has used me little, oy, woe to him! Because, when he'll be carried to his grave, whether he like it or not, he'll have to take me along!' "

At these words a loud wailing swept the women's gallery. The respectable dopes from other congregations sighed and groaned, oy-ed and ach-ed, coughed and heaved, blew their noses, hid their faces, and stealthily wiped their eyes with their sleeves.

Also the Milchigers were shaken up by the maggid's words. Some of the young bloods stood listening with dropped jaws and with wondering bulging eyes turned on the maggid. Others looked at one another with shining eyes, nodded their heads vigorously in agreement, their lips forming as if to tsk-tsk with delight. The older Milchigers were moved even more by the maggid's words. They gnashed their teeth in self-revulsion, snorted feelingly, and averted eyes that filled with tears, ashamed to cry openly.

Most affected of all was Oreh the Stork. He swayed his long body to and fro, whistled through his adenoids, wept copiously, and cried out as if he were talking to himself only, "It's the truth, every blessed word is true! In the end we'll all be rotting in the ground!"

Yisrolke the Rooster, on the other hand, thought enviously as he listened to the maggid, "Ah, if I only had his gift for words! What fine deals I could pull through!"

Shloime the Smack listened to the maggid with an enthusiastic expression. He had a handkerchief spread out on his knee ready for any emergency. He showed his agreement with the preacher by nodding his head vigorously, by blowing his nose and calling out with feeling every once in a while, "Oh little papa, oh my!"

Bentze, his son-in-law, was so wrought up that he did a lot of throat-clearing and was shaken by deep sighs. As for Getzel the Rabbit, he had his head buried in the sleeve of his caftan, weeping bitterly with his one good eye and casting stealthy glances about him to see if anyone was noticing that he was being pulled apart.

And the Blind Maggid continued preaching. His voice in turn blazed with anger, commanded sternly, and waxed soft and pleading with fatherly grief. He said that life in this vale of tears was nothing but a vanity of vanities and that the one true life was the eternal life which could be found only beyond the grave. For that reason, said he, each person, provided he was in his right mind, must prepare himself with sufficient sustenance against that dreadful day. That is, he should provide himself with nourishment not for the body that eventually will be eaten up by the worms in the grave, but with nourishment for the soul that was immortal.

"Oy, you idiots!" he cried out in such a terrible voice that his hearers shook with fright. "Oy, you idiots, tell me, what are you chasing after? What are you robbing for? Why do you snatch the very crumbs of bread out of one another's mouth? You lie in wait for poor people, you prey on helpless widows, you tear the very clothes off the backs of little orphans! And for what, I ask you, for what, ha? For what, you idiots?"

And he cried aloud with such vehemence that his reddened blind eyes seemed to move, to tremble.

"What will you do in the world of truth with all that you possess, I ask you? Oy, dear children, you'll be able to take nothing with you when your time comes to go there! Only a tallis and a winding sheet are you allowed to take with you from this world. For the rest—money, jewels and buildings—all that is false, false and wicked, a vanity of vanities! All that is false—false!"

And he brought his hand thundering down upon the reading desk.

Then in an imploring voice he continued:

"Children, oy children! Foolish little swallows! When you want to go on a day's journey, don't you make all the necessary preparations for it so that there may be nothing lacking while you're on the road? And yet see, when you have to prepare yourself for such a frightening long journey, not for one day and not for one year either but for an eternity, you forget to take along with you that which will be most necessary for you, without which it will go very hard with you, believe me! Yes, I mean *nebbech* good deeds! Oh children, woe is me! You're forgetting to take along with you the necessary good deeds for your far journey!"

The maggid fell silent, let his head sink over his white beard. He breathed heavily and his entire body trembled in agitation. The wailing of the women in the gallery grew ever louder. One woman screamed wildly. This had its effect on the menfolk below. One hid his face behind another's back and choked with sobs. Another screened his face with his sleeve, rubbed his nose vigorously and swallowed his tears. In no time at all, most of the Milchigers began to weep unashamedly as they kept their eyes fixed woefully on the maggid.

The old Blind Maggid's terrifying appearance and his fiery words, the lamentations of the women from the gallery above as if they came from Heaven itself, the groaning, sighing, and sobbing of the most hardened of men which swept like the wind through the synagogue, had an overwhelming effect on all the Milchigers. They were not accustomed to such emotional scenes. It made them think of death and of the hellish rods of wrath with which they would be flogged in the other world.

They suddenly began to feel very insignificant, weak, and helpless in the face of inevitable, terrifying death. Each one thought he already felt upon his skin the iron claws of the Angel of Death. Before their eyes loomed up the horrifying image of Gihenom with all its tortures, its fiery ordeals, and its boiling caldrons of pitch and sulphur. Ach, what miserable sinners they were!

Shloime the Smack dabbed his eyes with his handkerchief. All his crimes rose up to torment him. Only the day before he had accepted "merchandise" that had been stolen from a poor Jew. He now took a solemn vow that from that day on he would distribute a lot of charity among the needy and, if God would help and send a suitable husband for his youngest daughter, he might even, after the wedding was over, journey to the Holy Land to die there.

Bentze Pcheh snorted with emotion and constantly was clearing his throat. "After the maggid is through," he mused, "I'm going to invite him for the third Sabbath meal to my father-in-law's. There he'll find out what sort of a fellow I am! Goodness knows, he might even be thinking now that I too am an outcast of Israel and a horse thief! Pcheh!"

Getzel the Rabbit fell asleep from sheer delight, with his face on his arm. It was unbearably hot in the synagogue! Besides, he had found it so hard to resist the sweet slumber to which he usually succumbed after he had eaten the Sabbath cholent.

Oreh the Stork seemed to have gone entirely out of his mind. The maggid had so warmed him up with his preaching that he thrashed about with his head, his shoulders trembled, he beat his breast, and he groaned, "I'm a thief! The Devil blast my heart! Why, only today, on the Holy Sabbath itself, I made arrangements for a new 'job'!"

Only one person remained unmoved throughout it all. This was Yisrolke the Rooster. With his oxlike eyes he looked about him, saw how all the thieves were falling apart with penitential emotion. Smiling into his big black beard he ruminated:

"A foul disease take you, you mushy souls! I can see that every one of you is scared of death. But I, Yisrolke, spit on death and on all the stupid businesses in Gihenom! When I die I'll stop living, and as long as I'm alive—what the hell!"

Again the maggid spoke, this time in a pleading voice.

"Children, the High Holy Days are approaching! Passports from Heaven will be handed down to each one of us, to some for a generation and to others for only one year of life. Oy, oy!" He groaned aloud: "How many future widows there are now present in the synagogue! How many little orphans!"

The yowling that followed these words was indescribable. Strong men sobbed on top of their voices, the pious shrilled hysterically. But the maggid showed them no mercy. Words flew like sparks, darted like burning coals from his mouth, and scorched the hearts and minds of those who heard them.

"What about the little cheder children on whose Torah-study rests the world?" he cried out, and in such a voice of doom that even Yisrolke the Rooster shivered. "Yes, how many of these dear children, the pure little souls, do you suppose will be given heavenly passports as *corpses? Nebbech!* And I ask, for whose sins, blessed be Thy Name? For *your* crimes, for *your* sins! Repent, fathers and mothers of small children, repent!"

And the maggid flailed about threateningly with his hands, like a frightening specter come from another world.

The hoarse drunken voice of Oreh the Stork, now rang out:

"Oy vay! Now I know why my Berele died! He died because I, his father, am a thief!"

His face was twisted with grief and he beat his breast like the most unconsolable of penitents.

Everybody turned wonderingly to look at his grief-distorted face. Bentze and Shloime the Smack jumped to their feet and looked down at him from the Bima in confusion. Even the maggid turned inquiringly towards him with his unseeing eyes.

Yisrolke the Rooster grabbed him by the arm and snarled at him between clenched teeth: "Shut up, you're drunk!"

But Oreh flung him aside and shouted, "I will speak! I will repent! Let me alone, you thief!"

He ran wailing to the Bima. Everybody stepped aside, being too frightened and bewildered to stop him. Pandemonium reigned in the synagogue. He flung himself on the Blind Maggid's shoulder, kissed him and cried with the choked sobs of a child, "I am a thief, Rabbi," he moaned. "That's why my Berele died! We're all thieves here, woe is me!"

A great din broke out in the synagogue. Those nearest the door began to push their way closer to the Bima. Everybody shouted at Oreh at the same time:

"Sha! Sha! Shut up!"

Getzel the Rabbit started up from sleep and looked about him uncomprehendingly. Seeing that Oreh was weeping, he too rubbed his sleeve against his eye and twisted his lips in a manner as if he were going to cry.

Yisrolke the Rooster was now beside himself. He thundered at Oreh:

"Oreh, you idiot, get off the Bima! You're drunk! You don't know what you're talking about! Don't you believe a word he says, Rabbi! He's had too much to drink."

But Oreh, pressing his lips to the maggid's shoulder, continued to cry at the top of his voice:

"What a fine little head my Berele had! He certainly would have been a rabbi had he lived, but he went ahead and died! He died because I was a thief, because all of us here are thieves! Woe is me!"

Getzel the Rabbit nodded his head in agreement and brushed his eye with his sleeve.

"It's the truth, the truth!" he wailed. "I should know!"

Yisrolke jumped to his feet, spat out with contempt, and dashed out of the synagogue. Shloime the Smack and Bentze Pcheh stood on the Bima as if they had been turned to stone. They were simply ashamed to look anybody in the face. . . .

VI

A short while later, the synagogue was almost emptied. The trees in the orchard peeked serenely through the windows. There was again light and air in the room and a cooling breeze blew from without. Oreh was still sitting in his customary place, leaning his head against the wall with half-opened mouth and with shut eyes. He was snoring soundly and working his lips fitfully as he slept.

Yisrolke came in again with a smile on his face.

"Nu?" he asked ironically of no one in particular. "Is our synagogue still standing on its foundations? And you?" he asked of a young fellow whom he had noticed weeping bitterly before. "Did you too cry at the maggid's sermon?"

"Who me?" asked the young man scratching his head sheepishly. "Do you take me for a dope? Do you want to know who cried?" And he pointed to Avremele the Goat.

Avremele the Goat denied it heatedly. He too was no dope and he assured Yisrolke that the soles of his shoes did not swoon away every time he heard a maggid babble!

To his amusement, Yisrolke couldn't find one person who'd admit that he'd done anything but laugh while the maggid was preaching, although Yisrolke had seen them weep with his own eyes.

Yisrolke went over to Oreh and shook him rudely.

"Get up!" he cried. "I've brought you a stallion, three years old, a perfect eagle! Go and find a stall for him!"

Oreh jumped up and rubbed his eyes.

"Is it fresh merchandise?" he asked with great interest. "A stallion, did you say? Where, where is he?"

"Go to the Devil, you pious idiot you!" sneered Yisrolke the Rooster, and he gave him an exasperated clout on the shoulder. "Just look at him—a brand new penitent! The Devil take his soul!"

And he smiled into his beard.

Oreh looked at Yisrolke with bulging, uncomprehending eyes. He didn't know what the Rooster was talking about. The bystanders laughed and teased him, laughed at his penitence.

Oreh was overcome with confusion. He then began to recall the whole thing, but only vaguely, as if it all had taken place in a dream. And he felt ashamed. . . .

HE DID ALL HE COULD

Once there was a famous preacher who could move his audience to tears with his eloquence. On the occasion of the funeral of a prominent citizen, he delivered the eulogy. He elaborated on the life of the deceased with touching verve, referred to the purity of his character, to the nobility of his deeds, and to the tragedy of his sudden departure. Nonetheless, his hearers remained unmoved. Not even the mourners in the immediate family were seen to shed a tear.

"Rabbi," asked one of the preacher's admirers wonderingly, "how is it you haven't been able to wring a single tear out of the mourners?"

"My job is only to turn the faucet," answered the preacher. "Is it my fault if nothing comes out?"

WAITING FOR SANTY   A CHRISTMAS PLAYLET

BY S. J. PERELMAN
(WITH A BOW TO MR. CLIFFORD ODETS)

SCENE: *The sweatshop of S. Claus, a manufacturer of children's toys, on North Pole Street. Time: The night before Christmas.*

At rise, seven gnomes, Rankin, Panken, Rivkin, Riskin, Ruskin, Briskin, and Praskin, are discovered working furiously to fill orders piling up at stage right. The whir of lathes, the hum of motors, and the hiss of drying lacquer are so deafening that at times the dialogue cannot be heard, which is very vexing if you vex easily. (Note: The parts of Rankin, Panken, Rivkin, Riskin, Ruskin, Briskin, and Praskin are interchangeable, and may be secured directly from your dealer or the factory.)

RISKIN (*filing a Meccano girder, bitterly*)—A parasite, a leech, a bloodsucker—altogether a five-star nogoodnick! Starvation wages we get so he can ride around in a red team with reindeers!

RUSKIN (*jeering*)—Hey, Karl Marx, whyn'tcha hire a hall?

RISKIN (*sneering*)—Scab! Stool pigeon! Company spy! (*They tangle and rain blows on each other. While waiting for these to dry, each returns to his respective task.*)

BRISKIN (*sadly, to Panken*)—All day long I'm painting "Snow Queen" on these Flexible Flyers and my little Irving lays in a cold tenement with the gout.

PANKEN—You said before it was the mumps.

BRISKIN (*with a fatalistic shrug*)—The mumps—the gout—go argue with City Hall.

PANKEN (*kindly, passing him a bowl*)—Here, take a piece fruit.

BRISKIN (*chewing*)—It ain't bad, for wax fruit.

PANKEN (*with pride*)—I painted it myself.

BRISKIN (*rejecting the fruit*)—Ptoo! Slave psychology!

RIVKIN (*suddenly, half to himself, half to the Party*)—I got a belly full of stars, baby. You make me feel like I swallowed a Roman candle.

PRASKIN (*curiously*)—What's wrong with the kid?

RISKIN—What's wrong with all of us? The system! Two years he and Claus's daughter's been making googoo eyes behind the old man's back.

PRASKIN—So what?

RISKIN (*scornfully*)—So what? Economic determinism! What do you think the kid's name is—J. Pierpont Rivkin? He ain't even got for a bottle Dr. Brown's Celery Tonic. I tell you, it's like gall in my mouth two young people shouldn't have a room where they could make great music.

RANKIN (*warningly*)—Shhh! Here she comes now! (*Stella Claus enters, carrying a portable phonograph. She and Rivkin embrace, place a record on the turntable, and begin a very slow waltz, unmindful that the phonograph is playing "Cohen on the Telephone."*)

STELLA (*dreamily*)—Love me, sugar?

RIVKIN—I can't sleep, I can't eat, that's how I love you. You're a double malted with two scoops of whipped cream; you're the moon rising over Mosholu Parkway; you're a two weeks' vacation at Camp Nitgedaiget! I'd pull down the Chrysler Building to make a bobbie pin for your hair!

STELLA—I've got a stomach full of anguish. Oh, Rivvy, what'll we do?

PANKEN (*sympathetically*)—Here, try a piece fruit.

RIVKIN (*fiercely*)—Wax fruit—that's been my whole life! Imitations! Substitutes! Well, I'm through! Stella, tonight I'm telling your old man. He can't play mumblety-peg with two human beings! (*The tinkle of sleigh bells is heard offstage, followed by a voice shouting, "Whoa, Dasher! Whoa, Dancer!" A moment later S. Claus enters in a gust of mock snow. He is a pompous bourgeois of sixty-five who affects a white beard and a false air of benevolence. But tonight the ruddy color is missing from his cheeks, his step falters, and he moves heavily. The gnomes hastily replace the marzipan they have been filching.*)

STELLA (*anxiously*)—Papa! What did the specialist say to you?

CLAUS (*brokenly*)—The biggest professor in the country . . . the best cardiac man that money could buy. . . . I tell you I was like a wild man.

STELLA—Pull yourself together, Sam!

CLAUS—It's no use. Adhesions, diabetes, sleeping sickness, decalcomania—oh, my God! I got to cut out climbing in chimneys, he says—me, Sanford Claus, the biggest toy concern in the world!

STELLA (*soothingly*)—After all, it's only one man's opinion.

CLAUS—No, no, he cooked my goose. I'm like a broken uke after a Yosian picnic. Rivkin!

RIVKIN—Yes, Sam.

CLAUS—My boy, I had my eye on you for a long time. You and Stella thought you were too foxy for an old man, didn't you? Well, let bygones be bygones. Stella, do you love this gnome?

STELLA (*simply*)—He's the whole stage show at the Music Hall, Papa; he's Toscanini conducting Beethoven's Fifth; he's—

CLAUS (*curtly*)—Enough already. Take him. From now on he's a partner in the firm. (*As all exclaim, Claus holds up his hand for silence.*) And tonight he can take my route and make the deliveries. It's the least I could do for my own flesh and blood. (*As the happy couple kiss, Claus wipes away a suspicious moisture and turns to the other gnomes.*) Boys, do you know what day tomorrow is?

GNOMES (*crowding around expectantly*)—Christmas!

CLAUS—Correct. When you look in your envelopes tonight, you'll find a little present from me—a forty-percent pay cut. And the first one who opens his trap—gets this. (*As he holds up a tear-gas bomb and beams at them, the gnomes utter cries of joy, join hands, and dance around him shouting exultantly. All except Riskin and Briskin, that is, who exchange a quick glance and go underground.*)

CURTAIN

I'M TELLING YOU
—ARE YOU WRONG!

Contrary Fellows · SKEPTICS AND SCOFFERS

*When you're angry at the rabbi
you won't say, "Amen."*

There are certain individuals who always feel called upon to growl a challenging "No!" every time somebody says "Yes." We call them "contrary fellows," because they invariably interrupt one to rasp, "On the contrary!" Why they should feel such a compelling need to stand everything on its head is not so easy to understand. Who doesn't know some grown-ups who behave like spoiled brats? They are constantly straining to do or say some startling thing in order to draw attention to themselves. However, one must be careful to draw a distinction between the skepticism of the thinker and the neurotic scoffing of the frustrated. Criticism and perverseness are not quite the same things. Among intellectual pretenders, for instance, to be perverse is often considered as being original and brilliant, although it usually amounts to little more than bluff and chutzpah.

I recall the time when I was only a "green cucumber." I was talkative and loved to engage in discussion marathons with other equally talkative green cucumbers. Perhaps we argued with more heat than light, but it certainly was "profound" and "searching." At least, we thought so. Well, one night we sat around a table in Yiddish Bohemia's Café Royale, sipping tea with lemon from a glass, munching soggy Hungarian strudel and debating with equal sogginess on "things that really mattered." At the next table, listening to our conversation, sat a burly kibitzer. With a knowing, impudent look at us youngsters he kept on flicking the ashes from his cigarette into the empty saucer before him. Each time one of us warmed up and started to hammer home a point he'd interrupt rudely. "Applesauce!" he'd mutter coldly. That one word, and nothing more. Were he to have cried "Fire!" in a crowded theater the panic could have been no greater. The word simply paralyzed our tongues! Being young and tentative, what could we think? The devil only knew! Maybe this kibitzer was right? Maybe what we were saying was just "applesauce"? Embarrassed and ill-at-ease, we closed up like clams.

A little later we found out all about the fellow: he was just *an ignorant* nudnik, *and, if you were to ask us, a* no-goodnik *and* paskudnik *as well! He was a dress salesman with intellectual pretensions. And he took his "applesauce" revenge on us, no one could convince us otherwise, because he envied us for being "high-brows" while he was nothing but a "low-brow"* chutzpanik! *In fact, he even admitted with a chuckle that he didn't have the slightest idea what we were arguing about, nor did he care, for that matter! But no matter what it was we were talking about, of one thing he was sure—that it was all "applesauce"! And as they say in Yiddish, "Nu, go and do him something!"*

The plain fact is that Jews have a long intellectual tradition and have produced an astonishing number of men of talent in every field. This intellectual tradition runs deep in the plain Jewish folk too. They can boast of even a greater number of "geniuses," diamonds in the rough one might say, a swarm of three-quarter baked, half-baked, and quarter-baked intellectuals. For them, the urge to philosophize about life is like a nagging toothache. Just try and stop them!

In their ghetto past, Jews could never hope to be anything but partly baked. True, they had their religious Talmudic culture—about which most Gentiles haven't even an inkling—but poverty and lack of opportunity for a broader education kept them in a sort of twilight zone of culture. The old saying that a little knowledge is a dangerous thing applied readily to them. True, there were many fine minds that turned skeptical on a lot of matters, but they were objective truthseekers. The marginal intellectuals, on the other hand, developed a neurotic insecurity about themselves. And so they took a perverse pleasure in being contrary fellows. They became scoffers, compulsive and tiresome wits, explosive no-sayers, gadfly teasers, scornful dunderheads, and skeptics with an intellectual chip on their shoulders.

Perhaps I am exaggerating in thinking that the average Jew is at least a bit of a philosopher, even if he follows the most humble calling. Just try and get into a conversation with the plainest Jewish worker, peddler, or small shopkeeper, and what will you find? A lively interest in the affairs of the world, a grasp of philosophic ideas, a groping for absolute values. Not all the platitudes in which he smothers these can hide his intellectual curiosity. And if he is contrary? What of it? To be contrary is sometimes a virtue. The house wrecker too has his place in construction work.

N.A.

THE MODERN INTELLECTUAL
A JEWISH NEO-THOMIST'S SATIRE

BY FRANZ WERFEL

TRANSLATED FROM THE GERMAN BY GEOFFREY DUNLOP

"The intellect has emptied itself of all its content of Divinity—" the voice rose to breaking pitch—"Do you really think that Origen and St. Thomas, for instance, had any less brain than a modern experimental psychologist? Cleverness without God—that's your modern intellectual—or rather, it's your modern fool. There's no such thing as absolute intellect; it's a sheerly formal principle. I defined it once for myself as the subjugation of life to measurements. Technical! —that's what it is! Technical! Technique—the monstrous futile gyration of cleverness. Of course, I'm not so reactionary as to simply despise it all—railway viaducts and ferro-concrete, and cars and skyscrapers, hydraulic power, electric signs, Bleriot's aviation experiments, the Wright brothers, and so on. But even suppose I did? Mankind is accustomed to far greater miracles. The sun and the fixed stars aren't such bad electric signs. But all your modern intellectual wants is to drive the sense of wonder out of humanity. 'What's that shining thing?' you ask. Science says: 'An electric globe.'—'Why does it shine?'—'Because filaments shine.'—'Why?'—'Because an electric current of such and such intensity goes through them.'—'What's an electric current?'—'A substance of accumulated potentiality observed under certain conditions.'—Then all the human being can do is to make a little disappointed bow—and Science begins to sound a warning: 'Above all, my dear chap, no mystery! Miraculous is simply a vulgar word for the little spots I haven't managed to light up yet with my newest electric globe. Tomorrow, I shall explain a bit more clearly. But for heaven's sake don't you go looking for mysteries today; only be thankful that your house is better lighted than your grandfather's.'" Engländer, at this point, jumped up, his fat cheeks flushed with real anger. He yelled—

"But what I say is—it is miraculous!"

The noise made Ferdinand jump. Whenever he heard a loud voice, the terrified feeling came over him that someone in authority must be shouting at him. But Engländer did not notice the effect of his outburst; he was now addressing mankind.

"Aristotle, even, our Master, called mystery the source of all philosophy. But, unfortunately, Aristotle, our Master, was rather a dry old stick. If he hadn't been, he might have added—'There's a hierarchy of mysteries, my dear chap. To be lost in wonder at a vacuum-cleaner isn't quite the same thing as being lost in wonder at original sin.' See what I mean? But 'clever' people can only wonder at vacuum-cleaners. God knows where all this stinking rot began."

Engländer, whose bearing as a rule was most correct, for he did his best to hide his corpulence by an assumption of severe dignity, was so carried away by his theme that he thrust out a careless belly.

"Well, anyway, I know where it all started. The English! Naturally! The English were the people who launched all this modern intelligence stuff."

His plump, good-natured face was creased with hate. For Alfred Engländer, the "English" were an idée fixe. He detested them so heartily that he, whom fate had burdened with the odious name "Engländer," would have been only too willing to change it had he not been terrified lest people interpret his change of name as a flight from his Jewish nationality. Nothing would have made him more ashamed than that any such misunderstanding should arise, more especially since he was in love with the Catholic philosophy. No shadow of any suspicion that it sprang from some troubled source of opportunism or snobbery must be cast upon this pure enthusiasm. And this same complicated timidity explained why Engländer, whose knowledge of dogmatic and patristic theology was the admiration of many theologians, had never allowed himself to be baptized. If anyone asked him his reasons, he would answer that he did not feel sufficiently free to embrace a martyr's crown of misconstructions. So he kept his name and old religion which in many respects he still venerated. But whenever he happened to mention "the English," his eyes would dart forth hate.

"Of course—the English, and their American spawn! Some Wycliffe, some heretic or other. It began with the denial of a Sacrament. And where's it going to end? With the metaphysic of drainage!"

Suddenly, it came over him like a frenzy. He shut his eyes, stood still in the middle of the room, and began intoning, like a curate:

"Holy Capital,
> *Have mercy on us.*
Holy Dividends, its truly begotten son,
> *Have mercy on us.*
Holy business acumen of all the intelligent, third person of the Trinity,
> *Have mercy on us—*

*You blessed choirs of saints and holy spirits, Petrol, Cotton, Oil, Coal,
Leather, Rubber, Spare Parts,*
     Pray for us.
*You Holy Apostles and Evangelists of the Stock Exchange, the gold
market, and the modern science that goes with them,*
     Pray for us.
*All blessed hermits and solitaries of Trusts and Limited Companies
for jerry-building, with two w.c.'s, hot and cold water on every
floor, central heating and Rembrandt reproductions,*
     Pray for us!"

Beads of sweat stood out on his forehead; he paced the room, his
fists clenched.

> *A miracle cannot prove that which is impossible;*
> *it is useful only as a confirmation*
> *of that which is possible.—Moses ben Maimon (Maimonides)*

APHORISMS ACCORDING TO THE
HEBREW-YIDDISH ALPHABET

BY SHOLOM ALEICHEM

ALEF: *Adam*—the only happy man; he never had a mother-in-law.
BEYZ: *bankrot* (bankrupt)—a sickness you manage to survive.
 " *biecher* (books)—objects you always borrow but never buy.
GIML: *gemilas-chesed* (a loan)—something you never deny and
   never return.
 " *gelt* (money)—a thing everyone wants and no one has.
DALED: *dales* (destitution)—once upon a time it used to lie on a dung
   heap; nowadays it's dressed in velvet.
HEY: *hoffnung* (hope)—a liar.
 " *haskamah* (testimonial in a learned book)—"Lay off me now!"
VOV: *veksel* (a check)—a merchant's joke.

ZAYEN: *zalts* (salt)—a lot at the grocer's but damn little in the feuilletons.

CHES: *chupeh* (the marriage canopy)—you enter it living and you come out a corpse.

TES: *tug* (day)—by mistake there was such a newspaper [i.e., *Der Tug*, a New York Yiddish daily newspaper].

YUD: *Judenfrage* (the Jewish Question)—from what does a Jew make a living?

LAMED: *liebe* (love)—an article that's gone out of fashion.

" *leben* (life)—a drama for the wise, a game for the fool, a comedy for the rich, and a tragedy for the poor.

MEM: *maggid* (preacher)—a man who can't sleep because he's bothered by a Biblical quotation.

" *melamed* (a Hebrew teacher)—a Jew who deals with *goyim*.[1]

" *matzeyvo* (tombstone)—a slab of marble on which they carve lies.

NUN: *nadan* (a dowry)—a contribution.

SAMACH: *Seder* (the evening religious home-service on Pesach)—happens once a year for Jews and yet they insist on asking four questions.

AYEN: *egunah* (grass widow)—any lady writer on a Hebrew journal.

" *ershter April* (April First)—a joke that's repeated 365 times during the year.

PEY: *petch* (slaps in the face)—paid in cash.

FEY: *froien-tzimmer* (women)—you suffer before you get them, when you have them, and when you lose them.

TSADIK: *tsung* (tongue)—a dangerous enemy.

KUF: *kapital* (capital)—in Karl Marx it's on paper; at Brodsky's it's in the safe.

" *kadoches* (a fever)—in the cash box.

" *klugschaft* (wisdom)—something the other fellow lacks and we have.

REYSH: *rachiless* (gossip, slander)—a natural telephone.

SHIN: *shadchan* (a matchmaker, a matrimonial agent)—a dealer in livestock.

" *sholom aleichem* (peace be with you!)—a phrase that's sung every time to a different tune:

1. (as a greeting)—"Ah! Sholom! Aleichem!"
2. (blessing the new moon)—"Sholom aleichem?"

[1] *A* double-entendre *suggesting that the Jewish pupils know as much Hebrew as the goyim.*

3. (before reciting the Kiddush)—"Sholom aleichem."
4. (derisively)—"Sholom Aleichem? Why I heard him to begin with! May the devil take his father!"

May God protect you from goyishe *hands and from* yiddishe *tongues!*

THE HERESY OF THE WATER TAPS

BY JEAN RICHARD BLOCH
TRANSLATED FROM THE FRENCH BY CLIFTON P. FADIMAN

It is a matter of common knowledge that eunuchs never become entirely free from certain perturbations peculiar to their sex. Similarly, if your leg has acquired the odious habit of itching and someone happens to cut it off, its wooden substitute will continue to itch—and you to scratch. The final exhaustion of your bank account does not necessarily kill a taste for truffled partridge. So with religion. . . .

These are truths derived from experience—and one should not ignore experience. Had the Archbishop of Paris reminded himself of this in time, he would not have allowed such agitation to manifest itself when the great Heresy of the Water Taps broke out. Nor would the Consistory of the Ministers of the Reformed Church have allowed it to disturb their peace; nor the Chief Rabbi of France. . . .

This is how the affair was described to me by the little rabbi, Israel Cohen, who officiated with neither glory nor profit at the oratory of Trocadéro Passy. The little rabbi, Israel Cohen, was modest—and quite unconscious of his modesty. Quite simply, over our bocks of Zimmer beer, he told me the astonishing story which, in his own words, follows.

Have you ever visited my oratory? . . . It's a perfect copy of the Hammam, with this difference in favour of the bath establishment; that at my place the furnace is never going. Though my little bit of a synagogue is only about as large as a wafer, it gets as chilly as a catacomb.

At first I had a *chazan* who managed to stand it three months before going into a fit complicated by acute bronchitis. The result was that I myself had to make a fire out of old newspapers before I could dare to take off my overcoat. But one day when I almost set fire to the Temple I decided to abandon this method. Besides, my supply of old newspapers was running out.

I adopted the habit of saying my prayers while polishing the glossy oak benches with a soft flannel rag. Under my breath I cursed the idiotic munificence of Raphael Weill, the banker, who founded and endowed this useless synagogue eight days before his death just to spite his three renegade sons. Think of the services I could have given in the Marais neighbourhood, where ten thousand pious Jewish families are crowded together without either air or synagogue.

The twenty-four consecutive hours I had to spend in that solitude during the holiday constituted an immurement far more dreadful than anything ever invented by the Catholic monks. I never saw the holidays approaching without a feeling of terror. And when I emerged without strength, voiceless and chilled, the elegant automobiles of my congregants bespattered the modest garments which were all my 190 francs a month allowed me.

I informed the Central Consistory of these details and asked to be transferred. Their reply intimated that I possessed a certain mental simplicity if I imagined that it was their business to see that rabbis were provided with congregations. Undoubtedly, they said, M. de Rothschild ought to undertake to beat the drum up and down the Avenue Henri Martin just for the benefit of little Israel Cohen, a rabbi of twelve months' experience. They did not go so far as to say that I was entirely responsible for the difficulty, but they knew how to insinuate that there were certain devices commonly employed to lend the services a less austere appearance—devices which I had merely to avail myself of without asking anybody's permission.

This was just about the time when that fat rabbi from the East descended on Paris, you remember, the one who bragged so shamelessly and had such a purple neck. Remember him? Well, he brought along a complete scheme for the reform of the traditional services. The scheme had seventy different provisions, beginning with the recitation of the Pentateuch in blank verse and ending with a re-arrangement of the women's benches so as to make them face the men's.

The officials of the Chief Rabbi closed their eyes less in horror than in acquiescence and the little fellow opened up business not three hundred yards away from my little synagogue on the Rue Galilée, and what with his musical services on Sunday morning at the hour of the mass and his first communion for twelve-year-old bourgeoise heiresses, he managed to draw a capacity crowd for six months. Downright disgusting mummery, I call it! I mention this detail merely to indicate that tendency toward change in religious customs which was to culminate in the Heresy of the Water Taps.

On the seventeenth day of May, I was proceeding towards the Trocadéro, flourishing my stick gaily because—if you will excuse the professional image—the Avenue Kléber seemed to me like Zion crowned with flowers and singing in the light of a liquid silver Spring. I was happy, too, because I had changed my official stovepipe for a black straw hat. Just then—I think I'll have another beer—just then I saw a black frock coat plastered with a breastplate cravat of stiffly starched white cloth approaching me from across the Avenue. The person who inhabited the costume seemed to know me, for he accosted me without hesitation and held out his hand. He was a middle-aged man, quite rotund, and clean-shaven. He wore a black straw hat like mine, which he took off as he approached. I did not remember ever having met him.

He said, "Rabbi Israel Cohen, I believe?"

"The same," I replied, doffing my hat. He introduced himself. "I am Pastor Thomas Morin, minister of the Calvinist Reformed Church in the Rue Boissière. Delighted to meet you, my dear young colleague."

The words were accompanied with a somewhat ambiguous smile. I returned his greeting politely and waited for his next words. He put on his hat, rubbed his hands, and placed himself at my left.

"Would it inconvenience you if we walked together a bit?" he asked. I had no objection and so the two black coats proceeded side by side along the Avenue. He promptly broached his subject, rolling his ebony stick between the palms of his hands, and looking at me now and then with a sidewise glance.

"My dear young colleague—colleague in God——" he added with what I thought was a rather satirical smile, "we labour, do we not, under a common, or shall I say, a similar burden. Allow me to express the pleasure that the New Testament feels in meeting the Old. You are young and modest. We have heard quite a little about your courage. And that you know Hebrew and any number of Arabic and Syriac jargons. But you will grant all that has not enabled you to make much of an impression on your parishioners."

I did not feel called upon to reply to this all-too-clear insinuation. This fat individual really annoyed me. He continued, rubbing his hands with great pleasure: "Grant me that, Rabbi Cohen! As far as I am concerned I admit the same difficulty and, in a little while, the Abbé Joseph Patard will make a similar confession relative to his own flock."

I stopped short.

"The Abbé Patard?———"

"Yes, he is waiting for us at the Museum of Comparative Ethnography," declared the minister simply, giving me a side glance that felt as if he were shoving me with his elbow. "He trusts that you will honour us by giving us a few moments, Rabbi Cohen."

Well, you can understand that the whole thing took me quite by surprise. At the Seminary in the Rue Vauquelin we had learned all but two things—how to reawaken faith and how to behave in the face of another religion. I tried to carry it off by affecting an arrogant composure, but I felt that I was turning very red—a weakness of my complexion which I haven't been able to get rid of yet; and you know there's no idiocy a man will not agree to in order to excuse the colour of his ears.

"I shall be glad to accompany you, Monsieur . . . Monsieur Morin."

"Fine. That is what I told the great Abbé Patard, but he would not believe me. These Catholic priests see obstacles at every turn."

Well, when we entered the Trocadéro this stoutish clergyman had not yet done with his compliments nor I with my amazement. And there was a tall, lanky priest waiting for us, engaged in examining the antiquities of Yucatan. The contours of his shoulder blades caught the cassock at the bend. He turned, took off his hat solemnly, and then lowered his sharp nose till it pointed directly to his shoe tips.

I imagine the Calvinist minister was quite amused at our discomfiture, for he caressed his belly with a sort of slow enjoyment. Finally he started the conversation. It was agreed that he should be our spokesman.

"Rabbi Israel Cohen has consented to come, Father Patard, on my assuring him that we are to consider only topics likely to affect the future of the three faiths we stand for in our endeavours to benefit the souls of our parishioners, let us hope, and to diffuse more widely the doctrines of love, brotherhood . . . grace . . . salvation."

The last two nouns seemed to trouble him for a moment, but he finally got them out and turned to me a face literally beaming with guilelessness. The Abbé Patard raised his head with such a dry me-chanical gesture that I thought I heard his vertebrae creak. He tried to manufacture a smile out of the thousand little wrinkles that crimped his skin around the nose. I really couldn't say whether the colour of his face was usually as yellow as it was just then.

"Yes, Monsieur Cohen, you may well be amazed at our meeting. But the fact is that a great danger threatens the faith——"

"The various faiths of our faithful, Monsieur Cohen."

It was on the tip of my tongue to reply that any problem affecting a congregation could not possibly be of much interest to me, but I restrained myself just in time and merely bowed assent. The priest looked around uneasily. Then with short quick steps, he led us between the rear wall and a huge glass case entirely filled with images of Mexican deities. It was here, in the shadow and under the eyes of a gigantic Aztec idol, that our conventicle took place.

You know that my nature is neither over-imaginative nor over-enthusiastic. As is the case with the majority of my young colleagues, clarity and philology interest me far more than legend. Yet, my dear friend, will you believe me when I say that at that moment the little twenty-two-year-old rabbi felt himself standing on Mount Sinai? I could not help smiling at the emotion that stirred these worshippers of the Golden Calf. Involuntarily I recalled Isaiah's words in the nine-teenth chapter: "And I will set the Egyptians against the Egyptians: and they shall fight everyone against his brother." You will admit that there was something amusing in the idea of this young man being invited as a third by the two great enemy denominations of Western Europe.

Quite brusquely, the Abbé began to speak: "No doubt you are acquainted with Madame la Comtesse de Hauterive—or at least with her family?"

I will confess that I was entirely unaware of the existence of this lady. The clergyman, who had been watching me added: "You will identify her better, Monsieur Cohen, by her bapt— by her birth name: she is the daughter of Monsieur Julius Mayer, the banker, who owns that large new mansion—The Ranelagh."

"And mother of the wife of Monsieur Pelletier, the banker, who belongs to your denomination," continued Father Patard, not very graciously, turning to my frock-coated colleague. Here was a ray of light. I had completely forgotten the interwoven genealogies of this Frankfort family which had sought, in turn, money and titles of nobility. I ventured astutely: "Is Mademoiselle Pelletier thinking of contracting a union that would bring her back to one of the faiths of her forefathers?"

I was rewarded with an icy look from the minister of Calvin, which discouraged me from further jesting.

"No, Monsieur Cohen. The matter we have ventured to disturb you about is far more serious. This family depends on our threefold jurisdiction. You especially, sir [he was addressing me], can do a great deal through the influence that you must legitimately exercise over Madame Mayer, mother of Madame de Hauterive and grandmother of Madame Pelletier."

Why should I disillusion him by telling him that I had never even seen the good lady? After waiting a moment for a sign or a reply, he continued: "Now, you are probably aware that it is in this family——"

My countenance was quite impassive.

"You are not aware that this family is the origin of this ridiculous and blasphemous fashion which may well assume, unless we take precautions, an inordinate importance."

As you can easily imagine, I was burning with curiosity, but I merely heaved an eloquent sigh.

And so I learned of the disturbances which during the last two weeks had been agitating the aristocratic apartments of the Avenues Kléber, Victor Hugo, Henri Martin, Trocadéro, and others in that charming neighbourhood. The Comtesse de Hauterive had never really been a believer. But she displayed all the appearance of the most rigorous devotion. That is, until the Abbé Patard was appointed priest of her parish, the spineless fellow who had the misfortune to take his office seriously. He threatened to refuse the Comtesse absolution unless she made her real conduct and thought conform to this outward show. Well, war broke out between the two and one day——

"One day" (these are the clergyman's words, more or less) "when the Comte after being announced, entered the bathroom where the Comtesse his wife had been shutting herself up most of the day for nearly a week, he found her kneeling and praying—wasn't that it?" the minister asked, turning to the priest with a gesture in which the blackest malice was masked by tender condolence. The Abbé Patard nodded gruffly.

"He found her, then, kneeling and praying before a crucifix—you will pardon this detail, Monsieur Cohen?"

"Quite. Quite, Monsieur Morin," I said, "I am listening."

"A crucifix which hung on the wall of the bathroom just over the mixing tap—that's right, isn't it, Father Patard?—of the bathtub. The

Comte couldn't help remarking to the Comtesse—but only in jest, gentlemen, only in jest—that she seemed to be addressing her prayers to the water tap rather than to the crucifix. Whereupon without replying the Comtesse—with a gesture which you will understand, Monsieur Cohen, I cannot mention without a shudder—rose, removed the image of the Saviour, and smiling scornfully, deposited it on the dressing table. Then she returned to the bathtub and again set herself in an attitude of prayer—wasn't that how it was, Father Patard?—her knees on the marble floor, before the lone mixing tap."

My mouth must have been opened as wide as my straw hat.

"The Comte, of course, was shocked; but, assuming that his wife was joking, he began to point out the impropriety of this action, when she stood up—the Comtesse is still considered quite beautiful and very striking—when she stood up and interrupted him petulantly. She declared briefly that, one after another, all the religions she had tried had deceived her; that their priests lived in a perpetual betrayal of the principles they expounded; that the ministers of the religion which had commanded her faith before her marriage lacked even the slightest dignity—you will excuse me if the desire to be exact puts on my lips accusations of which I personally disapprove—in fact, were nothing but wretched—here followed a word of Hebrew slang which the Comte did not catch——"

I opened my mouth and allowed the word to escape mechanically: *"Schnorrers?"*

The triumphant satisfaction that spread over the seemingly contrite expression of the clergyman made me curse my naïveté and this awful blunder. I suppose I must have turned scarlet from the roots of my hair to the soles of my feet. This diabolical clergyman bowed and said sweetly: "You probably know better than I, Monsieur Cohen."

I could have strangled him. And then he continued with his false air of frankness: "She added that the priests of the creed she had adopted since her marriage to Monsieur Hauterive had offended her no less; that some of them lived in a sensual debauchery while others aspired merely to a profitable domination over the minds of others. But naturally I don't even wish to repeat such idle talk—and a great deal more that she said on the same subject," he added, observing with the corner of his eye the restless uneasiness of the Abbé Patard.

"It will be enough to know that besides these reasons—really not reasons at all—Madame de Hauterive alleged others which cannot help making one ponder over the state of decadence into which public morals have fallen."

I don't know why at that moment he should have cast a severe glance at me.

"She declared that, after all, the various religions contradicted each other; that she had no reasons to believe one in preference to another, that although everyone talked about God, no one had yet proved that he existed, and the disorder of the world rather argued the contrary; and that the only inference she had derived from observing the universal conduct of men and women was that they were all in quest of ease and pleasure.

"As for herself, she declared, her pleasure did not lie where one might suppose; and at this point she introduced" (it was still the clergyman who spoke) "several remarks most uncivil to her husband, the Comte, and which assuredly can have become the property of public gossip only through a devious route" (this to the priest).

"Under these circumstances, she had decided to pay no attention to anything outside of her own ease and would reserve her reverence exclusively for those marvellous mysteries which enabled her to surround herself with the comfort she sought. In this she claimed that she was merely complying with the fashion of her own social world and at the same time stripping it of the hypocrisy with which it was usually disguised.

"Finally suiting the action to the word, she began to pray to the water tap once more, then walked past the stupefied Comte to the electric switch, clasped her hands, bent down and touched it with her lips. Finally, on bended knees, she addressed a fervent prayer to the radiator. When the wretched Comte emerged from his bewilderment with the idea of forcing her to rise she was already withdrawing with dignity and giving orders to summon the servants. Now, are there any other details you might like to know, Monsieur Cohen?"

You can judge the state of amazement into which this story plunged me.

But I had no time to stop there, for the Abbé Joseph Patard had now drawn himself up and in a voice of thunder, which he tried vainly to soften, he proclaimed, pointing his index-finger at the clergyman:

"Know furthermore that these abominations might have remained forever concealed in the bosom of this impious woman if her own daughter, the wife of the banker Pelletier, perverted by the abjuration wherefor her parent and she herself will have to account before the tribunal of Divine Justice, had not hastened to follow her example——"

"If you please!" interrupted the pastor. . . .

". . . and if this example had not amid her own circle met with a success a thousand times regrettable for you, Monsieur Morin, and, I hope for the salvation of those sinful souls!"

"That's only too true, but——"

The pastor would not surrender. And at this point the priest lifted his two large bony hands, open wide, towards the sky: "What is it we see about us? Blasphemy, heresy, outrage going back generation after generation and striking the white hairs of Madame Julius Mayer, to whom our Church owes so much, and yours undoubtedly no less, Monsieur Cohen; from there, spreading in all directions, it strikes the neighbouring homes, Catholic, Apostolic, and Roman, as well as those subject to other religions! We are already losing our faithful by the score. Some of them brutally break all bonds connecting them with the religion of their fathers; others lean more moderately towards the heresy. But everywhere one encounters nothing but tolerance for these monstrosities. Even the most honest are merely content to smile. Brochures which the impious zeal of Madame de Hauterive causes to be printed are already circulating. They are being translated into various languages and we hear that abroad, in Spain, in England, even in Berlin, enthusiastic support will be given to this lunacy."

He tucked up his cassock vehemently and took out of his pocket a sheaf of little pale blue pamphlets, like those you may have seen afterwards. This was the first one I ever set my eyes on. The cover bore this legend:

FAITH IN THE ALL-POWERFUL FORCES

THE "ALL-IN-ALL"
or New Dogma of the Life and Death of Mankind
NEW LIGHT
on the true succession of prophets from Sakya Mouni to Edison
THE PRINCIPLES OF ALL THINGS
for the first time revealed and made manifest by a Society of the
Faithful
Science and Religion Henceforth Reconciled
Followed by fifty-two acts of devotion to the
POWERS OF THE HEARTH
(*Here was placed a design of a radiant water tap*)
PARIS, MECCA OF THE SCIENCES AND POWERS
Ten centimes the copy   MCMXII

And the slender column opened to that chant you may have heard so many times since:

> *O Fire, I revere you, Fire,*
> *You are the sun and you are God,*
> *You move about within our homes,*
> *Deprived of you, O Fire, I die.*
>
> *O Water, principle of all,*
> *O Power in which all things rest,*
> *Absolution, holy purity!*
> *Great Polymorphe, shadow or light.*
>
> *Light, mastered force, etc. . . .*

You may well wonder whether at first I believed a single word of these mad tales. I asked myself what sort of madmen these were. But my two colleagues gave me no time to answer my own question. They interrupted each other with increasing heat. Finally I gathered that the priest had hastened to the Archbishop, where his revelations, corroborated by testimony from three or four other sources, had stirred up considerable agitation. He had been commissioned to enter into negotiations with the representatives of cults similarly threatened. The pastor's experience had been practically identical.

The purpose of our conference, then, was to ascertain the extent of the damage. I foresaw with horror the moment when I would have to confess publicly my inability to estimate it—and to give the all-too-excellent reason. I was already cursing the ignorance in which the carelessness of the Central Consistory had placed me when our conversation suddenly took an unexpected turn.

The Abbé was engaged in a sort of harangue in the course of which he was endeavouring to depict the idolatry of these men and women training their children to follow the electric wires affixed to the walls of the apartment, to genuflect every seven steps and to recite appropriate prayers—all of which is, I admit, perfectly ridiculous. But he had the misfortune to conclude with a figure which though very happy from an artistic point of view was, nevertheless, an unpleasant mistake. It was something like this—the deuce! I can't seem to remember!—oh, yes:

"Well, gentlemen, it seems extremely urgent that we take action. The spirit of evil raises its head once more—ahem!—Madame de Hauterive, née Mayer" (I swallowed it) "desires to create a schism—a new reform movement. Against this new Calvin let us summon a new Ignatius Loyola!"

You will agree with me that these words were not—between our-selves—very tactful or appropriate. But the Abbé was a born sermon-iser. The pastor caught fire. At the mention of reform he held his breath and swelled like a pudding; at the mention of Calvin he turned scarlet; but when Loyola was named he jumped a foot in the air and jammed on his straw hat. I followed his example. He cried out sharply:

"Papist! What have you to do with our great Calvin? You and your whole Church are not good enough to wash the feet of this gentle-man's Jewish heiresses!"

"Sir!" cried the priest.

"Idolater! Simoniac! Bigot!"

"Rebel! Blasphemer!"

I did not stay to hear any more, but departed hastily. The noise had attracted the attention of the guard, who was asleep on a chair near the entrance. As I passed by, the good gendarme asked me: "What's going on?"

I gave myself the quite gratuitous pleasure of answering him: "Nothing much. The Four Gospels are merely having it out with the Apocrypha."

I have no idea what these words could have meant to him, for he dashed to the scene of the fray immediately. I have never seen my interlocutors again. Coming out of the place I asked myself whether I had not been the spectator of a ridiculous nightmare.

But I had to accept the facts. You recollect the progress of this extraordinary invention; the middle-class neighbourhood contaminated after the pseudo-aristocratic quarter; the Plaine Monceau and the Trinity behind the Bois and Champs Elysées; the heresy finally dying at the thresholds of districts where the bathtub is unknown, where one must work for one's daily bread and pay the collector for water.

You know, as well as I do, of those people who turned their pleasure trips into pilgrimages; great modern palaces transformed into temples where the rites of Steam Heat were celebrated on Mondays, where every evening before dining, they sang, standing bareheaded, the song of the Wire Filament Bulb, where they celebrated those mysterious and possibly disgusting mysteries of the Low Pressure Douche, which the police had vainly endeavoured to investigate.

And you recollect the impost publicly placed on the interiors of these household gods. And the fabulous prices attained in a few weeks by copper, aluminum, and nickel—metals declared fully as sacred as gold by the votaries of the new religion—and the particular devotion to Our Lady of the Four Cylinders, with the little altar erected two years ago in the middle of the Avenue de la Grande Armée to the demi-goddess called Spark Plugs.

And all the disgusting affectations which revealed the decay of the modern soul—those ambiguous gestures intended as salutation to the Elevator whenever one passes before the cage of this new god—and those electric switches of cut glass set in gold, before which the tongue of a light electric spark quivers night and day.

As for myself, good fortune sent me to Smyrna the following year. When I came back to France after an absence of ten years that was the state in which I found the country.

For faith decays to make way for a new faith. Belief must crop out somehow. When men, decadent and barren of ideals, reject all obligations, they come inevitably to adore their hip bath.

But what do you think of the conversation with my priest and my clergyman? Do you know that there was nothing to prevent the interview from becoming celebrated in ecclesiastical history under the name *Council of the Trocadéro,* with a zinc engraving of myself in the school text-books?

But it was preordained that the name Israel Cohen should not become famous just then. A lovely name, nevertheless—I have dreamed for a long time of making it illustrious, like Maimonides. Well, what would you have? I was born thirty years too soon. Our day belongs to the independent virtues.

Please don't hesitate too long about using that bell and let's have some more of this dark beer. I have become as the sands of Egypt after the seven lean kine. . . .

Man is like a musical clock—move him even slightly
and he begins to sing a new tune.—Ludwig Börne

A SERMON

The preacher held forth in the synagogue that Sabbath afternoon:
"My masters, people may be likened to horses. There are, you know, all kinds of horses. There is, for instance, the good horse who trots along willingly and no one has to drive him, not even show him the whip. Then there is the tolerable horse. He is a bit lazy. But once

you crack a whip over him he gets going. There is a third kind of horse who is lazy. You can crack a whip over him all you like, but he won't lift a hoof off the ground. Such a horse is absolutely useless.

"In the same way, my friends, there is the man who is pious and good. You don't have to preach at him, nor drive him to the service of the Lord. That, my friends, is a good horse. On the other hand, there is the man who stands in need of constant prodding and shaking. He has to be driven to do his duty. That's a tolerable kind of horse. Lastly, there is the man who, no matter how much you preach at him and exhort him, he will not lift a foot to go anywhere to do the service of the Lord. Believe me, my friends, that one is no horse at all!"

BUT YOU'VE GOT TO PRAY, NO?

BY I. L. PERETZ
TRANSLATED FROM THE YIDDISH BY NATHAN AUSUBEL

The happy day came at last for Berel the tailor when his son the doctor, was coming home for good. He'd build up a practice in his home town. People would ail. In short, there was nothing to worry about!

His son arrived on Friday, and on the Sabbath his father asked him to go along with him to the synagogue.

"I'm not going, Papa," said the doctor.

"You're not ashamed to be seen with me, are you, Son?"

"God forbid, Papa! What an idea!"

"Still in all, even if you are a doctor, do you think you no longer have to pray and praise God?"

"It's not that, Papa."

"What then, tell me! Are you tired, maybe? Are you sick, God forbid?"

"No, Papa, I'm not going."

"I'm curious to know why."

"Nu, sit down, Papa, and I'll tell you why."

The old man put down his *tallis* and sat down.

"Nu? Go ahead and tell me. I'd like to understand the matter!"

"Good! Try to imagine, Papa, that you're a rich man, so rich that a ruble has little value for you."

His father heaved a sigh. In order to make his son a doctor he had gotten himself in debt up to his ears. Once upon a time he had owned a little house—but now, no more house! Even his sewing machines he had sold! Now he was a lodger living among strangers.

"Nu?" said he, with a wave of his hand.

"In short, Papa, you're a rich man! Imagine that across the way from you there lives a widow, a weak, sick woman with small children, and she badly stands in need of aid."

"Of course, I'd help her!"

"Now tell me, would you hold back until the widow came around to you begging for help, swooning and spilling a river of tears?"

"God forbid! What for? If I knew——"

"Good! Now, take God. Tell me, is he better or worse than you?"

"What are you talking about? What a question to ask!"

"Nu, since God is better than you, doesn't he himself know what poor, weak, and ailing man needs? Do you think he'll wait for us to beg him that he should help us?"

"But——"

"I suppose you have in mind that we ought to praise God nevertheless."

"That's so!"

"Nu, Papa, how would you like it if someone should come and praise you right to your face: 'A fine tailor! a good tailor! an honest tailor! Ah, what a tailor! I'm telling you, a real tailor, the one and only tailor!'"

"Ach!" muttered the old man impatiently. "It would make me sick with embarrassment."

"Right! And do you know why? Because you're no fool! You couldn't find pleasure in silly praise. And don't forget, you're just a man, a weak man at that, whom criticism can hurt and praise can help!"

"But——"

"There is no but, Papa, no but! God is wiser than all of us; do you think he needs our praise? Do you think he requires us to clamor to him three times a day with our prayers? 'Ah, what a good tailor! A fine tailor!'"

"What are you talking about?"

"Nu, let it be then: 'A Good God! a fine God! Who has created Heaven and Earth!' What do you think—he doesn't know that himself?"

The old man fell into deep thought. Then he came to with a start.

"True. Everything you say, my Son, is right, but tell me—you've got to pray, no?"

A SHARE OF PARADISE

BY YEHOASH (SOLOMON BLOOMGARDEN)
TRANSLATED FROM THE YIDDISH BY NATHAN AUSUBEL

The official *apikoiros* or freethinker, without whom a Jewish community could hardly get along—just as it couldn't get along without a bathhouse, the town billy goat, or the town *meshuggener*—this official apikoiros in our town was Rabinovitch, the pharmacist, a confirmed bachelor of about forty-five.

His pharmacy was situated right opposite the synagogue. When the members of the congregation would stream out after the Friday night services they would see this contrary fellow sitting on his porch and smoking a cigar. If only he'd kept his mouth shut it would have been at least tolerable, but he actually saluted the worshipers with a hearty and cheerful *"gut shabbes!"* This piece of insolence stabbed everybody "to his seventh rib."

Had it been someone else, no doubt he would have been excommunicated, but since he was the only pharmacist in town and chockfull of medical knowledge besides, they had to tolerate him. It was the general opinion that he knew even more than the doctor himself. And on top of that he had a generous heart! When it came, for instance, to the distribution of *matzos* to the needy before Passover he was the first to extend a helping hand. He gave everyone who asked of him, although while doing so he'd abuse them good and proper and call them all the names in the cards. Nevertheless, all poor people knew that they had the standing privilege of getting medicine from him for nothing at any time. Such a man was Rabinovitch.

So the townfolk used to curse him silently in their hearts, but before him they would respectfully take off their hats and address him as *"Pani* Rabinovitch."

A steady customer of his was old Gitteh-Nesheh. She was a tiny bent woman of some seventy years. She was busy all the time making a "collection" for something or other. Her children who were in America sent her eight rubles every month which enabled her to live comfortably. She even had enough left to give Heshel, the *batlen,* his bath money every week and to buy the *yeshiva-bocherim* hot chick-peas every Friday. She was always collecting, here for an expectant mother, there for a dowerless bride, and sometimes "I can't tell you for whom." And everyone gave the old woman his contribution and with it his blessing, "May you live to a hundred and twenty, Gitteh-Nesheh!"

And Gitteh-Nesheh would smile and say: "My trousseau I already have, and when it will be His will, I'll be ready."

By her "trousseau" she meant her shroud, which she had made for herself ten years before and which she used to take out of her trunk the first of every month in order to give it a good airing.

She went to Rabinovitch for a contribution almost every day but from these visits she had to endure all kinds of aggravation. Sometimes he'd give her half a ruble on the condition that she would measure for him the goyisher cemetery and use the string for wicks in making candles for the synagogue. Sometimes he'd even ask if it was permitted to perform the ceremony of *kappara,* or redemption by a scapegoat, with a stork instead of a hen or rooster. And as he asked her this he'd roar with laughter.

"*Gevalt, Pani* Rabinovitch!" the old woman would rebuke him. "Have God in your heart! What will you do when the Day of Judgment arrives?"

At this, Rabinovitch would laugh still more, and the old woman would leave his pharmacy with a heavy heart. She was so sorry for him! Such a diamond of a man, and yet what a scoffer!

The grief all this caused Gitteh-Nesheh turned into genuine heartache when the terrible news got around town that Rabinovitch had desecrated God's holy name in a very revolting fashion.

Berel the chandler told how he had gone to buy some castor oil for his Peshkeh and while he was in the pharmacy waiting to be served he saw Rabinovitch sell to the town priest his entire share of Paradise *for two rubles!*

The townfolk were scandalized by this shameful deed and the rabbi rent his garments in mourning.

Gitteh-Nesheh felt as if a thunderbolt had struck her in the head. At the very time that the townfolk were causing a din over the pharmacist's sacrilege the heart of the old woman bled for him with compassion.

"God in Heaven! What is he going to do now without even a tiny bit of the World-to-Come!"

She tried to console herself with the hope that the merit of his benefactions would come to his aid in the hour of final accounting. And yet she could find no comfort in this thought. So she walked about all day weeping and wringing her hands. In her secret heart she had always been fond of this apikoiros.

At night she had frightful dreams. She saw how Rabinovitch, dressed in his shroud, was cringing under the rod of the Avenging Angel who looked strangely like Savitzky the Orthodox priest. All of a sudden someone laughed. Looking up, she saw the pharmacist balancing himself on the point of the church steeple. He held a stork in his hand and was performing with it the rite of the scapegoat. And as she looked closer at the bird she saw that it wasn't a stork at all but Heshel the batlen.

She awoke shaking. She could barely get out of bed, but in her heart there sprang up a heroic resolve: she was going to save the unfortunate pharmacist from the torments of *kaf-hakela,* the punish-ment of the sinful soul at the hands of the evil spirits in Gihenom.

She herself would be happy to contribute for him a tenth part of her own share of Paradise. The question, however, was where would she get the rest!

"What's the use of worrying?" she thought. "I'll find good people and I'll make a collection."

And from that day on began her labors of collecting fragments of Paradise for the atheist Rabinovitch.

At first people laughed at her. Who had ever heard of a thing like that: to make one a gift of Paradise and especially to such a *trefniak* like Rabinovitch! Furthermore, if the truth be told, no one felt he had too much of a share of Paradise for his own self, and then to go and give away yet a part of it!

But Gitteh-Nesheh used to plead so long and weep while doing so, and describe all her dreams, to which she would even add a lot of other terrifying visions that she herself cooked up, so that her plead-ings could have moved a stone. In the end, people gave: one a hun-dredth part of his share of celestial bliss, another a thousandth part—she wouldn't go away empty-handed.

And Gitteh-Nesheh pursued her labors patiently and tirelessly for a whole year. On the anniversary of the awful catastrophe she added up all the contributions. With a shining face she discovered that it all totaled up to a portion of Paradise of which even a saint wouldn't have to feel ashamed.

All the time that she was making her collection she had not said a word about it to Rabinovitch. In fact, she avoided him as much as possible. She pictured to herself what a happy surprise he'd have when she'd come to present him with the gift!

The following morning Gitteh-Nesheh arose early, radiant with inner happiness. With almost light, girlish steps she hurried to the pharmacy. She opened the door, her heart beating like a hammer under her lean ribs.

"Pani Rabinovitch," she called out to him breathlessly, "I have come to salute you with a *mazl tov.*"

"Who me?" smiled the freethinker. "Where's the bride?"

Gitteh-Nesheh did not hear his witticism, because it was no laughing matter, for in the palm of her hand she was carrying the fate of a human being.

"Pani Rabinovitch," she began, "for a whole year I have worked without rest making a collection, and people had pity on you and each one made a gift of whatever he could."

"For me?" gasped Rabinovitch. He looked at her as if she had gone out of her mind.

"Yes, for you! Jews are a compassionate people. No one refused to give. Know that I've gathered for you a full portion of bliss in the World-to-Come."

Rabinovitch exploded with a wild laughter, and he couldn't stop.

"What? . . . . Does it mean then? . . . . In other words— you——" mumbled Gitteh-Nesheh, not knowing what to say.

Rabinovitch laughed so hard that the tears ran down his cheeks. And as she looked at him Gitteh-Nesheh wrung her hands as if her only son had just died before her very eyes. And, weeping bitterly, she shuffled out of the pharmacy.

COLD LOGIC

BY HEINRICH HEINE

Dear reader, should you ever come to Amsterdam, you must have the guide show you the Spanish Synagogue. That is a fine building, the roof resting on four colossal pillars. In the center stands the pulpit from where they had once pronounced the curse of excommunication against a scorner of the Mosaic Law—the hidalgo Don Benedict de Spinoza. On that occasion they blew on a horn called the *shofar*. There must be a terrifying association with that horn. For I read in the *Autobiography* of Solomon Maimon how the Rabbi of Altona once tried to make him, Kant's pupil, to return to his old religion. But when Maimon showed himself stiff-necked and persisted in holding on to his philosophical heresies, the rabbi grew threatening and showed him the shofar with these ominous words:

"Do you know what that is?"

"That? That's the horn of a goat," replied Kant's pupil very calmly.

At this the rabbi collapsed to the floor in horror.

YOM KIPPUR FRESSERS

BY SAMUEL ORNITZ

"Aren't you going to *schule* [synagogue]?" mother asked. She has just finished lighting and blessing the candles. A *yahrzeit* (death anniversary) candle lamp burned on the shelf over the stove in father's memory. It was the eve of sacred Yom Kippur.

I hardly heard her question, so engrossed was I in a book on criminal law. The door opened and Maxie Freund pussyfooted into the kitchen. He had just passed his Regents' examination with great ease—after paying one of the examiners twenty-five dollars, thereby sparing himself another year's preparation. Big Jim Hallorhan put me next to the examiner, and I arranged the easing detail for Maxie.

Maxie greeted Uncle Philip, who was lying stretched out upon the couch, smoking a pipe. Philip now used a pipe because it was more economical than cigarettes. It seems the more money he made, the more frugal he became. . . . "Good evening, Herr Capitalist, may your fast be a light one." . . . "May your fasts be many and heavy," responded Philip. Maxie wished mother a good year and a light fast, and then saluted me with "Good evening, Judge." . . . Philip puffed stentoriously, blowing little clouds of smoke over his head. Mother remonstrated with him: "Philip, what will the neighbors think and say to see you smoking on Yom Kippur?" To which Philip replied, "Let them shut their eyes, the scared jackasses."

Mother again pleads, "Meyer, please go to schule. It is Yom Kippur. Every Jew, no matter what an *Epikaros* [Epicurean] he may be the rest of the year, goes to schule one day—on Yom Kippur. Please, if only for my sake, go to schule." . . . I tell mother that I plan to spend the holy day in study, as law school opens the following week. Whereupon Maxie interposes in the singsong of the Talmudist, "On the other hand, your honor, I think attendance at the synagogue may be properly classified as part of your preparation for lawyership." . . . "How do you make that out?" inquires Philip, who credits Maxie with sharp wits. And Maxie reasons in this wise: "To begin with it keeps him before the eyes of a lot of people. It stamps him a solid, respectable member of the community. It gives him a chance to impress a number of people. Everybody needs a lawyer some time, and the man before their eyes is the most likely one they'll think of when that time comes." So Philip says, "Get off to schule, Meyer. Hereafter be a regular attendant, mind. Maxie is right. Strut before them. They'll take you to be the man you say you are. Impress them. Make yourself their lawyer, the only lawyer they'll think of. Stick your oar into their congregational affairs. Advertise yourself. Start off with giving them free advice. They'll pay well later on. Do things for them. Get them used to having *you* do things for them." . . . After which I and Maxie became regular schule-goers.

Yom Kippur morning I accompanied mother to schule. I noticed a crowd in front of the Talkers' Café. The onlookers were highly scandalized and offended. The Ghetto freeminded elements were publicly eating on the most sacred of sacred fast days. The superstitious expected to see the traducers stricken on the spot. The tolerant deplored their bad taste. In the window a large poster invited the public to come to a Yom Kippur picnic at North Beach. The Talkers' Café was the only restaurant open in the entire East Side. The news of the open, defiant sacrilege spread, and, by noontime, when I left the schule for a breath of air, I found a dense mob in front of the café. Indignation grew as the hungry fasters beheld the impudent unbelievers dine with ostentation. . . . Soon Boolkie and his lads used the ready contents of overflowing garbage cans with which to pelt the men and women who went in and out of the café. The dodging and fleeing of the calumniators amused the crowd. Boolkie, spurred by popular approval, then hurled a cobblestone which smashed the large plateglass window. This was received with an uproar of acclaim. Then began a shower of stones, bricks and any missile that came to hand, and the café became untenable. When the freethinkers rushed out of the bombarded position the crowd pursued them until they were dispersed in all directions. A few were caught and severely drubbed and the café was completely wrecked.

By this time the exercise and excitement had made the gangsters good and hungry. They could get nothing to eat at home. They had just stoned men and women who dared to eat openly on a holy fast day, and they themselves were now thinking of ways and means of getting food. Everybody is agreed that consistency is the height of cruelty. . . . Big Joe reported that he had a line on a lot of good stuff. Mrs.

Weingrad, he said, was in schule and her ice-box was crammed full of "yum-yum, boys." And he licked his chops, making everybody's mouth water as he described each delectable, giving us to understand his representations were as per tasted sample. It was too much for Boolkie. He hastened a detail of youngsters to raid the ice-box and bring the stuff to a secluded backyard in Canal Street. They returned forthwith with a large roast duck, *gefülte fisch,* white holiday bread, the light and toothsome *challah,* a variety of fruit and a big honey cake. Everybody cried out, " 'Yum-yum, boys,' is right; Yum-yum." So the champions of the fast observance made an excellent meal from the Weingrads' larder, fattened for an after-the-fast feast.

All of which reminded me that I was ravenously hungry and there was nothing to be had at home. I met Lillie and asked her if she were hungry. She just laughed. Lillie never did anything. She was the kind that was always made to do the thing. I told her to slip up to the station of the Third Avenue elevated, where I would wait for her. She just laughed, as much as to imply, well, the sin is on you, you're making me do it.

We got off at Fourteenth Street, where there were a number of Gentile restaurants. We could not get into any one of them. They were packed with my hungry co-religionists, and the waiters told me that Yom Kippur was their busiest day of the year. We had to walk up to Twenty-eighth Street before we could find an eating place with a free table. How we enjoyed the hearty meal! A fast day always puts an edge on an appetite. . . . I hurried back to the synagogue and was in time for the solemn closing services. In all it was an interesting day.

INCREASED HORSE POWER

A Jewish rustic, whose soul was heavy with sin, decided to visit a rabbi in a neighboring town to ask for his intercession with God. When he returned home from this visit the rabbi of his own town asked him reproachfully:

"Isn't one rabbi enough for you? Must you have two?"

"You know how it is, Rabbi," answered the farmer. "Two horses can pull a wagon out of the mud better than one!"

Intellectuals always have microscopes
before their eyes.—Albert Einstein

An old Jew in Lithuania went to the village post office.
"When does the post leave for Gomel?" he inquired.
"Every day."
"Thursday too?"

One can positively never be deceived
if one mistrusts everything in the world,
even one's own skepticism.—Arthur Schnitzler

THE FOOL'S LIST

The caliph, who enjoyed scoffing at others, commanded his Jewish jester to write down all the foolish things everybody at court said or did.

"Is my name on your list?" the caliph once asked him.

"Indeed it is, O Caliph!" replied the jester.

"What have I said or done that is so foolish?" asked the caliph, offended.

"Only a week ago," replied the jester, "you gave ten thousand dinars to a Turk to buy you a string of pearls. How do you know he'll come back?"

"The Turk is honest!" the caliph insisted. "You'll see, he'll bring me the pearls before long. And if he does, what will you say then?"

"If he does," rejoined the jester, "then I'll take your name off my list of fools and put his on."

Chutzpaniks · IMPUDENT FELLOWS

When a chutzpanik *beats you up*
he yells "gevalt!"

FLEA SONG

BY YEHUDAH AL-CHARIZI (THIRTEENTH CENTURY)

You ruthless flea, who desecrate my couch,
    And draw my blood to sate your appetite,
You know not rest, on Sabbath day or feast—
    Your feast it is when you can pinch and bite.

My friends expound the law: to kill a flea
    Upon the Sabbath day a sin they call;
But I prefer that other law which says,
    Be sure a murderer's malice to forestall.

REST IN PEACE

To the proprietor's polite question, "Did you sleep well last night?" the irate guest retorted:

"How could I sleep? I found a dead bedbug on my pillow!"

"You're making a mountain out of a molehill, my friend," the innkeeper rebuked him with sarcasm. "Did the dead bedbug bite you?"

"Of course not! But you should have seen the grand funeral all his relatives and friends gave him!"

A chutzpanik can walk straight into Paradise.

TWO PLEASURES
TOLD BY YOINA THE SHADCHAN

BY Z. WENDROFF
TRANSLATED FROM THE YIDDISH BY NATHAN AUSUBEL

Do you want to know whether a *shadchan* ever collects a big broker's fee when he successfully sees through a match? Oy, oy, believe me, sometimes it adds up to hundreds of rubles! To talk about the important shadchan of national reputation is beside the point. For instance, it is told that when Leibele Brisker negotiated the match between the millionaire Brodsky from Kiev and Poliakov from Moscow he got nine thousand smackers for his fee—yes that's what he got! Why even I once got a cool thousand from two parties I brought together.

Sometimes it happens that the expected fee is smaller. Suddenly the proposition is dropped like a hot potato and for the same boy and girl you've now got to scratch out of somewhere two new and separate matches! Would you believe it, from one young fellow I collected my shadchan's fee three separate times over!

Let me tell you the odd story.

It was some time between Purim and Pesach—you know that's the worst time for a shadchan. People are too busy then with the holidays to bother their heads about marriage. One day, after the evening service in the synagogue, the thought began to gnaw away at my brain: where do I get a few rubles to pay for the barest necessities? About the expenses for Pesach I was even afraid to think. I racked my brains but I couldn't think of anything, not even how I might be able to make enough for a few postage stamps. Actually, there wasn't one householder in town with a marriageable son or daughter from whom I had not already taken money "for a postage stamp."

None the less, I had to lay my hands on a few groschen and right away too! How could I show my face at home without bringing even a loaf of bread? It suddenly occurred to me, why not call on Reb Hersch? True enough, his daughter was no more than a calf, barely seventeen years old at the time. But someone told me that he'd like to marry her off. Whatever it was, one thing was certain—Reb Hersch might be induced to give me enough for a "postage stamp."

So I went wading through the thick mud on the road to Reb

Hersch's house. I entered the dark vestibule and began groping for the doorknob. I felt along one wall, then another, and only when I reached the third wall did my fingers find a large iron knob. I opened the door and found myself standing in a dark storeroom. During the *Sukkos* festival it served as a *sukkah,* but for the rest of the year it was the storage place for barrels of cabbage, kegs of pickles, sacks of potatoes, and many other necessary articles for which there was no place in the kitchen.

I realized that I had blundered into the wrong place and began to grope my way out. But the Devil must have had a hand in it for I collided with a discarded double window and together with it I fell into a tub of water containing the day's wash.

I got up wringing wet and began to grope my way again with my hands extended before me like a blind man. But, forgetting my feet for a mere instant, I stumbled again and fell smack into a box of chicken feathers.

I pulled myself out as best as I could, and at long last found the door to the interior of the house. I entered the kitchen with my arms extended, the water dripping from me as from the roof during Pesach, and covered from head to foot with chicken feathers. You may believe me, I must have looked like a bird from the other side of the mythical Sambatyon River. When the youngest child of the house saw me she got frightened and began to bleat:

"Oy, Mama, I'm afraid! An eagle!"

"Don't be afraid, you little fool," her mama tried to soothe her. "That's no eagle—that's Reb Yoina. Can't you see his beard?"

Hearing this, her sisters exploded with laughter. The girls squeaked so that, honest, I felt like throwing up.

And there I stood, my face like fire.

"Nu, what idiotic things can happen to a human being?" I stammered lamely.

This too made the youngsters shriek with laughter and they simply wouldn't stop!

"What are you bleating at, you goats—at what? And you, my fine *kaleh maydel,*[1] aren't you ashamed of yourself?"

"I-I-I just can't stop! Hi-hi-hi!" shrieked the kaleh maydel.

"Nu, nu, enough! And you Reb Yoina, you'll do well to take off your overcoat and stand by the oven and dry up a bit."

I didn't have to be coaxed. I took off my wet garment and stood

---

[1]*Marriageable girl.*

dripping beside the hot oven. I'm telling you—you never saw so much steam in all your life, I'm willing to bet, except perhaps in a steam bath, as there came out of my clothes that time!

"Do you feel cold, Reb Yoina?" asked Reb Hersch. "Sit down at the table and have a glass of tea. A little brandy before, maybe? You should try and get a bit warm, ha?"

So we sat down at the table. I took a drop of brandy, drank two glasses of tea, but still I shivered.

One thing I know: that when you tremble with the cold the best thing to do is drink a glass of punch. Do you know what punch is? It's a sweet glass of tea with a pony of brandy in it. But how could I even think of making punch in *that* house? You don't know Sureh-Feigeh, Reb Hersch's wife! For a lump of sugar she's ready to jab your eyes out!

So I hung around the kitchen for a while, and, when no one was looking, I slipped three pieces of sugar into my glass and, to top it off, poured into it a nice drop of brandy! I wrapped my fingers around the glass so that Sureh-Feigeh shouldn't see what I had done. Quietly I crushed the sugar with my spoon against the wall of the glass and chatted with Reb Hersch.

"I'm telling you, Reb Hersch, have I got a match for you—one in the world!" I told him. "The boy is handsome—really very handsome! Do you want education? He's got education! Do you want good manners? He's got good manners! In short, he's got good looks, he's got education, he's got good manners. He's also got an income, and he's got—and—and—what else do you want?"

It was my rotten luck that Sureh-Feigeh should suddenly come near me. Naturally, I didn't want her to see the sugar in my glass of tea, and so, to remove all the tell-tale evidence, I began to crush the remaining bits of sugar with my spoon. Maybe I felt too strong that day, but I crushed so hard that the bottom of the glass fell out with the sugar.

Oy vay! You should have seen the hot tea pouring over the table-cloth and from the tablecloth onto my knees! Do you know, if at that moment the grave would have opened for me I would have jumped into it gladly. It wasn't so much that I scalded my legs with the hot tea as the shame I felt being caught red-handed by Sureh-Feigeh.

"Hm-m! How did sugar ever get into my glass?" I asked with pretended amazement.

You see I wanted her to think that Reb Hersch put it in the glass without my knowing it.

At this the youngsters exploded again with laughter.

But I want you to know that Reb Hersch is a very refined person; he didn't want to offend me. So he tried to brush the matter off:

"Nu, nu, it's nothing terrible," he said.

Sureh-Feigeh herself joked off the accident.

"Good! A glass broke so it's a sure sign that we'll soon break earthen pots for an engagement! Who's the groom's father, who?"

"The groom's father?" I answered, taking quick advantage of the opening. "You know him, he's a local man, Reb Tzemach Brantzitzer. You know, the one who holds a lease on the forest in Brantzitz."

"Nu, nu," muttered Reb Hersch with a deprecating wave of the hand. "Nothing to get excited about! And what does the boy do himself, tell me?"

"The boy works for his father."

"And how is he in . . . in——"

"Don't you worry, Reb Hersch! This is a young fellow who can satisfy both God and men!"

"I don't expect him to be too educated. For my part, I'd prefer if he didn't know too much about this modern foolishness. But what can I do? Go and start up with girls nowadays! They insist that the boys they marry must be modern. The most important thing, Reb Yoina, is that he should be decent, he should know how to behave properly in company and be a bit of a Jew besides. Do you understand what I mean?"

"He's exactly what you're looking for, Reb Hersch!"

To tell the truth—I can say it to you confidentially—I didn't have much confidence in this match myself. The young fellow was an empty pot. He had already been engaged once before, and to a girl I myself proposed to him. Actually, he was "no suit of clothes" for Reb Hersch's daughter. All I was interested in, naturally, was to get the money for a few "postage stamps," and, in order to realize that, I was quite ready to pair together a number eighteen with a number thirteen and call it a perfect match. I didn't hesitate to make the suggestion that I needed several rubles for some postage stamps, because I had to correspond with Reb Tzemach Brantzitzer.

But Reb Hersch didn't take kindly to the idea of writing. He had a better suggestion to make: since the match looked very attractive to him, he wanted me not to cause any long delay by writing but the very next morning I should go in person to Reb Tzemach and feel his fatherly pulse. I was to find out whether he would seriously consider the match. And if he did, I was to bring the lad down at once.

"I'll give you money for the journey," said Reb Hersch.

In short, I went to see Reb Tzemach and he agreed to the match. So I brought the young fellow back with me on the return trip, just as Reb Hersch had asked me to do. A day or two later he brought his mama down, and eight days after that earthen pots were broken at the engagement. I got one hundred and sixty rubles for my fee for the second time from Reb Tzemach. In addition, he sent me a gift of a cord of birch firewood.

You can see now why it was that I had a merry Pesach. That little pile of money all in a lump was nothing to sneeze at either. In fact, things got even jollier right after Pesach. Let me tell you about it, if you're interested.

The first days of Pesach the groom was to spend with the bride's family and the last days of the festival the bride was to celebrate with the groom's family. Two days before Pesach the groom arrived, and by the time the festival began the bride was all burned up for love of him. Her little sisters were also thoroughly smitten with him and her mother was passing out from *naches*.

Only Reb Hersch was dissatisfied with the groom. He remarked:

"There's something peculiar about the fellow . . . well, one might say he's a bit too gay! Too much ha, ha, ha with the girls in the corners, you know. We eat hot rolls and milk the morning of Pesach Eve and he makes wisecracks; I perform the rite of burning the leavened bread in the house and he gets a leer on his face. Very peculiar!"

Unlike her father, the bride was melting with pleasure over everything her intended said and did. What a scream of a fellow! What a wag! Did you see the funny imitation he gave of papa going from room to room with the feather duster and sweeping all the bread crumbs from the window sills at the ceremony of burning the unleavened bread! One could die laughing! He was just too comical for words! And oh how "modern" he was; she had never dreamed of having such luck, a blessing on him!

But how "modern" her intended really was she first discovered at the first *Seder* night.

Returning with his future father-in-law from the synagogue, the groom immediately buried his face in a newspaper he had brought with him from home. From time to time he winked to his intended, as if to say: "Nu, what have you got to say about these foolish ceremonies? We moderns don't believe in such things!"

When they sat down at the table for the Seder home service he put his newspaper near him and joined the others in reading the

Haggadah with an indulgent expression, as if to say, "I'm doing this only to please the old folks. Am I doing right, little pigeon?" And "the little pigeon" smiled back approvingly at him.

When Reb Hersch started filling the first of "the four cups" with wine the groom once more winked to the bride and demonstratively absorbed himself in the newspaper.

Reb Hersch had no sons. It was therefore customary for one of his daughters to recite the traditional Four Questions in the service. On this occasion he wanted to honor his future son-in-law with the recitation. A son-in-law is almost like a son, no?

So he looked at the fellow and said to him:

"Nu, *chosen bocher,*[1] how about putting away your newspaper and reciting for me the Four *Kashes?*"

Such an honor the fellow hadn't expected, and he plainly showed his displeasure.

What was he going to do—make himself foolish before his little pigeon? What would she think of him?

A clever idea struck him. He was going to get out of the mess with a joke. He winked to the kaleh, as if to say: "Just watch me, and you'll see what a piece of comical business I'm going to pull now!"

"The Four Kashes?" he began mockingly. "Why only four? I could put to you at least twenty-four questions. All right, let me ask. My first question is: Does a Jew get a sore on his rear end every Pesach Eve since he has to sit on cushions? My second question is: Why drink only twice—wouldn't it be easier to drink it down in one gulp? My third question is: Are we turkeys that we have to gobble up *knaydlach* on Pesach? My fourth question is:——"

But he never got around to finish the fourth question. At the first question Reb Hersch fixed on him eyes full of incredulity, at the second he grew as red as a beet, and barely had the fellow begun to ask the fourth when he let go at him—a smack on one cheek and a smack on the other. "Smack—smack, smack—smack," it went.

"That's my answer to your first question, you impudent lout!" shouted Reb Hersch [smack—smack]. "And there you have my answer to your second question, you brazen donkey [smack—smack]! And this one, you cheap scoffer, is my answer to your third question [smack—smack]! And now let me give you the answer, you miserable worm, to all your impudent, insolent, and insulting questions [smack—smack]!"

The bride's mother jumped up as if she had been scalded with

[1] *Marriageable lad.*

hot water. At each smack the girls let out a squeak. The bride fainted dead away. As for the groom—he, as the saying goes, "picked up hands and feet," and ran out of the house, forgetting even to take his newspaper with him.

When I first heard about it in the synagogue the following morning I got a twofold pleasure from it. First of all, I was glad that Reb Hersch was spared having that scamp as a son-in-law. Secondly, I could look forward to earning another broker's fee with a brand new match for the good-for-nothing!

FOR LOVE

A *shadchan* once came to a young man with a marriage proposal.

"I have a girl, a regular *tzatzkeh* for you!" he said. "But really, a beauty!"

"Don't talk nonsense!" answered the young man, annoyed.

"Nu," said the shadchan, "if you aren't interested in looks, maybe you're interested in a girl with money. I know one who'll bring you a dowry of five thousand rubles!"

"Leave me alone, please," begged the young man.

The shadchan sighed.

"You're certainly hard to please! . . . Good enough—I've another girl who has a dowry of twenty thousand rubles."

"See here!" snapped the young man. "Money is no object with me!"

"In that case then," said the shadchan hopefully, "you must be anxious to marry into a good family. Why, I've just the girl for you! She has four generations of rabbis among her ancestors!"

"Don't waste your breath!" interrupted the young man in disgust. "If ever I'll marry it will be only for love!"

"Oh, so you want love!" exclaimed the shadchan, his face brightening. "Why didn't you say so in the first place? I've that kind too!"

A-AH! PLEASURE!

Pleasures of the Rich

*When you've got a lot of money
you're both wise and handsome
—and my! how well you sing!*

In ghetto society, where almost everyone was poor, a rich Jew
was conspicuous by his rarity. It's easy to say: "a rich Jew"! Actually
he was only relatively rich as contrasted with the poverty of most of
his fellow Jews. There were only varying degrees of poverty in the
ghetto. A poor man standing on the bottommost rung of the ladder
of destitution would look up with dazzled eyes at the Jew holding on
precariously to the uppermost rung and he'd exclaim: "Ai-ai! Just
look—a nogid, a rich man!" That is undoubtedly the economic origin
for the quip often heard among American Jews, a carry-over from
other times.

"Tsk-tsk! Is he rich! A millionaire, I'm telling you!"

"A millionaire! You don't say so! Do you really think he's worth
as much as ten thousand dollars?"

Naturally, the special pleasures of any rich man are derived from
his possession of money. But in Jewish humor it isn't so much how
the rich man views his own privileged pleasures but what the poor
man conceives them to be. And the latter appraises them more in droll
pity than in envy, and often with satirical belittlement. The folk Jew,
for instance, asks: "What does Baron Rothschild do that we poor Jews
don't?" And he answers himself with a knowing wink: "What does he
do? Good God, he has nothing to do all day long! His servants do
everything for him. They help him put on his clothes so that he doesn't
even have to put his hand in cold water. He's got so many suits of
clothes and changes of underwear that he is kept busy dressing all the
time. He pulls on and he pulls off, pulls on and pulls off. Why, it's
enough to drive a person crazy!"

But one mustn't make the mistake of imagining that the realistic
Jew, who got his education in the hard school of the world for a very
high tuition fee, is not soberly aware of the power of money. In his
heart he may despise it as dross and capable of doing evil among men,
none the less, he gives the Devil his due. The Yiddish folksaying con-
cedes: "Money rules the world." This has its analogue in the terse
Americanism: "Money talks."

Apropos of the irreverent attitude Jewish tradition has toward *riches and rich men, in the writings of the Prophets and in several books of the Apocrypha the word "wicked" is sometimes used interchangeably with the word "rich." And as for the pleasures that money can buy, listen to dour Jesus Ben Sira, always with a jaundiced eye on the future: "When a man dies he inherits worms, maggots, lice, and other creeping things."*

The pleasures of the rich! "Pleasures you call them?" asks the poor Jew pityingly.

Nor, for that matter, are the pleasures of the poor treated with anything but facetious irony in Jewish humor. That is the folklore pattern which has gone over into literature as well. What it is trying to say is this: If the rich don't enjoy their pleasures, and if wealth cannot buy happiness, neither is poverty the virtue it is credited to be, and, believe me, it's no great pleasure either. The sly Yiddish saying puts it this way:

"What are three things hardest for man to bear?"

"Heart disease, stomach trouble, and worst of all—an empty purse."

N.A.

TWO GREAT MEN

BY S. AN-SKY (SOLOMON RAPPOPORT)
TRANSLATED FROM THE YIDDISH BY NATHAN AUSUBEL

Far, far away, on the other side of the ocean in the land of the English, there lived Reb Moishe Montefiore.[1] He was a great man in Israel, and his fame resounded from one end of the world to the other. He was royal counselor to the English Queen. Without his advice she wouldn't take a single step. The greatest princes and lords of the realm fell on their faces before him. Even rulers of other countries delighted in bestowing on him great honor.

Reb Moishe Montefiore possessed incalculable riches. He owned

[1]*Sir Moses Montefiore (1784–1885), famous Jewish philanthropist. He was Sheriff for the City of London at the time of Queen Victoria's coronation and subsequently acted as her close adviser. His intercession for the Jews during the ritual murder trial in Damascus in 1840 and his championing of the Jewish cause before Czar Nicholas I in 1846 turned him into a Jewish national hero in the eyes of the common folk. His power, benevolences, and devotion to his people made him the subject of many East European legends, of which this is one, treated in folkloristic literary form.*

many wells of quicksilver and they kept drawing from them full pails both day and night and yet they never reached bottom. And quicksilver, as everyone knows, is more valuable than ordinary silver. Some even say that it is more precious than gold. From all this one can well imagine how rich Reb Moishe Montefiore was!

He lived in a princely palace which was adorned with gold and silver, with precious stones and pearls. Hundreds of servants waited on him, and, when he wished to leave his home, it had to be in a golden carriage drawn by eight fiery horses. And before him hastened footrunners calling out: "Make way, make way for Milord Reb Moishe Montefiore!"

Let no one think though that Reb Moishe Montefiore acquired such celebrity throughout the whole world merely because of his great power and riches. It was mostly on account of his acts of loving-kindness and for his devoted efforts on behalf of all Israel. Whenever a misfortune befell Jews (may God protect them), whether it was a pogrom, a slanderous accusation, an expulsion, or some other evil decree, Reb Moishe immediately leaped forward like a lion to protect his brothers, even if he had to go to the other end of the world in order to do so. He'd hasten to the Queen and fall at her feet and implore her aid for his unfortunate brethren. He'd make journeys to the courts of the rulers of other countries, poured out his gold left and right, and could not rest until he had succeeded in voiding the hateful decree. At the same time he was also a great philanthropist. He built synagogues and *yeshivas,* supported thousands of Jews so they could sit undisturbed and study the Torah. He also helped the poor, raised up the fallen, and was a father to widows and orphans. And to all that he was *takkeh* very pious and with great devotion fulfilled all the precepts and commandments.

Just the same, since it isn't possible that there should be in the world one single person without some fault, Reb Moishe Montefiore also had a great shortcoming. What he lacked *nebbech* was learning in the Torah.

To be sure he was no ignoramus, God forbid! On the contrary, he had a good understanding of a page in the Talmud. Every day he'd study a special text, and not just so but *takkeh* with notes and commentaries, as it should be! Only . . . you see . . . there wasn't in his learning, how shall I say it, any subtlety, any depth. He lacked the required sharpness, the flame. . . .

Reb Moishe Montefiore understood this shortcoming but too well and therefore he took it greatly to heart.

II

At the very time when the fame of Reb Moishe Montefiore was resounding through the world, there lived in the city of Minsk, in Lithuania, the Gaon Reb Gershon Tanchum. He, too, was a great man in Israel and his fame was spread wide over all the world. He knew the whole Mishnah by heart. There wasn't one work of sacred lore that he hadn't read; there wasn't one piece of Talmud interpretation with which he was not familiar. Within him, too, gushed wells of quicksilver, only they were the quicksilver of wisdom. No matter how much he would draw from them they'd still remain full to the brim. He, too, built great palaces, but of thoughts and philosophic speculations, and with the greatest of ease he strolled about the orchards and vineyards of the most delightful tales in Talmud and Midrash. His intellectual treasures he, too, shared with others and with a full hand. All those who hungered and thirsted after the word of God he satisfied and slaked.

But as it was with Reb Moishe Montefiore so it was also with Reb Gershon Tanchum. He, too, lacked *something*. For all his wisdom and greatness, he was a wretched pauper. His income as rabbi was exactly two gulden a week, and, being blessed with many children, he suffered hunger and need.

III

The day came at last when the report about Reb Gershon Tanchum in Minsk reached the ears of Reb Moishe Montefiore in London. Thereupon, Reb Moishe promptly decided to engage him as his own private *melamed* to teach him Torah. And whenever Reb Moishe Montefiore decided to do something it wasn't very hard for him to carry it out, as you can well understand. So said, so done! He ordered that the eight fiery horses be harnessed to his golden carriage, and away he rode to Minsk. On the way, as was his custom, he threw from the window of his carriage heaps of gold pieces along both sides of the road. He didn't even bother to look back to see who was picking up the money; whether a Jew or a goy, it was all the same to him.

You ought to know that the distance between the country of the English and Minsk is very great indeed. But what did it matter when one rode in a carriage drawn by eight fleet horses? In a few days' time Reb Moishe Montefiore was already in Minsk.

He stopped his carriage right in the middle of the market place and inquired of the passers-by: "Where does Reb Gershon Tanchum live?" They pointed out to him a little old hut in an alley behind the synagogue courtyard. Reb Moishe Montefiore went in.

As he entered he saw Reb Gershon poring intently over a book of sacred lore. Reb Moishe Montefiore went over to him and said:

"*Rebbe!* I would like you to know that I am Moishe Montefiore!"

When Reb Gershon Tanchum heard these words he hastily arose and pronounced the benediction which one must always say on beholding a wise man: "Blessed art thou, O Lord our God, King of the Universe, who hast given of thy wisdom to mortals." Having said this he then welcomed his visitor. Reb Moishe Montefiore greeted him in turn and said:

"I want you to know, Reb Gershon Tanchum, that I have decided to take you for my rebbe. Your household I will furnish with all its needs, but you I'll take along with me. You'll live with me in my palace in London. You will sit at my table and will receive from me enough money for all your personal needs, for shoes and for clothes, also for a bath and for snuff."

Reb Gershon Tanchum heard him speak thus and did not know what to answer. How could he turn down Reb Moishe Montefiore when he had made a special trip for him in his golden carriage? Just the same, he answered him that he first had to talk it over with his wife and also get permission from the community.

When Reb Gershon had done all this, Reb Moishe Montefiore counted out ten thousand gold pieces for the household. Then he seated Reb Gershon Tanchum next to him in the golden carriage, and away they sped in a good hour.

IV

When they arrived in the country of the English the first thing Reb Moishe Montefiore did was to take Reb Gershon Tanchum over his estates. He showed him all his wells with quicksilver, all the towns and villages, fields and forests, orchards and vineyards he owned. He said to him:

"Rebbe! Lift up your eyes and look about you! Everything that you see, and more, is all mine!"

Reb Gershon Tanchum looked and was filled with wonder. It had never occurred to him that one person could possess so many estates.

Afterwards, Reb Moishe Montefiore led him into his palace and showed him through all the rooms. One room was more beautiful than the other and all were adorned with gold and silver, and precious stones and pearls, and on the walls hung the most priceless of tapestries. Reb Gershon Tanchum looked about him and was struck dumb with amazement. Such beauty he had never seen, not even in a dream.

Finally, Reb Moishe Montefiore led him into the largest room. It was lit up by the light which came from diamonds and precious stones. On the walls of the balcony were painted the sun and the moon and all the stars and they all turned round and round in accordance with the time of day. Across the entire length of the room stood a silver table covered with a cloth of gold. And on the table was served the finest foods and the most expensive wines in bottles of pure crystal. On one side of the table sat the foremost Gentile princes, counts, and lords, and on the other side the richest and foremost Jews in the kingdom of the English. A multitude of servants were waiting on them.

As soon as Reb Moishe Montefiore made his appearance, all the assembled rose to their feet, bowed low before him, and cried out as with one voice:

"Long live Milord Reb Moishe Montefiore!"

When Reb Gershon Tanchum saw what great honor they were all showing Reb Moishe Montefiore he was overawed. When the servants placed before him the most delicious foods he could not raise his spoon to his mouth, for his hands and feet shook with great fright before the riches, greatness, and honor of Reb Moishe Montefiore.

v

When the meal was over, the Gentile princes, counts, and lords made their departure. Then Reb Moishe Montefiore arose from his seat and called out with a grand air:

"And now let Reb Gershon Tanchum expound Torah for us!"

Reb Gershon Tanchum wanted to begin expounding Torah, but out of great fright he could not even open his mouth. Once more Reb Moishe Montefiore repeated his order:

"Let Reb Gershon Tanchum expound Torah for us!"

Hereupon, Reb Gershon Tanchum girded himself with courage and began to expound Torah in a low quivering voice. And as he spoke, Reb Moishe Montefiore listened to him, and the more he heard the more enthused he was over Reb Gershon's great learning.

And then Reb Gershon Tanchum mustered up new strength. All

of a sudden, he forgot about Reb Moishe Montefiore's vast estates. From his thoughts fled all the wells of quicksilver, all the fields and forests, the orchards and vineyards. His voice ceased its trembling. Soon he was lost in the vast forests of Talmudic interpretation. And Reb Moishe Montefiore listened to him and was staggered by the extent of his wisdom.

Once more Reb Gershon Tanchum girded himself with courage. He now forgot all about the palace and the magnificently decorated rooms, forgot all about the delicious foods, about the princes, the counts, and the lords. He forgot about all the honor that they accorded Reb Moishe Montefiore. Now his voice rose and grew in power. And as with the sweep of a bird he soared over the Paradise gardens of the Talmud. Reb Moishe Montefiore was already stirred by this illumination, and he listened to him with great awe.

Finally, when Reb Gershon Tanchum forgot completely about his surroundings he soared aloft to the highest mountain peaks of the Torah and then descended into its profoundest depths. And his face became aflame and his voice thundered like the roar of a lion.

Gripped with terror, Reb Moishe Montefiore could no longer sit in his place: his hands and feet began to shake. . . .

A rich man hates honor like a cat hates cream.

If you're lucky everybody says you're smart.

A NOGID'S LUCK

BY TASHRAK (ISRAEL J. ZEVIN)
TRANSLATED FROM THE YIDDISH BY NATHAN AUSUBEL

Rich Mr. Abraham Silverman, President of Congregation Anshe Glupsk, fell ill. The doctors prepared his closest of kin for his approaching end; his death was expected at any moment. The brothers of the congregation went about making the necessary preparations for the burial. They decided on the best cemetery plot for their honored president, for he was an outstanding community leader, a man of affairs, and a model citizen besides. Mr. Silverman was the sort of person who didn't like anyone to hold any grievances against him. He always paid his debts promptly, liked to have everything "clear and even" in all his relations with people.

But when he realized that the hour of his death was approaching, he started worrying how he could enter Heaven "clear and even" so that there also no one would have any grievance against him. He knew that even the holiest of saints have some sins on their consciences, sins that are recorded against their account in Heaven and for which they get their full measure of punishment.

Then a happy thought struck him: "Why can't I sell all my sins to another Jew? I'll even be largehanded with him! I'll give him as much as he'll ask, for I'd like to get to Heaven with a clean slate and go directly to my seat in Paradise."

Now in his Congregation Anshe Glupsk was a poor *melamed* who had one great aim in life, and that was to save a thousand dollars, buy himself a farm in the Catskills and till the soil. In this way, he thought, he'd be rid of his wretched Hebrew teaching once and for all. Unfortunately, it wasn't possible for him in his profession to put by even one thousand pennies in all the years. Nevertheless, he never gave up dreaming and talking about the farm he'd someday be able to buy.

It was this melamed that the *nogid,* Mr. Silverman, sent for.

"Reb Zalman," he said to him, "would you like to get well fixed in life? I'm going to give you the chance."

"May you live to be a hundred and twenty years, Mr. President!" the melamed answered fervently. "I'll never forget you! I'll study *Mishnayos* in your memory every day of my life and I'll recite Psalms for the peace of your soul too."

The half-lifeless lips of the nogid moved in a happy smile and he said to the melamed:

"I'm going to give you one thousand dollars, in cash too, but on one condition: provided you buy all my sins from me! You see, I want to get to Heaven with a clean soul!"

"What are you saying, Mr. Silverman!" gasped the melamed. "What could the sins of a good man like you amount to? I'm sure not more than ten cents! You're such an upright Jew, such a generous philanthropist, such an important contributor for the support of the synagogue, so many times called up to read from Scripture on the Sabbath, and as for meritorious deeds—why who can count them? How does a man like you come to sins?"

"Just the same, Reb Zalman, I'm offering you a thousand dollars if you'll agree to take over all my sins. Let's have the agreement quickly, time is short. We'll draw up a contract and after you have signed it, I'll give you the money."

The melamed was wide-eyed with amazement. He couldn't understand his luck! When he examined the ten yellow one hundred dollar bills that Mr. Silverman's manager gave him a few minutes later he was bowled over. "Long may you live!" he murmured, deeply moved. "I'll recite the *Kaddish* after you like for my own father!"

"I'll tell you what I'll do," added Mr. Silverman hastily, "I'll give you an extra hundred dollars if you'll agree to take over whatever sins I may commit until the moment of my death. You can see I haven't long to live, but I know that a human being is capable of sinning down to his last gasp. He can sin if not in his actions, at least with his tongue or even in his thoughts. Therefore, I'm more than ready to give you a hundred dollars, if you'll agree to be responsible for all my sins from now until the moment I die."

The melamed readily agreed, and, pocketing the extra hundred, he went home rejoicing.

II

When the melamed told his wife and children of his good fortune there was jubilation in their home.

"Basheh!" he cried gleefully. "I'm no more a melamed and you're no longer a street peddler! No longer will I have to grind away in *cheder* with the little bummers, and you won't have to sell hot chickpeas on the street anymore. Tomorrow you'll buy new clothes for the children. You'll also get them new shoes made of the very best leather. And now, wife, let's celebrate! Fix a fine dinner for us, buy a calf's tongue, some goose livers, chicken *pupiklech* and *gribbenes*. Get everything of the best; don't stint on money. And while you're cooking the dinner I'll go out and buy a bottle of wine."

Three hours later the melamed sat down to dinner with his family and devoured a feast he had never seen even in a dream.

But what should the happy, half-starved *schlemihl* do? He packed away so much food and poured into himself so much wine that he did not have strength enough to get up from the table. He fell asleep where he sat.

The following morning he awoke a very sick man. They called the doctor. After examining him the doctor said that the patient had overeaten and was suffering from a serious stomach upset. Despite all the medicines the doctor gave him the melamed felt worse and worse, and, when all hope was abandoned for him, he made ready to recite the Confession before death.

At this very time the great nogid, Mr. Silverman, underwent a remarkable change in his condition. Immediately after he had sold his sins to Reb Zalman, the melamed, he began to feel better. It could even be that the joy he felt upon his soul's purification brought about his recovery. The doctors were amazed as they watched his rapid improvement. The following morning they declared him to be out of danger.

But as he got better so the melamed grew worse. The very same day that the nogid got out of bed Reb Zalman heaved his last and they laid broken shards over his eyes.

III

When the melamed arrived in the World of Truth they brought him before the Heavenly Judgment Seat. They informed him that a big reckoning was to be added up against his account. First of all, there were his own sins, and then there were the sins of the nogid, Mr. Abraham Silverman, which he had bought.

When they piled up his own sins in the Heavenly Scales before his very eyes the melamed merely smiled. They were so few and such emaciated little sins! He had been tortured so much in the sinful world below and had so little opportunity to sin. But when he took a look at the sins he had bought from the nogid, Mr. Silverman, the great philanthropist, the upright man, the honest merchant and eminent president of Congregation Anshe Glupsk, he almost died a second time from fright! What a heap of sins, recorded on hundreds of account sheets! Who would have believed it of such a righteous man! Oy vay! Where did he ever find the time and the energy to commit them all? In the Heavenly Book of Accounts they were recorded not in ink but in red and black flames.

Could anybody have said of Mr. Silverman that he wasn't an honest merchant? Didn't he pay his bills regularly? Did he even once give false weight and measure? But ah! woe to him, he didn't pay the people who worked for him enough to make a living! He kept a sweatshop, forced them to slave for his profit from seven in the morning until eleven at night, so that in time they became estranged from their own families. And because fathers never had a chance to see and guide their children, the children followed evil paths. Therefore, all the sins of all the neglected children of all his workers were recorded in the Book of Accounts against him. And, although all these sins were not committed by Reb Zalman the melamed, nevertheless, by the strict interpretation of the law, they were charged against him.

"Five hundred years of Purgatory!" was the sentence pronounced by the angelic Chief Judge against the poor melamed. "And after you're through with this sentence you'll be flung into the bottom-most abyss of *Gihenom* for one hundred and seventy-five more years. Only after that will you be punished for your own sins. And for these sins the sentence is that you are to stand barefoot on the sharp points of nails for thirteen minutes and twenty seconds."

And no sooner was the sentence pronounced than the melamed was whisked away to Purgatory.

IV

As soon as the nogid got off his sickbed the first thing he did was to ask after Reb Zalman, the melamed. When they told him that he had died he raised his hands to Heaven, and murmured: "Blessed be the Just God! It is better for Reb Zalman that he died so fast, because that much sooner he'll be able to begin his punishment for my sins and the sooner he'll be purified."

Now everybody knows that it is the way of a businessman after he has had a profitable year to try to do even better the next year, either by cutting expenses or by increasing the profits, or by doing both. As time went on it began to sink in on Mr. Silverman that he had done a much better piece of business with the melamed than he had thought at first. Could anybody blame him if he were to try now to draw all the profit possible from his little deal with Reb Zalman?

He recalled that they had agreed that the melamed should take on himself all the sins that he, the nogid, would commit *until the moment of his death*. In other words, he, Mr. Silverman, had every right to sin as much as he liked because it wouldn't be he but Reb Zalman who'd be punished for it. Was there anything wrong if he were to enjoy himself a bit during his remaining life on earth? What a bargain—to have fun and yet not be charged with any sin!

With clean conscience Mr. Silverman had one marvelous time by day and by night. The members of the Congregation Anshe Glupsk were aghast.

"*Gevalt,* Brother President!" they cried. "Don't you know that you're doing everything that's forbidden? You eat *tréf,* you smoke on the Sabbath, and you do a lot of other horrible things for which you deserve being thrown out of the Congregation."

"I can do anything I like and yet I won't be punished for it!" answered the nogid triumphantly. "My soul is safe!"

V

With a sorrowful heart Reb Zalman the melamed began his five-hundred-year Purgatory sentence, and with bitterness he thought of the one hundred and seventy-five years of Gihenom he'd have to suffer after that for someone else's miserable sins. But after only one day he was called to the Judgment Seat to receive an additional sentence:

"For not saying the evening prayers on Thursday night and for eating dinner with an actress in a tréf restaurant you get an extra fifteen years of Purgatory."

"How so? When, why, and wherefore?" mumbled the bewildered melamed.

And the answer he got from the Heavenly Tribunal was as follows:

"Have you forgotten that for eleven hundred dollars you bought the nogid's sins, those he had already committed and those he was to commit until his death? Well, your nogid has decided to walk the path of evil and you'll have to suffer his punishment. You want proof? Here it is! Here's your contract, black on white!"

Again on the following day, he was hauled before the Judgment Seat and received an additional sentence.

"For playing poker on Sabbath eve, for smoking four cigars on Sabbath afternoon, and for eating two ham sandwiches the same afternoon you get an additional fourteen years and three months of Gihenom."

And from that time on they used to bring the melamed daily before the Heavenly Tribunal and each time would pronounce sentence on him for some newly committed sin of Mr. Silverman's. And each time it was a bigger sin, a heavier one, an uglier one—*feh!*

"Lord of the Universe!" was the anguished cry of the melamed. "If things go on this way I'll never be redeemed! Have pity on me, Holy Judges! Why is it coming to me? Where have I spent all my life on earth if not in Purgatory and Gihenom? I never had enough to eat and met with the greatest misfortunes at every step. I thought that with the wretched money I received from the nogid I'd at last free myself from my troubles. Instead the money has led me into greater misfortune! It's because of this cursed money that I'll continue to suffer for thousands of years more in Purgatory and in Gihenom. Have pity on me! It would be only right to bring the rich man here as soon as possible. If he remains alive God alone knows what sins he'll commit yet and it'll be I who'll have to suffer for them. Take pity on me, Holy Judges, and bring the nogid here!"

"No!" the Tribunal ruled. "He's too young to die yet. It's possible for him to live many years more. Why, don't you know, Reb Zalman, that only saints die young? That's the custom among men and a custom is more valid than law and even justice."

The melamed heaved a deep sigh and murmured: "Just like a nogid to have so much luck—to have this world, and the World-to-Come, too!"

Were the rich but able to hire others to die for them then the urimeleit *would be making a real nice living.*

It isn't enough for you to love money, it's also necessary that money should love you.—Baron Rothschild

CUTTING IN ON HIS RIGHTS

A wealthy, charitable merchant had many pensioners whom he supported with regular stipends. One poor man received from him ten rubles monthly. Rain, snow, or shine he always came for the money and always got it. In time, he began to take his allowance for granted as though it were an annuity for life.

Once, when he called for his ten rubles, the rich man's secretary gave him only five.

"You've made a mistake!" said the poor man. "I get ten, not five rubles a month."

"Of course you always got ten!" answered the secretary. "But you see, from now on, my employer can give you no more than five."

"What's the reason?"

"My employer is marrying off his youngest daughter, and the

dowry he gives her, the cost of her trousseau, and the wedding expenses are so great, he has to cut down on all his charities."

"Is that so!" cried the poor man, trembling with rage. "Then tell your employer that if he wants to marry off his daughter in such grand style he should do it with his own money, not with mine! Who does he think I am—Baron Rothschild?"

When you have mazl even your ox begins to calve.

A GLASS OF TEA

BY DER TUNKELER (JOSEPH TUNKEL)
TRANSLATED FROM THE YIDDISH BY NATHAN AUSUBEL

My acquaintance, the hero of this story, is David Palomishok who is a very stingy man. It stands to reason that in a time of inflation when prices zoom from minute to minute our hero is not at all happy about it, and much in his life becomes complicated because of it. It is about one of these complications I want to tell you now.

One fine afternoon, my acquaintance stood on Theater Place in Warsaw between the two confectionery shops, Semadeni and Centralna, and was thinking very seriously about a glass of tea. He had eaten some chopped herring for lunch. He felt very thirsty and he even suffered terribly from heartburn.

So he stood thinking, "This morning a glass of tea in the Semadeni shop costs two hundred marks, so I'd better try the Centralna."

He went into the Centralna and very discreetly inquired of the waiter, "Waiter, how much costs a glass of tea?"

"Two hundred and fifty marks."

So Palomishok left and remained standing undecided on Theater Place between the two confectionery shops.

At last he fell on a plan. He recalled that on Grzshibow Street there lived an acquaintance of his. This was the merchant, Motte Pzshpurke. He knew him to be a hospitable man. Madame Pzshpurke was also hospitable and was fond of intellectual people besides. Why not? If he called on them he'd surely be served a glass of fine tea and something sweet with it. As a steady visitor at their home he knew that their teatime was near.

There was one difficulty though. He had to take the tram to get there and the price of the tram ticket had already risen to two hundred marks. True, he could go there on foot but have you any idea how much a pair of soles cost today? Why they're dearer than a hundred tram tickets! It was quite a long way and he might get there after teatime!

So he got into a tram. He felt thirsty and distracted and he nervously started chewing on his tram ticket.

His fantasy wafted him away and he already saw himself sitting in the charming warm home of the Pzshpurkes. Madame hands him a glass of tea and he drinks it and munches on cookies. And he munches cookies, and he munches still more cookies.

And before he knew it and came to, he found that he had swallowed the tram ticket!

The conductor came up to him.

"Ticket, please?"

No ticket!

According to regulations he was fined four times as much as he had paid for the ticket. He tried to bargain with the conductor but it didn't help him any. So, as he paid the eight hundred marks, he thought:

"Because of this unexpected expense I'm going to drink two glasses of tea and with a lot of cookies and with a lot of candy too! Let's reckon three hundred marks for each glass of tea and one thousand marks for the pastry and candy. So I'll still break even."

When he entered the Pzshpurkes' home he was met by Madame Pzshpurke, who was dressed to go out in her hat and coat and was just pulling on her gloves.

"Ach, *Pan* Palomishok, God has brought you here! I want you to escort me to a meeting. Our Society for Aid to Poor Expectant Mothers is holding a special meeting. At the same time I want to ask you for a contribution. Nu? Out with your wallet! You've no idea how much money we need."

Palomishok started to bargain. Madame asked one thousand marks, he wanted to give only five hundred. They finally agreed on eight hundred and then they left for the meeting.

Madame Pzshpurke wanted a droshky. Palomishok was a gentleman and couldn't refuse and so he hailed a droshky. Madame seated herself in the carriage, but Palomishok started bargaining with the driver. It almost looked as though Madame would have to get out of the droshky, but being a gentleman he settled for nine thousand marks.

Throughout the drive he sat very perturbed, making mental calculations:

"Now let's see: two hundred marks a tram ticket, eight hundred marks fine, eight hundred marks contribution, nine thousand marks the droshky and, devil take it, I haven't had one glass of tea yet!"

"About what are you thinking so hard, *Pani* Palomishok?" the lady asked him.

"Oh, it's just a mood," mumbled Palomishok.

"I admire moody people very much," Madame Pzshpurke confessed.

Arrived at their destination, Palomishok escorted his lady to the door and she entered. He remained standing on the street. He felt now as if a *Gihenom* was raging inside his brain. And he began to reconsider the situation all over again:

"Now that I think of it, I know somebody else in the neighborhood. That's Nache Pendersohn, the rich man. In his house they serve tea with rum and cognac and tortes and strawberries with cream. If I should visit there and pour down my gullet three glasses of fine tea with rum and eat several pieces of torte, and tuck away a dish of strawberries with cream I'll come out about even with my expenses."

So he went to see his rich acquaintance.

Nache Pendersohn lived on the fifth floor. Fortunately, there was a lift in the house. He got in and pressed the button. On the way up, the lift stopped suddenly, hanging suspended between the third and fourth floors. The electric light in the lift went out and he remained in complete darkness.

Palomishok began to grope about and while he did so his glasses fell off his nose and a lens broke. He shouted for help and before long the corridors rang out with his cries. The house watchman came running, bringing with him the manager, and the manager went for a mechanic. After much excitement and effort they pulled the lift, together with Palomishok, down in the cellar.

For his pains in helping to free Palomishok the house manager requested two thousand marks, the mechanic three thousand, and the watchman one thousand. Finally he bargained them down to five thousand marks for all the three. After paying the money he again reconsidered the situation: "Now I'm going to drink four glasses of tea—one with rum, one with cream, one with cognac, and one with cordial. And tortes I'll eat, and strawberries with cream I'll eat. In fact, I'll remain for supper too. That way I'll come out about even again."

So he walked up to the fifth floor to call on his rich acquaintance.

On the third stair landing whom should he see coming down the stairs but the Pendersohns. They were smartly dressed and quite obviously on their way to some important engagement.

"Oh Pan Palomishok!" they called out. "What are you doing in our house. You're probably coming to see us, no? Unfortunately, we're on our way to the theater. A pity, what a pity!"

"That's all right, it's perfectly all right. Don't trouble yourself! As a matter of fact, I was just on my way to the fourth floor. I've some business to transact with someone there," babbled Palomishok, improvising a lie.

Madame Pendersohn threw him a sly but mysterious smile. Her husband said,

"In that case, *auf wiedersehen,* Pan Palomishok. Come to see *us* soon."

So they went down and he went up to the fourth floor.

He found himself standing at a door on whose brass plate he read:

JACOB BLUFF
DOCTOR OF VENEREAL DISEASES
Visiting hours from 2–4 and from 6–8

Now he knew why Madame Pendersohn had smiled. "To all the nine devils! Now I'll no longer be able to show my face there, and it's all over with the fine tea with rum forever and ever."

When the steps of the Pendersohns could no longer be heard Palomishok went down the stairs again and out into the courtyard. His eye fell on the house pump and suddenly he awoke to the fact that he was drenched in sweat and dying of thirst. So he bent his head under the faucet and guzzled cold water as if he would never stop drinking.

His thirst slaked at last, he went out into the street, but a gloom, a deadly gloom like a worm was gnawing at his heart. . . .

Three days later Palomishok was confined to bed with an icebag on his head and a thermometer stuck under his tongue. The doctor said that he had pneumonia and that drinking too much water while overheated had brought it on.

The heart grows hard quicker in riches
than an egg in boiling water.—Ludwig Börne

A GUIDE FOR BECOMING RICH

"How did you become so rich?" a self-made man was asked once.

"I lived by two rules of conduct," answered the rich man. "What I had to do tomorrow I did today, and what I had to eat today I ate tomorrow."

THE ACADEMY

BY SHOLEM ASCH

TRANSLATED FROM THE YIDDISH BY NATHAN AUSUBEL

Reb Anshel-Leib was the foremost Jew in town. His possessions included the Gasteniner Forest, which had belonged to his father before him, and the brick house in town with the two wings, which he himself had built. Like every Jew who prospers he had (may no evil eye fall on them) many children: six sons and six daughters. In addition, he had income aplenty and a handsome face, and on top of that, he belonged to the finest family in town.

Reb Moishe-Ber, who was Reb Anshel-Leib's father, had also been a prominent Jew, in fact even more prominent than Reb Anshel-Leib himself, and much more of a Talmud scholar besides. And children (may no evil eye fall on them) he also had many: six sons and six daughters. He too had income aplenty and a handsome face, and belonged to the finest family in town. But there was one difference between father and son: the more children Reb Moishe-Ber had the more joy he had from them, the more weddings, the more circumcisions. However, the more children Reb Anshel-Leib had the more grief, the more *tzoress,* the more humiliations he suffered on account of them.

I found Reb Anshel-Leib in his study when I called on him. He sat in an armchair, his fine beard resting impressively on his white starched shirt. Above his head hung the picture of his father, Reb Moishe-Ber. He too had a fine beard resting impressively on his white starched shirt. But around the old Jew in the photograph clustered a swarm of sons and of daughters, of sons-in-law and of daughters-in-law, of grandchildren and of great-grandchildren. The old Jew in the photograph was virtually "drowning" in a sea of children and grandchildren that had sprung up from his seed. It was the opposite however with his son, Reb Anshel-Leib. He sat solitary and alone with his fine beard. And this is what he told me:

"You ask me why I'm groaning, why I'm so sad? With an income you say, I'm well provided, and if I, Reb Moishe-Leib, groan and complain what should others do? That's what you said to me. Nu, what shall I answer you? I'm asking you, why shouldn't I groan? What sort of satisfaction do I have from my life? Look closely at the picture over my head. As you see, when my father was my age he already had (may no evil eye fall on them) five married daughters and six daughters-in-law. Every Sabbath afternoon his house overflowed with the throng of grandchildren that would come to bid him *'Gut Shabbes.'* And when it came to the Seder on Passover or the feast on Purim, when all of us, together with our wives and children and grandchildren, gathered at the house of our father (peace be to his memory), there wasn't enough room for all of us. There were too few tables, too few chairs to sit on. The waiters and the musicians were busy every minute of the time. We even kept our own midwife, and work she had 'way above her head.' And if God helped and my father bought another forest, why he'd marry off another child without delay. He'd set one up in business, celebrate a circumcision for another. Money earned provided a dowry for a daughter. And so, indeed, God blessed him with children and provided a livelihood for all of them. The more candles he donated to the synagogue the more riches poured into the household. Festivities were always going on in our family: here a grandchild became *bar mitzvah,* there a son became engaged to be married, still another went to look over a prospective bride. There was always the sound of music in our house, always festivities going on.

"Now take me. God helped me as He had helped my father (peace be to his memory). I too am blessed with six sons and six daughters, but what sort of happiness have I had from them? When they were small we had our hands full with Gymnasia troubles. Just as they had to get chicken pox, measles, and toothache, so they had to go through the Gymnasia disease. God! How much money that cost me! And how many times on account of it I was put to shame and the peace of the Sabbath was ruined for me, may the one and only God have mercy on me! Well and good! But no sooner were we through with the Gymnasia disease than the university plague started. They wouldn't take them in; they'd accept Jews with gold medals only. In short, my children didn't get any gold medals and if you don't get any gold medals you can't live!

" 'Now take me. I didn't get any gold medal and just the same I'm alive with God's help,' I'd argue with them. 'You see I got married and I've children and I've an income with the help of the Lord of the Universe. Nu, so you didn't get any gold medal—get married then!' I pleaded with them. But no, it had to be the university! And if not here then it was going to be in a foreign country, even if they had to go as far as the Dark Mountains, but somehow they'd find it!

"Well, they started running out of my house just as if it was from the plague. God protect us! In short, one fine morning I look around me and I find that I have no one to sit with at the table. One child had gone off to Berne, one to Paris, and another carried himself off to a country that's so far away the Devil only knows where it is! Yes, all of them went away, from the oldest to the youngest. That one has already gone, this one is leaving today, and the other one will go tomorrow. I'm telling you, down to the smallest Gymnasia student. And everyone of them was studying. All of Germany, the whole world even, they wanted to learn about and bring home to me—'and you Papa, send money!'

"God helped at last and the first one came back. My Adolph, the oldest one, came back. He was a finished doctor with a diploma inscribed from that university abroad saying that he was a finished doctor. But as to earning any money? Says he to me, 'Papa, wish me mazl tov; I've got the diploma!' Says I to him, 'What sort of pleasure will I get out of that? My father married off his eldest son to Reb Dovid Kaliter's daughter and, it seems, I'm marrying off my eldest son to a paper diploma!' So he says to me, 'Papa, you'll have pleasure yet from me.' So I says to him, 'When are you going to earn some money, my son?' So he says to me, 'As for money, Papa, that's still far off. First of all, I've got to pass a state examination, and that's a very hard thing. Even after I'll have passed the state examination I'll still not be earning any money. That's because I didn't study to be a doctor in order to make a career out of it, but for the sake of knowledge. Science is what interests me!'

"I listened to him and said nothing.

"My second son I married off to the University of Liège. He returned home a finished engineer. I asked my son, 'Have you got a diploma?' So he answered, 'Yes, Papa, I have a diploma.' So I ask him, 'What exactly is it that you've learned, my son?' So he says: 'Papa, I learned how to build bridges, how to construct a suspension bridge between one mountain peak and another; that's what you need when you build a railroad.' So I say to my son, 'I like your kind of work very much; it's a very useful thing. Now tell me, my child, when are you going to begin earning some money?' So he answers me, 'As for earning money, Papa, that's still far off. First of all, I have to take a state examination. After that I'll have to find some company that constructs railroads. But since in our country the government itself builds the railroads, I've first got to get a government post. But since the government doesn't employ Jews, I'd have to become a Christian, God forbid! And since to become a Christian, God forbid, I don't want, I'll never be able to get a government post. And since I'll never be able to get a government post I won't be able to earn any money.' So I ask my son, 'Did you have to learn such a profession? Why didn't you learn something from which you could make some money?' So he answers, 'Papa, I didn't learn a trade but a science. I like science.'

"Again I listened and said nothing.

"Then my eldest daughter came home. 'Daughter, to whom did you get married?' I ask her. 'To the Sorbonne in Paris, Papa,' she replies. Says I, 'I like the match you've made. What did you learn, my child?' So she takes out a whole book in French and shows it to me. 'This, Papa, I wrote to become a doctor of philosophy.' When I heard her say this I got frightened. 'Do you mean to say, Daughter, that you wrote this whole book in French?' 'Yes,' says she. 'And will it help you get a husband, Daughter?' I ask her.

"At this she got angry and left the room. You hear, at first, before this one here went abroad, all sorts of young men were after her; the matchmakers almost tore down my doors. But ever since she came back from Paris and the news got around that she had written a whole book in French it all died down. The young men who come here have great respect for her; as a matter of fact they're afraid of her! The matchmakers avoid me now, and why shouldn't they? With whom can she get married since she has written a whole book in French? You can imagine how educated a young man would have to be to marry her! They surely are afraid of her! And so, as you see, she got married to the French book.

"Another son of mine, a mathematician, came home and he can't even add up the cubic feet of wood I sell. He says he knows everything about mathematics, but what I need him for he never even learned.

"Right after him another daughter came home. She had studied business economics in Leipzig. She became a doctor of business economics. I ask her, 'Daughter, would you like to go into business?' 'God forbid!' she throws up her hands in horror. 'What! Do you want me to become a shopkeeper?' 'Why then, Daughter, did you study to become a doctor of business economics?' 'I just studied it for the knowledge.' For the knowledge? I myself, a merchant, am always running away from this 'knowledge.' Whenever I find the time I pick up some book of sacred lore to study, and here she comes along and studies business economics for the sake of knowledge!

"When dinnertime comes an entire academy sits around my table. Here you have a doctor and there an engineer; here a lady philosopher and there a lady doctor of business economics. All the branches of knowledge in the world my children have studied, and they have diplomas from every kind of university. Still in all, not one of them earns a groschen or gets married. They sit on my poor shoulders and live off my poor forest. I haven't even got anybody to reckon for me how many cubic feet of wood I'm selling. I haven't even got anyone to help me in the business, to look after the forest which stands in need of the work of all of us. And as I look around me and see at my table the doctors and the lawyers and the engineers and the philosophers and watch the little ones grow up also to become doctors and lawyers with diplomas, terror seizes me. Am I, a poor Jew, obligated to support an entire academy? Where will I find the means for all that? All from the forest? Even Korah's treasures wouldn't be enough!"

HE WOULDN'T BE A JEW

BY AN ELDER OF ZION

Last Thursday evening about eleven-thirty o'clock I was walking down Jefferson Davis Avenue, the fashionable residential street of Bienville, swinging my cane, and looking at the constellation Orion.

Suddenly down the quiet deserted street I saw a man striding along furiously through the shadows of the trees. When he came up to me, he peered hard into my face and stopped. I stopped, too, and the man stood glaring at me with the most intense hatred. I was, I confess, somewhat taken aback. I had never seen the man before. He was a young man, about thirty or forty years old. He wore a black coat with a brown fur collar, tan gloves, and an Ascot tie. He was, I should say, about five or six feet tall.

"Look here," he said, in a loud voice, "I won't be a Jew. There's no sense in it. I'm sick of it. I won't be a Jew and that's the end of it. Leave me alone!"

"All right," I said, and began to walk off.

"Look here," he said still more loudly, coming after me. "I've got enough of it. My hair is blond and straight." He took off his hat. "My nose is straight. My shoulders are square. I play football, baseball, soccer and squash. There's no sense in it."

"All right," I said, and began to walk off.

"Look here," he said, clutching my coat lapel. "I won't be bull-dozed. I am an American. I pay my income tax. I serve on the jury. I vote for Sheriff, alderman, mayor and President. I was over there fighting with the Rainbow Division in the Great War. I am a Demo-crat."

"All right," I said.

"I studied anthropology," he said, shaking his fist in my face. "I've got Ethiopian blood in my veins, Aramaic blood, Babylonian blood, Assyrian blood, Canaanitish blood, Egyptian blood, Greek blood, Moorish blood, Tartar blood, Dutch blood, Spanish blood, Polish blood and what all not. It's a farce."

"All right," I said.

"I don't know a word of Hebrew," he said, stamping his feet. "I don't know ten words of Yiddish. I speak English with a Harvard accent. I read Shakespeare and Milton and Dryden and Pope and Tennyson and Browning and Alfred Noyes and what all not. I listen to Brahms and Beethoven and Bach. I subscribe to *The American Mercury* and *The Atlantic Monthly*. I own the sixteenth edition of *The Encyclopedia Britannica*."

"All right," I said.

"My house is no different from anyone else's house," he said, banging his fist violently in his palm. "I own a Buick, a Frigidaire, an Atwater Kent. I have a bridge set, a gate-leg table, and a sun parlor. There are hooked rugs on my floor and a colonial knocker on my door."

"All right," I said.

"I don't believe in God," he shouted, punching me in the ribs. "I don't believe in the Bible. I don't believe in the Ten Commandments. I eat oysters, I eat ham and eggs, I don't fast, I don't keep the Sabbath, I don't go to Temple, I'm an agnostic. I'm a skeptic. I don't believe in sects. I'm an internationalist. I'm a universalist. I'm a modern man with twentieth-century ideas. I'm just a plain human being."

"All right," I said.

"I am vice-president of a Gentile bank," he said, jumping up and down on the sidewalk. "My partners are Gentiles. I make my money in lumber, no honester, no crookeder than anybody else. I'm on the membership committee of the Allstyne Luncheon Club, I'm on the greens committee of the Bienville Country Club, I'm on the house committee of the Corinthian Sodality. My wife is a Gentile and a D. A. R. My children have blue eyes. My son is going to St. Mark's, my daughter is going to Rosemary Hall. It's nonsense. I can read Greek at sight. I'm an excellent trapshot. I can play the mandolin. What's Jewish about that? I don't wear a beard. My manners are flawless. There's no point in it. I'm an Elk, I'm a Mason, I'm a Moose. It's sheer idiocy. How am I a Jew? There's no sense to it. I won't be a Jew and that settles it. Leave me alone."

"All right," I said.

"I'm not a Jew, I'm not a Jew, I'm not a Jew," he shouted, swinging his arms wildly. "Do you hear me? I'm not a Jew! What do you say to that?"

"All right," I said, and began to walk off.

He leaped after me and seized me by both shoulders.

"Who are you to tell me what I am?" he yelled, shaking me violently, his face white with passion. "Who are you to tell me what I am and what I am not? . . . Just because you have a long white beard, you think . . . Look here, I could be a Jew if I wanted to. . . . Listen here, goddam you, listen to this . . . I'm every bit as good a Jew as you are right this minute, I bet. . . ."

"All right," I said.

He danced about me in a frenzy, broken words and strange gurglings in his throat, his head bobbing up and down, his eyes popping, his cheeks puffed out like toy balloons with rage. I did not know what the man wanted, and I was frightened.

I wrenched myself away, and began to run down the street.

I had not taken three steps when I heard a loud report behind me. I turned around. The street was empty. I saw something that looked like a cloud or a wisp of smoke disappearing over the top of the sycamore tree above me. Evidently he had exploded.

The street was quite deserted. I looked at my watch. It was two minutes past twelve.

So I continued my walk down Jefferson Davis Avenue, swinging my cane, and looking at the constellation Orion.

Pleasures of the Poor

To have money is not so ai-ai-ai!
but not to have money is oy-oy-oy!

THE IMMORTAL ORANGE

BY ZALMAN SCHNEOUR
TRANSLATED FROM THE YIDDISH BY HANNAH BERMAN

Two boxes of oranges going across the blue ocean. The oranges are Algerian, globular, juicy, heavy, with a glowing red peel—the colour of African dawns.

The oranges in the first box boast: "We are going to Warsaw, the ancient Polish capital. Oh, what white teeth will bite into us, what fine aristocratic tongues will relish us!"

The oranges in the second box keep silent; snuggle one against the other, and blush for shame. They know—thanks be to God—that their destination is a little village somewhere in Lithuania, and God knows into what beggarly hands they will fall. No, it was not worth drinking so thirstily the warmth of the African sun, the cool dews of the Algerian nights, the perfumes of the blossoming French orange groves. Nimble brown hands of young mulatto girls cut them down off the trees, and flung them into bamboo baskets. Was it worth while?

But we shall see who came off best: the oranges that went to Warsaw, or those that arrived late at Shklov—a remote village in Lithuania. And we shall draw the moral.

So the first lot of oranges arrived at Warsaw and the fruit merchants set them out in pyramids. They glowed like balls of fire out of the window. But that did not last long. They were sold the same day. The tumultuous, thirsty street soon swallowed them up. Tired folk thrust them into their pockets, pulled off their juicy, golden peel with dirty fingers, and flung it on the slush-covered pavements. They swallowed the oranges as they walked along, like dogs, without saying grace. The refreshing juice bespattered dusty beards, greasy coats. Their place in the shop is already taken by other fruits and even vegetables. No feeling for birth and breeding! Only bits of their beautiful peel still lay about in the streets, like the cold rays of a far-off, glowing sun. But no one understood that these were greetings from distant sunny lands, from eternally-blue skies. They were trampled underfoot, horses stamped on them, and the street sweeper came with his broom, and swept them, ruthlessly, into the rubbish box. That was the end of the oranges! The end of something that had flourished somewhere, and drawn sustenance between perfumed leaves, and fell into bamboo baskets under a hot, luxuriant sky.

The second box of oranges arrived a few days later at Shklov. They were dragged along in little peasant wagons, and jolted in Jewish carts, until they had the honour of being shown into their new surroundings.

The wife of the spice-merchant of Shklov called over her husband:

"Come on, my smart fellow. Open the oranges for the *Purim* presents."

Eli, the spice-merchant, despite his wife's sarcasm, was an expert at unpacking. He worked at the box of oranges for a couple of hours. Patiently, carefully he worked around the lid with his chisel, like a goldsmith at a precious case of jewels. His wife stood beside him, giving advice. At last the box was opened, and out of the bits of blue tissue paper gleamed the little cheeks of the oranges, and there was a burst of heavy, festive fragrance.

In a little while, the oranges lay set out in the little shop window, peeping out on the muddy market-place, the grey, lowering sky, the little heaps of snow in the gutters, the fur-clad, White Russian peasants in their yellow-patched, sheepskin jerkins. Everything around them was so strange, northern, chilly, half-decayed. And the oranges with their festive perfume and their bright colour were so rich and strange and new in such an unfamiliar, poor *milieu,* like a royal garment in a beggar's tavern.

Aunt Feiga arrives with her woollen shawl about her head, and a basket in her hand. She sees the freshly-unpacked fruit, and goes in to buy. *Purim* gifts. And here begins the *immortality* of the orange!

Poor and grey is Lithuanian life. And the little natural wealth that sometimes falls into this place is used up a little at a time, reasonably, and with all the five senses. Not a drop goes to waste of the beautiful fruit that has strayed in here. No, if the orange had been no more than the wandering spirit of a sinful soul it would have found salvation at the home of Aunt Feiga.

II

"Then you won't take eight *kopecks* either? Good day!"
The spice-merchant's wife knows full well that Aunt Feiga has

no other place where she can buy; yet she pulls her back by the shawl:

"May all Jews have a pleasant Purim as surely as I am selling you golden fruit . . . I only want to make a start."

"We only want to make a start!" repeats Eli, the spice-merchant, the experienced opener of orange boxes.

A *rouble* more or a *rouble* less. Aunt Feiga selects the best, the heaviest orange, wraps it up, and drops it carefully into the basket, between eggs, onions, goodies for Purim, and all sorts. Aunt Feiga comes home, and the little ones clamour round her, from the eleven-year-old *Gemarrah* student to the littlest one who is just learning the alphabet, and who have all been given a holiday from school for the eve of Purim. They immediately start turning out their mother's basket.

"Mother, what have you brought? What have you brought?"

The mother silences them. One gets a smack in the face, because of the holiday; another a thump; and a third a tweak of the ear.

"What has happened here! Look at the locusts swarming around me!"

Yet she shows them what she has brought.

"There! Look, you devils, scamps!"

Among the small town Lithuanian goodies, *the orange* glows like a harbinger of wealth and happiness. The children are taken aback. They still remember last Purim, a shadow of the fragrance of such a fruit. Now it has come back to life with the same fragrance and roundness. Here it is! They will not see the like of it again till this time next year.

They snatch at it with thin little hands; they smell it; they marvel at it.

"Oh, how delicious!" cries the youngest child. "Oh, how it smells!"

"It grows in Palestine," puts in the *Gemarrah* student, and somehow feels proud and grave.

Aunt Feiga locks it into the drawer. But the round, fragrant, flaming fruit lives in the imagination of the children, like a sweet dream. It shines rich and new among the hard green apples and pickled cucumbers that the children have been seeing all the winter.

When the Purim feast begins, the orange sits at the head of the table, among a host of little tarts and jellies, and figs and sweets, and shines like a huge coral bead in a multi-coloured mosaic.

Aunt Feiga covers it with a cloth, and gives it to the Purim gift-bearer to take away. The orange sticks the top of its head out of the cloth, as one might say: "Here I am. I am whole. A pleasant festival, children!" The children follow him on his travels with longing eyes. They know, that it will have to pass through many transmigrations, poor thing, until it is brought back to them by the beadle.

And so it was. One aunt exchanges the orange for a lemon, and sends it to another relative. And Aunt Feiga has the lemon. So she sends the lemon to another relative, and there it again meets the orange, and they exchange places. And Aunt Feiga gets her precious orange back again.

The cloth is removed. The orange, the cunning devil, sits in his former place, like the *King of Bagdad,* and rules over little cakes, and sweets and raisins. The cold of the Purim night lies on him like a dew. He seems to be smiling a little wearily, a little chilled after his long journeyings in so strange, snow-covered, and unfamiliar a night:

"You see, children, I've come back! You needn't have been afraid."

III

When Purim is over, the orange lies in the drawer, still whole, and feels happy. If relatives call, and Sabbath dainties are served up, the orange has first place on the table, like ⌐ prince among plebeian apples and walnuts. People turn him over, ask how much he cost, and give their opinion about him, like wealthy folk who are used to such fruits, and he is put back on his plate. The apples and the nuts disappear one by one, and the orange always escapes from the hands of the relatives, and remains whole. Relatives in Shklov are no gluttons—God forbid! They know what must be left for good manners.

"When the month of *Adar* comes we have jollifications . . ." About ten days after Purim there is a betrothal contract drawn up in Aunt Feiga's home. Aunt Feiga has betrothed her eldest daughter to a respectable young man. And again the orange lies on top, right under the hanging lamp, just as if he were the object of the whole party. True, one cheek is a bit withered by now, like that of an old general, but for all that, he still looks majestic. He lights up the table with his luxuriant, exotic strangeness. The youngsters, from the ABC boy to the eleven-year-old Gemarrah student, have already hinted repeatedly to their father and their mother that it is high time they had a taste of the orange. . . . Say the blessing for a new sort of fruit—that was all they wanted, only to say the blessing for a new sort of fruit. . . . But Aunt Feiga gave them a good scolding: "Idlers, gluttons! When the

time comes to say the blessing over new fruit, we shall send a special
messenger to notify you. . . . Your father and mother won't eat it up
themselves. You needn't be afraid of that."

The youngsters were all atremble at the betrothal party lest the
bridegroom should want to say the blessing for new fruit. Who can say
what a bridegroom might want at his betrothal party? Mother always
gives him the best portions.

But the bridegroom belongs to Shklov. He knows that an orange
has not been made for a bridegroom to eat at his betrothal party, but
only to decorate the table. So he holds it in his hand just for a minute,
and his Adam's apple runs into his chin and runs out again. And the
orange again is left intact.

But at last the longed-for Friday evening arrives. The orange is
no longer so globular as it had been, nor so fragrant. His youth has
gone. But it does not matter. It is still an orange. After the Sabbath
meal the mood is exalted. No notification has been sent by special
messenger; but the youngsters know instinctively that this time *the
blessing over the new fruit will be said*. But they pretend to know
nothing. One might think there was no such thing as an orange in this
world.

Said Aunt Feiga to Uncle Uri:

"Uri, share out the orange among the children. How long is it
to lie here?"

Uncle Uri, a bearded Jew with crooked eyes, an experienced
orange-eater who has probably eaten half a dozen oranges, or more, in
the course of his life, sat down at the head of the table, opened up the
big blade of his pocket-knife—an old "wreck"—and started the
operation. The children stand round the table watching their father
with reverend awe, as one watches a rare magic-maker, though they
would love to see the inside of the orange and taste it as well. They
are only human beings, after all, with desires. . . . But Uncle Uri
has lots of time. Carefully and calmly he cuts straight lines across the
fruit, from "pole" to "pole." First he cuts four such lines, then eight,
one exactly like the other. (You must admit that he is a master at that
sort of thing!) And then he begins to peel the orange.

Everybody listens to the crackling of the fleshy, elastic peel.
Slowly the geometrically-true pieces of red peel come off. But, here and
there, the orange has become slightly wilted, and little bits of the juicy
"flesh" come away with the peel. Uncle Uri says "Phut!" just as if it
hurts him, thrusts the blade of his knife into the orange, and operates
on the danger spot. The orange rolls out of its yellowish-white, fra-

grant swaddling-clothes, and is artistically divided up by the Uncle into equal half-moons, piece by piece.

"Children," cries the newly-engaged girl, placing a big glass on the table, "don't forget the pips. Throw them in here. They will be soaked and planted . . ."

She addresses her little brothers, but she means her father as well.

The youngsters undertake to assist their sister in her house-keeping enthusiasm, which seems to hold out a promising prospect. And they turn their eyes on the tender, rosy half-moons on the plate.

The first blessing is the prerogative of Uncle Uri himself. He chews one bite, and swallows it with enthusiasm, closing one crooked eye, and lifting the other to the ceiling, and shaking his head:

"A *tasty* orange! Children, come over here . . ."

The youngest-born goes first. This is his privilege. Whenever there is anything nice going, he is always first after his father. He says the blessing at the top of his voice, with a little squeak, flings the half-moon into his mouth, and gulps it down.

"Don't gulp! . . ." says Uncle Uri very patiently. "No one is going to take it away from you."

"And where is the pip?" asks his betrothed sister, pushing forward the glass.

"Yes, that's right. Where is the pip?" Uncle Uri backs her up.

"Swallowed it . . ." says the youngster, frightened, and flushes to his ears.

"Swallowed it?"

"Ye-e-s."

And the tears come into the little one's eyes. He looks round at his older brothers. . . . They keep quiet.

But it is too late. . . . He knows. . . . No father can help him now. They will tease the life out of him. From this day on he has a new nickname: "Little pip."

Then the remaining portions of the orange are shared out in order, from the bottom upwards, till it comes to the turn of the Gemarrah student. He takes his portion, toys with it a while, and bites into it, feeling that it tastes nice, and also that it is a sweet greeting from Palestine of which he has dreamed often at *Cheder*. Oranges surely grow only in Palestine. . . .

"And a blessing?" says Uncle Uri, catching him out, and fixing him with his crooked eyes.

"Blessed art Thou . . ." the Gemarrah student murmurs, abashed; and the bit of orange sticks in his throat. His greeting from Palestine has had all the joy taken out of it.

But Uncle Uri was not yet satisfied. No. He lectured the Gemarrah student to the effect that he might go and learn from his youngest brother how to say a blessing. Yes, he might take a lesson from him. He could assure him that he would one day light the stove for his youngest brother. Yes, that he would, light his stove for him. And . . .

But he suddenly remembered:

"Feiga, why don't you taste a bit of orange?"

It was a good thing that he remembered; otherwise, who knows when he would have finished his lecture?

"It doesn't matter," Aunt Feiga replied. Nevertheless, she came up, said the blessing, and enjoyed it: "Oh, oh, what lovely things there are in the world!" And then they started a discussion about oranges.

Aunt Feiga said that if she were rich, she would eat every day— half an orange. A whole orange was beyond her comprehension. How could anyone go and eat up a whole orange costing eight and a half *kopecks?*—But Uncle Uri did things on a bigger scale. He had after all been once to the Fair at Nijni-Novgorod. So he smiled out of his crooked eyes: No, if he were rich he would have the juice squeezed out of—three oranges at once, and drink it out of a glass. There!

His wife and children were astounded at the richness of his imagination, and pictured to themselves a full glass of rosy, thick orange juice, with a white froth on top, and a pip floating about in the froth. . . .

They all sat round the table in silence for a while, gazing with dreamy eyes at the yellow moist pips which the betrothed girl had collected from all those who had a share of the orange. She poured water over them, and counted them through the glass, one, two, three, four. . . . She had nine in all. Yes. Next week she would plant them in the flower-pots; and after her wedding, she would take them with her to her own home. She would place them in her windows, and would let them grow under inverted glasses. . . .

You no doubt think that this is the end. Well, you have forgotten that an orange also has a peel. . . .

IV

One of the youngsters made a discovery—when you squeeze a bit of orange peel over against the lamp, a whole fountain of transparent, thin little fragrant drops squirts out, and when you squirt these into the eyes of one of your brothers, he starts to squint. . . . But before he had time to develop his discovery, he got a smack on his hand. And all the bits of peel vanished into Aunt Feiga's apron.

"There is no trick too small for them to play, the devils. Just as if it were potato-peelings. . . . If she could only get a little more, she could make preserves. . . . Yes, preserves. . : ."

But that was only talk. By the time she could collect enough orange peel to make preserves the Messiah would have come.

So she placed the peel overnight in the warm stove to dry. The golden red bits of peel, that only yesterday had looked so fresh and juicy, were now wilted, blackish-brown, curled up and hard, like old parchment. Aunt Feiga took her sharp kitchen-knife, and cut the peel into long strips, then into small oblongs. . . . She put them into a bottle, poured brandy on them, strewed them with soft sugar, and put it away to stand. The brandy revived the dried-up bits of orange peel, they swelled out, blossomed forth, took on again their one-time bloom. You pour out a tiny glassful, sip it, and taste the genuine flavour and bouquet of orange peel.

Relatives come to pay you a visit, they pronounce a blessing, take a sip, and feel refreshed, and it is agreed unanimously that it is very good for the stomach. And the women question Aunt Feiga how she came to think of such a clever thing. . . .

"Look," said Uncle Zhama to Michla his wife, "you let everything go to waste. Surely you had an orange as well for *Purim!* Where is the peel? Nothing. Thrown it away."

Uncle Uri interrupts him:

"Don't worry, Zhama, let us have another sip."

And he smiles out of his crooked eyes at his "virtuous woman," Aunt Feiga.

The bottle is tied up again with a piece of white cloth about the cork, so that it should not evaporate. And it is put away in the cupboard so that it should draw for a long time. And the bottle stands there, all alone, like a pious woman, a deserted wife, in a hood. . . .

Passover comes, and Jews go through the formality of selling their leaven to Alexieka the water-carrier, with the dirty, flaxen hair; so the bottle of orange-brandy-water too falls into Gentile hands. All that week it stands there, sold, a forbidden thing, and scarcely lives to see the day when it is once more redeemed, so that Jews with grey beards and Jewish women in pious wigs should pronounce the blessing over it, and tell each other about Aunt Feiga's amazing capacity.

Sometimes a bottle like that stands for years. From time to time you add fresh brandy, and it is tasted very rarely, until the bits of orange peel at the bottom of the bottle begin to lose their strength, become sodden and pale. Then Uncle Uri knocks them out on a plate.

This is always done on a Saturday night, after the blessing at the termination of the Sabbath, when the spirit of exaltation has vanished, and the week-day drabness creeps out of every little corner. Then Uncle Uri looks for something of a pick-me-up, and remembers the faded, brandy-soaked, sugared bits of orange peel.

He turns the wide, respectable bottle bottom up—begging your pardon, and smacks it firmly but gently on the bottom.

"Phut, phut, phu-ut . . ." the bottle resounds complainingly, penetrating with hollow dullness all over the room, into the week-day, post-Sabbath shadows.

There is a sound, like a deep, frightened sigh, an echo from a dried-up ancient well. The bottle seems to cry aloud that the soul is being knocked out of it, its last breath. . . . And at the same time, sticky, golden-yellow, appetising bits of peel fall out of the neck.

Then all is silent. Uncle Uri pronounces the blessing over the leavings, tastes, and then hands them round.

The children agree that though they are a little harsh, one still detects the taste of the one-time Purim orange, peace unto it.

But at the very moment that the last vestige of the famous orange is disappearing from Uncle Uri's house, the heirs of the orange—the sodden, swollen-up little pips—have long since shot up in the flower-pots at the home of Uncle Uri's married daughter. Three or four spiky, sticky little leaves have sprouted out from each little pip.

The overturned, perspiring glasses were removed long ago. They are getting accustomed quite nicely to the climate of Shklov, and are sprouting slowly, with the reserved, green little smile that they had brought with them and secreted within themselves.

The young wife looks after them, waters them daily. And *God knows what may grow out of them one day.*

When does a poor man eat chicken?
When he is sick, or else—when the chicken is.

WHY TREES GROW ON WINDOWS

The poor Talmud scholar didn't know where the frost was greater, inside or outside his house.

"Just look at the windowpanes!" remarked his wife, bitterly. "The cold has planted a whole forest of trees on them."

"If I were you, I wouldn't make sport of the trees in the windowpanes," chided her husband. "I know a nice parable about them.

"When trees were created there were two kinds: fruit trees and shade trees.

" 'Woe is us!' complained the shade trees. 'No one will pay any attention to us because we bear no fruit.'

" 'Never fear!' they were comforted. 'We'll see to it the people will pay attention to you! You'll have the sole right to appear on the windows of the poor who can't afford to keep their houses warm.' "

Every poor man has a dry throat and wet boots.

THE GRAMOPHONE

BY Z. WENDROFF

TRANSLATED FROM THE YIDDISH BY NATHAN AUSUBEL

Bertzik definitely made up his mind—he had to bring a gift home to his father!

He had been away working in Warsaw for three years. To write home about the honor and esteem in which he was held by his employer, to boast before every fellow townsman about his promotions, to send to all his girl friends his picture postcard on which he looked so well scrubbed and dressed up, just like the dandy portrayed on the hairdresser's sign—and after all that to come home with empty hands! That he wouldn't do under any circumstances, even if he had to pawn his brand new summer suit!

Bertzik figured: "And if I am bringing home a gift for my father why shouldn't it be a gramophone?"

Bertzik knew that for a nice tune his father would give away his very soul. On account of his love for singing, his father once left home on the morning of *Rosh-Hashanah* Eve and went to Goluchov to hear the celebrated Goluchover *chazan* whose singing made everyone who heard him weep. This journey almost led to a divorce between him and Bertzik's mother. Just the same, his love for singing and for music never diminished.

As soon as a new chazan arrived in town his father remained

glued to the inn where he and his choir were rehearsing their musical service for the *Mussaf* prayers. On *Shabbes* he didn't step out of the synagogue until after the chazan was done with the singing of *Adon Olam*. After the service he'd pull home with him for refreshment the chazan with his whole gang of ravenous choir boys.

Bertzik's mother got angry, thrashed about in a fit, scolded her husband and asked him with cutting irony whether he expected her to feed the entirely unexpected crew with the flesh from her body or did he prefer to do it with his own bones? But this didn't bother him at all. He walked about in a state of blissful ecstasy, all braided up in a festive mood like the Shabbes *challeh*. He rubbed his hands with delight because he had heard some traditional synagogical chant and was still going to hear an enchanting Wallachian Jewish folk tune.

Bertzik's father didn't think it at all undignified or beneath him to stand like any street urchin outside Melech *Klezmer's* window and listen to him play his gay "Wedding Supper March" or his sorrowful *Bazetsen* fantasy for the ceremony of "covering the bride." Why, even when a hurdy-gurdy would stray into town the occasion became a regular *yom-tov* for his father.

Taking all these facts into consideration, thought Bertzik, could there be a more desirable gift for his father than a gramophone?

Naturally, he'd have to buy along with it some Jewish records: cantorial renditions of liturgical chants by the world celebrated singers Sirota, Kwartin, Gutman, and Grundshtein. In addition, it wouldn't hurt at all to throw in a couple of Yiddish records, such as: *Dos Tallisl* [The Little Prayer Shawl], *A Breevele der Mamen* [A Letter to Mother], *Ich dank dir Gott vos ich bin a Yid* [I Thank You God Because I'm a Jew], and similar popular songs.

And Bertzik really "let go" and spent all of twenty-two smackers for a gramophone, and eighteen more for records. Then he started for home, satisfied not so much because on this trip he was going to be introduced to a prospective *kaleh* as for the fact that he was bringing so much pleasure for his father.

II

After the business of embracing and kissing was over with, Bertzik washed off the dust of his journey. He then distributed the gifts he had brought for everybody in the family, and after he was through with that he put his hands behind his back and, smiling broadly, he asked:

"Nu, *tatte*, just guess for the fun of it—what sort of gift do you think I've brought you?"

"A tobacco holder, I'm sure," answered Michel-Behr smilingly. "What sort of a gift would that be from Warsaw?"

"What then? Maybe you brought me a watch chain? And who knows, maybe even a watch!"

"And something better you can't imagine?" drawled Bertzik, his face radiant with the anticipation of his father's joy.

"Nu, come to the point. Tell me what it is! Is it a dressing gown, a custom-made *yarmulka* or silver brocaded edging for my *tallis*?"

"Hi-hi-hi! No! It's a gra-mo-phone!" called out Bertzik expansively, looking around with self-importance at everybody.

"Ah, there you are! Only a Warsawer could do a thing like that!" murmured the others with admiration.

"A what?" gasped Michel-Behr. "A gramophone! Do you mean like that picture they show in the newspapers? The one with a trumpet on top?"

The words choked in Michel-Behr's throat out of sheer joy.

"*Takkeh* the same!" agreed Bertzik. "And *takkeh* a fine instrument too! A genuine Sirena!"

"Nu, show me, let's see already, let's hear 'words' from the garmophone!"

"Gramophone, tatte, gramophone!" Bertzik tried to correct him.

"Good, so let it be garmophone, as long as you show it to me," murmured Michel-Behr, prancing with anticipation.

"Don't be in such a hurry, tatte," Bertzik rebuked his father in a cool voice. "I would like you to understand that a gramophone is a delicate thing; you've got to know how to go about it . . . for instance the way you put on the records. . . ."

"Enough of talk," cried Michel-Behr, jumping out of his skin. "Let's see the thing already!"

"You take a double record . . . from one side, let's say. . . ."

"What's the use of telling me all that—show me better!" his father pleaded.

"First you put on the record, then you turn the crank. . . ."

"Do you want to show or don't you? Where is it?"

Without undue haste Bertzik untied the string around the wooden box he had brought. Then he pried open the lid and carefully took out a small gramophone which he placed on the table.

No sooner had Bertzik done that than his father put his ear to the horn and listened raptly.

"But I don't hear a thing!" he complained.

Bertzik doubled up with laughter.

"Hi-hi-hi! That's what I'd call small-town ignorance!" said Bertzik with lordly scorn. "He thinks that as soon as you put it down it's got to play already!"

He'd show Michel-Behr how it was done!

In another minute the gramophone was blaring forth for all it was worth.

At the first scratching of the needle on the record Michel-Behr made a sour face. So that's what it was, huh? But no sooner did he hear the mighty roar of the singer and on top of that heard the machine pronounce Hebrew as if right out of the prayer book itself, his eyes almost popped out of his head with rapture.

Like one in a trance he turned around the gramophone, stuck his nose curiously into the trumpet, put his ear to the box, listened intently, drummed with his fingers, and was beside himself with joy:

"*Gevalt! Gevalt!*" he jubilated. "My, what people can do, what they can think up! As I'm a Jew, it sings! What a voice! What Hebrew!"

"Pay attention, tatte, listen carefully!" Bertzik tried to stem the flood of his father's enthusiasm. "This is the celebrated chazan Sirota that's singing."

"Sirota? You mean the *real* Sirota? . . . . I'm listening, I'm listening!"

And Michel-Behr stood with flushed face and sparkling eyes beside the gramophone. He moved his lips in the words of the liturgy, trying to keep pace with the voice in the gramophone.

After Bertzik had played all of the cantorial records he said to Michel-Behr:

"Hold on, tatte! I'll play you now 'A Breevele der Mamen,' really a fine piece!"

They played all the records over and over again until finally Bertzik's mother grew angry.

"Let there be an end with your hurdy-gurdy! Supper is already as cold as ice!"

From that day on there began what was to be known as the "Gramophone Epoch" in Michel-Behr's household.

Barely had dawn begun to break and the whole family was still asleep when Michel-Behr would jump out of bed and start playing the gramophone. And no sooner did night fall when he began to hurry home from his little shop in the market place.

"What's the use of sitting here—for the big profits I'm going to make?" he'd ask apologetically, thus laying the groundwork for his hasty departure.

"What's driving you home so, what? You're lonesome for the gramophone, what?" jeered his wife fully understanding what monkey-shines he was about.

Michel-Behr meandered over to the door of the shop and when he thought his wife wasn't looking he slipped out. A short while later the sounds of "A Breevele der Mamen" were echoing all over town.

In no time at all the neighbors came running up and Michel-Behr then played all the records for them, to the very last one.

When his wife came home from the store, hungry and cold, she began to grumble.

"Just look what a crowd is here! There's enough cigarette smoke to choke you! Playing they want? May it play in their heads yet! Let it play and fiddle in your heart, and may it never stop, oy, Tatte in Heaven!"

Michel-Behr was already used to her scolding so he pretended he hadn't heard her. He kept on playing the gramophone until all the neighbors had left. He remained sitting alone beside it until he dozed off.

When Michel-Behr and the rest of the town had learned all his records by heart he stealthily began taking coins out of the cash drawer. When he had enough money saved he'd commission Tevia the driver to buy him some new records in the city.

"See that they give you records by the best *chazzonim*. They should be hearty, you know, they should give one a tickle!" he'd caution Tevia each time. "And if you come across a good *Chassidic* tune it won't be bad either."

When his wife finally caught on what a shambles he was making of their finances she put the cash box under closer scrutiny. Frustrated in this direction, Michel-Behr began to borrow a ruble here, a ruble there. He'd even surreptitiously take things from the house and pawn them, and with the money he'd buy records. His wife soon discovered this piece of duplicity and demanded an end to everything: she wanted a divorce!

But Michel-Behr remained deaf to everything except to the play-ing of his "garmophone."

Once, when she entered the shop she discovered that Michel-Behr had taken the last three-kopeck piece out of the cash box, that three-kopeck piece she had intended to go toward the rent. And her Michel-Behr had gone and handed it to Tevia for records!

The blood rushed to her face, and boiling over with indignation she ran home. As soon as she came in she grabbed up a slab of firewood and, before Michel-Behr had time to stop her, the room was strewn with pieces of broken gramophone and records.

Michel-Behr stood mute, regarding the ruins with bulging eyes. Then he stamped his feet and cried out with fury:

"What have you done? It's murder! To the rabbi, you bandit, you! I want a divorce!"

Be gay, you beggars—tzoress don't cost a kopeck!

It's much better to be dead drunk than dead hungry.

MOSES LUMP

BY HEINRICH HEINE
TRANSLATED FROM THE GERMAN BY NATHAN AUSUBEL

In the Bäckerbreitengang in Hamburg there lives a man by the name of Moses Lump.[1] They also call him Moses Lümpchen, and for short—Lümpchen. All week long in wind and foul weather he runs around with a pack on his back in order to earn a few marks. Yet, when he comes home on Friday evening he finds the Sabbath lamp with the seven lights all lit up and a white cloth spread on the table. He puts his pack and all his cares away and sits down at the table with his crooked wife and even more crooked daughter. He eats with them the fish that has been cooked in appetizing white garlic sauce. And as he eats he sings the superb songs of King David, rejoices with an overflowing heart over the exodus of the Children of Israel from Egypt, rejoices too that all the scoundrels that did them harm, perished in the end, and that King Pharaoh, Nebuchadnezzar, Haman, Antiochus, Titus, and all the other villains of the same stripe, are dead, but that he, Lümpchen, is still alive and is now eating fish with his wife and daughter! And I want to tell you, Herr Doktor, the fish

[1] *In German the word* Lump *means "beggar" or "rascal."*

is delicious and the man is happy. He has no need of tormenting himself with culture. He sits there in his green dressing gown like Diogenes inside his barrel, enjoying himself in his religion. Delighted, he looks at the lamp that he himself has polished more than once. And I'm telling you: were the lights to grow dim and the (Gentile) *Shabbes-*woman whose job it is to put them out were not at hand, and were Rothschild the Great to come in just at that moment surrounded by all his brokers, commission agents, shippers, and office managers—men with whose aid he has conquered the world—and were he to say, "Moses Lump, ask for any favor you like and I shall grant it to you," well, Herr Doktor, I'm convinced that Moses Lump would answer casual-like: "All right, put those lights out for me!" Astonished, Rothschild the Great would then say: "Ah! if I weren't Rothschild, how I'd like to be just such a Lümpchen!"

AUNT ESTHER'S GALOSHES

BY ETHEL ROSENBERG

A week later, on the first gray December Friday morning, the bell rings in the Pasternak house. Mrs. Pasternak wonders, who can be at the door at this hour? She opens the door, and there is her Aunt Esther, come from the East Side on one of her rare visits to Brooklyn.

"Mamma *tira,*" Mrs. Bender says to her niece, "I wouldn't stay long. I'm going right home." Then she walks slowly into the kitchen and sits down heavily.

"But for lunch you'll stay, *Tante?*" Mrs. Pasternak asks, smiling.

That is a question for you. Esther Bender doesn't often go visiting, but when she does it is not a casual thing. This is a fact that the Pasternaks realize and appreciate. After all, Mrs. Bender is an old woman, and a big woman. The trip from her room on the East Side to her niece's home in Brooklyn—up the steps of the El, down the steps to the subway, up the steps again in Brooklyn, and that long walk from the station—is a real undertaking. Listen, you're young yet, you don't know what it is. Wait. You'll come to it too. So does it pay to take such a trip for nothing? Mrs. Pasternak's aunt doesn't need much urging.

"For lunch I'll stay, but right after we eat, I'll go home."

Mrs. Pasternak makes no comment. After all, her aunt has been visiting her for the past forty years, and her opening line has never varied. The moment she puts her foot across the threshold she carefully assures everyone within hearing distance that she can't stay, that she must go right home.

"So take off your galoshes at least," Mrs. Pasternak says.

"Why? After lunch I'm going home, so might as well leave them on already."

"It's starting to snow again?" Mrs. Pasternak goes to the kitchen window to peer through the steaming panes.

"Aaah," Mrs. Bender says. "In the winter time is always something. Better to wear the galoshes and be prepared."

"You'll have maybe a glass tea till lunch, Tante?" Mrs. Pasternak asks. This is a perfunctory question because the water is already beginning to boil in the kettle.

"Let be tea," Mrs. Bender says agreeably. "So, how are the children? How is Julius?"

"How is Julius?" Mrs. Pasternak shrugs. "Like always."

Mrs. Bender accepts this answer calmly.

"How is Yetta?" she asks. "She'll come in later?"

Mrs. Pasternak raises her eyebrows and shakes her head.

"*Friday* she'll come in?" she says.

Secretly Mrs. Pasternak feels the same way. After all, who in his right mind goes visiting on a Friday? But somehow Mrs. Pasternak gets her work done, guest or no guest. The chicken is in the pot; the fish is ready for chopping; the *lukshon kugel* is baking. The Friday routine is running smoothly.

"Hannah is going with somebody yet?" Mrs. Bender asks idly, as Mrs. Pasternak flits from sink to stove to closet and back.

"Yes," Mrs. Pasternak says absently, wondering if it might not be a good idea to bake a honey cake, now that her aunt is here. Mrs. Bender is very partial to Mrs. Pasternak's honey cake. "A nice boy, very quiet."

"You don't tell me." Mrs. Bender is thoughtful. "So how long are they going?"

"Ask me," Mrs. Pasternak shrugs. Will I have enough peanuts, she ponders, or should I run downstairs to the store . . . no, I'll make out with as much as I have.

"So I'm asking you," Mrs. Bender says in a reproachful voice. "You live in the same house, and you don't know how long she is going?"

Thus reproved, Mrs. Pasternak drops the cake momentarily to do some rapid figuring.

"Now," she counts aloud, "is December . . ."

"December," her aunt says impatiently, "you can't figure, it's not even a week yet."

". . . so they started to go the end of August. So that's September, October, November . . . three months," Mrs. Pasternak says triumphantly.

"Three months?" Mrs. Bender says judiciously. "So did he say something yet?"

"What should he say?" Mrs. Pasternak asks, pulling out a round baking tin.

"Frieda," her aunt says sharply, "I don't understand you. Three months they are going, you don't know the boy is serious, or he's taking Hannah's time for nothing. . . ."

"Tante," Mrs. Pasternak answers, "what is three months today to the young people? Listen, you'll eat an egg with the lunch?"

"Whatever you'll put on the table," her aunt brushes this aside. "It's too bad I wouldn't see Yetta. I would like to have a talk with her."

"So maybe she'll fall in for a few minutes later," Mrs. Pasternak replies. "Maybe I should poach the egg for you?"

"Let be poached," Mrs. Bender agrees. "It's a shame I shouldn't see her," she reflects. "But after lunch I am positively going home."

After lunch Mrs. Bender pulls herself together preparatory to leaving. But you know how it is when you start talking. What with one thing and another the time passes so quickly the afternoon disappears.

"You're here already, so might as well stay for supper and see Julius," Mrs. Pasternak says hospitably. Anyway, now there is certainly no question of Mrs. Bender's leaving—she will travel on the Sabbath eve? What are you talking?

When Mr. Pasternak comes home, he greets the company cheerfully.

"Oho!" he says. "I see the *m'shpucha* is here."

Mrs. Bender laughs heartily. No matter what Mr. Pasternak says, she laughs. She is a simple woman who regards Mr. Pasternak as a wit and a wise man—Julius, the philosopher, she calls him.

"Right after supper tomorrow night, if we live and all is well, and nothing happens," she tells him, "I am going home."

"Go with health," Mr. Pasternak says, smiling good-naturedly. "Meanwhile is still Friday's supper to eat yet."

After supper, Mr. Pasternak urges the company into the living room, but Mrs. Bender refuses. She can't sit so comfortably on the soft chairs.

"I'll sit down so I'll forget to get up," she laughs.

Mr. Pasternak looks at her speculatively.

"Maybe you are going to bed with your boots on?" he asks.

"Why not?" Mrs. Bender teases him.

"Because," Mr. Pasternak grins, "this is only for generals."

Mrs. Pasternak looks at her husband.

"Julius, with the jokes," she says dryly.

Her aunt laughs heartily.

"Listen to him, the philosopher," she says. "Don't worry, Julius. So it is possible I will take them off yet before I go to bed."

Taking off the galoshes requires a peculiar technique in Mrs. Bender's case. First she must divest herself of her sweater; this must be followed by pulling her dress up over her head. And then, breathless from all this exertion, she must rest.

"What's the matter, Tante?" Mrs. Pasternak asks kindly. (Mr. Pasternak has been banished to the day bed in the living room, although Mrs. Bender protests, "I wouldn't hear of it. *I* will sleep in the living room."

"Ridiculous," Mrs. Pasternak says.

"I will sleep in the living room," Mr. Pasternak tells Mrs. Bender, "otherwise you will be talking long distance all night."

"Listen to him," Mrs. Bender cries happily. But it is just as well that the two women are sharing the bedroom, for Mrs. Bender needs plenty of time and conversation to ease herself into bed.)

Now she is catching her breath.

"You're all right?" Mrs. Pasternak repeats.

"I'm all right," her aunt answers. "You think it's good to be so big like I am? I look at you and I envy you, how fast you can creep into bed. Me, till I move, is like moving a property." She sighs heavily.

"Tante, so take off the galoshes already," Mrs. Pasternak reminds her aunt.

"You talk like a child," Mrs. Bender says. "How can I take off the galoshes before I take off my corset?" Her fingers fumbled with the laces, pulling them loose. As each hook burst apart, little sighs of relief come softly from Mrs. Bender's lips. Mrs. Pasternak, watching the process, unconsciously sighs with her aunt. Finally the last hook is unlaced; with a tremendous gasp of deliverance, Mrs. Bender tosses the corset onto a chair.

"Tante"—Mrs. Pasternak sits up in bed—"*two* corsets you're wearing?"

Mrs. Bender nods sadly.

"The big one," she says simply, "is for me. The little one," she says, her fingers busy with the hooks in back, "is for my stomach."

"Oh," Mrs. Pasternak, enlightened, shakes her head wisely.

At long last Mrs. Bender is a free woman. Now she gets into the nightgown which Mrs. Pasternak has prepared for such occasions.

"Tante," Mrs. Pasternak says gently, pointing to her aunt's feet, "so now maybe you will take off your galoshes?"

"Look at that," Mrs. Bender cries. "I almost forgot them." She bends over heavily. After a few moments of puffing and struggling, the galoshes are yanked off. Mrs. Bender is actually ready for bed. She climbs in like a tidal wave, and Mrs. Pasternak is thrown into the breakers for a moment. When she comes up for air, the two women talk quietly at random until they drift off to sleep. Friday is at an end.

The next morning Mrs. Pasternak slips out of bed before her aunt is awake. She therefore does not witness the reverse process of last night's scene. If Mrs. Bender undressing is an impressive sight, Mrs. Bender dressing is equally awesome. Her first act, on getting up, is to struggle into her galoshes. Then, her nightgown removed, her stomach is captured and imprisoned in the special belt. This is followed by a determined assault on Mrs. Bender's body, which puts up a fight, but slowly, inexorably yields to the greater strength of Mrs. Bender's will. Finally Mrs. Bender is fully dressed.

"Tante," Mrs. Pasternak calls, "we'll be late for *shul*."

"I'm coming, I'm coming," Mrs. Bender calls back.

"Julius," Mrs. Pasternak says, "go see if Yetta will be ready soon. Tell her we are eating breakfast already."

Mr. Pasternak obediently repairs to the Rivkin door.

"Yetta," he says, poking his head through the open doorway, "you're ready? We're going right away."

"I'm coming, I'm coming," his sister calls.

And so the family goes to *shul*, the ladies without their pocketbooks and in their best hats, naturally. And of course Mrs. Bender wears a dainty handkerchief at her wrist.

"Yetta," Mrs. Bender says, "you're coming in later to see me?"

"What's the matter?" Mr. Pasternak kids her. "Now you are the invisible woman?"

"The invisible woman," Mrs. Bender laughs. "Oh, is this a Julius!"

"Julius, with his jokes," his sister says.

"I hear Hannah is going with a boy," Mrs. Bender says.

Mrs. Rivkin nods proudly.

"So quiet, he can hardly talk a word," Mrs. Rivkin boasts. If Howie could hear this description of himself he would be very surprised.

"You like him," Mrs. Bender states.

"I like him," Mrs. Rivkin agrees. "What's not to like?"

"Ladies," Mr. Pasternak says, "here we are. So if you will excuse me. . . ." And off he goes to his side of the congregation to discuss business and high finance with his cronies. The ladies get together and talk about this one (she should be well and have years) and that one (it shouldn't happen to us and to all our loved ones and all our friends and our acquaintances what happened to her). In a short while, conversation gives way to prayer, and services begin. The old people file out of the *shul* with a feeling of fullness and well-being. Some gather in small groups for the last bit of snatched talk; others hurry home for lunch. What a satisfactory way to spend the Sabbath morning! For all of them, but particularly Mrs. Bender, this is always the high point of their week.

"Yetta, might as well come in for lunch in my house," Mrs. Pasternak urges her sister-in-law hospitably.

"Not today," Mrs. Rivkin says. "Thank you just the same, but Hannah is coming home for lunch today."

"She isn't meeting Howie?" Mrs. Pasternak asks, surprised.

"Why isn't she meeting Howie?" Mrs. Rivkin says. "She is meeting him five o'clock by the lions. But first she wants to come home and change."

"By the lions? What kind of lions?" Mrs. Bender asks. She has never been in mid-town Manhattan in her life.

"By the public library on Forty-second Street," Mrs Rivkin says, "is two statues from lions. That's where they meet sometimes."

"Oh," Mrs. Bender says doubtfully, "on Forty-second Street." Mr. Pasternak eyes her quizzically.

"So now she told you," he sings to her, "do you know?"

Mrs. Bender pushes him playfully.

"Philosopher," she cries, "you're making fun from the old tante?"

Back at the house, Mrs. Rivkin bustles energetically into her apartment.

"I'll see you later," she calls to Mrs. Bender, who nods her head and enters the Pasternak home. It is then that Mrs. Pasternak notices for the first time that her aunt is wearing her galoshes.

"Tante," she cries, "on such a golden day you're wearing your galoshes?"

"I figure I'm leaving right after supper," Mrs. Bender says logically. "So I'm going to take off my corset to put on my galoshes later? It's too much trouble. I put them on so it will be for the day already."

"A whole day you'll wear galoshes," Mrs Pasternak says. "Foolish. So heavy on the feet. I would put them on for you."

"God forbid. Why should you bend?" Mrs. Bender says. "So it will be a little heavy on the feet. So long as it isn't heavy on the heart."

"Julius," Mrs. Pasternak reprimands her husband, "you'll put your nose in the paper later. Now is time to eat lunch."

After lunch, Mrs. Rivkin comes in bearing half a honey cake wrapped carefully in a fresh white linen napkin.

"For the company," she says cheerfully, "some *lekuch mit nis.*"

"If I knew you were making honey cake with nuts," Mrs. Pasternak sighs, "so I wouldn't bake yesterday."

"Don't worry," Mr. Pasternak assures his wife, "for honey cake you will get customers in this house."

Mrs. Bender laughs.

"Between you and me, Julius," she says, "will two cakes be enough?"

"I'm wondering," Mr. Pasternak answers. His wife cuts a few slices and stores them away in the breadbox. "For Morris," she explains to her aunt. "Morris likes a good piece honey cake once in a while."

"Where is Hannah?" Mrs. Bender asks. "She can't come in a minute to say hello?"

"She's coming, she's coming," Mrs. Rivkin says. "She just has to fix her hair a little. After all, to go meet a boy you have to look nice."

"Why not?" Mrs. Bender says. She is about to go deeper into the subject when Hannah appears. She kisses Mrs. Bender warmly, leaving a smudge of lipstick on the old lady's face.

"I'm sorry I can't stay long, Aunt Esther, but I have a date."

"I hear you are going with this date three months already," Mrs. Bender says, eying Hannah keenly. Hannah recoils automatically. She has a feeling she knows what is coming.

"That's right," she says. "I know Howie about three months already."

"So what's going to be?"

"I'm sure I don't know what you mean," Hannah says stiffly, knowing only too well what Mrs. Bender means.

"She means," Hannah's mother says, "what's the matter Howie doesn't say anything." She turns unhappily to Mrs. Bender. "The mamma can't say anything, God forbid."

"Mamma," Hannah says, in a tone of one who has been making this statement very often of late, "I only know Howie three months. We're not serious, or anything. . . ."

Mrs. Bender bristles.

"What's the matter you're not serious?" she asks hotly. "Three months is long enough to go. Time isn't standing still," she warns Hannah. "Why should he take your time for nothing?"

"He isn't taking my time," Hannah says, with great dignity. "I happen to enjoy his company."

Mrs. Bender disregards this as utter nonsense. She gets down to the practical immediately.

"Does he at least make a living?" she asks. "Can he support a wife?"

Hannah is on the verge of a complete frustration.

"Really, Aunt Esther," she says coldly, "I think it's customary to be *asked* before you start assuming whether a man can support you or not."

Mrs. Bender looks at Hannah speculatively, then at Mrs. Rivkin.

"I'll tell you," she says finally, "this one," indicating Hannah, "is a soft one. If you ask me, the boy will never marry Hannah. Just from listening I can tell you. A boy needs a push," she says vigorously. "To me he sounds like he likes a good time with no responsibilities. If you would take my advice," she tells Mrs. Rivkin, who leans forward eagerly to receive it, "you would forget about him and go to a *shadchan.*"

"A marriage broker!" Hannah says, outraged. "Honestly!" Her voice is edged with tears.

"What's the matter?" Mrs. Bender asks, surprised. "What's so terrible? I didn't get married through a shadchan?"

Mr. Pasternak, who is very fond of his niece, comes to her rescue.

"Hannah," he says gently, "it's getting late. Fix your face a little and go meet Howie."

She looks at him thankfully.

"I have to rush," she says, taking his cue. "Good-by, Aunt Esther," she says politely. "It was nice seeing you again."

"You take my advice, Hannah," Mrs. Bender says. "Don't waste your time, remember."

"I'll remember," Hannah says helplessly.

"I'll walk with you to the door," Mr. Pasternak whispers. "I'm going downstairs a little to see Morris, ladies," he says aloud. "Maybe I will also torture Kugel a little bit. So if you'll excuse me. . . ."

"We'll excuse you," they say, anxious to get on with their "woman talk," as Mr. Pasternak designates it.

"Listen, Hannah," Mr. Pasternak says kindly, patting her hand, "don't take it to heart. Believe me, she means it only for your own good."

"I know," Hannah says, "but after all . . ." She stops because her voice is threatening to go out of control again.

"Forget about it," he tells her. "Howie is a nice boy—go, enjoy yourself, have a good time."

"I will," Hannah promises, and is gone.

Women, Mr. Pasternak muses, women.

The three women are not concerned with Mr. Pasternak's musings. At the moment they are interested in pursuing further the proposition Mrs. Bender has set forth.

"What's so terrible?" Mrs. Bender is asking in a strong voice. "I didn't live forty years with my husband, may he rest in peace? A good husband, a good provider," she says, counting his virtues on her fingers, "a good father. What's the matter?"

"So who can talk to Hannah?" Mrs. Rivkin says. "Like you burned her with fire when you told her from a shadchan."

"After all," Mrs. Pasternak demurs, "she is still a young girl, and she is going with a boy. . . ."

"And to her a shadchan sounds already like it's a business," Mrs. Rivkin interrupts.

Mrs. Bender looks annoyed.

"Yetta," she says, "between you and me and the lamppost, marriage isn't a business? In my time," she warms up to her subject, "a girl didn't run around. The father and mother looked for a good steady boy, they looked from what family he comes. . . . Today with the young people is right away love. Who cares for the family? Who cares if he'll be a good provider? In my time, was no love, wasn't divorces, either."

"Why was no love?" Mrs. Pasternak protests, thinking back nostalgically to herself and her husband in the days of their warm, passionate youth. "Was love since Adam and Eve."

"Frieda," Mrs. Bender says impatiently, "you know like I do, in the old days the marriages were arranged. What's the shame? How many girls you see today can't get a fellow. . . . Listen, Mathilda's daughter didn't sit until she was forty, she wouldn't go to a shadchan? You think Mathilda listened to her?"

"I heard Mathilda paid two hundred dollars for Sam," Mrs. Rivkin says with interest.

"So she paid two hundred dollars," Mrs. Bender answers. "So what's the matter with them? They live like two little pigeons."

"Tante," Mrs. Pasternak says reasonably, "what makes Hannah to go to a shadchan? She has a boy, a nice quiet boy, maybe you'll see him yet, so what more does she need?"

"She needs somebody to give him a push, that's what she needs. Hannah is a girl who would go and go and not say a word, maybe she'll hurt the boy's feelings."

"So what can I do?" Mrs. Rivkin asks unhappily. "So I can't open my mouth. Right away Hannah tells me, 'Ma, you want to drive him away?' Can you imagine?"

"So if you can't ask him his intentions, what do you need him?" Mrs. Bender says vigorously. "By me that wouldn't go. A mother shouldn't be able to ask a boy his intentions!" she says indignantly.

"Well," Mrs. Pasternak says, getting up from the chair, "I better start fixing supper. You'll have supper here, Yetta?"

"No," Mrs. Rivkin says, getting up from her chair too. "I have to go over to see Rebecca, I promised her yet last week. So I'll grab a bite in the house. Well, Tante," she says to Mrs. Bender, "when will I see you?"

"Who knows?" the old lady replies. "I'm leaving right after supper."

"Well, take care of yourself," Mrs. Rivkin says. "So with God's help maybe we'll see you again soon."

"Go with health," Mrs. Bender says.

After the meal, Mrs. Bender makes a heroic attempt to leave.

"Now," she says, struggling up from the table, "I am really going."

"Julius," Mrs. Pasternak says, "I think that was the bell, or not?"

"It was the bell," Mr. Pasternak agrees. "I'll answer." He comes back with a small birdlike woman in tow.

"Look who is here," he says. "The cousin from Brownsville."

"Jenny," Mrs. Bender cries rapturously.

"Esther," Jenny says joyfully. "What are you doing here?"

"What are *you* doing here?" Mrs. Bender counters. They both talk at once. Listen, how long is it they didn't see each other . . . the family news they must catch up with . . . don't ask. This one has to discuss the daughter-in-law and how blind the son is; that one has to compare her grandchildren (how smart! how sweet! how beautiful! the father's eyes it has, or clever like the mother!) with the other one's grandchildren; one has to bring in the latest symptoms in her illness (you don't know what it is and you shouldn't have to know). By the time they look around, it's late.

"Look at the clock," Mrs. Bender gasps. "That's the right time? It couldn't be."

"Why couldn't it be?" Mr. Pasternak asks. "Time marches on!" he says impressively.

"I have to go myself," Jenny says reluctantly. "Good-by, Esther. Remember me to the family. Take care of yourself. Let me hear from you once in a while."

And after another half hour of good-bys and last-minute tidbits at the door, the Brownsville cousin finally leaves. But not Mrs. Bender.

"Listen," Mr. Pasternak says, "till you'll walk to the station, and wait for the train. . . ."

"And she has to change trains yet . . ." Mrs. Pasternak agrees.

"All right," Mrs. Bender says weakly, "but tomorrow morning right after breakfast I'm going. You hear, Frieda?"

"I hear." Mrs. Pasternak bends down. "Do me a favor already," she says. "Two days you're wearing your galoshes. Take them off your feet already."

The next morning is Sunday, but all three are up early. Mr. Pasternak likes to get started promptly on the Sunday paper; he is a thorough, painstaking reader, and the Sunday paper is fat with features. Mrs. Pasternak wants to get started on the *blintzes* in case, as she puts it, "the children will fall in." Mrs. Bender wants to go home. She gets up out of bed, and before she fights her way into her belt and corset she pulls her galoshes on.

After breakfast, Mr. Pasternak goes down to get his paper. Mrs. Pasternak gets busy on the blintzes. Now between us, it shouldn't go any further, you hear? Mrs. Bender is not only blessed with a big appetite, but she is a terrible *nasher*. And with all this activity going on, how can she tear herself away? She lingers, and lingering protests she must leave, lingers further, and wails positively that she must go.

"Where is the rush?" Mrs. Pasternak persuades her busily. "Might as well stay already for lunch. I have delicious sour cream for the blintzes. I made a few extra so you'll have some to take home with you."

It takes a little convincing—not much, just a polite little—and Mrs. Bender agrees to stay for lunch. Mr. Pasternak entertains the ladies by reading tidbits from the paper, though after a while Mrs. Pasternak says impatiently, "Julius, I don't know if I'm coming or going. Who can work and listen to you at the same time?" Mr. Pasternak is momentarily aggrieved. He is not the kind of man who ordinarily reads the paper aloud. He is only trying to be helpful. But he understands that his wife is under a strain and holds his peace. After all, Mrs. Bender has been here since Friday. Morris, like every Sunday, is invited for lunch. And Mrs. Pasternak is fussy; she likes everything just so . . . Listen, it's work.

Finally they sit down to lunch. Mrs. Pasternak piles the plates high with generous portions, but Mrs. Bender has an appetite, I'm telling you—knock on wood. Before they look around, the blintzes are all gone.

And Mrs. Bender intends to be gone, too. She is going home. Since early Friday morning she has been visiting the Pasternaks, most of the time with her galoshes on. Now it is Sunday afternoon. She is definitely going home. She gets into her coat and hat; she and her niece walk to the door, busy remembering each other to various sections of the family. At that moment, when Mrs. Pasternak opens the door and says, "Well, Tante, keep well and go with God," at that moment, Howie Weissman comes bounding up the steps.

"Hello, Mrs. Pasternak," he greets her pleasantly. "How are you?"

"Howie!" Mrs. Pasternak says. Mrs. Bender's ears come to attention.

"This is Hannah's Howie?" she asks. Howie looks a little wary at these words.

"This is my aunt, Mrs. Bender," Mrs. Pasternak introduces him.

"How do you do?" he says politely. Mrs. Bender studies him closely.

"A pleasure," she tells him absently. She is measuring him to see if he will make a good husband. It is a look that Howie shrinks from automatically.

"It was nice meeting you," he says hastily, ringing the Rivkin bell. Hannah answers the door, in time to hear Mrs. Bender ask Mrs. Pasternak, "So did Hannah meet his people yet, Frieda?" Mrs. Pasternak shakes her head.

"Good-by, Aunt Esther," she says firmly. "Let me hear from you how you got home."

Mrs. Bender shakes her head too, as she descends the steps with a heavy tread.

"What's the matter she didn't see his people yet?" she mutters loudly. Hannah stands red-faced in the open doorway. She is afraid to look at Howie.

"Come in, Howie," she says, her voice almost inaudible. He pushes the door shut behind them, and reaches for the acutely embarrassed girl.

"Take it easy, kid," he says softly in her ear. She turns her head to answer, but Howie covers her lips swiftly with his. He is not in a mood for conversation. He wraps his arms around Hannah and pulls her closer.

"Howie," Hannah whispers, after a moment, "we'd better go in. My mother will be wondering what's happened to us."

"Let her wonder," Howie says, aroused. Whenever I get a little more personal, he thinks, Hannah figures out a way to stop me. She can't kid me, he says to himself speculatively, she likes it, or she would if she could let herself go. But she's scared. This pleases Howie obscurely, at the same time that it irritates him. It is proof to him of her sweet innocence, a factor not overwhelmingly present in other girls he has dated. He remembers, even as he is kissing Hannah, a discussion they had when he had casually slipped his arm around her the first time.

"Don't you agree," she'd said, sitting stiffly against his arm, afraid to relax, "that a man and woman can be good platonic friends?"

For a full moment, Howie had been stunned. My God, she's a *baby*, he thought to himself in dismay. I'd better get out of here, but quick. And then Hannah had turned with her big serious eyes to see why Howie hadn't answered, and he'd kissed her.

Since then, Howie thinks, this relationship has been like no other I've ever had. I can't let her alone, and I can't get anywhere either.

"Howie," Hannah says, pushing away and fixing her hair nervously, "*please*. My mother will come looking for us if we don't go into the living room now."

Howie shrugs.

"O.K.," he says in resignation. As he follows her into the other room he thinks, she really is a sweet kid. A nice, *protected*, sweet kid, he thinks wryly. God, what a *protected* kid! Say, what was it the old lady said, going down the steps, something about Hannah meeting his parents? Howie has a quick picture of what would happen. His mother would start carrying on—"You're too *young* to be thinking of marriage, Howie"—and she'd start to cry. And who is thinking of marriage, Howie says honestly to himself. But try telling that to his mother. Every time he looks at a girl, his mother begins to worry. As long as he can remember, it's been that way. That's why he hasn't even told her he's been dating the same girl for three months. She'd throw a fit. . . . Now with Pop, it's different, he thinks. You can talk to him. . . .

"Howie," Mrs. Rivkin says, "maybe you'll have a cup of coffee?"

"No, thanks, Mrs. Rivkin," he says politely. "By the way," he adds, just to keep the conversational ball rolling, "I just met Mrs. Pasternak's aunt in the hall."

"You did?" Mrs. Rivkin cries in delight. "Isn't that wonderful? I'm so glad. She was so anxious to meet you. She thinks," Mrs. Rivkin says casually, "that people should marry when they are young, they shouldn't go around too long together."

Hannah is up in arms immediately.

"If we're going, Howie," she says desperately, "we'd better get started."

Howie stands up with alacrity.

"You bet," he says. "Well, so long, Mrs. Rivkin."

"Have a good time, children," Mrs. Rivkin answers serenely. Listen, she thinks grimly, Hannah likes it or she doesn't like it, still it doesn't hurt to throw in a word. Howie is no dumbbell; he'll understand, don't worry.

THE STRIKE OF THE SCHNORRERS

BY MORDCHE SPEKTOR

TRANSLATED FROM THE YIDDISH BY NATHAN AUSUBEL

Once, in my youth, I was invited to a wedding. It was none of those denatured weddings at which the powder pours from the décolleté women and girls, none of those weddings attended by frock-coated and white-gloved gentlemen with nasty-smelling pomaded side whiskers. No, I wasn't invited to a wedding of the sort where one had to eat according to a printed card: fish à la Leviathan, bouillon à la Vistula, roast à la Jacques Lebaudy, salad à la Green Gall, and wine from Sobieski's times (i.e., this year's adulterated bilge served up in dirty, dust-covered bottles).

Absolutely not! I was invited instead to an honest-to-goodness Jewish *chasseneh* at which the guests came dressed in the same clothes that they wore when they went to the synagogue on *Shabbes* and on holy days. It was the genuine article, where you started out with *lekech* and strudel, and then followed up with Sabbath fish eaten with fresh little rolls, "golden" broth, stuffed chickens, and roast ducks, and then washed it all down with excellent wine from large clean bottles. In short, it was a wedding with all the time-honored usages and customs, including a feast in honor of the groom and a meal for the *uremileit* as well.

At the weddings of his children it was Reb Yitzchok-Eisik Berkower's invariable custom to give a dinner for the uremileit. That's the way it was observed in every good Jewish home according to ancient tradition and commandment. And now, when he was about to celebrate the marriage of his youngest daughter, his *mizinke,* he invited all the uremileit of the neighboring town of Lipowitz to a feast in the village where he had lived all his life.

The day of the wedding arrived at last. But when the clock struck two the uremileit had not showed up yet. How could it be? Already bright and early that morning Chaskel, the servant, had gone to fetch them in three large wagons. Something unusual must have happened, since Lipowitz lay only five versts away! Needless to say, all the relatives and wedding guests were getting impatient waiting for the *chupeh.*

At last Chaskel came pounding in on a nag that he had unhitched from his cart, but alas! without the uremileit.

"Why do you come back alone?" asked Reb Yitzchok-Eisik in astonishment.

"The uremileit don't want to come," replied Chaskel and clambered off his nag.

"What do you mean 'they don't want'?" the bystanders asked incredulously.

"They say everyone of them must get a ruble or none of them will show up for the wedding."

We all had to laugh. Who had ever heard of such a thing!

"There has been another wedding today in Lipowitz and also with a meal for uremileit," Chaskel told us. "The uremileit ate heartily and drank well, and now they talked it over and came to an understanding. They won't leave their town unless everyone of them gets paid a ruble. The nastiest of all the rebels among the uremileit are Shmelke the cripple, you know the one with the two crutches, Avrom-Moishe the long *ganef,* Feitel the lame, and Yaykel with the flat nose. The others might have been willing to come, but those rascals wouldn't let them! What could I do? I negotiated with them for a full hour and got nowheres. Now, I ask you, what shall I do?"

All of us wedding guests went into an uproar of laughter over this strike by the *schnorrers.* Only our host, Reb Yitzchok-Eisik, boiled with anger.

"Nu! Didn't you negotiate with them? Didn't they want to make it any cheaper?" he asked Chaskel.

"I bargained with them a whole hour but they didn't want to take a kopeck less."

"*Takkeh!* Since when has this article become so dear?" asked Reb Yitzchok-Eisik with a bitter laugh. "And why did you leave the wagons in Lipowitz? We can get along perfectly well without schnorrers!"

"I didn't know what to do! I was afraid you'd give me a scolding, but I'll go now and bring the wagons back."

"Wait a little while. What's the hurry? We've got time yet."

And Reb Yitzchok-Eisik began to discuss the matter with his guests.

"What can this mean? Who in the world has ever heard such a thing: that uremileit should present conditions to *me*, should negotiate with *me*, that they should eat and drink well, and on top of that *I* should make each one of them a present! A ruble each—nothing less! Otherwise, they won't come! Ha-ha-ha! And if I were to distribute two gulden among them it wouldn't be worth their while, eh? Imagine what big expenses they must have! That's what I'd call *schnorrer-chutzpah!* For my part I can do very well without them! Come on, you musicians, play us a tune! Where's the *shammes?* It's time to 'cover' the bride!"

But right away he countermanded his own orders.

"Let's wait a bit longer. It's early yet. . . . What, in Heaven's Name, have I done to deserve that my happiness should be marred so? How can I marry off my daughter without a feast for the uremileit? I know what—I'll give each of them half a ruble. What do I care about money? But what do they mean by negotiating with me? I know I've done my duty. If they don't want it, it's all right with me. They'll be sorry for it, never you fear! Such a wedding they won't have every day. We can perfectly well get along without them."

Then the shammes came and asked:

"Nu? Can we start 'covering' the bride?"

"Yes, you can! But hold on, let's wait a little bit longer."

The wedding guests grew more and more impatient. It was their opinion that the best thing to do was to forget all about the schnorrers. But Reb Yitzchok-Eisik suddenly got a new inspiration. A look of determination came into his face. His anger vanished, and, turning to me and two other friends among the guests, he asked us to go to Lipowitz and make one more effort to persuade the uremileit.

"He has no sense!" said he with annoyance about his servant Chaskel. "One can't rely on him in such matters."

A cart was quickly readied and we rode forth in buoyant spirits. Chaskel again got on his nag and brought up the rear.

All the way to Lipowitz we held our sides laughing at the conspiracy. A union of schnorrers! How do you like that? I had already heard about a strike of workers who refused to work unless they obtained higher wages and better working conditions. But a strike of schnorrers, of schnorrers who demanded higher alms only because they had to eat for nothing at a feast! Is there any event like this in all of world history?

In about twenty minutes we rode into town. In the market place I saw standing three large farm wagons bedded with fresh straw. The small horses were unharnessed and eating out of their feed bags. Almost a hundred uremileit clustered around the wagons—the mutes, the lame, the blind, and in addition well-nigh half the population of the town made up of riff-raff and idlers. All were shouting and yelling at one time.

Shmelke the cripple was sitting on a wagon and beating with his crutches against the sideboards of the vehicle. And Avrom-Moishe, the long *ganef,* with a red kerchief around his neck, sat next to him. These two leaders of the revolt were addressing themselves to the people—that is, to the schnorrers.

"Very good!" cried Avrom-Moishe, the long *ganef,* when he caught sight of us and Chaskel. "They've come to beg us—wait and see!"

"Yes, they'll beg us!" echoed the cripple, beating his crutches against the wagon.

We then asked them, "Why don't you want to come to the wedding? And how about the feast? Never fear, you'll get your presents!"

"How much?" they all yelled with one voice.

"What do you mean 'how much'? What you'll get you'll take!"

"Will you give everyone a ruble? If not, we don't go!"

"There'll be a hole in the sky if you don't go!" jeered a bystander.

The schnorrers answered this jibe in a frontal attack with their sticks and a neat little skirmish followed:

Avrom-Moishe, the long *ganef,* drew himself up to his full height and shouted:

"Quiet! *Sha! Sha!* Quiet! Unfortunate cripples! Who can understand a single word! Pay attention when people speak!"

So saying he turned to us and said:

"I want you to know, dear brothers, that we won't move from this spot until you promise a ruble to every man of us. We are not worried at all! Without us Reb Yitzchok-Eisik won't celebrate the marriage of his youngest daughter. And where, let me ask you, can he find now other uremileit? He certainly's not going to Linetz! That'll cost him a lot dearer, and worse yet the wedding will have to be postponed."

"What do you think—just because we're uremileit you can do with us what you please?" shouted another rebel, climbing onto the top of a wagon wheel. He was blind in one eye and advertised the fact by means of a dirty rag over the socket. "No one can force us to go, neither the chief of police nor the governor-general! Remember—everybody a ruble or no one goes!"

"A r-r-r-ru-ruble!" cried a stuttering schnorrer.

"A ruble!" called out the one with the flattened nose.

"A ruble! A ruble!" cried two jolly schnorrers as they leaped into the air.

And then in chorus the entire band roared: "Hand over a ruble! A ruble!"

In their outcries, in their shouting lay so much bitterness and defiance. It seemed as if all the stored-up anguish of their wretched lives was now gushing forth at last. Ever before they had kept silent, were forced to be silent. For the groschen that was flung at them, or for a crust of bread, or for an already gnawed-off bone, they had to swallow so many insults! This, therefore, was the first time that their troubled hearts could beat freely, the one and only time in their lives! And so they reveled in the pleasure that was the lot of only the well-fed and vented their wrath against the servants of the rich and against the caprices of their masters. With the outcry of "ruble" they wished to relieve their schnorrer-hearts from all their despair, resentment, and humiliation. For the first time they enjoyed the dignified awareness that even well-fed happy people had to come to them for something that they had in their power to give. And they were eager to taste to the brim of this proud sensation of triumph.

And as we were negotiating with them, a new message came from Reb Yitzchok-Eisik: the schnorrers were to come right away. He promised that everyone would get his ruble.

A wild jubilation followed. The uremileit clambered into the three wagons. One yelled: "Look out—my sick hand!" Another: "A-ah! My poor leg!" But just the same the jolly schnorrers sang and leaped about with abandon. The horses were hitched to the wagons, and in a spirit of revelry they started out for the wedding. The riff-raff sent them off with a jeering burst of hurrahs; they yelled and whistled and threw stones at them. But the schnorrers behaved instead as if they were being pelted with roses and were being sent off with delightful music. That overjoyed they felt over their victory!

For the first time in their lives certainly, and probably for the last time as well, they spoke now in loud firm voices, for they had achieved what they wanted.

After the chupeh the wedding guests sat down to the feast; the uremileit were served at separate tables. Reb Yitzchok-Eisik himself and other members of his family waited on them and placed before them food and drink.

"*Le'chayim!* Long life to you, Reb Yitzchok-Eisik!" the uremileit toasted their host. "May you enjoy *naches* from your children and get to be a millionaire!"

"Le'chayim, le'chayim, Jews!" replied Reb Yitzchok-Eisik. "Drink in health! May the dear God help all Israel and also you!"

After the wedding feast the musicians played merry Jewish dance tunes and Reb Yitzchok-Eisik danced with the uremileit a lively hop and a farandole.

And Reb Yitzchok-Eisik had never felt happier in his life. He kicked up his heels in the round dance and the long tails of his silk *kapote* spread out like an eagle's wings. His eyes shone with tears of joy and higher and higher, even as high as the seventh heaven, soared his thoughts. He cried and laughed like a child and was always fluttering around the uremileit, embracing and kissing them as if they were his own flesh and blood.

"Brothers!" he called out as he danced. "We must be jolly! We must behave like Jews! Musicians play us a jolly tune! More lively, Jews! Come on—put some sparks into it!"

And so the uremileit and the wedding guests clapped time with their hands to the musicians' lusty dance tune.

Yes takkeh—that's how a Jew makes merry, that's how a Jew celebrates a chasseneh!

YENTE TELEBENDE

BY B. KOVNER (JACOB ADLER)
TRANSLATED FROM THE YIDDISH BY NATHAN AUSUBEL

All year round my Yente is as healthy as an oak. Healthier even! But when the *Shevuos* holiday comes around she suddenly gets sick, critically sick. All that's lacking is to make final arrangements with the Burial Society.

"What ails you, Yente?" I ask her casually.

"*Oy* Mendel!" she wails. "I'm passing out! I won't live through it all! My heart pounds, my pulse races, I've no appetite, there's a pain in my shoulder, and my back aches, Mendel! I'm telling you, Mendel, you're going to become a widower!"

From what she said I already surmised that it had something to do with her going away to the Catskill Mountains, that it concerned ten dollars a week for board, new dresses, blouses, shoes, socks, "wrappers," sweaters, underwear, a sailor hat, and a lot of other rags.

May your enemies and my enemies combined have as much strength to survive as I have the means to send Yente to the country! But go and argue with her when I see with my own eyes how my Yente is passing out like a light.

"*Nu,*" I said with a resigned sigh, "get ready for the mountains, Yente."

As I said these words I saw Yente take on a new lease on life. Her eyes began to sparkle.

"What, again to the mountains?" she said with annoyance. "Spend my vacation with those Brownsville *yachnes*? They shouldn't live so long! This year I've decided to go on a farm in Pikefield."

"Good! Let be Pikefield—as long as you go."

"Is that so! Don't you think I know that you're dying to get rid of me, ha? So that you can drag yourself around all night long with the blonde from Sheriff Street? Just look at him—he wants to be a free bird!"

"So don't go," I said.

"What do you mean, 'don't go'? What about my heart that's pounding so and my pulse that's racing like an express train? Is that nothing to you?"

"So who's stopping you? Go!"

"It's easy for you to say 'go'! And what about the children? Where will I leave Sadie?"

"Take her along."

"And Pinyale?"

"Take him along too."

"And Feivele?"

"Him too."

"And Isaackel?"

"Of course, take all the children!"

"Is that so! So you should be a free birdie! So you should have a good time and pretend you are a 'tsingleman'! No siree, you're not going to bluff me, Mendel. Yente's brains haven't dried up yet!"

"All right! So stay at home. Who's asking you to go?"

"Listen to him! And you think it's nothing that I have a pain in my shoulder, that I feel a stabbing in my back, that my heart pounds and my pulse races?"

"All that is mud, Yente," said I, "nothing but mud."

"And what about that I've got no appetite?"

"That too is mud."

"And what about that I feel nauseous enough to pass out?"

"So who's stopping you? Go to the country."

"But I'm afraid, Mendel, that you'll go crazy from pleasure!"

"Nu, so don't go. Stay at home!"

"But I *am* sick."

"In that case, go! Who's stopping you?"

"And do you think it's nothing to take all the children along? Some pleasure you can have taking care of four brats!"

"All right then, so don't go."

In this way we were at each other for two days and two nights. And she finally decided to go to the country, but without the children. They'd remain with me at home.

"Very good," I agreed. "I'm satisfied, but go."

"If I'll go, who'll take care of the children?" she asked. "After all, you've occasionally got to cook a spoonful of something for them, shampoo a little head, wash a little face, mend a little sock. They're children, after all—may a toothache gnaw their papa!"

"In that case, I'll hire a maid for them."

"What? A maid yet you'll take into the house? You should live to see that day! Don't think I don't know that you're trying to get rid of me!"

"If you're that scared why don't you remain at home?"

"Remain at home when I'm sick?"

"So go!"

"And you'll take a maid into the house yet?"

"So don't go!"

Do you want to know what the end was? The end was that Yente opened up on me with all the curses in her well-stocked arsenal and I had to run out of the house.

II

For several weeks Yente shuffled about the house in her bedroom slippers with a cold compress tied about her head, and with disheveled hair. She mumbled, "Decent husbands—may they have stabbing pains in the sides!—when their wives fall sick they do something about it, but I have a stone for a husband. Nothing bothers him."

"Is it my fault that you don't want to go to the country?" I asked wearily.

And the debate about going to the country was continued.

"What do you mean I don't want to go to the country?" she raged. "I should go and you should take in a maid? My enemies shouldn't live to see that day!"

"In that case, take the children along so I won't have to hire a maid. I'll lock up and become a boarder somewhere to some missus."

"Is that so, a boarder to a missus, you want to be! Treat her every night to the moving pictures, ha, take her every Sunday in Bronx Park and have a good time while I'm away? No sir, Mendel! You won't take any maid in the house, and you won't be a boarder to a missus, either!"

"Stay at home then and we won't have any of this trouble."

These words seemed to strike Yente in a very sore spot for she unscrewed her abusive little mouth at me:

"Nu, may you not meet with an easy death! A person sees how I hardly breathe, how I hardly drag along my legs, so he tells me to stay at home! Why did Sarah with the wart on the tip of her nose, who's as healthy as a nut, why did she go to the country, and why did Chaya with the freckles also go, and sallow Becky with the bald head is also going the day after tomorrow? But I, sick and run down, I've got to remain at home and sleep on the roof!"

"For God's sake, who doesn't let you go?"

"I know you're trying to get rid of me! You'd like to marry a better-looking woman, one who's younger and healthier than I. You should live so long if you'll be able to get a better-looking one or one who's younger and healthier than I!"

"So what do you want of me? It can only be one of two things: either you go or you don't go."

"What do you mean 'don't go'? Lord of the Universe! May I sit *shiva* for you already! And what about the children, ha? With whom will I leave the children? If they were orphans I could put them in an orphan asylum, and settled! But when they have a father, who will take them?"

"Take them along then. I'll eat in a restaurant."

"Ha! So you should spoil your stomach and get sick!"

"All right then, I'll find board and lodging with my landswoman on Pitt Street."

"Is she the one whose husband ran away? Is she the young woman with the broad shoulders?"

"That's right."

"With the dimples in the cheeks?"

"Yes."

"You don't say so! Well you should live long enough to have that pleasure!"

"In that case I'll eat at my cousin's on Columbia Street."

"You mean your blond cousin?"

"Yes."

"You mean the one that's always laughing?"

"Yes."

"No sir, Mendel, you can do that only after I'm dead."

"Where the devil shall I eat then?" I asked, completely out of patience.

"Six feet deep!" screamed Yente.

In conclusion, Yente finally decided to go to the country and take the children along with her. And I? I was to eat at my mother-in-law's! . . .

III

"Mendel, what are you standing around there doing nothing? Come on, help me pack and then dress the children. Time doesn't stand still, you know, Mendel. Get a move on you, will you? Pack up for me the blue wrapper with the little white squares and the white wrapper with the little blue squares."

"Already packed," said I.

"How about the brown shawl and the red sweater?"

"Already packed."

"And the brown stockings?"

"Also packed."

"And the woollen underwear?"

"Packed."

"And the striped skirt with the belt."

"Also packed."

"And the linen coat, did you pack that?"

"Packed."

"Good! Now help me dress the children."

"But they've got to be washed first," I protested.

"I'll wash them when we get to the country," Yente assured me.

"But Yente, just look at their dirty little noses, their smudged little faces!"

"That," said Yente, "that's mud."

"Of course," I agreed, "it certainly is mud!"

"Mendel!" she shouted at me, "are you beginning again with your tricks? Dress them, I'm telling you, or I'll fiddle up a wretched morning for you."

"Where are the things?" I asked her resignedly, my heart trembling for fear that she might change her mind and not go.

"What's the matter, you're blind, or what? Don't you see the things lying over there?"

"Whose is the little red cap?"

"The little red cap is Pinya's. Put it on him."

"It's on."

"Now put on his white shoes and the black socks."

"On."

"Now wipe his little nose."

"It's wiped."

"And now drive him out of the house," ordered Yente.

"He's out."

"You've done well, Mendel. Now take the little leather hat and put it on Isaac."

"It's done."

"Now dress him in the little white suit with the brown shoes."

"That's done too."

"Now wipe his little nose."

"It's no use, I've tried it already."

"Rub well!" commanded Yente.

"I've rubbed and it doesn't help."

"Then use the brush."

"I've already done that."

"Then let him go! God forbid, you might ruin his little nose yet."

"All right, I've let him go."

"Now give him a slice of bread with jelly and drive him out of the house."

"Already drove him."

"And now look to Sadie. First thing you do is put on her the pink dress with the sailor collar. Then her black socks with the red shoes and the little straw hat with the red ribbon."

"Done."

"Now blow her nose and give her a slice of bread with mustard."

"I gave."

"Drive her out of the house then."

"Already done."

"Look to Feivel next. Get a move on you, Mendel. Time doesn't stand still!"

Finished with the children, Yente started to abuse me because I had spilled some jelly into the satchel and right on her white silk blouse.

When two o'clock came we made a dash for the streetcar. I went bathed in perspiration, holding in one hand the big satchel and with the other clutching at Pinya. Yente had stuck under each of my armpits a box of crackers for the children to chew on the way. Yente herself carried a leather bag in one hand and in the other hand a basket. After her came Sadie struggling with a bag of bananas, a jar of jelly, and a bag of sandwiches. Isaac trailed after her with a bottle of milk, and Feivel with his mother's umbrella brought up the rear.

When we got into the streetcar my brats grabbed the best seats, right next to the window, and then they started a spitting contest through it. Yente yelled, "You little devils, you'll fall out of the window. Mendel watch them!"

The conductor came to collect his fares. He asked for two whole fares and two half-fares, but Yente flatly declared that more than thirteen cents she wouldn't spend: ten cents for us two and three cents for Sadie.

The passengers rocked with laughter listening to her. Yente turned fiercely on them and called them anti-Semites to their faces. In the meantime, while she wasn't looking, I paid the conductor what he asked for. This made Yente very angry, because I was throwing away my good money.

Suddenly Yente let out a blood-curdling yell:

"Mendel, look out—Pinya's fallen out of the window!"

And saying this she fell into a faint.

I got good and frightened, began to shout in a voice I didn't recognize as my own: "Pinya, Pinya!" My fright was so great that the words stuck in my throat and I almost choked on them.

But suddenly—well, would you imagine? I give a look and there sits my Pinya next to a sport with Palm Beach trousers! As I live and breathe he was making a pogrom on the man's white pants with his bread and jelly!

Thank God! we barely succeeded in reviving Yente, and we arrived at the station just at the moment the train was to pull out.

That shrew there dries up her husband's brains!

Love is blind, but jealousy sees too much.

GOOD AND—

"How are things?"

"Good!"

"Good? You seem to have plenty of troubles."

"No—it's always good! In the summer I'm good and hot; in the winter I'm good and cold. My roof leaks so that when it rains I get good and wet. Furthermore, that nag of a wife always makes me good and mad! When I'm home I feel good and buried. Believe me, I'm good and tired of it all!"

MUSHROOMS IN BRONX PARK

BY MICHAEL GOLD

Every Sunday morning in summer my father itched to be off somewhere. He did not want to stay in town on his one free day. But my mother hated trips. When he rode to Coney Island to swim in the ocean my mother never went along. She hated the pushing and excitement of a million frantic people.

"It's a madhouse," she grumbled. "Why must I fight a lot of hooligans because it is Sunday? I can rest better sitting here on my own stoop."

She made my father angry. He loved swimming; he could swim way out beyond the lifelines. And he loved, too, as much as I did, the razzle-dazzle, the mechanical blare, the gaudy savage joys of Coney Island.

"But the fare is cheap, only a nickel," he said. "Where else can one go for a nickel?"

"I don't care," said my mother, "it's a madhouse. Coney Island is a place for monkeys."

"Bah!" my father sneered. "You are an old Baba grandmother. You would like to sit by the stove all your life!"

"No," said my mother, calmly, "in Hungary I went to places. I used to walk there in the fields and the woods. But Coney Island is different. It has no fields."

"*Nu,*" said my father, irritably, "let us go to the fields then. I will take you to Bronx Park next Sunday."

"Has it a forest there?" asked my mother.

"Yes, it has a forest," said my father.

"Nu, we will see then," said my mother, casually, "maybe I will go."

She was not enthusiastic. My mother had the peasant's aversion to travel. In her Hungarian village no one ever traveled far, except to America. The East Side was her village now, and she saw no reason for leaving it even on Sunday. She still lives on the East Side, on the same street, in the same tenement, an unhurried peasant. She has never been out of New York City. There are millions of such peasants in New York.

Sunday came. My mother had evidently decided to make the trip to Bronx Park. She rose at six to get things ready. She ironed a dress for Esther, a waist for me; she darned our stockings, and packed a lunch of salami sandwiches, pickles, cake, oranges, and hard-boiled eggs. Then she swept the house, cooked breakfast, and woke us.

"Stand up!" she said, yanking off our bedclothes.

"Why so early?" my father groaned sleepily.

"We are going to Bronx Park," said my mother. "Have you forgotten?"

At breakfast my sister and I were crazy with excitement over the trip. My mother had to slap us. She was flustered and grumbly; the thought of travel confused her.

In the elevated train her face flushed purple with heat and bewilderment. No wonder; the train was worse than a cattle car. It was crowded with people to the point of nausea. Excited screaming mothers, fathers sagging under enormous lunch baskets, children yelling, puking, and running under everyone's legs, an old graybeard fighting with the conductor, a gang of tough Irish kids in baseball suits who persisted in swinging from the straps—sweating bodies and exasperated nerves—grinding lurching train, sudden stops when a hundred bodies battered into each other, bedlam of legs and arms, sneezing, spitting, cursing, sighing—a super-tenement on wheels.

Northward to the Bronx! And at every station new mobs of frenzied sweating families loaded with lunch baskets and babies burst through the doors. There was no room for them, but they made it for themselves by standing on our feet.

My father cursed each time a fat wet matron flopped in his lap or trod on his corns.

This was New York on Sunday. All the trains and streetcars were crowded like this. Seven million people rushing to find a breath of fresh air! *"Pfui!"* said my father.

"In Roumania it is a little walk to the country," he said. "Here it is a fight for one's life. What a crazy land!"

But my mother became happier as the train rolled on. She leaned out of the window and smiled. In the streets below, the solid palisades of tenement had disappeared. There were small houses, each set among green weedy lots, and there were trees.

"It's a pleasure to see green things again," she said. "Look, another tree! I am glad we came, Herman! When we come to Bronx Park I will take off my shoes and walk in the grass. I haven't done it for fifteen years."

"They will arrest you," snarled my father, as he glared at the fat Jewish woman standing next to him, who persisted in grabbing him around the neck each time the train lurched.

"I want to pick daisies!" cried my little sister.

"Yes, yes, my darling," said my mother, fondly, "daisies and mushrooms, too. I will show you how to find mushrooms. It is more fun than picking daisies."

At last the Bronx Park! My father bought us popcorn to eat, and red balloons. Then we walked through some green fields. My mother sighed as she sniffed the fragrant air.

"Ach," said my happy mother, "it's like Hungary! There is much room, and the sky is so big and blue! One can breathe here!"

So we walked until we came to a menagerie. Here we saw a gang of crazy monkeys in a cage. They were playing tag. We fed them peanuts and watched them crack open the shells. Then we saw a lion, two tigers, a white bear, some snakes, birds, and an elephant. All of them we gave peanuts.

Then we walked far into a big lonesome country. It had a big field with no one in it. It had a forest at one end. We looked for signs: KEEP OFF THE GRASS. There were no signs. So we walked into the middle of the field, and found a wonderful tree. This tree we made our own.

We spread newspapers under the tree, and my mother laid out the lunch. We were hungry after our long ride and walk. So we ate the salami sandwiches and other good things.

My father drank two bottles of beer. Then he stretched on his back, smoked his pipe, and looked at the sky. He sang Roumanian shepherd songs. Then he fell asleep, and snored.

My mother cleaned away the newspapers. Then she looked to see if no policeman was near. There was no policeman. So she took off her shoes and stockings and walked around on the grass.

My sister and I left her and went hunting for daisies. We found some and brought them to her. She wove for us two daisy crowns out of them, the sort children wear in Hungary.

Then my mother took our hands. "Come," she said, in a whisper, "while poppa sleeps we will go into the forest and hunt mushrooms."

My father heard the whisper. His snores abruptly ended.

"Don't get lost," he mumbled, not opening his sleepy eyes.

"Pooh," said my mother, "lost in a forest? Me?"

"All right," said my father, turning on his side and snoring again.

In the forest everything suddenly became cool and green. It was like going into a mysterious house. The trees were like walls, their leaves made a ceiling. Clear, sweet voices sang through the house. These were the birds. The birds lived in the house. Little ants and beetles ran about under our feet. They lived on the floor of the house.

I smelled queer, garlicky smells. I saw a large gold coin lying in a bed of green. I looked closer, and knew I was fooled. It was sunlight. The sun made other golden lines and circles. I heard running water.

My mother walked in front of us. Her face looked younger. She stopped mysteriously every few minutes, and sniffed the air.

"I am smelling out the mushrooms," she explained. "I know how to do that. I learned it in Hungary. Each mushroom has its own smell. The best ones grow under oak trees."

"I want to pick some," said Esther.

"No!" said my mother, sharply, "you must never do that. You are an American child, and don't know about these things. Some mushrooms are poison! They will kill you! Never pick them!"

"Do they come on strings?" I asked.

"Those are the grocery store mushrooms," explained my mother. "Ach, America, the thief, where children only see dry, dead mushrooms in grocery stores! Wait, I will show you!"

There was a flush of excitement on her black, gypsy face. We were surprised at our mother. She was always so slow-moving and careful. Now she jumped over big rocks and puddles and laughed like a girl.

"Stop! I think there are mushrooms under those leaves!" she said. "Let me scratch a little and find out. Yes, yes! do you see? My nose is still sharp after all these years! What a pretty silver cap it has! It is a birch mushroom. Its parents are those birch trees. When mushrooms grow near pine trees they are green, and taste of pine. But the oak mushroom is the finest of all. It is a beautiful brown."

She broke off pieces of the mushroom for us to nibble. "It is better with salt," she said. "But how good it is! It is not like the rubbish they grow here in cellars! No, the American mushrooms have no worth. They taste and look like paper. A real mushroom should taste of its own earth or tree. In Hungary we know that!"

We followed her, as she poked around under the trees and bushes for her beloved mushrooms. She found many, and lifted her skirt to make a bag for them. Each new mushroom reminded her of Hungary and of things she had never told us. She talked in a low, caressing voice. She stooped to the mushrooms, and her eyes shone like a child's.

"Ach, how people love the mushrooms in Hungary! In the season everyone is in the forest with a big basket to hunt. We had our own favorite spots where we went year after year. We never plucked mushrooms, but cut them close to the roots, like this. It means they will grow again next year. Two other Jewish girls and I always went hunting together."

"Momma, can mushrooms talk to each other?"

"Some people say so. Some people say that at night mushrooms not only talk, but dance with each other. They turn into jolly old men with beards. In the morning they become mushrooms again.

"Birds talk to each other, too, people say. I used to know the names of all the birds, and their songs. I knew good snakes and bad, and killed the bad ones with a stick. I knew where to find blueberries and huckleberries. I could walk twenty miles in a forest and find my way back. Once, two girls and I were lost in a forest for days and found our way back. Ach, what fun there was in Hungary!"

Suddenly my mother flung her arms around each of us, and kissed Esther and me.

"*Ach, Gott!*" she cried, "I'm so happy in a forest! You American children don't know what it means! I am happy!"

> "*Poverty is no disgrace,*" *runs the saying,*
> *but that's the only good thing you can say about poverty.*

FREE

BY SHOLOM ALEICHEM

If one has no means of livelihood, he is free to die of hunger.

If one is unemployed, he is free to knock his head against the wall.

If one breaks a leg, he is free to walk on crutches.

If one gets married and hasn't enough to support his wife, he is free to go begging alms with her from house to house.

If one dies, he is free to get buried.

Jewish Food

When a woman can't make a kugel—*divorce her!*

By the way, have you ever heard of Culinary Judaism? No?

To tell you the truth, I hadn't either, until I heard a quip about it made by an eminent neurologist. He remarked that regardless whether Synagogue Judaism will survive the corrosions of time and change, of one thing though he was certain—that Culinary Judaism would endure. In fact, it would be the catalyst to bind together all Jews in an indestructible brotherhood.

This tasty discovery he made after observing that many American Jews, who had completely given up attending synagogue and whose other ties to the Jewish people had become tenuous, had the conviction that by being passionate eaters of Jewish cooking they were thereby proving their loyalty to their Jewish identity. A slice of hot noodle kugel, as it were, should make all in Israel brothers!

The religious symbols of Culinary Judaism are too numerous to mention. But it might well be worth one's while to reflect on the celestial arcana which reside in bagel with lox spread out on a layer of Philadelphia cream cheese, in kasha knishes which melt in the mouth like manna but then sink like lumps of lead in the pit of the stomach, or in gefillte fish swimming in sauce and spiced with onion and pepper.

For a dish of delicious gefillte fish, as mama selig used to make it in the good old days, the faithful of Culinary Judaism are ready to go to the other end of Hoboken. For a crunchy bagel with lox they'll get up bright and early on a Sunday morning to drive twenty miles to the nearest Jewish dairy restaurant way off in Hartford. For a pastrami sandwich with a large dill pickle and coleslaw on the side, washed down by hot tea with lemon drunk from a glass and with lump sugar in the mouth, they'll move even to Pitkin Avenue in Brownsville.

I recall the time in Paris when, in taking leave of a fellow American shortly before my return home, he said to me almost tearfully: "Good-by and bon voyage! But before you go I want to ask a favor of you. Promise me, that when you get back to New York you'll go into a good Jewish delicatessen and order a nice juicy corned-beef sandwich on Jewish rye bread. Eat it with a large half-sour pickle and, as you eat it—my God! think of me!"

His passionate plea has lingered in my memory. Twenty years have passed, but every time I happen to be eating a corned-beef sandwich in some Jewish delicatessen the devout face of that Culinary Jew almost drooling at the mouth rises to haunt me and to give me heartburn.

The strenuous devotion the Culinary Jew shows for his delicious faith one brings only to the higher values. There is even a ritual to satisfy his spiritual craving. For instance, by virtue of lapping up a plateful of mandlen floating like pond lilies in chicken broth on Friday night, he feels as though he were participating in the reception of the mystic Sabbath Bride as visioned by the medieval cabalists. And as for a strip of helzel, which is stuffed chicken neck—holy, thrice holy!

It has been observed by doctors that Jews, largely those belonging to the well-fed classes, suffer disproportionately to other groups from gastrointestinal disorders. They are tireless consumers of hot water before breakfast, of seltzer water, epsom salts, milk of magnesia, citrate of magnesia, bicarbonate of soda, Ex-Lax, Tums, Pluto Water, and what not. They are only too often afflicted with gallstones, peptic ulcers, and liver trouble.

Of course, there is a reason for everything, also for the specific character of Jewish cooking. For centuries most Jews lived in stony ghettos where no green thing ever showed its natural face. So they became estranged from many vegetables and fruits. Since they were very poor, the principal articles of their diet consisted of herring— the poor Jew's meat—of cheese, potatoes, onions, garlic, dried beans, and bread—especially bread. Meat, poultry, and fish were usually *reserved for the Sabbath and religious festivals. Oddly enough, this unbalanced diet didn't seem to bother most poor Jews very much, they had so little to eat that whatever they ate they digested well. Only one trouble: there wasn't enough to eat!*

However, as soon as Jews began leaving the ghettos in droves for America little more than half a century ago, there emerged a sizable middle class and an even larger lower middle class. Yet, in the hour of their well-being, many could not forget their herring days when there was never enough to eat. Their innards now cried out hungrily for the fleshpots and the rich foods they had always yearned for in the days of their poverty. Into this hunger also entered an element of conspicuous mastication. In the olden days, one of the few ways the new rich could demonstrate their prosperity for the awestruck poor to see and envy was to eat "good" and "a lot." And so now many of the well-to-do started to eat with more enthusiasm and ostentation than good judgment. Worse yet, the tyranny of habit and tradition as fixed in the unbalanced diet of the ghetto was carried over into the new life. Many Jews still were not on speaking terms with green vegetables and put on weight from a diet dominant in starches, sweets, and fats. And that is precisely the juncture where doctors, pills, colonic irrigations, surgery, and mineral-water spas entered!

N.A.

THE GASTRONOMY OF THE JEWS
A REMINISCENCE OF MY YOUTH

BY MORITZ G. SAPHIR
TRANSLATED FROM THE GERMAN BY NATHAN AUSUBEL

We Viennese journalists write a lot about everything and a little about nothing. Both we and the ducks say: "You never can tell what's going to make you fat!" Because we are able to speak about nothing, we therefore can easily chatter about everything. . . .

Vogl's Jewish Restaurant is so highly praised and recommended by everybody that you feel like calling out with the poet: "There, oh, there, I want to go!"

At the mere mention of Vogl's my stomach begins to indulge in some youthful reminiscences. Who doesn't know that man's stomach has a better memory than his heart? The memory of the heart is called "gratitude." the memory of the stomach is called "lust." I'm now feeling downright lustful for the "fleshpots of Egypt." My stomach is stirred by dreams of *scholet* and *kugel,* by yearning after *ganef* and *belek* and still other savory dishes. These dishes are especially tasty with Babylonian harp accompaniment and even more so when they are penetrated by the subtle fragrance of that variety of Jerusalem oleander known to modern man as garlic. It was with this irresistible magic trick that King Solomon was able to attract the Queen of Sheba to himself.

Lucullus greatly advanced the art of gastronomy. Pompey was also no mongrel dog at it; he rewarded M. Asidium Lucro, who invented the technique of stuffing peacocks, with the sum of 60,000 sesterces. Apicius initiated the art of stuffing pigs with figs. Bittelius was the first to introduce nightingale-tongue pie; he paid 2,000 sesterces for a single Swedish nightingale. Yet none of these virtuosi of cookery and the gut had the slightest idea what the highly individual and piquant Jewish cooking tasted like. The Protector Cromwell once ate at the table of the celebrated Menasseh ben Israel and stated afterwards that never before had he found food so "delightful!" He really said, "delightful!" From this we can deduce that garlic must have had a hand in it.

If I'm going to describe here several of the favorite Jewish dishes, especially those dishes that are traditional for the Sabbath table, and known among the Romans as *mensae secundae,* then of course only "typical" Jews will understand me. In any case, it is precisely for them that I'm writing this article, because I really and truly love typical Jews. Let me be correctly understood. I mean that, if I had to choose between the old-fashioned Jews and the modern Jews, I'd choose the old-fashioned ones—they are the "typical" Jews. As for the modern Jews, they are "walking-stick Jews."

The typical old-fashioned Jew is an honest fellow; he says firmly and directly: "I am a Jew!" On such a Jew you can rely in time of need because he is a firm and determined fellow. But the modern "walking-stick Jews" bend and cringe. When it doesn't suit their interest to bend on one side they bend on the other. And should it again get a little uncomfortable for them, they bend again to the other side. I like everything that's thoroughgoing, by which I mean I like everything that's genuine. I like a typical Jew, a typical Christian, a typical Turk, etc., which only means I like a genuine Jew, a genuine Christian and a genuine Turk. However, let's get back to my typical Jews and to their typical cookery.

Our new emancipated age has already made many concessions.

That's why, for example, you can find menus with the entry: "Brown carp with Jewish sauce." Or even: "Jewish fish." Yes, these "Jewish fish" you'll find in one and the same column with "Trout," "Lachs," and so forth. A great advance, you'll admit! By themselves these "Jewish fish" have only a surface resemblance to genuine Jewish fish. One mustn't forget that there are also false imitations of Jewish fish.

Take, for instance, "sour Jewish fish"—it's world famous! I once gave a "Sour Jewish Fish Dinner" in Munich. Present were Gutzkow, Spindler, Lewald, Feldmann, Esslair, Urban, Jermann, Dettinger, etc. I placed before them a bowl of "sour Jewish fish heads" and, in honor of the occasion, I made the following speech:

"Gentlemen! I've invited you all to a 'sour Jewish fish head' dinner. For this tête-à-tête we're now gathered and we'll soon get to work upon head-and-neck. Before we do so, permit me to make a brief speech. The Jews and fish have great sympathy for each other. Jews gladly eat fish, and fish gladly eat Jews, which we know for a fact from the story of that celebrated fish who enjoyed a whole Jew with all his skin and hair for *déjeuner à la fourchette*. Fortunately, he spat him out again unharmed. And because the Jews know that fish gladly eat Jews, that is why they're so afraid of the water. If Jews like fish so much it is for the reason that, when they wanted to cross the Red Sea, the fish all at one time suddenly began to swallow up the water. This enabled the Jews to go across and remain dry. Finally, when Pharaoh and the Egyptians came by, the fish once more and all together spat out the water and thus drowned the Jews' pursuers.

"For that reason, on every Sabbath and holy day the Jews, to show their gratitude, invite the fish to be their honored guests. But so often have the Jews themselves been invited as honored guests only to be 'scaled off,' that they accord the same treatment to their guests, the fish. They proceed to scale them, pull out their insides, and then cook them the way they like. Observe gentlemen, these are excellent Jewish fish heads! Sweeten your life and dip a head in sour sauce! To make the sour sauce sweet you must put into it raisins, currants, sweet almonds, nuts, a bit of celery and spices. That's what is meant by the expression 'to tamper with the sour sauce in such a way so that it shouldn't be entirely bitter.' It's the sour sauce that makes Jewish fish heads so truly appetizing and irresistible!

"Well then, gentlemen, set to—head to head! The marinated heads look at the intellectual heads and the intellectual heads look at the marinated heads, and they both say to each other: 'When such heads as ours celebrate—what a loss it is for our century!'

"All right then, here are fish with Jewish sauce, and here are Jews with fish sauce! Who's still timid? Ah! 'You are a fishmonger?' asks Hamlet. In the end everyone is a fishmonger, a fisherman; he angles away all year round and casts his nets but winds up with a catch of rotten fish. Then let us go on fishing, let us fish for sour fish and allow us to think as we do so: 'He who is fated to meet with misfortune swallows a fishbone inside a goose liver and suffocates; but he who is lucky, even a Jewish head won't harm him. All right then, let's get down to headwork!"

Ad vocem "fish," it would be in place to mention here that the legend of the Ring and the Fish (*The Ring of Polycrates*) was already mentioned in the Talmud, to be exact in *Midrash Tanhuma,* under the name of "Doge Demalche." It is the same with the materials for the legend, "The Bail," which is found in the great midrash to the *Book of Ecclesiastes,* a copy of which Rabbi Menachem Confaro owns. Also the old basic legend of "The Women of Weinsberg" is recounted in the midrash to *The Song of Songs.* Better yet, the story of the lawsuit over the borrowed money found in a sack, which is included in *Don Quixote,* Part VII, is narrated in the Talmud, in the section concerning vows, and goes under the title "Kanna debe Rabbe."

None the less, sour Jewish fish are only the prolegomena to the Jewish table. An aphoristic description of several Jewish national dishes will follow here. National dishes! In order to understand them one has to be a scholar; to describe them, a genius; to enjoy them in a consecrated spirit, a Jew; but to lend them dignity—an apostate *meshumed!*[1]

So where do we begin? Which of the flowers that bloom in my memory will I pluck first for my little Paradise garden of descriptive art? Oh, thou lovely violet in the Valley of Jeshurun, you come first, you with the mysterious fragrance, oh,

Scholet Egg!

What is a *scholet* egg? It is the egg of Columbus. If you're already acquainted with it, it's nothing; but when it's first revealed to you, it rends the soul like a flash of lightning!

The scholet egg is the overture to the Sabbath meal. You take an earthen pot, a pot *tout simple.* In this pot you place some ashes, ashes tout simple, and in these ashes you deposit a number of eggs. Then you put a cover on the pot and close it hermetically, but if you cannot make it airtight you take some soft dough instead and you close up all

[1] *Moritz Saphir is indulging here in a bit of self-irony; he himself was an apostate* meshumed *from Judaism.* ED.

the chinks between the cover and the pot. And when the eggs in the ashes in the aforementioned pot get on as well as we ourselves would under the same circumstances, the pot with the ashes is placed in the oven on Friday before sundown and remains there until Saturday noon. And then on Saturday noon, when the community *Shabbes* oven is opened, they take the pot out of the oven, the ashes out of the pot, and the egg out of the ashes, and that's when it becomes a

Scholet Egg!

This scholet egg is not only cleverer but also better than the hen itself! It is a phoenix that has risen out of the ashes. The outer envelope is judiciously brown; when you peel off the earthly shell then there emerges its soul, the scholet egg, like the bridegroom coming out of the bride's chamber—*brilliant et radieux!* This inner egg is now purified and free of all the heavier substances; it is reflectively brown and full of wisdom-wrinkles; it is concentrated in itself; it has had a long and good experience; only the essence of its existence remains; it is the Egg of the Egg; it is the concept of the egg apprehended in the act of becoming a hen, roasted *in flagrante* and then eaten. Usually the egg becomes very small, reduced at least to a half of its size when it is only boiled. This scholet egg makes one think of a trill by Mlle. Lind, or better yet, of a pirouette by Elssler. He who has eaten this trill and pirouette knows exactly what a scholet egg tastes like.

Just as the hen comes right after the egg so the scholet egg is appropriately followed by

Scholet

Heine and Börne write "schalet." I have no idea what authority they have for spelling it so. I myself write "scholet"! It could even be that when Heine and Börne ate it they exclaimed "Ah!" That's perhaps why they write "schalet." But you see, I called out "Oh!" when I ate it, and so that's why I spell it "scholet."

Scholet is the union of the classical with the romantic: you take classical barley and romantic peas and you mix them together, like you mix the poetry of Tieck with Shakespeare; then you crown the whole business with a diameter of beef. Naturally, before you place it in the community oven on Friday, you put in fat and a dash of *odeur de garlic.* You let it simmer until Saturday noon in order to give the romantic and the classical elements a chance to amalgamate and to suck in the principles of the beef, and thus resolve itself into an original philosophical system. This system is called "scholet." In order to fully enjoy it one has first to rid oneself of all prejudices and emancipate one's stomach of all preconceptions; the tongue must be free of all anti-Jewish feeling, and the palate must be elevated to the "Pinnacles of Time" and to the "Watch Towers of Culture." The German has his pumpernickel, the Englishman has pudding, the Italian has macaroni, and the Jew has his scholet. It is just like the fate of the Jew: it is neither cooked nor roasted, is accorded no rights of citizenship in the cookbook, and is not allowed even in the same guild with other foods. It is possible that Schiller may have eaten scholet when he wrote:

"The genius evokes the good out of the bad!"

Right after scholet in rank, social standing, and riches comes

Kugel!

This is a food belonging to the flour family. Because the sphere is the most perfect of all geometric forms, therefore this dish is made in a round shape—that of the *Kugel* or cannonball. More than once the fighting courage of the seed of Jacob has been impugned by slanderers who say, "They're afraid of the kugel, the cannonball!" For that reason many Jews go through battle practice every Sabbath by advancing in the face of the kugel with serenity and bravery.

The ingredients that go into the making of one of these cannonballs are flour and chicken fat and still another "something," a nameless "something" that probably is generated by the oven itself and which penetrates into the kugel. Perhaps it's some sort of natural element, a certain kind of alcohol or a phosphoric acid salt. Undoubtedly it must be phosphoric acid salt which is so economical to use.

One can very well see by this that I am treating kugel strictly from the viewpoint of natural history. And should the whole matter not appear too slippery "round" for you, the next object of investigation by the natural philosophers should be, by all means, the kugel!

A bastard child of scholet and kugel is

The Ganef!

A *ganef!* That's kugel that has been ennobled and blended with the fragrance of scholet! In short, the kugel as epic!

The meaning of ganef is "thief." This dish is called ganef because it is made in the shape of a coarse doughy mess filled in the middle with rice, beans, breast of goose, goose livers, and other delicacies. For twenty-four hours it is confined in a sealed oven. During this time it is occupied in absorbing, indeed in stealing, all the fat, all the good smells, all the tastiness of the various things in it. Then like a person that has gone through a transformation and has acquired borrowed good traits from others, this mess finally emerges out of the pot and into the world as a "heart ganef." In order to be able to eat and digest a ganef one has to have the stomach of a Jew who grew up in Russia, and then, as a grown man, traded with oil of roses in Turkey, and finally spent six weeks as an invited guest in Berlin. Such a man, and such a man only, is competent to eat a ganef on the Sabbath Day.

Right after the ganef follows that Greek epigram of Jewish cooking

Gefüllt Hälsel[1]

This is the neck of a goose, or rather, the skin of the gooseneck stuffed with groats and flour and a number of other delicacies. It is sewed up at both ends and then smothered in its own fat. When Lord Byron was writing his Hebrew Melodies, for the two weeks they took him to compose he ate Gefüllt Hälsel. That was because while eating Gefüllt Hälsel, he could hear the whispering of the cypresses of Babylon, could make out the lament of the waves on the Jordan, could discern the wail of the harps of the grieving Exiles with the yoke around their necks while their own groat-stuffed Gefüllt Hälsel still bore the wounds of the slaughterer's knife.

Finally, in the third category of Jewish national dishes come *dicht mit reis, besteckte belek, gänsekrees mit penetzlich,* and so on. These are the entr'actes, the inexpressibles, the untranslatables, the unexplainables. Their charm lies in their mystery, their mystery lies in their magic, and their magic lies in a *je ne sais quoi*. Their *je ne sais quoi,* however, finally passes into a *je sais très bien quoi*. In English this *quoi* is called "garlic," in Italian it is *aglio,* in French *ail,* but in German—oh, in German! I'm almost consumed with shame to say it—in German they call it—yes—*Knoblauch!*

What's that? Did I really say *"Knoblauch"*? Oh no, no! "It is not the nightingale!" It is not *Knoblauch*—God forbid!—it is *Läuchel, Ramthonwürzel, Saftkraut, Salsekraut, Hermsel,* etc.—please, by every other name but not *Knoblauch!*

Oh, you slandered species of the leek—how sadly misunderstood you are! Every art has its perceptive side, including the art of Jewish cooking, whose perceptiveness may be described as *auch,* always *auch,* i.e., *Aschlauch* (shallott), *Schnittlauch* (chives) and *Knoblauch* (garlic). Can it be anything else but prejudice against garlic? The *Laurus nobilis,* for instance, has leaves like cobbler's leather, and yet one crowns poets with it! But garlic, on the other hand, has a fine aroma and taste, and, in addition, an open crown of flowers. Why, King David, before he played his harp, would sit down to eat some garlic! Then take the Prophetess Deborah, before she started chanting her

[1]*This is the German name; in Yiddish it is* gefillt helsel. ED.

inspired songs, she too had to have some garlic. And the poet Homer, he never started out on a journey without taking a good supply of garlic along with him. Ah! then take us—yes, us blasé ones! Why, we stink so from *patschouli* and musk and yet we dare despise the pure natural *odeur* of garlic!

Is it any wonder that the great singer of the *Song of Songs* who ate onion and garlic, was forced to comment: "All is vanity!"

And finally, I hope that when Herr Vogl, who, like God the Father, feeds all hungry Jews in his *restaurant du peuple,* I hope that, when he reads this gastronomical treatise, he will be so moved that, out of gratitude, he'll throw a fiery cannonball kugel right into the office of *The Humorist,* where I work. Also, that he will tell his Jewish fish: "Hurry over now to Moritz Saphir as my emissaries and speak up for me!"

IN PRAISE OF SCHALET

BY HEINRICH HEINE
TRANSLATED FROM THE GERMAN BY NATHAN AUSUBEL

At this opportunity I cannot help but mention that during my stay in Frankfurt Börne invited me to eat the Sabbath midday meal with him at a friend's house. This friend, of course, in loyal observance of Jewish customs, placed before me a dish of the celebrated *Schalet.* I was delighted with this dish, which probably dates back to ancient Egypt and is as venerable as the pyramids. . . . I'm surprised that he [Börne] didn't see fit to make any mention in his writings with what appetite, with what enthusiasm, with what fervor, indeed, with what conviction, I once gulped down a helping of the ancient Jewish dish, schalet, at Doctor St——'s!

This dish is really first-rate and it is deeply to be regretted that the Christian Church, which borrowed so much that was good from ancient Judaism, should have failed to adopt schalet as its own. Maybe it has put it off for some future day when it will fall on hard times? . . . Then it will seize upon schalet! Whereupon, the back-sliding nations will once again and with new appetite return to its fold. When that will happen the Jews, at the very least, will adopt Christianity out of conviction . . . because, as I clearly see it, it is schalet alone which holds them together in their old faith. Börne assures me that, no sooner will the renegades who will go over to the new faith get a whiff of schalet than they'll begin to feel homesick again for the synagogue.

SHABBES-SOUP

BY HERMANN HEIJERMANS
TRANSLATED FROM THE GERMAN BY NATHAN AUSUBEL

Maupie and Zelik came in about the same time. Because the marine auction had ended late Maupie had not been to the Friday night service in the synagogue. The candles in the room burned in festive welcome, in candlesticks, on the mantelpiece, and in the chandelier above the table. The aroma of cooking, of steaming soup and of a fatty smell, oppressively mingled with the heat of the Dutch tile stove and with the finely curling vapor rising from a smoking kerosene lamp.

"My God, how hot it is here!" complained Zelik who was still perspiring from his walk along the Breestraat.

"*Gut shabbes,* Tante Serre. Gut shabbes, Bekkie, my Bekkie-chen!" said Maupie with friendly smiles. "I already smell the soup from here!"

"Couldn't you open the window a bit?" puffed Zelik mopping his brow.

"It's drawing too much," said Mother irritably.

"Drawing? Drawing? How can a draught get here anyway?" persisted Zelik. "There isn't a draught in all Amsterdam today."

"When the window is up the cold cuts so into my back! Is it warm here, Maupie?"

"Neh!" chuckled Maupie. "Zelik has so much fat on him, Tante Serre, he gets hot easily."

"It's stifling enough here to choke! Who says it's drawing here? Just give it a try!"

"But what can I do if it draws! He thinks he knows better. He thinks he knows everything!" his mother muttered angrily.

"If Tante doesn't object," Bekkie ventured, "since they're coming directly from the fresh air. I mean if they'll just sit down for a while they won't feel so hot."

Zelik and Maupie took off their jackets and sat down at the table in their shirtsleeves, both with their hats on. Assisted by Bekkie,

Mother also shuffled up to the table and Bekkie then went to fetch her coal-heated footstool.

The light fell starkly on all the faces, on the anxious, pained face of Mother, looking sallow under her *sheitel*. Her eyes blinked lifeless and tired, the lids constantly drooping over them like faded Venetian blinds. She held her head tilted on a side just as if it were dried up, too heavy for the thin, emaciated neck to support. Her mouth remained always open like that of a sick person; it looked like a dark gash between her jaws as she sucked in with a gasping sound the hot air in the room. Over the white shimmer of the tablecloth and the soft, quiet sparkle of the round plates her bowed head cast a shadow as it sank weakly over her heaving breast gasping for air. It was a tired face, like that of one who was dying, the parchmentlike wrinkled skin on her neck looked like the skin of an old bat.

Opposite her sat her nephew Maupie. His hands lay folded under the light of the lamp, his face was smooth-shaved and there was a brownish smudge in the corner of his mouth where he had held his cigar. His strong hooked nose stood out in the light. His lips were screwed up in a friendly pouting. The lively eyes were shaded by the brim of an odd black hat that hardly covered the head on account of his luxuriant mop of hair which was black and thick and at the temples was peppered with fine gray hair.

At the side facing the door sat Zelik, looking perspired and flushed, with an expressionless face. There were glints of gold in his red whiskers. Drops of sweat stood out on his forehead and on the sides of his pug nose among the freckles.

Starkly fell the light on the faces, on the false sheitel, on Maupie's odd little hat and on Zelik's shiny high silk hat. The men sat leaning their elbows on the white tablecloth, red hands laid on white cloth next to tin knives and forks and tumblers. In a dish was piled a heap of brown bread sprinkled with poppy seeds. Nearby stood the salt-cellar and a thick yellowish pickle cut in slices. Clumsily low hung the ceiling over the flowered tablecloth and made the air oppressive for Zelik and Maupie and Bekkie and Tante Serre. And in this manner they were ready to eat the shabbes meal and to sing *zemiros,* the table songs of praise to God.

Bekkie stood bent over the side of the oven, whose fire was already gone out. She took the soup out of the dark interior and filled the first plate for Tante Serre. In the meantime Zelik pronounced the benediction, babbling the words like one who has to chew a hot potato quickly! The end of the challeh he cut into four parts, dipped each piece in salt, his little eyes blinking dreamily as he did so. Maupie took his piece of challeh from Zelik's warm hand and hummed along with him while he cast a glance at Tante Serre's plate of soup and at Bekkie's hand ladling the soup at the oven. Then Zelik's *bar-mitzvah becher* made the rounds after the *Kiddush,* filled with the wine that Bekkie had drawn, and each took a little sip, Bekkie the most because the others drank up what remained. Zelik smacked his lips for he liked everything sweet. As for Maupie, he slobbered up soup.

"M-m! What fine soup! Soup you don't get in a thousand years!" he assured everyone. He buried his face in the plate, and with relish carefully sipped the soup, making an unpleasant sucking sound as he drew it in. Bekkie, who was now able to sit down, greeted them all with a swelling nasal sniffing through the steam of her plate: "Enjoy your meal!" Zelik and Tante Serre and Maupie returned her greeting.

The light in the room beamed yellow on the four eaters, on Maupie's raven hair, on Zelik's half-bald head, which he bared after reciting Kiddush, on the false sheitel of the old woman, and on Bekkie's shining black hair.

"*Ja, ja*—what a fine soup!" said Zelik. "Really, it's one fine bit of soup!"

The sweat broke out on him and purple glowed his immature face under the nimbus of his curly red hair.

On the other hand it wasn't real soup weather at all, a little too warm for soup no doubt. But a shabbes meal without soup was no shabbes meal! And then one had to keep in mind what kind of soup it was too—Bekkie's soup! She put her very *soul* into it!

Bekkie's soup consisted namely of "thread" noodles and Spanish peas. And a lot more! Ordinarily the consistency of thread noodles and Spanish peas was a bit soggy . . . wasn't liquid enough. Bekkie's soup, however, was made of thread noodles, Spanish peas, nutmeg, and a lot of saffron and pepper. But still that wasn't all. Her soup was her soul, unfathomable like every mystery. On the surface floated fatty "golden-eyes" enriched by choice marrow-bones, dumplings and the soup meat that was cooked with it. Bekkie's heart seemed to jubilate through her soup just as if it too were smothered with thread-noodles, Spanish peas, nutmeg, saffron, pepper, marrowbones, dumplings and soup meat. But most wonderful of all, the highest aspiration of her young womanhood took on new life in her soup. At such a time a superhuman ecstasy flooded her soul.

Every Friday afternoon her soupy exertions fagged her out completely, just as if she had done some heavy exhausting toil. She then felt depleted like an exorcist after he had communicated with a spirit. Bekkie's soup was a smooth, fatty-flowing nectar. The fragrance of nutmeg and saffron steamed from it, the peas bubbled up like buds, the pepper playing merry pranks among them, sufficiently titillating and tickling to make one swoon with delight.

Yet Bekkie's soul, that appeared in the light of her eyes, in the sound of her voice, and in the down on her throat, winged like the irresistible warblings of larks in the ether together with the aroma of nutmeg and saffron and flowed along gently with the little "eyes" of fat in the soup. Without Bekkie's soul, her soup would have been just soup. It was this magical substance which transformed ordinary soup into shabbes soup, into a soup of such classic taste that Zelik with sweating rapture sat drawing it in with slow deliberateness. His stumps of teeth ground eagerly into the hot dumplings made of chopped meat. Saffron was in it, nutmeg was in it, and pepper was in it, and each spoon shoveled greedily into his mouth was full of the miraculous and of Bekkie's own soul.

And thus he sat, quietly drawing the fragrance into his nostrils, relishing it and blowing slowly on the soup in his spoon to cool it off. He was bathed in perspiration like an old cheese crust lying under a glass cover on a hot summer day. Happiness was inside of him. The dream he had in the synagogue had now turned into reality. Whenever he looked up he saw Bekkie's fat lips shining with a fatty joy in her spoon. The slobbering sound of sipping soup, of sucking it in and of lip smacking, filled the room like the calls of clucking hens. Mother, painfully preoccupied with her throat, sipped her soup with little starts, more often than not spilling half of what was in her spoon back into her plate. The spoons kept dipping into the plates, rummaged for the noodles and brought them up to eager lips.

"It's just as if a little angel had pissed on your tongue," said Maupie, licking his lips and with gusto renewing his clucking. The strong hawklike nose bent sharply into his plate.

" 'N all my life never tasted such wonderful soup!" answered Bekkie, her mouth full of noodles.

" 'T's good!" agreed Zelik, perspiring so hard that his shirt clung wet against the hair on his chest. He suddenly thought of shabbes soup in the wintertime, when every spoonful brought even greater joy. Following this line of thought he said puffing gently, "And still enough, I like soup on a cold winter day a lot more. . . . It's not so agreeable

on a hot summer day. . . . It makes me sweat more than sunstroke.
. . . In wintertime give me lentil soup with dumplings and with the
end of a wurst. . . ."

"What? you'd like lentil soup!" asked Bekkie angrily. "You big
fool, you——"

"*Nu,* not in summer, but on a winter's day——"

"Lentil soup!" said Maupie, slobbering soup mightily. "Did you
say lentil soup? Why don't you speak of *Pesach* soup with *matzo* balls
and tender young chervil? Lentil soup! *Och!* Don't make me throw
up! I feel hot enough as it is."

"Everyone to his own taste," replied Zelik, skimming the surface
of his soup for the fatty "eyes." He regarded them with his own small
foolish eyes and then discreetly smelled them. "You know how it is;
one loves the mother and the other the daughter. You're *meshuggeh* for
Pesach soup . . . I'm meshuggeh for lentil soup . . . for my part
you can give me on a cold winter day a little plate of lentil soup. . . ."

"What's Pesach soup got to do with lentil soup! Don't get excited!
Better make yourself a new coat!" scolded Mother with vexation at
her forty-year-old Zelikie. She always treated him like a child and
could hardly endure him.

But Maupie didn't wish to give up so fast.

II

"Chervil soup isn't a good dish . . . no good for my health.
. . . Give me better barley soup with calf's foot in it. *Adenom!*
You've got something to lick when you get through!"

Mother laid down her spoon, breathing heavily. She didn't think
much of calf's leg meat.

". . . When I cook barley soup I always put in a chunk of soup
meat. . . ."

The spoons were being raised and lowered from the plates to the
lips. The heads of the eaters clustered together underneath the glare
of the burning lamp. Zelik got through first and started sucking on a
marrowbone, making such noises as if he were moaning on a mirliton.
He now felt the need of praising Bekkie.

"There's nothing better than this soup," said he, sucking in air
so that the marrow sprayed from his mouth, "nothing finer! For this
alone one should thank God that one is a Jew. . . ."

His sticky fingers gripped the bone as his lips were sucking in the
marrow just as if he were a child and it was the teat of his mother's

breast he was drawing on. But it was of no avail, for the bone had a hole in it. The slender marrow end quivered like a fine nerve in the bone hollow.

"Do you think that a *goyeh* could cook such soup as this, such blessed soup?" he asked. "What do *goyim* know about such things? Christian soup! Och!"

Maupie tilted his plate and tried to scoop up the remaining soup between the bones.

"Pork they can eat," he agreed with relish as he plunged the end of his spoon between his lips. "But if it's soup you want, shabbes-soup, then you've got to go to Jews."

"Och, don't talk nonsense!" said Bekkie, feeling flattered. "There are plenty of Christian women who know how to cook soup."

"Boils they can!" broke out Maupie shaking his head in disagreement.

"Maupie's right," winked Mother approvingly. She had a high estimate of his opinions because he was such a *chochem*. "Maupie's right. Goyim can't cook!"

"Nu, Tante Serre, in that case I'd like to know how you know all that?" asked Bekkie, swallowing a spoonful of her soup. "Have you ever eaten at a goyeh's that you know? Otherwise how could you know?"

This question caused Mother to shake her head in deep pain. The spoonful of soup shook in her hand so that half of it fell back into the plate.

"Have I eaten at a goyeh's, you ask me? I'd first bite off my tongue before I'd take a drink of water from a goyeh!"

"Do give me another bit of soup!" asked Zelik who had at last succeeded cleaning out the hollow of his marrowbone with his little finger. "And while you're at it put in some more dumplings."

"As much as you like," winked Bekkie with a devoted air and refilled his plate, putting into it a lot of solid substance which was at the bottom of the pot and to which she knew Zelik was partial.

Mother still continued fussing over her first portion of soup. Maupie, leaning on the table with his elbows opposite her, made another try at the soup.

A short time before, he had gone on a journey and had eaten at a kosher hotel.

"The soup they served me there I'll never forget—just plain canal-water! Pure canal-water, I'm telling you . . . with neither a lick of vegetables nor meat in it . . . and for that I had to pay kosher money!

But there's one fine cook—Rachel! How is Rachel's chervil soup, Bek? If I eat her chervil soup for two days I can fast three *Yom Kippurs*. . . ."

Mother was now only half listening, drew her breath with difficulty, her mouth wide open and almost shaping itself in a square. She too began to perspire at last, beads standing out on her forehead. The emaciated hands got busy wiping the damp off her face.

"What good strong soup this is!" she murmured with difficulty. "Fine soup! See, it's making me sweat!"

"Well, that's what I've been saying," grumbled Zelik.

He now unbuttoned his vest all the way down.

"Maupie, do me a favor and open the window."

Maupie got up willingly. Through the open window penetrated the stifling hot air from the twilit courtyard. The vegetation in the tiny garden hardly was stirring. In the courtyard, right near the window, stood a wooden *pissoir* which adjoined the rear of a box factory. It was clogged and overflowed because the workers had thrown into it their tobacco quids and other refuse.

"*Meshuggaas!*" complained Zelik. "The idea of serving such hot soup on a summer day!"

"For my part, I'll put it on ice for you, och!" said Bekkie incredulously. "Cold soup! *Very* tasty!"

"*Nee!* You don't have to do *that!*" apologized Zelik, with blown-up cheeks, stuffing into his mouth some more soup on which he was blowing to cool it off. "Don't make it cold but lukewarm."

Maupie unbuttoned his vest so that his fat little potbelly bulged out of his trousers belt.

"Maupie is also getting hot," laughed Bekkie. "Isakie! would you like another little plate of soup?"

"Nee, I shouldn't have anymore," protested Maupie with a warding-off gesture of his hand around his plate, at the bottom of which the gnawed-off bones glistened like butter among the remaining strands of thread noodles.

"You mean to say you don't want anymore?" asked Bekkie coaxingly in a singsong, holding the soup ladle over his plate.

"Whenever I eat so much soup I've no appetite left for the *tzimmes* and the meat course," Maupie insisted, spreading his fingers over the plate.

"Nu, come on, take another little plateful! Just see what bones there are!"

"Nee, honest I can't! Let me alone! Let me alone! It will be no sin on my part to pass it up."

During all this conversation Zelik went on happily slobbering up more soup. He broke crumbs of *challeh* into his plate. Then he went fishing with his spoon for them. Under the table he discreetly unbuttoned the top of his trousers which was pressing uncomfortably against his distended stomach. Now he could sit *tov-tov* and comfortable and enjoy himself.

Maupie, in the act of exploring a tasty bone and dabbing some horse-radish on its specks of meat, glanced at Tante Serre's old wizened face peering at him from under her false sheitel. Feeling contentment, he laughed in order to cheer her up. But the old lady, overburdened and quarrelsome, remained unresponsive.

"Don't you dare joke with an elderly person!" she severely admonished him with a whistling sound in her throat behind her plate of soup. "I'm again having such an awful pain in my stomach!"

"If someone younger had told me that," leered Maupie gnawing away at his bone, "I'd be led to think that she was pregnant."

"Go on—make fun of me . . . make fun of me. . . . If you had my pain you'd be whistling a different tune. Ever since David *olim besholim* died I haven't known one moment of health. . . . *Adoishem!* What a pain I feel inside! . . . O! . . . O! . . . O! . . . ."

"Och! *nebbech!*" said Bekkie shaking her head with compassion and without putting her spoon down. "Do you feel the stitches again?"

"Why don't you consult a doctor?" asked Maupie licking his bone.

"No doctor . . . no doctor!" wailed the old woman, wringing her hands against her body. "They know a lot about their own health! I swallow and I swallow all kinds of pills and it helps me *nix*. . . . O! . . . O! . . . O! . . . For my body I don't want doctors anymore!"

" 'T could come from the soup!" ventured Zelik, swallowing his last spoonful of soup. He had more than once been through this before.

"From the soup did you say? From the soup! Who ever heard that you get pains in the belly from soup?" asked Mother peevishly. "Better go and close the window. The cold that blows on my back is too awful . . . too awful!"

"Must we have this sort of rumpus every night?" asked Zelik angrily.

The lingering illness that year in and year out had made her act fretful and peevish in the crowded little dining room more than once struck evil sparks in his otherwise stolid and childlike soul.

"Go ahead and raise children until they grow up!" scolded Mother angrily. "Rumpus! Rumpus! Och! What an ungrateful dog!"

Bekkie decided that it wasn't fitting that she should say anything.

When all was said and done, did Tante Serre find any pleasure in her pains in the belly? Maupie, who was now through polishing up his bone, wiped his fingers on the edge of the tablecloth and spoke amiable words in order to put an end to the quarrel.

"That was one fine soup, Bekkie! Why, the fat's still pasted on my gums! Just look! Look here, Bekkie!" and Maupie opened wide his mouth.

"Better leave me alone, you big fool!" laughed Bekkie as she started clearing off the table.

A JEWISH BEGGAR'S COMPLAINT
AN ANONYMOUS HEBREW POEM OF
THE FRENCH LORRAINE IN THE MIDDLE AGES

> *Greens on Sunday,*
> *Crumbs and water Monday,*
> *Onions Tuesday,*
> *Left-over onions Wednesday,*
> *Stale lentils Thursday,*
> *Left-over lentils Friday;*
> *While on the Sabbath it seems best*
> *From meat and wine to take a rest.*

FOODS

BY SAMMY LEVENSON

Purim and *Homentaschen* brought this on.

As I was picking the savory poppy seeds from my teeth, I remembered other flavors and odors that were part of our traditional Jewish past; the taste sensations that were part of Momma's household, and I feel like Pavlov's dog as my mouth recalls:

Matzohs gently coated in chicken fat over which a good healthy *tsibbeleh* had been rubbed. This rubbing the half-onion over the matzoh became in itself an experience in ecstatic anticipation. I've never sampled marijuana but I can't imagine that it would produce a more glowing sensation than golden chicken fat on hemstitched boards.

But this voluptuous experience must have been a sin, because, just as you were reaching the climax of sense experience, the matzoh would snap, and the reality of a dimly lighted slum kitchen would burst in upon this little piece of heaven.

The dietitians have definitely outlawed some specific delights of Jewish children. At the age of three, I had already experienced an exquisite heartburn from a red-skinned *Retach*. Let the dietitians eat pablum and skins of baked potatoes! For me, life was just a bowl of *Retach*. And I had a better complexion than the dietitian.

The child was ushered into the world with an array of herring. A *Briss* meant HERRING. For months before the great day our house was inhabited by pickled herrings. Jars, big ones, little ones, glass and clay ones. Eyes, herring eyes, staring at you through windows, in clothing closets, in kitchen closets, on fire escapes—the phosphorescent glow of herrings swinging on onion-hoops. (Notes from a psychiatrist's casebook.)

What better lunch for a school child than cold *koogle* from the previous night with a crust that looked like the scales of a prehistoric mammal, with a side dish of yesterdays *tsimmes* and a seeded roll oozing *hock-flaish* in all directions. For dessert, a penny for a "twist" and back to school raring to go—to sleep. You can imagine the enthusiasm of forty-two such well-oiled scholars for the remainder of the afternoon. What with the noon sun pouring through the windows and the teacher's sweet and gentle voice, the odds were 30 to 1 against arithmetic; and the unceasing parade to the watertrough and other places.

During a holiday, there were special delicacies.
Momma's home-baked *choleh* which was so arranged that you didn't have to slice it. There were bulges all around which you just pulled out of their sockets with ease and *toonked* into nice, oily soup with big eyes that looked up at you from the plate. The sought-after prize in the soup, like the trinket in the cracker-jack box, was a small unhatched egg which Momma had found in the chicken. There was one egg and eight children. What a strain on Momma's impartiality to choose the deserving child. The *ayeleh* usually went to the girls because of some folk-theory about fertility.

Soup could offer a variety of surprises—*kreplach* (meat balls with sport jackets), exquisitely shaped by the sculptural genius of a *balabusteh,* who always planned the structure of the *kreple* so that a tempting bit of the buried treasure should show through, just enough to make the mouth water.

Or soup might contain *lokshen,* which hung like weeping willows over the *flaishigeh leffel.* The excess lokshen could either be sucked into the mouth or bitten into.

What better contribution to *fressen* have we given the world than the incomparable *kishkeh* (sections of fire hose)? They tell me my *zadeh* stuffed his own kishkeh with cow's kishkeh to the age of 94. He carried around a permanent heartburn which kept his body warm and protected him from the severe Russian winters.

THE GOURMAND AND THE LATE RISER

BY M. SCHLESINGER

My piteous plight oft makes me weep—
I cannot eat when I'm asleep.

NUTTOSE AND PROTOSE

BY MOISHE NADIR (ISAAC REISS)
TRANSLATED FROM THE YIDDISH BY NATHAN AUSUBEL

Do you mean to say you don't know what "nuttose" and "protose" are? Never heard of them? Ach, my dear friend! If only I too had never heard about them I wouldn't be where I am now. I'd be a free man like all other people and not have to rot in prison—ech, heh-heh!

You hear me sigh, eh? Of course I sigh! Why shouldn't I sigh when I recall that only several months ago I was young, vigorous, and full of life and hope about the future. And now I am a criminal . . . charged with attempted murder . . . rejected by both God and man! Pardon my tears, I beg you. . . . I can't help myself!

Nu, already! Now I'm a bit calmer and so I'm going to tell you how this great misfortune happened to me.

As you look at me I'm a healthy man with a good appetite. For me to tuck away a three-pound steak used to be a mere nothing. I could grind away nine, ten cutlets with one tooth. I was always a great meat eater . . . of all kinds of meat. Steak—all right let it be steak! Veal—let it be veal! Lamb chops—let it be lamb chops! Goulash—let it be goulash! Chicken—nu, so let it be chicken! You can see that meat was my principal food. Four times a day I used to eat meat: sour meat, sweet meat, pickled meat, raw meat, pastrami, corned beef, rolled beef, frankfurters, meat cooked with peppers, meat with olives, meat with sour apples, meat with ketchup—in short, as long as it was meat! I'm not going to detain you long, but I just want to tell you that I was one terrific meat eater. I couldn't get along without a piece of meat. And it was no wonder. If a person works in a metal factory and keeps pounding all day with a big hammer and you almost bang out of yourself every drop of life and strength and you sweat like anything—is it any wonder that one's got to have a piece of meat?

So you will ask: who didn't let me eat a piece of meat? So listen, that's just what I *takkeh* want to tell you. I want to tell you what made me become a vegetarian and begin to nourish myself on nuts, peanuts, and raisins. The devil, I say, take all nuts, peanuts, and raisins, and may they burn and burn and burn, and may they never stop burning! Just listen to this story! A fellow comes along with long hair, a goatlike tuft of beard, and canvas pants, and asks me whether I ate meat.

So I answer: "Albetcha, what else?"

So he says: "If that's the case, then you're a cannibal! You're digging," says he, "your grave with your own teeth."

So I say: "What are you muttering under your nose? Cannibal, gannibal and shmannibal! Grave-shmave! As long, I'm telling you, as a man lives, he's got to, says I, he's got to eat a good piece of meat."

Says he: "You know what your stomach is? A cemetery, that's what it is! And the blood," says he, "of innocent chickens will fall on your head!"

Says I: "You're a *meshuggener!*"

Says he: "Ha ha! *I* am the meshuggener? *Meshuggeh*," says he "are those who say that I'm meshuggeh. By the way," says he, "give me thirty cents, so I'll give you a book which preaches our ideals."

Says I: "Thirty cents! Why, for thirty cents I could almost buy a good tenderloin steak!"

Says he: "Nu, so give me seventy cents and I'll add another book to it. This book proves that all people who eat meat die young from blood poisoning which comes from the stomach. Here," says he, "is a piktcha!"

And he showed me a piktcha of a corpse with a steak stuck in his mouth.

The whole business was getting to be a nuisance so I bought from him the two books and *takkeh* the same day I discovered that meat is a deadly poison and that in the whole world there was only *one* thing that could be compared to meat, but no druggesman wanted to sell it because it was too strong a poison. At the end of the book I read that the best foods one can get in Verimkroit's Vegetarian Restaurant where you can also get all kinds of vegetarian leaflets cheap.

In short, when suppertime came I went to Verimkroit's Restaurant, sat down at a table and waited for the waiter.

Soon there came over to me a pale coughing long drink of water who looked like a middle-aged scallion.

"For how much do you want to eat?" he asked me. "For thirty or for forty?"

"I eat only for one," says I. "At the very best I can eat," says I, "only for two, but not for thirty."

He gave a yawn, the waiter did, and said, "I want to know whether you want to eat regla for thirty cents, or special for forty . . . with protose."

Says I: "Let it be for forty with . . . how do you call it, portis? As long as it's tasty, who cares?"

So he disappeared, the waiter did, for almost half an hour. He finally came back carrying a tiny bowl in which lay *epis* a pale sickly lump.

"What sort of a dish is that?" I ask and take a sip of water quickly.

"Nuttose—NUTT-OSE!" he answered proudly and walked away.

He soon returned to ask me: "Do you want to eat a steak of nuttose or of protose?"

"Let be for a tchenge," says I, "protose!"

Again he disappeared somewheres and came back with a small plate on which lay *epis* a brown mystery cuddling between two lettuce leaves.

"Nu," says he, yawning over my head, "now what sort of soup will you have?"

"What sort of soups have you got?" I ask.

"We have," says he, "two kinds of soups. One soup is made of nuttose and the other of protose."

I'm telling you my hands and feet got cold hearing him say that. I finally got strength to mutter:

"All right, I'll take nuttose."

Again he yawned over my head, the waiter did, and he said:

"I'd advise you not to take nuttose . . . but protose. Protose, you know, is healthier than nuttose. Besides that," says he, "we have no more nuttose, so you'll have to take protose."

"Let it be protose," says I, in order to get rid of that *nudnik*.

He finally brought me a little soup plate with some cloudy liquid in which swam around two homeless onions, like ships lost in the Mediterranean.

"Now what are you going to have for an entree?" he asked.

"What sort of entree have you got?" I asked him.

"We have," says he, "two kinds of entrees. One is of nuttose and the other is of protose."

"Protose," I muttered. I was certain that *epis* was going to happen now.

Again he yawned over my head and said to me, "I wouldn't advise you to take protose. Take nuttose. Nuttose is healthier than protose. Besides that," says he, "we haven't any more entrees of protose, only of nuttose. You'll take nuttose, heh?"

"So give nuttose!"

He yawned and went away, the waiter did. Soon he came back carrying a dish with three cooked raisins and a suspicion of a boiled fig.

"And now," says he, "what'll you have for a drink? We have," says he, "two kinds of drinks: one is of nuttose and the other is of protose. Only," says he, "I wouldn't advise you to take nuttose, but protose, because protose," says he, "is a lot healthier than nuttose, although nuttose is also a healthy dish. But how can it compare to protose! Because protose," says he, "contains more fat than nuttose. Besides that," says he, "we're all out of nuttose tea; we only have protose tea. Before," says he, "we also had nuttose tea, but we used up all the nuttose and all that's left is protose. Now take me, I personally," says he, "like protose better because nuttose . . ."

Now, my friend, do you understand why I'm now in jail charged with attempted murder?

WHAT'S THERE TO LAUGH AT?

Shmendriks and
Shmiggeges · FOOLS AND SIMPLETONS

*If the fool weren't mine—
wouldn't I laugh too?*

*As if it weren't enough of a handicap in this world just to be a
Jew, imagine being a Jew and a luckless* schlimazl *too! However, most
intolerable of all was to be at one and the same time a Jew, and a
luckless* schlimazl—*and a fool!*

*Now, clinically speaking, a Jew often enough acquired this triple
distinction. More likely than not it was because it was his misfortune
to be a Jew in the first place. When a Jew had no luck—and so many
Jews had no luck!—he often felt like a fool; and after he was thoroughly indoctrinated with that conviction, he even began to act like
one. There is nothing that can rob a man of his self-esteem and good
judgment as much as continual failure in life. For every "successful"
Jew in the ghetto there were at least a thousand hopeless ones. And
perhaps so much of their so-called foolishness came from unworldli-
ness and ignorance. Many of them lacked any contact with practical
experience, the source of all common sense. Perhaps that is what made
for so many fools in spite of the fact that Jews are famed for being
clever people.*

*The plight of the fool in the highly competitive life of the ghetto
was calamitous. Whether natural-born or cultivated by circumstance,
the fool was foredoomed. The precariousness of Jewish existence
demanded more than usual wisdom and resourcefulness, and many
Jews were fortunate enough to acquire these. Perhaps this is why Jews
have always placed such an excessively high premium on wisdom! Of
course, where poverty was as general as it was among Jews, a fool remained a permanent dependent. He was a millstone around the neck
of his parents and overdrew on their family loyalty. Not being an
earner, he was only an extra mouth to feed, and his parents would
sound the bitter rebuke to fate: "Oy, dear God, if the fool weren't
mine—wouldn't I laugh too?"*

But actually, what was there to laugh at?

*Compassion, not derision, is the key in which laughter at the fool
is pitched in Jewish humor. Is it the poor fool's fault that he's a fool,*

nebbech? *As if to say: "Brother, aren't you and I lucky to have been born clever, otherwise we might have been fools, like this one?" In fact, Jewish tradition encourages all wise men to be fools sometimes as a moral corrective, because if a man is wise all the time, he's just one big* shmiggege!

Quite often, Jewish preoccupation with fools in humorous literature is a didactic one. It is concerned not so much with mocking at those unfortunates as in using them as whipping posts for the stupidities of the rest of the clever ones.

To indicate the great importance given by Jews to the subject of fools, the following is only a partial list of synonyms for the word, probably the choicest collection in any language: naar, lekish, lekishber, cham, chammer, shmendrik, shmiggege, lemishke, ferd, lemech, tam, vaizoso, goilem (golem), shoiteh, shmoiger, eyzel, yold, shvantz, idioht, *and quite a few unprintable ones.*

Perhaps the classic Jewish joke about fools is the one which tells of the small dealer in wheat who went to Minsk to sell his grain. Before leaving, he faithfully promised his wife to send her a telegram if he succeeded in making a profitable transaction. Having, with God's help, closed his deal, he went to the telegraph office and sat down to compose his telegram. He wrote:

"Sold wheat profitably return tomorrow embrace lovingly Itzik"
As he was about to hand the text to the clerk he hesitated.

"Now why do I have to write 'profitably'? Certainly, my wife knows that I am no shmendrik to sell my wheat at a loss!"

So he crossed out the word "profitably."

Then he went over the telegram more carefully.

"Tsk-tsk! What have I done? Doesn't my wife know already that I went to town to sell my wheat? So why the devil do I write the words 'sold wheat'?"

He crossed out "sold wheat."

Made doubly cautious now by his errors he reread the telegram.

"God in Heaven! What am I jabbering about? What makes me write 'return tomorrow'? When then should I return—next month? My wife will suppose I've gone out of my mind and imagine I'm Rothschild!"

Without hesitation he crossed out "return tomorrow."

Then with an eagle eye he went over the telegram once more.

"Goilem that I am! Why do I have to write 'embrace lovingly'? How else do I embrace my wife? And why should I embrace her today of all days? Is it her birthday, or Yom Kippur, *or something?"*

He crossed out "embrace lovingly."

Looking down at the telegram, he noticed that there was only one word left now—"Itzik."

"Nu? *What do you say to my cleverness? Why do I have to sign 'Itzik'? Who else would be sending my wife a telegram?"*

And he crossed out the word "Itzik."

Now he scanned the telegram, and, finding that he had crossed out every word, a light dawned on him.

"By *my* bubba's *mustache! Do I really have to send this telegram? Money doesn't grow on trees, Itzik!"*

So he tore up the telegram and went away rejoicing that by his cleverness he had saved himself fifty kopecks.

N.A.

TWO STRANGERS CAME TO TOWN

BY ISAAC MEIER DICK

TRANSLATED FROM THE YIDDISH BY NATHAN AUSUBEL

It happened in 1830. One Friday morning, there arrived in the town of Durachesok[1] a small cart carrying a single passenger, who took a room in the largest inn. The innkeeper, to be sure, received him most hospitably. He greeted him with a hearty *sholom aleichem,* then put to him the time-honored Jewish question: "From where does a Jew come?"

"I'm the Shtoperker *chazan,* Reb Zundl Kreihuhn,"[2] the stranger answered. "I'm making now a tour over the whole countryside, singing in all the important synagogues. In fact, I'm planning to sing the service in your town this very *Shabbes.*"

The innkeeper, who happened to be a great enthusiast of cantorial singing, was delighted with this unexpected bit of news.

"If that's the case," he replied, "then please don't delay but go right over to the *Parnass* of the town and get his permission to sing the Shabbes service in the Great Synagogue. Rest assured, you'll be received very cordially. I want you to know that our townsfolk are always eager to hear good singing and they pay generously every

[1] *In Russian the name implies The Town of Fools.*
[2] *"Crowcock" in Yiddish.*

chazán who shows up in town, especially one who's as famous as you are. My, my! who hasn't heard of Reb Zundl, the Shtoperker chazan!"

With such an enthusiastic reception, the chazan put on his best clothes and went off to see the parnass, without any loss of time.

No sooner had he walked out of the inn and showed himself on the street than the whole town began to boil with the news that an important person, either a chazan or a preacher, had come to town. The stranger stopped to inquire of several passers-by, "Can you tell me, my good friend, where is the house of the parnass?"

And he uttered these words with such a refined and grand air that everyone was impressed.

Naturally, there was no one in town who wanted to be left out in the cold concerning any bit of information about this unusual visitor. They all hurried to the inn. But before the innkeeper had a chance to satisfy their curiosity a cart with a second visitor suddenly rattled up to the door of the inn.

The new arrival looked very important indeed. He was big and fat, with a face as plump and ruddy as the sun at dusk. He had a long grey beard, wore a coat with wide sleeves, a round hat, a *Chassid's* sash around the waist of his *kapote,* and he gripped a thick bamboo cane in his hand.

Seeing such an important-looking guest, the innkeeper ran out to welcome him and extended his hand to him with a hearty sholom aleichem! The stranger inquired whether he could engage a comfortable room since he planned to celebrate Shabbes in Durachesok.

"I've just the room for you!" replied the innkeeper eagerly, and he ordered the servant to carry up the traveler's baggage. This consisted of a heavy carpet-bag and a big chest on which was painted in large red letters the name: Reb Borech Baal-Shem.[1]

Seeing this inscription, the servant quickly ran to the innkeeper and whispered breathlessly into his ear:

"Master, this guest here is a wonder-worker!"

"What? A wonder-worker!" cried the astonished innkeeper. "Imagine! There are still people in God's world who can perform a wonder or two! *Nu,* believe me, I'm glad that he has chosen to honor us with his presence. Now my Rivtcha won't have to travel to the other end of nowhere looking for a wonder-worker!"

Without loss of time the innkeeper hastened to tell his wife the good news. When she heard it she began to rejoice, just as though she were already holding in her hand the key with which to unlock the

[1] *Reb Borech the Wonder-Worker.*

fruitfulness of her womb. Rivtcha, may it not happen to any of us, was barren. So she was prepared to make a great fuss over the wonder-worker, as if he were the bridegroom awaited impatiently by the bride on the Sabbath of Hanukkah.

Right away she sent her husband up to the Baal-Shem with a tray of white rolls and coffee so that they'd be able to get acquainted with him before everybody else in town started to descend on him.

No question of it—there were plenty of Jews in town who desperately wanted to be helped! Besides some thousand barren women there were many abandoned wives and hopeless old maids and other kinds of *tzoress, nebbech!* That there were also general tzoress goes without saying. For instance, what tzoress they had from that nasty assessor, a regular bloodsucker he was! And, on top of that, the direst rumors were being heard that the authorities were about to open a secular school in town, a new menace to piety . . .

"Better see to it, husband mine," the innkeeper's wife admonished, "that you be the first to call on this wonder-worker! Maybe, with his aid we will be helped. How well I remember that my mother, a blessing to her memory, became pregnant with me only with the help of Reb Feivel Pintchevesher Baal-Shem."

When the innkeeper brought in the rolls and coffee, his guest reproached him: "Why did you have to go to all this trouble yourself? You've got a servant for that."

"Oh *Rebbe!*" cried the innkeeper, "please don't think that I don't know who you are! And don't think that I don't know how great will be my *mitzvah* to wait personally on such a great man as Your Honor!"

"Who do you take me for? Why do you call me 'Rebbe'?" asked the guest modestly.

"Good wine you can smell from afar," answered the innkeeper sagely. "I know you're the wonder-worker, Reb Borech!"

"Simply amazing!" marveled Reb Borech Baal-Shem. "Simply amazing! One just can't hide oneself from the world! But when all is said and done, you must have a good instinct if you can smell a pleasant fragrance from afar."

"To tell you the truth," answered the innkeeper, "a hungry man smells a good dish quicker than one who has a full belly."

Hearing these words, Reb Borech turned his eyes to heaven and replied:

"What this means is that the Creator, Blessed be He, sends flax to the spinner and wine to the drinker."

The door suddenly opened and the innkeeper's wife came in, carrying a tray with a bottle of schnapps and slices of cake.

"Do you see, Leml," she twitted her husband, "nothing good ever comes out of being in a hurry! See—you forgot to take along the schnapps."

Rivtcha, the innkeeper's wife, was not more than thirty. She was a handsome lusty woman with fiery eyes which could have melted an icicle. That's why the wonder-worker became a bit flustered. Although he had a pious mien, he was a lecherous fellow and had never in his life denied himself any pleasure in the world. When Rivtcha entered the room he found it more pleasant to look at her than at the sheepish face of Reb Leml. When she started to leave, he motioned to her that she should remain. She, of course, wished for herself nothing better than that, and remained standing respectfully at the door with downcast eyes, as the Shunnamite once stood before Elisha.

"Good that you have come!" he said to her. "If not, I'd have been obliged to send for you. You probably know already who I am. If you'll tell me what your wish is then we'll be able to come to an understanding."

"Oh, Rebbe!" she burst out. "What do you mean 'understand each other'? One doesn't have to be too smart for that! My wish is that you should send us a child and we'll surely know how to reward you because, God be praised, we have the means to do so."

"If that's the case, then tell me: have you ever had a child before?"

Rivtcha hung her head sadly.

"I've never conceived," she replied.

She began to dab at her eyes.

"How old were you when you got married?" Reb Borech went on.

"Eighteen miserable years!"

"Eighteen years! Tsk-tsk!" said he commiseratingly. "Why, at eighteen years other women are already rocking the cradle with their second child! You waited too long, became an old maid! Ach! That's what you get for being too choosy!"

"As a matter of fact, my parents weren't choosy at all," said Rivtcha plaintively, "but it took some time before they could find a husband for me. You know you can't find many men willing to take girls who have grown up in inns and taverns. Because my parents ran an inn for the Polish gentry we were gossiped about a lot; there are always slanderous tongues wagging!"

"Nu, let's put all that aside!" the wonder-worker interrupted her. "What I would like to know is: have there been *epis* any barren women in your family?"

"Oh, for saying that may you have a lot of *naches* from your own children!" cried Rivtcha. "You've guessed like an angel! My mother, a blessing to her memory, was for a time barren and probably would have remained so always were it not for the wonder-worker, Reb Feivel Pintchevesher. Yes indeed, above everything in the world was He whose name I dare not mention, and right after Him came the wonder-worker, through whose caress I was born. On the other hand, I ought to tell you that a great-grandmother of mine was barren and died barren (may I be spared a like fate!)."

The wonder-worker nodded his head and said:

"Just the same, be sure that in another year you'll be suckling your own babe. I'm going to give you an amulet and, in addition, I'll tell you about *epis* something that you'll have to do. You're going to give birth to a boy! You must name him Samuel, like our mother Hannah named her first-born."

"Oy, we should only live to see that happy event!" cried Rivtcha, jumping for joy. "Let his name be anything you like, Rebbe!"

This most important conversation between Reb Borech and the innkeeper's wife probably would not have come to an end just then had the servant not come up to inform his master that the chazan was back already from the parnass. He was feeling very jolly and had asked to see him right away.

The report about the chazan, that he had received the parnass's permission to sing the service in the Great Synagogue, and that he wished to see Reb Leml, diverted Reb Borech's thoughts into other channels.

As Reb Leml was about to leave the room Reb Borech detained him. His wife, in the meantime, hastened out, fired by the great hope that soon her dearest wish would be fulfilled. In fact, she dwelled on the matter so enthusiastically that she was certain she was already feeling the kick of the child in her womb.

When Reb Leml and the wonder-worker were left alone, Reb Borech asked:

"Tell me, Reb Leml, what sort of a chazan is this man who has asked to see you."

"We have a new chazan in town for this Shabbes," the innkeeper replied. "You may have heard of him? His name is Reb Zundl Kreihuhn; he's the Shtoperker chazan."

"Is that so!" exclaimed the wonder-worker with astonishment. "Is that so! So Reb Zundl is going to sing in your town! I'm delighted to hear that, delighted! I want to tell you he's someone worth listening to. He's a great singer and just as great a prayer leader. His voice is sweet as sugar and gladdens both the heart and the soul. On top of all that, he's really a very distinguished man, a fine Torah scholar and a God-fearing Jew! You can well believe me, it happens but seldom that all these wonderful qualities should be combined in one chazan. If what you tell me is true, that this chazan is really Reb Zundl Kreihuhn, then I've no right to detain you any longer. Nu, hurry, hurry down to him! But first I must caution you about one thing: whatever you do, don't tell anybody that I'm Reb Borech Baal-Shem! If people find out who I am they won't leave me in peace, and I want to get a good rest on Shabbes!"

"When are you planning to leave, Rebbe?" Reb Leml asked.

"On Sunday," answered Reb Borech.

"Now that I think of it, you should have warned my wife not to say a word about you," said Reb Leml in some distress. "I myself surely won't tell anybody."

"Nu, so I beg you *takkeh* to caution your wife in my name."

"And that I'll takkeh do," Reb Leml assured him, and he hurried out of the room.

When Reb Leml came down he found his wife deep in the midst of preparing diapers and little coverlets for the baby that the wonder-worker had promised her. And while doing this she held forth rapturously before a growing crowd of women that surrounded her. She recited all the great wonders performed by Reb Borech, repeated word for word what she had said to him and what he had said to her, and how amazed she was that he knew right away what she had come to ask him for before she could even say a word!

And so there she stood, patting her belly before everybody, as Tamar did when she got acquainted with Yehudah. And she kept on shouting like one possessed:

"Gevalt! I'm going to give birth to a *gaon* [genius]! I've a *tzaddik* in my belly!"

All that Friday, the inn was bubbling like a kettle. People kept coming in all the time to get either a peep or a smell of the chazan and the Baal-Shem. Seeing that it was no use trying any longer to be secretive about the Baal-Shem, the innkeeper went on to relate to the crowd wonders upon wonders about his eminent guest.

"He's a godly man, I'm telling you! He doesn't only see the outsides of people, like you and me, he can see what's doing inside your very heart! I saw it myself—he proved it on me personally! Praise and thanks be to His dear Name that I stood the test! All you have to do is to look at him. You can see with your own eyes how the holy *Shechinah* rests on his face! He looks like an angel of God!

"He recalled to me and my wife things that had taken place in our lives that we had almost forgotten about. It's perfectly clear to me now why he turned his face away from Berkeh, my kindhearted servant, when he went out to help bring in his baggage. Yes, from afar this godly man smelled that there was something *tréf* in Berkeh!

"Now I can very well understand that Reb Zundl Kreihuhn, the Shtoperker chazan must be epis one fine diamond of a Jew because, when I was telling Reb Borech that Reb Zundl would sing for our townsfolk on Shabbes, he began to rejoice! He said that a kosher Jew like him was hard to find and he went on to praise him very highly. He lauded his singing to the skies. He said it was as dazzling as the largest diamonds that the angels set into their crowns out of the prayers Jews send winging to the Almighty."

The innkeeper's praise certainly sent the chazan's prestige soaring very high. Few now had any doubts about his great cantorial gifts. Why in the world should they? First of all, would the Baal-Shem praise a chazan without cause? Second of all, would a wonder-worker like that want to make a liar out of himself? It was almost Sabbath Eve by now, and soon enough they'd be able to hear for themselves how the Shtoperker sang. Yes, the chazan must takkeh have one fine "instrument" in his throat!

However, there were some people in town who continued to have their doubts about the Baal-Shem and didn't put much stock in the reports about his miraculous powers. One of the most vocal of these doubters was the *melamed,* who taught the innkeeper's young nephew whom Reb Leml had been raising to be his *kaddish.*[1] Of course, with the coming of the wonder-worker Reb Leml was already beginning to consider that he no longer needed an adopted kaddish! Why, wasn't

---

[1]*According to orthodox Jewish practice, only a male child can recite the Kaddish, the mourner's prayer for the dead, which has to be repeated daily during eleven months of mourning. Since this is considered of enormous importance for the peace of the deceased one's soul, it was quite common in former days for sonless couples to adopt and raise an orphaned boy, usually a relation, who was then referred to as their "kaddish." Thus kaddish (holy) has two meanings: the prayer for the dead, and a son, natural or adopted, who will recite the Kaddish after a deceased parent.* ED.

he going to get one of his own now? The melamed felt very resentful at this threat to his livelihood and heaped nothing but scorn and ridicule on the Baal-Shem. This conduct on the melamed's part naturally made Reb Leml very angry. He set about giving him and the other skeptics a good piece of his mind.

At that juncture the chazan, with *payyes* that were still moist, returned from the *mikveh*.

"You've come just in time, Reb Zundl!" called out Reb Leml joyfully to him. "We're having quite an argument about Cabala and about a certain wonder-worker. Let's hear what you think about it."

"Oh that!" parried the chazan, "why that's a short question that requires a long answer, and there's no time for it now. The choir boys are already waiting for me to rehearse with them. Nonetheless, I'll say this in passing, that we Jews, who are believing sons of believing fathers, must have faith in the accepted fact that our great men performed wondrous deeds by means of the Cabala. You'll find the proof of that in the Talmud and in the performances of the Holy Ari.[1] Of course I can't say that much about our modern wonder-workers!"

"If that's the case, I'm very anxious to hear what you think of Reb Borech Baal-Shem."

"Why epis do you ask about him?" asked the chazan in surprise.

"I'm asking because at this very moment he's stopping in this inn."

"Is that so!" exclaimed the chazan with some alarm. "So this swindler has come here too! Ach! and you have the *mazl* to have him for your guest! I warn you to be very careful with him! He can easily make a fool out of you and of everybody else in town, just as he has done in other places. He's a rogue of the first order! He talks well and smoothly and he is so clever that he can take in practically anybody you like. In fact, he looks to me like an awful ignoramus, and for that reason he takkeh poses as a cabalist! He wears this pretension of being a master of hidden wisdom like an overcoat to cover up his ignorance and his vices. Oy, I'm really sorry that I wasn't around when he came! Believe me, I wouldn't have let you take him into your house."

"But Reb Zundl!" answered the innkeeper much astonished, "if you only knew what Reb Borech said about you, you wouldn't have spoken in such a harsh way. I want you to know that he praised you highly, but very highly! He said that you were a great chazan, a kosher Jew, and a scholar!"

[1] *Rabbi Isaac Luria, a noted cabalist of sixteenth-century Safed in Palestine.* ב.

The chazan burst out laughing.

"Now you see, when a swindler like that praises me I don't feel flattered at all. I don't need his praise and I don't need his judgment. In a few hours from now you'll hear for yourselves what sort of a chazan I am. And as for my Torah learning—how can such an ignoramus set himself up as a judge? I've come here to sing and not to show off my learning! Rest assured though, about his 'merchandise' none of you has the faintest idea. Since you do consider me a kosher Jew, as you've told me, then take my advice and guard yourself against him like against a *meshuggener* dog!"

After this brief discussion, the chazan went into his room to make his arrangements with the choir boys. His abuse of the Baal-Shem gave encouragement to the melamed and the other skeptics, so they began to rant against him still louder and heaped even more ridicule upon Reb Borech and upon all other cabalists. This only upset Reb Leml, and especially his wife, Rivtcha, who expected to be delivered very soon.

The melamed grew more belligerent from minute to minute. He finally insisted that Reb Leml take him up to the Baal-Shem's room and he'd prove to Reb Leml's own satisfaction what a big ignoramus and fraud that wonder-worker was!

In the end, Red Leml gave in to his demand.

"Very well, let's go up to the Baal-Shem," said he, "and I'll introduce you to him. I'll tell him you're my melamed and that you wish to discourse on matters of Torah with him."

Unfortunately, the melamed had the heart of a chicken. Although he used to laugh at ghosts, nonetheless, he was afraid to sleep alone in a room. He'd even mock at dreams, yet this didn't stop him from fasting devoutly after he had had a nightmare.

No sooner did they come into the wonder-worker's room than the melamed's hands and feet began to shake. In the middle of the room he saw standing the Baal-Shem, his face hidden in the folds of his *tallis,* his eyes turned to the wall, and staring so intently heavenward, that he did not even notice their coming in. There he stood, swaying to and fro as though he were in the midst of his devotions and looking like one who has just renounced this sinful world and gone soaring in spirit to the celestial regions.

From time to time he cried out in a hoarse voice the names of some obscure-sounding evil spirits—demons and devils.

"Shut up you—get inside!" he yelled to one demon. "And you, too, shut up Pargud! Also you, Udial, keep your mouth shut!"

Right after that he cupped his hand over his right ear, as if he wanted to hear what someone invisible was saying. Then, appearing outraged, he began to repeat words he presumably had heard:

"What! You mean that swindler? . . . . A rogue of the first order! . . . . Guard yourself against him like against a meshuggener dog! . . . . Enough now—making such vile accusations against a kosher Jew and a scholar! . . . . Oh, Angel Gabriel, you who once shut the jaws of lions so that they shouldn't bite the prophet Daniel, shut the mouth of this base slanderer! Let not the entire town suffer on account of this good-for-nothing! It's enough that he alone should be punished! This I beg of you, Gabriel, as I would beg of an old and true friend!"

These words the wonder-worker uttered in a tremulous voice and with the exaltation of prophetic vision.

The melamed and the Reb Leml listened to him in stunned silence. They understood only too well the nature of his cries, knew that he had repeated word for word what the chazan had said about him before. This was the Baal-Shem's way of rebuking his defamers and at the same time showing how magnanimous he could be.

The melamed and Reb Leml remained standing on one spot, congealed with fright. Now they could see clearly what a great prophet the Baal-Shem was! Did anybody need other proof? And besides, my oh my! didn't they see for themselves what a hail fellow he was with all those terrible demons and devils, even with the Angel Gabriel himself? And because of that they remained rooted to the spot. They wanted to run away but all their strength had left them and their feet refused to obey them.

They remained standing thus until the Baal-Shem got over his godly ecstasy. Then he turned around and was amazed to find them there. He asked them in a most friendly way how long they had been standing there and what they wanted of him.

Reb Leml barely had the strength to mumble:

"This, Rebbe, is the melamed who works for me. He's teaching my brother's boy whom I'm raising to be my kaddish. Well, he's asked me to bring him up here so that he might have the honor of saying 'sholom aleichem' to you."

"Very nice of him!" Reb Borech answered, and graciously extended his left hand to him in greeting.

One can well understand why out of great fright the melamed, in a manner of speaking, was reduced to a heap of dead man's bones. He didn't even have the strength to clasp the wonder-worker's extended hand, just stood like a corpse unable to move hand or foot.

"What's the matter with both of you? Epis you look upset!" murmured Reb Borech innocently.

"We feel that way, Rebbe, because we've been standing here and listening to you for more than a half hour," blurted out Reb Leml. "What's more, we've heard something that never before in our lives have we heard the like! Truth to tell, both of us almost fainted away!"

"What! You mean to say you've been here for such a long time?" cried the Baal-Shem amazed. "Surely you must have heard with whom I was talking! And you probably understand, too, about what I was talking! Well, know that in Heaven they are very angry at the Jews of your town. That's because in one of your houses such wicked words were spoken about a kosher Jew and a scholar! Positively nothing like that can be allowed to go unpunished!

"In fact, we even find it written in the *Talmud* and in the *Midrash* that the Creator, blessed be He, is quicker to forgive an offense against His honor than an offense against His holy men. Of course, the first to be punished, Reb Leml, should have been your own household, because it was in your house that the evil words were spoken. But, because I've always been a man who bears no grudge against anyone, I've been able to straighten everything out by cabalistic means. Nobody's going to be harmed, not even that rogue who spoke such vile slanders against me.

"True, the chazan wasn't the only one to speak falsehoods. There were others, too, including this melamed who's standing right here. Still in all, I'll be content to bring down God's punishment on the chazan alone because it was he who spoke more wickedly about me than anyone else did. Therefore, because he called me a 'meshuggener dog' and himself barked at me like a dog, let him become meshuggeh like a meshuggener dog and let him bark and howl like a dog!"

Reb Leml and the melamed barely managed to muster strength enough to leave the Baal-Shem's presence. They came down the stairs looking as white as the whitewashed walls. The melamed began to beat his breast and recited the penitential prayer, "Ours is the transgression!" That was out of contrition because he had spoken evil of such a holy man as Reb Borech. Reb Leml, in turn, went about patting his little belly with great self-importance and telling everybody with elation what he had seen and heard in the Baal-Shem's room.

"Mind you!" marveled Reb Leml to those who crowded around him. "This wonder-worker, upstairs in his room, repeated word for word what had been said about him right here below. It was just as if he had been present! But to me it's no longer any mystery. I've discovered that Reb Borech is a person who speaks with angels and demons just as simply and in as matter-of-fact way as I speak with you. At the very moment we came in we found him in the midst of a conversation with them. Just ask the melamed, good health to him, if that wasn't so! Ask him what he said about the Baal-Shem only an hour ago! Go ahead—ask him!"

The melamed, who nebbech wasn't quite over the great anguish and fear that the Baal-Shem had flung him into, had to confess before everyone present that this wonder-worker was indeed a wonder-worker.

"Now one can see," he admitted ruefully, "that our own sins pursue us everywhere we go and that slander has the power to penetrate through walls even! How lucky we are that this wonder-worker is such a great-hearted man! If he wasn't, believe me more than one person would have been punished! Certainly, I would have been the first bcause I uttered plenty of slanders!"

These words of the melamed caused a sensation among all those who heard him and, in no time at all, among the rest of the townsfolk. Every house buzzed with the account of the remarkable happenings. It threw everyone into a somber Yom Kippur mood. Each person separately began to search his soul and take stock of all his deeds and misdeeds. More than half of the town's Jews finally hurried over to the wonder-worker to ask from him a penance for the expiation of their sins.

In all this excitement they pretty near came to forgetting about the chazan, were it not for a certain incident. This cast the town into an even greater turmoil than had the Baal-Shem's conversation with the angels, the devils, and the demons.

Barely had the melamed finished talking when one of his pupils, a boy of ten or so, ran in breathlessly to tell him that from the room where the chazan was quartered he had heard barking and howling, like that of a big dog. "Is that the way, Rebbe, he's rehearsing to sing in synagogue on Shabbes?" the boy asked innocently.

The crowd listened with mounting incredulity and amazement. Reb Leml himself got so frightened that his hair almost stood on end:

"*Ut!* There you have a clear answer!" he finally managed to stammer. "Let's hope that the chazan will be the only one to be punished and that the rest of us will get by unharmed. We can learn from it a good lesson: that the tongue was made to hold between the teeth and not to wag evil against others. I want you to know that I am a good judge of people. As soon as I clapped my eyes on Reb Borech the Baal-Shem I knew that he was a godly person!"

However, there was still one skeptic around. Only a little while before he had given his full support to the melamed's doubts. He said now:

"If I were you, Reb Leml, I wouldn't put too much stock in what a little snip like that gabbles. How do you know he didn't imagine it all? We've got to hear it with our own ears and see it with our own eyes to be convinced. Let's all go and look into the chazan's window!"

The crowd hung back out of fear. Still enough, there were several brave souls who volunteered to go, and they pulled the reluctant melamed along with them.

They looked into the chazan's room, and what they saw and heard—ach! may all good people be spared such an experience! Right in the middle of the room they saw the chazan. He was down on all fours, looking angrily around him with wild rolling eyes. His hair hung matted-like down his face. His mouth was wide open in a snarl, his tongue hung out, and he drooled just like a dog. From time to time he gnashed his teeth and leaped backwards towards the door. Each time he touched the door with his rear end he bounded forward again and started to bark and howl ever louder and louder. It wasn't long before he began to leap about crazily until he finally broke the bowl and pitcher; and the broken fragments he bit with his teeth and trampled upon with his feet.

The whole town soon began to boil over with this astounding news. Everybody came running up to watch the chazan's strange cavortings. Later, of course, each one embroidered in his own way what he had seen and heard.

From minute to minute the Baal-Shem grew holier and holier in the eyes of the townsfolk. In the brief course of only a half hour he had gone through an amazing transformation: from a baal-shem to a prophet, from a prophet to a worker of miracles, from a miracle worker to a godly man, from a godly man to an angel, and from an angel to a partner of the Creator Himself!

The townsfolk soon descended on the Baal-Shem like an avalanche, some to get his blessing, others to ask for an amulet, or to request a penance for their sins, or to implore for miraculous cures for their illnesses. But it wasn't so easy to get to him because there was a mighty shoving and pushing and elbowing all around him.

At first the Baal-Shem refused to let anyone even come near him, but in the end he relented, allowing only the richest men in town to enter his room.

Of course, the first blessing and the first amulet he gave to Rivtcha, the innkeeper's wife. After her he attended to her good friends, and they paid him generously for everything. Everyone who came in to see him stood in awe of him. As they talked with him they could plainly hear the chazan's barking, and they trembled in their *pupiks*.

The melamed acted like a scared rabbit. He was frightened more than anybody else. It wasn't long before he began to imagine that his own voice had grown epis peculiar, similar to the voice of a dog. Terrified, he pressed his lips tight together and locked his jaws with his fingers so that he shouldn't, God forbid, start to bark or whine. He also clutched his stick more firmly to prevent his falling on all fours like the chazan. All the time he kept on imagining that an irresistible force was drawing him down on all fours. For that reason, to avoid such a horrible fate, he eagerly emptied his pockets of his last ruble to give to the Baal-Shem for a peace offering.

That night, after duly greeting the Sabbath Bride with appropriate prayer and song, the town rabbi called together the dignitaries of the town and spoke to them as follows:

"Brothers! I want you to know that we have no right to close our eyes to what is happening in our midst. The Baal-Shem himself has testified about the chazan that he is one fine kosher Jew, and a scholar at that! Why has the chazan come to our town? He has come here in order to earn his livelihood. Unfortunately, he has nebbech fallen into great misfortune so that now he lives among us as a meshuggener dog! I'm not even going to try to deny it, he has earned his punishment well and kosher. One must guard oneself against talking any foolishness like that, one must never laugh at the hidden mysteries! Just the same, it's a great pity on the poor fellow; he has, after all, nebbech a wife and children! How long must he be tormented for his sin, anyway? My advice, therefore, is: that we all go together to Reb Borech Baal-Shem and promise him a handsome gift of money, and that we respectfully beg him to send up his prayers in intercession for the unfortunate chazan so that, God willing, he may be able to depart from our town in peace, like a human being."

The communal officials readily agreed to this and they accompanied the rabbi to the inn.

They found the Baal-Shem in his room where he had been conducting the Friday night services with a special *minyan* of worshipful believers. With great inner concentration and rapture he was intoning the Sabbath prayer, "Sholom-Aleichem." His callers waited for a long time until he was finished and had opened his eyes.

After they had explained the object of their visit, Reb Borech said to them:

"You mustn't, God forbid, consider me a vengeful person! All the evil the chazan spoke against me I pardoned right away. All my life I've tried to be big-hearted. In fact, had I not prayed in your behalf every single Jew in this town would have perished! You know how it is, we Jews accept responsibility one for the other. The chazan still owes me thanks because I interceded in his behalf and got him off with a trifling punishment, and for a short time too. God alone knows I didn't do what I did out of vengeance but only in order to remove from him the mark of slanderer. I just want to say this much: were it not for my intercession Heaven would have decreed against the chazan that, upon his death, his soul would have had to enter into a dog and dwell there for many a year. This way he'll get over the punishment in a short time while he is still alive. But, seeing that you've come to me to ask a favor for him, I'll not let you go with empty hands. For your sake, and in honor of this Holy Shabbes day, I'll try to lighten his punishment still more, although I cannot let him off completely.

"Therefore, I, Reb Borech Baal-Shem, decree that the chazan stop crawling on all fours right away, and that he let up his howling and his barking like a dog!

"I regret to say, though, that he won't be able to talk like a human being until after Shabbes. And as for singing at the synagogue, ach! he won't be able to do that until a month has passed! Do you want to know why? It's because they're angry at him up there in Heaven, because every time he sings the service he tries to please the women. And that's a terrible sin, as you know! Of course, he'll have to stammer a bit for quite a while because, after all, he has sinned a great deal with his tongue.

"Now I think I've said enough, my masters. Hurry home before the Sabbath candles burn down! Here is my tallis! Spread it out over the unfortunate chazan and he'll give up being a dog and will return to his human form. Now go, and may peace be with you!"

So they took Reb Borech's tallis and hurried over to the chazan. They spread the tallis over him, just as the Baal-Shem had told them to. And lo and behold! Miracles and wonders! Before their very eyes they saw the chazan change! He grew calmer and more human from minute to minute. Within the space of half an hour he was already standing upright on his feet. When they placed a chair before him he was able to sit down, although he had to grip the arms for support. And when he had come to even more he started to put to rights his disheveled beard and payyes. He wiped his perspired face and even tried to say epis, but it just didn't work! However, he had by this time already collected his wits to such an extent that he was able to make himself understood by means of signs. For instance, when he wanted them to give him a schnapps he gave himself a quick fillip in the Adam's apple. When he wanted to eat he shoved his finger in his mouth. When he wanted to sleep he put his hand to his cheek, nodding his head drowsily sideways.

In short, in the course of only a few hours he had become human just like you and me. However, one human characteristic was lacking —he had lost his power of speech. Not the slightest doglike sign was left on him except that. On Shabbes, after synagogue, when he sat down to the feast he fell upon the food like a hungry dog and gorged himself until he was ready to burst. He broke the dishes from which he ate into the bargain. All these things were reported right away to the Baal-Shem, but he made nothing of them.

"If he behaves that way," said Reb Borech, "it is a well-deserved punishment for gorging himself like a pig at all the weddings and circumcision parties where he sings. You know how it is, they are now making the debtor pay off all his debts. Know, that up above they behave exactly the way we do down here below. What do you think happens when a criminal falls into the hands of the police for committing a crime? They settle accounts with him not only for that particular crime but for all his other crimes as well."

When this got abroad, it raised the prestige of the Baal-Shem even more, if such a thing could be possible. They believed in him now like in a prophet—what am I saying?—like in a *tzaddik* who simply has no peer!

That night at the conclusion of the Sabbath, they flocked to him in even greater numbers, bringing more money and more gifts.

He, in turn, distributed among them many amulets and promises of positive cures. Many Gentile women also came to ask the Baal-Shem to help them in their tzoress. They too brought him money and gifts and, when they left, glowed with enthusiasm over him because he had guessed their secret wishes and had given them good advice and promises.

The following morning, on Sunday, the Baal-Shem made ready to leave town. The communal authorities rewarded him handsomely for the great services he had rendered the town in sparing it so much misfortune. However, the largest contribution he received was from Reb Leml, the innkeeper, because now he was at last assured of a son.

At parting, in the presence of everybody, the melamed humbly begged his forgiveness. "I know," he told him, "that I deserve the same punishment the chazan got, but your holiness has served as my shield and buckler. Because of that, and from this day on, I'll be a firm believer in Cabala and in the wondrous powers of a Baal-Shem!"

And, as the melamed spoke, the Baal-Shem stroked his beard with pleasure and smiled benignly. He said to the melamed in farewell:

"May you be washed clean of your sin and may it be forgiven you!"

A great throng of men and women escorted him out of the town, and at the moment of parting, they assured him that they'd do no harm to the chazan. On the contrary, they'd pay him as if he had really sung the service in the synagogue. Besides that, they'd take good care of him until he'd begin to speak again. Then they'd send him home at the town's expense.

And they kept their word because, besides being great believers, they were also honest people.

By the time Wednesday arrived the chazan was already able to talk. He then confirmed that everything the Baal-Shem had said about him was true. Then he departed for home with a nice fat groschen tucked away in his pocket.

Several weeks later, two strangers happened to stop at Reb Leml's inn. They observed the Sabbath there and told their host a marvelous story about a Baal-Shem and a chazan that had taken place only a couple of weeks before in their town, Lachmotz.

And that is how Reb Leml came to discover that exactly the same thing had happened in Lachmotz that had happened in Durachesok. And when they got down to talking about particulars it became as clear as the nose on his face that the two rascals were the identical birds.

Everybody now understood how they had been swindled and that the Baal-Shem was no genuine Baal-Shem and the chazan was no genuine chazan. They all nebbech hung their noses from shame and vexation!

Reb Leml's wife, of course, gave up being with child. The husbands who had left their wives continued to stay away. The sick thought it over and went to the doctor for treatment. In fact, they all felt ashamed now because their town was called Durachesok—the town of fools! People from other towns made sport of them and applied to them the well-known saying:

"They fit the name of their town just as their town fits them."

*A lot of people talk foolishness
because there are* nebbech *bigger fools
who listen to them.*

You don't get poor from taking.

WELL-TRAINED PILLS

A sick sage went to the chemist's with some prescriptions from his doctor. The chemist explained to him:

"You have three kinds of pills here: one to soothe your nerves, another to take away your headache, and the third to stop your stomach cramps."

The sage was filled with wonder.

"Please tell me—how on earth can those little pills know just where to go?"

MY FIRST DEPOSIT

BY MOISHE NADIR (ISAAC REISS)
TRANSLATED FROM THE YIDDISH BY NATHAN AUSUBEL

I don't know how it happened, how I ever got the idea of taking my hard-earned money and depositing it in a bank. Just the same it did happen. Right after Hanukkah I took my entire fortune—my twenty dollars—and carried it over to the bank. Instead of money, *real* money with which you can buy whatever you like, I got *epis* a green little book in a yellow envelope and—that's all! When I saw it my heart caved in and I was sorry for the whole business.

First of all I didn't like the snip that stood at the little window and took my money. A young nobody, not even married, albetcha! What, for instance, could I do to him if he took my money and ran away? Then I didn't like the way he treated me: he took my money, grabbed up *epis* a little book, scribbled in it the Devil knows what, smacked it down in front of me through the little window, and squeaked, "Next!"

I took a look inside the book, and I got a creeping chill down my spine! What sort of a writing was that, what sort? And how would he ever be able to read it again? And how does he know that it makes twenty? "Ai!" I thought, "Epis I don't like the whole business." And I ran back to the little window, shoved aside the man standing in the line, and called out to that little nothing inside, "Hey!" I yelled. "I've just handed you twenty dollars!"

"So what do you want?" he asks me, and went on sharpening a pencil.

"I want," said I, "that you shouldn't be so fresh! If not, you're going to get such a smack that the Devil will take you!"

So what do you think he answers? "Mister," says he, "what do you want? I gave you a bankbook, no? Dasall!"

"It'sanuff!" says I. "I don't want to talk to you any more, you bloodsucker what you are! I already see," says I, "that I've fallen into the right hands, so give me back," says I, "the money and don't be my son-in-law!"

" 'T'simpossible!" says he to me.

"I'll soon give you a 't'simpossible," says I, "that the good year will take you! Swindler that you are!" says I. "With me," says I, "you're not going to make such tricks! Hand over the money," says I, "before I call the police and before," says I, "I yell gevalt!" And before he could say anything I began to yell at the top of my voice: *"Ge-va-lt! Ge-va-lt!"*

When he heard me yell like that he got soft like butter, that little nobody did. He began to explain to me that he couldn't give me back the money right away, that I'd have to wait two weeks. 'T'sarule such!

"If that's the case," says I, "so read to me what you wrote in the little book. Let me see," says I, "if you know what you wrote there. Epis," says I, "you wrote it too fast. It's hard for me to believe," says I, "that you could write down so much money so fast."

He took the little book from me and read: "Twenty dollars."

"All right," says I. "Now remember! It's twenty dollars! And let all these people standing around here be my witnesses. Folks," says I, "be my witnesses that I've just put in this bank two ten dollar smackers!"

Then I took my little book and went home.

Well, you can understand that sleep was out of the question for me that night. All night long I was dreaming that robbers held up the bank and cleaned out its last penny. Several times I awoke and yelled, "Gevalt!" As soon as it grew light the first thing I did was to jump on the streetcar and hurry over to the bank.

I found it the same as before; there had been no robbery. A stone rolled off my heart.

But as I stood looking over the bank it suddenly struck me that the iron bars outside the windows were a little weak. They ought to put in new bars, I thought. So I stood with my lunch box in my hand and waited for the bank president to come.

As soon as I saw him go in I pulled him aside and told him about the bars. "According to my opinion," says I, "the whole building is too weak and the whole thing should be rebuilt. You've got to see," says I, "that the whole building should be made of marble, because marble," says I, "is hard stuff!"

"All right," says he to me. "Thanks for your advice."

"Remember then, for heaven's sake—a new building made of marble! And new bars! 'Tshould be well protected. I've come down extra from Brownsville," says I, "because," says I, "I dreamed that we were robbed."

Then I rushed off to work.

Late that afternoon, when the time came for me to go home, I thought to myself, "I'll pass by the bank and see what's news. You can never tell how a thing will turn out—'samerica, after all!"

When I came to the bank and took a look, I saw epis a fellow was flying out of the bank and running away like mad. So naturally I began to run after him and yell "Gevalt!" Finally a policeman caught up with him. And who do you think it turned out to be? It was a man who worked in the bank and he was running to catch the streetcar because his wife had just given birth to a baby.

A little ashamed at my mistake I went home, but sleep well I couldn't this time either.

All night long I was dreaming that the little clerk who took my money was running away with a sack of money in his hand and I was chasing him. I yelled "Gevalt!" in my sleep and threw my arms around all night long with such strength that I almost killed the baby.

Early next morning I went to see a *landsman* of mine who happened to live right opposite the bank. I promised to pay him thirty per cent of my money if he kept an eye on the bank. "Watch it!" I begged him. "Sit and watch! Don't take," says I, "an eye off the bank. And as soon," says I, "that God will help me and the two weeks will be over, I'll grab my twenty dollars, and then," says I, "let all banks burn! Never again," says I, "will I darken their doorsteps again!"

Two days passed. Suddenly I read in the papers that a bank, somewhere in the Bronx, was held up. So I ran quickly to the president of my bank.

" 'T'sbitter!" I tell him.

"What's the trouble?" he asked me.

"Holdups!" says I.

"There'll be no holdups here!" says he. "My bank is protected."

"*Nu,*" says I, "and what, for instance, will you do if your little cashier grabs ahold of the money and runs away?"

"Mister," says he, "you don't know what you're talking about."

"Nu? have it your way," says I. "So I don't know what I'm talking about . . . but new bars you've got to put up, no?"

"No," says he.

"Nu," says I, "are you going to rebuild the bank or are you not?"

So what do you think he answers to that? "Please, mister, stop bothering me."

So I says, "Since new bars you haven't put up, and you haven't even started rebuilding the bank, and your handsome little cashier you haven't even fired yet, so please be so good and hand over—give me back the money!"

"You've got to wait until the two weeks are up," says he.

"All right," says I, "I'll wait. But it's going to be right outside the bank—that's where I'm going to wait. By me you're going to chew the dirt . . . believe me, you're not going to get any satisfaction. Even if I should know that my children would remain without a papa, I'll not move from the spot until I'll get my money back. I'll watch," says I, "and my landsman who lives across the way will watch too. It's going to be real lively, that I promise you. Yeh, that's the sort of man I am! I'll stand right outside," says I, "in the biggest frosts, and just let me see," says I, "and do me something! Nu, go ahead and do me something!"

"You're a funny man," says he to me. "Come inside the bank and I'll give you back your twenty dollars."

"No sirree!" says I. "Such monkey business don't go with me. Just because you want to give me back the money I won't take. You can't," says I, "force me to take!"

"All right," says he, "so don't take."

"Never mind," says I. "If I'll want to I'll take and you can't stop me."

"Please, mister," says he, "go away and stop pestering me."

"All right," says I, "I'm going. But remember, I'm going to stand right outside. In the biggest frosts I'm going to stand right outside and watch my money. And my innocent blood," says I, "and the blood of my innocent orphans will fall," says I, "on your head. Bandit what you are!" I yelled. "The 'lectri-chair is too good for you! Bummer you! Murderer! GE-VALT!"

Oy, did I yell!

You ask what the end was? The end was that they gave me back the twenty dollars, but on my way home from the bank someone picked my pocket.

From that time on I swore that my foot would never cross the door of a bank. Reg'la bandits, I'm telling you! Pickpockets! Oy, those banks—they should only burn!

A Jew, when he's smart—oy, is he smart!
And when he's a fool—oy, is he a fool!

RABBI ITZIK THE FOOL

BY YEHUDAH STEINBERG
TRANSLATED FROM THE YIDDISH BY NATHAN AUSUBEL

About Rabbi Itzik the Fool, the pious *Chassidim* are fond of relating that he was so simple-minded that he didn't even know that he was a *tzaddik*.[1] When he was told what a tzaddik he was he marveled greatly. What a silly idea! But he lacked the *chutzpah* to doubt what people told him. How could he possibly suspect any Jew of telling a lie? "Likely as not God rewards me because of the great merit of my ancestors," was the way he used to explain away the matter.

It is told how once the *rebbetzin* complained to Rabbi Itzik that they were badly in need of *parnosseh,* and his *gabbai* also complained about his poverty. Now the Fool wanted to bless the rebbetzin and the gabbai so that God should give them both parnosseh. But the gabbai reminded him that it wasn't in the power of a tzaddik to make divine intercession for his own household. So the Fool replied with the utmost simplicity: "That being the case, I'll go and look for some other tzaddik to bless you."

Now the rebbetzin and the gabbai talked it over and decided that Rabbi Itzik would do better to visit those towns where his disciples

[1] *A saint.*

lived in large numbers. He would give them his blessings and they, in turn, would give him their gifts. Thus he would earn enough money for parnosseh.

"Why not?" agreed the Fool. "Parnosseh is something that every Jew has got to have, and to go out into the world in order to meet and talk with God's Jews is very very definitely a fine thing!"

So the gabbai hired a cart for a whole week and they set out for a distant town. The gabbai thought: "Even as the tidings of fragrant oil is carried afar so are the fair names of the tzaddikim held in great esteem in far-off places. Their fame is greater there than in towns nearby."

Moreover, the gabbai was afraid that Rabbi Itzik would only make enough to sustain himself for one week, and then, likely as not, with his habitual lack of concern for the future, he'd return home thinking that he had sufficient money.

And so they journeyed, the Fool, the gabbai, and the driver, towards the distant town until they arrived only two miles from their destination. The gabbai advised that it would be wise to stop and rest a bit before entering the town. But on the sly he bid the driver to hasten ahead and let everyone know that the great tzaddik, Rabbi Itzik the Fool, had arrived and was waiting to be welcomed by the disciples.

The driver carried out his errand and returned instantly. The Fool then began to hurry on the driver for he was afraid he might arrive too late for the *Mincha* prayers. But the gabbai did not seem to be in any hurry. Looking up the hillside, he saw how there was descending upon them a great multitude of carts with many Jews in them. No doubt it must be the disciples coming down to welcome Rabbi Itzik, he thought. So the three of them got into their cart and drove on.

When the Fool raised his eyes and saw carts on every side of him he was filled with wonder.

"Where are you all going?" he asked a Jew in one of the carts rattling by.

"We're on our way to welcome a tzaddik," was the answer.

"To welcome a tzaddik!" joyfully exclaimed Rabbi Itzik. "Why, is there a tzaddik around? I didn't even know! Driver turn the cart around! Maybe we'll be lucky enough to be among the first to greet him!"

The driver scratched his head perplexed and looked questioningly at the gabbai. In the meantime several carts drove up and a number of Chassidim jumped out and ran up to Rabbi Itzik.

"Just look what kosher Jews these are!" thought the Fool, rejoicing. "They're so pious that, out of respect for the tzaddik, they're going to meet him on foot. Great indeed will be their merit in the World-to-Come! I too will get out of the cart and walk with them to greet the tzaddik."

And so he clambered out of the cart and joined the Chassidim on foot.

He ran ahead and when the Chassidim saw this they ran with him. And many others ran behind him and on every side of him.

"Where are you running, *Rebbe?*" a disciple asked him timidly.

"What do you mean, where," replied Rabbi Itzik, all out of breath. "Why, to welcome the tzaddik, of course!"

"Tzaddik! What tzaddik?" asked the bewildered disciple.

"That's just it—you tell me!"

And that's the story the Chassidim tell about the devout tzaddik, Rabbi Itzik the Fool.

He who in his life has never made a fool of himself has also never been wise.—Heinrich Heine

DIVISION OF LABOR: *One chops wood, and the other one yells: "Oy!"*

Every fool is clever—for himself.

THE TWELVE WIDOWS

FROM THE TALMUD

Once there were thirteen brothers. Twelve of them died, and only one remained. As the twelve widows were left childless they demanded that their brother-in-law marry them, according to the injunction of Jewish law. However, he refused, so the twelve widows went to complain against him before Rabbi Yehudah "the Prince."

"Why don't you do what the law requires of you?" Rabbi Yehudah asked him.

"I'm not rich enough to support all these women," the brother-in-law answered.

"All we ask is that he support each one of us for one month of the year," the twelve young widows said with one voice.

The man half consented.

"But who will support them in a leap year?" he asked. "Who will feed them in the thirteenth month of Ve'Adar?"

"I will feed them for the extra leap-year month," volunteered Rabbi Yehudah.

He then blessed all the widows that they might be fruitful and bear many children, and they went away.

Three years later, the twelve women assembled before the house of Rabbi Yehudah. Each one brought three little children that had been born to her in the meantime and the twelve mothers with their thirty-six children stood and waited. Rabbi Yehudah's servants reported to him:

"Rabbi, a whole townful of women and children have come to inquire about your health!"

Rabbi Yehudah looked out of the window and saw the multitude.

"What can I do for you?" he asked.

"It's leap year and this is the month of Ve'Adar!" the twelve mothers cried with one voice.

*Better to lose to a wise man
than to win from a fool.*

THE LOAN

BY ABRAHAM REISEN
TRANSLATED FROM THE YIDDISH BY NATHAN AUSUBEL

The most important fair in Klemenke is that of *Ulas*. The Jews of the town wait for Ulas with beating heart and high hopes. "Ulas," say the merchants and shopkeepers in Klemenke, "is one of God's blessings." Were it not for Ulas, Klemenke would have ceased being Klemenke a long time ago and America would have lured away all the Jews still remaining there.

However, for Ulas one has got to have the right "tools"! The shopkeepers have got to have merchandise, and the merchants money. Without these tools, Ulas is just plain mud!

And so it happened that Chaim, the grain merchant, walked around more dead than alive. All told, only three days remained before Ulas and yet he didn't have a single kopeck. In the market place the other grain merchants were already dashing about, their cap visors askew, thick cigarets hanging from the corners of their mouths, and dangling their walking sticks. They were talking excitedly about the fair.

"In three days from now! . . ." exclaimed one with delightful anticipation.

"Ps-sh!" murmured another ecstatically. "In three days from now will things hum!"

And Chaim blanched. He felt like praying that the fair should turn out a failure, that it should rain or snow or storm on that day so that not even a *meshuggener* dog would show up. But Chaim knew very well that Ulas was no "timid little boy," Ulas wasn't afraid even of the worst snowstorm. In short, Ulas always remained Ulas!

Chaim almost became goggle-eyed looking for a loan. Where in Heaven's name could he get a loan? A twenty-fiver even!

He asked everyone, but from each one he got the mirthful answer: "Are you *meshuggeh* or something? Money for the fair—indeed!"

And it appeared to Chaim that he was *takkeh* going crazy!

"Why don't you walk over to Leibe-Beres?" his wife counseled him, for she shared his woe.

"In fact, I was thinking of that myself," replied Chaim thoughtfully.

"Only what? . . ." his wife asked, puzzled.

Chaim wanted to answer her, "I can't go to him; I haven't the courage," but he thought it wasn't proper to admit such a thing to his wife.

So he answered instead, "The Devil take him—he won't lend!"

"Does it hurt to try?" she coaxed him.

Chaim began to think it over. He takkeh did not have any alternative, and, to be sure, Leibe-Beres was a wealthy man and did live on the same street with him. Practically a neighbor! Besides, did Leibe-Beres need money for the fair? He himself was a lumber dealer.

"Hand me my *Shabbesdiggen* coat," he said to his wife with a resolute air.

"What then?" observed his wife. "The best thing is to go and see him."

Chaim went to the broken little mirror that was nailed to the wall. He studied his reflection, patted his beard with both hands and curled his *payyes*. Then he took his hat off and gave it a brush with his sleeve to get the dust off.

"Look at the back and see if there's any whitewash on it!" he told his wife.

"What a question if there is!" his wife answered, and with both hands began beating the back of his coat.

"Seems to me we once had a piece of brush. Where can it be, ha?"

"You must have seen it in a dream," answered his wife as she continued pounding him on the back. *"Nu,* it has come off a bit!"

"You've banged enough!" growled Chaim almost angrily. "I'll go now."

With a sigh he put on his Shabbesdiggen overcoat.

"He should live so if he will lend me!" he muttered, and left the house.

On his way to Leibe-Beres' house Chaim's heart quaked. For all the years that Leibe-Beres had been living on his street he had visited him no more than twice. Chaim felt that the visit he was now going to make would resolve itself into a sort of examination. The elaborate vestibule, the rooms full of light, the large mirrors, the soft chairs, and Leibe-Beres himself with his long broad beard, his stern rich man's eyes, and then his wife, their merry children, even the servant girl who had become fixed in his memory from those two visits—all of their images frightened him. He asked himself, "Where the devil are you going? Are you crazy? Better go back!" And then he'd stop and he'd remain standing a minute, undecided, right in the middle of the street. But the thought of approaching Ulas and that he had nothing with which to do business in his granary drove him on.

"Oh, he's not going to lend me! It's no use hoping!" he thought.

And as he walked on he poised himself for the blow. He had the feeling that if he'd allow his self-esteem to deflate any more he wouldn't be able to open his mouth to ask for the money. To bolster his spirits he tried to take a more hopeful view of things:

"If I'll find him in a good humor, it could be he might agree to lend. Why should he be afraid to lend me a few rubles until after the fair? I'm going to tell him that, as soon as I sell my grain, I'll return him the money right away. Why, I'll take a solemn oath by my wife and children! . . . . He'll believe me . . . and takkeh I intend to return it to him!"

But this line of reasoning did not succeed in increasing his self-esteem. He began to look for another hope, for another means to buoy up his spirits:

"He's not such a bad fellow, after all! Then again, he knows me for a long time. It's already twenty years since he and I are living on the same street."

Chaim recalled that only two weeks before, when Leibe-Beres passed by his little office in the market place, Chaim was standing outside his door and he greeted him with a friendly "good morning" in the manner appropriate for a rich man. ("I could swear that I even shook his hand!") Leibe-Beres had responded to his greeting graciously. He had even stopped to inquire just as one does of a good acquaintance, "How are you, Chaim?"

Chaim struggled hard to remember. He recalled that he had answered the rich man, "Thank you for asking. Not too bad . . . one does business."

And, recalling it, Chaim was pleased with the answer he had given him.

"And I answered him as I would an equal," he thought pridefully.

And Chaim resolved that now too he was going to talk to him man to man, with dignity. Debase himself—never!

From a distance Chaim could already see Leibe-Beres' house. He coughed and cleared his throat, smoothed his beard, and glanced hastily at his coat to see how it looked.

"It's still a fine coat," he reassured himself in order to give himself courage and to add to his self-respect. But, when he stood before Leibe-Beres' large house and saw the brilliant illumination which poured into the street through the eight big windows, his heart jumped a beat.

"*Oy,* Lord of the Universe, help me!" he uttered a stifled cry, but immediately after he felt ashamed and he tried to take it all back.

"*Et,* foolishness!"

He turned the doorknob, and his involuntary prayer came rolling even more vehemently off his tongue.

"Help me, Almighty God!"

Leibe-Beres was sitting at a large table that was covered with a white cloth. He was drinking tea and chatting amiably with his children.

"Some Jew has come, *tatte,*" a little boy of twelve called out loudly when he caught sight of Chaim at the door.

"*Takkeh* a Jew!" another little boy echoed gaily, turning on Chaim his mischievous black eyes.

They all turned to stare at Chaim, who soon began to feel that in another moment he'd fall down in a faint. "It won't look very nice if I faint," he admonished himself. Without even a good evening he advanced and stammered:

"I'll tell you, I happened to be passing by and I saw you sitting at the table. . . . That meant, of course, that you were at home. . . . Nu, so I figured, 'I ought to go in . . . after all . . . we're neighbors!' "

"Why not?" Leibe-Beres replied, smiling amiably. "You're always a welcome guest here. . . . Sit down!"

The rich man's answer greatly reassured Chaim, and, without taking his eyes off the two little boys, he sat down in silence.

"Leah! Hand Reb Chaim a glass of tea!" Leibe-Beres called out to the servant girl.

"Quite a kindhearted man!" thought Chaim, "May the Almighty help him!"

He looked gratefully at the rich man. He felt like falling on his thick neck and showering kisses on him.

"Nu, what are you doing?" Leibe-Beres asked.

"God be praised, one lives!"

The servant girl placed a glass of tea before Chaim. He said to her, "Thank you," and immediately regretted it. He had heard that it wasn't proper to thank a servant. He flushed and bit his lips.

"Put some preserves into your tea!" Leibe-Beres urged him.

"A fine person—really a fine person!" thought Chaim quite surprised. "Now I know he'll surely lend!"

"Are you doing any business?" asked Leibe-Beres.

"Why sure!" replied Chaim airily. "I've business. . . . Thank God no worse than other merchants!"

"How are oats on the market?" the rich man asked him suddenly.

Of late the price of oats had declined, but Chaim heard himself say instead, with the tone of voice of a man of affairs, "Quite high!"

"I suppose you stocked up on oats in advance?" further inquired the rich man.

"I have a nice pile of oats . . . didn't cost me dear . . . in fact, quite cheap!" answered Chaim vaingloriously. But he forgot while saying this that for several weeks not a grain of anything was to be found in his granary.

"Are you planning to speculate?" asked Leibe-Beres. "Do you have enough money?"

"Thank God!" Chaim answered with pride. "I've never yet suffered from a lack of money."

"Woe is me! What am I saying?" thought Chaim getting frightened at his own words. "How can I ask him now for a loan?" He was about to take back what he had said when Leibe-Beres interrupted him:

"So it means that you're doing good business, that you're a bit of a *nogid!*"

Chaim wanted to say: "May my enemies have such riches as I!" But looking at the rich man's beaming face and at the blue jug of preserves standing on the table he answered proudly, "God be praised, I've nothing to complain about!"

"There goes your loan!" jeered a voice inside of him, just as if someone had crashed a stone against the back of his head. Idiot! Imbecile! Why are you bragging? Why don't you tell him instead that you badly need a twenty-fiver for Ulas? Beg him he should save you! Tell him that you're falling by the wayside, that . . . !"

But Chaim fell into a more cheerful and happy tone as he continued speaking, boasted more and more about his big deals and chatted with the rich man as one does with an equal.

But suddenly he began to feel uneasy. He shouldn't have conducted himself the way he did, he shouldn't have talked the way he did! How much better he'd have done had he talked about the fair, and then about the loan! Now it was too late!

"I've never yet suffered from a lack of money."

Ach! Chaim threw a despairing look at Leibe-Beres' merry face. He looked at the two little boys who were sitting opposite him and with laughing mischievous eyes were staring at him and kept on whispering to each other in an odd way and were smiling in an even odder way.

A cold sweat covered him. He got up to go.

"What, you're already leaving?" asked Leibe-Beres politely.

"Now! I still have a chance to ask him for the loan!" the idea to save himself seethed within Chaim. But, looking at the boys with the mischievous eyes that regarded him with such cunning, he replied grandly:

"I'm sorry, but I've got to go! You know how it is—business affairs. I'm pressed for time!"

As he walked to the door, Chaim experienced the most curious sensation: that the two little boys with the mischievous eyes were sticking their tongues out at him behind his back and that Leibe-Beres himself was highly amused and kept on urging them by means of signs: "Show more of your tongues! More!"

And Chaim felt a sharp burning in his back. He walked out hastily.

It's not that it is so good with money,
but that it's so bad without it.

A fool goes to the steam-bath
and forgets to wash his face.

A fool grows without the help of rain.

THE GIFT

Once, in an obscure little Polish town, there was a wheat merchant whose name was Shmul. His one great dream in life was for once to be able to attend the great fair at Danzig. He had heard how overnight one could become a *nogid* there with some lucky deal.

At last his great chance came and he was able to go to the annual fair in Danzig. The Lord was with him and he did good business, may it happen thus to all Jews! Elated by his success, he decided he'd bring home a gift for his wife Surele. But it was to be no ordinary gift—it had to be something *very* special. So he looked about, went from shop to shop and from stall to stall, yet he could find nothing one could consider very unusual.

But one day, as he was passing one of the city squares, he suddenly noticed a fortune-telling gypsy and on his shoulder was perched a strange green bird that had a long beak. Shmul had never seen the likes of it before. So he stopped to gape at it. He wondered what on earth that bird was. But suddenly—good God! was he hearing right or was he imagining it all?—the bird began to talk, and in good German too!

A fever gripped Shmul. He had to have that bird, come what may! And it suddenly occurred to him that there could be no more unusual gift for his Surele than that wonderful bird. So he bought it, and paid good money for it too.

But since the fair wasn't over yet and he had some business to settle, Shmul decided to send the bird on ahead of him by post. With it he sent a letter to Surele telling her he was sending it as his gift to her and giving her instructions what to feed the creature and how often. But did he tell her the bird could speak and in German too? Certainly not! Let her find out for herself and get the surprise of her life the way he did!

When Surele received the gift she was struck dumb with amazement. What on earth was this green creature with the awful-looking beak? It was neither *kotchkeh* nor chicken nor *schmaltz-herring!* "Nu, what do you say to that *schlimazl* of mine—to send that horrible thing to me, and for a gift too! Why, it's enough to throw up!"

All in a dither she grabbed up the cage with the bird and ran off with it to the rabbi: maybe he could tell her what the creature was?

When the rabbi looked at the bird he was taken aback.

"Nu, Rabbi, what do you think it is?"

The rabbi put on his silver-rimmed spectacles, stroked his long beard thoughtfully, and began to examine the creature carefully from every side. And when he was through he furrowed his brow in perplexity.

"To tell you the truth, Surele, I really can't tell you what this beast is. Never in my life have I seen anything like it. But I'll tell you what. Maybe I'll find something about it in my books."

So the rabbi consulted his books and after careful meditation he said to Surele:

"My daughter, I think I know what the creature is! It's a rare fowl—a green goose! That happens one in a million. Since tomorrow is a feast day you might as well have the *shochet* kill it for you. Eat it in good health!"

And Surele went home and did as the rabbi told her. She had the green goose killed, and she and her children ate it in good health.

The day came at last when Shmul came home. The first question he asked was about the bird.

"Oh, you mean the green goose? Don't send me such gifts again, *schlemihl!* Why it was as tough as leather, and it tasted—may my worst enemy not taste such a thing!"

When Shmul found out what had happened to his wonderful bird he began to tremble with rage. Quickly he ran to the rabbi.

"Rabbi!" he cried indignantly. "I ask you, how could you tell Surele that the bird I sent her was a green goose? Why, that was a parrot, a wonderful bird! I paid good money for it!"

"A parrot!" marveled the rabbi. "Oh, then I made a mistake! I was sure it was a green goose. But what I'd like to know is: what's so wonderful about a parrot?"

"But Rabbi, you don't understand," Shmul almost wept. "Why that bird was highly educated and he could talk!"

"Talk, did you say?" gasped the rabbi incredulously.

"Yes, talk, and in German too!" added Shmul.

For a moment the rabbi remained silent. Then reflectively stroking his beard he said apologetically, "Nu, if the bird was really so educated and could talk, and in German too, as you say, why the devil didn't it speak up and tell us what it was?"

IT WORKED LIKE A CHARM

A Jewish innkeeper on the estate of a Polish lord came to his wonder-working rabbi.

"Rebbe, I'm in great trouble!" he complained. "I've come to you with two requests. One is that you should make my landowner learn to appreciate me and to be good to me, for he treats me miserably. My other request is that you should make my wife, who is barren, bear children."

The rabbi nodded and said, "Here, my son, are two amulets. This one you wear to help you with the landowner; the other is for your childless wife."

The innkeeper thanked the rabbi, put the amulets into his pocket, and rode home.

Unfortunately, he got the amulets mixed up, so he put around his wife's neck the amulet intended to make the landowner appreciate and be good to him. The amulet to be blessed with children he put around his own neck.

So what happened? When the Polish lord looked upon his Jewish tenant's wife he began to appreciate her and was good to her. Naturally, he softened in his attitude toward the husband, too.

Children soon followed. And the innkeeper cried out, "Truly, my rebbe is a wonder-working rebbe! Both of his amulets worked perfectly!"

One fool can ask more questions than ten wise men can answer.

A TALE WITHOUT AN END

BY ELIEZER STEINBERG
TRANSLATED FROM THE YIDDISH BY JOSEPH LEFTWICH

I have a tale to tell
Of a donkey that under its burden fell.
The owner belabored it with a stick.
"Get up, you brute," he said, "up you get, quick."
But the donkey lay there submissively.
All donkeys submissive beasts must be.
"Now that's enough," the neighbours cried,
"You'll kill the poor donkey, with your stick on its hide."
"It isn't your donkey," the owner said,
"I must get my load delivered, will you carry it instead?
Perhaps you will carry the donkey as well?
With such kind-hearted people one never can tell."
"You'll break your stick on the donkey," the neighbours cried.
"I've got plenty more sticks," the owner replied,
"Did you think I keep the beast because of its beauty?
I house it and feed it and it must do its duty."
Then all the neighbours beg the donkey to rise.
"Not till he stops hitting me," the donkey replies.
So the donkey gets thrashed because he won't rise.
And he won't rise because he gets thrashed, so on
*   the ground he stubbornly lies,*
And from stick after stick the blows descend.
I told you this is a tale without an end.

Better the company of a wise man in Gihenom
than a fool in Gan-Eden.

The wish to be wiser than everybody else
is the biggest foolishness.—Sholom Aleichem

GEVALT!
IT'S NOT SO GOOD!

Schlimazls · THE LUCKLESS

When a schlimazl *kills a chicken—it walks.*
When he winds a clock—it stops.

"Jewish luck!" That's an exclamation one often hears on the lips of Jews. It is usually accompanied by a sigh and an ironic shrug of the shoulder.

Mazl, *is the Yiddish word for good luck, and* schlimazl *is the one for bad luck, as well as for the person who has it. The philosophy of mazl is neatly expressed by a nameless folk sage: "From mazl to schlimazl is just one little step, but from schlimazl to mazl—oy, is it far!"*

Naturally, the people most preoccupied with the question of luck are those who don't have it—the poor. Those who prosper ascribe it to their own superior gifts. Since, as a people, Jews haven't prospered overly much, the matter of mazl has always absorbed them, probably because there were always so many schlimazls among Jews. Like daydreaming children, they were constantly talking about mazl.

These schlimazls and their almost as numerous cousins, the schlemihls, *swarmed in the ghetto anthills. The schlemihls were those bungling, butterfingered incompetents endowed with a Charlie Chaplin genius for getting into deep waters. Like lightning rods, the schlimazls and schlemihls seemed to attract to themselves every bolt of misfortune. A lack of productive skills deprived them of the necessary worldliness and common sense required for practical living, and so we find these grownup misfits aptly described in that folklore nursery rhyme:*

"Schlimazl,[1] where are you going?"
"To the poor man, of course!"

Did you think perhaps that you can find schlemihls and schlimazls only among human beings? Well, you're wrong! You can find these misfits among Jewish animals too.

"What! Are there Jewish animals?"

Of course not! There's no such thing as a Jewish zoology, although there's a Jewish zoo in Jerusalem and the animals there bear sonorous Hebrew names. What made "Jewish" the few domestic animals ghetto Jews adopted into their close-knit family life was their owners' highly

[1]*Here it means "bad luck."*

subjective feeling about them. They imaginatively endowed them with some of their own Jewish characteristics and problems. Jewish humorists were quick to recognize the satirical possibilities in this folk attitude. Because the fable and the parable have been part of the Jewish literary pattern since the Talmudic Age, these writers turned their stories of "Jewish" animals into thinly disguised allegories about life and character in the ghetto.

In this section about animals, you will find stories about a Jewish cat, a Jewish dog, and a Jewish calf. Each of these creatures shares the misfortunes of the Jewish people: being either a schlimazl, a schlemihl, or nebbech all at the same time. The Jewish cat is made to meow in a minor oy-oy-oy! The Jewish dog Rabchik, barks at fate in a doleful Book of Lamentations ai-ai-ai! And the gentle non-resistance-to-evil calf, a purebred Tolstoyan, meh-mehs a resigned Jewish ach! which is two thousand years old.

N.A.

AVROM THE COBBLER

BY ABRAHAM REISEN
TRANSLATED FROM THE YIDDISH BY NATHAN AUSUBEL

Avrom the cobbler was a lanky old man with a long beard and still longer *payyes*. He also had a high forehead. Were a stranger to meet him some morning while he was on his way from the synagogue with his large *tallis* sack tucked under his arm, he'd surely think that this was the rabbi of the town, or, at very least, a prominent member of the community. True, Avrom had no mean opinion of himself and didn't at all feel that his dignity was being lessened by his humble trade. Ever since he had heard a *maggid* say that Rabbi Yochanan ha-Sandler, the great sage of the Talmud, had also been a shoemaker, he was mighty proud of his trade. Whenever the subject of shoemaking was discussed he'd always step forward as champion to refute all its detractors. And his defense he'd always wind up with the following persuasive words:

"What more do you need? Do you happen to know that Rabbi Yochanan, the great sage of the Talmud, was also a shoemaker? He, too, sewed with shoemaker's thread. . . ."

He'd say this with a laugh, but he'd soon regret his levity. Good Heavens! How dared he belittle a sage of the Talmud! And so that Rabbi Yochanan shouldn't feel offended by what he'd said, over there

in the World-to-Come, he'd hastily add, "Of course, he himself didn't
do any sewing but he surely must have employed workmen who did!"

Nevertheless, it helped Avrom but little, his defense of cobbling
and his boasting about his illustrious colleague, Rabbi Yochanan. He
was not even esteemed by other workers, not because he was a shoemaker but because he was only half a shoemaker. In town they called
him a *"latutnik,"* a man who lays *lattes,* or patches. He never made
whole shoes or boots, only laid patches. To be sure, he even boasted
that long, long ago he used to make whole shoes, but ever since the
wretched newfangled fashion of making shoes with "narrow noses" was
introduced he had given up making shoes. What, was he going to make
a fool of himself? Just the same, he made up for that by laying a patch
that was "one in the world." Why, even the town's shoemakers, who
always used to tear down one another, never had the nerve to pick
flaws in one of Avrom's patches. Still in all, no one in town ever
made a fuss over him. On the contrary, at every opportunity they'd
joke about him. His pride suffered from this and he'd find the chance,
sooner or later, to avenge himself on all of them.

The coming of this chance he awaited every year with great
impatience. He was sure it would come. It had to come! Almighty
God was not going to change the order of Creation. Autumn had to
come every year and it always would bring rain. In autumn, Avrom
knew, it had to rain. He had already lived so many years and it had
never happened yet that it shouldn't rain in autumn. Avrom also
knew that the rain made a great deal of mud in town. Such a mud he
had to have for his livelihood and which he prayed that God would
send. Just as the peasant prays to God to send him rain so that he
might have bread, so also did Avrom pray to God, but not for bread
alone. He prayed for mud so that he'd be able to square accounts with
those fellow townsmen who made sport of him.

During the Sukkos Festival, while Avrom sat in the foliage be-
decked *sukka,* a cold autumnal rain began to fall. But Avrom was
in no hurry to come into the house. Old Pesheh began calling him
in a loud voice.

"*Meshuggener* you! In such a downpour who in his right mind
sits in a sukka? Do you want to be more pious than the rabbi?"

"Don't you worry, don't you worry," he'd say to her comfortingly,
and with a satisfied expression he'd come into the house. "I'm not
afraid of today's rain. From such a rain as this the mud will form.
Narrelleh, do you hear—mud!"

"*Nu,* thank God *takkeh* for the mud!" answered Pesheh with a pious expression. She reminded herself that their entire livelihood came from the autumnal mud.

And so Avrom finished the feast indoors, but his eyes were glued to the window and kept on roving along the street. His heart grew big for joy, seeing how the earth was softening up like mush under the rain.

Whenever the sun peeped out from behind the rain clouds for a fleeting moment Avrom became frightened. It looked to him as if it were trying to snatch the bread from his mouth. Luckily, the autumnal sun didn't shine for long; the clouds soon concealed it, and once more Avrom became lighthearted.

And God heard Avrom's prayers. All Sukkos it rained and rained. Jewish children were grieving because the Holy Day was ruined for them; they could not play outside even for a little while, but Avrom was powerfully glad with it. Under his eyes the sticky autumnal mud was already shaping up. Stranded in the middle of the street, women would stand bewildered, not knowing what to do. Some even left their shoes behind. Small children were carried across and the menfolk tried to show off with their skill as they navigated through the street.

"Ha, ha, ha!" Avrom laughed at the sun. Such a little disk of fire won't have the strength to dry up such an ocean of mud! Even if it shouldn't rain any more, it still would take several months before it would dry up. Avrom found additional comfort in the thought that there would be plenty of rain yet. This he based on the unchanging rule: in the fall it's got to rain!

Avrom rested up during the holidays, stored up strength for the days ahead. He knew that right after Sukkos he'd have to work hard every day until late in the night. They would simply swamp him with work.

Sure enough, the morning after Sukkos a regular country fair started in his hut and it lasted for three whole months. They brought him shoes from all sides. The mud was deep and everyone wanted to have whole shoes. Besides, when the mud lies on the ground, shoes tear quicker.

Avrom kept well in mind that during this "country fair" he had to make enough to live on for the rest of the year. Of course, he had shoes to patch even in the dry season. But at such times he was no great shakes to anyone. At such times the high and mighty shoemakers who made boots with the "narrow noses" found themselves without work. And they felt no shame at all in drawing away part of his livelihood. And that's why in the muddy season he felt as if he were sitting on top of the world, and he tore the hide off his customers. He overcharged without feeling a single twinge of conscience. For a pair of new soles you couldn't bargain down a broken groschen, regardless of who you were, whether a relation or a poor neighbor. And should someone have the temerity to argue with him and say, "See here, Reb Avrom, what's the idea of charging so much?" Avrom would answer coldly, "Who's forcing you? If it's too dear, why don't you bring your shoes to Beril the Shoemaker. He's also a pretty good shoemaker you know. After all, it's he who makes shoes with the 'narrow noses'!"

These last words Avrom would utter in an ironic tone, just as if he were saying, "Not all the time do you need Beril the shoemaker, as you see—you've got to have me too, sometimes!" He wanted to be sure whether they takkeh really needed him. And casting a hasty glance through the window, he was filled with even greater self-esteem. He said to himself, "My, my, just see how the street is flooded with soupy mud—almost good enough to jump in and drown yourself! Oy, do you need me!" And he smiled into his beard and didn't even cast a look at the customer standing at his side with a pair of shoes and trying to bargain down ten kopecks from the price. Avrom gloated: now was the time to settle accounts with his enemies! And he took his revenge by striking hard bargains with them.

It was in this manner that Avrom the cobbler lived to a ripe old age. He steadily continued to draw his sustenance from the town mud, and he thanked God who had created the world with such wisdom that he had appointed a time every year for mud to flood the town and to rot away shoe leather. In his eyes, mud had the most wonderful charm, perhaps even more than the azure sky had for a poet. Whenever he'd pass through the market place on his way to buy pieces of leather in the tanner's shop, he'd look with deep pride on the mud-covered streets through which even the most eminent residents were walking gingerly, holding up the hems of their long kapotes and cursing under their breaths, "N-n-nu! some mud! May God protect us from it!"

Of course they didn't like *it* a bit, thought Avrom with sarcasm. They could get along without *it*. But as for him was *it* his worry?

Whenever one of his customers would come to him and complain that he could no longer endure the mud and express the hope that it was high time that God should show some pity and dry it up, Avrom would get very angry. That is, he'd feel angry but wouldn't show it. For daring to complain about the mud he'd "punish" the customer by charging him two kopecks more for each patch. He'd think to himself vengefully: "That's what you get for talking foolishness!"

Once, in the middle of the summer—it was still a long way off to Avrom's patch season—as he was walking across the market place, he saw a big heap of stones lying smack in the middle of the square. The thing seemed odd to him. What could it mean? He went over to a shopkeeper.

"Why do they need so many stones?" he asked him.

"So many stones!" the shopkeeper mimicked him. "Do you call that many? You just wait and you'll see ten times as many, a hundred times as many."

"But what will so many stones be used for?"

"Do you live in this town or don't you?" replied the shopkeeper with some irritation. "You know as well as I that they'll soon pave our streets, first of all the market place, then the rest of the town."

"Pave? Did you say pave? What do you mean, pave?" asked Avrom scratching the back of his head as if he had just recalled a frightful thing.

"Do you know what they say in Russian: *'starai yak malai!'* " (an old man is like a child) muttered the shopkeeper with a smile. "You don't understand, what? With these stones that you see here they're going to pave the streets of the whole town so that there'll no longer be any mud."

Avrom didn't need any further explanations. The shopkeeper's last words, "so that there'll no longer be any mud," struck him like a thunderbolt. Nevertheless, he didn't quite grasp the whole thing. Like a crushed man he turned to go home. On the way he kept on talking to himself and gesticulating with his hands, "What do they mean: 'so that there'll no longer be any more mud'? How could it be that all the mud in town should suddenly dry up?"

He now recalled what one of his customers had once told him, "There are in the world big cities where all the streets are paved, and it's always dry there."

He entered his house with a dazed look on his face.

"No more mud!" he mumbled. "They no longer need me!"

His wife Pesheh didn't understand what he was talking about. She thought he had suddenly gone out of his mind.

"What are you saying?" she scolded him. "What mud are you talking about? Do you expect mud in the middle of summer? Don't you have enough mud in autumn?"

"Listen, Pesheh, those bandits want that there should be no mud in autumn, do you understand? They want to leave us without bread in our old age!"

"What bandits are you babbling about?" cried Pesheh, now really frightened.

Avrom himself didn't know who the bandits were, but his anger seethed within him and he blurted out:

" 'They' don't like mud! Do you understand? 'They' are big aristocrats. 'They' think 'they' are on the same level with the big cities and so 'they' have decided to pave the streets of the town. Now what do you say to that?"

"*Oy vay!* A cannon ball has struck me!" wailed Pesheh wringing her hands. "Now we're done for! How are we going to live now?"

"Why don't you go and ask 'them'?" snapped Avrom with bitterness. "Do you think they're worried about us? Do you imagine that after Sukkos everybody in town brings me shoes to mend out of pity? If they can get along without me you can be sure they'll gladly do so, the bandits!"

"The way you talk, one would think that people will stop tearing shoes," argued Pesheh in a tone of voice in which there still lingered a ray of hope.

"You talk like a fool! Tear shoes they will. Shoes tear even on pavements, but it won't be the same as before. On stone only the soles and heels get rubbed off, but in mud the whole shoe rots. And that's what counts mostly."

Every single day Avrom would walk to the market place to find out how things were getting on with regard to paving, and, as the heap of stones grew, so grew the wound in his heart, and he began to shuffle about like a sick man.

Just the same, he didn't abandon hope; they were not going to pave the streets so fast! He found a precedent for that: he remembered that when they were going to build the bathhouse they also piled up stones and bricks. Any day, they said, they were going to start building. Nonetheless, the matter dragged on for a nice number of years without anything happening. And Avrom would console himself with the thought that they were not going to start paving during his lifetime.

But that proved to be cold comfort. One beautiful morning that very same summer, as he was walking through the market place he suddenly noticed that a crowd had gathered. He had a foreboding that it meant nothing good for him. He elbowed his way through the crowd and what he saw made him tremble in every limb. Laborers with sledge hammers were pounding on the stones, filling the air with a thundering noise. The crowd of bystanders looked on and rejoiced.

"Now it will be a real pleasure," said one.

"And what a pleasure!" echoed another. "It's no small matter; we'll be rid of the mud!"

The town wag noticed Avrom in the crowd and he started to tease him:

"Do you see what they're doing, Reb Avrom? You know, that's going to cost you a pretty kopeck."

"What's one thing got to do with the other?" asked Avrom lamely, pretending not to see the connection. "What has paving streets got to do with my work?"

"It's got to do plenty!" relentlessly went on the wag. "On nice dry pavements our boots won't tear so and you'll have fewer patches to lay on."

"Nu, so he'll sew new boots!" another wag continued the drollery.

"New boots he *nebbech* can't make. How does he come to that? He's a born latutnik!"

"Don't worry, he'll learn how! Take a look at his high forehead!"

Everybody laughed.

At this point Avrom could no longer restrain his anger. The rascals had at last gotten under his skin and so he exploded:

"Good-for-nothings!" he roared. "What do you think, you're going to make over the world? You should be sick so long as there'll still be mud! You wait and see—you'll come yet with your rotten boots for me to fix! I'll rip the hide off you then, the hide!"

"Hurrah!" yelled some scalawag.

The merriment swept through the crowd and they lustily took up the cry:

"Hurrah! . . . . No more mud! . . . . There'll be no more mud! . . . . No mud! . . . . Hurrah!"

When autumn came around again, the paving of the streets was still unfinished. The mud lay as deep as before, but Avrom could no longer take the same pleasure in it and in earning a heap of ten-kopeck pieces. The last incident in the market place had had a shattering impact on him. After that he went about for several weeks looking haggard and ill. Then he was put to bed and died.

Those who were present at his death later told with a laugh that his last words were:

"Bandits! No more mud!"

A year later the paving of the streets was finished. When Pesheh saw this she sighed and murmured:

"Oy, Avrom, Avrom! If you were to rise from your grave now and take a look at what has become of the mud you'd positively lie down and die a second time! . . . ."

> *"A poor man has no mazl," says the world.*
> *If he had mazl would he be a poor man?*

THE HERRING MARTYR

A small Jewish trader lost his shirt in the herring market. So he gathered up his four barrels of herring and carted them home.

All along the way he sat hunched up in his driver's seat, his head sunk gloomily on his breast. Suddenly he lifted his eyes and saw a wayside shrine. It held a statue of St. Sebastian with woebegone look and downcast head.

The herring-dealer drew up his cart and sat regarding the holy image for a moment. Then, heaving a deep sigh, he muttered commiseratingly:

"Poor man! So you too were in the herring business!"

THE ESSRIG

BY AARON D. OGUS
TRANSLATED FROM THE YIDDISH BY NATHAN AUSUBEL

That year the price of an *essrig*[1] was very high. Not only was it dear but *takkeh* scarce; you coudn't get one for love or money! That year the essrig crop in Eretz Yisroel, and in other countries where it is raised, was a very poor one. In fact, that holy fruit which was obtainable was withered, spotted, and wormy. An extra fine specimen was out of the question. It was as if Satan (may his name be blotted out!) had purposely put his foot out to trip up Jews so that they wouldn't be able to fulfill the great *mitzvah* of reciting the blessing over the essrig.

[1]*The* essrig *or* ethrog, *a fragrant, sweetish thick-skinned fruit of the orange and lemon family, is sometimes as much as six inches long. It is used with the* lulav *(palm branch) in religious ceremony during* Sukkos.

And so it happened that in Lapinishok, a small town in Lithuania, the scarcity of the blessed fruit created a terrible sensation, a sensation which they haven't gotten over to this very day.

As small and poverty-stricken as was the Jewish community of Lapinishok, nonetheless, every year when Sukkos time came around there was more than one essrig to be found in town. Now take the rabbi. Everybody knew what a great pauper he was. Just the same, he always bought an essrig for his own use. Reb Yose, the tavern keeper, one of the most prosperous men in town and a pillar of the community, also was in the habit of buying an essrig. Or even take Simcha Pipatch, the *nogid* who had started out as a wagoner, he didn't hesitate to spend a ruble or two on an essrig every year. Perhaps he bought the essrig not so much because it was a mitzvah but to show off his silver essrig box at the synagogue and to tell everybody that he bought it way off in Warsaw, and what he paid for it—don't ask! Poorer householders would buy an essrig in partnership. And, of course, it goes without saying that the synagogue also purchased an essrig for general community use.

But that essrig-lean year was very disastrous for Lapinishok. Where, how, and with what were they to get an essrig?

Borech the *Soifer,* who always supplied the fragrant fruit to the community and to the Jewish farmers in the neighboring villages, had already smelled the oncoming crisis before Rosh Hashanah yet. So he wrote to his essrig dealer in Vilna that he should put aside for him a few perfect specimens. He got a reply informing him that if he wanted first-grade merchandise it would cost him not less than fifteen rubles apiece, and money in advance, right away too! If not, he wouldn't be able to get even a smell of one later.

Fifteen rubles an essrig! May he, Borech the Soifer, and all Lapinishok be spared such a pleasure!

Borech the Soifer was a man with many trades and few blessings. He was not only a soifer, but a *shadchan,* and a piece of *maggid.* He sold tallis fringes, prayer books, Hanukkah candles, and, in addition, lottery tickets. But from all these sources of livelihood he remained a first-class pauper, and as many trades as he had so many times a day "he died of hunger." The best time in the year for him was the Sukkos Festival. From the sale of *essrogim* he'd make enough for holiday expenses, buy himself or his wife or a child a winter coat, and even have enough money left to buy half a cord of wood. When, therefore, he read the answer of the essrig dealer from Vilna he was dumfounded.

Reb Borech brought the letter to the synagogue and showed it to the rabbi and all the officials of the congregation. Naturally, some gave the traditional advice: "If you have no essrig, you make no blessing!" Others merely shrugged their shoulders, repeating the old pun: "What'll happen to all Israel will also happen to Reb Israel."

However, there were a number of skeptics, merchants by calling, who cynically stated that the whole story about the scarcity on the essrig market was a transparent lie. It all added up to, they said, that the big essrig merchants created a false scarcity in order to boost their prices, but later on it would only slam back into their own faces and they'd go begging for customers.

The danger that threatened the community didn't seem to disturb anybody. Only Borech the Soifer kept it well in mind. How could he forget when such an important part of his livelihood depended on the sale of essrogim? Therefore, he could not rest. He wrote to another essrig dealer and that one answered him that he couldn't supply him with any perfect specimens, even if he were to pay a hundred rubles apiece. However, if he was willing to take an inferior grade of essrig he could supply him with a small number, provided he'd pay twelve rubles a piece, but for selling them to him so cheap Reb Borech would have to pay cash.

In the meantime, the day before *Yom Kippur* edged up and still not a sight or smell of an essrig. Reb Borech then ran in panic to the rabbi and told him how critically the matter stood.

The rabbi then called a meeting and explained to everybody that they must no longer sleep on the matter. He reproached them for taking things too lightly. After all, they had to consider that the mitzvah of performing the essrig ceremony was intimately tied up with all the other six hundred and thirteen mitzvahs. Accordingly, the community should see to it that it shouldn't remain, God forbid, without an essrig!

Several of the richest men in town then and there formed a partnership to buy one essrig. It was also decided that the community as a whole put up the money for another essrig. Right after Yom Kippur, Reb Borech the Soifer, was to make a special trip to the city to purchase the two essrogim. They didn't have to be perfect specimens, as long as they were kosher.

The day after Yom Kippur, Reb Borech made his journey to the city, but when he got there there wasn't a blessed essrig to be gotten anywhere, not even if it were to serve as a cure for a dying man. He returned downcast and with empty hands.

In the meantime, it was already a day before Sukkos Eve and

the slaughterer's knife, so to speak, was already at the throat. But no essrig! Suddenly, the wild rumor spread in Lapinishok that in Turbanovke, a tiny hamlet not far from Lapinishok, two essrogim were to be found. One essrig the Turbanovke community itself had bought; the other, one of the householders had received from "the real place"—from Eretz Yisroel itself, where the most perfect essrogim grow. When the rabbi and the elders heard of this they hurriedly sent a special messenger to Turbanovke to plead with the rabbi there that he should use his influence with the householder having the Eretz Yisroel essrig to surrender it to the Lapinishoker community. This way each town would be able to fulfill the mitzvah with one essrig each. Would it be right for Jews to abandon each other in time of need?

It so happened that the Turbanovker with the Eretz Yisroel essrig was a moneylender and loved his money more than life itself. So he wasn't at all lazy and sang out for his essrig all of fifty rubles. He knew very well that he had the Lapinishokers in his power because they had no other alternative. So why not take the hide off them? He argued that the pleasure he'd get from reciting the first blessing over the essrig was well worth to him hundreds of rubles; but seeing how an entire community of Jews would, God forbid, remain without an essrig, he would renounce all thought of material profit and sell his essrig for a mere fifty rubles.

When the messenger returned with the answer the whole town was flung into dismay. Fifty rubles to the Jews of Lapinishok looked twice as big as Rothschild's fortune! How in the world would they be able to raise such a sum?

It was already the Eve of Sukkos and the matter could no longer be delayed. The rabbi again called a meeting and took counsel with the others about how to raise the money for the essrig. It was decided that they should raise it with the sale of "honors." Thus the rabbi himself agreed to give three rubles for the honor of reciting the first blessing over the essrig. And other honors were bought up for smaller sums, one even paying ten kopecks for getting the stem of the essrig when the festival was over. The purchaser of the stem was Channa-Dvoireh who kept a dry-goods shop. She got it for her only daughter, Tzirele, who was about to give birth. Two of Channa-Dvoireh's daughters (may it not happen to any human being!) had already died from difficult deliveries, and so Tzirele remained like a single eye in her head. It was Tzirele's first pregnancy and her mother had forebodings that the same disaster would occur. So she put a protective wall of amulets and incantations around Tzirele. And who in Lapinishok didn't know that when a pregnant woman bites off the stem of an ess-rig she is certain to have an easy delivery? Channa-Dvoireh, therefore, lost no time in buying a lien on the stem ahead of time because it would be the only one in town and she was greatly afraid that someone else would snatch it right from under her nose.

By the time the last "honor" was sold it was already midafter-noon. Quickly they collected all the money and sent it with a covering note to the Turbanovke moneylender asking him to give the essrig to the messenger. Now this messenger was a *goy,* for they could send no Jew, the hour being so late that he might, God forbid, yet desecrate the Holy Day by traveling back to Lapinishok after sundown.

The *Ma'ariv* service being completed, the congregation gathered at the rabbi's house and waited for the goy to return with the essrig. The messenger, however, was late in coming and the crowd grew very uneasy. Goodness knows what he did on the way! He might even have gone into a tavern and guzzled up the money! Who knows, he might even have lost the essrig! It could even be that someone stole it from him. Ai, the things that go on in this world!

Hosannah and halleluja! The messenger arrived at last! With trembling hands the rabbi began to untie the package the messenger had brought. Impatiently all craned their necks to see what sort of beauty their fifty rubles had bought. But a wail and a yammer! When the rabbi took the essrig from the box, he found it crushed, practically split in two halves and the juice running out of it.

"Mikhail! What's that you've brought us?" was the outcry.

And Mikhail answered that he was curious to know what the Jew of Turbanovke had sent with him. They should believe him, all he did was to untie the package and to give the "lemon" a squeeze.

"Some *squeeze* that was!" yelled the congregation.

They argued with him: "Listen here, you bandit, you murderer, you have slaughtered a whole town of people!" So all the goy does is to cross himself and swear that he hadn't tasted the thing, not even a lick! Furthermore, he hadn't handled any pork that day, and so help him God, it was kosher!

Nu, go and argue with him! Try and teach him Judaism! You can yell today and you can yell tomorrow, it can't be helped now!

So what do you think happened? Lapinishok remained without an essrig, Borech the Soifer without his livelihood, the rabbi without the mitzvah of reciting the first blessing, and Tzirele, Channa-Dvoireh's daughter, without her stem. *Oy vay!*

PACKAGE TZORESS

BY M. VULFARTS

TRANSLATED FROM THE YIDDISH BY NATHAN AUSUBEL

You're looking at me, ha? You think I'm happy, eh? No one can compare with me, what?

True, blessed be His Name, I've *takkeh* lived to see the happy day when I'm about to go to Eretz Yisroel! I've even obtained "the wishing ring," meaning of course the entry certificate, the train ticket, and the steamship ticket. But what's the good of them all if I've got to go through yet all the trials of the Messiah—the *tzoress* of Jewish packages?

When a Jew travels to Eretz Yisroel he stops belonging to himself, he must take on the job of "Jewish mail carrier," he's got to carry with him all kinds of packages from relatives living in the lands of the Dispersion to their kin in the Holy Land.

As soon as they got a whiff of the rumor that I was getting ready to leave for Eretz Yisroel, the entire Jewish population of my town descended on me to bid me bon voyage, but they made sure to bring with them gifts of "good things" intended for their relatives.

For instance, a woman came to see me lugging with her a heavy package. I had never seen her before in my life. Her face was full of smiles. She started out by discussing politics, Eretz Yisroel, certificates, orange groves, Englishmen, and tzoress from children. Eventually she led me on "to the Path of the Just," revealed to me that she had a son in Eretz Yisroel and that she wanted me to bring him her heartfelt regards and to hand him "this little *pekeleh*."

What did "this little pekeleh" consist of?

Some homemade cakes baked out of dough that had twenty eggs in it, a pot of goose *schmaltz,* several lengths of wurst, two jars of preserves (one with cherry juice and the other with raspberry), a few *tayglach* (moist and dry), several kilos of hard candy, six pairs of socks, bars of chocolate, conserves, and finally, a bottle of homemade wine. That's all!

In passing, she begged me that in getting off the train to go on board the ship I should be most careful with "the little pekeleh" so that nothing should break.

Fool that I am, I was weak and let her talk me into it! I took the pekeleh from her and was certain that this would be my first as well as last pekeleh I'd ever have to take with me to the Holy Land. But barely had she finished giving me her instructions when a father aided by his son staggered in, dragging between them a basket that I judged to weigh at least one hundred kilos.

"A handsome good evening to you!" the old man greeted me effusively, wiping the perspiration off his face; he was thoroughly winded, I could see. "I've heard," said he, "that you're going to Eretz Yisroel tomorrow morning. Well, I've *takkeh* a daughter there. She lives in Kfar Saba and with mazl she's at last become a bride."

"*Mazl tov!*" said I.

"Thank you!" he replied. "You see, she's getting married in two weeks. Of course, we don't want to give you too much trouble but we'll be grateful to you if you'll be good enough to take to her this 'bit of trousseau.' "

Right after, an elderly pair dropped in. They declared themselves to be blood relations of mine and showered me with compliments on account of my good character. In the end it turned out that they had a grandson in Eretz Yisroel. He was an electrician, and, as he had left behind him his tools, they asked me whether I'd be good enough to bring him his few little *instrumentelech*. They had made out of them a "little pekeleh" so small you could hardly see it!

In no time at all, my house filled with relatives who had relatives in Eretz Yisroel. All came to bid me a happy journey and not one failed to bring along a little pekeleh of tzoress. One came in, another went out; no one asked very much from me. All he wanted me to do was to take along with me his pekeleh. That's all! After all, what was it? Just a mere nothing—a little pekeleh!

At the end of three hours my living room was turned into a storeroom, piled from floor to ceiling with packages, boxes, baskets, and trunks; I simply could find no place where I could sit down. For a mad second I had a hallucination: I was under the delusion that I had wandered into the baggage room of a large railroad station.

I broke into a cold sweat. What earthly good would my certificate of entry be, should they decide to keep me out of Eretz Yisroel on account of these *pekelech!* Sure! Go and carry on a debate with the Children of Israel! Say to them:

"*Gevalt,* Jews! Bandits! What the devil do you take me for? An express company? A communal expediter? A baggage wagon? Have pity! Let me alone!"

Unfortunately, I didn't feel courageous enough to tell them that, seeing that I was one and they were many. What then should I do? The thought occurred to me that I might do wisely if I said good-by to all these Jews and took fond farewell of their packages and made a quiet getaway. But how could I do that when I could no longer tell apart my own packages and baskets from theirs? Only three hours were left until my departure. And having insufficient time to go through carefully all the baggage, I was forced to take along the entire "transport" of pekelech.

What shall I tell you? I was more dead than alive when I managed at last to get on the train with my baggage!

Wherever I found a vacant spot I deposited my pekelech—under the benches, on the benches, and over the benches, in the passageway and everywhere else possible.

When the conductor came in to examine the tickets and looked around him, he stopped openmouthed, struck dumb apparently.

"Whose baggage is this?" he roared like a wounded lion.

"Not mine!" said I.

"What do you mean *not yours?* Whose else?"

"On every package you will find carefully written down the names and addresses of the sender and the receiver," I argued weakly, from tzoress it seems.

"Who cares about names and addresses!" the conductor went on heatedly. "All I want to know is who's carrying with him all this bag-gage?"

"Carry?" I replied meekly. "Yes, I'm carrying them. I'm the car-rier of all these Dispersion packages to Eretz Yisroel!"

"In that case," said the conductor solemnly, like a judge passing sentence on a criminal he had just found guilty, "because you failed to check your baggage in the proper way you will have the goodness to pay a fine of 369 zlotys and 80 groschen."

"What's that? Three hundred and sixty-nine zlotys and 80 groschen! Can't you make it a little cheaper?"

"If you'll argue any more I'll put you and all your packages, boxes, baskets, and trunks off the train at the very next station!"

What could I do? I paid and held my tongue.

The train moved on and I recovered a bit. I wanted to find out how many pieces of baggage I was carrying. And as I looked up on the racks I suddenly saw that a gooey red liquid was dripping down. I started to feel the pekeleh from where it flowed. *Vay is mir!* A ruin! A wreck! The juice was escaping from the jars of preserves, and the wine was flowing out of the bottle. All the glass was broken!

My fellow passengers advised me not to fool around with the broken jars and the bottle. If I hoped to get off "dry," they said, I should throw out of the window all the "wet" stuff! What alternative did I have? I flung at least ten broken jars and bottles out of the window, getting quite a few glass splinters into my fingers, so that they bled.

Now everything would have turned out right, had it not been for the bomb—yes, the *bomb!*

Shortly before we reached the station at the frontier all passengers got their baggage ready for customs inspection. Naturally, everybody felt strained and nervous, and there was quite a bit of crowding. Suddenly something shot out of my pekelech with such explosive force that all the windows on the train rattled. Women started to faint, children screamed—the din was indescribable! I was even accused of trying to smuggle bombs into Palestine! Imagine that!

To my mazl, when the conductor opened one pekeleh which contained six bottles of mead, the corks of several of them popped out with a frightful report. That was the bomb!

I barely managed to get on the ship with my "transport." And when finally I got to Eretz Yisroel my tzoress started anew. I discovered that two of my own trunks, which contained my best clothes and my underwear, had disappeared, together with fourteen pekelech I was carrying for "relatives." Most of the remaining packages got so thoroughly wet and stained en route that it was no longer possible to decipher the names and addresses of the senders and the receivers. The bride's trousseau looked like a geographic map, full of juice, mead, and tayglach stains.

And tzoress, believe me, were plenty!

My own relatives back home write me that they cannot go out of their houses without being molested. People stop them on the street and say:

"Send our regards to that so-and-so, your relative in Eretz Yisroel, that pekeleh-grabber! That *ganef!* That swindler! Tell him for us that he's not going to get away with it so easily!"

Every day, here in Eretz Yisroel, I get letters. All Eretz Yisroel is writing to me, from Kfar Gileadi, Rosh Pinah, Ain-Zatim, Nes Tziona, Benyemina, Kiriat Enavim, and Kfar Saba, to wit:

Why did I swindle packages intended for them out of their relatives? Therefore, they want, if possible, to settle the matter in a peaceful way: I should better return the pekelech right away! If not, they'd take me into court and bring suit against me. A *shacher-macher* like me should know that Eretz Yisroel was no haven for thieves and swindlers but for honest, decent people!

Nu, let me ask you, what do you now say to my pack of pekelech tzoress?

THE CONSIDERATE BEGGAR

A merchant was carrying some goods to market in his wagon. On the way he met a beggar trudging along with a heavy pack on his shoulders. The merchant felt sorry for him and asked him to get into the wagon.

As they rode on in silence the merchant saw that the beggar was sitting with his pack still on his shoulders.

"Why don't you put your pack down?" he asked in surprise.

"Bless you," said the man, "it's enough that you're carrying me! Do I have to burden you with my pack besides?"

LUCK

BY JACOB STEINBERG
TRANSLATED FROM THE YIDDISH BY JOSEPH LEFTWICH

A lot of blind beggars on the roadside.
A jester comes by, and stops in his stride.
Here's a gold piece, he cries, and hurries on.
And all the blind beggars search to see where it's gone.
Each thinks the gold has been found by one of the rest.
While all the time the whole thing was a jest.

WHAT A LIFE!

An unlucky merchant in an impoverished village once came to his rabbi and complained, "Holy Rabbi, I am in the most desperate circumstances! My wife abuses me because my childen cry for bread and I can no longer provide for them. Advise me—what shall I do?"

The rabbi pondered the matter and then answered, "My son, I advise you to become a trader in flour and in shrouds. As you well know, those who live have to eat bread and those who die have to wear shrouds. You can't fail in such a business!"

Overjoyed, the poor man went away and followed the rabbi's counsel. But after a while he came running again to the rabbi in great distress.

"Rabbi," he complained, "I followed your advice and traded in flour and in shrouds, but, if anything, I'm worse off now than I ever was before! Why is that?"

The rabbi was perplexed. "But surely people must live and people must die!"

"Oh no! Not the people in these parts," said the merchant gloomily. "The trouble is, here they don't live, and they don't die. They just drag themselves around."

THE SQUASH

BY DOVID BERGELSON
TRANSLATED FROM THE YIDDISH BY NATHAN AUSUBEL

Now take, for instance, Beila-Henia, Moishe the *Tuter's* wife. Until she got married she worked as a servant in the house of the rich widow. She was ugly as sin, had a small narrow face that was pitted full of pockmarks. Just the same, from the time she was a little girl, she had made up her mind that she'd marry only a man of refinement and Torah learning. In fact, she balked at the idea of taking Moishe the Smith, whose nickname was "Tuter" (Tartar), for her husband.

This high-and-mighty air of hers simply galled the "Tuter." As the saying goes, "it crept right into his liver." What a nerve!

"Such an ugly thing, and it's she who doesn't want me yet!"

For that he got even with her after they were married: he beat her all the time. Even so she spurned him.

The last time he gave her a trouncing was on the festival of *Simchas Torah.*

It felt that day as if it were going to rain, yet no rain fell. Outside it was merely wintry raw, chill and gray. In the rabbi's house they all sat around the table. The door stood open. In the half circular ring of houses outside women sat on their porches, watching the communal bigwigs hunched around the rabbi and Mottel the Redhead, the newly chosen *gabbai*. The menfolk drank *brazhek,* sang convivial songs, and playfully threw melon rinds straight into Yoina the Long's beard. Out of deep affection for Yoina the Long they called out to him: "Oh Yoina! Yoina the Long! The Devil take your father!"

But Yoina the Long pretended not to hear them. He stood up in all his lankiness under the rain of melon rind, and with his grating voice like a *chazan* he bellowed a folksong to the tune of the "Prayer for Rain," sung during the Feast of Tabernacles.

Suddenly, a quick cry of fear rang out in town. And in a flash someone came dashing in to the rabbi's, crying, "He's again beating his wife!"

"Who? Moishe the Tuter?"

"The Devil take his *tréfeneh* guts!"

Like one man, everybody rushed out of doors. They saw how Moishe the Tuter was chasing after his wife, Beila-Henia, all over the market square. He was a muscular giant, his sleeves rolled up just as on weekdays when he stood in his smithy, hammering iron sheeting onto the peasants' wagons. In contrast to him, Beila-Henia appeared small and bony like a scrawny hen. Despite her homeliness, everybody in town knew that she kept a mirror at her bedside; it was quite broken, with the red paint on its back side rubbed off. Oh, how she liked to look at herself in the mirror! Nonetheless, while running away from the Tuter she didn't forget to hide her heavily pock-marked face in her spotless white kerchief. Her guilty eyes couldn't look any man in the face; she felt abashed just as if she had been caught red-handed in some sinful act. Quickly she now ran toward the house of the rich widow where she had served until her marriage to the Tuter. Everybody stood watching her, waiting until the door was bolted securely behind her.

"Finished!" they said with a sigh of relief.

II

The rich widow's house looks imposing, ancestral, and very old. It has a flat white roof, firm whitewashed walls, and old acacia trees growing before its large eight-paned windows. The slightest breeze makes these old trees rustle; they quiver pensively under the over-clouded November sky. And all around huddle the ramshackle houses of the poor, already sick and tired of the same old story about the big house which they keep on whispering to one another:

It's a story about a wealthy man of long ago who had built this house, a story about his son who has already been dead a long time, and now only the son's widow is living there. She prefers talking Russian to Yiddish and never shows her face in the synagogue. And oh my—what people she entertains! She receives frequent visits from the doctor, the tax collector, and the village police chief!

Everywhere it is muddy and wet. Empty fields, stretching upwards along a mountain slope, lie abandoned and waste, showing only their faded stubble. All the time they are wrapped in mist and in a seemingly endless winter. It is so silent there.

Only occasionally a wagon passes through the town and without stopping, for life there is constricted and empty. The clang-clang of the wagon bells rings out in a hollow sound and quickly dies out. And once again the tiny town hunches itself up and its silence grows heavier.

The houses of the poor stand up to their bellies in mud and they listen intently. Suddenly there is heard the scrunch-scrunch of boots in the mud. It is Moishe the Tuter who is out walking. Once more he is seen wandering about, and in broad daylight too, among the poor shops, although he possibly couldn't have business with any of them. Studying the toes of his boots, he falls into deep thought. This leads him only into a great rage and grief. In the end he spits out and curses, "The Devil take her father!"

But the "her" he is cursing is not Beila-Henia but the rich widow with whom she has taken refuge. Why doesn't she return him his wife? Ever since Simchas Torah she has kept Beila-Henia in her house, and doesn't want to send her back to him. Each time he goes there to make inquiries she sends out word to him:

"I'll give you fifty rubles if you'll agree to give Beila-Henia a divorce!"

The Tuter is a little afraid of the rich widow and of her big house. Doesn't the police chief visit there often? Every time he goes to demand the return of his wife he's made to stand in the vestibule near the street door; he's got to wait a long long time, just like a pauper who's come to beg for alms.

By the time he's asked in, Beila-Henia has already fled from the kitchen and has gone to hide herself in her mistress's bedroom. The baby's nurse, a chunky peasant-woman with a flattened nose and the lips of a *nasher*, suddenly comes in. She stares hard at Moishe the Tuter with her little bashful eyes, and in the meantime keeps on rocking the baby in her arms. Of course, she doesn't want to say anything to him. She's only come to take a good look at him, to see what sort of a mug he's got, that Jew on whose account pock-marked Beila-Henia is so scared that she's gone to hide herself in the mistress's bedroom!

After long waiting, the mistress herself comes out but only to abuse him. *Oy,* what a mouthpiece she's got—like on screws! The Tuter says nothing but looks at her all the time with the eyes of any angry, helpless man who's been robbed.

"May she get a boil in her windpipe!" he fumes inwardly.

The Tuter is already fed up with the whole business. He walks away and goes to his smithy. But he finds he can't keep his mind on his work. Nor can he expect to find any comfort at home—there is simply no one to talk to! And all the time he feels a sour taste in his mouth, just like after the brashok he drank on Simchas Torah. On top of it all, the weather has to be so nasty! She has brought him no children either, oh that pock-marked mouse! The Devil take her father! Him he'll visit after he has exhausted every possibility of a reconciliation.

Why not? He'll give her a divorce!

To the divorce proceedings came the rich widow too. She stood at Beila-Henia's side at the rabbi's. She wore a black headdress. Each time the Tuter repeated after the rabbi the words of the divorce formula she listened intently and nodded her head with the air of an expert who is on guard to make sure that no one is going to defraud her. She had a pleased look on her face, as if it were well worth to her the fifty rubles she was paying the Tuter in order to free Beila-Henia of him.

The Tuter had a sister living in town. She "threw cards" for the peasants and made predictions about stolen objects, namely, whether they'd ever be recovered or not. Throughout the divorce proceedings she stood outside the rabbi's house. A peasant's kerchief was tied around her head. Around her there gathered a circle of the curious. Women and children listened to her as she showered curses on Beila-Henia and on her protector, the rich widow:

"May the earth swallow up both of them! May they die an unnatural death! Let it happen today yet, O God in Heaven! May they get boils in their bowels!"

In the meantime, she kept her eyes fixed on the rabbi's house to see how the divorce business was getting along. She looked as if she were muttering prayers to herself.

Everybody's eyes were fixed on the door of the rabbi's house when it finally opened. And as soon as the people inside came out, it became quite clear that something very unusual had just taken place. So people came running up from every direction. Those who were last to arrive asked what had happened. They were told: "Nothing! just nothing!" All that had happened, of course, was that, having been duly divorced, the Tuter then proceeded to slap Beila-Henia's face for the last time.

III

The Tuter sold his smithy and, in parting, spat heartily on the whole town. *Nu,* go ahead and be a prophet whereto he has disappeared! It's already summer now and there's not a trace of him.

Beila-Henia is free at last.

On Friday afternoon, when the boys are let out early from *cheder,* they go peeping into the rich widow's yard through the cracks in the wooden fence. There they see Beila-Henia sitting on the ground not far from the kitchen door, busily engaged at her polishing. Near her stand two samovars and much copper and brassware. Suddenly the children, from the other side of the fence, start hooting at her:

"Beila-Henia the pock-marked! Watch out, Beila-Henia—here comes the Tuter!"

And, frightened by their own yelling, they turn and scamper off quickly.

Nowadays, whenever two little sisters fall out and go at each other's hair, the one who gets the worst of the fight squeals at the other, "You Beila-Henia, you! You pock-marked mouse!"

And passing by just then, Beila-Henia hears the abuse and tries to hide her pock-marked face in her spotless white kerchief.

When she arrives home at the wealthy widow's she gets into a corner and for a long time studies her face in her small broken mirror. And what she sees are pockmarks, many, many pockmarks, and two cross-eyes looking in opposite directions.

But her thoughts are suddenly interrupted. The guests are already assembled in the dining room. Her mistress is calling her. So she quickly hides the mirror, as guiltily as if she had done some forbidden thing.

"Coming, coming!" she calls out as she hurries to the dining room.

She's afraid to look all the male guests in the face. To be sure, everyone knows why at first she had refused to marry the Tuter, that ever since she was a little girl she had made up her mind that the man she'd marry would have to be refined and learned. Now that the guests are in a gay mood they all laugh at her, crack nuts and jokes at her expense:

"Nu, what's the news? When is Beila-Henia going to marry her rabbi?"

In the house of the rich widow there are employed a cook, a parlormaid, a Gentile servant girl, and a nurse. Everyone of them is dying to get married. Whenever a *challeh* is drawn out perfect from the oven and every time they render chicken or goose fat for their mistress they superstitiously wish for themselves a husband. And to every wedding in town they all come out to gape and gossip; the older the bride the greater their interest. So they stand and listen to the playing of the musicians as they precede some poor graying bride to the *chupeh* and they loiter around the brilliantly lighted home of the bride all night long, and first turn their steps homeward at break of day.

They go to bed in the servants' quarters but they find it hard to fall asleep. So they start talking, and they talk and talk so long and ardently about getting married that they end by quarreling. The parlormaid throws it up to the cook that her husband was nothing but a lowdown *ganef* and had died in prison. In turn the cook screams that she very well knows who it was that the parlormaid used to steal out to meet behind the fence every night that past winter. The Gentile servant girl and the nurse somehow get tangled up in the argument and soon no one knows who it was exactly that started the whole squabble.

The next morning they are all still angry at one another. They yammer at one and the same time. The cook spits in Beila-Henia's face. She is aflame and furious and forgets all about the pot that's boiling over on the oven. When she sees her mistress hurry into the kitchen to quell the commotion and to take Beila-Henia's part, the cook shouts, "Why should such a piece of dirt talk it into herself that she'll marry only a learned Jew?"

The yawping lasts an interminable while and keeps flaring up anew.

True, Beila-Henia suffered keenly on account of her quarrels with the other servants, but in the end her happiness came. She had always been slow-witted, and her thoughts were hopelessly confused. She could never think logically about her own self, nor about her happiness. Nonetheless, her happiness came.

IV

The sun sends its rays pouring down to earth like through a sieve. The day is summery and hot. Carts rattle by, a multitude of cries grate on the ear, people swarm hither and thither. There's a fair, a great market day in town. From the peasants' wagons hang garlands of onions. Eggs, they say, are selling for next to nothing. And carts keep on coming and carts keep on departing endlessly.

On one of these carts sits an old Jew. He is dressed in his Sabbath *kapote* and wears a velvet hat with a rubbed-off brim. This is old Dovid-Layzer, the *melamed* from the neighboring town. All the time his shoulders shake to the heaving and rattling of the wagon. He draws with a sage air upon his short pipe and smiles into his yellow-gray mustache. Dovid-Layzer, the melamed, has come to the fair to buy a tub and a *lokshen* board because the old ones are already broken. The neighbor, who has been baking bread for him for the past ten years, ever since his old woman died, tells him that he needs new ones.

Dovid-Layzer is a quiet sort, doesn't like to stick his nose in any community or synagogue squabbles. That's why, in the course of time, he has developed a great capacity for keeping silent and for smiling sagely into his little gray beard and into his yellow-gray mustache.

Nu, so he keeps silent, old Dovid-Layzer does—hasn't opened his mouth for a long time already. But about eleven o'clock in the morning, as he draws near the old Kantikazever synagogue he hears a lively melody floating out towards him. When he enters he almost melts with happiness—people have recognized him, still remember him!

As they pump his hand and salute him with a hearty *sholom aleichem* he doesn't say a word but keeps on smiling with a quiet joy. Out of his throat, encrusted with the tobacco smoke of a lifetime and with the long silence he has kept, there emerges a peculiar grunt, like the sound a mute makes to express his deep satisfaction: "Cheh-cheh-cheh!"

The expression on his face is sly and mischievous, as if he has just played a practical joke. So they thought, did they, that he had been dead a long time already! Cheh-cheh-cheh! Now he has proved to them, performed a clever trick, showed them all that he was still alive and about! And after the service is over and they all drink with him *le'chayim*—to life—they discover to their surprise that he has been a widower for these past ten years. At this they begin to preach at him:

"*Feh!* Reb Dovid-Layzer! How come that such a pious man as

you should do an awful thing like that—be without a wife for so long? Why that's a sin!"

Yoina the Long wrinkles his forehead for a long time and thoughtfully rubs his itching back against the wall. Then he gets up suddenly, saying he has to leave for a moment: "I have to talk over something with my old woman."

Right after that Yoina the Long's wife hurries over to the rich widow and enters by the back door.

This day Beila-Henia's pock-marked face is flushed with excitement. She has put on her new calico frock which she has made especially for Rosh-Hashanah. Her thoughts are in a whirl. The long market day has turned out for her like a radiant sunburst. Her overflowing heart comes pretty near bursting from joy. The negotiations with Reb Dovid-Layzer have almost reached the concluding point. Yoina the Long's wife is expected to arrive at any moment to report his final decision—"yes," or "no!"

That evening she sidles into the rabbi's house on some pretext and watches them put up the chupeh. She looks on Reb Dovid-Layzer for the first time. He pleases her. All around him crowd the respectable householders of the town while he keeps on sagely pulling on his short pipe and smiling into his yellow-gray mustache. It is just as if some old cronies of his were tickling him and he lets them do it and enjoys every bit of it. . . .

On the day after the wedding, Reb Dovid-Layzer returned to his home in the neighboring town and left Beila-Henia behind at the rich widow's. Everybody thought: that wasn't such a nice thing to do! Beila-Henia was afraid that perhaps they were laughing at her. She was simply ashamed to look people in the eye! No question, she felt deeply humiliated. The rich widow said crossly, *"Takkeh* only among very pious Jews are such odd things done!"

She never liked pious Jews too much, this rich widow! She waited one week and then she waited another, and when no word came from Reb Dovid-Layzer she engaged a peasant cart and put Beila-Henia and her bundle into it.

"Haida! Go home to your new husband!"

v

Dejectedly Beila-Henia climbed into the peasant's cart. As they pulled out she heard behind her the mocking laughter of her fellow servants.

The town where Reb Dovid-Layzer lived was entirely strange to her. It nestled at the bottom slope of a hill near a lake. By the time she arrived it was already wrapped in the darkening shadows of twilight.

Women, whom she was seeing for the first time in her life, were going out to meet the cattle returning from the pasture, and each singled out her own cow and drove it into the shed. The menfolk were on their way to the synagogue for the *Ma'ariv* service and stopped to gape at Beila-Henia driving up in the peasant cart. They all stood and waited to see before whose house she'd stop! It so happened that the peasant who was driving her knew his way about town. As he turned into a narrow alley in which stood two tumble-down houses he called out to several women of his acquaintance:

"I'm bringing Dovid-Layzerov's wife."

Beila-Henia immediately sensed that something important was going on inside the house before which the driver pulled up his cart. When she stopped at the threshold she saw Reb Dovid-Layzer sitting around the table with all his pupils. They were paying him their tuition fees in whole rubles and in forty-kopeck pieces. Then he assigned to them the prayers they were to memorize, pointing to various places in their tattered prayer books. This done, he dismissed them for the day.

When Beila-Henia finally mustered up enough courage to enter, the melamed did not even honor her with a glance. Smiling into his yellow-gray mustache, he arose from his seat, turned his back on her, and, with his usual sage air, began to pull on his short, half-extinguished pipe. With pleasure he gave a cough, as if he were addressing himself to someone, *"Pche!"*

And just as he did on all other days at dusk he went off to the synagogue for evening prayers. When he returned he found his small hut spick and span and everything in order: the bed was made, the rubbish under the table had been swept up, and on the hot oven the old sooty kettle was boiling merrily.

Afterwards he sipped his tea before the kerosene lamp which threw a feeble light on the table. And he continued to smile his everlasting deaf-mute smile.

Beila-Henia's coming had pleased him immensely! Perhaps he might even have addressed a word or two to her, but he didn't have the faintest idea what her name was. On top of it all she was quite clearly the bashful kind. She chose to sit in the kitchen all the time opposite the burning oven. Even after he had snuffed out the lamp and gone to bed, she remained sitting in the kitchen, her hands folded on her breast and looking intently into the dying fire in the oven.

From that day on Reb Dovid-Layzer stopped putting the tuition money into his own waistcoat pocket. He deposited it instead on the crooked little window in the kitchen. And Beila-Henia took the money and went to market and bought with it all she needed. Now all the women in her husband's town soon knew that she was pock-marked. But they also knew that she had a fine husband and so they would ask her respectfully with the deference of one equal to another, "What do you think, Beila-Henia, are these fish fresh or not?"

Beila-Henia would answer briefly and to the point. Like her husband, she too hardly ever spoke. But for that, oh could she cook! Old Dovid-Layzer was filled with wonder.

"She certainly learned how to cook over there, at the rich widow's!"

Both dug their spoons into the same bowl and yet they bashfully averted their eyes from each other. Nor did they ever make conversation.

However, once it happened that, while she was out marketing, Beila-Henia bought a big yellow squash—a real *metzieh!* It was so heavy she had some trouble lugging it home. She cooked it in a lot of butter, mixed it with millet, and seasoned it with all the condiments they were in the habit of using in the rich widow's kitchen.

When old Dovid-Layzer returned from the synagogue he smelled right away the aroma of the appetizing dish. And he was filled with genuine wonder: "Just look! How did *she* find out that I love squash?"

The first helping she gave him he fairly swallowed in no time; he didn't eat—he gulped it down. And he licked his shiny, moist fingers when he got through. He looked at her with his hungry eyes. She could see he wanted more more! So she handed him a second helping, and after that a third. And still he ate ravenously and his hunger was not appeased. For the first time he spoke to her at last: "What a fine dish! Really good squash!"

Beila-Henia's pock-marked face was suffused with blushes. She was so overcome she had to step into the kitchen to collect herself. For the first time in her life she had tasted true happiness, and it went to her head like strong drink.

When evening came Dovid-Layzer got drowsy a little earlier than usual. Then he felt a chill and he began to shake so that Beila-Henia had to cover him with both featherbeds. Then his stomach was affected; during the night he suffered such severe cramps that Beila-

Henia got frighted and called in the neighbors. They placed warm pot-covers on his belly and hot bottles to his feet. Then they called in the *Feldsherr,* who drummed on his hot belly with his cold fingers and peered into his face like a billy goat.

When the day broke they thought he was feeling better; he had dozed off. But only an hour later a new clamor was raised. That was the end.

Hurriedly they lit candles and placed them at his feet. Pious Jews came hurrying from the *mikveh* with moist sidelocks. Out of thick prayer books they began to intone something. Dovid-Layzer's sister-in-law, Keila-Malkeh, carried on like one demented. When they were carrying out the body on the short, narrow burial board, she struggled frantically to get to it. She tried to follow the funeral procession of menfolk to the cemetery. The restraining hands of the other women drew her back into the house. Everybody tried to talk at once.

And all this time Beila-Henia remained sitting alone in the kitchen. Her guilty eyes felt ashamed to look people in the face.

VI

Ever since the funeral Dovid-Layzer's sister-in-law, Keila-Malkeh, and her husband Yoizef have been occupying the house. Beila-Henia herself lives in the kitchen, in her corner near the oven, out of everybody's way.

Every time she hears Keila-Malkeh and her husband whispering in their room she becomes frightened and turns her eyes guiltily to right and to left. She strains with all her might to hear what they are saying. She's afraid they're planning to turn her out of the house. No one has any idea how she manages to sustain herself. Some say she has a neat little pile salted away from the money she must have put by through all the years she worked as a servant in the rich widow's house.

It is the first of the month of Elul. The worshipers have just gotten through with the morning prayers in the two synagogues. Beila-Henia makes her way to the cemetery to pray at the grave of her departed husband.

Beila-Henia hasn't changed any. She's still a silent one, still small and bony like a scrawny hen. As of old, she still hides her pock-marked face in her spotless white kerchief. Her guilty eyes are still ashamed to look menfolk in the face.

She makes her way to the cemetery all alone and by a devious roundabout way. For a long time she has sat behind the cemetery fence, looking fearfully in every direction, looking like a night bird that has lost its way. And from the other side of the fence she hears the wailing of widows, lashing themselves into a frenzy of grief before the graves of their departed mates!

Finally, everything grows quiet; the lamentations subside. The women, red-eyed from weeping, start to leave the cemetery. Then they lock up the funeral chapel. It's then only that Beila-Henia musters enough courage to go stealing past the cemetery fence.

Solitary she stands among the deserted graves. She stands for hours at the feet of Dovid-Layzer's grave. She wants so badly to tell him something, but she doesn't know what. All in all, he had been her husband for only three months. When she tries to recall his face she can see him only as he looked that last time when he glutted himself with the three helpings of squash that she had served him. She recalls how ravenously he shoveled it down, although it was too hot even to put it in one's mouth, remembers how he licked his buttery shiny fingers and exulted, "What a fine dish! Really good squash!"

And now he was lying dead in the cemetery! Among all the most respected Jews of the town he was lying. She looks long and reverently on his tombstone, and recalls now most vividly how he looked.

Suddenly, she begins to intone to herself in the manner of all pious women when they are at their devotions. It is a chant in a minor wail, a slowly sung and long-drawn-out lamentation, as is fitting for mourning the dead.

"So you liked squash! . . . . Nu, so I cooked for you squash! . . ."

All around her Beila-Henia hears the murmur of the trees in the little cemetery woods. Grasshoppers leap about in the uncut grass among the graves. In the air there still vibrates the sighs of weeping women, the echoes of distant sorrows. The tombstones stretch in straight rows, abandoned and hushed. If you look at them you get the illusion that they are keeping to themselves some deep mournful secret, that they are listening intently. And over them still is floating Beila-Henia's low wailing plaint:

"So you liked squash! . . . . Nu, so I cooked for you squash! . . ."

May God spare me from having an only child and an only shirt!

Jewish Luck

When a Jew gets a boil,
He has no onion for it.
When he gets an onion,
He has no boil for it.

SCHLIMAZL

BY ABRAHAM IBN EZRA (TWELFTH CENTURY)

My labor's vain,
No wealth I gain.
My fate since birth
Is gloom on earth.

If I sold shrouds,
No one would die.
If I sold lamps,
Then in the sky,
The sun for spite
Would shine by night.

WHEN NATURE TAKES ITS COURSE

A man and his wife who had raised nine children once went to the rabbi to ask for a divorce. When the question arose of dividing the children between them the wife argued, "I want five children to stay with me."

"Why should I take only four? I want five, and you can take four," rejoined the husband.

To postpone the settlement of an argument which seemed impossible to solve, the rabbi said, "I suggest that you live together another year and in the meantime have another child. Then you will have ten and you will be able to divide your children evenly."

The couple did as the rabbi suggested.

A year later, the husband visited the rabbi to report.

"We'll have to live together another year," said the man ruefully.

"Why so?" asked the rabbi. "Didn't your wife give birth?"

"Yes, she did, Rabbi. But you see, it's twins!"

When good mazl *comes in
draw up a chair for him.*

*There are always kindhearted people:
anyone who is lucky enough to be unlucky will find help,
but certainly not before.—Ludwig Börne*

Only schlimazls *believe in mazl.*

THE DREAM

BY BAR-HEBRAEUS [THIRTEENTH CENTURY]

A poor man once dreamed that he was frying dung. He went to an interpreter of dreams to explain it to him.

"Give me a *zuza* [a small coin] and I'll interpret it for you," said the soothsayer.

"If I had a zuza would I fry dung?" cried the man scornfully. "I'd buy a fish and fry that!"

WHOSE GOOD FORTUNE?

In a certain town in Poland the congregation treated their rabbi without much consideration. They paid him a wretched salary and he collected it irregularly at that. His life was bitter and he never had enough to make ends meet.

One day, driven by desperation, he came to the heads of the community and said, "I'm in great need. My wife is sick, my children are hungry. I've got to have a hundred rubles right away!"

After much debate they decided to make him the loan.

"But on one condition," they said, "that we deduct the hundred rubles from your salary after Passover."

The rabbi consented. Then he said grimly, "If I survive until after Passover you can consider it your good luck—you'll be able to collect from me. On the other hand, should I die before—believe me, I'll consider it my good luck!"

HE DID FAR TOO MUCH

A poor, harassed man came running to the rabbi.

"Help me, Rabbi, I'm in great trouble!" he cried. "I'm without means and cannot support my wife and seven children. What's more, every blessed year my wife brings me a new child. Advise me, Rabbi, what shall I do?"

"Do? Take my advice and do nothing!" replied the rabbi.

Schlemihls

What a capable fellow!
He falls on his back
and breaks his nose!

A PACK OF TROUBLES FOR ONE CENT
A STORY TOLD BY MY GROCERYMAN

BY TASHRAK (ISRAEL J. ZEVIN)
TRANSLATED FROM THE YIDDISH BY NATHAN AUSUBEL

TROUBLE NUMBER ONE

Once, on a fine afternoon, as the storytellers like to say, a boy threw a circular into my grocery store. Since there were no customers to wait on at the time, I picked it up and began reading it. It announced a big sale of pianos. "The finest pianos almost for nothing!" it said. "We will send you a piano without cost, and if you like it you'll name your own price and the piano is yours. Drop us a postal card and we'll send you free a beautiful album with the pictures of all the world-famous pianists."

I thought to myself, "Do I need a piano? I need it like a hole in the head! Still enough I'd like to have that free album with the pictures. It'll make a nice present for my sister's boy because he studies how to play on the piano."

So I bought a postal card for a penny and wrote away to the piano dealer he should send me his album.

A day hadn't passed but who should come into my store but a "gentleman"! He looked well-fed, had a round little "corporation," a ruddy face and large black mustaches that were turned up. He showed me my postal card and right away I began to feel uncomfortable.

I felt heartily ashamed of myself. How could I have *dared* fool such a gentleman? He certainly must have thought that I wanted to buy a piano. So I said to him, said I:

"Please excuse me, mister. I assure you I didn't meant to trouble you. Since I saw you were giving away albums for nothing, I thought I'd like to have one too."

And as I said this I felt as if my face was changing color.

"It's all right!" the gentleman assured me. "It's no trouble at all. On the contrary, it'll be a pleasure for me to get acquainted with you. You'll get your album, never fear. It's a fine album, bound in leather and stamped in gold. But first, I'd like to recommend to you a piano— a beautiful piano, a first-class bargain! The regular price is seven hundred dollars, but we'll sell it to you for only two hundred and twenty-five."

"I'm very sorry," I replied, "but I don't need a piano. What can a groceryman do with a piano? Besides, my wife can't play."

"Don't you worry about that," said the gentleman. "Our firm will furnish your wife with a teacher who charges very little. You'll see what a pleasure you'll have when your wife will play the piano for you! You'll know then what 'living' really means!"

He continued talking this way for a long time. Ach, what a little *mamzer* of a tongue he had! Smooth as silk, and like chloroform too! Just another instant and I would have given in to him and taken the piano. But perhaps because he spoke a little too much I had time to cool off a bit. I even got up enough courage to say to him that he was wasting his time and that it was no use talking to me any more, because my wife was much too busy with the household and with helping me in the store to have time to take piano lessons.

What I said didn't seem to make the slightest impression on him. He continued to shower me with his arguments why I should buy a piano, but apparently he began to realize that he couldn't do anything with me, for he took out his card. *"Nu,"* he said, "I hope that someday we'll do business."

"You should be sick so long!" I thought to myself. "Did you ever see such a *nudnik*? First he promises me an album, then he tries to sell me a piano!"

TROUBLE NUMBER TWO

From that day on I took a vow that never again would I waste a cent on a postal card which only brings me trouble!

Three days after I got rid of the piano agent I got a call from another gentleman. He was short and dressed like a sport with a soft green felt hat. He addressed me familiarly by my name.

"How are things?" he asked.

"Pretty good," I answered. "But tell me please, with whom have I the honor to speak?"

He took out his card and introduced himself: "My name is Barney Tzapelman. I'm an agent of player pianos. I've been informed that you're interested in buying a piano for your wife. Since I'm told she has no time to learn to play I'll make you a proposition. I'll sell you a piano that plays by itself. All you have to do is to put in a roll, turn a lever and it plays!"

"Aha!" I said to myself. "This fine fellow here must have been sent by the first 'gentleman.' It's one and the same gang, I'll bet."

"We'll send you the piano free of charge," said the agent, with the air of a philanthropist.

"What do you mean, 'free of charge'?" I asked.

"You don't have to pay a cent in advance," he explained. "You keep the piano a week's time, and if you are pleased with it you can pay for it in small monthly installments."

I didn't say anything and racked my brain how I could get rid of him. And right in the middle of it who should have to come in but my Tillie!

When he saw my wife, the agent bowed to her and showered her with compliments. Then he began to chew the whole story all over again. He told her that he wanted to send us a player piano free of charge, but that I wasn't a good sport at all and didn't want to accept his present.

You know how my Tillie is. She's a decent, good sort, but after all she is a woman, and she was flattered by that bluffer's compliments. She beamed at him and enjoyed herself. I felt as if I was getting a bit angry with her. Here comes along a nudnik who twists my head off with his tricks, and I try to get rid of him, and there she comes and encourages him to stay!

"Nu," said he to me, "are you going to give me your order? If I had such a beautiful wife as you, would I hesitate for a minute? I'd order a player piano right away!"

That really made me mad! What's his business whether my wife is beautiful or ugly? So I cut him short:

"Say mister, I want you to know that such a thing as a piano don't interest me at all. I haven't even room where to place one. So be so good and let me alone! You're wasting your time and my time."

My Tillie even tried to say a good word for him. My conduct didn't seem refined enough for her. But I made myself busy in a barrel of herring and paid no attention to him. Seeing how matters stood, the agent said good-bye and carried himself off.

"An idiot!" I thought. "He thinks he understands his business. Boils, he understands!"

TROUBLE NUMBER THREE

When the player piano agent left I felt upset for quite a while. Wasn't it ridiculous—to cause myself so much trouble with a one-cent postal card? Now I was more certain than ever that he had been sent by the first piano agent. Somewhere I've heard that when these agents pounce on the name and address of a person whom they can sell something they don't let him alone. The first one passes on the name and address to a second, the second to a third, and so forth. Each one tries his luck with the prospect, maybe he'll be able to sell him.

Therefore, you mustn't think I was surprised when only about five minutes after the second agent had left a middle-aged Jew with a black beard bounces in.

"Are you a *landsman* from Grodno?" he asked me.

"No," said I. "I am from Liadi."

"And I thought you were my landsman!" he said, looking disappointed.

The man had such friendly homey ways about him that I began to like him.

He talked to me about the grocery business and about the high cost of living. Afterwards he touched on his own business. He was an agent of phonographs, he said, and he sold all of his machines for a third of their regular price. That was because, he explained, he bought his merchandise direct from the factory. He showed me a little booklet in which were pictures of various styles of phonographs. I saw that they interested Tillie very much.

"I'll tell you what," the man proposed to me. "If you like I'll make you a present of a phonograph."

"What do you mean, a present?" I asked him. "You want to be paid for it, don't you?"

"Not one cent!" he assured me. "Not a cent now and not a cent later. I'll give you a brand-new phonograph, straight from the factory, and entirely free. I'll tell you what I'll do, I'll give you a certificate that the phonograph is your property. Nobody'll be able to take it away from you and nobody'll come to bother you for money. It's as free as the air on the street and as the water in the river. Nu, could it be better?"

I looked at Tillie and Tillie looked at me, and we both felt uneasy. *Takkeh,* say yourself, wouldn't you be suspicious if a stranger came and made such a proposition to you?

The phonograph agent continued to talk to me and tried to make the matter a little clearer to me.

"It's true," he said, "that the phonograph costs me twenty dollars. But, you see, it pays me to make you a present of it because I expect you to buy your records from me."

"Eheh!" I said to myself triumphantly. "So it's no longer for nothing! A fine present, indeed—it's a present with a string attached."

Since Tillie was so anxious to have the phonograph I gave in. Why shouldn't we have a phonograph, I ask you? It's good once in a while in a free moment to wind up the machine and listen to a bit of music. When do you suppose has a groceryman or a groceryman's wife the time to go to the theatre or to a concert? Why not? Let's have a bit of pleasure in the house! With the sort of life we lead the soul could easily get rusty.

In short, I ordered from the agent three dollars' worth of records, and he promised to send me the phonograph.

"After all," I thought, "the cent that I spent on the postal card was not entirely wasted."

But don't you jump to conclusions! My real troubles were first to begin. Listen to what I'm going to tell you.

TROUBLE NUMBER FOUR

The phonograph arrived. Tillie and I had a lot of fun with it. Our records consisted of The Blind Chazan's "Our Father, Our King," Shmulevitch's "Herring," Sousa's "March," "Yisrolik Come Home," and Aronson's "A Letter to the Kaleh." We played them for ourselves and for our customers so often that the songs began to crawl from our gullets. Even the best piece of music gets boring when you play it all the time, or ten times a day the way we did. So we decided to buy several new records.

After a couple of weeks, who should show up but a new agent, also of phonographs!

"I already have a phonograph," I told him.

"Would you mind showing it to me? I'd very much like to see it," he coaxed me.

So I took him into my rooms in the rear of the store and showed it to him.

The agent examined the phonograph with the air of a judge of phonographs.

"A fine phonograph," he said. "How much did you pay for it, at least forty dollars, no?"

"I got it for nothing," I told him. "An agent made me a gift of it on condition that I buy records from him."

"Aw, go on!" said the agent. "You're making fun of me! The regular price of such a phonograph is forty dollars. Sometimes, if you're lucky, you might get it for thirty. I'll tell you what I'm going to do with you. I'll pay you twenty dollars for the phonograph. No? All right, I'll give you twenty-five dollars, then."

At first I thought that he was joking, but he assured me that he was in earnest. He made me a proposition: If I'd like to get a better phonograph he'd give me one for fifty dollars that regularly sold for seventy-five. More than that, he'd buy mine for twenty-five dollars, so that actually the seventy-five-dollar machine would cost me only twenty-five dollars.

Oy, was this an agent! Compared to him, all other agents were like babies. Why, do you know, he was so smooth that he could convince you that there was a tenement house in your belly!

We finally made a deal: I gave him my old machine and in addition twenty-five dollars in cash.

Of course the new phonograph really wasn't worth more than twenty-five dollars and he must have made at least ten dollars profit on it, not counting the value of my old phonograph which he got for nothing. And don't think either that the second phonograph agent wasn't the right-hand man of the first one, who had given me the phonograph! That mamzer! As if he didn't know that sooner or later he'd get his phonograph back!

But all this I didn't find out right away, but later.

TROUBLE NUMBER FIVE

Less than a week had gone by when an agent of books blew in. He was a tall young fellow with red hair and sharp eyes. As a talker he was pretty weak. But oh, did he have leechy ways about him—a leech from Leeches' Land. Why, he didn't understand the meaning of the word "no"! As many times as I told him that I did not need any books he ignored me. He put on his little hat of deafness and didn't give a tumble to what I was saying. But he, on his part, drowned me in a flood of words.

That was a musical library that he wanted to sell me, he told me. In it I'd find the pictures and life stories of all the great musicians in the world. I'd also find there the stories of all the operas and a lot of other valuable things besides. He had heard that I was a great music lover. That's why he came to offer me his musical library, twenty volumes, all told, beautifully bound in leather and stamped with gold. All I had to pay was three dollars a month. The books cost, all told, only a hundred and fifty dollars, but he assured me that he had inside information that the company would positively fold up in two months, so the books would remain with me for only six dollars!

Nu, let me tell you, my friend, that once you get drawn into these things you get soaked in them like a sot in whiskey. To make a long story short, I was persuaded to sign the contract that the agent pushed under my nose and while I did that I rejoiced inside of me: "Huh! This set of books is worth the six dollars even if I did nothing more with them than tear out the pages and wrap herring in them!"

But no sooner did the agent leave than I had a change of heart. I was sorry about the whole business. What the devil did I need the books for? Who was going to read them? Let's even say that they were a great bargain for the six dollars that I was going to pay for them. But what was I going to do if, instead of folding up in two months the company pulled through? Then I'd have to keep on paying three dollars a month, and month after month!

A little upset I went to see the man in the cigar store across the way. I begged him to write for me a letter in English to the company, asking that they should be so kind and tear up my contract because I suddenly found out that I had no use for the books. I sent away the letter and slept quite peacefully that night.

Several days later an expressman pulled up to my door and delivered a long narrow crate. He gave me his receipt book and asked me to sign. I thought it was only a box of soap or sardines, so I signed.

After the expressman had gone I opened the box.

"*Oy vay!*" cried Tillie. "Look what they sent us—the books!"

"It must be a mistake," I said turning pale. "I'll write to the company and ask them to take the books back."

I did so right away but before they could answer my second letter I got an answer to the first. This is what it said:

Dear Sir:

We regret that we cannot cancel your order. Our agents work very hard and we pay them for every order they bring in. Naturally, we cannot tear up your contract. However, we know that your credit is good, so if you would like to pay for the books in cash, we'll give you a discount of ten per cent. The books have already been sent to you by express.

Ai-ai, did that agent sell me a bargain! I'd have to pay for it four whole years! I first offered him ten dollars and later increased it to fifteen if only he'd free me from the deal. Of course he refused, but gave me the cold comfort that after I'd be through paying for the books he'd surely get me a buyer for them. And he could even see where I was going to make a handsome profit on them!

As time went by I saw that the book company had absolutely no intention of going bankrupt. Why should it? As long as there were such dopes in the world as I they'd have no need to.

TROUBLES—A REGULAR FLOOD

From then on there fell on me fresh troubles, one on top of the other.

My name and address, I'd like you to know, was given out all over America. There isn't a day when I don't receive all kinds of catalogues of musical instruments, phonographs, pianos, and musical albums.

One day recently, the letter carrier brought me a large package. I opened it and found a beautiful leather-bound book that was full of music notes. I didn't have the slightest idea who had sent it to me.

"At last," I rejoiced, "someone has sent me something that won't cost me any money!" I then gave the book to Tillie and she in turn gave it to her cousin who's taking piano lessons.

Her cousin naturally, was very happy to get our gift.

Five days later I received the following letter:

Dear Sir:

Knowing that you are a music lover, we are taking the liberty of sending you our new collection of classical music. We hope that you will like the book, and if you do you will please send us your check for only three dollars. Should the book not meet with your approval, you, of course, can send it back at our expense.

Nu? How do you like such a deal? How could I ask my wife's cousin to give me back the book? There was nothing else for me to do but to pay the three dollars.

You think that's all? In today's mail I got a letter in which I found six concert tickets. The letter read:

Dear Sir:

Since we know that you are a great lover of musical art we hope that you will support a young and talented musician by attending a benefit recital given by him in Beethoven Hall. We are enclosing six tickets for which you will please remit to us six dollars.

Now you can see what a mess of trouble I've gotten into with that damned one cent postal card that I sent away for the free album that I never got!

Do you think I'll ever write another postal card?

He who has been bitten by a snake will be scared by a piece of rope.

THE GIFT OF THE EMPEROR

BY LEO KATZ
TRANSLATED FROM THE GERMAN BY SYBILLE BEDFORD

Mordche, who was *shames* at the middle synagogue and taught Hebrew to women and young girls on the side, would never have dreamt of entering into direct correspondence with the Emperor. He often thought of the Emperor, Franz Joseph, though; and a picture of the Emperor hung in his room, as it did in most houses in Sereth.

Even on this very Sunday afternoon, in the main street of Mihaleni—which was a Rumanian border town and therefore outside the territory of the Austro-Hungarian monarchy—Mordche was thinking about the Emperor and his multifarious businesses. On Sunday afternoons in summer, and often in winter too, many of the inhabitants of Sereth would drive the four miles out to the small Rumanian frontier town. There they would drink wine and eat meat grilled over charcoal. The taverns of Mihaleni were always full, and there were a great many taverns in Mihaleni.

Mordche, as has been said, had two jobs, but he did not earn enough to be able to walk into a tavern, as he longed to, and stand up at the bar and say to the proprietor or proprietress, "Let's see what your vinegar tastes like." It would annoy them to hear their wine called vinegar, but they had to be polite to a paying customer, and in spite of their irritation they'd smile and serve him his glass of wine. But when you have no money, you aren't entitled to say anything.

Why had he come to Mihaleni then? Well, his neighbor, Dudl Schmotscheck, had pointed to the empty seat on his wagon-box and called out, "Come on, Mordche, sit next to me. It won't hurt you to ride over with us."

Often an acquaintance would notice him in the street in Mihaleni and offer him a glass of wine. But today he had already been walking up and down the long street for hours. The voices coming out of the drinking places sounded as though everybody had their tongues well soaked, but nobody seemed to remember Mordche. Wandering about in the streets on a hot day, all alone, with nothing to quench your thirst, and seeing others enjoying themselves in plenty, produces dismal thoughts.

I can't understand the Emperor, thought Mordche. At home, in Sereth, under his government, meat and wine are three times as expensive as in Mihaleni. But you are not allowed to bring anything in from Mihaleni. On the other hand, if you go there yourself you can eat and drink as much as you want to. Wouldn't it be better then for the Emperor if the meat and wine were brought home before they were eaten and drunk, so that the tavernkeepers of Sereth would make the profit instead of those in Mihaleni? The Emperor's attention ought to be called to this. But after all, was that Mordche's worry? The Emperor had been sitting on the throne for sixty years now, carrying on his businesses with the army and tobacco and cigarettes, with law courts and taxes. He had never told Mordche how many candles to light in the synagogue; so why should Mordche give him advice about allowing Rumanian wine and meat into Sereth?

Just then a stranger came up to Mordche and said, "Reb Mordche, will you drink a glass of wine with me?"

This did not surprise Mordche. As *shames* of a synagogue, he was used to seeing strange faces and being spoken to by strangers. Someone traveling through might want to honor his late father's or mother's memorial day. He would ask Mordche to provide the candles and buy some brandy so that they could drink to the health of the deceased's soul after *kaddish*. Mordche never asked these people's family names or places of origin, but only their mothers' names and those of the deceased. That was the regulation.

So when this stranger asked Mordche to have a drink of wine, he did not say no. They went into a tavern and the stranger ordered two glasses of wine. These were hardly emptied before he had them filled up a second, a third, and even a fourth time. The stranger also invited Mordche to help himself to his heart's desire from the meat dishes at the bar. Mordche wondered, however, whether the stranger would also let him have a few pennies to buy some candy to take home for the children. They sold a Turkish honey called *rahat* at Mihaleni, and *halvah,* a stuff made of nuts and sugar.

Then he heard the stranger saying: "Would you be kind enough to keep this package for me until I come back? I have to go somewhere on some urgent business."

He handed Mordche a package and a crown piece, and added, "In case I'm late, which is not likely, don't worry but just take the package home with you and I'll call for it there."

"But you don't know me at all," said Mordche.

"Who doesn't know Mordche *shames?*"

Mordche felt very much flattered by these words. He took the package, and went off to the delicatessen to buy a few pennies worth of candy for his children. He had not had such a lucky day in a long while. The delicatessen man, who knew him, was not a little amazed by Mordche's extravagance when he saw him buy thirty cents' worth of *halvah* and *rahat.* This was the maximum amount you were allowed to take across the border without paying duty.

As he still had seventy cents left from the crown, Mordche was even tempted to go to another tavern in order to say, "Let me have a look at your vinegar." But he gave up the idea. If God had sent him such a wonderful day, he should not be too reckless about it and attract public attention. In his happiness, Mordche had forgotten only one thing—which was that he was on the wrong side of the border and therefore he had to be careful about packages.

It was getting late now. Several people with buggies offered him a ride but Mordche refused them all and continued to wait for the stranger. Dusk set in. It came time for the evening prayer. Mordche said the prayer behind the tavern, but the stranger still did not appear. The last wagon had left Mihaleni for Sereth. Alone, with the package under his arm, Mordche went toward the customs station. After all, he thought, there was no harm in walking a few miles on a summer evening; it even did you good after eating so much meat and drinking so much wine.

Nothing ever escaped those faithful servants of His Imperial Majesty, the border guards. How often had Mordche crossed the border on foot or sitting on the box of some buggy without being asked whether he had anything dutiable or prohibited with him.

The chief inspector, in a green uniform, noticed the package under Mordche's arm and asked him, "Have you anything to declare?" Mordche showed him the bit of candy he was taking home to his children. He had quite forgotten about the package he was carrying for the stranger.

"And you haven't anything else to declare?"

"What should someone like me have to declare?"

The chief inspector ordered Mordche to follow him into the customs house. Inside, his voice changed:

"Give me that package."

Only now did Mordche remember that he had another package. He started to explain, telling about the wonderful day God had sent him, about the stranger he had met who had bought him meat and wine and given him a whole crown into the bargain; in short, he wanted to talk about all the good things that had happened to him on this summer afternoon. But the inspector ordered him to be silent.

He opened the package. It was wrapped in several layers of paper. In the end it turned out that it contained Russian snuff. Now Mordche did not know much about the Emperor's business, but he did know that the Emperor dealt in snuff among other things. No snuff other than that made in, and shipped from, the factories of His Majesty, Emperor Franz Joseph I, was allowed to be sold in the stores in Sereth—and the same was said to be the case in all other cities and villages of his realm. Like all Jews in Sereth, Mordche was a good patriot. But like all Jews, he had to admit that the snuff produced by the Russian Czar was incomparably superior to that of the Emperor Franz Joseph. This was why everybody preferred Russian snuff to Austrian. And its price was twenty times as high. Mordche also knew that the smuggling of Russian snuff was strictly forbidden and severely punished.

So when Mordche saw this amount of snuff in his package—or rather in the package that the stranger had asked him to hold—he was seized by such fear as he had only experienced once before in his life, when his phylacteries had accidentally slipped from his hands and fallen to the floor. He had had to fast for forty days to expiate that sin. But fasting saved money. Would the customs officers settle for a penalty of fasting? He wanted to propose this to them immediately, because he was afraid that the fine would be so large that he would have nothing left of the change from his crown.

The chief inspector did not grant Mordche so much as a look. He pressed a button. Another inspector appeared who was asked to call in the head of the customs station, Chief Commissioner Womula. Soon the room was filled with all the other officials. The tobacco was weighed and it turned out to amount to five pounds, four and six-sevenths ounces.

The Chief Commissioner said, "Man, do you realize what you've done? Do you know what the penalty for this is?"

"I didn't know anything about it," said Mordche. "A stranger gave me the package to hold for him. I don't know whether I have the right to leave it with you. I should talk it over with our rabbi first."

"Is your rabbi mixed up in this, too?"

"God forbid! Only, because the stranger gave me a crown, I have to ask the rabbi whether that made me a hired watchman, and therefore duty-bound to hold on to, and watch the package until the stranger asks for it back, or whether the crown could be considered a present, in which case I would be an unpaid watchman and have no obligation."

Mordche pulled at his beard and went on, "You see, gentleman, the case can be looked at this way and that. It all depends on the interpretation. Now, in the tract *Babamizia,* for instance—"

The Chief Commissioner interrupted him, "My dear sir, you are now in the Royal Imperial Customs House. There is no question of interpretation around here. You don't seem to be aware of what you've done."

Chief Commissioner Womula was a decent man. He believed Mordche's story. But what could he do? Snuff was a Royal Imperial monopoly and could not be imported into the territory of the Monarchy. Smuggling one pound of snuff was punished at the rate of a fine of a hundred-and-twenty-thousand crowns or a year in prison. He wanted to help the poor man, but it was impossible to suspend the proceedings, because Mordche had been asked twice by the inspector, in accordance with the regulations, whether he had anything to declare, and had twice answered no. The Commissioner by no means wanted to send him to prison for years, but he did have to take some official action. He knew that he would never lay eyes on the stranger who had given the package to Mordche. Smugglers were up to all kinds of tricks and always involved simple people in them.

At last he said to Mordche, "What you are going to talk over with your rabbi is your own business. As far as I'm concerned, I have to do my duty and fine you a large sum of money."

"Do I have to give you all the money I have?" Mordche asked in fright. "I've got seventy cents and I won't get another penny before Tuesday. My wife can't borrow anything anywhere because nobody'll lend her anything. Suppose I give you fifty cents and you let me keep the other twenty, because I'd like to give them to my wife."

The officers all laughed. "You can keep your seventy cents," said the Commissioner. He did some figuring. Then he said, "Your fine adds up to two-hundred-and-eighty-six-thousand-three-hundred-and-twenty crowns. This sum is to be remitted to the tax collector at Sereth as quickly as possible."

Mordche heaved a sigh of relief. Fifty cents would have hit him hard, and the blow would have been even harder had they asked him for six crowns. That was his average weekly earnings, and he had to feed his wife, his six children, and himself on it. But two-hundred-and-eighty-six-thousand-three-hundred-and-twenty crowns—he could not conceive of such a sum; he could not even imagine that the Emperor himself with all his various businesses had that much money.

So he asked, "Will you give me a certificate that I can show to the stranger when he comes which will show him that—God forbid—I didn't take his package. And may I also ask you if I can't have a little bit of this snuff for my box? If I could only have such fine Russian snuff in my box when I offer it to the gentlemen at the synagogue on Saturday. . . ."

The Chief Commissioner suppressed a smile and said, "I must draw your attention once more to the fact that the fine is to be remitted as soon as possible, and that until then all your assets, movable and immovable, as well as your income, are placed under official supervision and cannot be disposed of. It is therefore to your own interest to pay the sum to the tax collector at the earliest possible. . . ." Unobserved by the other officers, the Commissioner shook a little snuff into Mordche's box.

Happy and satisfied as he had not been for a long time, Mordche took the road home from Mihaleni to Sereth. He felt like Forefather Jacob after God had appeared to him in a dream on his journey to Haran. No, he thought, I have no obligation towards the stranger. The crown was a present, not payment for holding the package.

Next day, Mordche told everybody at the synagogue and in the street about the luck that had come his way, adding that he'd been fined a sum he could not even remember. Some of his listeners did not take the matter as lightly as Mordche. To have anything to do with a government was always a bad business, especially when it came to customs matters, about which the Emperor was very strict. Others thought that they knew the stranger. He was from Czernowitz, they said, and one of the smugglers of Russian snuff. But Mordche had already lost all interest in the matter. When a few days later the mailman brought him an official envelope, Mordche showed it around everywhere proudly. The Emperor was asking him for two-hundred-and-eighty-six-thousand-three-hundred-and-twenty crowns, and at the earliest possible, too. And there was a lot in it about movable and immovable assets, remittances, income, inheritance, liquidation and confiscation. Mordche didn't understand a word of it, and didn't try to either.

Every month a man in a green uniform would appear at Mordche the *shames'* house, with a paper form in his hand, and ask, "Are you ready to acquit yourself completely of the sum you owe the Imperial Treasury, or at least a substantial fraction thereof? If not, you will have to pay a bailiff's fee of one crown and six cents at once."

Mordche would answer that he was not in the position to pay the bailiff's fee of one crown and six cents, whereupon the man in the green uniform would ask him to sign a statement to the effect that he was unwilling to pay either the total sum, an installment on it, or even the bailiff's fee of one crown and six cents. Mordche always said on this occasion, "I want to, but I can't."

So the summer passed, then came the fall and made way for winter, and spring was setting in already, when the man in the green uniform appeared at Mordche's house for what was probably the eighth time. But this time things did not proceed with such formality. He informed Mordche that six dollars had arrived for him from America. Mordche was surprised at first. For more than ten years now his sister in New York had sent him six dollars each year at about this time. But it had always been Justfan, the mailman, who brought him the six dollars—or rather the six dollars already changed into Austrian money. The mailman would count out thirty crowns on the table and Mordche would always give him the five-cent delivery fee and then another five cents for a tip. Then, invariably, a discussion would follow on the blessings of the mails, which took six dollars in New York and paid out thirty silver crowns in Sereth.

Did he also owe him a five-cent delivery fee, Mordche asked the man in the green uniform? And he was ready to part with another five cents for a tip, in return for which he expected to be paid his sister's six dollars, changed into thirty crowns.

The man in the green uniform answered: "As your entire movable and immovable assets, as well as your income, principal and auxiliary, are under government sequestration, the government has confiscated these thirty crowns as the first installment on the sum you owe the Imperial Treasury. As your debt amounted to two-hundred-and-eighty-six-thousand-three-hundred-and-twenty crowns plus eight crowns and forty-eight cents accumulated bailiff's fees, your total debt now amounts to two-hundred-and-eighty-six-thousand-three-hundred-and-twenty-eight crowns and forty-eight cents. From this total, thirty crowns are deducted, which reduces your debt to the government to two-hundred-and-eighty-six-thousand-two-hundred-and-ninety-eight crowns and forty-eight cents.

"You see, Mr. Lew," he added, "your debt is shrinking very slowly. Have you got only one sister in America? Now if you had several and they sent you presents more often, you'd make quicker progress."

With these words, the man in the green uniform left Mordche the *shames'* dwelling.

Mourning reigned in Mordche's house. "It is said that joy comes with the arrival of the month of *Adar*," Mordche said to his wife, "but sorrow has come to us. What shall we do?"

The question was a difficult one. The thirty crowns Mordche received every year from his sister for Passover formed a substantial part of his income. They paid for the repairing and mending of the old shoes and clothes given to Mordche for his family during the year. As Mordche had realized long ago, people only gave away what they could no longer use themselves. He did not mind his children wearing grown-ups' shoes, if only they hadn't been so full of holes. Fortunately, Berl the shoemaker was a friend of his and would fix the shoes for a small sum. It was for this and the mending of the old clothes that the New York sister's thirty crowns were destined. And now all of a sudden the Emperor had taken the thirty crowns away. Despair was great in Mordche's house. But Mordche was a pious Jew who never lost his trust in God.

"I'm sure the Emperor would never have done this," he said to his wife, "if he knew our situation. They call him the Merciful Emperor. The question is how to tell him about this."

Mordche went from one lawyer to another. They all listened and they all gave him the same answer—there was nothing to be done in this kind of matter, and Mordche should consider himself lucky that the Treasury had shown him such leniency and had not thrown him into jail.

In the synagogue Mordche said to everybody, but especially to himself: "It's impossible, it just can't be that such a rich man as the Emperor, with so many businesses and on top of them all a printing press where he can make all the banknotes and coins he wants—for who can stop him?—it can't be that a man like that should take away six dollars from me, a poor *shames,* whose sister worked so hard for them." But the people who listened to Mordche offered him neither sympathy nor advice; instead, they warned him not to make seditious speeches.

On his return from the synagogue, he found Deaf Abraham, the corner scribe, waiting for him at home. Abraham was called the Deaf because his father had been deaf. Abraham's own hearing was normal. Deaf Abraham was considered Mordche's enemy because six years ago both he and Mordche had simultaneously applied for the post of *shames* at the synagogue, and Mordche had got the job. But now when Mordche was in need, it turned out that Abraham had secretly remained his friend.

"Mordche," said Abraham, "I heard of your great misfortune. I know it is as deep as the sea, but a pious Jew must never despair. We will both sit down and write a letter to the Emperor. Now show me all your papers."

Mordche found the letter that Justfan, the mailman, had delivered to him shortly after that fatal Sunday. Deaf Abraham read the document carefully, then shook his head. He understood its contents, and especially the terms, "movable and immovable assets," just as little as Mordche had.

"Listen, Mordche," he said, "go across to Nute Bender at the stationer's and buy a sheet of letter paper, a white envelope and a three-cent stamp."

Meanwhile Mordche's wife, Gittel, made potato soup, and Abraham was asked to stay to dinner. Mordche brought the paper. And after dinner Deaf Abraham examined his quills, chose the best one, and began to compose the following letter to the Emperor:

Dear Gracious Emperor: You do not know me. But your picture has been hanging on my wall for a hundred and twenty years next to the pictures of our Jewish benefactors, Baron Hirsch and Montefiore. My name is Mordche Lew, or more exactly, Mordche shames. *A* shames *has a sacred calling. But may God keep all Jews and all decent human beings from being* shameses. *There is no salary, and when there aren't enough candles it's my fault. If there's no money for wood in the synagogue, whose fault is it? Mordche* shames'. *If one of the worship-*

pers hasn't made enough money, he'll give me only six cents instead of ten cents a week, sometimes only five—and if he hasn't made anything at all that week, I haven't the heart to remind him. I am happy and satisfied when I make as much as six crowns a week as shames *and as helper to the teacher Jankel.*

As shames *it's my duty, to which I am accustomed, to obey everyone, to carry out any commission. Mordche, they say, take these fish home for me. Mordche, go get me my coat; it's going to rain. Mordche, take this note over to the wealthy Reb Shlomo. So the stranger at Mihaleni told me to keep his package until he would come for it. How was I to know what was in the package? A* shames *has to do what he is told and not ask questions.*

Mr. Emperor, you can ask anyone you please whether I ever dealt in snuff in all my life. In fact, I never dealt in anything. The stranger seemed a decent man and gave me a whole crown for a present. If I had known there was snuff in the package, I would have said: Gentlemen of the frontier, this package contains snuff but it does not belong to me. As soon as the stranger calls for it I will send him to you. But since I didn't know, I didn't say anything. So they fined me two-hundred-and-eighty-six-thousand-three-hundred-and-twenty crowns. If the employees of Your Majesty thought this was right, it must probably be so. And I accepted the responsibility. And I signed every month what I was asked to sign. But suddenly I was struck as though I had been hit over the head with a club. The thirty crowns that I wait and hope for all year long, the way I do for the Messiah, were taken away from me. It cannot be possible that you, my gracious Mr. Emperor, need my thirty crowns. And now I don't know how I'll get my poor children's shoes fixed. Don't think that the thirty crowns would make me a rich man. I have such worries that I wouldn't wish even half of them on my enemies. I beg you obediently to write to Sereth that they should return my thirty crowns and if possible that they should also not bother me about the matter of the snuff.

Your deeply sorrowing Mordche Lew, shames, *and his deeply sorrowing family.*

Mordche signed the letter. It was put into the envelope and addressed: "The Emperor Franz Joseph I in Vienna," and underneath Deaf Abraham added, "Very Urgent."

Berl the shoemaker was let in on the secret of the letter. Deaf Abraham guaranteed that this letter, which would have moved a stone, would not fail to have its effect on the Emperor. If the Emperor did not return the whole thirty crowns, Abraham said, he would at least send back fifteen. In view of the prospect offered by this letter, Berl the shoemaker agreed, in spite of all the difficulties that it might cause for him, to fix Mordche's shoes on credit until the money came from the Emperor.

Weeks of waiting passed. It was after Passover, and Whitsun was approaching. The newspaper reported various things from Vienna. The whole country, they said, was preparing to celebrate the sixtieth anniversary of His Majesty, Emperor Franz Joseph I's ascent to the throne. Beaming with joy, Deaf Abraham brought this news to Mordche *shames'* home.

"If the Emperor is going to celebrate his sixtieth jubilee," he said, "he won't bother much about thirty crowns. I think our prospects are favorable."

Then there came more news: the Emperor had added two new provinces to the Monarchy, Bosnia and Herzegovina. Deaf Abraham rushed again to Mordche and said: "Now I think there can't be any doubt left that the Emperor will pay back your thirty crowns. If he's acquired two new provinces, he must be richer than ever."

This time Mordche was skeptical. "It is my experience," he said, "that the richer people get, the less they understand the poor."

Deaf Abraham already looked upon the affair as his own. "With you it's a question of thirty crowns," he would say to Mordche, "and I can understand that the thirty crowns hurt you because you haven't got them and you can't pay what you owe shoemaker Berl; but with me it's a question of justice. When I write a letter I want it to have effect."

Deaf Abraham was not only a scribe; he was also the proprietor of the refreshment counter at the Sereth railroad station. His refreshment counter consisted of a handbasket containing a bottle of brandy and a few pieces of pastry. Four times a day he went to the station, twice before the arrival and twice before the departure of the trains. This gave him a chance to talk to many people, and now he turned all his conversation to the subject of the Emperor. Abraham inquired about everything: how much the Emperor's fortune was estimated to be, his profit from the sales of cigarettes and tobacco, his income from taxes, his expenses for the army and police, and for his personal needs. Did the Emperor eat a great deal, Abraham wanted to know, did he drink, and above all did he play cards? For Deaf Abraham had a fundamental theory—that human nature sets a limit upon eating and drinking; a rich man may eat and drink as much as he likes without risking his income or property; danger begins only when he falls victim to the passion for card-playing. Then he could lose his entire fortune down to his last under-pants in one night. Abraham felt greatly reassured when he was told that the Emperor was no card-player.

One day he turned up at Mordche *shames'* in a particularly cheerful mood. "Mordche," said he, "I have good news for you."

"Did an answer come from Vienna?"

"Not yet, but from what I've heard I no longer have much doubt that the Emperor will give back your thirty crowns."

"King Solomon, who was the wisest man in the world," answered Mordche *shames,* "said that a dead dog in my possession is better than a live lion in the bush."

"I don't see what the one has to do with the other. I'm talking to you about India and you answer me about Ethiopia. What have King Solomon's dead dog and live lion to do with our Emperor?"

"Too much. I'd rather have twenty crowns in my hand, or even fifteen, than the hope of getting all thirty."

"Mordche, why do you make a habit of not letting a person finish what he has to say? Listen to me. Yesterday at the station I met a traveling salesman from Vienna. He bought a glass of brandy from me and we got to talking. 'You're from Vienna,' I said, 'do you ever see the Emperor?' 'Almost every day,' he answered me. 'He goes for a drive in the streets in a beautiful carriage.' 'By himself, or with his wife and children?' I asked him. 'Our Emperor,' he answered, 'is the most unhappy man in the world. He is a widower and he has no children.' "

"No children?" cried Mordche in fright. "Whom is he going to leave his whole fortune to then?"

"That's just what I want to talk to you about. He's got a large country, and now he's added two new provinces to it, and he isn't a card-player. So what does he need your thirty crowns for? Do you understand now why my hopes and yours are justified?"

Mordche thought for a few moments. "An Emperor is not just anybody," he said. "He can't just go and die and leave a large country with a great network of businesses. He'll certainly pick out somebody to be his heir."

"Quite right. He's done that too, the salesman from Vienna told me. He's made some distant relative his heir. But you know, you feel differently toward your own flesh and blood than you do toward some distant tramp of a relative. Don't you know the story about the very rich man who had no children? One day his wife died. So he adopted a son and treated him like his own child and gave him the best education. Then one day—changeable as are the fortunes of man—a great misfortune befell the rich man. He was sentenced to death by hanging. They led him to the gallows. The whole town collected there weeping over his fate. His adopted son stood next to him. The judges were there, but no hangman could be found. The judges issued a proclamation: a thousand crowns to anyone willing to serve as hangman. Nobody came forward. Then the adopted son offered himself: 'Father,' said he, 'you will have to be hanged in any case. So why should a stranger and not I earn the money?' You see, Mordche, that's what an adopted son is. Now why, I ask you, would the Emperor be interested in leaving your thirty crowns to his adopted son—or the Heir to the Crown as they call him—in addition to a whole country with two new provinces and so many prosperous businesses? That's why I'm certain that he'll answer our letter favorably."

Like many other cities in the realm of His Majesty, Emperor Franz Joseph I, the city of Sereth prepared for the jubilee celebration of the Emperor's coronation. There was talk of an expected amnesty. It was rumored that the Emperor had decided, in connection with the jubilee, to cheapen the price of cigarettes, lower the tariff on flour and wine, and cut the tax on brandy. One Friday around noon, as Mordche was just about to go to the steam-bath, there appeared at his house a young man named Lewitzki who was orderly to the Provost Marshal of the district. Lewitzki was an impudent young fellow and sported the largest curled moustache in all Sereth. He considered his job more important than that of the Provost Marshal himself. Provost Marshals, he used to say, come and go; they depend on the whims of the Provincial Governor; but their orderly is securely ensconced in his office. And therefore Lewitzki addressed everybody in a familiar manner. He usually entered without knocking and his tone of voice was one of official command.

Thus Mordche was much surprised when Lewitzki greeted him with a civil good morning, gave him, Mordche the *shames*, his hand and said in the politest tone: "Mr. Mordche Lew, the Provost Marshal begs that you come to his office. He says he has an important communication for you from the Chancellory of His Majesty, our august Monarch, Franz Joseph. A joyful communication, the Provost Marshal asked me to inform you. It has something to do, he says, with the amnesty and with the magnanimity that the Emperor is now bestowing, and has for sixty years bestowed, upon everyone. So please come soon, and if it turns out to be something extra good, remember Gregory Lewitzki who has always been your friend."

Mordche was dazed with surprise. His children helped him to shine his shoes, while his wife got his Sabbath trousers and his Sabbath cloak out of the chest. He curled his ear-locks and put on the velvet hat his father-in-law had given him twenty years ago as a wedding present. Accompanied by the blessings of his family, he set out for the Provost Marshal's.

But first of all, he wished to tell his friend, benefactor, and helper, Deaf Abraham. At this time on Friday Abraham was always at the bathhouse where Mordche himself would have been had the Provost Marshal not summoned him. Mordche therefore made a detour across Volksgarten Street and Einbrunnen Alley and headed straight for Herman's bathhouse.

He knew the rules of the place well enough to know that no one in clothes was ever allowed inside—but who with a heart so full could be expected to care about rules and customs? He rushed past the bath manager, Herman, and Mikita his assistant, and burst straight into the steam room.

"Abraham, my friend," he cried, "do you hear me?" For it was impossible to make out anyone in the steam.

"Is that you, Mordche?"

"Yes, it is. The Emperor has answered."

"What does he say?"

"I don't know yet. Put on your clothes in a hurry. Lewitzki came for me. He said that the Chancellory has written that I'm going to get a jubilee present from the Emperor."

"What did he say about the thirty crowns?"

"I'm supposed to go to the Provost Marshal's immediately."

"Why did the Emperor write to the Provost Marshal when he could have written direct to you? But wait a minute, I'm going to get dressed and come with you."

"You're going? We're all going!" came a shout from the benches on which the bathers sat. In a minute the bathhouse was empty. Mordche went in front, followed by all the bath-house customers, many of them with their beards still dripping with moisture.

"Mordche," some of them begged, "put in a good word for us. Don't forget your friends and neighbors in the hour of your happiness."

The procession grew. Women left their stoves, children their play. Soon they all stood before the office of the Provost Marshal. Only Mordche was allowed in by Lewitzki. The others had to wait outside. Lewitzki locked the door behind him and accompanied Mordche to the Provost Marshal's private office.

He knocked on the door and cried in an official voice: "Mordche Lew, *shames!* Go in please!"

"Are you Mr. Mordche Lew?" asked the Provost Marshal.

"Don't you know me, Mr. Provost Marshal?"

"Of course I know you. But your identity has to be ascertained officially. You wrote a letter to His Majesty, the Emperor, concerning a fine of two-hundred-and-eighty-six-thousand-three-hundred-and-twenty crowns. Is that correct or isn't it?"

"Excuse me, Mr. Provost Marshal. I and my friend Deaf Abraham wrote to the Emperor that I'd been fined this sum—I don't really know how much it is—because of a package that didn't belong to me. And I wouldn't have bothered the Emperor about that, except that they took thirty crowns away from me. If Berl the shoemaker hadn't fixed our shoes in the expectation that the Emperor would return the thirty crowns he took away from me, my children would be running around barefoot right now."

"This is not a matter of thirty crowns," the Provost Marshal interrupted him. "His Majesty has graciously deigned to read your letter and has ordered his Chancellory to remit one-hundred-and-forty-three thousand-one-hundred-and-sixty crowns of your fine by way of grace. So that you now only owe the Imperial treasury another one-hundred-and-forty-three-thousand-one-hundred-and-sixty crowns plus accumulated fees, from which thirty crowns have been deducted. Will you be good enough to remit this remainder at once? For rarely has a subject been granted such a favor. Please sign this document signifying your grateful and obedient acceptance of this gift of one-hundred-and-forty-three-thousand-one-hundred-and-sixty crowns."

Mordche signed and waited.

"What are you waiting for?" asked the Provost Marshal.

"For the money," said he.

"What money?"

"The money I signed for and gratefully and obediently accepted. Or is it paid at the tax collector's?"

"Don't you understand Mr. Mordche? Half your fine has been remitted to you. The thirty crowns were deducted."

"And who's going to pay Berl the shoemaker for fixing the children's shoes?"

"Mr. Mordche, you will have to try to show yourself worthy of His Majesty's magnanimity by paying the remainder of your fine as quickly as possible."

With this the interview ended.

As Mordche came out of the Provost Marshal's office, he was surrounded by hundreds of people in a flash. "Is it true," he was asked, "what Lewitzki's been telling us? Is it true that the Emperor made you a gift of almost a hundred-and-fifty thousand crowns for his jubilee?"

"It's true," said Mordche, "but God in Heaven knows how I'm going to pay Berl the shoemaker who needs the money so badly. My poor thirty crowns for which my sister had to work so hard—but it's not for nothing that they say that the rich don't understand the poor."

"Long live His Majesty!" someone shouted, "long may he live!"

And the Sereth band, which had heard about the great event and was now assembled outside the building, struck up the Imperial hymn, "United fast with Hapsburg's crown, eternally Austria's fate will be."

THE HEAVY LOSER
OR A SCHLEMIHL IN THE GOLD RUSH

This letter is no mere invention of a writer of dialect humor. It is authentic down to its most bizarre misspelling and was printed originally in Publications of the American Jewish Historical Society *to afford its readers an insight into the life of the Jewish pioneers during the fabulous gold-rush days in California. Alexander Mayer, the writer of the letter, was an immigrant from the German Rhineland. Like thousands of other Americans of every national origin, he was dazzled by the glitter of "golden opportunities" in the Western frontier, and pell-mell left Philadelphia for the wide-open spaces. It goes without saying that not only was young Mayer a pipe-dreamer, he was also a first-class* schlemihl. *Whatever he laid his hands to prospered—with trouble. Though lured on by the most grandiose hopes, he had forebodings of disaster. He wrote to his "dear onckel" while en route to San Francisco; ". . . a man is bound to make money in California such an Expence it is Tremendous it is very likly if it goes that way I have not enough money to Go in the steerage. Since I heard such News I have got no appotide."*

Everybody in San Francisco was making money except Alexander Mayer. Something dreadful was always happening to him. If it wasn't a series of fires which brought him heavy losses, it was the most outrageous thefts; if it wasn't an earthquake, it was the most cutthroat competition. If you were to take him seriously you'd think the city was just full of Jewish traders and shopkeepers. He complained: "There are so many jehudem (Jews) Here in Business and Every One Want

to Sell." You'd naturally think he'd buy his return passage to Philadel-
phia for "130 doll." On the contrary, he went wild with hopefulness.
After a fire he wrote to his friend Edwin in Philadelphia on May 12,
1851, "Dear Edwin, I had britty heavy Losses in this Fire. from 4 to
5000. . . . Try Yourself and come here if your Parents let you go. I
think we can make money. You & Me." N.A.

SAN FRANCISCO June 30th 1851

Mr L Mayer
  Philadelphia
    Pa
DEAR UNCLE.

    Enclosed Please find a Bill of Laiding for One Hundred Aunzes
of Gold Dust. shipped by the Pacific Mail Steamship Co. which I paid
for Freight & Box 34^{50}/$_{100}$ I am in Hopes that you are in Receit of
my Last Letter and Tow Packages sent by Adams & Co^s. Express.
The Claims Against the Insurance Co. Damaged by ship Masonic &
Mazatlan, And I am in Hopes that the Same will be Paid, and also
I think that we are Entitled to get the whole Amount of the Bills. It
is not my fault that this Goods got Burned up The Porte Warden
Said that Day and Ordered the Said Goods to Auction by the Next
Week And the Fire Consumed the Goods on the Same Day or at
least the Same Night. Dear Uncle it is hard for me to write you Again
about my Misfortune I had on the 22nd of June. A Large Fire took
Place again. And I am an Heavy Looser again. I can not Blame myself, I have not neglect a Minute to Move. And I worked till the Last
Minute. I know I have been in my Store and the Fire Men Scrimed I
shall go out of the Store the fire is Behind me. I thought then it is the
best for me to go out the Store. Rather let them Goods Burne then
my self, I know You dont want medo that

    Even I had a great many Goods out of my Store a great many
Burned up and some I safed. and Good many getting Stolen. it is
Likely that I get some back again, A Person at Home cannot Imagin
this fire's what takes Place Here. I know very well that Day I would
been glad to give One Hundred Dolls for a Dray $100 pr Load I could
not get any to safe my Life, The whate I have saved I had the Goods
Laying were other People had theirs Laying. and mine Caught fire,
and others did not. I put the fire out with my Hands, and then I
hollerd out I give any Men $5. to Carry a Load or at Least an Armfull
away or Else every thing would went to the Devil. If it goes that way
after while I could not Buy me a Pair Shoes. I had 5 Packages down

from the Palatine when the Fire took place. the most of this I have saved the Parrasols I did not loose One 3 or four got brock it is astonishing such Article to safe like they got Handlet about. the Market is full with Parrosols and Carpet Bags Since the Last 3 weeks. This June fire I shall recolect for atime hence The May Fire I did not mind so much. as I do this. I wrote you in May for Some Goods to sent me, I am in hopes thate You did note sent them. it might be good andit might not. and in the Same time I wrote you that I will be Home by next fall. But you need not Expect me in the least: I shall stay Here now And try to make up my Losses. My wish is only to bring back Again whate I brought Here there fore it is impossible for me to tell when I go back Again. You may Really Belive me Since I left Philadelphia I look ten years Older. In all my Days alife I have not been so down Hearted as I have been for the Last 6 weeks. Some of this Days I shall write more definete whate Stock I have got on Hand and whate I have lossed by the Two fires Lazard & Goldman have lossed Heavy also. there fore look out for Straus & Goldman if you have sold them any thing. Potsdamer & Rosenboum Lossed $14.000 again they been living 4 squares further down where I lived for Safity they Moved their Goods, Some Men had their goods Laying along side P & R. did not Burne up and their Goods Burned up? a Man got one Misfortune then Comes one after the other. Edwin you write me in Your Last Letter Keep on I shall keep on with my Segars. I done so. I thought so myself. I should have a Profit. Now I got a good price John Fire have not been Perticular about the price Cleared them out all of them except Some boxes for me to Smock. the Segars which you sent me by the Barque Palatine I have not Opened them Yet I stored them. and some more Goods Besides. About the Market I Can not write You much the Market Dull and prices Low. This fires dont affect any the Market. Contary it makes every think quired. This week I have seen selling at Auction Some Prints at 5½ ¢ pr yard home cost 9¢. and Some 4 to 4½ Home cost 7 to 7¼ My Candles I tried them at Auction 20 Boxes I had Sold for 32½¢ pr lbs Simon Shloss sold some for 37½ but cost at Home 42½ the Real Sperm that is the way it goes here. If I would want to keep mine I could Solt them by a Couple of Boxes at 35¢. Ed you wrote me about Mr Finks Papers I shall attent to it I shall go up to Sacromanto City Soon and try to find Woodward out and do my best. The Expense I make I shall charge to Mr Fink it cost me at least $20. to go up. I was Sorrow to hear that my Aunt was sick But I am glad that She has recovered her Healths again in my Gold Box I sent you oppened you will find

a Letter and a Specimen for my Aunt   the Specimen ways 2¾ aunz
Give my best Respects to Mr & Mrs Bomeisler Eveline Cha^r. Thea.
and all Inquiry friends. hoping that this Letter will find all of you in a
Perfect State of Healths, I am quit well hoping you do a Goods Buiss-
ness at Home and not Loose much I remain Yours Truely A Mayer
Give my best respects to Tomi Lipper   Mr Bodenheim and Sharff
are going away from Here do. they go to Europe   they come Prob-
abley to Philadelphia they come to see You   they live here by next
Mail. Simon Shloss is Selling off fast and intents to go Home Soon
a great many will go back again next fall. Stein lossed some by the last
fire too. in the Last fire were Tow jehudem Burned to deaths again
they stoot in their Store to save their goods   And a Mr Polock from
Phila^a. was shot from another Men. the Same Day the fire took place
I expect You know him. he was quit a Gentleman   He is a Brother of
Mrs. Binswanger   His Business were Gambling. that is all the News
I can write You Except they Catch the Man who put they City in fire
again a Neger   he was instructid of a Women   a Low Live they
arrest both of them. that is a great Country   I hope you can read this
and remain Yours &c. &c. &c.

(*signed*) A. MAYER

Jewish Animals

*One could live—
but they don't let you!*

A JEWISH CAT

BY S. J. AGNON
TRANSLATED FROM THE HEBREW BY I. M. LASK

One Thursday Tsirel Treine took the knife to cut up the meat
and found that her hand wouldn't obey her. What's this, Tsirel Treine,
said she to herself, all these chickens that you prepared today, and the
New Moon feast you prepared for the fine folk of the town, without
anything wrong with your hand, and now it has to go and trouble you?
She spat behind her, stuck the knife in the poultry and carved them
up into pieces, putting each piece in the pot, took the innards of the

chickens and set them on the floor so that Lasunka could come and take her due.

But Lasunka never came. Tsirel Treine laughed to herself, saying Oho, Lasunka, proud you're becoming, eh? Well, we'll see who needs who? And in this Tsirel Treine erred, thinking that Lasunka required her; this was not so, for had it not been for Lasunka the meat would have been spoilt through lying about, but Lasunka's movements forced her to be spry.

Just then she heard Esther Malka calling, Tsirel Treine, have you prepared everything? Tsirel Treine lifted up her knife and called back, Mistress, mistress. Into the kitchen came Esther Malka and asked, What is it, a problem for the rabbi again? Tsirel Treine turned her eyes on Esther Malka and said, Lasunka's not here. Silly, replied Esther Malka, wait until she smells the innards and she'll be here quick enough. Then Tsirel Treine pointed with the knife in her hand to the offal on the floor and silently shook her head.

Esther Malka went red in the face trying to remember when and where she had last seen Lasunka. Why, she cried at length in grief, I haven't seen her at all today. And either of the two turned her pale startled face to t'other. And since they saw no reason for hope their sudden grief increased. If she wasn't in the house where could she be? Never had she been seen under a neighbor's rooftree. Lasunka was an aristocrat and knew her place, which was in front of the fire smoothing her fur on wintry days, and sunning herself in the open during summer. Observe, Lasunka used to seem to remark; everything there is in the house can equally well be found in the open. For your stove and mice in the house there are your sun and birds in the open. And therein Lasunka laid herself open to the charge of the heresy of dualism, for she did not know that Man is likewise the handiwork of the Holy and Blest One, so that if he did stoke the stove and warm up the house, it was all equally of His blessed light

And now Esther Malka remembered that her husband would be returning from the House of Study and, sitting down to eat, would wish to feed pieces to Lasunka—and she would not be there. So Esther Malka stretched out her two hands and cried, Lasunka, Lasunka, where are you, Lasunka? Tsirel Treine, seeing the sorrow of Esther Malka, said to herself, Seeing that the mistress takes on so, it's a sign that I shan't be held responsible for Lasunka but she will be; it isn't from me the master will demand Lasunka but from her. And she straightway, having found herself some comfort, returned to her work.

And so Esther Malka was left standing and scratching her head, as was her habit when confronted by matters beyond her understanding. Since she saw no way out she said to herself, Lasunka won't be found so quickly, so what am I to do but see that Israel Solomon is delayed and doesn't sit down to eat at once. For Esther Malka waited on Time to do its work. It was like the case of the tollkeeper to whom the lord of the manor gave a dog to be taught to pray in the prayer book. If I refuse, thought the tollkeeper, he'll kill me out of hand, so instead I'll fix him a time; meanwhile either I'll die or he'll die or the dog'll die.

After Tsirel Treine had scrubbed the pot and wiped the knife she went out into the street and asked the passers-by, Maybe you've seen Lasunka? And she stood asking, Have you seen Lasunka, have you seen Lasunka? And straightway everybody knew that Lasunka had run away. Folk began joking and said, Now Reb Israel Solomon will have to feed his leavings to the mice.

But when they thought the matter over they began wondering what Lasunka could have seen to run away. Particularly on a Thursday when kitchens are full of chicken gizzards and innards. One man in the street came out, after the fashion of such, with the explanation, Why, it's plain as plain can be; this is the month of Adar, which comes out the same time as what the gentiles call March; and it's a widespread custom throughout the cat world that in the month of March cats go out climbing on the roofs; rest assured Lasunka hasn't cut herself off from the rest of the cat community.

It happened that just then along came a village Jew who had been expelled from his inn, and now came to beg Reb Israel Solomon to intercede with the lord of the manor on his behalf. Said he, Stop your joking. Who knows what this vanished Lasunka was ere she was a cat, or what incarnation she might have been? And all the townsfolk cried out in wonder, An incarnation now?

The village Jew looked all round him first, and then whispered, I'll tell you. Probably Lasunka was Reb Israel Solomon's beadle in an earlier incarnation, and Reb Israel Solomon didn't treat him properly; just as he oppresses all his servants, so he oppressed that selfsame beadle. And when that beadle came to die it was decreed on high that he must return to This World, as it says in Proverbs "to punish the just is not good"; and our sages of blessed memory said in the Talmud, "Nobody on account of whom a fellow man is punished is brought within the bounds of the Holy and Blest One"; and therefore he descended and was incarnated in a cat; and now that Reb

Israel Solomon has righted in Lasunka what he wronged toward the beadle, and the soul has been righted and the days of the incarnation are at an end, that selfsame soul no longer has any business to attend to in this Lower World; and therefore Lasunka has vanished, and I tell you there's no hope whatsoever of finding her.

When Reb Israel Solomon heard that Lasunka had vanished he quivered at the tidings as at a blow. Nonetheless he did not put any blame on the folk of his household; but the sorrow glistening in his eyes seemed to speak all the iniquities in the world. You might have thought that whoever did not return Lasunka to him must have smuggled her away. And on the Sabbath Eve he felt her absence even more. Reb Israel Solomon was accustomed, when he entered his house on Sabbath Eve and began repeating the "Peace be unto you, angels of peace, ministering angels," to have Lasunka jumping up toward him and catching the tassels of his girdle; the savor of the hallowing wine and the fish made her very wise, as it says in the Talmud that wine and scents make one clearheaded. He in turn would amuse himself watching her motions and jumping, and with a sweet voice would sing "Who shall find a woman of valor."

But this Sabbath Reb Israel Solomon entered his home as one might enter a house of mourning, the Merciful One prevent us and deliver us; he repeated the "Peace be unto you" in a low voice, and hallowed the wine in so dejected a tone that Tsirel Treine's eyes filled with tears and she vowed a half-pound of candles to the synagogue when Lasunka would be found. She also thought upon going to Issachar Demon so that he might tell her where Lasunka was.

Reb Israel Solomon broke bread and dipped it in salt, sat back comfortably in his chair and stretched out his legs, expecting that they would meet Lasunka's plump body; but they remained hanging stretched. And to whom might Reb Israel Solomon be then compared? To a man falling in dream from the roof into a deep pit; although he is not injured the feeling of tumbling shakes him up.

That night Reb Israel Solomon paid no attention to the guest he had brought home with him for the Sabbath. The guest, seeing that the house was full of good cheer and the household vessels bore witness that the master of the house must be wealthy, sat wondering why the faces of the household folk should be so downcast, and all the more so on the Sabbath. Seeing that the great trouble of that poor fellow was how to make a living he could not so much as imagine that there might be any other worry. But being modest and humble he did not even dare to open his mouth and ask.

Instead he remembered that in the countries of the west there is a wealthy Jew who cannot eat unless he be told something new; all the desirable things of earth are worthless to him compared with travelers' tales, and whoever brought him news of something fresh was well entreated by him. And he thought to himself, How many tales I have heard on my travels, like the story of the gluttonous preacher, and the story of the horses that went astray, and the story of the reprover who stuck his head inside the Holy Ark during his sermon and stole the holy vessels. And these tales are so well fitted to cheer downcast spirits, like those two men in the Talmud who diverted the sorrowful; and if the master of the house were to hear them he would pay me well, so that I could buy grain and send it to my wife to do business with; but what can be done when poverty puts me out of my mind, so that I can't even open my mouth before such great folk.

Directly after the Sabbath night Havdala ceremony Tsirel Treine put on her weekday clothes and went off to Issachar Demon. She found Issachar sitting on a clay bench plaiting twigs for a besom. As she came in he dropped the twigs and shaded his eyes with his hand to see who had entered. Recognizing her he rubbed his two hands together and asked, Well, Tsirel Treine, what news have you to tell? I wish there weren't any news, she replied. Haven't you heard that Lasunka's run away? Then you're the only person as doesn't know.

To which Issachar replied proudly, If I'm not told I don't know anything. And while speaking he held his ear to the oven wall as though he was told everything from thence. The oven creaked and Tsirel Treine jumped. Don't be afraid, silly, Issachar scolded her. Some dead bird fell down from the chimney. I'm no Master of the Holy Names nor do I practice witchcraft.

She took heart and told him the whole story. I see, said Issachar, that you were told before I was, so why have you troubled to come to me? And Tsirel Treine began fearing to utter a word lest she spoil everything. I don't need your chatter, added Issachar, and you don't have to tell me anything. And while speaking he bent a number of rods into all manner of peculiar shapes. Tsirel Treine stood in despair, not yet certain what she should do. A sudden thought occurred to her; she put her hand in her pocket and began jingling the coins she had there, in order to let Issachar know she didn't want him to have all his trouble for nothing; and she called him Reb Issachar in order to flatter him. Where's there a Reb Issachar? Issachar scolded her again. Who's Reb Issachar here? Do you think I'm a Master of the Names? If you annoy me I'll tell you a Master of the Names saw that Lasunka of yours and killed her so's to turn her skin into parchment for charms.

At this Tsirel Treine's legs began trembling, and she came over weak; and if she hadn't remembered that all the prospects of finding Lasunka depended upon that seance she'd have tumbled over backward. And there was an angry silence until the wind could be heard blowing amid the twigs. Issachar rose and said, Do you know what the rods are twittering? She'll be back, whisper the rods; She'll be back, whisper the rods. Tsirel Treine took out four groschen to pay him and hurried out before he'd have time to prophesy otherwise. Once she was outside she said to herself, Womenfolk are highty-flighty and forgetful. Why didn't I ask him when? She was in two minds whether to return or not; but going back is a bad sign, may it be for the foes of Israel. So she up wi' her legs and went back to her mistress' house, half hoping, half annoyed.

As long as the mice had been afraid of Lasunka you never even heard the whisper of a mouse; but now she had vanished they could be heard all over the house. Once it even happened that Reb Israel Solomon woke thinking the beadle had knocked him up, and went to the House of Study before the stove had so much as been stoked. All that time, they say, there was no end to the turmoil and disturbance in Reb Israel Solomon's house. There was a complete set of the Babylonian Talmud there which he had inherited from his fathers, and which had never passed through the hands of the censor. The mice made a conspiracy against it and turned it into a pile of paper scraps. There were manuscripts in the house which the great ones of the age had left with him when they had been suspected of belonging to the sect of Sabbethai Zevi; the mice conspired against them and turned them as well into a pile of paper scraps. Tsirel Treine, in haste to fulfill her vow, bought half a pound of candles; but before ever she had a chance of taking them to the synagogue there was not even as much left of them as the tail of a wick. His in-law, Simeon Nathan, sent him his own cat, Shinra, which killed many of them. Thereupon the folk of Shebush, growing jealous of Simeon Nathan, wished to send their own cats as gifts to Reb Israel Solomon; but all this happened in the month of March, when the cats go up on the roofs about their lawful occasions, and you couldn't find a cat for a guinea. The scamps and loafers went up on the roofs after them, and came back with scratched faces and eyes and torn clothes and empty hands.

Meanwhile Shinra took up her residence with Reb Israel Solomon, at whose home they gave her food and drink while she did her duty by him. And she too kept Tsirel Treine lively, while Esther

Malka secretly began to hope that her husband would stop grieving for Lasunka. But Reb Israel Solomon couldn't even let his eyes rest on Shinra. He knew, did Reb Israel Solomon, that Lasunka wasn't dead; a dead thing or person is sure to pass out of mind, but Lasunka still kept her place in his heart.

Now the village Jew already spoken of would often come to beseech Reb Israel Solomon to entreat with the Lord of Shebush for an inn to be leased to him, but Reb Israel Solomon wouldn't take any notice of him. Throughout those days Reb Israel Solomon disregarded all the affairs of the community, and did not even attend to wheat money for the poor. As long as the community could get on without Reb Israel Solomon it was not so hard, but as soon as it proved impossible to go further without Reb Israel Solomon, matters became very serious indeed.

It happened that gentiles came to return the Jews the fine clothes they were wont to borrow on their Sabbaths when they go to their churches, and they reported that the chief of all their priests was coming to Shebush from the metropolis. How can we honor this great bishop, asked the Jews, when he comes to Shebush? It is a time-old custom that when a prince comes to a town the Jews go out to meet him with the Scrolls of the Torah, and the gentiles, pardon the allusion, with bread and salt. They go with theirs and we come with ours.

There were such present as protested against that selfsame custom, saying, God forbid that we should drag about the Scrolls of the Torah for the sake of an evil and vicious oppressor of Jews; and what'll we do if his wicked mind tempts him to do to the Written Torah what his comrade, may his name be blotted out, did to the Oral Torah when he went and burnt all those sets of the Talmud? But the others repeated, A Jewish custom's the law and a custom can't be changed. But in order to prevent any quarrels we'll take out spoilt Scrolls and array them in expensive covers and holy vessels, and the bishop won't know.

And something similar was told them by a certain Sephardic Jew who came to sell raisins for Passover wine, and related how in his city it was the custom, when a pasha came to the town, to take the silver cases (in which the Sephardim keep their Scrolls of the Law) without any scrolls inside, and bring them out to greet him. But once when the pasha had to come there was a certain convert who came to the pasha and said to him, Don't imagine for a moment that those Jews give you the honor you deserve. And how do you know? he asked. Tomorrow, answered he, they will come out to meet you with their Scrolls. Tell them to open their cases and you'll see they're empty.

On the morrow the pasha came to the town and all Israel came out to meet him; and he at once ordered them to open their cases. But what had the Holy and Blest One done? He had prepared the remedy before the blow. The night before, the beadle of the synagogue had dreamt of all this, and had gone and put the books back in their places; and so when the evildoer opened the cases he found them full of Scrolls. Thereupon the pasha hewed the evildoer in little pieces, but always favored Israel thereafter.

At which Shebush said, We'll do the same. As the Talmud says, Miracles aren't to be depended on. They sent to Reb Israel Solomon but received no reply; they sent again and still received no reply. So they visited him to hear what he thought. Just then Pinye Pest passed by. Reb Israel Solomon saw him and banged on the windowpane. Enter Pinye. Pinye, said Reb Israel Solomon, Well? What are *you* doing? I swear by my beard, said Pinye, seizing it, that I shan't depart from the world until I've brought her to you. So seeing how troubled and despondent Reb Israel Solomon was they decided to hold a second meeting.

And what were the gentiles doing meanwhile? They were draining the puddles in the streets and repairing the roads and sweeping away the snow and whitewashing the outsides of their houses. Gentlefolk among them came and borrowed fine shawls and cloths of the Jews for to adorn their windows, and Shebush, the city, was bright and lively. Her houses hummed and her streets were full. Women were selling crucifixes in the streets, and all manner of sweetmeats made to look like the great bishop robed in his vestments, with little angels dancing and prancing round about him.

Those cakes were baked by the aunts of the town priest, for it is the custom of their priests, who do not marry, that they keep their aunts in their homes to look after the household. And they were busy cleaning and polishing their ikons and images, and framed them in silk and set a big box in the hands of the chief image, so that it should open the hearts of the gentiles to give much charity. And at the entry to the town they put up poles on either side, joined by planks on which they hung all kinds of flags and a silken canopy beneath it, so that the bishop might enter with fitting ceremony and honor.

But the Children of Israel remained at home in sorrow and concern, taking no steps to entreat the bishop with honor when he might arrive in Shebush, even though this might lead the Gentiles to say, You hate your fellow men; here's our bishop come to town and you haven't lifted a finger to receive him; and the following day he would deliver venomous sermons in order to harm them. There was never a Jew in Shebush at the time but grieved that Lasunka had run away.

On that day the village Jew of whom we have told went out of town. Said he to himself, there are many gentiles will be coming to town from the hamlets, and they'll be sure to bring poultry with them for sale, so I'll go along to meet them and buy a chicken for the Sabbath. But though he stood without the town he found nothing, for all the gentiles had already gone to church. When the Lord approves the paths of a man, said the village Jew to himself, he will not forsake him. With the words yet in mind and on the tip of his tongue he saw a cat before him, and he laughed and said, That's the Shebush saying, a cat or a cock, long as there's a fowl for the Sabbath. And he made a dash for the cat.

It stood calmly as though it were awaiting him. When he reached it, it scratched his hand and his face and fled. The village Jew took some of his spittle and rubbed it into the scratch saying, Lord of the Universe, come and have a look what you've done to me. Here I came out to buy a chicken and found a cat. I didn't keep any bad thoughts in mind about Your methods but said, I'll take the cat to town and they'll pay me for my trouble and I'll make Sabbath; but when I tried to catch it, it ran away, and what's more it scratched me across the face, and how shall I go back to town now? For he had recognized that the cat must be Lasunka.

While he was standing there he suddenly saw some poor man before him. You've set some fine marks on yourself, said he. Your mother wouldn't mix you up with anybody else now. That's right, said the villager, go mocking me when I'm in pain. God forbid, said the other. But I can tell you sure enough that this here's a queer town. Shebush piles up its troubles from all the world over. You're making two mistakes, my friend, said the villager. First of all I'm not from Shebush, and, second of all, Shebush enjoys a right good laugh. Well, says the other, a man can't know more than what his eyes tell him. One Sabbath not long ago I was the guest of a rich Jew named Reb Israel Solomon, and he's the warden of this town if you don't mind; and he couldn't even taste a crumb of bread because of the grief that reigned in his house.

Why, said the villager, even my botheration only comes about because of Reb Israel Solomon's sorrow. And what have you to do with Reb Israel Solomon? asked the other. Reb Israel Solomon, explained the villager, had a cat called Lasunka which has run away. And maybe you ask what I have to do with Lasunka? I'll tell you. You see these hands? They all but caught Lasunka. Do you see this face o' mine? Lasunka did that to me. And had I been worthy in the eyes of the All-Present I'd ha' caught her and brought her to Reb Israel Solomon, who'd then pay attention to my needs; but now I haven't been found worthy I stand here empty-handed.

The poor man began comforting him and he, his bitter mood being gone, said to the other, I see you're going back to town. But I must warn you that it's bad to go there because the townsfolk are angry with the Jews for not going out to greet that bishop o' theirs. And so maybe you're wondering what we're going to eat? Here's a spring, and I have something in my bag. So let's wash our hands and sit down.

When they sat down to eat Lasunka smelt the food. Said she to herself, That smell reminds me of eggs and onions; I'll go along and give a sniff. Out she jumped and went and stuck her head in the bag. And what did they do? The poor man threw the skirts of his overcoat over her, and the villager tied her legs together with his girdle. And once they had Lasunka safe and sound in their hands they up with their feet and ran towards town, shouting, Lasunka, Lasunka.

As soon as their voices were heard, all Shebush began wailing, Woe's us for we're lost; the townsfolk are coming to take our lives. And thereupon the butchers said to one another, why are we sitting quiet, waiting for them to come and break our necks like so many calves? If he can't save our lives, we'll save the Scrolls of the Torah. So they armed themselves with their cleavers and out they went. When they were out of the Jewish Quarter they saw two Jews running and yelling, Lasunka, Lasunka, and understood that Lasunka must have been found. Thereupon they too lifted up their voices for joy and ran along with them yelling, Lasunka, Lasunka.

At the fresh outcry the porters called to one another, How long shall we sit quiet and do nothing while Jews are suffering? So they clapped their hands and out they went as well. Once they were out they heard that Lasunka had been found. And straightway they raised their voices, began yelling Lasunka, Lasunka, and went along with the others in great joy.

When the smiths saw the porters starting out, they applied the argument to themselves, saying, If those porters can go off to see what can be done although they have nothing more than shoulders on which to carry loads, shall we sit with arms folded when we all have our hammers and sleds? Up they heaved their tools and out they too went. Once they were out they heard the meowing of Lasunka. And they too raised their voices and began shouting, Lasunka, Lasunka, and joined the procession and ran along with tremendous joy.

Thereupon the tanners said, How long are we going to let the other artisans crow over us and say, you smell too bad to be given a share in anything holy? Now we'll show what we can do. So out they all went in turn. Once they were out they heard the noise around Lasunka. And they too raised their voices, yelling, Lasunka, Lasunka, and began running happily along with the rest of the procession.

When the householders saw all the workmen and artisans going off they wailed, Woe's us for these ruffians who bring down the anger of the gentiles on us; now they'll say all the Jews are murderers. So there was weeping and wailing on the one side and joy and dancing on the other. But when a long while had passed without anybody having been hurt they said to one another, It's written in Leviticus, "Thou shalt not stand over the blood of thy fellow," and came out of their hiding places.

When they came out they saw Jews running along yelling, Lasunka, Lasunka; and they understood that Lasunka had been found. Then they too began clapping their hands and yelling, Lasunka, Lasunka, until their throats were hoarse and they were so breathless they could only gasp, La, La. When the children saw that their fathers had gone out they too went out after them, climbed up the newly erected gate of honor and there stood crying, la la la. The womenfolk, hearing their children's voices, and recognizing how joyful they sounded, said to one another, It seems as though the Holy and Blest One must have wrought a miracle. And at once they put on their finest clothes and went out into the open and began clapping their hands and calling, la la la. The fiddlers and music makers peeping out saw women dressed in their best and dancing, and said to themselves, There's gladness in town. So they took their instruments and went out blowing and drumming and fiddling for all they were worth, and took up their stand near the entrance to the town.

And there was never a Jew in Shebush but went out to meet and greet Lasunka. They were following two Jews and patting the bundle those two held, and stroking Lasunka through the bundle and calling her by all manner of pet names. The butchers went ahead clashing their cleavers and fighting imaginary duels; the smiths swung their hammers until the sparks flew; the porters flung up their ropes on high, caught them as they descended and flung them up again; and the music makers were making music. And just at that time the bishop came past and saw all the Jewish population jubilating. Said he, And all these have come in honor of me; and at once he turned a bright and cheerful face upon them and began to speak in praise of them. And what was more he repented his former ways and became a lover of Israel. When the fine folk of the town saw how greatly the bishop approved of the Jews they said, And that's not all the Jews have done in your honor; the fine clothes the townsfolk are wearing in your honor today were borrowed from the Jews without any charge or fee. And they even admitted that the curtains and shawls with which they had adorned their own houses were borrowed from the Jews.

Meanwhile the poor man and the village Jew came to Reb Israel Solomon, bringing him Lasunka, who lay down on the ground and cried meow. Tsirel Treine began hugging her and loosened her bonds and cheered her up and said, What's the matter, Lasunka? Aren't you Lasunka? Aren't you my pussy? And Esther Malka came along and spoke sweetly to her, saying, Lasunka, Lasunka, her voice promising the cat all manner of good things for the future; and she bent and looked into Lasunka's eyes with her own fine weary eyes; and although there was no happiness on her face you could see that a great load was off her mind.

When the cat arrived Reb Israel Solomon was sitting in his place by the stove reading new legends and stories; for ever since Lasunka had disappeared he had not been in a condition to study as much as a page of Gemara; and his pipe was out. Esther Malka entered with the brightest of faces. What's the matter, Esther Malka? asked Reb Israel Solomon. Come into the kitchen a moment, said she. And why, asked Reb Israel Solomon, should you want me to come into the kitchen all of a sudden? I noticed your pipe is out, she answered, and thought you might care to take yourself a coal from the kitchen. He peered into her face, then cried, Lasunka? And Esther Malka turned her laughing face from him and went out.

He rose and followed. Before he reached the kitchen door he heard a meow and recognized that it was the voice of Lasunka. He opened the door, saw Lasunka couched on the floor, stretched out his hand to stroke her back and said, *oti Lasunka,* meaning, she's a glutton. But realizing at once that he was making mock of the unfortunate, for her shape bore witness that she had long forgotten the entire lore of eating, he ordered them to bring her white bread and milk. Then he bent down to the hearth to take himself a coal.

Thereupon the poor man on the one side, and the villager on the

other, leapt forward to serve him. Reb Israel Solomon raised his eyebrows and asked, Who are these? These people, said Esther Malka,
are the fine fellows who brought back Lasunka. Reb Israel Solomon
looked at them again and said, I believe I've already seen you both.

Thereupon the village Jew began to tell him the whole story of
his inn. But Reb Israel Solomon said to him, My dear Jew, now's no
time for words; and he gave them a purse full of coins to share. Then
he took them into the winter house, opened the box filled with bottles
of brandy, poured them out two glasses and cut them two slices of
cake, gave one to each and said, Say the blessing, and invited them
to eat dinner with him. After they had eaten, drunk and said benediction they entered a House of Study and divided the money between
them. The poor man went to the meal sellers with his share, took
some sacks of meal with which he did business, and made much profit.
After a time his business began to grow. Then he sent meal to the
village Jew. The village Jew entered the business, left his inn, established his dwelling with that of his family in town like all the other
Jews, prayed with full congregation every day and brought up his sons
to a knowledge of Torah.

To return to Tsirel Treine, with whom we began. Tsirel Treine
remembered the prophecy of Issachar Demon that Lasunka would
certainly return; and now that she was back, she went to buy a besom
from him so that he should also derive some benefit. But Issachar
mocked her, saying, And do you suppose that I can take besoms out of
my beard and earlocks? Don't you know that I've sold all the besoms
I made; because of the great dust that was raised on Lasunka's account all Shebush began to choke with dust, and they haven't left me
as much as a single besom.

Now to return to Reb Israel Solomon. When Reb Israel Solomon
saw Lasunka eating and drinking as usual he felt a great pity for her
and asked cunningly, Well, Lasunka, will you forsake us again to
follow the evil desires of your heart? But Lasunka never left Reb
Israel Solomon again; for she recognized that all the things she had
thought pleasures, and in which she had steeped herself, were not
equal to a single hour of quiet with a dish of milk and slice of bread
or chickens' innards or fishguts lying on the floor before her. And she
already desired to forget all she had done, but penitent thoughts led
her to twitch up her lips and stick out her pointed tongue; while a sort
of satisfied smile hovered round her mouth by reason of the pleasures
of life whch she had tasted in her time.

Under the watchful eye of Tsirel Treine her strength returned and her belly grew sleek and round and full. And Lasunka then left behind all her youthful indiscretions, and no longer continued to meditate on unworthy matters, such as the heresy of dualism and the like.

And though she might have lost her speed she retained her stealth, and the dread of her remained so strong among the mice that they veritably lost their senses at her voice. And at the end of the appointed period her womb brought forth many tiny creatures the like of which she had never seen in all her life. But before long they had grown to delight the eye of everyone who saw them, with their charm and graceful movements. And she brought them up to do their duty and hunt mice and make an end of them in Shebush.

RABCHIK

A JEWISH DOG

BY SHOLOM ALEICHEM
TRANSLATED FROM THE YIDDISH BY NATHAN AUSUBEL

Rabchik was a spotted white dog. He wasn't by any means a big dog, only a medium-sized one. He was always quiet and well-behaved, and he wasn't the grabbing sort either. Unlike other dogs, he never tried to attack anybody when his back was turned, or to tear off the hem of his coat, or to bite him in the shins. As long as no one bothered him he was content. But, as if for spite, everyone who had God in his heart decided to make his life wretched. To give Rabchik a whack on his rump with a stick, or to kick him in his side, or to fling a stone at his head, or to empty a pail of slops on him—that was considered a joke by everyone who did it, in fact almost a *mitzvah*.

Whenever Rabchik received a blow he did not stand up like other dogs to sass back, to bark it out, or even to show his teeth. Definitely not! At each blow Rabchik would cringe with a yelp almost to the ground: *"Ai-ai!"* And with his tail dragging he'd run away to hide in a corner, to lose himself in his sad thoughts, and—to catch flies.

II

Who was Rabchik? Where did he come from? That's hard to know. It was quite possible that he had remained in the courtyard ever since the days of the old *poretz*. It could even be that he was a stray, had somehow lost his original master and, attaching himself to the new one, he had remained around ever since.

It could easily happen that you'd be walking down the street when suddenly you'd find a little dog on your heels. "What sort of a leech is this?" you'd wonder. And you'd raise your hand threateningly and say to the dog, *"Pshol von!"* But the dog wouldn't budge from the spot. He'd recoil like a human being would when dodging a blow, and he'd continue to follow you. Suddenly you'd bend down to the ground, would swing out with your arm, feigning to fling a stone at him. But it would be no use. You'd remain standing where you were, looking curiously at the dog; he'd remain standing where he was, looking back at you. So you'd peer into each other's eyes mutely. Then you'd spit out with annoyance and start walking off. But the little dog would still run after you. Now you'd begin to lose your temper. You'd grab up a stick and you'd go after him, really angry. So what would the dog do? He'd fall on a stratagem, would stretch himself out on the ground, belly up. He'd tremble and look you straight in the eye, as if to say, "Na! You want to hit—go ahead and hit!"

Now that's the sort of dog our Rabchik was.

III

Whatever else he may have been Rabchik was no *nasher*. Even "gold" could lie around the house and he wouldn't touch it! Rabchik knew that whatever food he found under the table belonged to him; anything else was not his business.

When he was younger, they say, he was quite a nervy fellow. He once tried to steal a goose foot from the salting board on which they made the meat kosher. When Breineh the cook, a woman with a dark mustache, caught him in the act she began to yell, "Isaac! Isaac!" Isaac came running in just as Rabchik tried to dash by him with the goose foot in his mouth. Thereupon, Isaac caught him in the door and pushed it hard against him, so that half of Rabchik stuck out from one side of the door and the other half of him stuck out from the other side. Oh, how they settled their account with him then! On his front half Isaac cudgeled him over the head with a stick and on his little rump Breineh beat him with a slab of firewood. And all the time she beat him she kept on yelling, "Isaac! Isaac!"

From that time on, whenever anyone came up to Rabchik and merely said the word "Isaac!" he'd become frightened and scurry away "where black pepper grows."

IV

The one who made his life most miserable was the peasant woman, Paraskeh. This Paraskeh used to do our laundry, whitewash the walls, and milk our cow.

What grudge she could have against Rabchik was very hard to understand. She was always ready to pick on him. Whenever she'd catch sight of him she'd flare up and shout: "The plague take you, you infidel dog!" And just as if he were doing it out of spite Rabchik liked to get tangled up in her feet.

When she was at her work Paraskeh used to wreak her vengeance on him, like we Jews usually do on the cursed memory of Haman. For instance, when she'd be doing the laundry she'd empty a tub of cold water on him. Rabchik didn't like that kind of a bath at all; he'd be busy for a long time afterwards shaking off the water. When she'd be at her whitewashing she'd splash his face with white lime so that for an hour on end he'd be busy trying to lick it off with his tongue. When she'd be milking the cow she'd honor him with a whack from a slab of firewood across his legs. That's how Rabchik learned to leap skillfully so that whenever he saw a chunk of wood flying at him he'd adroitly leap over it like a circus performer.

On one occasion he got the very devil from such "honor." Paraskeh flung a slab of wood at him which struck him in a foreleg. Rabchik began to yelp, no longer in his own voice but in a peculiar screech: "*Ai-ai-ai-ai-ai!*" People ran up to see what was the matter. When Rabchik saw so many people gather he began to whimper in order to gain their sympathy. He showed everyone separately his broken leg, as if to say, "Na! Just see what she did to me, that Paraskeh!" Rabchik expected, no doubt, that they'd all take his part and the very least they would do would be to chop Paraskeh's head off for what she had done to him.

Instead, everybody began to laugh. Breineh with the mustache dashed out of the kitchen with a ladle in her hand. She wiped her perspiring nose with her bare arm and exclaimed, "*Nu*, so she did break the *schlimazl's* leg! Serves him right!" Also, all the mischievous little rascals began to collect. They hooted and whistled at Rabchik. Then Paraskeh turned up carrying a pitcher of hot water which she promptly proceeded to pour over him. Rabchik raised a *gevalt* and a screeching "*ai-ai-ai! ai-ai-ai!*" He leaped and thrashed about, turned round and round and bit his own tail. The little imps only laughed the louder. Seeing how Rabchik was dancing crazily about on only three legs they jeered at him and beat him with their sticks. Rabchik squealed and started to run, stopping every little while to roll on the ground because of the pain. The boys ran after him and threw stones at him. They hooted and whistled, and continued to drive him before them until they reached at last the edge of the town on the other side of the water mills. There they left him.

V

Rabchik ran on and on. He made up his mind: never, never would he come back to town, never as long as he lived! And he ran without knowing where he was running, nor caring either. Wherever his eyes would lead him and his legs would carry him, there he'd go. And after he had been running for a long time he at last reached a village. There he was met by all the dogs in the place. They smelled him all over.

"Blessed be thy coming!" they all greeted him ceremoniously. "And from where does a dog come? And what sort of a *tzatzke* do you have on your rump? *Epis* as if someone has burnt out a piece of hide right in the middle of it."

"*Ech!* Better don't ask!" answered Rabchik with a doleful expression. "There's a lot to tell but nothing really to listen to. Do tell me, is it possible for me to spend the night with you?"

"*Och!* With the greatest of pleasure!" replied the village dogs. "The out-of-doors is plenty big and the under-the-skies is even bigger."

"And how is it with you about eats?" inquired Rabchik discreetly. "With what do you still your hunger when the stomach demands nourishment?"

"*Et!* We've nothing to complain of!" answered the village dogs. "Slop pails are found everywhere. And when the Lord created meat he added bones to it. We should worry! Let our masters eat the meat and leave us the bones, as long as—how do you say it?—you can fill your gut."

"Nu, and what sort of masters have you got?" continued Rabchik with a twist to his tail in the manner of a dog making an investigation.

"The masters? Our masters are like all masters!" replied the village dogs evasively.

"Nu, and how about Paraskeh?"

"Paraskeh? What Paraskeh?"

"Why, Paraskeh! You know, the one who does washing, who

whitewashes the walls and milks the cow! You mean to say you don't know Paraskeh?"

The village dogs stared at Rabchik, thinking that he had gone out of his mind. "What are you Paraskehing about, anyway?" they asked. Again they smelled him all over and then trotted off, one by one, each to his dung heap.

"*Ut!* What happy dogs!" thought Rabchik enviously, as he stretched himself out on God's earth under God's heaven. He wanted to take a nap but he couldn't sleep. First of all it was on account of his scalded hide; it hurt and itched terribly! And the flies annoyed him no end; it was simply impossible to drive them off. Secondly, there was a growling in his belly. *Ach!* If only he had something to chew on! Looked very much like he'd have to wait until morning. And a third reason why he couldn't fall asleep was his thoughts. His mind was full of all that the village dogs had told him. Could it be that among them there were no Isaacs who squeezed the door against dogs and then beat them with a slab of wood? How strange! Nor were there any Paraskehs who scalded one with boiling water, no mischievous boys who threw sticks and stones after them, who hooted and whistled and chased them out of the village. "What happy dogs there are in this world! And there was I thinking all along that my town was the whole world! You see how it is—a worm lies buried in a jar of horse-radish and says to itself, 'There certainly doesn't exist any life sweeter than this!' "

Rabchik finally dozed off. And as he slept he had a dream, and in his dream he saw a slop pail. It was a big one, too, and full of bread crumbs, chicken intestines, buckwheat gruel mixed with millet and potatoes, and then bones, oh so many bones! A whole treasure! Knucklebones, rib bones, marrowbones, fishbones, and unchewed heads of herring! Rabchik was both enchanted and bewildered; he hardly knew where to begin first.

"A hearty appetite!" the village dogs called out to him, looking on from a distance as he was girding himself for the feast.

"Won't you join me?" asked Rabchik just out of politeness.

"Eat hearty!" replied the village dogs affably.

Suddenly he heard a voice roaring into his ear: "Isaac!"

Rabchik awoke with a great start at that. *Ach!* It was all only a dream! . . . .

When morning came Rabchik made the rounds of all the yards looking for a slop pail, a piece of crust, even a little bone. But wherever he went he found himself shut out by some other dog.

"Could a fellow get some breakfast here?" asked Rabchik timidly.

"Here? Oh no! In the next yard maybe."

And Rabchik kept on running from yard to yard. Everywhere he heard the same tune. So he thought the whole matter over: what would he get from being so polite? Might it not be better to go straight over, grab what he could, and make a quick getaway?

Nu, so he tried, and got properly punished by the village dogs for grabbing. At first they looked angrily at him, growled and showed their teeth. Then several leaped on him at the same time, bit and tore at him and made a wreck of his tail. This job done, they escorted him out of the village with great ceremony.

VI

With his injured tail between his legs Rabchik set out for the next village. But when he reached his destination the same old story was repeated. At first they welcomed him pleasantly. "A fine guest, why not?" But, when he tried to edge near the pail of slops, they started looking angrily at him. They growled and showed their teeth, then bit and tore at him, and barked, "Get out of here!" from every side.

Rabchik now felt sick and tired of being unwanted, of knocking around from one place to another. So he thought it over. "It's perfectly clear: people are bad, but then again dogs are no better either. Now wouldn't it be preferable to live in the forest among the wild beasts?"

And thus reflecting, Rabchik made his way into the forest.

He wandered and he wandered, one solitary dog alone in the forest. One day passed, then another, and a third, until Rabchik finally began to feel that his belly was contracting more and more and that his intestines were shriveling up. He was feeling faint from hunger and thirst. "Nu?" he said to himself bitterly, "so all that's left for me to do is to stretch out right in the middle of the forest and breathe my last!" Ha! But as if just for spite, he had a strong desire to go on living and living!

So once more Rabchik hung his tail between his hind legs, stretched his forelegs, hung out his tongue, and lay down under a tree to think through his confused doggy thoughts: "Oy, if I could only get a piece of bread or a bit of meat, a bone even, and oy, for a sip of water!" And from great *tzoress* Rabchik became a thinker, a regular philosopher! He began to philosophize:

"Why am I, a dog, punished more severely than all the other creatures in the world? There, for instance, is a little bird; watch it fly straight to its nest! There you have a lizard; see how it crawls into its hole! And right here are a worm, a beetle, and an ant—each of them has a home, each of them finds his nourishment, only I, miserable dog that I am! . . . . Bow-wow-wow!"

"Who's barking here in the forest?" howled a wolf who happened to be passing by just then; his tongue was hanging out from sheer hunger.

Never before in his life had Rabchik seen a wolf. He thought it was a dog. So he slowly rose to his feet, being in no great hurry, stretched himself, and then trotted over to the wolf.

"Who are you?" asked the wolf contemptuously. "What's your name? Where do you come from? What are you doing here?"

Rabchik was delighted that at last he had met with a fellow creature, someone to whom he could pour out all his tzoress. And so he unburdened his bitter heart to him.

"I'll tell you the truth," said Rabchik as he ended his sad tale, "I feel so wretched that I'd positively be overjoyed were I to meet here with a lion, a bear, or even a wolf."

"So what would be?" asked the wolf with a *paskudneh* smile.

"Nothing," replied Rabchik. "In any case, I'm fated to die. Better let a wolf devour me than that I should perish of hunger among my own kind, among dogs!"

"Nu?" said the wolf, flexing his muscles and sharpening his teeth with pleasurable anticipation. "I want you to know that I'm a wolf and I would very much like to tear you limb from limb and eat you for my breakfast. I'm awfully hungry for it's already eight days since last I had a morsel in my mouth."

Hearing these words, Rabchik felt terror creeping over him so that his ragged hide began to quiver.

"My lord, the king! Dear Reb Velvel!"[1] answered Rabchik trying to speak with a piteous expression and a tearful voice. "May God send you along a better breakfast than I! Lord preserve you, what do you suppose you can get out of me? Only hide and bones, I assure you. Take my advice and let me go. Have pity on my unhappy dog's life!"

And thus saying, Rabchik lowered his tail, twisted his little rump, crawled on his belly, and went through such hideous antics and grimaces that the wolf began to feel nauseous.

"Pick up that paskudneh tail of yours," snarled the wolf, "and go and carry yourself off to the devil—you dog of dogs! And furthermore, don't let me ever see your *tréfeneh* mug again!"

[1]Velvel *is a Yiddish variant of the Jewish masculine name* Volf (*Wolf*).

More dead than alive, Rabchik started to run. He ran so fast that he didn't feel the ground under him. He was afraid even to look around. So he fled, away, away from the forest—and back to town!

VII

As he trotted into town Rabchik avoided the house and yard where he had grown up, although it was precisely there where his heart drew him most, despite the fact that it was where he had been cruelly beaten, where they had broken his poor leg and scalded his rump. Instead he made his way into the market place to the butcher shops, to join his own kind—the dogs there.

"Well, well, just look who's here! From where does a dog come?" the butchers' dogs greeted him with a yawn as they made ready to retire for the night.

"I'm *takkeh* a local dog," replied Rabchik. "What, you don't recognize me? Why I am Rabchik!"

"Rabchik? Rabchik? A familiar name!" said the butchers' dogs, pretending not to recall who he was.

"What sort of a scar do you have on your rump?" Tzutzik, a small dog, asked him and, so saying leaped at him with great insolence.

"No doubt it's an identification mark, or maybe it was done just to make him look more beautiful. You mean to say you can't figure that out?" jeered Ravdek, a red dog with a furry hide.

"When it has to do with scars, just ask me and I'll tell you what it is," said Sirko, a grey dog, an old bachelor who had only one eye and one ear. "I'm sure the scar this fellow has he must have gotten in battles with other dogs."

"Why do you all talk?" called out Zhuk, a black dog without a tail. "Better let Rabchik talk himself. Let him tell us."

And Rabchik stretched himself out on the ground and began to tell about everything that had happened to him, not leaving out a single detail. They all listened to him except Ravdek, who considered himself quite a wit. Every other minute he'd interrupt him with a joke.

"Shut up, Ravdek," called out Zhuk, the black dog without a tail, opening his mouth wide in a long yawn. "Go on, Rabchik, tell, tell! We like to listen to stories after dinner!"

And Rabchik continued to tell his sad tale in a dispirited voice, but no one paid any attention to him. Tzutzik talked quietly with Sirko, Ravdek cracked jokes, and Zhuk snored like ten soldiers. Every so often he started up from sleep, yawned, and urged, "Go on Rabchik, tell, tell! We like to listen to stories after dinner!"

VIII

Bright and early the following morning Rabchik was already up and going. He stood at a discreet distance watching the butchers hacking up the meat. There he saw an entire forequarter of a cow, suspended neck down with the blood running from it. Here lay a rump, a choice chunk of meat, juicy, deeply cushioned with fat. Rabchik devoured it with his eyes and swallowed saliva. The meat choppers hacked the meat into pieces. Every once in a while they'd throw a handful of skin or a bone to their dogs. And the dogs leaped high, trying to catch them in midair. Rabchik saw how hard they tried to be clever, jumping skillfully at the right instant in the right place. They didn't let a single bone pass them by. When each dog got his portion he stepped to a side, stretched himself grandly on the ground and started his feast. Every once in a while each dog would look at the others as if to boast:

"Just look at this bone! Some bone, eh? That's my bone and it's I who am chewing it!"

The other dogs pretended to look elsewhere, but at the same time they said to themselves:

"May you choke on it! May it make you sick! Just look at him! All morning he keeps on *fressing* and fressing. And we have to look on while he eats—may the worms eat him!"

One of the dogs, carrying a piece of hide in his mouth, looked for a quiet spot so that nobody should watch him chew on it; he was probably afraid of the evil eye.

Another dog stood watching an angry butcher who was quarreling with the other butchers and abusing them heartily. The dog wagged his tail flatteringly to him and called out to the other dogs.

"See this butcher? He looks angry, doesn't he? Let me have such a good year what a fine man he is! I'm telling you—one diamond in the world! A character of pure gold! He's the kind that takes real pity on a dog—he's positively 'a friend of the dogs.' Wait, you'll soon see a bone flying with a chunk of meat on it. *Hop!*"

So saying, he leaped into the air and snapped shut his jaws so that the others would think that he had caught a fat morsel.

"Ach! What a flatterer and a liar! What a braggart! The Devil take him!" called out a dog standing on the side.

Still another dog stationed himself near a meat-chopping block. When the butcher happened to turn away for a moment up leaped this dog upon the block and began licking it up with his tongue. What a barking started among the other dogs; they were thus informing the butcher that a *ganef* was at work. "Why, that dog has gone and *nashed* a piece of meat! Such a piece of gold we should have! May we not live to see all kinds of good things if with our own eyes we didn't see that ganef steal! May we drop dead on the spot, may we choke on the next bone we chew, if we tell a lie!"

"Feh! It's enough to throw up!" cried out an old dog. Of course, he himself wouldn't have had anything against having a lick of that block!

And seeing and hearing all this, Rabchik began to consider his situation: What would he get out of it all by just standing and looking on? All the dogs were jumping and barking—why shouldn't he do likewise? But before even he had a chance to try, several dogs were on top of him, their teeth fastened in his throat and snapping and tearing at him. They bit him on his still fresh wounds, where it hurt so!

Rabchik lowered his tail, crawled away into a corner, stretched out his neck, and began to whine.

"What are you crying about?" Zhuk asked him as he licked his chops, for he had just finished his breakfast.

"Why shouldn't I cry?" moaned Rabchik. "I'm the most unlucky dog among all the dogs in the world! I had foolishly thought that here, among my own kind, I could at least get epis to eat. Believe me, I wouldn't go crawling where I'm not wanted if I wasn't so terribly hungry! My life is simply ebbing out of me!"

"I believe you," said Zhuk with a sigh. "Believe me, I know what hunger is! I can place myself in your sad situation very well. Unfortunately, I cannot help you at all. That's the custom here: every butcher has his own dog, and every dog has his own butcher."

"Do you takkeh think that it's right so?" asked Rabchik bitterly. "Where is justice? What about dogmanity? Ach, that a dog should be so abandoned by other dogs! And oh, that one who is hungry should starve to death among those who are sated!"

"Alas! I can help you only with a sigh," sighed Zhuk with feeling.

He yawned heartily, and, with his good breakfast tucked away in his belly, he made ready to doze off.

"If that's the case," said Rabchik, finally plucking up courage, "then I'll go directly to the butchers. Maybe I'll be able to bark up a butcher, somehow."

"With the greatest of pleasure," answered Zhuk, "as long as you don't go to my butcher. Because, I warn you, should you dare go to my butcher I'll bite off your tail!"

IX

Then Rabchik went directly to the butchers, by-passed and avoided all the other dogs. At first he tried to flatter the butchers, jumped up before them and wagged his tail. But what kind of *mazl* has a schlimazl? One of the butchers, a lusty fellow with broad shoulders, just for a joke threw his meat chopper at him. It was Rabchik's good fortune that he had learned how to jump well. Otherwise he would have been cut in half.

"You dance quite well!" said Ravdek to him with a leer. "A lot better than our Tzutzik. Here, Tzutzik, just come over here and you'll see how one should dance!"

Tzutzik came running up. He leaped straight at Rabchik. But Rabchik could no longer endure his insolence. He gripped Tzutzik with his teeth, threw him down, and bit savagely into his little belly. On him he vented all his pent-up bitterness, and when he was through he fled as fast as his legs could carry him.

Solitary and woebegone, he dragged himself through the fields, and when at last he came to the road he stretched himself out right in the middle of it, and for very shame he hid his face between his paws and did not want to look at the light of day. It didn't bother him even that the flies swarmed over him and bit him. Good! Let them bite, let them peck at him! What difference would it make? . . . .

"It's the end of everything!" thought Rabchik sadly. "If a dog cannot live even a single day among other dogs, among his very own kind, then may the whole world go to the devil! . . . ."

It is the way of a dog that if he is hit by a stone he bites a fellow dog.—The Zohar

THE LITTLE CALF

BY MENDELE MOICHER SFORIM (S. J. ABRAMOVITCH)
TRANSLATED FROM THE YIDDISH BY NATHAN AUSUBEL

Once, on an early winter morning, as I lay cuddled up under the quilt half-asleep and with no thought of getting up to go to *cheder*, I suddenly felt someone shaking me and calling to me:

"Hurry . . . get up! Quicker . . . quicker!"

More dead than alive I raised myself in bed. It was my twelve-year-old sister who was waking me. Her face was shining, her eyes had a peculiar sparkle. She wanted to tell me something but couldn't, so breathless she was. Mutely she pointed to something in a corner of the room.

I took a quick look. *Oy, gevalt!* A little calf!

Barefoot as I was, and dressed only in my nightshirt, with the palm of my hand pressed piously to the top of my head because I didn't want to take the time to look for my *yarmulka,* I jumped out of bed and ran quickly to the calf.

The joy in me was indescribable. It was as if the whole world were mine, as if all creation were sharing with me my happiness. Suddenly, the sun seemed to shine differently than on other days, the morning felt milder, friendlier than usual. A holiday spirit rested on everything. The whole radiant universe seemed to be full of the calf. *"Gut yom-tov!"* it said, *"mazl tov* to you and to the little calf!"

I squatted on my knees and from a respectful distance I looked the little calf over. It was a nice one, with a red face and a white spot on its forehead like a silver cockade. Really, one of God's wonders!

Little by little I inched nearer, trying to get acquainted with it at closer range. Finally I gave it a caress here, a feel there, probing cautiously with one finger and, while doing so, looking it straight in the eye. It wasn't long before I became an intimate *shmelke* with it, and I extended to it a hearty *sholom aleichem,* but *takkeh* with the whole hand, with all my five fingers!

It was clear to me that the little calf hadn't learned yet the meaning of sholom aleichem, or how you ate it. It looked as if it felt offended by something because, suddenly gathering all its strength, it began to struggle to its feet. Slowly, very slowly, it tried to raise itself on its hind legs, supporting itself by its forelegs on which it was still kneeling. A little later it was fully up and its four little legs wobbled under it like the legs of a shaky table. It stood in this position for quite a while, clumsily shaking, bulging its large calf eyes at everything. Suddenly it whisked its tail and began going gallop-gallop around the room.

What a noise, what a din! The *milchiger* bench, the one with the broken leg, toppled over. That frightened the hens who went flying crazily over the table and benches and ended by breaking a glass full of seeds standing in a dish. When my mother, who then happened to be with the mama cow in the barn, heard the tararam she came running breathlessly into the house and let out her anger on my poor head.

Oy, what a day I had then! It was a day solely of slaps and whacks, both at home and later in cheder. Believe me, I earned plenty!

When I left home that morning to go to cheder my head was simply full of the calf. To everybody I met on the way, I blurted out the glad news: "Our cow's given birth to a calf!" I praised the little calf to the sky before all the boys I knew and beamed with pleasure like one who had real cause for celebration. Heh, heh! let them envy me! To any boy I felt like, I promised to let him have a look at the calf. I'd even allow him to play with it for a while. From one boy I got in advance several brass buttons ripped from a soldier's uniform; they had the Imperial double eagle on them. I swore to him "on my word as a Jew" that the honor of the first ride on the calf would belong to him, and to him only.

It goes without saying that, out of my great joy and because of my many business transactions that morning, I came late to cheder and got properly punished for it too.

Slaps, to be sure may be slaps, but a calf is still a calf! My *Gemara* lay open before me, but all that peered out at me from the printed Hebrew text were the bulging eyes of my little calf. There went whirling through my brain the image of its adorable chin, so beautiful, so chiseled! Then its ears, so tiny, so alert! And, oh, its precious little head and, ah, its dear little neck! Our teacher drilled with us, whining in a Talmudic singsong. But in my ears all I heard was the ma-a-ing of the mother cow for its calf. When the teacher got up from his chair, all I saw was the little calf struggling to its feet. When the teacher stretched out his hand, all I could see was the little calf pertly wiggling its tail and galloping about: hutz-hutz-hutz! And then—smack! went the teacher's heavy hand on my cheek! Yes, the teacher was real angry. "*Nu,* my fine scholar," he jeered at me, "where in the text do we hold now?" "Hold?" he asked yet! I was holding my cheek!

When I came home that day my first concern was the calf. Softly, on tiptoe, I stole over to it. To protect it against the Evil Eye my mother had hidden it in a corner. I began with a look, an eating-up with the eyes out of the hunger of my love. Then I caressed it, felt it all over, and finally I threw my arms around it and hugged it with all my might. I wound up perhaps a little roughly: I gave the calf such a squeeze that it suddenly leaped up and began dashing about like mad all over the room. It turned everything upside down, a regular Sodom and Gomorrah! My, what pitch and sulphur there rained down on me—fiery slaps, that is! It was something terrible!

My love for the calf grew from day to day, and she too grew, and with it came increasing heartache and trouble for me. My blood ran cold as I listened to the talk at home about what they were going to do to the poor little thing, how they planned to have her slaughtered *nebbech!* Ach, how they haggled over the price with the butcher! And there she stood and kept on looking and looking so trustingly like a member of the family! She licked my mother's hand so sweetly, so lovingly! And there they were, putting a price on her licker, on her dear little tongue! It was takkeh an outrage, a gevalt!

How my heart bled for the calf! Gevalt, what a pity! It made me angry, it burned me up! Gevalt, what did they want nebbech from its life?

I went about all upset. I had grief coming to me from both ends. I was simply ashamed to look both the calf and my mother, pardon the comparison, in the eye.

God alone knows what this would have led to if something that we hadn't at all expected suddenly happened.

II

It was a winter night, frosty and windy; the frost scorched like flame, the wind was blustering. It blew, it whistled, rip-skrip, like at a wedding attended by a thousand devils. Columns of snow swirled and danced, spiraling crazily through the streets. The shingles on the roofs banged and rattled; there was a howling in the chimneys and a rattling of the windowpanes. No living creature, not even a single Jewish barnyard animal, could be seen about. It was as if they had all been moved out, and those that remained, woe to them, lay buried up to their ears in the drifted snow.

Our cow, "a mama of a baby," so to speak, spent the night in the dark shed lying in all the wet and dung. It blew there from above and it blew there from under, and from all sides as well. It was almost enough to die of the cold. And what did the poor cow do? It kept on chewing the cud. It shook with a strangling cough all the time and heaved soft, deep sighs. These sighs carried quite a distance. We even heard them in the house.

Quite early the following morning I was wakened from sleep by a bitter outcry, by a yammering and a wailing. It was as if they were mourning for the dead.

I listened to my mother's tearful lamentations.

"What's the matter?" I asked.

"The cow died!"

The whole household was downcast. Grief had fallen on everyone. Even the rooster stood with bowed head, didn't lead his hens as usual from under the oven. One of the hens kept on clucking and looking for a spot where she could lie down to lay her egg, but there was no one to cover her with the sieve. Another hen dashed out from under the bed, hendum-pendum, and flew onto a chair, her little head thrown saucily on the side. Very proudly she clucked, "Mazl tov, I've laid an egg; I've been delivered in a good hour!" All stood around glumly, including the neighbors. My mother then eulogized the cow, told about her many virtues, about the marvelous cheese and butter made from her milk, and all kinds of wonderful traits of hers about which I had never heard before.

"Listen to a story!" she began in a wailing singsong. "Bright and early this morning I open this very door here and go out to milk the cow like any good housewife would, with the milk pail in my hand. Straw for the animal the peasant who helps me hadn't brought yet. The frost, a fright! I call out, 'Mine-mine-mine!' The cow doesn't answer. I go closer and give a look—oy! It was as if a thunderbolt had struck me down: there she lay, dead! Well what do you say to that, right after calving, an animal goes ahead and dies!"

In the very middle of my mother's funeral oration the calf came flying in from the alcove—hutz-hutz-hutz!—with her tail pertly turned at an angle, her head thrown back. "Meh-meh!" she cried on top of her voice. Looking at the orphan nebbech everybody's heart ached. All understood the meaning of her "meh"; the poor little thing was mooing nebbech after her mother's teats; she simply wanted to be fed. It stood mooing, imploring her mama to give her a washing with her tongue. The neighbors blew their noses and dabbed at their eyes and got ready to say something eloquent. One of them, who was as learned as a scholar and who gushed all the time with the sayings of the holy sages, beat everyone to it. She let herself really go:

"He Who is eternal, Whose Name I'm not even worthy to mention," she began in a pious singsong, pressing her little lips tight and screwing up her face, "the Almighty, He is just and His judgment is just. May she, the cow, be as a burnt offering for us, may she bring forgiveness, purify us and all Israel of all impurities and of all evil! My advice is that the little calf, because she is the first fruit of her mother's body, should remain living. Raise it, and He Who nourishes all living things from the small worm to the weasel beast will help to nurture it, sometimes with potato peelings, sometimes with a bit of bran, from this a bit, from that a bit—you know, how much does a little calf need, anyway? You understand, a little calf grows some-day into a cow, and a cow is a good animal, is always useful, especially these days, and more so for Jews, ach-ach-ach!"

All the women mumbled their agreement. My mother let herself be persuaded.

And so the little calf remained among the living, and a stone rolled off my heart.

The story with our cow and her unusual death, stirred up the whole town. Many people came out of curiosity just to look at the calf.

III

At first the little calf nebbech longed for her mother's teats. Sometimes we were able to quiet her with a bit of bran, sometimes with a crust of bread, with a handful of hay. Little teeth she had, eight front ones; I myself counted them. They were pretty and white already at birth. As she ate she mooed from time to time, sniffed, poked about, and smelled. Whatever came handy to her mouth, whether a towel, a tablecloth, a yarmulka—that too was "merchandise" for her. Once she almost strangled herself with a *cholent* rag. It was lucky that my mother looked around in time because she wanted to put the cholent into the oven at that moment. And if we stood all that from the calf and didn't try to get rid of her it was only on account of the merit of her mama, that wonderful cow, may she enjoy her peace wherever she is!

I was the only one who takkeh really and truly loved her from the depths of my heart. How I pitied her! She was nebbech, poor thing, so lonely—an orphan! If someone, out of the kindness of his heart, tried to give her a blow or a kick I rushed forward to take her part, and believe me, I got my portion of abuse for the effort! That only drew me closer to the calf because we both were being treated rudely, because both of us had to suffer at the hands of others who were stronger than we.

From what I could judge, the little calf liked me too. She'd allow me to stroke her over the head and to pull her by the ears while she blinked at me with her sad eyes, licking me with her tongue in a friendly fashion, just as though she were trying to complain to me about some-thing, wanted to tell me something. I was sure I understood what she was feeling and what she was trying to tell me with her caressing tongue.

And so I was drawn mightily to the little calf and she and I became devoted friends.

IV

It was after *Pesach;* vacation was over. We little boys went back to cheder, and the little calves too went back to the herd. Our teacher took up his rod, the herdsman took up his whip. The *melamed* began to drill with us, also the cowherd did the same with his animals.

The teacher's assistant dragged or carried to cheder the tiny tots who were still half-dazed with sleep. But our little calf, strong and frisky as she was and big enough to run on her own little legs, was kept at home. She went around all day long doing nothing. "Why?" "Because she's still too young to drive to pasture with the rest of the herd," said the cowherd. "What does it matter? So she'll learn her Torah and making with the mouth a little later! In the meantime, let her grow up at home until the right time will come for her to take her place in the herd."

What else could one do? The calf remained nebbech at home and had to stand for a lot from everybody. Believe me, she licked no honey! My mother didn't give her any hay to eat. The only hay she showed her was the letter "hay" in the Hebrew prayer book! My, what she had to suffer! Someone would stuff her mouth full of *shihi-pihi*. Still another tried to teach her etiquette. And from all these favors she nebbech always remained hungry and grew scrawny.

To her luck my melamed suddenly found that he had reached the bottom of his sack of Torah for me. So I began to study by myself in the House of Study. In other words, with regard to learning they put me on my honor. In time the care of the little calf was entrusted entirely to me, and so I began to raise her in a good hour.

A new world opened up for both of us, a world that was radiant and beautiful and free from care. Never before had either of us really seen that world, neither I nor the little calf who had always been kept in the house or in the shed.

"Come, my beloved!" I said to her in the words of the Sabbath Eve hymn, as I led her by the rope around her neck into the open. "Come, my friend, let us flee to the green pasture, there to graze!"

Ai-ai, was it good over there! A pleasure! Everything lived, everything was in motion, moving hither and thither. Until that time God's creatures had been perfect strangers for me. Birds of all kinds, all sorts of beetles, grasshoppers, and crickets flew about and leaped merrily into the air. What a singing, what a humming and a strumming! They were all playing in a heavenly concert! The air was sweet with spices, and the eyes were dazzled by the flash of a myriad colors among the flowers.

It was so easy to breathe, so free! Something inside of me gave me a shove—hop-hop-hop! So I gave a jump and out of great pleasure did a somersault several times. And then I stretched myself on the soft moss, belly up. The radiant sun looked straight into my face; it shone and it smiled, as if to say: "Nu, *yingele,* it's good, eh?" As if by a will working outside of me, my mouth opened and I began to sing the melody of a *Shabbes* prayer in my shrill little treble. As I sang the little calf looked at me and let out a "meh," as if to say, *"Sha,* what's all the singing about?"

The little calf got all absorbed in her crunching which she did with real pleasure. I looked and looked at her, lost in thought. And as I looked I suddenly saw standing before me our Father Jacob as he was grazing the sheep of Laban the Aramean. And I also saw his meeting with Rachel at the well—the well over there—and how they embraced and kissed each other out of their great love.

We started our grazing on the green hill not far from the town, and afterwards we strayed far, far away, ever looking for a more and still more beautiful spot.

Just try and imagine a forest. Tall pine trees stretch in even rows and their tips reach high into the heavens. At the bottom they are smooth and bare, but on the top they wear green hats—a sea of flashing green—through which the slanting rays of the sun break through and light up the velvet grass on the ground with bands of golden light. At the approach to the forest, stand small but thickly grown copses of young saplings, all kinds of juicy little trees, scattered here and there among patches of fragrant herbs. All around extend green fields as far as the horizon, so that the eye cannot take it all in. The rolling country descends gradually into the valley. Down its gentle incline rushes a gurgling stream with crystal-clear water. It leaps playfully about like a child that is playing hide-and-seek among the willows. How it darts and leaps down the hill, dashing from stone to stone and constantly gurgling, bul-bul-bul!

Besides me and the little calf there was nobody else. Every once in a while a bird would come flying over, perch itself on a branch, and eye me stealthily. No doubt it was wondering what sort of a creature I was. The next instant it would give a quick bow with its head, twitch its tiny tail, shake its wings and —good health be yours!—away, away it sped!

On the opposite side of the valley a stork suddenly came flying and alighted on its long red legs. It stretched its long silver-white neck and red beak toward the sky. Thus it stood for a while motionless. Suddenly it began to klip-klap, klap-klip with its beak and it sped across the swamp.

From time to time I heard echoes of sound reverberating somewhere in the forest. There was wafted to me the rattling of carts on the road that passed through it. Purring for sheer pleasure, I looked at the little calf and thought:

"Oh, how good it is for both of us! We have each other to thank because we're here. If not for me, little calf, you'd now be locked up in the shed. And if not for you I'd now be a prisoner in the House of Study."

This is how I spent a good part of each day, drawing *naches* from God's delightful world and from the little calf which in the meantime had become very much attached to me. The two of us grew to be, so to speak, *pani-bratzi*, like blood brothers! It was something to look at and marvel over with what joy she would play with me, with what rapture she would suddenly, for no reason I could see, throw up her little rear end and start running. Takkeh it was *epis* like a child when it comes to its mother! She would stretch out her neck, bend her head down to me, as if to say, "Na! Go ahead and scratch me!"

By the time the summer had come to an end both of us had changed a lot. The little calf had taken on flesh. She had shed her fuzzy hair and gotten a smooth shiny hide. I, too, grew in strength, got a tanned skin and a ravenous appetite. My studies at that time were as tasteless to me as hay and potato peelings were to the little calf after she came home from her delicious cropping in the pasture.

V

About the little calf there is not much more to say. In God's good time, if she'll remain alive, she'll yet be a cow. The question now is quite another: Young man—meaning me—what's going to become of you? What sort of good can come out of your roaming through field and forest?

This is how my kin preached at me. They put to me the question, but they answered it for me takkeh themselves: "If you want that something decent should come out of you there's only one thing left for you to do—enter the *Yeshiva!*"

How my heart ached to part with the little calf, to part with God's beautiful world that had breathed a new soul into me! Just the same, I was torn by another desire: Is there anybody who is against his becoming a somebody, who is averse to making something out of his life! "Ach, Ruler of the Universe!" I said to myself, "I'd be content, if only it were possible to take the little calf along with me to the Yeshiva!"

And later, when I was already a student at the Yeshiva, living its rigorous life, sometimes sleeping on a hard bench, and sometimes on the cold ground with my fist as a pillow, there would open for me in my mind's eye wondrously beautiful images of trees, of fields, of shimmering green wild flowers, hills, and valleys, a golden sun, and a clear blue sky. In my head played a finch, in my ears hummed an insect. All kinds of fragrances, probably of herbs, floated to my nostrils. I imagined that under my head lay a little pillow filled with moss, and over me, it seemed, crawled a whole army of ants. It drew me, oh how it drew my soul always there, there!

"*Mama-léb!*" I wrote home one summer day, "I like studying very much. I'm making good progress, God be praised! Only what then? I so long for home, for you, Mama, and for everyone else [I was ashamed to include the little calf]. Oy Mama, just let me come home for a few days! Really, it won't cost anything; I'll come all the way on foot. Really, it's not so bad! So what? All boys in our Yeshiva go home on foot. And what sort of a going it is too! Barefoot! With sticks in their hands and their bundles thrown over their shoulders. I have about eighteen groschen in cash left over yet from *Purim,* which I earned reading the Book of Esther for the cook in the home where I eat free on *Shabbes,* and for delivering the Purim gift of the householder to his father-in-law. So let me come, *mameniu,* oy, I beg you!"

And not waiting for her answer, and going just as I was, I started out for home several days later, naturally on foot.

If ever there was in the world a happy person, it was I. True enough, I saw merchants riding in covered wagons, Christian gentry rolling by in their carriages, but what sort of pleasure could their comfortable riding be compared to the carefree strolling on foot of a little *Yeshiva-bocher* like me who had just wrenched himself loose from a life full of mold and stagnation, who had emerged suddenly into the fresh air, into the world of freedom and light? It was like the coming to life of one who had been dead!

I started out on my journey early in the morning, avoiding the highway and deliberately choosing footpaths across the wheat and corn fields. I arrived home when it was time to recite the *Mincha* prayers and when the cows were on their way home from the pasture.

Suddenly I saw my little calf! Heh-heh-heh! What a calf—may no evil eye fall on it!

I went and stood face to face with her.

"Sholom aleichem, little calf!" said I, trying to pat her.

Immediately she lowered her head without even looking at me and started threatening me with her little pointed horns, as if to say, "Don't you dare touch me! What sort of relation of mine are you anyway to pat me? Are you maybe my uncle?"

It takkeh made me a little resentful. But, no matter, I thought to myself, I ought to try again.

"Mine-mine-mine!" I called, grasping the calf by her nose and holding a handful of grass before her. In other words, *"Na!* A present from me!"

She sniffed the grass, poked around with her nose a bit, and looked at me with surprise, as if to say, *"Epis* familiar; Seems to me it's he. And yet, it's not he;"

"So you don't recognize me! Ai-ai!" I smiled a twisted smile, with gall, that is.

For a while I stood regarding the calf. How handsome, healthy, and well-fleshed she was! How lively and fresh she looked! And then, comparing her to my own scrawny, emaciated body and my pale worn face, with all its Yeshiva-bocher air of neglect, unwillingly I heaved a sigh out of the depths of my heart.

Apparently recognizing me by my voice, the calf soon became more familiar with me. With a friendly air she stretched out her neck to me so that I should scratch it as was her habit formerly. She stood looking at me with half-closed eyes, softly mooing to me, "H-m-m!" I knew very well what she meant, what she was trying to say to me: "Where did you suddenly disappear? And at the same time takkeh what a pity! H-m-m! Oy, how terrible you look nebbech!"

VI

To live with my poor mama, an abandoned widow with a flock of little orphans, was simply out of the question. So I said a sad good-by to all my dearest ones, my little calf included. I then bid farewell to the beautiful fields and to the shimmering green forest and started back on foot to the Yeshiva.

The following year was a bitter one for me in the Yeshiva, much worse than before. It was a year without "days." There were not enough householders who cared to invite me to their tables for a day each, as was the custom. So I suffered hunger. It was my good fortune that many other poor students at the Yeshiva also had to suffer the pangs of hunger. For me that sharing of misery was half a consolation, but what a sorry one!

After a long silence my mother wrote me finally:

"Mazl tov to you, dear son, also mazl tov to me in honor of my cow! Your calf has calved, and so she has become a cow. And now she'll give us cheese and butter. There's plenty of *milchigs* now in the house, a bit to sell and also a bit to keep for ourselves.

"O Lord of the Universe! May I live to have naches from you too, soon! Amen! Really a good cow. But what then? I have tzoress from her. She doesn't allow herself to be milked. She throws herself around, bellows, and is torn with longing. She's simply dying for her little calf which we took away from her. Did you ever hear that a cow shouldn't be able to forget her little calf! It's like a mama grieving for her child!

"She was already *meshuggeh* when she was yet a calf. You were the only one who could do anything with her. Now just see how well you taught her! You should have taught her less and have studied more yourself. Study well, dear son, study, so that in God's own time you'll become a somebody! Ach, what a wonderful little calf she bore! Takkeh one in the world. The butcher gave me a good price for it. And from this money I'm now sending you a few gulden. Na! May you too have some pleasure on account of the pains you once took with your calf.

"Furthermore, I'm writing you to let you know that. . . ."

Enough! I didn't care to finish the rest of the letter. It grew dark before my eyes. I became dizzy. Feh! In fact, I felt so badly that they had to douse me with a full pail of water.

My fellow students stood around me and showered me with questions: "What's the trouble? . . . . Did anybody in your family fall sick, God forbid? . . . . Or die, may his hour not have struck yet?"

But I kept silent, clutching my heart because of the pain. Nu, go ahead and tell them and become the butt of their jokes! Sure, spin them a yarn about a little calf! Tell them that I fainted from pity for an animal with which I was fated, for the first time in both of our young lives, to look upon God's beautiful world together! Nu, go ahead and tell them that my heart was bleeding out of pity for a dumb beast, a mother of a firstling, yearning for her child that had been slaughtered nebbech!

Enough, more than enough, were for me my mother's few words

They made my blood boil, stimulated my overwrought imagination, and robbed me of sleep at night.

No sooner I would lie down—aha! How do you do? And the play would start. And there passed across my mind's stage my little calf, now already a mama, with her child, a little calf, takkeh a diamond! The little calf wouldn't leave her mama in peace; suckled from her udder and twisted her little tail about in a curl. Her mama was full of bliss, she lowered her head to her child, licked it, licked it all the time and softly mooed to it out of her overflowing love. Everything sparkled and shimmered. And in my heart too I felt so light, so blissful! But suddenly, everything changed! It grew dark before my eyes, the images vanished and the bright colors faded. Everything turned to nothingness!

I tossed about. I turned myself on the other side. Kling-kling! A little bell tinkled in my ears. Heh-heh! Again the play went on!

This time the scene was a very sad one. The little calf was struggling, struggling to tear itself out of the butcher's hands. She fled with a bitter cry, the butcher after her. Sensing that the Angel of Death was after her, and yet desperately wanting to live, she ran away nebbech, helter-skelter in a panic, tried to hide herself, trembled and mooed piteously, and begged for mercy. "Save me!" she moaned. But the butcher paid no heed to her cries. He seized and bound her legs with rope. She quivered, she shrieked, *"Meh-meh!"* ("Mama!" that is!) But it was all in vain. Her mama was in the field, did not hear the bitter cry of her dear child, did not hear the child's farewell to her before she died.

There was a violent palpitation of red and blue in the air; I was blinded. Everything got tangled up and confused in my mind. I felt myself all over, wiped my face, thought that I was wiping off blood, little spurts of blood. . . .

A cold sweat broke out on my body which now felt like a broken shard. There was no longer any difference between the reality and the dream. It was all confusion—chaos!

I felt a splitting pain in my head! Ai, my poor head!

THE HORSE THAT DRANK WHISKY

Once a rabbi went on a journey with his *shammes*. Their cart was drawn by a lively horse of which the rabbi was very fond.

When they came to a roadside inn the rabbi went in to rest. In the meantime, a horse trader passed by and, seeing the shammes stand before his cart, he soon made friends with him. He plied him with drink and, as the shammes was fond of "the bitter drop," he let himself be coaxed, and soon was as drunk as Lot. In that condition it was easy for the horse trader to induce him to sell him the horse for a song.

Although drunk, the shammes was frightened by what he had done. What would the rabbi say when he came out of the inn? An idea occurred to him. He placed himself between the empty shafts of the cart and started to chew hay.

When the rabbi came out he was struck speechless by what he saw.

"What's the meaning of this?" he finally managed to stammer. "Where's the horse?"

"The horse? That's me!" replied the shammes, and he uttered a loud neigh.

"What on earth are you doing?" murmured the rabbi, frightened to death. "Have you gone out of your mind?"

"Don't be angry with me, Rabbi," pleaded the shammes. "Years ago a great misfortune happened to me. I was a young man then, a little wild and foolish as young men usually are, and, may God forgive me, I sinned with a woman. So to punish me, what did God do? He turned me into a horse—your horse. For twenty long years you have been my master, Rabbi, little suspecting who I really was. Well now, it seems my punishment is over. I'm again, praise God, a man!"

When the rabbi heard the story of his shammes he began to tremble and prayed for God's mercy. However, there was a practical difficulty to attend to—he could not continue his journey without a horse, so he went into the market place to buy one.

Suddenly, he stood face to face with his old horse. It was munching a wisp of hay at the horse trader's. Going up to it in alarm, the rabbi bent over and whispered into its ear, "For God's sake, shammes! So soon again!"

When you're told you're dead—lie down!

BORES AND PESTS

Nudniks, Phudniks, and Trombeniks

ADVICE TO NUDNIKS: *Silence is restful:*
it gives rest to the heart, the larynx, the tongue,
the lips, and the mouth.—*The Zohar*

Actually, there are two kinds of bores—the quiet ones and the chatterboxes. But you will have to go a long way from Capetown to Brooklyn before you'll find a nudnik who doesn't talk. A nudnik simply has got to talk! Because, for one thing, he's a Jew, and a Jew, like the Frenchman, the Italian, and the Slav, is conditioned to be articulate. For another, if a nudnik kept silent—God forbid—he'd either have to be sick or else he would not bore you. And in that case he'd stop being a bona fide nudnik.

A nudnik's got to talk—and a lot!

The word "nudnik" is derived from the Russian word "nudna" which, paraphrased freely into plain English, would mean something like "It's enough to throw up!" That is the effect of the nudnik upon his victim.

Now the question occurs: Why are nudniks nudniks? Furthermore, why is so much attention given them in Jewish humorous literature, especially in the Yiddish language?

The answer is quite simple: Jews, especially ghetto Jews of East European origin, talk a great deal. In the first place, that is because the Slavic peoples among whom they lived were voluble talkers. They also have a lively temperament and an intense curiosity about people and things. Then, too, talk is one of the more enjoyable compulsions of frustration; it is a substitute for action. And since frustration has been one of the cornerstones of Jewish destiny, talkativeness has evolved through the centuries as a national Jewish trait.

In every ghetto in the world there was a lot of time to kill in the company of fellow Jews who also had a wealth of time to whittle away. So everybody sat comfortably around the synagogue stove, or in the steam bath, or the market place, in order to spend the time of day, and often it was all the time of day. And so they'd sit and talk, eaten up by boredom, and still talk and talk about heaven and earth until weariness and hunger would set in at last.

And that's how nudniks became nudniks.

Nor must we forget that, by and large, Jews have been made articulate by twenty-five hundred years of Talmudic disputation and hairsplitting. In individuals who wear their self-importance décolleté, it makes for a certain amount of exhibitionism. They have a positive life-and-death urgency to show off their learning and wit before others. And so they talk, or they write—all a part of the selfsame nudnik business. Talk and argument are excellent means for driving away tedium, time, and trouble. And goodness knows that other peoples are just like Jews in this respect. Only their boredom hasn't a Yiddish accent, if that makes any difference.

Take the phudnik, *for example. He is really a high-class bore! Very very modern and stuffed full of culture and emptiness. To get right down to a definition, a phudnik is a nudnik with a Ph.D. It's a portmanteau word, as you see— Ph.D.-nik. Although he first acquired his name in America the phudnik has had an ancient and honorable tradition. He has existed among Jews since the Talmudic schoolmen debated with one another in Sura, Pumpeditha, and Jerusalem. He may have been recognized formerly as a specimen, and labeled accordingly under other unflattering descriptives, such as pedant, dry-as-dust intellectual, and learned fool. But, in reality he remained the same gabbing grandpa, wearing a different* yarmulka *in each case.*

What is the inner drive of a phudnik?

To be profound by being overwhelmingly trivial. He has the need to be recognized and esteemed as a superior person. But, by trying too hard to be profound he only becomes inane and banal. To his misfortune, he doesn't know when to stop talking or writing. Nor does one have the police force adequate to ward him off or to free oneself from his clutches. His victim has got to be forearmed with stoicism and the glazed stare of a deaf person.

Then there is still another variety of bore, the trombenik. *He is exclusively an American product, the Jewish prototype of Babbitt in most respects. But he's also a publicity hound, and an insufferable nudnik into the bargain. That's the complete trombenik!*

There is a colorful origin to the word "trombenik." It is derived from the Yiddish word "tromba," which means "a brass horn." A trombenik constantly toots his own horn and the sound he produces is brassy and raucous. He is like a rooster who has to strut, flap his wings, and shrill forth his cockadoodle in order that the whole world might hear and admire him. If he weren't such a fraud, if he didn't have so much gall—would he then be a trombenik? What's more—and if he weren't blessed with such leathery lungs and a powerful pair of elbows—would anybody pay attention to him? Nu, that's why he is a trombenik—a nudnik plus!

What do you suppose is a Tooter?

A Tooter means "tartar" in Yiddish. And specifically it refers to wild unruly boys.

And a pippernooter? *A little mischievous imp, always fun-loving and sometimes sadistic.*

His name was derived from the pippernooter, a small brat's stiletto. It consisted of a needle or nail stuck into a stick with sharp point protruding. The scamp's strategy was to sidle up to another child with casual innocence and then suddenly jab him with it. His one reward for the effort: a howl of pain from his victim.

N.A.

THE TECHNICAL EXPERT

BY LEO KATZ

The ship, a steamer of 7,000 tons, carried 1,100 passengers. Hardly any had ever seen the sea before. For fourteen days the ship danced on the waves. Most of the passengers found this hard to endure. The blue of the sea or its beauty, so celebrated by the poets, was little in evidence. The water looked gray, mean, and hostile.

And then a day came when land was sighted. The passengers felt like the sailors on Columbus' ships. When the cry of "Land!" rang out, sickness was forgotten, the weak became strong, and new hope arose.

Several hours later one found oneself on board an immigrants' train that was crossing the northern and middle-western part of the United States at a not excessive speed and depositing the newcomers at every station.

"Just look at the cows!" cried one man. "Horns, exactly like ours."

"What did you think, American cows wore high hats?"

The train rolled through cities where on all sides you saw wash hanging out to dry on long clothes-lines. It was as if the Americans had put on a show of fresh laundry in honor of the newcomers and future citizens.

The journey from Boston to Chicago lasted sixty hours, with the number of passengers diminishing steadily. Finally, my journey ended. In Chicago, relatives took me to a house near Humboldt Park. At ten in the morning I found myself in a warm and pleasant room, with a storm raging outside and snowflakes whirling at the windows. I thought of my fellow-travelers. I was sure that someone had exclaimed, "Just look, snowflakes exactly like the ones at home!"

The news of a greenhorn's arrival spread through the whole house. Neighbors came running in to greet the newcomer. One of the neighbors who came in was a man of fifty who had been in the United States over thirty years. He pushed the many guests aside, went straight to the newcomer, and said: "Just let me talk to the greenhorn. Nobody else around here has as much experience of this country as I have and nobody else has traveled around as much."

Turning to the newcomer, he said, "How do you do, greenhorn? Before you do anything else, notice one thing: America is not Europe. I can still see Europe as though I'd left it only yesterday—little houses with thatched roofs, little kerosene lamps, sometimes only candles, and sometimes not even that. A person could spit wherever he pleased, and white bread was only for holidays. Yes sir, believe me, that's the way it was. But what's the use of telling you that, you come from there.

"You'll be amazed at what you see here. Over there you only kept your pants up with suspenders. Belts like we have here were unknown. You had to put your shirt on over your head. You had long under-drawers with strings hanging down behind. And wide shoes.

"Yes sir, that's the way it was. But *I* lost my greenness very soon. There are many people who stay green forever."

The attempts of the other guests to halt this flood of talk were of no avail. He was so filled with his mission, with his desire to smooth the newcomer's path in America, that nothing could stop him. The others had to give up. Most of them soon departed, leaving him alone in the room with the newcomer. And now the lesson really began:

"With you in Europe everything has a lot of serious difficulties connected with it. You can't make a light without matches. But here, believe it or not—do you see this button?"

"I do."

"What is a button like that used for?"

"I don't know."

"Of course, how should a European greenhorn know? Do you see this lamp here? Take a good look at it. Does it have any sort of wick? Do you see any kerosene? Does it stink? Not at all. Press this button, don't be afraid. Nothing will happen. In America everything is safe. Press like this, straight in. Look at the lamp. What do you say now? Did you ever see such a light before? It's too bad it's not night time. Just a moment—Bessie, will you draw the curtain over the window? Now, what do you think of that light? Without matches, without kerosene, without even touching the lamp itself. Press the button again. Do you see me? I don't see you either. Black as night. So, greenhorn!

"Let's go into the kitchen for a moment. Remember the way it was at home? I ask you whether you remember, when as a matter of fact you've just come from there. Of course you remember. You had to bring water from the well in buckets. And there would be a big barrel in the kitchen to pour the water into—for cooking, dishwashing, drinking, everything. Where do you see a barrel here? Have you yet seen a well in America? Believe me, I've been here more than thirty years and I haven't seen a well yet. They're needless. Who uses them? Do you see this brass faucet in the wall? Turn it, don't be afraid. Everything is safe in America. What do you think of that? Water comes out of the wall. And not only here, but in every house, in every apartment—the same thing. Water comes out of the wall. Cold water from one side, hot water from the other. Yes sir. And they drink seltzer here out of bottles, all flavors.

"And look here. What's that? A stove—correct. But where do you see wood or coal? Nothing of the sort. You don't have to split wood here the way you do in Europe, and blow till you're out of breath. Just press the button and it lights. You can make it larger, you can make it smaller. You can put milk on to boil when you want to do any cooking, and you can go away without fear of having it boil over. And where does it all come from? Out of that hole. Here you just put a quarter in and the quarter makes it burn. That's America. Money takes care of everything. All you need is quarters, and then everything comes by itself.

"And who do you think discovered all this—the buttons that make light, the faucets that give water without stopping if you need it, the boxes with quarters that give gas, all America with its English language and the dollars you have to work so hard for? Yes sir. That Columbus was a genius, a real American even if he was born in the old country."

After these words my teacher took me by the right hand and led me out of the kitchen into another room.

"This," he said, "is the dining-room. Look out of the window.

Do you see all that snow? Do you hear the storm howling? On days like this in Europe you wrap yourself in a sheepskin, fill the oven full of wood, and still can't warm yourself up. Do you feel cold here? No sir. Even if you said so, I wouldn't believe you. And where does it all come from? Steam heat. They keep a fire going in the cellar and up here, on the second floor, it's warm. Now what do you say? Nothing, I should think so. But that isn't anything, yet.

"Look to the right. What's hanging on the wall there? Take a good look at it. Don't be afraid. Everything is safe in America. Don't take it down. If you take it down, someone you don't see will immediately say, 'Operator.' And then you have to say a name and a number into this hole. And then you hear another voice say, 'Hello, Mister or Missus—whatever the man or woman's name is—speaking.' Back home when you want to talk to someone you have to send somebody to ask him over or you have to be kind enough, in case of storm or rain, to go and see him yourself. Here it can rain and storm as much as it wants to, snow can pile up over your knees and up to the windows. But if I want to talk to somebody living on another street, all I have to do is pick up this tube here. The operator immediately answers and I tell her a number, and a voice answers me from that other street. And we talk to each other, I tell you, just the way you and I are talking now. The only difference is that you first say hello."

I had listened patiently until now to the explanation of all these technological achievements and submitted without a murmur to the lesson. I had been rendered speechless by hearing that Columbus had discovered the electric light, the gas meter, plumbing, America, and the English language. But when it came to the telephone I felt compelled to express doubt. I permitted myself to interrupt.

"Listen to me, dear friend," I said to him. "I've believed everything you've said. You've proved to me that whatever you say is so. But that you can hear from one house to another in the middle of this storm and all the noise in the streets—no, I don't believe that. You might just as well try to convince me that ice can be made in the summertime. I am a greenhorn, it is true, but still I haven't lost my mind."

These words made him excited. "Unfortunately I can't prove it about the ice just now. But even so, a time will come for that. In the summer, when it's so hot you sweat water from yourself like the faucet in the wall, then I'll show you what America can do. We can make ice here on the hottest day the way we couldn't even make it back home in the heaviest frost.

"As for the telephone, you'll see that today. Not today, right now. Yes sir. We're near Humboldt Park here. From here to Blue Island it's two miles, maybe more. Yes sir. Back home when the cantor used to sing in synagogue you could hear his strong voice for a quarter of a mile at the most. But I'll show you that you can hear from Blue Island to here better than from the kitchen to the dining-room. And you don't have to strain yourself at all. You talk as if to the wall and you hear it as if it were a human voice. Wait a minute, I'll show it to you right away."

The man disappeared. Two minutes later he returned with his wife, whom he had fetched from her kitchen. He had his overcoat and rubbers on.

His wife cried, "Are you crazy? In this storm and snow? You can prove it to him in the afternoon."

"No, what Sam says has to be proved immediately. Let a greenhorn see what Columbus could do."

Then he turned to me: "Listen, when you hear it ringing, run over and pick up the receiver—this tube—with your left hand. Put it to your left ear and with your mouth say into this hole here, 'Hello!' And then—but I don't want to tell you in advance. You'll hear it for yourself."

Then he turned to his wife: "The greenhorn won't know how to handle it. As soon as the phone rings you come in and show him how. But let him pick up the receiver, not you. And make sure he says hello the right way."

With these words the man disappeared into the storm and snow.

While we waited, his wife ran from one neighbor to another and told them how the greenhorn was being Americanized. "Come over," she said to them, "you'll have a nice show." The room was soon filled and everything was tense with expectation.

After about half an hour the telephone rang. The wife was taken by surprise. She pulled me by the hand, but in her surprise she cried "Hello!" into the telephone herself. But then she handed the receiver over to me, saying, "Say hello loud."

I did as I had been told. From the other side I heard the familiar voice: "Do you hear me, greenhorn?"

I answered, "No."

The voice got louder. "Do you hear me, greenhorn?"

"No."

The voice became so loud that I felt a violent pain in my ear.

"No," I answered.

The man began to despair. His voice took on a hoarse undertone. The words were always the same: "Do you hear me, greenhorn?" And my answer was always the same: "No."

Half an hour later the man returned, snow-covered and tired but with a smile on his lips.

"I admit it was stupid of me," he said. "How could I expect a greenhorn to learn and grasp in the very first day what I myself only learned gradually in the course of years? Don't be afraid, greenhorn, take it easy and you'll get used to things here, your greenness will wear off. You mustn't lose patience."

A pseudo-scholar is like a donkey
that carries a load of books.—The Zohar

WHEN A CHAIRMAN GETS STARTED

The chairman arose to introduce the lecturer of the evening to his fellow lodge members.

"Tonight," said he, "we are going to hear about the Book of Proverbs from our distinguished guest."

And the chairman rambled on and on telling all he knew about the Book of Proverbs. When he had finally finished, the lecturer arose and said:

"Ladies and gentlemen! Since your chairman has already covered the Book of Proverbs, my lecture tonight will deal with the Book of Lamentations."

You can tell an ass by his long ears—a fool by his long tongue.

THE MOUTH AND THE EARS

BY SHEM-TOB PALQUERA (THIRTEENTH CENTURY)

My friend, speak always once, but listen twice,
This, I would have you know, is sound advice:
For God hath given you and all your peers
A single mouth, friend, but a pair of ears.

THE RABBI'S ELOQUENCE

The preacher was rambling on and on without coming to the point, and the audience was growing restless and bored.

Suddenly, a loud snoring was heard in the synagogue.

"Shammes!" cried the preacher, angrily. "Wake that man up and ask him to leave!"

"Rabbi!" retorted the shammes. "Why don't you throw him out yourself? It was your sermon that put him to sleep in the first place!"

THE GIFT

BY DER TUNKELER [JOSEPH TUNKEL]
TRANSLATED FROM THE YIDDISH BY NATHAN AUSUBEL

On account of a certain business matter I blundered into a small town in Holland. The name of the town was Zagril, an hour's journey from Amsterdam. It was an obscure town, so obscure that it was a matter of wonder to me how anyone got there in the first place. I had an engagement in Zagril with a lady, but she was delayed and sent word to me that she'd arrive a few days later.

To spend profitably the time I had to wait I decided to go to Amsterdam for a day. I'd leave early to give me time enough to walk through the city's streets, to visit the museums and other places of interest. That same evening I planned to return to Zagril.

So I got up bright and early and took along all the necessary articles for such a journey: a towel, a bar of soap, my fountain pen, my notebook, a book to read, a toothbrush, two handkerchiefs, and my cigarette case and matches. All these articles I tucked away in my thirty-seven pockets. With my raincoat on my left arm and my umbrella hanging from my right, I went off to Amsterdam in holiday mood.

Connoisseurs among tourists say that there can be no greater pleasure on any journey than to get off on the spur of the moment in a strange city where nobody knows you and you know nobody. You meander about, observe, gawk, look about you, lose your way just for the fun of it, and enjoy every moment of it.

I did exactly that. I got out of the railroad station at Amsterdam and began to wander through the city squares, streets, and market places, and finally wound up in the museums. I picked up novelties here and there: albums with views of Amsterdam, a couple of ties, a walking stick, a pair of wooden shoes, an ash tray with a picture of Amsterdam harbor on it, a traveling cap, a guide of Amsterdam with a map, and a lot of other things which I packed into my already bulging pockets. What packages couldn't go into the pockets I hung by their strings on the buttons of my coat so that I swelled up like a balloon.

By noon I was already fagged out. Footsore from dragging myself around all over the city, worn out from the packages I was loaded with, I decided to return to the station and take the train back to Zagril where I would lunch.

I had no sooner taken a few steps in the direction of the railroad station when I suddenly found a lanky individual with a portfolio under his arm blocking my way. He addressed me in a feminine voice and in a fancy German:

"Pardon me, but aren't you Der Tunkeler?"

"Yes."

"Do you recognize me? I recognized you right away."

"No."

"I'm Schwemel! Don't you remember Schwemel? We went to day school together in Vilna? Why, we were even friends!"

"A-a-ah!" I exclaimed, recognizing him.

That was really Schwemel, Menachem Schwemel, the day pupil who was my classmate in Vilna. The same Schwemel, the same cataract on his left eye, the same feminine voice, the same elongated goat's face with his *shofar* beak, the same long neck with the bulging Adam's apple. Now he had acquired a pointed beard which made his face look even more goatlike, almost Mephistophelian. The same long, thin, knock-kneed legs that seemed to stem directly from his curving shoulders. Were you to put a period under him he'd look like a question mark.

"Well, well, so you're now visiting us in Holland!" he said to me in a plain Litvak Yiddish this time.

"Yes," I answered. "I'm staying in Zagril. I'm on business there for a few days, so I took the opportunity to look at Amsterdam for a couple of hours."

"Very good, very good!" said he, rubbing his bony hands. "According to statistics, such a chance meeting as ours occurs once in a million. M-m-nieh! I'm not going to let you go. You've got to lunch with me. I have a wife and a home here and you're going to be an honored guest of mine. I know my wife will be very happy to see you. You know it's no small thing, a friend of one's youth! Statistically speaking, a meeting between friends of one's youth occurs once in three million."

I must confess that I was delighted with his invitation. The prospect of being in a home where I'd have an opportunity of resting up from my morning's sight-seeing pleased me, and I went along with him.

"Well, well, so you're in Holland," he marveled as we sat at lunch, stabbing his nose into his bowl of soup because he was so shortsighted. "Do you remember how we both started out for America at the same time? You got there, all right, but I got stuck in Amsterdam because I didn't have enough money to go farther. But I don't regret it a bit. I'm quite comfortably settled here. Statistically speaking, my economic status is two in one hundred. I have a position in the Royal Bureau of Statistics; you know I hold the degree of Doctor of Statistics. It might interest you to know that I've published my doctoral dissertation in two parts in Dutch. The book has enjoyed great success. Such success only one book out of 3617 enjoys. I'll prove it to you in just a moment. In fact, I'm going to make you a gift of the book to remember me by."

He wiped his lips with his napkin, went up to his bookcase in which I saw a pile of freshly printed books with red covers. He pulled out two volumes which he handed to me. I glanced at the title page and the words looked foreign and incomprehensible. But my friend did me the kindness to translate the title for me from the Dutch. It was *Sources for the Statistics of Stomach Typhus Among the Netherlandish Tribes During the Early Middle Ages*. I could see the book was full of figures, tables, diagrams, and graphs.

"Would you like to have both volumes of my work?" he asked.

"Oh yes! With the greatest pleasure! I'll always treasure them," I murmured my gratitude.

"In that case, let me inscribe the books."

So he pulled out his fountain pen and inscribed the following words on the title page:

> *My friend! Remember statistics!*
> *It is the mother of wisdom.*
> *A gift in remembrance of our meeting.*
> *[signed] Doctor Menachem Schwemel.*

He drew himself up to his full height and, lifting both volumes with the elaborate ceremoniousness of a Spanish grandee about to present his donna with a bouquet of flowers, he offered them to me. "Allow me," said he.

I too stood up and with even greater ceremoniousness accepted his gift.

"Thank you very much," I said, but what I was actually thinking was: "How will I carry these two books when I'm so overloaded with my packages?"

After lunch we took friendly farewell of each other. I executed a masterly piece of strategy by forgetting the books in the foyer. That is, so I thought. But going down the stairs, I heard Doctor Schwemel's voice calling after me:

"The books! The books! You've forgotten the books!"

"Ai, ai, ai!" I shuddered with chagrin at my absent-mindedness. "Every time I travel I get my wits scrambled so. Of late, I've been suffering from acute absent-mindedness."

"That's nothing to worry about," Dr. Schwemel said, trying to calm me, and he shoved the books under my arm. "That you are distracted only shows that you are a spiritual person preoccupied with your thoughts. Statistics prove that the number of absent-minded people is highest among intellectuals and the proportion of——"

What alternative did I have? So I grabbed the books from him in the same way that you snatch a child from a fire, and I went away.

I staggered down the street like an overloaded ass, with bulging pockets and with packages and boxes in my arms. I was annoyed that on top of all that I had to lug with me a two-volume work in Dutch about the statistics of stomach typhus!

I went into a park and seated myself on a bench. Stealthily I placed the books on the bench, got up, and fled. But soon the park watchman caught up with me, handed me the valuable treasure and stuck his hand out for *trinkgeld*.

I gave him several coins and continued on my way. I then found myself in a quiet street and, when I thought that no one was looking, I dropped the books into the canal. But a boatman saw them and showed great skill in the way he retrieved them for me. For this I thanked him heartily and gave him several coins trinkgeld.

By this time I already had lost hope of ever ridding myself of this pesty gift. I began to consider seriously that if I was to continue "losing" the books every little while I'd remain without a coin in my pocket. So I staggered on, bending underneath the burden of my packages.

At last I came to the Judenstrasse. It was a summer twilight and the sun sank with the same splendor that it sinks with on all the Jewish streets and ghettos of the world. In the same way the sun goes down on the Place de Rivoli in Paris, on Dzika Street in Warsaw, on Hester Street in New York, on Frying Pan Alley in Whitechapel, and on other Jewish streets and ghettos. Workers were on their way home from work, children dashed hither and thither and got tangled up between the feet of the passers-by. Some were running races and others were dancing to the music of a hurdy-gurdy that an old Dutch woman was grinding. It was noisy, Jewish-like, although the cries and the curses were in Dutch.

All of a sudden I noticed a lusty woman in a *sheitel* wearing an oilcloth apron. She was selling *matjes* herring from a pail. Around her had gathered a crowd of customers. For each customer the woman pulled a herring from the pail, skinned it first on the right side then on the left in almost the same way that one skins a banana. And when the herring remained bare and glistening with fat, she picked it up by the tail and dunked it in a bowl of sliced onions so that when she pulled it out again it was covered with pieces of onion, like flypaper with flies on a hot summer day. The customer delicately lifted the herring by the tail, threw his head back and, holding the herring above his mouth like a bunch of grapes, devoured it with a few well-timed bites.

Watching people eat herring made my mouth water. I too asked for a herring. However, I had no desire to eat it on the street, and so in pantomime language I asked the woman with the sheitel to wrap it up for me in paper so that I could take it back with me to Zagril. Unfortunately, the woman didn't have any wrapping paper handy since most of her customers ate their herring on the spot. Instantly recalling the two books, I got an inspiration. I went and tore out a few pages from the back of one volume. (I had enough ingrained piety for all books not to tear out the title page with the inscription.) The woman wrapped the onion herring in the pages I gave her, tied a string around it and gave it to me to hang on the last remaining button of my raincoat. Out of gratitude I left her the two books as a gift. M-m-nieh! Let her have plenty of paper to wrap herring in! Besides, I thought that a very good way of getting rid of the pesty things.

Lightheartedly, now, and also with baggage a little lighter, I went to the railroad station. To my luck the train had already left, and all on account of my piddling around with the herring! There wouldn't be another train for an hour.

What was there for me to do? To while away the time I rambled again through the streets, curious to see how the city looked at nightfall. Here and there electric lights were already turned on in houses, on street signs, and in the trams.

I made my way to the business and amusement center of the town where the lights were brightest.

On Rembrandt Platz I suddenly heard a familiar feminine voice calling me. I turned around, and sure enough, there stood Doctor Schwemel!

"What, you haven't gone yet?" he asked me in surprise.

"No, I just missed the train."

"So you missed the train, eh?" he echoed reflectively. "Statistically speaking, one out of 8701 misses the train. When does your next train leave?"

"In an hour."

"First rate!" said my Doctor Schwemel, looking very pleased. "Come, let's go to my house for supper. Have I a little herring! I'm telling you it's fit to recite a benediction in Hebrew over it! Statistically speaking, such a fine herring you'll find only one in 110. You've never seen such a herring in Poland, that I can tell you! Since it's my luck to meet with you again, let's break a herring together! What do you say? After supper, since I've time, I'll walk you back to the station."

I agreed. It was better to spend the hour in a home than drag myself around the streets, especially since I felt so exhausted.

My old school friend's wife served us the herring. Stuffing his mouth with chunks of it and squinting his nearsighted eyes at the tip of his fork, he casually asked:

"And where, may I ask, are my books?"

"What do you mean, where? They're here!" I replied and vaguely began to look among my packages.

"It's a waste of your effort," he advised me, fixing me with a cynical look. "Why, you've lost them!"

"What do you mean I've lost them? I've been guarding them like the apple of my eye."

"Ach, are you an absent-minded man!" he reproached me in a friendly way. "You probably lost them and somebody found them and gave them to a woman herring-vendor on the street."

I felt that I was turning color. I lost my power of speech, so great was my embarrassment. It was my good luck indeed that Doctor Schwemel droned on in an endless monologue.

"It was certainly a remarkable coincidence!" he assured me.

"Such a coincidence, statistically speaking, occurs only once in a million. You see at that very moment of all times I had to pass by a herring vendor and I had to feel like eating a herring. Suddenly, I give a look. Two books are lying on the pavement. I could swear they were familiar books. I open them—my books! *Sources for the Statistics of Stomach Typhus Among the Netherlandish Tribes During the Early Middle Ages.* You guessed it: they were the same books that I gave you as a gift at lunchtime! All I found missing were several pages at the end of one book. You can't believe it? Here are the books!" And he unwrapped a package and handed me the two books.

I must confess that when he confronted me with the books I felt exactly like a murderer when they exhibit his bloodstained knife in court.

"Good God!" I exclaimed, aghast, "I can't see how I could have lost them. It's clear I'm even more absent-minded than I thought I was. I know I deserve to be skinned and quartered for it. I'm an unfortunate person; my absent-mindedness will yet lead me into serious trouble!"

"Don't take it so hard!" Doctor Schwemel tried to console me. "No harm has been done; we'll set everything right. Here! Take two other books. Why only two? I'll give you four—two whole sets! It'll be with you now as with the Patriarch Jacob in the Bible. If you'll lose one set you'll have another set left!"

He pulled out of the mountain of books two sets and then sat down to inscribe them.

So, thank God, I was already the proud owner of four books instead of two! And in order that I shouldn't forget them anywhere, upon leaving me at the station Doctor Schwemel shoved them under my arm.

I thought to myself: "Lord of the Universe, why should I be stricken with this pestilence of books? What for do I need four books of statistics about medieval stomach typhus written in Dutch? So many people are walking the streets and riding in trams and in trains, yet not one of them is carrying any books on stomach typhus statistics! Never fear! As soon as I take my seat in the train compartment I'll know what to do with them."

At last the train moved out of the depot and I was on my way to Zagril.

It wasn't so easy for me to shove the books under the seat, especially with all the passengers watching. But quietly, stealthily, I shoved them to one side with my foot. When the train came to a stop in Zagril,

I leaped out and started to run like a political assassin who has just thrown a bomb.

The following morning the postman brought me a letter with a package and asked me to pay him three gulden. I was under the impression that it had been sent to me by the person for whom I was waiting in Zagril. I readily paid the three gulden, then I opened the letter which came with the package. It read as follows:

> *Honored Friend:*
>
> *Your absent-mindedness is truly phenomenal. It confounds every reckoning of statistics. You forgot the books on the train, and since the name of the publisher, that is my own, was printed in the books, the railroad administration returned the books to me. Knowing how deeply you must suffer over their loss, I've decided to send you a new package with three sets, all properly inscribed. Please accept this modest gift from me and may it remain a souvenir of our meeting in Holland.*
>
> *Your devoted,*
>
> *Menachem Schwemel*
> *Doctor of Statistics*

Now dear reader, be smart and make a guess! What, in your opinion is Doctor Schwemel? Is he a graphomaniac? A fool? An eccentric pest? Or is he just a sly wag who played a neat little trick on me?

Man knows much more than he understands.

Some scholars are like bank tellers
who carry the keys to the strongbox
that contains great sums of money
that don't belong to them.—Ludwig Börne

IT MUST HAVE BEEN A LIE

A chatterbox once came to the Vilna Gaon and dinned into his ears all kinds of foolish gossip. He talked interminably. The rabbi couldn't get in a word edgewise, neither could he get rid of the bore. So he sat glum and silent, resigned to the presence of his tormentor.

Suddenly the man said, "Let me tell you now, Rabbi Elijah, what I once heard the Rabbi of Prague say about you."

Quick as a flash Rabbi Elijah struck back at him. "It's a lie, a big lie!" he cried.

The visitor was aghast.

"What do you mean, 'lie,' " he stammered. "How do you know it's a lie when you haven't even heard what I was going to say?"

"I say it's a lie!" insisted the rabbi, stubbornly. "With a man like you who talks and talks, I'm certain the Rabbi of Prague couldn't have gotten in edgewise a word about me or about anybody else!"

One jackass can make more noise than a thousand nightingales.

REASON IS THE HIGHEST PRINCIPLE

BY HEINRICH HEINE
TRANSLATED FROM THE GERMAN BY CHARLES G. LELAND

During the night which I passed at Goslar, a remarkably curious occurrence befell me. Even now, I cannot think of it without terror. I am not by nature cowardly, but I fear *ghosts* almost as much as the "Austrian Observer." What is fear? Does it come from the understanding or from the natural disposition? This was a point which I frequently disputed with Dr. Saul Ascher, when we accidentally met in the Café Royal, in Berlin, where I for a long time dined. The doctor invariably maintained, that we feared anything, because we recognized it as fearful, owing to certain determinate conclusions of the reason. Only the reason was an active power—not the disposition. While I ate and drank to my heart's content, the doctor demonstrated to me the advantages of reason. Towards the end of his dissertation, he was accustomed to look at his watch and remark conclusively, "Reason is the highest principle!"

Reason! Never do I hear this word without recalling Dr. Saul Ascher, with his abstract legs, his tight fitting transcendental-gray long coat, and his immovably icy face, which resembled a confused amalgam of geometrical problems. This man, deep in the fifties, was a personified straight line. In his striving for the positive, the poor man had philosophised everything beautiful out of existence, and with it, everything like sunshine, religion, and flowers, so that there remained nothing for him, but a cold positive grave. The Apollo Belvedere and Christianity were the two especial objects of his malice, and he had even published a pamphlet against the latter, in which he had demonstrated its unreasonableness and untenableness. In addition to this, he had, however, written a great number of books, in all of which, Reason shone forth in all its peculiar excellence, and as the poor doctor meant what he said in all seriousness, they were, so far, deserving of respect. But the great joke consisted precisely in this, that the doctor invariably cut such a seriously-absurd figure in not comprehending that which every child comprehends, simply because it is a child. I visited the doctor several times in his own house, where I found him in company with very pretty girls, for Reason, it seems, however abstract, does not prohibit the enjoyment of the things of this world. Once, however, when I called, his servant told me that the "Herr Doctor" had just died. I experienced as much emotion on this occasion, as if I had been told that the "Herr Doctor" had just stepped out.

To return to Goslar. "The highest principle is Reason," said I, consolingly to myself as I slid into bed. But it availed me nothing. I had just been reading in Varnhagen von Ense's *German Narrations,* which I had brought with me from Clausthal, that terrible tale of a son, who when about to murder his father, was warned in the night by the ghost of his mother. The wonderful truthfulness with which this story is depicted, caused while reading it, a shudder of horror in all my veins. Ghost stories invariably thrill us with additional horror when read during a journey and by night in a town, in a house, and in a chamber where we have never before been. We involuntarily reflect, "How many horrors may have been perpetrated on this very spot where I now lie?" Meanwhile, the moon shone into my room in a doubtful, suspicious manner; all kinds of uncalled for shapes quivered on the walls, and as I laid me down and glanced fearfully around, I beheld—

There is nothing so "uncanny" as when a man sees his own face by moonlight in a mirror. At the same instant there struck a deep-booming, yawning bell, and that so slowly and wearily that I firmly believed that it had been full twelve hours striking, and that it was now time to begin over again. Between the last and next to the last tones, there struck in very abruptly, as if irritated and scolding, another bell, who was apparently out of patience with the slowness of her friend. As the two iron tongues were silenced, and the stillness of death sank over the whole house, I suddenly seemed to hear, in the corridor before my chamber, something halting and waddling along, like the unsteady steps of a man. At last the door slowly opened, and there entered deliberately the late departed Dr. Saul Ascher. A cold fever drizzled through marrow and vein—I trembled like an ivy leaf, and scarcely dared I gaze upon the ghost. He appeared as usual, with the same transcendental-gray long coat, the same abstract legs, and the same mathematical face; only this latter was a little yellower than usual, and the mouth, which formerly described two angles of 22½ degrees, was pinched together, and the circles around the eyes had a somewhat greater radius. Tottering, and supporting himself as usual upon his Malacca cane, he approached me, and said, in his usual drawling dialect, but in a friendly manner: "Do not be afraid, nor believe that I am a ghost. It is a deception of your imagination, if you believe that you see me as a ghost. What is a ghost? Define one. Deduce for me the conditions of the possibility of a ghost. In what reasonable connection does such an apparition coincide with reason itself? *Reason,* I say, *reason!*" Here the ghost proceeded to analyze reason, cited from Kant's Critic of Pure Reason, part 2, 1st section, chap. 3, the distinction between phenomena and nouomena, then proceeded to construct a hypothetical system of ghosts, piled one syllogism on another, and concluded with the logical proof that there are absolutely no ghosts. Meanwhile the cold sweat beaded over me, my teeth clattered like castanets, and from very agony of soul I nodded an unconditional assent to every assertion which the phantom Doctor alleged against the absurdity of being afraid of ghosts, and which he demonstrated with such zeal, that finally, in a moment of abstraction, instead of his gold watch, he drew a handful of grave worms from his vest pocket, and remarking his error, replaced them with a ridiculous but terrified haste. "Reason is the highest——" Here the clock struck *one,* and the ghost vanished.

POOR MAIMONIDES!

A learned pretender came to an eminent Talmudic scholar and dinned into his ears his own unoriginal views on the Prophets. His patience finally strained, the scholar muttered with faint sarcasm, "It's too bad, too bad that you did not live in the days of Maimonides!"

"Thank you, Rabbi, thank you!" murmured the pretender, overcome by the compliment. "But tell me, please—what would have happened had I known Maimonides?"

"Had you known Maimonides you'd have bored him—not me!" snapped the scholar.

A bad wheel creaks the loudest.

If all men were students of philosophy,
the social order would be destroyed
and the human race quickly exterminated. . . .
     —Moses ben Maimon (Maimonides)

Imagine a bedbug completely flattened out,
living on the surface of a globe.
This bedbug may be gifted with analysis,
he may study physics, he may even write a book.
His universe will be two-dimensional.—Albert Einstein

THE EDUCATED FOOL

BY THE PREACHER OF DUBNO [DUBNER MAGGID]

The king of a great country had an only son, but as he was a fool his father took the matter gravely to heart.

"What would happen were I to die?" he thought in dismay. "How can I possibly leave my kingdom in the hands of such a *schlemihl* and ignoramus?"

So he called a council of his ministers and they thrashed the matter out. They advised him to send his heir to a certain university in a foreign land. From the great savants who taught there, they were sure, he would acquire a little wisdom and learning.

The king took their advice and sent his son to study in that university. At parting he said to him:

"Be sure, my son, not to come back until you're an educated man."

Several years passed. The king's son studied hard. At last he grew tired of learning so much, and he wrote to his father one letter after another, imploring:

"Dear Father, I have already learned everything there is to be learned. As there is no further wisdom for me to acquire I beg you to let me come home."

After several such letters the king became convinced that it was high time to call his heir home. So he sent several of his ministers to fetch him.

The king was overjoyed at their reunion, and he ordered that a feast be prepared in honor of his son who had come back to him a mature and learned man. To the feast he invited all his ministers, nobles, and generals. When they were all high in their cups, one of the ministers wished to inquire into the prince's newly acquired wisdom.

"Do tell us," he asked, "what did you learn at the university?"

The prince replied, "I studied algebra, geometry, astronomy, and mathematics."

Unnoticed, his questioner took a ring off his finger and held it in his clenched fist.

"Guess what I hold in my hand," he asked.

The prince regarded his fist sagely and answered, "I should judge, according to the sciences I have studied, that the object you hold in your hand is round and has a hole in the center."

The minister was filled with amazement. The prince really had become a sage!

"Now, Your Highness, will you be good enough to name this object?" he asked.

"According to the sciences I have studied," replied the prince, "I cannot name it, but my own common sense tells me that it must be a cart wheel."

MORAL: You can educate a fool but you can't make him think.

Some people may be compared to new shoes:
the cheaper they are the louder they squeak.

Every dog feels important on his own dunghill.

The best part about telling the truth
is that you don't have to remember what you said.

Love your neighbor—even when he plays the trombone.

Tooters—Pippernooters

When a mother yells, "Mamzer!"
at her child—you can believe her.

MY PINYA

BY B. KOVNER [JACOB ADLER]
TRANSLATED FROM THE YIDDISH BY NATHAN AUSUBEL

I

My Pinya is a fine little fellow. He has only one fault—he's crazy about mud! For mud he'd give away his papa and his mama.

When the weather is wet and muddy you can't find him in the house, but if the day is nice and sunny you can't budge him to go outside. No matter how much I beg him it's no use. I say to him, "Pinya, little Pinyale, my little *kaddish,* what are you hanging around the house for, why don't you go out a bit and play?" I might as well talk to the wall. He hangs around the house and gnaws at my poor brain like a maggot.

He sticks his nose into all the pots, loots the icebox, climbs on all the walls. And what doesn't he put his little paws on: an apple, a turnip, a hunk of bread, an onion—as long as it's edible he's not too particular.

He has only two passions: eating and mud!

But the most important to him is mud. There he feels fully at home.

Just to look at him not even the greatest biologist would be able to determine that the child had human ancestors. Just about as much mud as there is in the world can be found on my little Pinya. He's a chunk of mud on two little legs. . . .

II

My wife Yente says to me:

"Go ahead, Mendel, and take Pinya to school. You know he won't go himself. Do you remember the trouble we had with him last year? Go ahead and take him. He's bummed around enough on the street, he's crawled under every express wagon and rolled in all the gutters."

"Pinya doesn't need to be taken," I answered. "He'll go by himself. Pinya is an obedient child; if he's told to go he'll go."

"You're talking from the heat, Mendel!" cried Yente on top of her voice. "He won't go! Pinya's not the kind of child who likes to go by himself. He won't go unless you force him. Rely on Pinya's sense of right—that's silly!"

"All right," I said. "Get him ready."

So Yente ran out into the street and soon came back dragging my reluctant Pinya by the hand. She wiped his little nose with her apron and pulled his old cap with the ragged visor down on his head.

"Take him, Mendel!" she commanded.

When Pinya heard what it was all about he became mulish and wouldn't go.

Yente pleaded with him:

"Pinyale dear, Pinyale darling, if you'll go to school with papa like a good boy I'll give you a lollipop, an ice-cream sandwich; papa will take you to the moving pictures—but go to school!"

Pinya didn't want to. Yente gave him a kiss on his forehead and continued to plead with him:

"Pinyale, my dear boy, birdie mine! Here's a penny . . . a nickel . . . there, you have a quarter—but go to school!"

Pinya whimpered doggedly.

When Yente saw that, she grew angry.

"Pinya!" she yelled. "You'll be sorry for this, I'm telling you!" And she plucked at his right ear so that Pinya winced.

But still he refused to surrender.

Yente began to yell. "Pinya I'll murder you, I'll cripple you!" And she poked him in the ribs.

But Pinya remained mute.

This made Yente even more angry. She turned furiously on me.

"Mendel, may you suffocate, you dolt, why do you keep quiet. You're a papa, no?"

So I went over to Pinya, took him by the hand and asked him straight to the point, "What do you want?"

"I want a hammer and nails," he answered, also straight to the point. "If you don't give them to me I don't go to school!"

I lost patience, took hold of him, and pushed him out of the house. He resisted, so I dragged him away by force while Yente followed behind abusing me. Why did I torture *nebbech* the poor child? Why didn't I let him go?

So I let him go. And without a moment's hesitation Pinya ran away.

Yente now reversed her tune: Why did I let him go? Right away, that very moment, I should run after him!

So I ran after him and caught him and once more began dragging him to school.

Pinya began to slither about like a snake struggling to free himself from my grip. But I held him firmly by the hand and would not let him go.

Again Yente reviled me: What did I want to do, anyway—dislocate his little arm? It would be she and nobody else who'd have her hands full should it happen.

"Well, what do you want me to do, anyway?" I asked, exasperated.

"Let go of the child; he'll go to school by himself."

Again I let him go, and again he ran away!

So Yente bawled me out why I didn't run and catch him.

So I ran after Pinya and caught him. After that I paid as much attention to Yente's orders as Haman does to the noisy *gragers* the children sound on Purim when the Book of Esther is read in the synagogue. I dragged Pinya off to school. The teacher told me to leave him there; she'd pacify him, she assured me grimly.

I wiped the sweat from my face and went home, with Yente still behind me, abusing me for torturing the poor child so.

Only twenty minutes had passed when—aha, my heart told me something like that would happen! The teacher sent a little *boychik* to find out where Pinya was.

"Where Pinya is?" we asked in surprise. "Why, in school, of course!"

"He's not in school," said the boychik. "The minute you left he ran away."

Yente and I dashed out to look for Pinya. She instructed me, "If you catch him make a cripple of him!"

"With pleasure!" I answered.

And we agreed that I should look for Pinya on one street and she on another and we'd meet at the El station after.

At that moment a milk wagon rattled by. We took a look. There, hanging on to the back of the wagon with his feet dragging on the ground, was little Pinya!

When Pinya caught sight of us he let go his grip on the wagon and scampered away.

We found him at last towards nightfall near a livery stable, all covered with mud, without his cap and with a blackened eye.

III

I asked my neighbor, Abie the carpenter, "What do you think I ought to do with Pinya? What shall I make of him?"

"Take my advice, Reb Mendel," my neighbor replied. "Make a musician out of him. It's very nice when a child knows how to play. It's very refined. When company comes he can entertain and give papa and mama great *naches,* and by the way, your Pinya has a very good ear."

"How do you know my Pinya has a good ear?"

"I'm sure he has; he shows many signs of that. When it thunders he hears it, when an express wagon rattles by he hears it, when an automobile honks he hears it, when the fire engines clang by he hears that too. That's a sign that he has a good ear."

"If that's the case, then what kind of instrument shall I let him learn to play?"

"The violin! The violin is a beautiful instrument. All the great violinists like Mischa Elman and Zimbalist play the violin."

"That may very well be, only I don't like the violin; it's too quiet an instrument."

"So teach him the flute! That's a lovely instrument and cheap, too. For two dollars and fifty cents you can buy him a flute."

"Feh, a flute's not for Pinya! Anybody can play on the flute; it's just like a whistle."

"Well, what else?"

"My plan is to teach him the trombone or the trumpet. I like instruments that let themselves be heard from. That's why I got married to Yente."

"I'll tell you what, Reb Mendel: You ask Pinya himself what instrument he'd like to play."

"That's a fine idea," I agreed.

My Yente ran down the stairs into the street and soon came back pulling Pinya by the ear.

When I put the question to him Pinya answered without hesitation: "I don't like a trombone and I don't like a trumpet and I don't like a violin and I don't like a flute either. I want a kettledrum, a big, big kettledrum with brass dishes on it."

I could see that Pinya knew what he wanted and that he had a good ear. So I went to Brownsville and found for him a teacher, and then I went together with him to a music store and bought for Pinya a little kettledrum with two brass dishes on it. I arranged with the teacher that he was to give Pinya one lesson a week, on every Tuesday.

Last Tuesday, around seven o'clock in the evening, the teacher came to give Pinya his first lesson. He brought along with him his own drum, as big as he was himself, and with brass dishes as well. He placed his kettledrum beside Pinya's and thrust a big drumstick into Pinya's hand; they both began to pound away on the kettledrums so that the whole house shook. It didn't take two minutes before the whole block was full of people.

Don't ask me what followed. The janitor came running up; he looked pale and scared to death.

"What's going on? What's happened?" he gasped.

"Nothing, just nothing," I told him. "My Pinya's taking his first lesson on the kettledrum today. I'm going to make a musician out of him."

The janitor spat out with contempt.

"He'll be some musician! It can make a person deaf."

"If you don't like it, you can move," I advised him.

So he began to abuse me on all the instruments he knew, but at that moment my Yente sprang into the breach and he was obliged to retreat. He left, slamming the door behind him.

Yente yelled after him, "Slam your head in the ground, you!"

What's the use of saying anything more? For more than an hour on the clock, Pinya and his teacher banged away on their kettledrums. Before he left, the teacher said that Pinya looked very promising, that he was very musical but that he had to practice, the more the better.

When the teacher left, Pinya began to practice his lesson with such enthusiasm that he almost busted the kettledrum. All the neighbors raised a yell. They shouted from all the windows that Pinya's playing was making them nervous, that he didn't let them sleep. But Pinya ignored them and continued to pound the daylights out of his drum. Four hours he sat there drumming, and he resumed it again in the morning, and so for the entire week.

"I've got to practice," said Pinya with a light in his eye. "The teacher will come soon to give me another lesson, so I'd better be prepared."

What else is there left for me to say? Since he took his first lesson Pinya has forced three families to move, and, by the looks of things, after he has taken his second lesson we'll be the only family left in the whole tenement house. The neighbors tell me that the janitor is also looking for another job.

Well, as you see Pinya's already provided with a future.

IV

In the morning, as soon as I opened my eyes, I heard Pinya cry.

"What are you crying about, Pinya?" I asked him. "Do you have a toothache?"

Pinya said nothing.

"Are you hungry, maybe?" I continued.

Still Pinya didn't answer.

"Maybe you want a penny?" I asked soothingly.

Pinya was dumb.

"Pinyale darling, why do you cry. Say something!"

Sha, silence! Pinya doesn't talk.

Out of patience, Yente began to yell, "Stop it, Mendel! What's the idea of carrying on a debate with Pinya? With Pinya he wants to start up yet! Rip an ear off him! Give it to him with a strap! He'll find his tongue then, all right!"

And Yente grabbed up a strap and threateningly descended on Pinya. But it didn't have the slightest effect on him. He did what he wanted: he said nothing.

Yente now opened up on him with the real language: "I'm telling you, Pinya, you'll earn for yourself a black year this way, you and your father rolled together. So open your yap, what do you want?"

And so saying, she gave him such a pinch that poor little Pinya gave a convulsive shake.

When Pinya saw how he was playing with fire and that he would come out of his mama's hands a permanent cripple, he blurted out:

"I want a flag!"

Seeing that what Pinya asked for was just and reasonable, for it was *Simchas Torah,* Yente shouted at me, "What are you standing there like a *goilem,* Mendel? Go right down to the candy store and buy him a flag."

Five minutes later Pinya was already clutching a green flag in his little paw.

"Lunatic!" cried Yente to me. "What's the idea of buying him a green flag? What are we anyway—Irishers? Run down quickly and change the flag! What do you say to him? Gets an Irish flag for Simchas Torah!"

So I ran down and exchanged the green flag for a yellow one.

When Yente saw the yellow flag she almost got a fit of apoplexy.

"Mendel!" she shouted. "May a misfortune strike you! You ox, you horse's head! You couldn't find any other flag except a yellow one? What do you say to that—a Chinese flag he got! What are you, a Chinaman? Run right down and bring Pinya another flag."

So I ran down and brought up a red flag.

"Have you gone crazy or something?" screamed Yente at me. "Why does Pinya need a red flag? What is he—a socialist? Go right down and bring up another flag."

"There are no others," I said, "except a blue-and-white one."

"All right, let it be a red one then," said Yente sick and tired of the whole matter.

When Feivel and Isaac saw that Pinya had a flag they started whimpering—they too wanted flags. First of all, Yente cursed them good and proper. Then she gave them some awful pinches. Finally, she gave each one of them a penny so that they could buy flags themselves.

Feivel bought for his penny a whistle and Isaac a lollipop. Later, when Yente discovered what they had done, she gave them a good hiding.

Do you think it bothered them? Not a bit! Feivel kept on whistling on his whistle and Isaac sucked on his lollipop.

That night Yente said to me, "Mendel, go and wipe Pinya's little nose and take him with you to the synagogue so he can watch the procession with the Holy Scrolls. Let him see how Jews dance and rejoice over their Torah. Let him know that he's a Jew, woe to him!"

So I took hold of Pinya, blew his nose for him and then took him with me to the Congregation Anshe Fife where Barney the expressman was *chazan*. I lifted up Pinya and put him down on a window ledge. Then I lighted the little candle on his flag.

But Pinya remained Pinya. In two minutes' time the flags of all the other children were ablaze; Pinya had put them all on fire. And from those flags that he didn't succeed in burning he twisted off the red jelly apples.

On our return from the synagogue, Yente eagerly asked him, "*Nu*, Pinya, were you at the synagogue?"

"Sure," answered Pinya gleefully.

"Tell me, what did you do there?"

"I had a good time—I burned all the other boys' flags! I took away their jelly apples."

And proudly he pulled out of his pockets four sticky jelly apples and showed them to Yente.

> *When you get a paddling you become a prophet:*
> *although you lie face down*
> *you know pretty well what's going on above.*

ANGELS IN CHAYDER

BY LOUIS GOLDING

The vicissitudes of school and Angel Street represented only the secular side of Philip's existence. The Jewish, the clerical side, claimed his servitude as soon as he pushed open the door of the house. The whole day, of course, was punctuated with greater or lesser ceremonies; but a considerable portion of it, at least of that part not taken up by school, was spent in his father's *chayder*. Beyond chayder, to gather together and confirm the saintliness ardently desired and pursued for him by his father, lay the synagogue in Doomington Road, the *Polisher Shool*.

The room in which the chayder was housed was distinctly dismal, despite the fountain of spiritual light playing perpetually there, the fountain whereof Reb Monash himself was the head. It lay between the "parlour," a chilly room upholstered in yellow plush, which was on the right as you passed into the "lobby," and the kitchen in the recesses of the house, to enter which you descended two invisible steps. Beyond the window of the chayder and beyond the yard, hung a grim, blank-windowed hat-and-cap factory.

Low forms, where the two dozen scholars were disposed, ran round the four walls of the room. Before a table facing the window Reb Monash sat, in the additional shadow cast by the large oblong of cardboard which occupied a fourth of the window-space so as to hide the damage caused by a malicious gentile stone. More for minatory gesture than for punishment, a bone-handled walking-stick lay to his hand, along the table. Facing the door a large cupboard stood invariably open. Here on the lowest shelf were the prayer books, from the first page of which the youngest scholars learned their Hebrew capitals. Here also were the penny exercise books where the scholars proficient in the cursive script wrote letters of a totally imaginary politeness to their parents. "My dear and most esteemed Father and Mother," they ran, "I am full of concern for your health. Reb Monash joins me in respectful greeting. The High Festivals are approaching, God be thanked, and I trust the Above One will bless our ways with milk and honey and will much increase our progeny, even as the sands on the shore. Believe I am your to-death-devoted son."

Upon one wall hung a chart where an adventurous red line traced the forty years' wandering of the Jewish race between the House of Bondage and the Promised Land. A portrait of Dr. Theodor Herzl, every feature cleverly pricked out in Hebrew letters, hung opposite. There were enlargements from photographs of Mr. and Mrs. Massel, and portraits of Heine and Disraeli, which had been hung not without compunction, although each had made so generous a death-bed recantation of his errors.

The payment to Reb Monash for a week's tuition ranged between one shilling and eighteenpence. He sometimes accepted ninepence, but on the condition that other parents should not be informed and the market be thus demoralized. He even accepted no payment at all, in cases of extreme indigence, where it meant that a scion of Israel would otherwise run riot in pagan ignorance. The attendances of his pupils were as follows: In the week-days, a few frantic minutes between morning and afternoon school for the recital of *Minchah,* the midday prayer, and more importantly, several long hours in the evening; on the Saturday, once, after dinner.

During the evening session, while the maturer boys were biting their pens over their letters home, and the boys less mature were transcribing for page after page a sample line in Reb Monash's own script, *rebbie* himself dealt with the infants, five, four, three years old. Patiently, gently, the meat skewer he used as a pointer moved from capital to capital. (A safe way to win temporary harbourage in *rebbie's* good graces was to provide him with a new pointer.)

"*Aleph!*" said Reb Monash. "*Aleph!*" piped the little voice. "*Bazel*" "*Bazel*" "*Gimmel, daled!*" "*Gimmel, daled!*"

With the young he had enormous patience. When at last they knew all the letters in their consecutive order, his pointer would dart bewilderingly from letter to letter.

"Lange mem, tsadik, coff. . . ."

Ignorance, up to a certain age, Reb Monash could condone. It was inattention against which he maintained a fiery crusade.

"What, thou canst not distinguish between *baze* and *shloss mem?* Playest thou then alleys already? Thou art a lump-gentile, a *shtik-goy!*" After the youngsters had been thus instructed, a snap of his prayer book was the signal for a deathly calm. All the exercise books were closed and put away upon their shelf. Everybody sat down upon the benches round the wall and each face assumed a look of virtue bordering upon imbecility. Reb Monash then produced a thin note-book where in three columns down each page he had written a large number of Hebrew words. These words had, excepting rarely, no connection with each other. One leaped abruptly from "pepper" to "son-in-law" and thence to "chair," "snake," "pomegranate," and "yesterday."

Starting with any boy indiscriminately he read out word after word, receiving an English or Yiddish equivalent. Here again, to introduce a complexity, he suddenly interrupted the written order of the words, or, indeed, himself gave the profane equivalent of the vocabulary and demanded the "Holy Speech" in return. With as little warning he transferred his attention to another of his scholars, and woe upon him if the black crime of inattention had sent his wits scattering, woe if his lips could not repeat the word just translated! A silence intense as the silence of the antechamber where the High Priest three times demands from Radames his defence, occupied the breathless chayder during the process of "Hebrew."

Yet for all his sallies and alarms the tragedy of Reb Monash was no more apparent than in the heart-broken monotone in which he uttered his list of inconsequent words. All the ghettos of Russia had known the silver of his voice. If there had been sorrows of Israel none had told them more poignantly; if Zion still were to raise tall towers, none so joyfully had prophesied her new splendours. Still in many synagogues beyond the *Polisher Shool* his oratory was in demand. But the glow of his old dreams? Was it because no single reality had called him to concrete endeavours, that no single dream had found fulfilment?

But all this lay deep down, deeper than himself dared to pursue.

"Pilpelim?" "Pepper!"

"Lo mit a vov?" "To him!"

"Philip, where holds one?"

". . . er . . . er . . ."

"What! thou knowest not?"

"Yes, *tatte*, yes . . . *odom*, a man!"

Reb Monash's lips set tight. Philip's back curved under his father's fist. He pressed his head down upon his neck. He knew that the nearer he attained to immobility, the sooner would his punishment be over.

Reb Monash sat down again.

"*Roshoh?*" he asked significantly.

"Evil one!"

"*Boruch?*" to point the contrast.

"Blessed!" the voice translated.

And so till "Hebrew" was at an end. Then followed translation from the week's portion of the Pentateuch; and perhaps if one or two scholars of such holy state remained under his care, an excursion into the Talmud.

The combination of Miss Tibbet and chayder left Philip limp with fatigue and dejection. Life under Miss Tibbet was clockwork, barren of adventure and hope. Chayder was a cycle that each year returned to the same spot through a round of indignities and petty tyrannies. All its nightly incidents were the same as last week's and last year's and seemed destined to reduplication world without end. Walls seemed to rise frowning before him wherever he looked. It was hard to breathe. Were these days the pattern of all the days he should ever know, till he died at last and half-hearted funeral eulogies were uttered over his coffin?

Yet now and again there were incidents which slightly relieved the tedium of existence. As for instance when the notorious Jakey arrived in chayder about an hour late one stifling summer evening. Jakey was in truth a desperate character. His stockings lay invariably over his boots, and the boots themselves knew no other fastening than string. Among the layers of dirt on his face his right eye or his left emerged livid in purple and salmon hues. On numerous occasions he had "wagged" school in order to play pitch and toss with coins, derived who knew whence? in the company of stalwarts fifteen years old, three years his senior.

It was in fact during the solemn stillness of "Hebrew" that he arrived. Upon his appearance the hush was intensified into something acute as shrill sound or pain. Slowly, with tight-browed condemnation, Reb Monash turned his head to the truant. "So thou art come!" he said. "Enter! we are incomplete without thee!" With withering courtesy he motioned him to the end of a bench. Nonchalantly moving the tip of his tongue from one cheek to the other Jakey sat down.

"*Nu,* Jakele, what hast thou for thyself to say?" he asked, still couchant, as it were, upon his chair. Jakey for several seconds longer kept his tongue in his left cheek. He lifted his brows in interested contemplation:

"I had the stomach-ache!" he suggested, clasping his hands against his liver as a piece of convincing byplay.

"*Ligner!*" thundered Reb Monash. "Thou art sound as a Hottentot!"

Jakey withdrew one hand from his stomach, and lifted a thumb to his mouth.

"My muvver's dying!" he said after further meditation.

Reb Monash quivered with wrath.

"Such a year upon thee! Long live thy mother, but thou, thou art a proselytized one!"

He advanced to make Jakey more immediately aware of the jeopardy into which his soul had fallen. Jakey looked up shiftily, his eyes watchful. Reb Monash's fist came down upon empty air. Swift as a lizard Jakey darted across to the table. He stood there, Reb Monash's bone-handled stick uplifted. A murmur of horror went round the chayder. Reb Monash with a shout of anger advanced raging. And then it was that his own stick, the symbol of more absolute authority than the Shah's, was brought down upon his own shoulder. There was a silence. Then immediately a tremendous hubbub filled the room. Reb Monash sank into his chair. A few of the youngest lads lifted up their voices and wept. A boy in a corner was giggling nervously.

"Where is he? Where is he?" asked Reb Monash weakly. An enormity had been perpetrated unknown in the annals of chayders. And in *his,* Reb Monash's, where discipline and holiness were equal stars.

" 'E's ran away! I seen 'im!" the cry rose.

Reb Monash grimly took up once more his book of Hebrew words. The long monotone began again.

"*Ishoh?*" "A woman!"

"*Sachin?*" "A knife!"

The door was flung open. A storm of flying apron-strings filled the threshold, and a cloud of loose hair. It was the mother of Jakey.

"Reb Monash, what is for such a thing?" she demanded indignantly. "One might think a policeman, not a rebbie. My poor Jakele, gentle as a dove, a credit in Israel! What for a new thing is this?"

Reb Monash lifted his hands deprecatingly. "What say you, Mrs. Gerber? An hour later he comes. . . ."

She gave him no time to continue. "And then to lay about him with a walking-stick! A Tartar, not a Jew! Never a word of complaint from God or man about my poor orphan and . . . to come to chayder . . . and a pogrom! *Oi, a shkandal!* A walking-stick like a tree! A moujik, God should so help me, not a rebbie! Poor Jakele, crying his heart out like a dove! I'll take him away from a so crooked chayder!"

"But that concerns me little!" broke in Reb Monash. "For each one that goes, come four each time!" (This confident mathematic invariably puzzled Philip. He knew how necessary to the Massel family was an increased income. Why should not Reb Monash dismiss his whole chayder and then automatically increase his clientèle fourfold?)

"Like a tree a walking-stick!" continued Mrs. Gerber. She flounced through the door. "Such a year! Such a black year shall seize you!" she spat. The door closed with a loud bang. It was impossible to sit down under it. Not only to have been assaulted, but to be accused of being the assailant was too much to bear. Reb Monash took his skull-cap, his *yamelke,* from his head, placed it on the mantelshelf, and assumed his silk hat.

"Learn over your passages!" he rapped out as he followed furiously to the house of Jakey.

There was subdued whispering at first.

"Wot a lark!" said some one. "Oo—aye! Wot a lark!" some one else repeated. Then every one laughed. Philip was hilarious. It really was too funny—Jakey the dove!

"I've got the stomach-ache, rebbie!"

"No you've not, you mean your muvver's dying!"

Some one lifted the walking-stick. Barney did a *pas seul* in the corner. The gaiety of the situation intoxicated everybody. Philip was swept off his feet by the general merriment. He reached up for his father's skull-cap, put it on and looked round solemnly. Barney imitated Mrs. Gerber with great distinction.

"A moujik, not a rebbie!"

At this moment the door opened. Reb Monash's face looked round glowering below his silk hat. Quick as thought Philip covered the borrowed skull-cap, knowing there was no time to replace it, with his own cap. He felt the unfortunate load pressing guiltily against his head.

Reb Monash took off his silk hat and looked round for the yamelke.

"Where's my yamelke?" he demanded fiercely.

"Dunno!" a murmur rose.

"Did I not place it on the mantelshelf?"

"Didn' see yer!"

"Dost thou know?"

"No, rebbie!"

"Dost thou, Philip?"

"No, *tatte!*"

"Dost thou, Barney?"

"No, rebbie!"

"Empty ye out all your pockets!"

The yamelke was nowhere to be found. It was a very hot evening and it produced on Philip an unholy delight to see his father sitting there in the close heat, with bright red carpet slippers, thin black trousers, a thin alpaca coat—and to crown all, the stately and stuffy tall hat, malevolent and quite definitely absurd.

It was towards the end of the evening that Philip lifted his cap to scratch his head over some knotty point in the *chumish*, the Pentateuch, they were translating. He had wholly forgotten the abstracted yamelke, so, whilst his own cap fell with a soft slur on the table before him, the yamelke sat revealed like a toad under a lifted stone.

Reb Monash looked up. It was too late to hide the yamelke. Reb Monash's eyes glinted unpleasantly. Chayder drew to an immediate end.

HEBREW LESSON

The Hebrew teacher was guiding little Stanley through the intricacies of the holy tongue. He helped him along with outrageously open hints, for the boy's mind hovered less over Mount Sinai and more over the Yankee Stadium, where the Giants and the Cards were playing a "double-header" that afternoon.

"What does the Hebrew word *isha* [a wife] mean?" asked the teacher.

"I don't remember," answered Stanley in confusion.

"Let me give you a hint—*isha*, a w—!"

"A wall!" hopefully experimented Stanley.

"Dumbbell! Try to pay attention—*isha*, a w—!"

"A wart!"

"Idiot! How could the word 'wart' get into the Five Books of

Moses? Now pay attention! Once again, and watch my lips—*isha,* a w—w—!"

"A w-whip!"

"It's no use!" groaned the rabbi, utterly discouraged. "Now listen carefully, Stanley! We'll start all over again. *Isha* is—what your grandfather had, what your father has, what your uncle has, well—what I too have."

" I know. I know!" cried Stanley triumphantly. *"Isha* is a hernia!"

THE THEATER

BY JACOB GROPPER
TRANSLATED FROM THE YIDDISH BY JOSEPH LEFTWICH

There's in the barn a theater.
Admission buttons four.
Who doesn't pay won't be let in.
He'll stop outside the door.

And if he is caught stealing in,
Not paying what he owes,
He'll get a thrashing and will go
Flying out on his nose.

Only you, because you give us
Often a lovely treat,
We shall allow you in for nothing,
And give you a front seat.

All the players in a row
Up on the stage stand.
Mendel is leading the chorus.
Berl Klotz is the band.

I turn my jacket inside out,
Wear my hat upside down,
And crack a lot of funny jokes,
Behaving like a clown.

A few of us are wearing masks.
Try to guess whose is whose.
Baruch sings like a woman would,
Hersh cackles like a goose.

Such a lot more things we can do.
You will love it, I know.
It's worth the buttons that you pay.
Do come and see the show.

Now we're starting our theater.
Four buttons to come in.
Only two for mother-o'-pearl ones.
Quick, before we begin.

Hurry up, before we get started.
We don't intend to wait.
And if you don't get inside now,
You'll find you've come too late.

THE AWAKENING

BY ISAAK BABEL
TRANSLATED FROM THE RUSSIAN BY ESTER AND JOSEF RIWKIN

All the men of our circle, brokers, shopkeepers, employees of banks and shipping companies, had their children take music lessons. It was a regular mania. Our fathers in their impotent longing for success had invented a lottery pool. But *this* gamble had children for its stakes. More than other cities, Odessa had been afflicted with the craze. In the course of a dozen years, our city had supplied the concert halls of the entire world with child prodigies. Both Mischa Elman and Gabrilovitch came from Odessa, and it was there that Jascha Heifetz made his debut.

As soon as a boy reached the age of four or five, his mother would take the puny creature to see Zagoursky. Zagoursky had started a factory of child prodigies, a factory of Jewish dwarfs in lace collars and patent leather shoes. He dragged them from the bedbug-infested hovels of the Moldavanka, out of the stinking yards of the Old Market. Zagoursky taught them the elements of music. Then they were shipped to Professor Auer in Petersburg.

A powerful harmony vibrated in the souls of these agonized brats with blue, puffed heads. They were to become famous virtuosos! And so my father, too, decided to run after Heifetz and Mischa Elman. I was almost fourteen and had already outstripped the age of child prodigies, but I was so small and delicate that I might easily pass for eight years old. And in that lay all our hope.

I was taken to see Zagoursky. As a favor to my grandmother, he agreed to charge the small sum of one rouble a lesson. My grandfather Levi-Yitzhak was the town's laughingstock and pride. Attired in a top hat and a pair of long woollen drawers, he used to meander through the streets and dissolve doubts about the most obscure problems. He was asked why the Jacobins betrayed Robespierre, how artificial silk is manufactured, the nature of a goblin, and the meaning of a Caesarean operation. My grandfather was a match for all these questions. So out of respect for his wisdom and madness, Zagoursky charged us only a rouble a lesson. And it was only out of fear of grandfather that he took pains with me, for there was nothing to take pains about. The sounds that crawled from my violin grated like iron filings. I was the first to have my heart lacerated by those sounds—but my father refused to give up his idea. At home they could think only of Mischa Elman, whom the Czar himself had exempted from military service, and of Gabrilovitch, who had been presented to the king of England and had played at Buckingham Palace. Gabrilovitch's parents had purchased two mansions in Petersburg. The child prodigies brought fortune to their families. My father would have put up with poverty, but he yearned for glory.

Poor people who ate at our table spurred him on. "It's impossible," they whispered in his ear, "it's impossible that the grandchild of such a grandfather shouldn't. . . ."

But I had other ideas. While practicing, I used to put a volume of Dumas or Turgenev on the music stand, and while scraping God knows what, I devoured page after page. In the daytime I would tell the kids of the quarter fanciful stories, and during the night I spent my time writing. Authorship was hereditary in our family. When Levi-Yitzhak approached old age, he began a story entitled "The Headless Man," and worked on it all through his remaining days. I continued on his path.

Three times a week I would drag myself, loaded down with my violin case and music books, to Witte Street, formerly the Street of the Nobles, where Zagoursky had his apartment. There, lined up along the walls, stood hysterically inflamed Jewish women. To their feeble knees they hugged violins, much larger than their children, destined to be heard in Buckingham Palace.

The door of the professor's sanctum would open. Big-headed, freckled children would come staggering out of Zagoursky's study; they had necks as slender as flower stalks and a flush of stupor on their cheeks. The door would shut again, swallowing the next gnome. Behind the partition, the professor, with a ribbon tied in a bow in his reddish locks, skipped around, sang, and waved his baton with a great display of energy. Promoter of a monstrous sweepstakes, he had fits of inspiration and peopled the Moldavanka and the back-alleys of the Old Market with the ghosts of pizzicati and cantilenas. These melodies, later on, were polished to a diabolical sparkle by the hands of Professor Auer.

I felt out of place in the midst of this sect. A dwarf among dwarfs, I had heard another note in the voice of my ancestors.

It was some time before I took the first step to freedom. But one day I left home with my violin case, music, and a dozen roubles, the monthly cost of my lessons. I went down Nejinskaya Street. To reach Zagoursky's, I ought to have turned into the Street of the Nobles; instead, I mounted the Tirapolskaya and found myself at the waterfront. From that time on, my study hours were wafted away at those docks. Zagoursky's studio never saw me again. My pal Nemanov and I fell into the habit of going aboard the steamer "Kensington" to visit an old sailor, Mr. Trottiburn. Nemanov was my junior by twelve months, but ever since the age of eight he had devoted himself to a kaleidoscopically wonderful trade. He had a genius for business and eventually realized his promise. He is now a New York millionaire and an executive of General Motors. Nemanov took me along because I always gave in to his wishes. He used to buy contraband pipes from Mr. Trottiburn. These pipes were made in Lincoln by the old sailor's brother.

"Gentlemen," Mr. Trottiburn would address us, "remember my words: every man must take pleasure in making his own children. . . . To smoke a machine-made pipe is as bad as sucking an enema. . . . Have you heard of Benvenuto Cellini? . . . He was a craftsman, a master. My brother, who lives at Lincoln, could tell you the story of Cellini. My brother sticks to his trade. He has only one conviction, and that is that every man ought to make his own children. . . ."

Nemanov sold Trottiburn's pipes to bankers, foreign consuls, and rich Greeks. He made a good profit.

The pipes of the Lincoln craftsman had a breath of poetry about them. There was in each of them an idea, a drop of eternity. In their stems a little yellow eye glowed; their cases were lined with satin. I often tried to imagine the life that Matthew Trottiburn, the last of the pipe artists and rebel against the tide of events, led in old England.

"Impossible, gentlemen, to refute the fact that every man ought to make his own children. . . ."

The heavy waves near the jetty bore me farther and farther away from my home, heavy with the odor of onions and Jewish fate. I left the docks and made the beach beyond the jetty my new stamping-ground. There the urchins of Primorskaya Street spent their days on a tiny shelf of sand. From morning till night they strolled about naked, diving under the wharfs and stealing coconuts for their dinner while waiting for the better days when the barges of Kherson and Kamenka would come, loaded with watermelons which could be split open against the mooring-posts.

The dream of learning how to swim obsessed me. I was ashamed to confess to those bronzed children that, born in Odessa, I had not seen the sea until the age of ten, and that at fourteen I still did not know how to swim.

How late in life to learn such essential things! My childhood had been spent nailed to the Talmud, and I had lived the life of a sage. But while growing up, I began to climb trees.

I couldn't possibly learn how to swim. The hydrophobia of my ancestors, Spanish rabbis and Frankfort brokers, dragged me to the bottom of the sea. The water did not bear me up in the least. Completely exhausted and saturated with salt water, I used to stagger out of the sea toward my violin and music.

I had become welded to the symbols of my crime and always lugged them around with me. The contest between the rabbis and the sea continued until the moment the local Neptune, Efim Nikititch Smolitch, a proofreader of the *Odessa News*, took pity on me. His athletic chest harbored tender feelings for us Jewish boys. Nikititch reigned over a horde of rachitic, twisted waifs. He picked them up in the Moldavanka slums, led them to the seashore, dug them into the sand, made them do gymnastic exercises, dived with them, taught them songs, and, while they were being grilled in the perpendicular rays of the sun, told them stories of fishes and animals. To grown-ups, Nikititch would explain that he was a natural philosopher. Listening to his talk, the Jewish kids would burst sides laughing—they squealed and rubbed against his side like puppies. The sun sprinkled them with evanescent, lizard-like stains.

Nikititch had silently observed my duel with the sea. As soon as he understood that there was no hope left and that I was never to learn how to swim, he gathered me into his flock of protégés. His gay heart, free of all greed, of all anguish, was entirely given to us. . . . This man with copper-colored shoulders, with the head of an aging gladiator, and bronzed, slightly bandy legs, would lie there on the sands beyond the jetty, like the king of those waters, iridescent with gasoline and watermelons, looming among us children, ultimate sprouts of a tribe that cannot learn how to die.

For Nikititch I felt a love such as only a boy suffering from headaches and hysteria might feel for an athlete. I did not leave his side for an instant and was always on the alert to do him every possible favor.

He said to me: "Don't get excited. Strengthen your nerves. Swimming will come later, of itself. . . . What's this story of yours about the waves not holding you up? And why shouldn't they hold you up?"

Nikititch felt how I was drawn to him, and he made a favorite of me. He invited me to his attic. It was large and clean and covered with rugs, and he showed me his dogs, his pigeons, his hedgehog, and his tortoise. In return for these marvels, I presented him with the tragedy of my literary cravings.

"I suspected you of scribbling," said Nikititch. "One can see it in your eyes. . . . Most of the time you don't look at anything. . . ."

He read my manuscript, shrugged his shoulders, passed his hand over his gray, tufted hair, and paced the attic.

"Can't escape it," he said, drawling his syllables and with a pause between each word. "There's a divine spark in you. . . ."

We came out into the street. Nikititch stopped, struck the sidewalk violently with his cane, and looked straight at me.

"What is it you lack? . . . It's not being young that's a misfortune—you'll get over that with age. . . . What you lack is a feeling for nature. . . ."

He pointed with his cane to a tree with a reddish trunk and low spreading foliage.

"What's the name of that tree?"

I had no idea.

"What grows on this shrub?"

I did not know that either.

We were crossing the Alexandrovsky Square. Nikititch pointed out all the trees with his stick, caught hold of my shoulder when a bird flew by and forced me to listen to its call.

"What bird is that singing?"

I could not answer. I did not know the names of the trees, where the birds migrate to, where the sun rises, nor the hour when the dew falls.

"And you dare to write! One who has not lived with nature like a stone or an animal can't compose even two lines of any value in his lifetime. Your landscapes remind me of a description of a stage setting. What the devil were your parents dreaming of these fourteen years?"

What had they dreamt of? . . . Of unpaid notes, Mischa Elman's elegant mansion. . . . But I didn't tell this to Nikititch.

At home I wasn't able to eat my dinner. . . . A feeling for nature. My God, why had I never thought of it? . . . Where could I find a man to explain to me the calls of the birds and the names of the trees? What did I know about it? . . . I could recognize lilac, and that only when in flower. Lilac and acacia. The Derebasovskaya and Gretcheskaya Streets were planted with acacias.

During the meal my father told still another story about Jascha Heifetz. On his way to see Robine, he had met Mendelsohn, Jascha's uncle. Just think, the boy earned eight hundred roubles a night. Calculate how much that would make at the rate of fifteen concerts a month.

I calculated: twelve thousand roubles a month. As I was going through the multiplication and was carrying four, I glanced out the window. Across the small courtyard, Mr. Zagoursky, my professor of music, advanced majestically leaning on a cane. He wore a gently flowing cloak, and his reddish locks stuck out like a fringe beneath his soft felt hat.

He had taken a long time to find me out. Over three months had passed since the day I had deposited my violin on the sand beyond the jetty. . . .

Zagoursky strode to the entrance door. I made a dash for the rear door, but the day before it had been nailed down as a protection against thieves. No escape. I shut myself in the toilet. Half an hour later, the whole family had gathered in front of the toilet door. The women were weeping. My aunt Bobka rubbed her fat shoulders against the doorframe and groaned. My father kept silent. Then he began speaking in a voice that was low and more distinct than ever before in his life:

"I am an officer," he said. "I have an estate. I hunt. The peasants pay me rent. I have placed my son in the cadet corps. I have no further trouble with my son. . . ."

He grew silent. The women whined. Then a terrific blow shook the toilet door, my father was pounding it with his whole body, taking a run each time to ram it down.

"I am an officer," he howled. "I hunt. . . . I'll kill him. . . . It's the end. . . ."

The hook gave way, the door was now held by a slide-bolt fixed by a single nail. The women were rolling on the ground, screaming, clutching at my father's feet. Half-mad, he tried to free himself. His mother, an old woman, hobbled up, attracted by the noise.

"My child," she said to him in Yiddish. "Great is our sorrow. It has no bounds. Only blood is lacking in our house. I do not wish to see blood in our house. . . ."

My father groaned. I heard him walk away with dragging steps. The slide-bolt hung by a single nail.

I stayed in my fortress till late at night. When everybody had gone to bed, my aunt Bobka led me off to my grandmother's. It was a long walk. The moonlight fell in petrified designs on the unknown shrubs and the nameless trees. An invisible bird whistled, then stopped or perhaps fell asleep. . . . What bird was it? What was it called? . . . Does the dew fall in the evening? . . . Where is the Big Dipper? Where does the sun rise?

We were skirting Potchtovaya Street. Bobka gripped my hand tightly to prevent my running away. She was right. I was thinking of flight.

THE REWARDS OF FIDELITY

A teacher of Scripture once asked a merchant who had just moved to town to entrust his boy to his teaching. Among his other virtues, the teacher said:

"Praise God, I'm not just a teacher of Scripture since yesterday! As you look at me, I have been in this profession for twenty-five years."

"That, my friend, is a very bad sign as to your teaching ability."

"Why so?"

"To me, may no evil eye fall on you, you look well fed and just bursting with health. There is an old tradition among us Jews that a really good teacher of Scripture, who drills devotedly with his children, after several years begins to suffer from heart disease, gall-bladder trouble, ulcers, and consumption!"

MY BROTHER ELIYAHU'S DRINK

BY SHOLOM ALEICHEM
TRANSLATED FROM THE YIDDISH BY NATHAN AUSUBEL

"One ruble will make a hundred! Everyone can earn a hundred rubles a month and more after he gets acquainted with the contents of our book, which, all in all, costs only one ruble plus postage! Hurry! Buy! Or you'll be too late!"

This was the advertisement my brother Eliyahu read in the newspaper right after he went off eating *kest*.[1]

And my brother Eliyahu went off kest not because the end of the period had come. Actually his wife's parents had promised him kest for three full years, but they didn't keep him even three quarters of a year. And the reason for it was that a misfortune had happened to his rich father-in-law: Yoineh the Baker had bankrupted, and from a rich man he had become a pauper. How this disaster came about I've already told you. Tell a story twice I never do unless you'll beg me to. This time even begging won't help because I'm very busy. I'm earning money! I'm peddling a drink that my brother makes himself, with his own hands. He learned how to make it from a book that altogether costs a ruble, and with it one can earn a hundred rubles a month and more! As soon as my brother Eliyahu read that there was such a book in the world he right away sent off a ruble (his last one, too) by mail and he told mother the good news that she wouldn't have to worry any more.

"Thank God, Mama, we're saved! With *parnosseh* we're already provided that much!" And he put his finger to his neck.

"What's happened?" asked mama. "Did you get a job?"

"Even better than a job!" answered my brother Eliyahu with shining eyes. It was from joy, I could see. He told her to wait a few more days until the book would arrive.

"Book! What book?" asked my mother.

"It's a wonderful book!" my brother Eliyahu assured her, and he asked her whether she'd be satisfied with a hundred rubles a month. My mother laughed at him and told him that for her part she'd be satisfied with a hundred rubles a year as long as it was certain. To this my brother Eliyahu replied that she had no idea what it was all about, and he hurried to the post office. Every single day he went to the post office to ask whether the book had arrived yet. It was more than a week since he had sent off the ruble and yet no book had come! In the meantime one had to live! "And you can't spit out the soul" so says my mother.

II

Sha! The book has arrived! As soon as we got it unwrapped my brother Eliyahu sat down to read it. My, my, what he read there! How

---

[1] *Young newlyweds were usually supported by the bride's parents for one or more years.* ED.

many ways to earn money through all kinds of recipes! There was a recipe for earning a hundred rubles a month by making the very best quality inks. A recipe for earning a hundred rubles a month by making good black shoe polish. A recipe for earning a hundred rubles a month by driving out mice, cockroaches, and other ugly things. A recipe for earning a hundred rubles a month, and more, by making liqueurs, sweet brandies, lemonade, soda water, *kvass,* and even cheaper drinks.

My brother Eliyahu stopped at the last recipes. First of all he thought he could earn more than a hundred rubles a month with them. That's what it said in the book, black on white! Secondly, it wouldn't be necessary to *patchkeh* around with ink, and with shoe polish, nor would he have anything to do with mice, cockroaches, and other ugly things. The question only was what sort of a drink should he make? For liqueur and sweet brandies you've got to have Rothschild's fortune. For lemonade and soda water you've got to have a certain machine that costs—who knows how much!

So only one thing remained: kvass! Kvass is the sort of drink which costs cheap and sells a lot. Especially on a hot summer day, like today. From kvass, you should know, Borech the *kvassnik* in our town became a rich man. He makes bottled kvass. His kvass has a reputation in the world. It shoots from his kvass bottles like from a cannon. What's the sense of it, why does it shoot? That no one knows. That's Borech's secret. Some people say that he puts *epis* something inside that makes them shoot. Others say that it's a raisin. And still others that it's hops. When the summer comes around he finds he hasn't enough hands—so much money he earns!

The kvass that my brother Eliyahu makes according to the recipe is no bottled kvass, and it doesn't shoot either. Our kvass is a different sort of a drink. How it's made I can't tell you. My brother Eliyahu doesn't let anyone be around when he makes it. When he pours water everybody can see. But when he's right in the middle of making it he locks himself up in my mother's room. Not I, nor my mother, nor my brother's wife Brocheh—no one has the privilege to be there.

But if you promise that you'll keep it a secret I can tell you what goes into the drink. Don't I know what things he gets ready! You'll find there lemon rinds, thin honey, and a thing that they call *krima tarterum* and which is sourer than vinegar. And the rest—just water.

Water is there more than anything else. More water, more kvass? All that is stirred up well with a plain stick, that's how it's written in the book, and the drink is ready. After that it's poured into a large pitcher and they throw a piece of ice in it. Ice is what counts. Without ice the whole drink is worth ninety-nine diseases. This I'm telling you not from the book, but I once tasted a little kvass that had no ice in it, and I thought that was going to be the end of me!

III

After the first barrel of kvass was made it was decided that I should be the one to go out on the street and sell it. Who else, if not I? It wouldn't look nice for my brother Eliyahu. After all, he's a married man. My mother? Out of the question! How could we allow my mother to go around all over the market place with a pitcher yelling, "Kvass, kvass, Jews, kvass!" So everybody agreed that that was to be my job. I thought so myself. I was happy when I heard the news.

Then my brother Eliyahu began to teach me what I should do. The pitcher I should hold in one hand by a string, the glass in the other hand, and in order that the people should stop I should sing out loud and clear this way:

> *Jews, a drink!*
> *A kopeck a glass!*
> *Cold and sweet—*
> *A real refresher!*

A voice, I've long ago told you, I have a good one. It's a soprano voice which I inherited from my father, peace be to his name! So I sang out on the top of my voice and twisted the words about so that they stood on their head:

> *Sweet kvass a glass!*
> *A kopeck a Jew!*
> *Refresh and a cold—*
> *Enough to drown!*

I don't know whether my singing pleased so much or whether the drink was *takkeh* so good. Or was it because it was such a hot day! The first pitcher I sold out in half an hour and came home with almost five gulden. My brother Eliyahu gave the money to my mother, and for me he filled the pitcher again right away. He said that if I could sell five, six pitchers a day we'll be earning exactly a hundred rubles a month. Now be so good and take off from the reckoning the four days of *Shabbes* during the month and you'll find out yourself how much the drink cost us, and what per cent profit we earned.

The drink cost us very cheap, one could say almost nothing. All the money went for ice. For that reason I had to sell my pitcher of kvass as quickly as I could. That was so that we could use the piece of ice in the next pitcher and then again in the next one and then again in the one after that. Therefore, I had to hurry with my pitcher but *takkeh* run! After me ran other boys, a whole gang. They mimicked the way I sang, but I paid no attention to them. I tried to empty my pitcher as fast as possible and then run home for a refill.

How much I earned that first day I don't know myself. All I know is that my brother Eliyahu and his wife Brocheh and my mother had a lot of praise for me. At supper I got a slice of canteloupe and a slice of watermelon and two Hungarian plums. I don't even have to mention kvass: we all drank kvass like water. My mother made my bed on the floor and before I went to sleep she asked me whether my feet didn't hurt, God forbid.

My brother Eliyahu laughed at her. He said that I'm the sort of boy who never has any pains.

"Sure," said I. "If you want proof of that I'll go out right away in the middle of the night with another pitcher of kvass."

All three of them laughed, but I saw tears in my mother's eyes. Nu, that's an old story, a mother's got to cry! What I would like to know is: do all mothers cry all the time like my mother?

IV

May no evil eye fall on us, but things do go well with us, "through door and through gate" as they say. One day is hotter than the other. It just burns! People pass out from the heat, children drop like flies. If not for the glass of kvass they'd burn to a cinder. Without exaggeration, I run home to refill my pitcher at least ten times a day! My brother Eliyahu squints into the barrel with one eye and says that he sees it's already "dawning" there. So he gets a plan and pours a few pails of water into the barrel.

I fell on this plan even before he did. I've got to confess to you that I played that trick several times already. Almost every day I'd drop in on our neighbor Pessi and pour out for her a glass of our own drink. I gave two glasses to her husband Moishe the bookbinder; he's a good man. And I also gave each of the children a glass. Let them know, too, what sort of a drink we're making! Their blind uncle I also gave a glass to taste. A pity, he's *nebbech* a cripple! All my acquaintances I gave kvass. For nothing, without a kopeck *gelt!* But so that there shouldn't be any loss I poured water into the pitcher. For every glass of kvass that I gave away for nothing I poured in two glasses of water.

We also did the same thing at home. For instance, when my brother Eliyahu was through drinking a glass of kvass he poured into the barrel a glass of water. He was right, too. It would be a sin to throw away a kopeck! My sister-in-law Brocheh drank several glasses of kvass at a time (she loved my brother Eliyahu's kvass something terrible!), so she immediately made up for it with water. My mother had a glass of kvass once in a while (but her you've got to beg; alone she won't take!), so right away we poured in a glass of water. In short not a drop got lost and we made, may no evil eye fall on us, good money.

My mother has already paid off a lot of debts. She has redeemed a few of the things she's pawned that we need most, for instance, our bedding. In the house suddenly appeared a table, a chair. On Shabbes we had fish and meat and white braided *challeh*. They promised me, with God's help, a pair of new boots for the Holy Days. The way it looks to me, nobody has it as good as I!

V

Nu, go and be a prophet and guess that such a misfortune should happen to us, that our drink would be condemned! All that was left to do was to pour it into the slop pail! It's my luck that I wasn't taken away by the police. Just listen to a story!

One day I strayed with my pitcher of kvass into our neighbor Pessi's house. The whole gang there took a glass of kvass each, and I, too, had one with them. I figured that I had missing twelve or thirteen glasses. So I hopped into the shed where they kept the water, but, instead of reaching for the water trough, I went by mistake to the washtub where they had just done the laundry and I scooped out from it fifteen or twenty glasses into my pitcher. Then I returned to the street with a new song that I myself had made up:

> *Jews, a drink!*
> *Taste of Gan-Eden!*
> *Such a year on me,*
> *On you and on all of us!*

So a Jew stopped me, paid me a kopeck, and asked me to pour him a glass of kvass. He drank up the whole glass but he screwed up his face.

"Little boy!" said he. "What sort of a drink is this!"

I paid no attention to him because there were two other Jews waiting for me to pour drinks for them. One of them sipped half a glass, the other about a third. They paid, spat out, and went away. Another came along, he put the glass to his lips, tasted it, and said that it had a soapy taste and that, so it seemed to him, it was also salty. Still another took just one look at his glass and gave it back to me.

"What's that you're selling?" he asked me.

"It's a kind of drink," I replied.

"A drink?" he barked at me. "You mean a ge-shtink not a drink!"

One man came over, gave a taste, and splashed the kvass right into my face. In another minute a whole crowd was standing around me. Everybody was talking at the same time, making with the hands and getting excited. When a policeman saw the crowd gather he came over and asked, "What's going on here?"

So they told him. So he came over to me, looked into my pitcher, and asked that I give him some to taste. I went ahead and poured him out a glass of kvass. The policeman gave a sip, spat out, and got good and mad.

"Where did you get such slop?" he asked me.

"That's from a book," I told him. "My brother's work. My brother makes it himself."

"Who is your brother?" he asked me.

"My brother Eliyahu," I tell him.

"What Eliyahu?" he asks me.

"Don't talk, you little fool, against your own brother!" several Jews said to me almost at once, speaking half Yiddish and half Hebrew so the policeman shouldn't understand.

A terrible din started. Every minute new people joined the crowd. The policeman held me by the hand and wanted to take us (that is, me and my drink) right to the police station. At this the noise got even worse. "An orphan! . . . *nebbech,* an orphan!" I heard on every side. My heart told me that things were going bad for me. I looked at the crowd around me. "Jews, have pity!" I cried. Someone wanted to slip a coin to the policeman, but the policeman wouldn't take. So an old Jew with cunning eyes said to me, in disguised language, half in Yiddish and half in the holy tongue:

"Mottel, tear your hand out of the policeman's, and pick up your legs and run!"

So I pulled my hand away suddenly, "took my feet on my shoulders," and ran home!

More dead than alive I burst into the house.

"Where's the pitcher?" asked my brother Eliyahu.

"With the police!" I answered and flung myself at my mother with a sob.

SAVED BY THE SALE

BY YURI SUHL

Friday was pay-day, the most wonderful day of the week. I quivered with excitement at the thought of receiving my first salary in America, and the meat blocks quivered under the block brush as I scrubbed them to a white surface.

Around one in the afternoon Mr. Resnik left for the slaughterhouse to pick out his meat for Saturday night. He said he'd be back at four o'clock, by which time he expected to find the store spick-and-span: the ice-box scrubbed, the meat grinder stripped and washed, the knives and cleavers shining down from the hooks. He didn't expect any customers for the two left-over chickens that hung forlornly on the window rack, but if somebody showed up to buy them I should sell them as a bargain and get rid of them.

When his hand was on the doorknob, he turned around and dropped a subtle hint: "Make a nice job on the store, Sol. Today is pay-day. When I come back I'll give you a check."

A check!

Throughout the morning, as I sat on the small stool in the back room plucking chickens, or as I rode the bicycle to and from the store, my first week as butcher boy passed before me in review. Measured in terms of days it was a short procession: Monday, Tuesday, Wednesday, Thursday, Friday. But looked at in terms of experience acquired, it was a long and endless parade of confusion and hope, of despair and delight, of grappling with dead chickens whose feathers stuck tenaciously and wouldn't budge unless the skin went with them, of a bicycle that threw me like a wild broncho, of a boss who kept complaining: "Oi, Sol, Sol, what shall I do with you?"

Now the feathers were cooperating beautifully, the bicycle was well behaved, the customers were already calling me by my first name instead of: "Hey, boytchik!" and when Mr. Resnik sent me into the ice-box for the shoulder of lamb, I didn't come back with a shoulder of veal.

And soon, very soon, I would reap the reward for it all—eight American dollars! I broke them up into white rolls and saw myself taking over a whole bakery. I added two more dollars and had a brandnew suit (not exactly custom tailored). But best of all I liked to see myself walking into Shirley's candy store, putting down a dollar bill on the counter and saying: "I'll have the best banana split in the house."

Would Mr. Resnik pay me in singles or in a five and three singles? It was a matter of speculation, of course. But no more. Now I knew it would be a check. A check had to be cashed and I knew right away where I'd cash it. At Morris Finkel's drugstore where my father cashed his weekly fifteen dollar check—where all the immigrants in the neighborhood cashed their checks because they trusted him. And they liked him because he was one of them who had made good. They all knew that he had come from Rumania a poor boy in rags and half-starved; that he had worked as pants presser by day and studied at night until he became a pharmacist. But that wasn't all. He was also a notary public and spoke five different languages: Russian, Polish, German, Rumanian and Yiddish. "Doctor Finkel," they called him, and although he protested mildly that he was only a druggist, they insisted on calling him doctor and there was nothing he could do about it.

They brought him their legal documents for interpretation as though they were medical prescriptions; and they brought their medical prescriptions to him with the belief that if he personally prepared them the chances for the patient's recovery were as good as assured. His drugstore was partly Hias [Hebrew Immigrant Aid Society], partly Ellis Island, partly a family relations court and sometimes a drugstore, too. And, of course, he cashed checks for nothing.

Long before Mr. Resnik returned from the slaughter-house, the store was thoroughly cleaned. I looked at the clock in the window. It was three. A whole hour between me and the check. An hour can be interminably long when you wait for your first pay in America. I felt too exhilarated to sit still, so I made a personal tour of inspection around the store. I wanted to make sure that nothing would mar the smile of satisfaction on Mr. Resnik's face.

A chicken feather had eluded my vigilance and hid behind the broom in the back room. It was promptly ferreted out of its hiding place. A little bump of sawdust on the floor had been spared by the rake. I flattened it out. A small blood-speck on the ice-box mirror. Off with it!

Suddenly my eyes beheld the only dismaying sight in the store: the two unsold, half-plucked chickens that hung from the hooks of the window racks. If I could only get rid of them, I sighed. What a wonderful surprise that would make for Mr. Resnik! What a perfect finish to my first week's work in America! I looked at the two miserable, blue-skinned fowl hanging stiffly from the hooks, and hated them. They presented a challenge to me which I could not meet.

I walked up to the window and instinctively my right arm swung out at one of them, as though it were a punching bag. The chicken swung right back at me, scratching my face with its dead claws. I stepped back a little and waited for it to come into position. Then I let go with another jab. Still the fowl came back for more. I punched the other one and it, too, began swinging as though it had come to life again. Now both of them were flying back and forth and I stood there, slightly hunched, fists ready, punching now one, now the other, unaware that I had already attracted a half dozen curious spectators.

Kids pouring out of a nearby public school swarmed up close to the window, flattening their noses against it. They laughed, shouted, waved their hands and stamped their feet. When one of the chickens was punched clear off the hook and hit the window, a roar went up from them and they began to count: one, two, three, as a referee does over a floored prize-fighter.

I forgot about the store, the check, Mr. Resnik and my job. I was now in the ring at Madison Square Garden, the only boxer in the world to take on two opponents at the same time.

The show was at its peak, with a record crowd spilling over the edge of the sidewalk, when a tall policeman, pushing his club ahead of him, came up.

I stopped punching the chickens and wondered what to tell the cop if he questioned me. Then Mr. Resnik himself appeared. His face pale with panic, he charged frantically into the crowd, waving his hands in all directions, as though he were swimming up to the store rather than pushing himself toward it. The cop got there first and only after explaining that he was the proprietor was Mr. Resnik admitted into his own store.

"Sol, what happened?" he sputtered out. "Where is the accident?"

I wanted to say something, but I felt as though my tongue had swollen to an enormous size. I had a mouthful of tongue that wouldn't let a word pass through. So I pointed to the chickens that were still swaying wearily, as though unable to steady themselves after the ordeal.

"For Godsakes," Mr. Resnik began to shake me by the shoulder. "Whatsematter? What happened?"

"Nothing. Nothing happened," I managed to squeeze the words past my swollen tongue. "I played with the chickens, I just punched them a little."

Mr. Resnik glanced at the two swaying fowl and gave me that startled look you give a person when you suddenly doubt his sanity.

Then he shrugged, sighed and threw his hands up, all at the same time. The cop was bored with the whole thing and went out to disperse the crowd.

Mr. Resnik took his chin into his hand and reflected on my fate. The way he dropped his hand a moment later I knew that I was doomed. It was like dropping an ax.

He reached for the check-book, made out a check for eight dollars and, handing it to me, said: "You don't have to come in to work on Saturday night. I don't think you'll make a good butcher boy. Maybe you should go to a factory and learn a trade."

Outside a few people were still standing in front of the window, letting their curiosity wring the last drops of interest out of my tragic folly. Among them was a short, scrawny-faced woman.

Mr. Resnik took the two chickens off the hook and was about to storage them in the ice-box when the door opened and the scrawny-faced woman came in. Mr. Resnik turned to face her.

"Are these chickens for sale?" the woman inquired in a high-pitched voice.

"Sure, sure," Mr. Resnik's face brightened a little. "I'll make them a bargain for you," and he put them quickly on the scale lest the woman change her mind.

He mentioned a price and the woman agreed to it.

"Sol," Mr. Resnik commanded, "get me a big bag, quick!"

I dashed into the back room and nearly tripped over myself getting that bag. After the woman had paid, she turned to me, patted my back a little and said: "You sure are a smart butcher boy getting your customers that way. I was on my way to get a leg of lamb for Sunday, but I stopped to watch you and decided to get chicken instead."

Mr. Resnik grinned a proud grin, as though he had had a share in this unusual sale. After all, I was his butcher boy, wasn't I?

When the woman was gone he turned to me and said: "All right, Sol, I'll give you another chance. But next time if you have to punch the chickens be careful with the neck. It's a good thing it was a Gentile customer. They don't bother much with stuffed neck. But a Jewish woman looks for the neck first."

"Yes, Mr. Resnik," I said. "I'll be careful."

I said: *"A guten Shabbes,"* and went away.

As I boarded the trolley-car I suddenly remembered the check and quickly put my hand into my pocket. It was there. It was like getting paid twice.

THE JESTING
PHILOSOPHER

Synagogue-Stove Sages

*Life isn't more than a dream,
but please don't wake me!*

The average Jew is a bit of a jester: laughter helps ease his burden. He is also quite a bit of a philosopher: adversity makes one think. As soon as any person begins to recognize that life has limitations and that human beings are as stuffed full of absurdities as the pomegranate is full of seeds, he straightway becomes a jesting philosopher.

The Jew's jesting is largely cerebral and his philosophy home-spun. He is in fact a kinsman of the American cracker-barrel philosopher; but since his hangout in the past has been the synagogue and not the village general store, he well deserves the title of synagogue-stove philosopher.

Huddling around the cosy warmth of the synagogue stove and of one another's gregarious loneliness the poor Jews in the ghetto ranged like soaring eagles over the chaos that is life. They touched on every problem, personal, communal, national, and international with the air of spoofing authority that comes quite naturally to simple people who always find the short cut to the most complicated problem. It's the kernel and not the outer husks that they seek for in truth. With ironic amusement they viewed the mess that the powerful of the earth, the learned, and the wise made out of human affairs. And so their waggish and sometimes gadfly observations would begin with the speculative formula: "Now if I were the Emperor. . . . Now if I were Rothschild. . . . Now if I were the Rabbi. . . ." Naturally, invested with those suppositional powers, they proceeded to stand everything reverential and conventional on its head. Yet, underneath all the merrymaking, one could discern the sober face of the little man resenting the shambles the bigwigs were making out of his hard-earned world. Were you to ask for his frank opinion he wouldn't hesitate to tell you that if you gave him the power to run the world he'd do a much better job.

The synagogue-stove philosopher was very much preoccupied with his fate as Jew in the world. From long experience he had discovered for his own guidance that "whatever happens to all of Israel also happens to Reb Israel." He was never allowed to forget that he was a Jew, nor for that matter did he want to. He tried to understand his

*own precarious position in the world, and he had a nagging curiosity
to find out why his enemies were so insistent on using him as a scapegoat for their own crimes. He viewed it all with wry and sometimes
bitter laughter and his indignation was thus made endurable.*

*There is the fable which stingingly telescopes the fate of the Jew
as his persecutors might see it:*

*A lamb once fell into the river and began to drown. With the
agony of death upon him he cried aloud: "Woe is me! The world is
coming to an end!"*

*Now it happened that the lamb's enemy, the fox, was standing at
the bank of the river watching. When he heard the lamb's outcry he
laughed loud and long.*

*"Ho-ho-ho! My friend, you're mistaken! It isn't the world that
is coming to an end! All I see is a poor lamb drowning!"*

*Apparently, the Jewish lamb has shown no enthusiasm for drown-
ing. As far as he is concerned if he drowns the whole world goes under.
The jesting philosopher would rather drown his mortal enemy, the
anti-Semitic fox, in the torrent of his ridicule.*

N.A.

REB ANSHEL THE GOLDEN
A FAIRY TALE FOR GROWN-UPS

BY YEHUDAH STEINBERG
TRANSLATED FROM THE YIDDISH BY NATHAN AUSUBEL

Once, on a Sabbath eve, two *urimeleit*[1] were sitting against the
west wall on the poor man's bench in the synagogue waiting for the
service to come to an end. No question about it—someone would
invite them home for the *Shabbes* meal! One of the two was a cripple
who limped along on crutches. The other had a scar across his face and

[1]*Literally "poor people," (uriman, singular). While the Yiddish word
for "beggar" is baytler and a baytler, too, is an uriman, the urimeleit in the East European ghettos represented a large class of "respectable" paupers, reduced by the economic stagnation of the ghetto to
going from house to house asking for alms in order to keep their families alive. To reduce the humiliation of their involuntary calling, they'd
wander off to Jewish communities where they were not known. Their
knapsacks slung over their shoulders were mute witnesses of their plight.
All they could ever hope for was a night's lodging, a crust of bread, and
a coin. And when their knapsacks would be filled they'd trudge home
again and rejoin their hungry wives and children. ED.*

looked cross-eyed; also one side of his beard was shorter than the other. Evil tongues among urimeleit wagged that that was a souvenir from his wife, who had plucked out one side of his beard, but fortunately for him, before she could begin work on the other side, she suddenly went and died.

The two urimeleit looked about them in the synagogue and saw that they were the only urimeleit there, and because of that they were filled with self-importance. Just think of it! Only two urimeleit in an entire synagogue full of householders! How they were all going to fall over one another for the honor of having them for their Shabbes guests! And as the two sat there they began to speculate into whose hospitable hands they might possibly fall.

"I'd like my host to be an uriman himself," said the one with the scar on his face. "You see, if the host is rich, a *nogid* (may God not punish me for the words!), right after the blessing over the *challeh* twists, the servants snatch them away. Then the maid places tiny bits of twist on a tray. Let me tell you, the rich man's challeh is merely emptiness blown up! Just feathers! It can never still your hunger. All in the nogid's household are well fed. That's why they can't imagine that someone else may be hungry. Although they lay before your eyes all sorts of good things, nonetheless you go away hungry. But oh! if you're lucky enough to eat at the table of an uriman! Whatever they serve you, you eat heartily and you leave with a full belly."

"You talk like a snip even though you've had the privilege of laying your wife in her grave," mocked the one with the crutches.

Actually, the uriman with the scar appeared like a boy next to the cripple. He was small and thin, in his middle thirties, and he piped in a soprano voice. The cripple, on the other hand, was tall and broad-shouldered and boomed in such a low voice that it seemed to come up from his stomach.

"For my part, I'd prefer to be the guest of a nogid," said the cripple. "Rich folks, you know, lead a monotonous existence doing nothing all week long. When they meet with a stranger they like to question him: Where from? . . . . Where to? . . . . What's news in the world? And when it comes to news they like to hear about everything under the sun, except of course, about themselves."

"*Nu,* so what?"

"Don't you see? You can go on eating while you tell them news, and they put down their spoons and open wide their mouths and ears."

And thus it happened that God heard the urimeleit's wishes and He fulfilled each of them.

After the evening service the worshipers bid each other *gut Shabbes*. Then they turned to look on the poor-man's bench at the west wall.

"Not one decent-looking stranger to invite home for Shabbes!" each one complained to himself. "If not some Jew from the Holy Land, or an unfortunate man from Brisk whose house has burned down, or a *goy* who has become a convert to Judaism, or a grandson of some eminent Chassidic *tzaddik*—who the devil cares, as long as it is a decent Jew! But what's the use, there isn't such a bird here!"

Everyone who looked at the two urimeleit on the poor man's bench turned up his nose: "Pfui! Call these proper guests for Shabbes!"

But what other choice was there? What was one to do? So they reluctantly used the urimeleit for the pious purpose they were intended.

The cripple was taken home by a nogid, Yossel Manufactur-shtchik. But it so happened that on this particular night the nogid felt very sleepy, so he got through with the Shabbes meal in a hurry, and then, without any ceremony, sent his guest to bed.

The uriman with the scar on his face fell to the lot of a poor man, a clerk in the tax collector's office. He ate heartily of the Shabbes meal and was also invited to stay overnight.

The following noon Yossel Manufacturshtchik sat down to the Shabbes feast. He was well rested from a long winter's night sleep. He was a wealthy man, was the proprietor of a large shop in town; more precisely speaking, it was his wife who owned the shop. That was some shop! You could walk into it as naked as your mother bore you and walk out dressed from head to toe like a count. There was only one thing the matter with it—you had to pay for the things!

Yossel Manufacturshtchik liked to entertain a stranger even on weekdays, because from plain folks one could hear all kinds of interesting stories about the great wide world which never in his life had he seen except occasionally in a dream. Not once in his life had he ever been outside his village, not even to buy merchandise, since his wife saw to that. On weekdays, when there were no customers to attend to, he'd pass the time of day with the other shopkeepers, would listen to their yarns or spin some himself. Of stories he was never short, and when he exhausted the stock of those he knew he thought up new ones. After telling but once a story that he had thought up himself he no longer felt that it was thought up, he hadn't the slightest doubt that he had heard it somewhere. That was the sort of person he was. To listen to wonderful tales was a weakness of almost everybody in town, only in the case of Yossel it reached the acuteness of a disease.

As Yossel sat down with his guest to the Shabbes feast that noon he began to ply him with questions.

"From where does a Jew come?"

"*Et!* From where doesn't a Jew come? Naturally, from the wide world."

"And what's news in the world?"

"What news can there be? Only wars."

"Tsk-tsk! Is that so! Who with whom, tell me? And where?"

"What do you mean who with whom? Everybody with everybody! What do you mean where? Everywhere! America with China, Turkey with England! There're no more rifles left, so help me! They're blowing entire mountains and islands into dust!"

"Is that so! Ai-ai-ai! Nu, and what about Jews, what about *parnosseh?*"

"Jews? Parnosseh? Of course there are Jews in the world! There are all kinds of Jews like this and Jews like that."

"Are there rich Jews in the world? I mean *really* rich Jews?"

"What a question—are there rich Jews! You surely must have heard of Reb Anshel the Golden."[1]

"What Reb Anshel are you talking about?" asked Yossel, putting down his spoon.

"What! you never heard of Reb Anshel the Golden?" asked the cripple in astonishment, furiously ladling spoonful after spoonful of soup into his mouth. "Really, you mean to tell me you've never heard of him?"

"As true as pork is forbidden, I'm telling you I never heard of him! When I say 'no' I mean 'no.' "

The cripple couldn't get over his astonishment. He just couldn't believe it! He began to work more furiously with the spoon, lapping up the soup, just as if his life depended on counting a certain number of spoonfuls.

Finally, he got through, wiped his mustache, and began to talk:

"I'd like you to know that Reb Anshel the Golden is an enormous millionaire—*enormous!* His horses are quartered in a stable of gold and *takkeh* on account of this golden stable they call him Reb Anshel the Golden. He himself, I want you to know, lives in an amber palace. He never uses a lamp, oh no! In the middle of the room hangs a sort of diamond which lights up the whole house. After all, why should he use up kerosene for nothing every night? It would be a real sin to waste it!"

[1] *Reb Meyer Anshel (or Amshel) Rothschild of Frankfort-am-Main (1743–1812), the founder of the Rothschild banking house.* ED.

And as he listened to the cripple talk, Yossel could hardly draw breath from sheer amazement.

"But do you think that's all? You can hardly imagine what a charitable man Reb Anshel is. I was his guest for the Shabbes feast not so long ago. Ach, the sorts of fish, the kinds of *tzimmes!* It's enough to break your brains! And when I got through eating I had to take away with me as a gift the golden spoon with which I had eaten. 'What are you saying, Reb Anshel?' I argued with him. 'May good health be yours, but won't it look as if I had stolen it?'

" '*Et,*' said he. 'That's my custom. Every guest of mine has to take his spoon home with him.' So what do you think I did? I sold the spoon and with the money I married off my daughter!"

"Ai-ai-ai!" murmured Yossel, his mouth agape.

"But that's not all!" continued the cripple. "Just listen to what comes next. Reb Anshel the Golden does so many acts of loving-kindness, distributes so many alms, not only among Jews but even among *goyim,* that he is bepinned and behung with so many medals and with so many orders that he simply has no more room on his chest for them. They practically bend him down to the ground, those medals of his! And for that reason takkeh he has stopped handing out alms, so that, God forbid! he shouldn't get another medal. Why, he purposely took the leashes off his dogs so that they shouldn't let a uriman come into his courtyard. But since Reb Anshel is the sort of a person that cannot live without doing good, and since his wife (may it not happen to ours, dear God!) was barren, he fell upon a plan. He put on the rags of an uriman and started out into the wide world. He went from house to house begging alms and, whenever he found an unfortunate person, he gave him a heap of money and then disappeared. For instance, if a poor man invites him for supper, he drops a bag of money when no one is looking, and if they give it back to him he says, 'It's not mine.' On the other hand, should they try not to return the bag of money to him he writes it down in his notebook: 'This so-and-so uriman is a *ganef.*' If it happens that a rich man treats him to a good supper he writes home to his managers: 'Give a lot of credit to this and this one.' And that's the way he gets around everywhere and nobody knows who he is!"

"Ai-ai-ai!" cried Yossel in amazement. "All the things that go on in this world!"

Yossel fell into deep thought. Suddenly he started up as if from sleep: "Do tell me, Uncle (may good health be yours!), since you've eaten the Shabbes feast with Reb Anshel, give me some sign by which

I could recognize him if he comes my way. You know how things are! One can never tell, he might come around our way sometime."

"He's got a scar right here on his face," replied the cripple on a sudden inspiration.

Throughout all of that Shabbes day Yossel kept on talking of Reb Anshel the Golden. The following morning, bright and early, standing before his shop door, he told all he had learned about him to his clerks and the other shopkeepers. Of course, he told it better and with more precise details than he had heard the story from the cripple. He told them exactly how many ships of Reb Anshel's sailed on the ocean, how many kings owed him money, how many thousands his coachman got for wages, and a lot of other facts that the cripple had neglected to tell him. But knowledge of the scar on his face by which Reb Anshel could be recognized he confided only to his shop clerks. "You know how things are. Let them know; they're much more in the shop than I."

II

The uriman with the scar spent a very wretched Shabbes. And it was even worse Sunday morning; the frost was biting, the snow lay in deep drifts, and, to top all that, he walked practically barefooted, and his *kapote* was full of holes. As he wandered through the streets he doubled up with the cold, staggering against the wind and snow. When he passed a large shop displaying fur coats he stopped without realizing that he had done so.

"Ach! How good it would feel to be wrapped up in such soft thick fur! To be well wrapped in it . . . one's hands deep in one's pockets . . . it would have the feel of Paradise! Even for one hour . . . even for fifteen minutes . . . even five minutes!"

A thought suddenly struck him: "These coats are for sale! I've the right to go inside the store and try on a fur coat. I'd ask the price, bargain long and stubbornly, and not come to terms. In that way I'll keep the coat on for a while and thaw out a bit."

This plan delighted him no end, and so he went inside the shop and asked to try on a good fur coat.

The clerks winked to one another; they found it hard to keep back their laughter. They then started flinging witticisms about with tongue in cheek: "What sort of a fur coat does Your Honor wish? For what price, Your Lordship?" One asked him in elegant language: "Does Your Highness wish to pay for the coat in gold ducats?"

But when the clerk Itzl, who had happened to be busy elsewhere, took a look at the "customer" he became petrified. He ran breathlessly to his employer and whispered into his ear, "Take a look at that uriman! Do you see what I see? Look at his scar!"

"Nu? So what if he has a scar! How many people do you think are there in the world with scars? Idiot, you!" his employer replied with feigned impatience, trying hard to suppress his own excitement. "You know there are no two scars alike."

"Takkeh because no two scars are alike, I'm pointing it out to you," the clerk answered. "This uriman ate the Shabbes meal at my neighbor's, he claims he lost there a little purse with money."

Yossel Manufacturshtchik leaped up from his chair and began to stare hard at the uriman.

"Go Itzl and give him a good fur coat, and when he asks the price don't be afraid to lay it on good and thick. There's no doubt in my mind who he is."

The clerk let the uriman try on an excellent fur coat. The uriman cuddled himself snugly into it. There was a rush of warmth through his body. He didn't feel like taking it off again.

"What's the price?" he asked.

Yossel Manufacturshtchik eagerly drew up a chair for him.

"Don't you worry about the price! We'll have no trouble coming to an agreement," he answered him. "But be so good. . . . I've got to keep a record of everything. . . . What is your name, Your Highness?"

"My name is Anshel, only. . . ."

A delicious shudder ran down Yossel's spine.

"That's *he*—definitely *he!*" he jubilated inside. "A kosher good fortune has walked into my store!"

Yossel became so excited he couldn't stand still.

An idea suddenly struck him. "Perhaps you'd like to have breakfast with me?" he asked the uriman most respectfully.

"Ach! Why not?" replied the uriman overjoyed. "I'll eat if you'll only give. My morning prayers I've already said."

Yossel led the uriman into the dining room in the back of the store. At Yossel's wink they set before the uriman a tin of sardines, a slice of lemon, and a fresh white *bulke*. The uriman almost melted with pleasure at the sight and smell of the food. What a delicious breakfast that was! Only one thing was wrong with it—that slice of lemon! Everybody knows that something sour increases the appetite. And *oy!* was the bulke crisp and fresh! It simply melted in the mouth! Reb Anshel felt that he could go on eating bulke forever. . . .

"Won't you buy other clothes from me? Why only a fur coat?" his host asked the uriman with an ingratiating smile.

"But I have no money!"

"So what! A promissory note from you isn't enough?"

It didn't take more than five minutes and Anshel was dressed up in new clothes from head to foot. When he looked at himself in the mirror he wanted to take off his hat out of respect for the gentleman. He fumbled *nebbech* for the visor of his cap but he couldn't find it. What was his amazement then to discover that there was no cap. In its stead they had put a beaver hat on his head!

For the time being the entire incident naturally was held in the utmost secrecy. The fewer people in town that knew about it the better, decided Yossel. Only the clerks and his wife shared the secret with him. But *such* a secret could not be kept for long! In no time at all, all the Jews of the town had crowded outside Yossel's shop, waited impatiently, pressed against one another, hoping at least to get a glimpse of the wonderful Reb Anshel the Golden who, as everybody already knew, was wandering through the world disguised as an uriman. Only the cold and the wet had forced him to reveal his true identity to Yossel Manufacturshtchik.

"Rest assured," the shopkeepers gossiped, but not without envy, "our Yossel is going to lick a nice bone from all this!"

"It wouldn't by any means be a bad idea," said one shopkeeper, "to slip Reb Anshel an unsigned note. Let him be warned that that Yossel *Schacher-Macher* is skinning him alive."

III

After an excellent supper, as the uriman lay stretched out luxuriously on his soft bed he racked his brains to find some sense in what was happening to him. He finally came to the following conclusions:

First of all, Reb Yossel, the shopkeeper, was one fine Jew, and oy was he hospitable to strangers! Furthermore, he must surely be coining money like a mint in his shop, otherwise why should he trust a traveling uriman like himself on whom he had never before in his life clapped eyes? And, on top of that, why should he treat him to a first-class breakfast? Believe you me, everybody in the world should be fighting to get in that shop! And still another reason Reb Anshel found to explain Reb Yossel's unheard-of generosity. He must be nothing less than a tzaddik! Have you any idea how many kinds of dishes he serves urimeleit? You can eat there until you're ready to burst!

And just as marvelous, Reb Anshel discovered that new clothes and a warm fur coat—all without holes—could be a real pleasure, and for an uriman even more than for a rich man. The reason for it being that an uriman nebbech always finds himself tramping in the open through rain and snow and wind, and the cold gets into his bones a lot quicker.

And Reb Anshel decided that Reb Yossel was a very clever Jew, a *chochem* of the old cut. Why then did he advise him to remain in that town for the rest of his life? A very sensible idea it was too! Why should he prefer another town? Were there anywhere in the world such hospitable men as here?

In the meantime, all sorts of marvelous stories were being told in town about Reb Anshel the Golden. One man even swore that, just as he knew his own ten fingers, he knew for a fact that when a certain uriman left his daughter's dowry with Reb Anshel for safekeeping he not only got it back but with it also enough to pay all the wedding expenses, and, in addition, a costly wedding gift.

When the urimeleit of the town heard of this they began to descend upon Reb Anshel with their daughters' dowries for safekeeping. This reached such a point that also many rich men began to figure out how they too might be considered urimeleit and get pleasure and profit out of Reb Anshel. They too deposited their daughters' considerable dowries with him.

Needless to say, Reb Anshel was enchanted. The whole business had only one little fault: from the vague way the dowry depositors spoke, it appeared that they expected to return someday and get their money back. "If they expect to get it back later why do they give it to me now?" he marveled. "And on the other hand, it won't be so bad either, for not all of them will ask for their money the same day. Some of it will surely remain with me. And perhaps new depositors will come along as time goes on."

Suddenly an idea struck him. To go begging for alms in town now was out of .the question. Besides, he hated to leave the cozy warmth of the house for the cold outside. But why in God's name couldn't he ask for alms from those who came to see him? Of course they'd give him! These were decent folks with Jewish hearts!

"Ach! Why not?" everybody he asked for alms said with alacrity. "We're also Jews, even though we are little people. Compared to Reb Anshel the Golden, what are we all? Ants, little ants, standing next to a bear! But each one must give according to his ability."

And each one gave according to his ability, and even more. How could one make the piteous face of a gypsy when Reb Anshel himself asked for alms, God knows for whom and for what? Maybe it was for marrying off dowerless girls, or to aid the poor sick, or for the pious act of burying a dead person with no relations. Have you any idea for what purposes such a nogid like Reb Anshel could ask an alms?

When night came and all had left, Reb Anshel sat down to count his alms. He felt highly pleased. Such alms he had never seen even in a dream. But the dowry monies he didn't want to count; he didn't get much pleasure from them. In fact, they filled him with anxiety. What, after all, would he do if all of them should come demanding their money back at the same time? Ah! but how different it was with the alms money! "That's mine for keeps," he comforted himself. And that's why he counted the alms money over and over again, and each time with greater pleasure. And as he counted, he thought, "What a fine way this is—to sit at home and shovel in so many alms! Not until today did I have sense enough to try out this new method which is both easier and more profitable."

And he resolved never again to go dragging his feet from house to house, begging for alms. Whenever he'd want alms he'd collect it at home, right there in his room, where it was so warm and cozy and where they served him such delicious food and drink and, into the bargain, showered so much money on him!

IV

All the matchmakers in town soon began to rack their brains for Reb Anshel the Golden. What do you mean, a widower like that shouldn't be able to find a bride right here in town? True enough, if you consider his riches, his treasures (and if he's so rich, no doubt he's also a scholar, for what rich man isn't a scholar?), there's no girl in town worthy of him. But that's why he is Reb Anshel the Golden with his many good deeds like a tzaddik. On the contrary, out of just plain pity he'd want to marry a poor girl, and, compared to him, who is not poor? Not even the wealthiest man in town! That being the case, it would be well worth while to feel his pulse in the matter. Could there be any doubt about it? Why then do you think he settled down among us, left his marble palaces and his golden stables and lives here in a tiny room? If not for pity, why do you think he is doing it?

All the marriageable girls in town were buzzing away excitedly about the golden widower.

"His fine character lies written all over his face!" one of them said with enthusiasm.

"You see, on his face a scar is becoming!" another said. "It makes him look charming! It could even be that he made it himself on purpose."

"What penetrating eyes he's got!" said a third. "With one glance he looks at two people."

"Yes indeed, his eyes draw you like magnets."

"Golden eyes, they are!"

"He's altogether a man of gold!"

"Happy is she who will fall into his arms as his wife!"

There were even some daring rich men who wished to send a *shadchan* to Reb Anshel, but no shadchan had the courage to approach him. However, there was one who feared neither man nor God. Why, he could even pair together a lazy donkey with a sleeping bear, and for that very reason he was known as "Donkey-Bear." Well, this shadchan was ready to undertake this piece of business.

And everything turned out as easy as Donkey-Bear had hoped it would. Reb Anshel the Golden was so humble that at first he did not dare believe that there was one girl in town who'd care to have him.

"You want me to marry?" he asked astounded. "Why not? To get married is a pious Jewish act, but which man in town here will agree to give me his daughter?"

For the first time in his life Donkey-Bear was obliged to swear on the truth he was saying: "By my life, by my wife and children, over a Holy Book, I swear, Reb Anshel, that if you wanted all the girls in town, all of them without exception would go under one *chupeh* with you! How is it possible not to want such a nogid, such an eminent person (may no evil eye fall on you!) as you? Maybe you want a poor girl? Maybe you want a rich girl? Of the very richest? Or maybe perhaps you want the rabbi's daughter? Perhaps you prefer 'Mamselle'? You can have her too. She's the doctor's daughter. Is she educated? Ai, ai, ai! A *gevalt,* I'm telling you! She wears glasses, too, and she carries a walking stick like a regular man! Here you are, I'm leaving you a list of eligibles. Beside every girl's name you'll find an estimate of her father's wealth and the amount of the promised dowry. And there you have a list of the eligible daughters of urimeleit who can boast of eminent ancestors. You'll find my daughter among them, too. But you're free to choose anyone you like. Tomorrow you'll give me your answer. Ach, I almost forgot to tell you. On my list, against each girl's name you'll find three checks for beauties, two checks for pretty ones, and one check for quite pretty ones! But I promise you won't find an ugly one in the whole lot."

Reb Anshel began carefully to study the list, and from among all the names he finally chose a mate. And he came to his choice this way:

"They're eager to have me, says Donkey-Bear, every one of them. Rich men, I can see, are fewer than urimeleit. Rich men, of eminent ancestry are even fewer. Rich men of eminent ancestry with beautiful daughters are very, very few. But paupers, common people with 'quite pretty' daughters I see are a great many. If I should take a 'quite pretty' girl whose father is an uriman, then all the others in her class will be green-eyed with envy. They'll nebbech take it to heart! So wouldn't it be more humane and sensible to marry a beauty whose father is a nogid and comes of eminent ancestry as well? Then there'll be very few who'll envy."

Nu, with the choice of a bride Reb Anshel was all through. But there was still another matter that puzzled him greatly. He had heard from Donkey-Bear's own lips that he, Anshel, was a great nogid. Since Donkey-Bear was a very clever fellow who knew everything, he most likely knew what he was talking about. "And would you believe it, I had no idea about that until today! True enough, I've a lot of money on my hands already. Nu, so what? Someday I'll have to return it all, except the alms money. Who can tell what the future will bring? In that case to marry a nogid's daughter wouldn't be a bad thing at all!"

Overjoyed by his discovery, he ate his supper with hearty appetite and lay down to sleep—a nogid!

V

Reb Anshel got married with *mazl* to the most beautiful girl in town. In the main he was very pleased with his bride. He found only one little fault with her—her long name, "Ye-li-za-ve-ta." A regular rigmarole, a black year take it! He didn't pronounce the name once without stumbling. What the devil did she need such a name for? Wouldn't "Yachne" be better and shorter? The bride, on the other hand, got mulish and wanted nothing less than that he trim the tip of his beard. The black pepper take them! What have the women got against beards, anyway? " 'That one,' my first wife, (may my words not be held against her in the World-to-Come!) she plucked out one end of my beard with her bare hands. And now this one here is picking on the other end of my beard, wants to make an end of it, supposedly with scissors. A misfortune, really! It breaks my heart! Have you any idea how many years my beard has been growing?"

But, besides this grievance, everything was perfection itself. He led a carefree, delightful existence. True, his father-in-law didn't pay him the promised dowry yet. What was the sense of paying him the dowry, his father-in-law figured. He had been planning to borrow money from him anyway right after the wedding, so why go through the fool's play of giving and taking back? It would save Anshel the trouble that way.

Reb Anshel led a much happier life with his second wife than with "that one." Only now he realized how much easier and pleasanter it was to be a nogid than an uriman. He had business dealings with all the important merchants, for his fame extended beyond the town and through the entire region. Everybody talked about his great riches and even more about his many philanthropies. But the most lavish praise he got was for his simple, unpretentious ways. People marveled: "Can you imagine! A man is so rich and, just the same, he acts so humble that, compared to him, any small shopkeeper would appear proud!"

Many merchants came to Reb Anshel for advice and they'd ask him to judge between them whenever they had any disputes. And when they'd leave they'd pummel their brains to fathom the deep wisdom that lay in his decisions. They used to say in town, "Reb Anshel the Golden talks profoundly. It would almost look as if he didn't answer your question. . . . His words sound just like a puzzle. . . . Sometimes even foolish. . . . But when you rack your brains good and hard you're bound to find some deep meaning in it."

Naturally, people racked their brains and they did find deep meanings in Reb Anshel's vague words.

As time went on Reb Anshel's fame spread through all the world. There wasn't a single place where people hadn't heard of him. They even wrote about him in all the newspapers, told how much capital he had and all about his "ideals and aspirations."

Once there fell into Reb Anshel's hands a Yiddish newspaper. This was quite accidental because it isn't in the nature of a nogid to want to read a Yiddish newspaper. What was his amazement to see his likeness, as real as life, printed there!

"Now what do you say to that!" he marveled. "Just see how well they've gotten me down, even to the scar across my face!"

Then he read what they wrote about him.

"His benevolences are so numerous that they cannot be counted, and he gives everything in secret. No person ever finds out when and to whom he gives. Not only does he give his money to the poor, but he rips the hide off all the rich men who come to fawn on him. Every time someone comes to see him he's got to leave an alms. And oy is he a chochem! And oy, how well-read he is! What good common sense he has!"

Reb Anshel's face shone for very joy. "That I was so smart I never imagined. True, I never considered myself a fool, although 'she' (may her pious ancestors stand her in good stead in Paradise!) tried so hard to make me out a dumb calf; (may my words not harm her wherever she may be!) but she certainly had *chutzpah!* Whenever she'd get angry with me she'd say whatever came to her lips. Still in all, who'd ever dream that I, Anshel the pauper, was a chochem and a scholar! The world, it seems, knows a man better than he does himself!"

The more his fortune increased the greater the chochem he was considered. His witticisms were repeated with ecstasy by everybody in town.

One day, as he stood at his window yawning, he suddenly heard a noise outside the door. An uriman was trying to enter, but the servants wouldn't let him in. And as Reb Anshel saw this he recalled his old comrades of the road, and a yearning for them came over him. Oy, if he could only exchange a few words with an uriman, at least show off for him with his great mazl! He therefore ordered the servants to let the uriman come in.

When they were alone in his room, the uriman stood hunched up with respect before him, hardly daring to lift his eyes from the floor. "It isn't Your Excellency I wanted to see," he mumbled, "I'm looking for Anshel the uriman."

"Nu, that's me!" replied Reb Anshel.

"No, that can't be! The Anshel I know looked different. That one was cross-eyed and your eyes are straight. That Anshel had a scar across his face and you have a mazl wrinkle on your cheek."

And as the two looked at each other they suddenly recognized each other.

"Oy! Cripple! What are you doing here?"

"Just look takkeh if it isn't Anshele himself! How are you making out, Anshele?"

"Heh-heh—how I'm making out? What a question! You see, Cripple, I decided to change my trade and I became a nogid. And let me tell you, I haven't done so badly. Take my advice, Cripple. What's the use of being a pauper? Believe me it's a lot easier to be a nogid."

"It came easy to you, all right," answered the cripple, "but do you know why? It's because of me, and of me alone. Not that I had any intention to do you a good turn. I only felt like emptying my little sack of lies before a certain householder at whose table I ate that Shabbes, you remember when. I stuffed him full of stories about Reb Anshel the Golden of Frankfort, and when the fellow asked for signs by which he could recognize him I suddenly got the bright idea to describe you to him."

"Is that so?" said Reb Anshel, roaring with merriment. "Nu, I suppose now you're going to tell him the truth."

"And if I did tell him the truth who'd believe me, you idiot? It's no use, brother! You're a nogid now and you'll croak a nogid! Even if you were to tell them the truth yourself no one would believe you."

"They may not believe me but they'll believe you," insisted Reb Anshel. "If they believed you before they'll surely believe you now, too."

"No, it's absolutely no use! First of all, people believe a lie quicker than a truth. A lie always sounds more attractive than a truth. If it rings better you believe in it quicker. Secondly, people have made up their minds that you are a very rich man. They don't need your money, they need you. Merely on account of your reputation as a nogid they make their livelihood, have enough for breakfast and supper, furnish dowries for their daughters and provide work to others. Were you to tell them now that you're only Anshel the pauper, I'm sure they'd kill you, and they'd be right, too!"

"You're takkeh right! It's a pity on them. It wouldn't be nice of me now to tell the truth, especially when I've become a chochem (you know, I've become a chochem recently—all the newspapers say so!). Nu, I ask you, does a chochem act as foolishly as that?"

"Right you are, chochem mine! Now I'd like to know what you're going to give me for all I've done for you?"

"What shall I give you? If you like, I'll give you a job in one of my businesses."

"Do you think I'm *meshuggeh* or something? If you'll give me a job I'll have to work."

"What then shall I do for you?"

"I'll tell you what: Since you've no children of your own why not make me your heir?"

"What an idea! Do you think you're going to live longer than I?"

"Of course I will! It's simply because being that you're a nogid, doctors treat you when you're sick and me they don't because I haven't any money."

"And the way I've been thinking it'll be the other way around!

In fact, I've even been promising myself that after your death I'll study *Mishnayos* in memory of you. Did you have an idea that I knew Mishnayos? Eh, you didn't! Well, I do! How, do you ask? Just so, by myself. I don't know how, when, or where, but I know Mishnayos."

And so the two good old comrades had a long cozy chat, and when they had nothing more to say they separated.

It so happened that it turned out just as the cripple said it would: Reb Anshel didn't live much longer. A chochem, you see, and yet a fool! For he went ahead and died. After the funeral, they opened his will and to their astonishment they read that Reb Anshel left his entire fortune to an uriman, a cripple. He didn't even know his real name, for he knew him only by his nickname, "Cripple." But, in order to prevent any other cripple from claiming the fortune, he wrote down the sign by which he would definitely be recognized: "He is a terrible liar. Therefore, should a cripple come forward and make any claims as my heir, he should be given an examination in lie telling. The cripple who tells the biggest lie you'll know is the genuine heir."

The townfolk followed the instructions in the will to the letter. They let it be announced from the pulpits in all the synagogues and houses of study that anyone so blessed by God (magnified be His Name!) that he was both a cripple and a liar, should come forward to be examined by Reb Anshel's executors.

In no time at all an army of cripples, some real, and some fakers, descended upon the town. The matter didn't pass without much quarreling and scuffling. The feigned cripples fell upon the real cripples and abused them angrily! "You ganef, you *mamzer!*" shrilled nebbech a real cripple, with righteous indignation. "Why do you fake so? You're no cripple! Only yesterday I saw you dancing with the girls at the wedding!"

"The Devil take your father!" answered the other calmly. "Takkeh that's why you saw me dance—because I'm a cripple! It's easier for me to hop than to walk, no?"

That day, when mothers let their children out to play in the street they cautioned them, *"Kinderlach,* limp up a bit! If they'll ask you, you should say, 'We are nebbech cripples,' and if they'll ask you 'Is it day now?' You should answer, 'No, it's night!' And if they'll ask you: 'Are *tatte-mame* alive?' You should answer: 'No, they're nebbech dead!' "

Who could have anything against those mothers nebbech? They dared hope that maybe perhaps their children would become heirs.

Hopes are very good things for poor people, and besides they cost nothing!

The whole town suddenly began to limp. Jews coming from the synagogue and Jews going to market—all went limping about. Even the town doctor and the rabbinical judge started to limp. And each went in search of the other and met him on the way. The judge was on his way to the doctor to ask him to prescribe for his left foot that had suddenly gone bad on him, and the doctor went to inquire of the judge whether it was permitted a cripple to limp along beyond the proscribed limits for Shabbes.

But not all the proof required rested on being a cripple alone. There was the lie test too. Reb Anshel's executors called the cripples one by one. Then the lies flew thick and fast. One told them that he had seen a young couple who had gone to the rabbi for a divorce. The husband argued that his wife's father had chiseled off one hundred smackers from the dowry. So the rabbi asked him, "What fee will you pay me for divorcing you?" "Twenty-five rubles," answered the husband. Without hesitation the rabbi counted out seventy-five rubles and gave them to the young man. *"Na!"* said he. "Together with the twenty-five rubles you'd pay me for divorcing you, you'll have the hundred you're complaining about."

The crowd who listened laughed. "Not bad for a lie, but not good enough. Let's hear others."

Another cripple came forward and told how he saw two *melamedim* standing with a householder and quarreling. One *melamed* argued, "Let him teach your child and not me. He knows a lot more than I." And the other shouted, "Don't you believe him, that ganef, that liar! It is he who should teach your child. I don't have in my head what he has under his nail!" And when the townfolks heard of their amazing honesty they ran quickly and paid up all the back tuition fees they still owed them and the difference between all the fees that they had bargained down. Nu, it's enough to say that the two melamedim became stone rich that day!

The crowd turned up their noses. "That's a *melamedisher* lie! The nerve of him to drag in yet a respectable householder!" In fact a lot of them takkeh became very angry.

Ach! What lies they told that day! One said that he knew a usurer who on his deathbed had sent for all the clients he had cheated and gave back to each one what he had overcharged. There was only one fault to his repentance—his fortune wasn't big enough to return what he owed everybody. Another swore that he once knew an honest agent. Still another insisted that he knew a young woman who hated jewelry and pretty clothes. Only towards the end a cripple pushed his way through the crowd. Everyone could see that he was a genuine cripple.

It grew very still. Everybody had a feeling that this cripple was going to tell an honest-to-goodness lie.

"My Masters," he began gravely, "hear what I'm going to tell you. I want you to know that Reb Anshel the Golden (on him be peace!) was a terrible *kabtzen,* a wretched pauper, and oy, was he foolish—like a calf! No, I meant like an honest Jew!"

The crowd shook with laughter. "Bravo, bravo!" they cried. "That's what you could call a lie! You couldn't tell a bigger lie if you wanted to! This cripple must be the real heir!"

When the bookkeepers opened the account books they discovered that the entire fortune that remained barely covered Reb Anshel's debts. All that remained was a bag of money, of coins worn thin from much use. This was the alms money that Reb Anshel had saved. And so the cripple inherited it.

The crowd felt abashed and were filled with wonder. And as they started going away the cripple stopped them. "My Masters!" he cried. "Since a lie is so highly prized by you, then you've got to reward me for mine!"

"For what lie? You've been rewarded already! Aren't you the heir of the whole bag of alms?"

"No! That was for an old lie. The alms, you see, belong to me anyway because they're already in my hands, but I've yet to tell you an older lie still."

The cripple then told them the story of Reb Anshel from the very beginning.

Everybody exchanged astonished glances. For several minutes no one said a word. It was quite clear that they wanted to convince themselves that the cripple wasn't fooling them. But when he was through they all cried out with one voice:

"Liar! Who do you think you're fooling? What sort of humbug are you telling? Do you think you're smarter than the whole town?"

"Nu, folks! Don't you see the fellow is a *meshuggener?* Let's drive him out of town!"

"A meshuggener! really a meshuggener!" roared the crowd with one voice.

God loves the poor but helps the rich.

Most people, when in prosperity, are so overbrimming with wisdom (however inexperienced they may be), that they take every offer of advice as a personal insult, whereas in adversity they know not where to turn, but beg and pray for counsel from every passer-by.
—Baruch Spinoza

THE ARTFULNESS OF YOSHKE "LIAR"

In a little town there lived a man whom everybody nicknamed Yoshke "Liar," because he used to invent the most unbelievable stories about what he saw and heard in the wide world. Yoshke was constantly wandering forth, would go on long journeys on foot to Bucharest and Stambul and other distant places. He'd always return in tatters, looking woebegone. But he'd tell the most wonderful stories in the synagogue and the bathhouse and wherever else the local Jews met. His tales were so tall that nobody believed them.

"Why does the poor *schlimazl* have to wander away from home all the time?" someone asked the rabbi. "Wouldn't it be better if he stayed at home and invented his tall tales about Stambul while he sat in his own kitchen instead of knocking around in all far-off places where he is not wanted?"

"I'm sure there is some logic to our Yoshke's odd doings," answered the rabbi. "Let's look at it this way. Suppose, as you say, he sat at home in his own kitchen and invented his stories about Rome and Stambul over a nice, comfortable glass of tea. He'd think maybe there was a chance that they could happen. As you very well know, life can be stranger than anything you can invent out of your imagination. So Yoshke goes there to make sure that his stories are impossible. Then he can peacefully return home and not be uneasy that somebody might catch him at a truth!"

The liar fools himself most of all
when he imagines people believe him.

Everyone sits in the prison of his own ideas.—Albert Einstein

GOD AS TRADER

Wertheim, the Berlin stockbroker, who was seventy-two years old, lay seriously ill. An old crony visited him.

"Wait, Wertheim, you'll live yet to be eighty," he comforted him. "God will see to that."

"What do you think, God can't add?" muttered Wertheim scornfully. "If he can get me at seventy-two, why should he wait until I'm eighty?"

The longest road leads to the pocket.

A human being is nebbech *no more than a human being.*

Life is the cheapest bargain
—you get it for nothing.

One hour in Paradise isn't bad either.

HOW THE CZAR FOOLED MONTEFIORE

BY MENDELE MOICHER SFORIM
TRANSLATED FROM THE YIDDISH BY NATHAN AUSUBEL

It was wintertime, Saturday night after the *Habdalah* benediction. On the *lutchnik* under the chimney, a fire was crackling merrily. From time to time dry kindling wood was thrown in to revive it.

Opposite the fire at a table, pressed against the warm *hruba,* the household was gathered. The neighbor from next door came in packed tight as a drum with news. While words were being exchanged, nimble fingers got busy stripping feathers. And when everybody fell silent, one of the children read aloud in a Yiddish translation the story of Joseph and his Brethren. The great physical prowess of Judah stirred both pleasure and wonder in the hearers. My, my! Just one shout of his was almost enough to turn all of Egypt into a shambles!

All this time, the cat lay stretched out near the oven, licking her paw and twiddling her ears, by all appearances also with pleasure. The fire in the oven was ablaze, for supper was being cooked. But to still the pangs of hunger before supper was ready, a pot of potatoes had been put on the stove to boil and it was now simmering.

Back and forth across the room, still dressed in his Sabbath *kapote,* and singing "Elijah the Prophet" with great feeling, strode Reb Chaim. And as he concluded the words, "May he speedily come to us with Messiah, son of David," he came over to us. At that instant the door opened and some villagers piled in. The house resounded with hearty greetings: "A good week! . . . a good year!"

It's easily understood that when well-brought-up people try to outdo each other in courtesies at an open door in the wintertime, the people inside are just about ready to die of exposure. Then the elaborate amenities in getting seated; it took a long time and not before there was much moving about, motioning, pleading, and getting tangled up with each other.

Sureh, Reb Chaim's wife, treated the guests very hospitably with drinks of *shpetzies,* a concoction of herbs, compared to which tea was mere dishwater. She also served lumps of rock candy compared to which the sugar of today is just plain dirt.

And so they sat around, blew on the drink to cool it off and then sipped it. One lit his porcelain pipe, which had a silver cover and a long spiraled stem. Some coughed, others blew their noses or stroked their beards, and the conversation grew lively. It meandered this way and that way, about this a bit and about that a bit, until, in the end, the conversation switched to the burning question of the day:

"Ach! The Government's decree against Jewish clothing is really an ugly thing!" all agreed with a sigh. Imagine, that Jews should be forced to dress in the German style! A cap with a visor! It would certainly look queer, a fright! *Gevalt!* And for what, O Lord of the World, for what? What can "they," they over there, get out of it if Jews will go dressed in the German style? There must be some explanation for it!

"Do you know what people say? People say that there's a sly trick behind it all," muttered the man with the pipe. He drew on it deeply and let out smoke rings which grew ever larger as they floated through the air. "And who do you suppose is behind it? Montefiore!"

"God be with you, Reb Behr! What are you talking about?"

"Just that, what you're hearing! Certainly you're not going to doubt Reb Borech-Hillel's word? He's just come back from the fairs and with his own ears he heard——"

"I, too, heard something like that," interrupted a lively, convulsive Jew, chewing on his lip. "Ha, wait-wait! Do you want to know what I heard?"

"Oy, Reb Yossel, please don't interrupt!" the others begged him. "Sha! Nu, Reb Behr?"

"They're saying," began Reb Behr, unhurried, chewing on every word. "Yes, that's what it was. When Montefiore saw that it was feh! so he came with such a proposal to the Czar: 'O my lord King,' said he, 'I want you to sell me your Jews. I'll give you for them so many and so many millions.' "

"A hundred thousand millions, a hundred thousand of them, I heard!" again interrupted Reb Yossel. He was not so much concerned with giving the exact amount as to show off before everybody that he, too, knew what was going on in the world no less than others.

"So what's the difference?" muttered Reb Behr, turning up his nose disdainfully. And he continued his story: " 'Why not?' answered the Czar. So they takkeh on the spot drew up a contract and Montefiore laid down a deposit of a million smackers on the deal."

"No, that wasn't it! He laid down then and there in cold cash, a hundred thousand million!" again Reb Yossel interrupted, swaying excitedly to and fro as if he were holding a disputation with Reb Behr about a passage in the Talmud.

"Ai! Reb Yossel, please be quiet! Sha!" everybody begged him.

"In short, Montefiore laid down a million for the time being," continued Reb Behr slowly, unperturbed by Reb Yossel's challenges. "He obligated himself to pay the whole amount at the time when he would take over the merchandise, meaning all the Jews of the country. Then they went their ways. 'Farewell,' said Montefiore to the Czar. 'Depart in good health,' the Czar told him. After breakfast, as was the custom, the Czar went to the Senate in a merry mood. 'My lord the King,' his minister asked him, 'what is the reason that you're so merry today?' 'It's because so-and-so,' answered the Czar, with a pleased smile. 'I made a fine little deal today. I sold my little Jews for so much and so much.' 'My lord the King,' cried the minister, very much scared, 'what have you done? You've been swindled!' And soon takkeh he made him a reckoning that the percent which such goods, the Jews that is, would earn for him in a certain period of time amounted by at least a fiddle-with-a-bow more than the purchase price of all the goods.

" 'So what's to be done?' asked the Czar. 'An agreement is an agreement, you know, and the word of the Czar is as good as a decree. Nu, so advise me since you have the head of a minister, think up something.' 'My lord the King,' replied the minister, after he had thought for a while, 'I have a solution. Issue a decree, but takkeh right away, that all Jews should dress in German style.' 'Dress-shmresh! What's that got to do with it?' asked the Czar. 'Plenty!' replied the minister with a shrewd wink. 'As soon as the Jews dress German, will they look like Jews anymore? Do you get my idea?'

" 'Ai-ai, that's mighty clever of you!' cried the Czar, with enthusiasm. 'For that I'm going to present you with a gold medal.'

"So there you have it, my masters, the trick!" said Reb Behr, and he started to clean out the ashes from his pipe with a thin wire. "Exactly at the appointed time Montefiore arrived at the court of the Czar."

"No, that wasn't it, he didn't bust in on the Czar just like that! He had himself announced first," heatedly interrupted Reb Yossel, no longer able to restrain himself.

"Sha! Please Reb Yossel, don't interrupt!" everybody begged him, eager to hear the end of the story. "Nu, Reb Behr, go on, nu, nu!"

"So Montefiore came," Reb Behr took up where he left off, and he drawled his words out slowly, as if he wished to spite Reb Yossel. "So he came, just as I'm telling you, to close the deal. 'My lord King,' said he to the Czar. 'Here's the rest of your money, and let me take away my merchandise, the Jews that is, just as it is written in the agreement.' 'Sure, why not?' replied the Czar. 'Please go out and wherever you see a Jew, take him in the name of the God of Israel! He's your goods now.'

"Naturally, Montefiore didn't require to be coaxed too much and he went looking for his Jews. He came to one city—he saw no Jews! To another—no Jews! In short, he went to Berditchev—still no Jews! Not the sign of a Jew anywhere! Why? Because all Jews were dressed up in European style and looked like Germans."

"Ai-ai-ai!" gasped everybody in amazement. "Is that really what the world is saying, Reb Behr?"

"*Et!*" murmured Reb Chaim with a disparaging smile. "Not everything the world says is true!"

"Whether it's so or it's so, it's nonetheless revolting!" cried everybody with a groan. "No matter how you look at it, the decree is, tak-keh a decree! As for wearing the kapote German style, nu, that's not so terrible! We'll cut a slit in the back and the Devil won't take it that way either! But oy the cap with the visor! Lord of the Universe—the cap with the visor! Nu, Reb Chaim, how about it? Think up a way out of it, ha! Nu, what do you say, Reb Chaim?"

DISCRETION

When the Czar passed through the little Jewish town everybody turned out to welcome him and do him homage. Only one Jew failed to show up—Shmelke the Nitwit. He locked himself up in a clothes closet and wouldn't budge from there.

Later, when the Czar had left, he came out of hiding.

"What was the idea, Shmelke?" people asked him. "Why did you hide from the Czar?"

"Ai, what a danger I've just escaped!" rejoiced Shmelke. "For three years I haven't had money to pay the Czar his taxes. Can you imagine what he would have done to me if he had spotted me in the crowd?"

Out of the Spice Box

Tzoress *with soup are easier to swallow than tzoress without soup.*

Ingenious ideas usually come like the firemen—too late.

God is an honest payer—but a very slow one.

Barking dogs don't bite,
but they themselves don't know it.—Sholom Aleichem

WHY GET EXCITED?

Yossel, a small-town Jew who had a cousin in Brooklyn, decided to emigrate to America. On the third day out at sea a storm broke out. Great excitement raged on board ship. The captain shouted orders through a megaphone. Sailors lowered lifeboats, women screamed, children cried, dogs barked, while everybody else milled about the deck in great confusion. Only Yossel went about tranquilly watching the pandemonium with amusement.

"How can you be so unconcerned when the ship is sinking!" a fellow passenger upbraided him sharply.

"What are you excited about, uncle?" asked Yossel. "Does the ship belong to you?"

A good friend you get for nothing,
an enemy you've got to buy.

No choice is also a choice.

The rebbe *drinks up all the wine,*
then he tells everybody: "Be jolly!"

NATURE'S SECRETS

I

It was after the *Mincha* service at dusk on a hot *Shabbes* day, and as the old men in the synagogue waited for the *Ma'ariv* prayers to begin they sát around and whiled away the time in various speculations about God's wonders. Among them was Chaim, the retired *melamed,* of whom everybody used to say, "Ach, that Chaim, he certainly has a head on him; he knows everything!"

"Do tell us, Reb Chaim," asked one of the greybeards, "why is it that it's warm in summer and cold in winter?"

Reb Chaim wrinkled his forehead and stroked his beard thoughtfully.

"Let me answer your question with another question," he began. "When does one make the stove? In winter, of course! Everybody knows that. *Nu,* when you make the stove it gets warm inside, no? That's plain. But the question is: where does all that warmth go when you put the fire out? You know, it goes out of the stove and then out of the room. And then you've got to make the stove again! Nu, so answer me, where really goes all the warmth that you get out of making the stove? Well, it moves up into the air and rises higher and higher until it reaches the clouds. There it collects, and it keeps on growing and gets heavier and heavier from day to day. And when it gets so heavy that it can no longer remain suspended in the air it starts to sink. And it sinks ever lower and lower until it finally reaches the ground. And when it does that, it's warm again! You see, that's how summer comes!"

"That's clear!" answered the questioner. "You've already explained why it's hot in the summer. Now tell us, Reb Chaim, why is it cold in winter?"

"Tsk-tsk! What a question to ask!" the melamed chided him. "Everybody knows that in Nature all things are connected. When it's hot in summer it's because you make the stove in winter, and it's cold in winter because who the devil is *meshuggeh* enough to make the stove in summer?"

II

The old men were gathered around the synagogue stove as the rain came down in torrents. Someone expressed the wonder what it was that made it rain.

Reb Groinem the philosopher, as usual, was ready with an answer:

"Even a child knows that rain comes out of the clouds. You may compare the clouds to sponges that have soaked up a lot of water, and so these sponges float across the sky driven by the winds. From the right come sponges, from the left come sponges, and when they meet they strike and press against each other. And may I ask you what happens when you squeeze a sponge that's full of water? What comes out of it? Water, of course! And this water falls on the ground and that's how it rains."

This explanation of Reb Groinem was met with skeptical shrugs all around.

"It's all very well to philosophize," the old men argued. "But what concrete proof have you got for your theory?"

"Proof you want yet?" scornfully snorted Reb Groinem, the philosopher. "Do you need proof yet? Just look out of the window! It's raining, isn't it?"

TIRING WORK

"My rabbi, he's always deep in contemplation. Ach! What silence he keeps! He keeps silent so long that he grows tired. Then he rests a while, and after he's rested, he keeps silent some more!"

HOW LATE IS "LATE"?

A Jew hurried to the railroad station to catch a train for Vilna but the train pulled out just as he arrived.

Seeing this, he wrung his hands and moaned, "Woe is me that such a misfortune should happen to me! It was so important for me to catch that train."

"How late were you, uncle?" a by-stander inquired sympathetically.

"Just about thirty seconds."

"Not more? Heh! By the way you carry on I thought it must have been at least one hour!"

When you love your wife you love all her relations.

To a wedding you walk —to a divorce you run.

The longer a blind man lives the more he sees.—Sholom Aleichem

Those who have nothing are always eager
to share it with others.

NO PEACE FOR A RABBI

Squabbles with the congregation's leaders were driving the rabbi to distraction.

"If you're so unhappy why don't you find yourself another post?" suggested a colleague. "I hear there's a good pulpit vacant in Detroit."

The elderly rabbi shook his head wearily.

"Don't you know that there are seven purgatories in Gehenna? You must have wondered, why seven? Isn't one good purgatory enough to punish any hardened sinner? And the answer is 'no'! No matter how excruciating the torments are in any one purgatory the sinner is bound to get used to them. Once he's used to them he suffers less. But since God is just, what does he do? He has the devils carry the wretch to the next purgatory, where he has to start getting used to a new set of tortures.

"I'm in the same position. Whatever tortures I have to endure in this congregational purgatory I'm already accustomed to. Believe me, were I to take the Detroit pulpit I'd have to start a new purgatory all over again!"

Rich people swell up with pride.
Poor people swell up with hunger.
> —*Sholom Aleichem*

RETROSPECT

BY KARL KRAUS
TRANSLATED FROM THE GERMAN BY ALBERT BLOCH

What crazy existence is this we've led,
That so undermined us?
We have kept pace with progress and rushed straight ahead
And left ourselves behind us.

Money is round, so it rolls away.

Sell even the shirt off your back
if that'll make you rich.

When does a Jew sing?
When he is hungry.

When poor girls begin to dance
the musicians stop playing.

In order to become immortal our great writers
first have to die of hunger.—Moritz G. Saphir

The space in a needle's eye is sufficient for two friends, but the whole
world is scarcely big enough to hold two enemies.—Solomon ibn
Gabirol

We have far greater compassion for someone else's misfortune
than the pleasure we take in his good fortune.

A stale crust is more useful to the poor man
than a lot of fresh air.

If you begin to think of death
you're no longer sure of your life.

If you lie on the ground you can't fall.

THE PARABLE OF A BUNDLE OF STRAW

BY SHOLOM ALEICHEM

Once there was a tailor and he died. *Nu,* go ahead and weep over him! But his fellow tailors didn't want to weep over him. So the rabbi who conducted the burial service fell on a stratagem and told them the following parable:

"Once there was a bundle of straw. As long as it held together all went well. But (now just take a look at this poor dead corpse!) no sooner did the bundle of straw get untied than the individual straws began to fall away!

"Now brothers, you too may be compared to a bundle of straw. . . . Since one of you tailors has died, in that way untying the whole bundle of you—tailors will now keep on dying and dying!"

Oy, did the tailors weep!

> *If you have to hang*
> *—pick out a tall tree!*

If you are too sweet, they'll eat you up.

> *All brides are beautiful*
> *—all corpses are pious.*

Tzoress *are partial to wetness*
—to tears and brandy.

> *Blind is he who thinks he sees everything.*

WAR OF PERSUASION

The Battle of Tannenberg was at its height when a Czarist officer drew up his company and addressed them.

"The moment has come! We're going to charge the enemy. It'll now be man against man in hand-to-hand combat."

In the company was a Jewish soldier who hated the Czar and the war.

"Please, sir, show me my man!" he cried. "Maybe I can come to an understanding with him."

There's no ruble that's a mamzer.

If you want to get a reputation as a wise man, agree with everybody.

If you lend someone a
"fiver" and he avoids you
—you've gotten off cheap.

A smooth tongue is a fresser
—it gobbles up the truth.

COLLECTORS, ANCIENT AND MODERN

Two skeptical Talmudists were discussing the Golden Calf that Aaron made for the Children of Israel in the wilderness.

"Explain to me if you can," asked one, "how it was that since Aaron cast so much gold into the fire there came forth only a calf. You'd think that from so much gold at least an ox would have come forth."

"As I figure it," answered the other, "Aaron must have sent out collectors to gather up the gold among the people. What surprises me is that with all those collectors around it was actually a calf that came forth and not a *flea!*"

A stingy person and a fat cow are useful
only after they are dead.—Sholom Aleichem

A glass of tea you'll drink?
What does Rashi say? "A sick man you ask—a healthy one you give!"
—Sholom Aleichem

A drunk gets a red nose from white wine too.

SELF-APPRAISAL

BY GEORG BRANDES

I'm not a philosopher—for that I'm too small.
I'm not a critic—for that I'm too big.

It's Hard to Be a Jew

Dear God! You help complete strangers, so why not me?

THE HUSSAR WHO LOVED THREE JEWS

BY FERENC MOLNAR [NEUMANN]
TRANSLATED FROM THE HUNGARIAN BY JUNE BARROWS MUSSEY

"Well," the captain said, "it began with the Jews. I've been fond of two Jews in my life. One was the proprietor of the Café Mirabella, the other Lieutenant Rado, whose name was Roth, but when he became an active officer he changed his name to Rado, which sounded Hungarian. He was a thin, dark Jew boy, silent, punctual, orderly, a very good soldier. He stayed in the army because the officers liked him, and urged him to stay in the army when his year's service was up. Even though he was a Jew. But first I'll tell you quickly the story about the proprietor of the Café Mirabella. He was an elderly Jew. And you can write this one—not the one about Rado. Do you know where the Café Mirabella is?"

"In the Andrassy ut."

"Right. In a big, four-story corner building. They say it used to belong to another Jew by the name of Pollak. Well, one afternoon a Polish Jew with a beard and a long black caftan comes into this Pollak's Café Mirabella. The Mirabella was full of women in silks, drinking coffee. The man in the caftan sat down in the extreme corner at a small table, and waited. The waiter must have gone past ten times, but never asked what he wanted.

"Finally he called the waiter: 'A cup of coffee, please.' The waiter looked at him, and said, 'We haven't any coffee.' The man in the caftan looked at him wide-eyed. What, no coffee in a big café like that? He was beginning to suspect that they did not want to serve him because they were ashamed of his caftan in front of all the other, fashionable Jews.

"Going over to the cashier's desk, where the proprietor was standing, he greeted him civilly and inquired, 'If you please, is it true what the waiter tells me, that there isn't any coffee here?' The proprietor looked at him disdainfully, and said: 'Not for you.'

" 'Thank you,' said the man in the caftan, and went out. It was raining outside; that's important too. He stood in the rain outside the fashionable café for a while, and his heart ached. I know that, because he told me so himself. His heart ached because the Jewish café-owner was ashamed of him on account of the Jewish guests. 'If it had been an anti-Semite,' he said, 'I wouldn't have said a word.'

"He stood outside the café for a while, then went into the building and asked the doorman where the owner of the building lived. He lived on the second floor. He went up to see him. He told me they discussed the matter for about an hour.

"After an hour they telephoned a lawyer, for the man in the caftan had bought the building. He paid the full purchase price on the spot and then went downstairs with the lawyer to the café, and gave the proprietor notice. The proprietor was so astonished by the whole story that it was not until an hour later in the gambling room that he fainted away.

"This was about eight years ago; since that time the other man has owned the café, and has doubled his fortune. You can write the story, but make the title 'Anger Is a Bad Counselor.'

"I grew very fond of the fellow. There's a man for you. For years I went to the café every night, and we used to drink our brandy together. I used to make him tell me the story every week because it was such a wonderful one. Only I did feel sorry that he took to wearing a gray English tweed suit and a red tie. He really ought never to have taken off his caftan. But that's none of my business now. I mentioned it because he's one of my Jews."

"And Rado?"

"The other one. He did play a part in my life, the poor fellow. Rado was not a hussar, but an infantryman. But he was in the same town of Nagyvarad where I was. I used to sit with him a lot in the café; not so much in the restaurant. He was an excellent chess player. Well, if you please, down in Dalmatia or somewhere in one of those wild regions, they were having maneuvers. And the following business happened to Rado. During the maneuvers, that is, on duty as a lieutenant, he was going through some big woods, and after him his orderly, an honest Hungarian lad. They walked and walked, and then sat down to rest on some big stones or rocks.

"As they were sitting there, Rado's striker suddenly began to yell, because a viper had bitten him. They tell me the whole country is full of vipers down there. The boy yelled, and Rado was in a terrible fright, because he knew that one of these viper bites is deadly. The snake had caught the boy on the upper thigh, where it could reach him as he sat, deep under his hip. Notice that, because it's important too. Under the hip. A small patrol of officers came by, and they heard what had happened, but nobody could help. The poor fellow was yelling, because he too had heard that you could die of it. Several of them said you had to suck the blood out of the wound right away, and no harm would happen.

"Well, who was ready to do that? Nobody. Rado was very fond of the boy. That hardly needs mentioning; it's usually the way. Well, who was willing? Nobody was willing. They actually even smiled. Finally Rado forced himself to suck the blood from the poisoned bite. A hundred doctors afterward said that he saved his striker's life by doing it. It was in a bad place, as I told you—on the upper part of the thigh. The results in the town of Nagyvarad were most unfortunate. The officers said they wouldn't sit at the same table with Rado. You know how it usually is in a provincial town. The whole town knew about it. There was so much gossip that the officers' corps had to take up the case.

"And I can't blame those officers; from their standpoint they were perfectly right. No officer could go around among the enlisted men when he had kissed a buck private's backside, even if it was from the side. It was a disastrous situation.

"The officers were right, and poor Rado was right too. But I was young then, and very indignant at the strict orthodoxy of the officers. I had very acrimonious arguments with them, and even with my brother officers in the cavalry.

"Rado was nowhere to be found; he went to Budapest, for he was ashamed to be seen. I kept exposing myself more and more—you know, I had charged into it and got tangled up in it; in those days I still believed a fellow like Rado might shoot himself if he had to resign from the army. On his account I was at outs with everybody, and went to dinner alone for weeks. I couldn't do him any good. Rado was given to understand that he must immediately resign his commission and get out of the army, and within a month the affair was forgotten. The only thing not forgotten was that I had savagely upheld the opposite point of view, and now my position began to be untenable. . . ."

The following morning at nine the captain came banging at my door. He did this often, although he knew I was in the habit of going to bed at six in the morning. He sat down beside me.

"I told you recently that I had loved two Jews. I was wrong. I have loved three."

"And for that you waked me out of the midst of my dreams?"

"For that. The third one's name was Schurz. He was an old man. His profession was that of usurer."

"And you loved him? A usurer?"

"Very much."

"And . . . is that all?"

"No. I've got to explain why I loved him. I'm no anti-Semite, but when it's a question of a Jew a cavalry officer always has to explain why he's fond of him. There are Jews, though of course only a few, whom even our Imperial and Royal Majesty loves. But he always makes it a practice to say why. It's strange, but it's so; I can't help it.

"Just once I said something mildly disagreeable to a Jew, and was sorry afterward even for that. In case you're interested, it was my godchild. An honest, thirty-year-old bank clerk. He got himself baptized, adopted the Catholic faith, and chose me for his godfather.

"On the day before the ceremony he came to call on me, and asked: 'Will I be properly dressed if I go to church to be baptized tomorrow in a cutaway and dark striped trousers?'

" 'Right,' I told him.

" 'What sort of shoes should I wear?' he asked.

"I said, 'That I can't tell you, my boy, because I was barefoot when they baptized me.'

"But let's get back to old Schurz. As aforesaid, old Schurz was a usurer. In my opinion usurers are benefactors of humanity, and especially of the cavalry. You needn't gape at me like that. A cavalry officer has two indispensable attributes: his horse and his financial difficulties. Friends who occasionally help out a person with small loans are simply doctors prescribing a powder for a headache. Usurers —now there are the great surgeons, saving our lives with a major operation. I repeat for the third time, old Schurz was a usurer.

"I was a cardplayer by then. Schurz lived in the town of Arad, because a regiment of hussars was garrisoned there. A thoroughbred usurer loves neither the infantry nor the artillery. Only the cavalry. He not only lends money to the officers, but takes care of their other affairs.

"In general we took him for a decent fellow. The officers not only loved him, they trusted him. This went so far that when an officer was transferred to some other town, no matter where Fate sent him, he would continue to be a client of old Schurz for years. Some people, who wanted to be witty at all costs, called him Shylock. I always regarded that as base ingratitude.

"About that time I was transferred from Arad to Budapest. Here, of course, I played cards more than ever. I lost, and was in acute financial distress.

"I had a valuable old family ring, and decided to sell it. Obviously no one else but old Schurz was to be thought of. The matter was very pressing. I took the old ring, put it in its little old red leather case, wrapped it up, and sent it by mail with a short, categorical note to old Schurz at Arad.

"I wrote: 'Enclosed I send you my old family ring. If you want to give three thousand crowns for it, keep it. If you don't want to give that much, send the ring back at once. I won't take a penny less. No haggling.' Then I waited for an answer.

"In two days I got a telegram. Contrary to my instructions, old Schurz tried to bargain. He wired: 'Ring not worth three thousand. Give two thousand at most.'

"Furiously I answered: 'Price of ring three thousand. No haggling.'

"The next day came another telegram. The old fox went on bargaining: 'Offer twenty-five hundred, positively no more.'

"At this I lost patience, and wired: 'Ring three thousand. No haggling. Return immediately.'

"A few days passed, and I got a little package by mail from: Schurz. Contents: ring. I opened the parcel. There lay the case with the ring, carefully tied up and sealed. On top of the case was a note from old Schurz—to my annoyance, more haggling, as follows: 'As an expert I tell you that this ring is not worth three thousand crowns. You would never get that much for it anywhere in the world. However, because I like you, I raise my last offer from twenty-five hundred to twenty-eight hundred crowns. That is my final word. If you want to sell for that price, don't open the case, just send it back to me as is. I will send the money the following day. If you don't want to sell the ring even for twenty-eight hundred, keep your ring; I wouldn't buy it.'

"I was deeply embittered on reading this. I vowed I would not sell the ring any cheaper, would not send it back, and would try to sell it to someone else.

"Exasperated, I broke the seal and opened the red leather case. The ring was not there. In its place was a tiny paper with the following words: 'All right, all right, don't get excited, I will give you three thousand crowns.' "

I had almost fallen asleep in the middle of the story, but at this unexpected conclusion I awoke.

"How can one help loving a man like that?" said the Captain in a tone of honest enthusiasm.

GY-MA-NA-SI-A

BY SHOLOM ALEICHEM

TRANSLATED FROM THE YIDDISH BY FRANCES BUTWIN

Listen to me, your worst enemy can't do to you what you can do to yourself, especially if a woman—I mean a wife—interferes.

Why do I say this? I'm thinking of my own experience. Look at me, for instance. Well, what do you see? A man, you'd say—just an average man. You can't tell from my face whether I have money or not. It is possible that once I may have had some money, and not only money—for what is money?—but a decent livelihood, an honorable position, without rush and bustle and noise. No, the way I look at it, the quiet, unassuming way is best. I've always operated in a quiet, unspectacular way. In a quiet unspectacular way, I've gone broke twice. Quietly, and without fuss, I settled with my creditors and started all over again. . . .

But there is a God who rules over all of us, and through my own wife, He chastened me. She isn't here, so we can talk freely. To look at her you might say she is a wife like all wives. A pretty decent woman as women go. A big woman, God be praised, twice as big as I am, and not bad-looking. Really handsome, you might say, and not a fool either. She is smart—very smart, you might say—in fact, a woman with a masculine brain. And that's just the trouble. It's not so good when a woman has brains like a man. It doesn't matter how smart she is—after all, the good Lord created Adam first, and Eve after him! But try to point that out to her, and she answers, "If the Highest One wanted to create you first and then us—that's His affair. But if He saw fit to put more brains into my little toe than into your whole head, I'm not to blame for that either."

"How did we come around to that?" I ask.

"Very simply," says she. "Whenever there is a decision to be made around here, I am the one who has to rack her brains. Even when our boy has to be sent to the *Gymnasia,* I have to do the planning."

"Where is it written," I ask, "that he has to go to the Gymnasia? I'll be just as happy if he studies the Torah right here at home."

And she says, "I've told you a thousand times already that you won't succeed in setting me against the whole world. Nowadays the whole world sends it children to the Gymnasia."

"To my way of thinking," I say to her, "the whole world is crazy."

"And I suppose you are the only sane one," says she. "The world would come to a pretty pass if everybody did what you wanted."

And I tell her, "Everybody acts according to his way of thinking."

"May all my enemies and my friends' enemies," says my wife, "have in their pockets, in their chests, and in their cupboards as much as you have in your head! They'd starve to death."

"Pity the poor man," says I, "who has to listen to a woman's advice."

And she says, "Pity the poor woman who has a husband who needs her advice."

Well, try to argue with a woman. If you say this, she says that. If you say one word she gives you back twelve. And if you stop talking altogether she bursts into tears or better still falls in a faint. To make a long story short, she had her way. For let's not fool ourselves: if a woman makes up her mind, is there anything we can do?

Well, what shall I tell you? *Gy-ma-na-si-a!*

First of all we had to start getting him ready to enter the *Mladshi Prigotovitelnie,* the junior preparatory school. "What's there to worry about?" I said with a shrug. "A trifle like that—Mladshi Prigotovitelnie. It seems to me that any little schoolboy among us can put them all in the shade. Especially a child like ours!" If you travel the length and breadth of the Empire, you won't find another like him. I'm his own father and I may be prejudiced, but you can't get away from it— the child has a head on him. He's the talk of the province. . . .

Well, why should I make a long story out of it? He made his application, went for his examination, took his examination, and— he didn't pass! What happened? He failed in arithmetic. He's a little weak, they tell me, in figuring. In math-e-ma-tics, they call it. How do you like that? Here's a boy with such a head—he's the talk of a province—you can travel the length and breadth of the Empire. . . . And they tell me: math-e-ma-tics. At any rate, he failed. That made me good and mad. If he took that examination, he should have passed it. But after all, I'm a man, not a woman. So I thought it over: the devil take it! We Jews are used to such treatment. Let's forget the whole thing.

But try to convince *her* once she'd got that crazy idea into her head! She's made up her mind once for all—*Gy-ma-na-si-a!* So I plead with her. "Tell me," I say, "my dear wife, what does he need it for? Will it keep him out of the army? For that, the Lord has already provided. He's an only son. What then? To help him make a living? I can get along without it. What do I care if he becomes a storekeeper like me, or some other kind of businessman? And if it's his luck to become a millionaire or a banker, I'll bear up under that too." Thus I plead with her. But does it do any good?

"It's just as well," she tells me, "that he didn't get into the Mladshi Prigotovitelnie after all."

"Why?" I ask.

She says, "He might just as well go right into the Starshi Prigotovitelnie, the advanced preparatory school." "Well," I think, "why not? After all, with a head like that . . . you can travel the length and breadth . . ."

But what happened? When it came to the final test, he failed again! Not in math-e-ma-tics this time. Something new. His spelling is not what it might be. That is, he spells the words all right, but there is one letter on which he is a little weak. The letter *yati*. He puts it in all right, but the trouble is that he doesn't put it where it belongs. So I'm heart-broken! I don't know how I'll ever be able to go to Poltava or to Lodz for the fairs, if he doesn't learn to put the letter *yati* where they want him to. . . .

Anyway, when they told us the glad tidings, *she* almost had a fit. She rushed right off to the director and insisted that the boy could do it; he knew how to spell. Just let them try him out again right from the beginning. Naturally, they paid no attention to her. They gave him a *two*—the failing grade—and what kind of a *two? A two minus!* And go do something about it. Help! Murder! He failed again. So I say to her, "What do you want us to do? Commit suicide? We're Jews. We're used to such treatment."

At this, she flares up at me and starts to yell and to curse as only a woman can do. That doesn't bother me. The only one I feel sorry for is my boy, poor child. Think of it. All the other boys will be wearing uniforms with silver buttons and he won't. So I plead with him. "You dummy!" I say. "You fool! Is it a law that everybody has to go to Gymnasia? Silly child, somebody has to stay home, doesn't he? And besides. . . ."

But she doesn't let me finish. "Such comfort he offers! Who asked for your sympathy? What you can do instead is to go and find a good teacher for him, a tutor, a Russian tutor to teach him *gra-ma-ti-ka*, grammar."

Listen to her. She wants two tutors. One tutor and one *melamed* for Hebrew isn't enough for her. Well, we argued back and forth, but in the end she won the point. Because when she makes up her mind, is there anything I can do?

Well, what shall I say? We hired another tutor, a real Russian this time, because the examination in Grammar for First Class is a tough proposition. It's strong medicine to take, as strong as horse-radish. You can't trifle with *gra-ma-ti-ka* with the *bukva yati,* the letter *yati.* And what kind of tutor does the good Lord send us? I am ashamed to talk about it. He made life unbearable for us. He belittled us and made fun of us right to our faces. May he burn in hell! For instance, he couldn't find another word to practice on than garlic— *Tchasnok! Tchasnok, tchasnoka, tchasnoku, tchasnokoi.* . . . If it hadn't been for *her,* I'd have taken him by the collar and thrown him out together with his grammar. But to her it was worth going through. Why? Because the boy was going to know where to put a *yati* and where not to put it. Think of it! All winter we tortured him and it was not until late spring that he had to go to the slaughter. And when the time came, he made his application, took his examination, and this time he didn't fail. He got the best marks, a four and a five. Hurrah! Let's celebrate! *Mazl-tov!* Congratulations! But wait! Don't be in such a hurry. We don't know yet if he'll be admitted. We won't know till August. Why not? Go ask them. What can we do about it? It's *their* world. A Jew is used to such treatment. . . .

Comes August, my wife can't rest. She rushes around, from the director to the inspector, from the inspector to the director. "Why do you keep running, like a poisoned rat, from one hole to the next?" I ask her.

"What do you mean—why do I keep running?" she says to me. "Are you a stranger around here? Don't you know what goes on these days? Haven't you heard about quotas?"

And what finally happened? He *didn't* get in. Why not? Because he didn't get two *fives*. If he had gotten two fives, they told us, then *maybe* he would have got in. How do you like that? *Maybe*. Well, I'd just as soon forget what I got from her that day. But the one I felt sorry for was *him*. The poor boy. He lay there with his head in the pillow and wouldn't stop crying. So there was nothing else to do; we had to get another tutor, a student at the Gymnasia, and we started grooming him all over again, this time for second class. And that was a real task, because to get into the second class you had to know not only math-e-ma-tics and grammar, but geography and penmanship and I don't know what else besides. Though, if you ask me, for three groschen, you can have it all. Any Bible text our boys have to learn in *cheder* is harder than all their studies and much more to the point. But what can we do about it? A Jew is used to such treatment. . . .

There followed a round of lessons. We lived on lessons. When we got up in the morning—lessons. After we had finished the morning prayer and eaten—lessons. All day long—lessons and more lessons. Until late at night we could hear him reciting: "Nominative, genitive, dative, accusative. . . ." It rang in my ears, it pounded in my head. I couldn't eat. I couldn't sleep. "Look," I said, "you take an innocent creature and you torture him. It's a crime. The poor child will get sick."

And she exclaims, "Bite your tongue for these words!"

And once more he went to the slaughter, and this time he brought home nothing but *fives!* But, then, did you expect anything different? A head like his—you can travel the length and breadth of the Empire and you won't find another like it! It sounds good, doesn't it? Well, listen to this then. When they posted the names of the boys who were accepted, and we looked—ours wasn't there. Help! Murder! It's a disgrace, a crime! He had perfect marks. Watch her go! Watch her run! She'll show them. Well, she went, she showed them—and all they told her was to stop annoying them. In plain language, they showed her the door. And she came rushing into the house with a roar that could be heard in heaven.

"You!" she yelled. "A fine father you are! If you were a real father like other fathers, if you had an ounce of love for your child, you'd find some way. You'd see people. You'd do something. You'd use your influence, with the director, the inspector, somebody. . . ."

What do you think of that? There's a woman for you! "Is that all I have to do? Isn't it enough that I have to carry on my mind all the seasons, the markets, the fairs, and notes and receipts and checks and drafts, and I don't know how many more things? Maybe you want me to go bankrupt on account of your *Gy-ma-na-si-a* and your classes? You know what I think of them! You know where you can put them!"

After all, I'm only human and there is a limit to what a person can stand. So I let her have it. But it was she who had her way, not I. Because when she makes up her mind. . . .

And what did I do then? I began trying to use influence. I humbled myself, I underwent all sorts of humiliations; because everyone I came to asked me the same questions and everyone of them was correct. "Here you are, Reb Aaron," they said, "a person of some consequence, with an only son. What possesses you to go sticking your head where you're not wanted?"

Go tell them the whole story—that I have a wife—may she live to be a hundred and twenty years old—who has one obsession: *Gy-ma-na-si-a* and *Gy-ma-na-si-a* and *Gy-ma-na-si-a!* But I'm not such a half-wit either. With God's help I worked my way in where I wanted to be, right into the office of the director himself, and I sat down to talk it over with him. After all, thank the Lord, I know how to talk too. No one has to show me how.

"*Tchto was ugodno?*" he says to me. "What is your wish?" And he asks me to sit down.

I come close and whisper into his ear, "*Gospodin* Director," I say, "*mi ludi ne bogati,* we are not rich people, but we have a boy, an only child who," I say, "wants to study, and I want him to study too, and my wife," I say, "wants very much . . ."

So he says to me again, *"Tchto was ugodno?—What is your wish?"*

So I come a little closer and say to him, "Your honor, we are not rich people, but we have a boy, an only child, who," I say, "wants to study, and my wife," I say, "wants *very much* . . ." And I stretch out the *ve-ry* so he'll understand. But he's thick-headed and slow. He doesn't seem to know what I'm talking about. He repeats angrily, *"Tak tchtozhe was ugodno—*once and for all, what is your wish?"

So slowly, cautiously I put my hand into my pocket. Slowly, cautiously I pull it out again, and slowly and cautiously I say, "I beg your pardon, *Gospodin* Director, *mi ludi ne bogati*—we are not rich people, but we have a boy"—and I pause—"an only child"—and I pause again—"who wants to study." And I look meaningfully at the director. "And my wife," I almost whisper, "wants *very, very* much to have him study." And this time I stretch out the *ve-e-ry* even longer than before, and I put my hand into his. . . .

All at once he knew what I meant. He took a little book out of his drawer, and asked me what my name was, and what my boy's name was, and which class I wanted him to enter. I thought to myself, "That's the way to talk!" And I told him that my name was Katz, Aaron Katz, and my boy was named Moishe or Moshka, and I wanted him to enter third class. So he told me that seeing that my name was Katz, and my boy's name was Moishe or Moshka, and he wanted to enter the third class, I should bring him back in January and then he'd surely get in. You understand. An entirely different language. Apparently if you grease the axle the wheels will turn. The only trouble was that we still had to wait. But what could we do about it? They told us to wait, so we waited. A Jew is used to such treatment. . . .

Came January, and again a tumult, a clamor, a rushing around. Any day now a meeting would be held, a *soviet,* they called it. The director and the inspector and all the teachers of the Gymnasia were going to come together, and when the meeting was over we'd know if they were going to take him in. The day came; my wife wasn't home. There was no dinner, no samovar, not a thing in the house to eat. Where was she? She was at the Gymnasia. That is, not at the Gymnasia itself, but in front of it. All day long she trudged back and forth in the deep snow, back and forth, waiting for them to come out of the meeting. It's a bitter frost, the wind is sharp, it cuts your breath off. And she walks back and forth outside, waiting. What for? She must know that a promise is sacred . . . and specially since . . . you understand? But try to tell that to a woman!

Well, she waited an hour, she waited two, three, four hours. All the boys have gone home already, and still she waits. At last the door opens and one of the teachers comes out. She jumps at him and grabs him by the arm. Does he know how the meeting—the *soviet*—came out? So he says, why shouldn't he know? They decided to admit, all in all, eighty-five boys. Eighty-three Christians and two Jews. So she asks, who were the Jews? And he tells her a Shepselson and a Katz. When she hears the name Katz, she turns around and comes running home all out of breath, falls into the house in ecstasy. "Mazl-tov," she cries. "Oh, I thank Thee, Heavenly Father, I thank Thee! They've accepted him! They've accepted him!" And tears stand in her eyes. Naturally, I am pleased too, but do I have to start dancing to show my joy? After all, I'm a man, not a woman.

"It looks to me," my wife says, "as if you're not too excited about all this."

"What makes you think so?" I ask her.

"Oh," she says, "you're a cold, heartless person. If you only saw how eager the child is, you wouldn't be sitting there so calmly. You would have been on your way long ago to buy him a uniform, a cap, and a satchel for his books. And you'd be doing something about a celebration for our friends."

"Why a celebration all of a sudden?" I ask her. "Is the boy being confirmed, or getting married?" So she gets angry and stops talking to me altogether. And when a woman stops talking it's a thousand times worse than when she's cursing, because if she is cursing you, at least you hear a human voice. But this way it's like talking to a brick wall. Well, who do you think won out? She or I? Naturally, she did, because if she makes up her mind, is there anything I can do?

And so we had a celebration. We invited all our friends and relatives and we dressed the boy up from head to foot in a handsome uniform with shiny buttons and a cadet's cap with a metal gadget in front—just like a general. You should have seen him. He was a different lad altogether, with a new soul, a new life. He shone, like the sun in July! The guests drank toasts to him, wished that he might study in the best of health and go on and on to higher studies.

"That," I said, "is not so important. We can get along without that. Just let him go through the first few years of the Gymnasia," I said, "and with God's help I'll get him married off."

My wife smiles at the guests and gives me a funny look. "You can tell him that he's very much mistaken," she says. "He has old-fashioned ideas."

"And you can tell her," I say, "that I wish I had a hundred blessings for every way in which the old-fashioned ideas are better than the new-fangled ones."

And she says, "You can tell *him* that he is a. . . ."

At this everybody starts laughing. "Oh, Reb Aaron, Reb Aaron," they cry, "have you got a wife, God bless her! A Cossack, not a wife!"

On the strength of that everybody took another drink, somebody struck up a tune, the crowd made a ring with the two of us and our boy in the middle, and we lifted our feet and danced. We danced until dawn. As soon as it was light outside we took the boy and went straight to the Gymnasia. When we got there it was still early, the door was locked, there wasn't even a cur in sight. . . . We stood there until we were frozen stiff, and when the door was finally opened we went in and began to thaw out. Before long the youngsters began coming, with knapsacks full of books on their shoulders. Soon the place was full of them, talking, laughing, joking, shouting—like a circus. In the midst of all this a man comes up to us, obviously one of the teachers, with a sheet of paper in his hands.

"What are you here for?" he asks me.

So I point to the boy and tell him that I had just brought him to start cheder here, that is, the Gymnasia. So he asks me what class he's in and I say the third. He's just been admitted.

So he asks, "What's his name?"

And I tell him, "Katz. Moishe Katz. That is, Moshka Katz."

So he says, "Moshka Katz? There is no Moshka Katz in the third class. There *is* a Katz in the class," he says, "but not Moshka. Morduch. That's the only one. Morduch Katz."

So I say, "What do you mean—Morduch? Not Morduch—Moshka."

He says, "Morduch!" And he waves the paper in front of my face. I say "Moshka!" He says "Morduch!" Well, what shall I tell you? Moshka—Morduch, Morduch—Moshka. We Moshka'd and Morduch'ed until at last we found out what had happened. Would you believe it? They did take in a boy named Katz. But they made a mistake and took in a different Katz. There were two Katzes in our town.

Well, what shall I tell you? You should have seen the boy's face when we told him to take that gadget off his cap. A bride doesn't shed as many tears when she is led to the canopy as my boy did that day. I begged him to stop, I threatened him. It didn't help. "Look!"

I said to my wife. "See, what you've done to him! Didn't I tell you that this *Gy-ma-na-si-a* of yours would be the death of him yet? May God help us," I said, "I only hope we don't have more trouble on account of this. I hope he doesn't get sick."

"Let my enemies get sick, if they like," says she, "but my child *must* get into the Gymnasia! If he didn't get in now, he'll get in a year from now. If he didn't get in here, he'll get in somewhere else. But," she says, "he must get in—unless I die first and you bury me."

Did you ever hear the like of that? And who do you think won out? Let's not fool ourselves. If she makes up her mind, can I do anything?

Well, I won't take up much more of your time. We traveled from one end of the country to the other. Wherever there is a city, wherever there is a Gymnasia, there we went. We registered him, he took his examinations, he passed his examinations, he passed with top grades— and he *didn't* get in. Why not? Because of the quota. Always the quota.

I began to think that I had really gone crazy. "Fool!" I said to myself. "What is this? What are you flying around for, from one city to the next? What good will it ever do you? What do you need it for? And if he does get in, so what?" Well, you can say what you want, ambition is a great thing. It finally got me too. I became stubborn. I wouldn't give up. At last the Almighty had pity on me and sent across my path, in Poland somewhere, a certain Gymnasia, a *komertcheska,* they called it, a business school, where for every Christian they were willing to take in one Jew—a quota of fifty percent, that is. But here was the catch. Every Jew who wanted to have his son admitted had to bring along with him a Christian boy, and if he passed the examination, this Christian, that is, and if all his fees and expenses were paid, then there was a chance! In other words, you had not one headache, but two. It was bad enough to have my own son to worry about, but now I had to eat my heart out over somebody else's son too. For—woe is me!—if Esau fails to make the grade, then Jacob lies in the dust together with him.

So I set out to find a Christian youth, and what I went through before I found one! He was a shoemaker's boy, a shoemaker named Holiava. And then what do you think happened? The shoemaker's boy failed in his examinations. And in what? In religion. And my boy had to sit down and drill him in religion! You ask, how does my boy come to know religion? You don't have to ask. After all, with a head like his! As I told you, you can travel the length and breadth of the Empire. . . .

Well, in spite of that, at last God came to our aid. The lucky day arrived. They both got in. But do you think we're through? No. When it came to paying the fees, I look around; my man has vanished. What's the matter? He doesn't want his son to go to school with so many Jews. You can't budge him. He says, "What good is it to me? Aren't all schools open to me anyway? Can't my boy go to any school he wants to?" And can I contradict him?

"What do you want, *Panie* Holiava?" I say. And he says, "Nothing." I try this, I try that. I went to see some friends of his, drinking companions, we went into a tavern together, had a glass or two, maybe three. Well, before I lived to see him enrolled, my hair almost turned gray. But anyway, praise the Lord, my work was done.

When I came home I found a new headache. What now? My wife has made up her mind. After all, he is an only child, the apple of her eye. . . . Was it right to leave him out there all by himself?

"What," I ask, "are you driving at now?"

"What am I driving at?" she asks. "Don't you know what I'm driving at? I want to be with him."

"Oh," says I. "And the house?"

"The house," says she, "is nothing but a house."

And what do you think she did? She packed up and went over there to be with him, and I remained all alone at home. You can imagine what it must have been like. May my enemies live like that! My life was no life any more, my business was no business. Everything went wrong. And we kept writing letters to each other. I write to her. She answers. Letters go back and forth. "To my beloved and cherished wife—peace!" "Peace to my dear husband."

"In the name of God," I write to her, "what will be the outcome of all this? I am only human. And what's a house without a mistress? Listen to reason, my wife."

Well, she paid as much heed to my pleas as she might to the snows of last year. She won her point, not I. For if she makes up her mind— is there anything I can do?

Well, I'm coming to the end of my story. I was ruined. I went broke. I lost everything. My business disappeared, my last few remnants were sold. I was left penniless. I had no choice. I had to swallow my pride and move over there with them. There, I had to start all over again. I looked around, sniffed here and there and tried to figure out where I was in the world. At last I found something. I went into partnership with a merchant from Warsaw, a man of some means, a householder, a president of a synagogue, but at bottom a manipulator, a swindler, a pickpocket! He just about ruined me all over again. I couldn't hold up my head any more.

In the meanwhile, I come home one day and my boy opens the door for me. He has a strange look on his face. He is blushing and I see that the fancy gadget, the insignia, is gone from his cap. I say to him, "Look, Moishe, my boy, what happened to the gadget?"

He says to me, "What gadget?"

I say, "The insignia, the thing-a-ma-jig."

The boy turns redder still and says, "I tore it off."

"What do you mean, you tore it off?"

And he says, "I am free."

"What do you mean—you are free?"

And he tells me, "We're through. We are not going back to school any more."

So I say, "What do you mean *you're* not going any more?"

And he says, "We're all free. We didn't like the way they treated us. So we went out on strike. We all agreed not to go back."

"What do you mean—strike?" I shout. "What do you mean—agreed? Was it for this that I gave up my home and my business? Was it for this that I sacrificed myself? So that you could go out on strike? Woe is me. And woe is you. May God protect us. Who will suffer for it? We Jews."

That's the way I talk to him, warn him, lecture him, the way a father naturally does to a child. But I also have a wife, God bless her. She comes running in and lays down the law to me. I'm slightly backward, she tells me. I don't know what's going on in the world. We're living in a new era, she tells me. A better life, a newer life has come into existence, she tells me, where all are equal. There are no rich, no poor; no master, no slave; no lamb, no shears; no cats, no mice. . . .

"Tut-tut, my dear," I say to her. "Where did you learn all this funny talk? It sounds like a new language to me. By the same token, maybe you want to open up the chicken coops and let out all the chickens? Here, chickie-chickie! Shoo, chickie! You're free."

At this, she flares up at me. It's just as if I had poured a bucket full of boiling water at her. She went after me. . . . I had to listen to a whole sermon, from beginning to end. The only trouble is, there was no end. "Just a second," I beg. "Listen to me. Just a minute." And I beat my breast with my fist, as we do on *Yom Kippur:* "I have sinned, I have subverted, I have transgressed. Now let's call a halt."

But she pays no attention to me. "No," she says. And she wants to know "why" and "how" and "besides" and "for Heaven's sake," and

"what do I mean," and "how does it happen," and "who says so"?
And then a second time and a third time, and once again for good
measure. I was lucky to escape alive. . . .

Tell me, I beg you. Who ever invented wives?

You can't live from naches
and you don't die from tzoress.

You can't force people to learn,
but you can prevent them from learning.—*Ludwig Börne*

THE NEW POLICE CHIEF

BY ZALMAN SHNEOUR
TRANSLATED FROM THE YIDDISH BY JOSEPH LEFTWICH

That winter, a few months before the fire broke out, there was
a new Police Chief appointed in Shklov, a handsome fellow, with
copper-colored mustachios, carefully twirled up, and with a severe
angry look out of a pair of bold eyes, like Czar Nicholas I. Nicholas I's
portrait had hung for generations in the Shklov post office. And the old
postmaster remarked on the similarity, when the new Police Chief came
to pay him his first official visit. The young Police Chief was flattered
by the comparison. And he took to copying every detail of the Czar's
portrait. He began to comb up his side-whiskers from ear to temple.
And his eyes were always fierce, and his face impassive, as if he had a
permanent toothache, but didn't want to make a fuss about it. And he
lorded it over the Jews of Shklov.

The big landowners had for generations been in the habit of incit-
ing their dogs against the Jews, so that the fear of dogs was in their
blood. And in the same way they must have retained their fear of
Nicholas I, who had snatched schoolchildren away from their parents
to make soldiers of them. For as soon as the Jews saw the new Police
Chief, with his fierce eyes, and his turned-up, stiff mustachios, and his
side-whiskers carefully combed over his ears, their hearts began to
beat fast. They thought of the portrait that hung in the old post-office.

"He will be a hard master!" the Jews whispered among themselves
in the market-place.

And, indeed, the new Police Chief began at once to put things in order. The old wooden bridge across the big ditch had to be mended! It was mended immediately. Two lanterns, no less, had to be kept burning in the market-place till midnight. "Very well, your lordship! Here you are! Two lanterns, with paraffin lamps inside, and please don't shout!" All the lavatories had to be cleaned out, and carbolic put down. It was done! "Look! They've been cleaned, with lots of carbolic! Smell it, if you don't believe us!" The ice round the wells had to be hacked away because it was dangerous for children. "He! He! Look who's worrying about Jewish children!" But that, too, was done. They humored all his caprices. Anything for a quiet life! They were sure that he would tire of it in the end. That was the way of all new Police Chiefs in Shklov. When they first came they strutted about fiercely, issued orders, put things straight, intimidated everybody, in order to show their superiors in Mohilev how devoted they were to the Czar. Then they sampled a little Passover spirits, and some Jewish stuffed fish, and they grew more amiable. Their eyes brimmed over with kindness. And they took bribes. They sat day and night playing cards with the postmaster and sent their constables to do their work. And the constables were easy to handle.

Everybody thought it would be the same with the new Police Chief. But they were wrong. The more they gave way to him, the more demands he made. The next thing was that he insisted that the refuse heaps outside the shops should be swept away after each market day. Then he got annoyed because the slops were being poured down the steps into the middle of the streets. He ordered that every householder must dig a hole in his backyard and pour the slops down there. So all the Jews started digging holes behind their back walls.

But this time they swore and cursed as they dug, because the ground was frozen, and their forks and spades couldn't get a grip on it. And the Jews grumbled as they worked: "We've got to dig these holes to pour down the slops, but don't we wish it was a hole to bury him in!"

By this time the town realized that the new Police Chief meant business, that this wasn't only a sudden spurt of energy, a case of a new broom sweeping clean. He was going to keep on like this! No end to it! So at last the town decided to try whether he could be bribed.

There was one man in Shklov who was an old hand at bribing officials. That was Yoshe, the barber. He had been a great pal of the last Police Chief, who had been just as bad when he had first come to the town. Yoshe had put him in touch with the moneyed Jews, and after that he had become quite easy-going. Yoshe was sure to handle the new Police Chief just as successfully. It wouldn't be his own money he would be paying out, anyway!

But Yoshe, the barber, was a diplomat. He wasn't going to gate-crash into the new Police Chief's house. That would be too crude. He preferred to wait till the Police Chief came to his shop to have his mustachios trimmed. And then he lavished all his skill and care on him, used his finest pomades, and wouldn't take any pay for it.

"Your Excellency! I am honored to have your Excellency as a customer. I wouldn't dream of taking any pay for it! It's an honor, your Excellency!"

But the new Police Chief stared at Yoshe so coldly, that Yoshe felt a shudder running down his spine. Without knowing how it happened, he found himself accepting the coin that the Police Chief had flung down at the side of the mirror. And he felt an utter fool when he found himself standing there with his brush in his hand, when the Police Chief walked out without waiting to have his coat brushed, without saying good day to him!

Yoshe saw that he hadn't much chance with the new Police Chief. So he decided to try his hand on the women-folk, the weaker sex. The new Police Chief's wife was a young woman with a head of black hair and red blotches on her Tartar cheekbones. While the Police Chief was away worrying Jews in the market-place, Yoshe took her a couple of fat, plucked geese. "A present from your Jewish neighbors," he said. But the Police Chief's wife turned up her nose, and said to Yoshe in pure Petersburg:

"Oh, don't bother, please! I'd rather not!" And then she turned her back on him.

Yoshe was so upset at the failure of his mission that he told his wife to roast the two geese, and sighing heavily at the sad fate of the Jews, he ate them up all by himself. And as he was finishing off the last morsel, it occurred to him that it might be best to start at the bottom, with the new Police Chief's servant, Stefan, the door-keeper and messenger. He'd try him with some Jewish delicacy, and Stefan might pass it on to his Petersburg mistress, telling her how nice it tasted, and then she might want some as well.

Yoshe first made sure that there was nobody else at home, and then he went along to Stefan with some stuffed fish and a bottle of spirits.

"Here you are, Stefan!" said the barber. "This was left over from a Jewish wedding! Have it! It's nice!"

"He! He!" said Stefan with a chuckle, looking round cautiously to see that nobody was watching. Then he poured out a stiff dose of spirits, and was just about to dig his fingers into the fish, when the Police Chief's wife suddenly arrived, wearing a hat, and with her cheeks all red with frost. Stefan dropped the fish back into the pot and started tugging at the coat-tails of his tunic.

"What is all this!" cried the Police Chief's wife. "What do you mean by drinking in here!" And then when she saw the pot of stuffed fish, she turned up her nose very daintily, and said: "What's this nasty smell of onions. Pah!"

That's all she knew about Jewish fish!

Stefan who had only a minute ago been drinking the Jew's brandy and guffawing, suddenly turned on him. "Clear out!" he said to Yoshe, pointing to the door, as if he were a beggar.

So the barber, feeling very crestfallen, put the cover on the pot, and took it and himself off through all the doors of the new Police Chief's house; and, weeping over the failure of his mission, he sat down again, poor man, and ate up the fish too, all by himself, with plenty of horse-radish and tears to go with it.

And then he gave the community his considered opinion, which was: "He won't be tempted!" There was only one more method they could try—to go to the Police Chief direct and put the money into his own hand, let happen what may!

People did not like the idea of trusting Yoshe with the money. They saw what had happened to the two geese, and the fish, and the Passover spirit. Yoshe hadn't even returned the pot. But there was nobody else, so in the end they put the best face on it and agreed among themselves that the only way in which they could tell that the money had really reached the Police Chief was to wait and see. If Yoshe seemed to be on terms of friendship with the new Police Chief as he had been with the old, that would mean that he had paid over the money. But if Yoshe came back with his nose out of joint, they would know that the Police Chief had refused the bribe, and they wouldn't let Yoshe stick to the money! Oh, no!

That day, Yoshe came into the synagogue for the afternoon service with his face flaming, and his eyes glared. Without saying a word he pulled out the two twenty-five ruble pieces that had been entrusted to him, and handed them over to the Warden.

"What's this?" he was asked. "That's that!" he answered. So they asked him again: "What does it mean?" "That's what it means!" he said. And then he burst out that he wasn't going to have any more to do with this business. He was finished with it! And he wouldn't say another word.

It was not till the evening service that a few late-comers told the congregation that they had seen with their own eyes how Yoshe was escorted down the steps of the Police Chief's house by two policemen, with the door-keeper giving him a shove from behind, so that Yoshe suddenly went flying right into a heap of snow at the bottom of the steps, and his astrakhan cap was then flung after him. It seemed to have been the Police Chief's orders.

Everybody's heart sank. They saw that there was no way out now. They came to the conclusion that the authorities in Mohilev must have heard about the latitude which the last Police Chief had allowed the Jews of Shklov. They must have found out about all the good things he had been getting from the Jews, so the authorities had sent down someone who would not take bribes. Besides, there were a lot of young men going about in the town wearing peasant blouses, with printed papers hidden away under their girdles. Socialists, they were called. So somebody had been sent down to deal with them. The Jews doubted whether the new Police Chief would really be able to do anything with these wild fellows, but they were sure that ordinary simple Jews would get into trouble.

After Yoshe's discomfiture, things got worse. The Shklov police constables, who had always gone about in rags, with the buttons dropping off their tunics, were suddenly dressed up in new uniforms, with red stripes, and new peaked caps, with cockades. You could see them a mile off, and they went about the market-place poking their noses everywhere. They were different men now in their new uniforms. It wasn't safe to say a word to them! No matter what you did, they said it was wrong. For instance, a woman who sold pots and pans had a row with a woman who sold poultry, and they came to blows over it. A broody hen belonging to the poultry-woman had flown out of the cage on the stall of the other woman, and had smashed a new earthenware pot. Was that any business of the police? But the constable pushed his way through the crowd like a Cossack, and forced the two women apart, so that they both stood there and cursed him, and told him to go home and mind his own business. But Alexei pulled himself up to his full height and delivered a speech: "In the name of His Imperial Majesty!" And he ended up with: "It's the law!"

He loved mouthing the fine phrases. They filled him with ecstasy. They made him feel that he was the trusted servant of the Czar, and he was so moved with emotion that the tears actually stood in his eyes as he spoke, and his voice shook.

As if these things were not bad enough, the insurance agent had come to Shklov just then, and had persuaded Jews to take out insurance policies. And when he had succeeded in insuring most of the better-class Jews in Shklov and had nailed up the green plates on their walls, he had said, "Good day, gentlemen," and had walked off. A couple of weeks later another man from the insurance company turned up in Shklov. He came from the head office in Mohilev. He wasn't a Jew. He had a long neck and a pair of piercing eyes, and wore a high celluloid collar. He said that he was an inspector. And he walked into every Jewish house that had been insured, examined everything carefully, wrote down the names of the people, and made a lot of notes. He began with the new millionaire, and ended up with the coachmen's guild, which had also taken out a policy. That had been Sender Pardon's idea.

The things he wanted to know! When had they taken out their insurance policy? How much was it for? What did they do for a living? He examined the stoves, and wanted to know how often they had their chimneys swept. And then, when he had got all the information he wanted, people saw him with the new Police Chief. And then he, too, went away.

As soon as he had left, the Police Chief started a new game. His policemen went round to every Jew who was insured, and ordered his chimney swept again because otherwise he might have his chimney on fire. As if they were his chimneys!

People pointed out that the snow was still on the roofs, and that there was no danger of a fire breaking out while the snow was there. Besides, the chimney sweeps didn't like sweeping chimneys in the frost when the roofs were slippery. But the Police Chief wouldn't take no for an answer. He insisted that the chimneys must be swept.

Then he sent his policemen round to tell everyone who was insured to keep a barrelful of water in his yard. It might be needed. People pointed out that in winter the water would freeze in the barrels, and the pressure would burst the hoops. So he told them that if wooden hoops were not safe, they should get some old herring-barrels with iron hoops. There were plenty of old barrels like that lying about in the Jewish market, he said. The herring-dealer would be only too glad to get rid of them. And the market-place would look cleaner when they were out of the way. And the houses would be safer. You couldn't argue with him! He refused to leave it till the spring.

So people sighed and bought old herring-barrels. There was such a demand for herring-barrels with iron hoops that the herring-dealers walked about with their noses up in the air. And when the barrels were filled with water the whole town reeked of herrings. And that was in winter! Heaven knew what it was going to be like in the summer!

Zavel, the chimney sweep, did well out of it. He charged double his usual rates, because he had to climb up on roofs that were full of snow and ice. His teeth gleamed out of his sooty face. He found himself a rich man by the time he was finished with those chimneys.

The town came to the conclusion that it was the inspector from the insurance company who had arranged all this with the new Police Chief. He must have asked him to keep a strict watch on the Jewish houses, so that the insurance company wouldn't suffer any losses. People began to get quite nervous in case a fire should break out.

"Mark my words," people said to each other, "it's an insurance company for taking money, not for giving you any. We'll have to pay all our lives, and if there is a fire, God forbid, they'll refuse to pay us a penny! And the Police Chief will prosecute us into the bargain!"

A few Jews decided to back out of the arrangement. They refused to pay their premiums, and told the insurance company to take away the green metal plate with the golden anchor. They didn't want to be insured! People began to envy those who had refused to be taken in, and were not insured. And everybody cursed the new millionaire for having started the ball rolling.

Then the inspector came down again from Mohilev, with his high celluloid collar, and his piercing eyes; and he brought along with him the filled-in forms. "Your signature?" he asked. "Yes, my signature," he was told. "Then why don't you pay?" "Why don't we pay? You see, there is such a fuss made about it! We've got to buy herring-barrels, and have our chimneys swept in the middle of the winter. We are no longer the masters of our own houses. We are being watched at every step. The Police Chief is worrying us to death!"

"That isn't our concern," said the inspector. "The insurance company doesn't interfere with the Police Chief, and the Police Chief doesn't interfere with us. You can refuse to take the insurance money if you have a fire, but you can't refuse to pay your premiums. Here are your signatures. You have bound yourselves for so many years. If you don't pay your instalments regularly, the insurance company will bring an action against you, and demand full payment for the whole period of the insurance in one lump sum."

What a mess the Jewish insurance agent had got them into! He had gone round collecting signatures, had handed over a whole town-ful of Jews to a lot of heartless gentiles, and then he had disappeared! If ever he showed himself again in their town! They'd teach him!

But the agent never came near Shklov again. And the Jews moaned and groaned, paid their insurance money, and went in fear and trembling of the Police Chief. They had never been so careful before with live coals and matches. The chimneys were always kept clean, because if the slightest thing happened, if a spark flew out of the chimney, or a stack of hay started smouldering, or the chimney smoked more than usual, the new Police Chief came along at once with blazing eyes, shouting and storming. If the house was not insured it wasn't so bad. But if it was one of the insured houses, he rattled his sword, and cried:

"Hi, you, Isaac Berl, what's the game? Want to draw the in-surance money? We'll clap you in jail, that's what we'll do with you, you dirty Jew!"

That was the way he spoke to them. And if there happened to be a few non-Jews passing by, to hear what he was saying, he raised his voice properly, to teach them how Jews ought to be spoken to. The poor Jews didn't know which fire was worse, the fire in the chimney, or the fire that blazed in the Police Chief's eyes.

Understanding is something we are certain the other fellow hasn't got.

A LESSON FOR THE BISHOP

A bishop of the Russian Orthodox church once traveled abroad. At last he came to Berlin. As he walked through the streets a crowd of urchins followed at his heels. Seeing his black robe and long black beard, they took him for a Russian ghetto Jew. So they pelted him with stones and hooted him.

The bishop ran for his life, the urchins close behind him. When a Jewish shopkeeper saw this he drew the frightened bishop into the safety of his shop.

As the bishop wiped the mud from his face and robe, he ranted about the indignities he had suffered.

"This is no Christian country! It's fit only for barbarians!" he cried.

The Jew gave a bitter laugh.

"What do you find so funny?" asked the bishop, angrily.

"I laugh," answered the Jew, "because we Jews have been suffering the indignities you've just experienced, not just once, as you did today, but for two thousand years!"

First Christian: If I were of the race to which Christ belonged I wouldn't be ashamed but I'd boast of it.

Second Christian: I would too, provided Christ were the only member of that race.

—Heinrich Heine

THE FATE OF THE JEW-HATERS

BY HEINRICH HEINE

TRANSLATED FROM THE GERMAN BY NATHAN AUSUBEL

. . . Inside the synagogue is heard a remarkable nasal singing. The quavering voice appears to belong to an old man, and the melody, which is drenched in the sweetest plaintive sounds, swells gradually into the most terrible hatred.

"What sort of a song is that?" I asked my guide.

"That's a good song," he answered with a surly laugh. "It's a lyrical masterpiece that hardly finds its like in this year's almanac of the Muses. . . ."

You may know this song perhaps in its German version: *Wir sassen an den Flüssen Babels, unsere Harfen hingen an den trauerweiden.*[1] A magnificent poem! Old Rabbi Chaim sings it very well in his quavering thin voice; Mme. Sontag probably could sing it with finer voice but scarcely with so much expressiveness, with such deep feeling. . . . For the old man is filled with an unending hatred for the Babylonians and he weeps every day over the destruction of Jerusalem by Nebuchadnezzar. . . . The recollection of this misfortune he cannot

[1]*"By the rivers of Babylon, there we sat down, yea, we wept, when we remembered Zion. We hanged our harps upon the willows in the midst thereof."* (Psalm 137: 1–2)

drive out of his mind, although so many new disasters have happened since then. In fact, "only the other day" the Second Temple was destroyed by Titus the Wicked. . . .

I must point out, though, that in no way does Rabbi Chaim consider Titus as a *Delicium generis humani;* he regards him as a scoundrel with whom God's wrath finally caught up. . . . Namely, a small flea flew into his nose, grew larger and larger from day to day and gnawed around in his brain, causing him such indescribable agony that he could only find relief when he stood next to several hundred blacksmiths who went pounding on their anvils at one and the same time.

It is indeed remarkable that all the enemies of the Children of Israel should have come to such a bad end! You know yourself how it fared with Nebuchadnezzar; in his old age he turned into an ox and had to eat grass. Then take the Persian Minister of State, Haman! In the end wasn't he hanged in the capital city, Susa? And then you have Antiochus, the King of Syria! Didn't lice rot away his living flesh?

Those latter-day villains, the Jew-haters, ought to take these lessons to heart. . . . But it seems it's no use—the horrible example of others doesn't scare them in the least!

THE LADY OF ZION

BY ISRAEL ZANGWILL

There was a lady of Zion,
Who was offered a lift by a lion
She was mounting astride,
When he roared: "Step inside,
There is no room on top of a lion."

Responded that lady of Zion,
"Why should I go inside a lion?
I was promised a State
And a happier fate."
"L'état c'est dans moi," said the lion.

If my theory of relativity is proven correct, Germany will claim me as a German and France will declare I am a citizen of the world. Should my theory prove untrue, France will say that I am a German and Germany will declare that I am a Jew.—Albert Einstein

THE JEWS IN THE FREE CITY OF FRANKFURT

BY LUDWIG BÖRNE

TRANSLATED FROM THE GERMAN BY NATHAN AUSUBEL

In his very precise geography, Stein states that 10,000 Jews are to be found in Frankfurt, although actually less than 4,000 live there. Metaphorically speaking, he says so himself—that these less than 4,000 Jews make as much of a din as if they were 10,000!

In former days the Jews used to live in a street by themselves, and this place was definitely the most populated spot in the whole world, not even excepting Malta. They enjoyed the most tender care of their government. On Sundays they were not allowed to leave their street, in order to avoid getting beaten up by the Gentile drunks. They were prevented from marrying before the age of twenty-five, so that their children might be born strong and healthy. On holidays they were not allowed outside the ghetto gate until six o'clock in the evening, in order that they should be spared the excessive heat of the sun. The public promenades outside the city were forbidden them; instead it was found preferable to let them wander through the fields in order to awaken in them a taste for farming. Whenever a Jew happened to be walking in the street and a passing Christian called out to him: "*Mach' Mores, Jud!* [show your manners, Jew!]" he had to take off his hat. Apparently, it was by means of this polite attention that the brotherly love between the two religions was to be strengthened. . . .

AN INTERVIEW WITH AHASHUERUS

BY IRVING FINEMAN

"These Jews," said the king, slowly twirling the thin stem of his glass and gazing reflectively through the ruddy wine, "these Jews are a curious people."

On this I thought it best not to comment. A special correspondent, just arrived in Shushan for news of recent events, it behooved me to be diplomatic. And one expects an interview with a king to be a rather one-sided affair with few questions asked. I had found him resting after dinner in one of the smaller throne rooms—a genial, unassuming gentleman; but here, not five minutes after my introduction, he was talking about the Jews. I was getting fed up. Everywhere, in all the countries by the Mediterranean, this inexplicable preoccupation with the Jews and their Problem. Wherever men gathered—at dinners, or in the clubs, one heard endless discussions about Jews, pro and con. Articles in the magazines and books were being written. Were we never to hear the end of it? And here too. . . .

"Although," the king went on, "relatively they are really few in numbers, one seems to find them everywhere. Perhaps, on your way here, you stopped at one of Our summer resorts on the Mediterranean?"

I had, I admitted, spent a day at Philistia-by-the-Sea.

"Then," said the king, as he lit a fresh cigar and continued to sip his wine, "you know what We mean. They get in everywhere; their invasions are as insidious, as inexorable as the inundations of the tides. Like castles of sand on the beach, one exclusive hotel after the other has been overwhelmed by their inroads until there is hardly a quiet place left for a retiring, unostentatious heathen." The king knitted his brows in annoyance and puffed a great cloud of smoke.

I was a bit uneasy. The king's sudden tempers were notorious. Report had it he had had a once favored chancellor hanged because of a sudden whim. I coughed deprecatingly.

"One cannot," he continued, "but admire their push, their energy, their unbounded ambition to get ahead. Indeed, do We not teach Our own sons the creed of *Gogetter,* to strive valiantly, to accomplish? But one cannot help wishing these Jews were not so confoundedly—well, how shall We put it?—so overwhelmingly successful. Mind you We are not prejudiced. When you have been with Us a while you will see what a great influence they wield in Our kingdom and at Our court. Not a few of your colleagues, Our court scribes, you will find are Jews. The conductor of Our imperial symphony orchestra is a Jew. Our court costumer and Our Chancellor of the Exchequer, of course, are Jews. You have heard, We are sure, of Our great and wise Prime Minister, Prince Mordecai; and indeed Our own dear Queen Esther—" whereupon the king and I rose, clinked our glasses and drank to the Queen.

I murmured something about never having heard. . . .

The king held his refilled glass to the light. It was plain he had been imbibing rather freely. "Yes, indeed, bless her clever little heart. Mordecai's first cousin in fact. You shall meet her tomorrow at court.

The loveliest lady in all Our land. We can vouch for that. Took first prize in the national beauty contest at the Shushan Centennial. We were the judge. A Jewess, yes indeed. You would never think it to look at her—the loveliest and the cleverest. . . ." He smacked his lips and set down his glass. "Ah! but they are all clever, these curious people of hers. Confoundedly clever. . . ." The king was thoughtfully filling his glass.

It seemed an opportune moment to change the subject. I expressed my keen delight in the prospect of meeting the fair Queen Esther.

"As a writing fellow, you will, We are sure, be interested in Our Queen's romantic story." The king settled back in his throne, crossed his legs, put his fingertips together and gazed up at the crown suspended like a halo over his head. I smelled a good story and was cheered.

"It all began at the Centennial celebration in the third year of Our reign. Shushan had never seen the like of that celebration—nor had Babylon for that matter. We were determined then to put on the greatest exposition ever, and no expense was spared. It may as well be known that there had for some time been seen ominous signs of unrest among Our people. All sorts of strange gospels were in the air —about 'distribution of wealth,' about 'rights' and other balderdash. Our then Chancellor Haman was no fool. A surly, obstinate bismarckian, he made some mistakes and lost out in the end; but, mind you, no fool. A war, said Haman, would stop this nonsense, but just then, he felt, we were not diplomatically prepared. The next best measure, he advised, was to divert the people—give them a good time —make the Centennial a great national carnival. 'And incidentally,' said Haman, 'I would get rid of these radical Jews; they talk too much.' " The king earnestly tapped the arm of his throne.

I evaded the necessity of agreeing by taking another drink.

"In those days," said the king, "we must admit We hardly knew what a Jew looked like; they were the remnants of a tribe We had mopped up in one of Our campaigns. Haman had taken a profound dislike to these strange people, but We were not particularly concerned about them. We let that pass," the king sipped thoughtfully, "we let that pass and concentrated on the Centennial. That was a great success, as you may have heard. Lasted one hundred and eighty days— fine buildings, sumptuous displays, a circus, followed by seven days of free banquets with wine and music in the great court of Our palace, all on the most lavish scale and open to all Our kingdom, high and low alike. It worked; Our people enjoyed it immensely, and one heard little more talk about 'rights.' Yet trouble came, but from an unexpected quarter.

"It had always been the custom at previous expositions for the Queen to appear on a certain day before the populace and the assembled court of provincial princes in a special edifice built for the occasion. Bistha, Our court architect, had done a magnificent pavilion of bizarre design. Its tessellated floor was of yellow and black marble, its walls covered with fantastic blue hangings between green marble pillars. A monstrous throne of wrought gold inlaid with chrysoprase stood on a dais of ebony. Charbona, Our court jeweler, had contrived a remarkable costume designed to set off the handsome figure of the late Queen Vashti: a delicate net of fine gold threads with breast plates and girdle of jet encrusted with carved chrysoprase. The Queen was to enter the court with her train and the people were to enjoy the pomp from behind lines of gold cord. What a show that would have been! Vashti, it must be admitted, was a splendid creature. Everything was ready and the very day was at hand when Haman came to Us with the dreadful news that the Queen refused absolutely to take part in the ceremony. We were dumbfounded! Vashti, though frightfully good-looking, had never been proud, always a congenial soul and not too clever or vain. We had, it must be confessed, rather neglected her of late, what with affairs of state and the Centennial. But it was not pique. Oh, no.

"Something much more serious. According to Haman, Vashti had been badly infected with the prevalent radicalism, had clipped her hair, taken to wearing a mannish toga and said she no longer had any use for queenly fripperies. We tried, of course, to reason with her. She was quite impossible: said she would no longer be a party to an affair designed to dupe her oppressed people into forgetting their slavery by dazzling their eyes with extravagant display. And she ranted a lot about 'women's rights,' about 'a woman's place,' about no longer being 'merely a plaything' and other rot. We feared she might have been spreading this demoralizing propaganda at the teas for the visiting ladies from Media and Persia, over which she had been presiding. A 'feminist' she called herself! And We give you Our word she looked a fright, her lovely figure swathed in a shapeless sheet, her clipped hair all straight and not a drop of kohl on her eyelids. Needless to say, there was a dreadful scene and, with the palace full of princes from Media and Persia, you can very easily imagine how frightfully embarrassed We were."

The king puffed quickly at his cigar and took another drink. "It was all very exasperating. 'This,' said Haman, 'comes of not getting rid of those radical Jews. She got it from them.' We could not quite see the connection—nor do We to this day. Haman was always growling about the Jews, blaming them for everything. But if Our poor, misguided Vashti got her radical 'uplift' ideas from the Jews, We must say she neglected to learn their methods of putting them over. There Is, for example, Our dear Queen Esther," whereupon we both rose and drank the Queen's health. "Clever as she is," the king sighed as he sat down a bit unsteadily, "—diabolically clever she sometimes seems—she has kept her loveliness . . . as desirable as ever. . . . You shall see her. . . ." The king for a moment seemed lost in meditation. "It occurs to Us now in the light of past events that both Our queens may well have had the same objectives: the welfare of their people and the emancipation of women. You shall see how cleverly dear Esther attained these ends whereas Vashti in her uncompromising forthright manner failed miserably. These Jews have a way. . . ." mused the king.

"But to continue Our story: Jews or no Jews, the Queen, We saw, had to be handled firmly. This feminism had to be suppressed or there was no telling what might follow in the provinces after so exalted an example of rebellion. We promptly deposed Vashti; and then the Chancellor hit upon his clever scheme for choosing her successor. Well, it did seem a bright idea at the time, but the poor fellow unwittingly put a noose around his own neck. As part of his plan for diverting the populace, there was scheduled to be, after the carnival, a beauty contest in the capital, and for this the loveliest virgins were already being gathered by Our Chamberlain Hegai from the one hundred and twenty-seven provinces of Our kingdom. 'Why not,' said the Chancellor, 'choose the loveliest of these for your new Queen?' We liked the idea and acted on it. It stirred up a tremendous heart interest in the people, who promptly forgot the revolutionary Vashti in following the daily bulletins reporting the gradual elimination of various provincial candidates from the contest. Altogether it served many ends admirably. After a tiresome lot of perfuming and anointing with oil and myrrh, of dressing and parading, a number of preliminary heats reduced the contestants to a bare half dozen; but there was no doubt in Our mind immediately these appeared before Us as to which was the loveliest. We beckoned to her and asked her name. 'Esther,' she said simply. She was ravishing—she still is for that matter—as you shall see tomorrow."

I bowed and murmured my thanks.

"Ravishing," the king sipped his wine slowly, "in a slightly exotic way; but we never suspected. She had the manners of a well-bred Shushanite. An orphan she said she was. We made her Queen. The people cheered and dispersed—too tired, too surfeited to grumble about the additional taxes levied to pay for the great Centennial. You can imagine Our exchequer was sadly depleted."

The king had another flagon fetched and we filled our glasses.

"It was then," he continued, "We first began to notice these strange Jews. Haman was more persistent than ever. The Jews, he said, had in their insidious ways acquired considerable wealth. Why not, he counselled, get rid of these tiresome people and by confiscation pick up some needed funds? He complained, too, about the way they were getting the best jobs at court and that there was, so he said, an insolent old Jew lawyer called Mordecai always hanging about the palace gates waiting to be called in for consultation by the Queen. To tell the truth, We had little interest in these matters at the time. We were infatuated with Our ravishing Queen. We still are for that matter"; and dipping the end of a fresh cigar in his wine, the king stretched out his legs and puffed leisurely a while. "We told Haman to set his own date for the riot and not to annoy Us. But We were destined to have no peace.

"Some days later, Mordecai, a suave old fellow, asked for a private audience with Queen Esther, and soon after the Queen came to Us in great anxiety over his information regarding a plot against Us. It was planned by Our Chamberlains Bigthan and Theresh for the very next day, when We were to go hunting outside the city gates. A guard was set and the culprits discovered, just as old Mordecai had said. Haman later maintained, even at the foot of the gallows, that the whole thing was framed up by these Jews, that even Bigthan and Theresh, who were promptly put to death, were Jews, and willing victims of a monstrous scheme to overthrow him and put the Jews in Our favor. Haman was certainly a little cracked on the subject of the Jews. We can hardly believe they would deliberately go to such lengths, although We must admit they are a persistent people, these Jews, and cunning, devilish cunning. . . . Haman maintained, too, it was no accident that one night the Court Chronicle was brought to divert Us, sleep having deserted Us just after a sumptuous dinner at Queen Esther's apartments. We are, it is true, always prone to caprice after much wine, and the dear Queen had been very generous. But Haman maintained it was no accident that the bookmark lay on the very page recounting Mordecai's exploit and that, just when the Chancellor came to ask for the old fellow's life, We were prompted to play a little joke on Haman by way of rewarding Mordecai for his eminent service to Us. Eminent it was, We maintain, plot or no plot. Jew or no Jew, he had managed to put Us in his debt and was worthy of the reward. And Haman had begun to weary Us with his incessant talk of the doings of these Jews: how two out of every three of my servants were Jews; how Jews controlled all the banks in the kingdom, all the theatres and all the wine trade . . . perfectly ridiculous, you know, considering their numbers. We rewarded Mordecai and brought Haman down a peg but, all the same, it must be confessed We heartily looked forward to the day when the kingdom would be rid of these troublesome people, when the Chancellor would stop worrying and We would be left in peace. . . ." The king puffed slowly and blew a thick ring up through the crown over his head. "That is what We have always sought—peace and comfort." He sipped his wine, enjoying its fragrance as he rolled it under his tongue. "For peace, We have ever been willing to let well enough alone. We tried to make Haman see that. But, after all, his lack of equanimity may be understood, in the face of an upstart people with their strange almighty God and their genius for insinuating themselves into power. We had not then realized the extent of this insinuation. That was yet to come." He helped himself and me to more of the wine.

"It was early in the month of Sivan, some months before the date set for Haman's pogrom, that the Queen again asked Us to dine in her apartments. It has always been Our greatest joy to dine with the Queen, a perfect hostess, so charming, so gracious, so stimulating, so lovely—as you shall see—and clever, too, as We have told you, always interested in Our affairs of state. We were telling her of the distressing Jewish problem and remarking how it had wearied Us, how glad We should be when Adar had passed and with it these troublesome people; We were blithely teasing her about the number of servants she would have to replace if what Haman had said were true, when We suddenly perceived the tears silently flowing from her lovely eyes. 'Then I, too, shall have to go . . .' she cried—and let the cat out of the bag. We were stumped, dear fellow, simply stumped, as you can imagine." The king emptied his glass at a gulp and reached for more with an unsteady hand.

I could well imagine, I submitted.

"And not a little chagrined," he continued. "Fact is We were madly in love with her—still are for that matter—and felt all the more keenly the apparent deception. She tearfully denied the deception. She had, she admitted, changed her name from Hadassah before entering the contest; but what chance, she asked, would she have had with a Jewish name? Would Chamberlain Hegai, notoriously anti-Semitic, even have admitted her in the preliminaries? We had to admit she would never have been entered; and We were not a little amused to recall how profuse had been Hegai's recommendations of her—how he had boasted of her as his 'find.' When he later learned how he had been taken in he left Our court for sheer mortification." The king chuckled and slapped his knee. "It was clear she had been well coached by clever old Mordecai. It was true, she asserted and wept, she was an orphan. She had simply not mentioned her relationship to Mordecai. Would We, she pleaded, have so much as given her an audience had We known of her ancestry? She cried bitterly that her great happiness was at an end. We had to admit the charge was just. We never had liked foreigners. One does not stop to explain a prejudice, to justify it. Then can one justly accuse another of guile who has somehow circumvented an unreasoned objection? . . . Well, there We were. We loved Our dear Queen to distraction—and still do for that matter—and Haman persisted in making a perfect nuisance of himself with his tiresome protestations that We were being made the dupe of a Jewish clique. We wanted only to be left in peace with Our dear Queen. Haman saw only disaster in letting the Jews stay on. There was only one thing to be done with him. . . . Toward the end he tried to publish a book, a polemic, giving his version of the affair, which the Queen, of course, suppressed. Prince Mordecai is now getting out *The Book of Esther,* a charming story, colored a bit to be sure by the Jewish point of view—but then, where in history is one to seek the truth? . . . Poor Haman doubtless sincerely thought he had it. He died, on the very gallows he had reared for Mordecai, predicting the speedy downfall of Our kingdom. The poor fellow of course was wrong. . . ." The king looked at the end of his cigar and sighed.

I was relieved.

"The Jews remained and We have prospered. We have, need We say, been very very happy with Our beloved Esther, who has enjoyed privileges and powers no other queen has ever had. Our government is, as you know, the most stable in the world, Our credit the best. It is true these Jews have increased incredibly and Shushan is often referred to as New Jerusalem. We have nothing to regret, yet—" again the king sighed and looking straight at me said almost wistfully.

"yet one does miss a little the good old careless pagan days." Tears stood in the king's eyes, maudlin tears. There was no doubt the king was a bit tipsy. He leaned forward and put his hand on my shoulder.

"We have, We are sure, been saying some indiscreet things, We always do, you know, when We have had a bit too much. But We trust you not to publish these where the Queen," he staggered up and we drained our glasses, "where the Queen or Our Jewish princes may see them. That, you understand, would be troublesome."

I assured him he might rely on my discretion.

"We trust you," he said. "Have another drink. Do you know, dear fellow, when the editor of your Mediterranean Mercury submitted to Us the names of available interviewers, We chose yours because," he almost whispered, "it was the only pagan one among the lot. After all one does want once in a while to get away from these confoundedly earnest Jewish fellows and talk to a real honest-to-Baal pagan. It's a relief. Do have another drink." He patted my shoulder fraternally.

I did take another drink, but begged his indulgence and regretted the error, but really, and despite the name, for what's in a name, I said, "I must tell Your Majesty: I am a Jew." His face fell.

"Not really!" said the king, and put down his glass, shocked sober. "Really, dear fellow, so sorry—we mean—we hope we have not said anything to hurt your feelings. . . . We never would have guessed! Really you know you don't in the least look, or speak, or behave. . . . We mean . . . but really you know some of Our very best friends are . . . and the Queen too, We are sure, will be delighted to meet another of her clever people. We shall present you at court in the morning. . . ." He reached for his glass.

I bowed to the king. Dejected, he seemed to droop on his throne. I murmured my thanks and retired.

THIS MAN'S WORLD

BY BAR-HEBRAEUS (THIRTEENTH CENTURY)

A certain woman asked her neighbor, saying, "Why should a man have power to buy a handmaiden and to lie with her and to do whatever else he pleases with her, while a woman has no power to do any such things freely and openly?" And the neighbor answered her,

"That is because the kings, and the judges, and the lawgivers, are all men. Therefore, they have acted the parts of advocates of their own cause and have oppressed women."

THE PETITIONER

BY ABRAHAM IBN EZRA (TWELFTH CENTURY)

I call on my lord in the morning,
  But am told that on horseback he's sped;
I call once again in the evening,
  And hear that his lordship's abed.

But, whether his highness is riding,
  Or whether my lord is asleep,
I am perfectly sure disappointment
  Is the one single fruit I shall reap.

[General] *Juvan:* Jew! Do you know why you are the lowest of all men?

Feiwel: Everyone has a different reason.

Juvan: Because you cannot understand bloodlust.

Feiwel: Imagine! And I thought that was the reason why we were the chosen people!

From *Goat Song,* by Franz Werfel

What will induce the Jews to found their state and to settle in it? We can trust the anti-Semites to see to that.

—*Theodor Herzl*

The real exile of the Jews in Egypt was that they learned to endure it.

THE MOST HE COULD ASK FOR

During Napoleon's invasion of Russia in 1812 a Jewish soldier saved the life of General Kutuzov, the Russian commander.

"Ask of me any favor you like and I shall grant it!" exclaimed the grateful Russian.

"In that case," said the Jew, his face wreathed in smiles, "please change me to another company. My corporal does not like Jews."

"The Devil take you!" cried Kutuzov impatiently. "Why don't you ask to become a corporal yourself?"

DONNA CLARA

BY HEINRICH HEINE
TRANSLATED FROM THE GERMAN BY EMMA LAZARUS

*In the evening through her garden
Wanders the Alcalde's daughter;
Festal sounds of drum and trumpet
Ring out hither from the castle.*

*"I am weary of the dances,
Honeyed words of adulation
From the knights who still compare me
To the sun—with dainty phrases.*

*"Yes, of all things I am weary,
Since I first beheld by moonlight,
Him my cavalier, whose zither
Nightly draws me to my casement.*

*"As he stands, so slim and daring,
With his flaming eyes that sparkle
From his nobly-pallid features,
Truly he St. George resembles."*

*Thus went Donna Clara dreaming,
On the ground her eyes were fastened,
When she raised them, lo! before her
Stood the handsome, knightly stranger.*

*Pressing hands and whispering passion,
These twain wander in the moonlight.*

Gently doth the breeze caress them,
The enchanted roses greet them.

The enchanted roses greet them,
And they glow like love's own heralds;
"Tell me, tell me, my belovèd,
Wherefore, all at once thou blushest."

"Gnats were stinging me, my darling,
And I hate these gnats in summer,
E'en as though they were a rabble
Of vile Jews with long, hooked noses."

"Heed not gnats nor Jews, belovèd,"
Spake the knight with fond endearments.
From the almond-tree dropped downward
Myriad snowy flakes of blossoms.

Myriad snowy flakes of blossoms
Shed around them fragrant odors.
"Tell me, tell me, my belovèd,
Looks thy heart on me with favor?"

"Yes, I love thee, O my darling,
And I swear it by our Savior,
Whom the accursèd Jews did murder
Long ago with wicked malice."

"Heed thou neither Jews nor Savior,"
Spake the knight with fond endearments;
Far-off waved as in a vision
Gleaming lilies bathed in moonlight.

Gleaming lilies bathed in moonlight
Seemed to watch the stars above them.
"Tell me, tell me, my belovèd,
Didst thou not erewhile swear falsely?"

"Naught is false in me, my darling,
E'en as in my bosom floweth
Not a drop of blood that's Moorish,
Neither of foul Jewish current."

"Heed not Moors nor Jews, belovèd,"
Spake the knight with fond endearments.
Then towards a grove of myrtles
Leads he the Alcalde's daughter.

And with love's slight, subtle meshes,
He hath trapped her and entangled;
Brief their words, but long their kisses,
For their hearts are overflowing.'

What a melting bridal carol,
Sings the nightingale, the pure one!
How the fire-flies in the grasses
Trip their sparkling, torch-light dances!

In the grove the silence deepens;
Naught is heard save furtive rustling
Of the swaying myrtle branches,
And the breathing of the flowers.

But the sound of drum and trumpet
Burst forth sudden from the castle.
Rudely they awaken Clara,
Pillowed on her lover's bosom.

"Hark, they summon me, my darling.
But before I go, oh tell me,
Tell me what thy precious name is,
Which so closely thou hast hidden."

And the knight, with gentle laughter,
Kissed the fingers of his donna,
Kissed her lips and kissed her forehead,
And at last these words he uttered:

"I, Señora, your belovèd,
Am the son of the respected
Worthy, erudite Grand Rabbi,
Israel of Saragossa!"

TWO VIEWS ABOUT JEWS

BY LUDWIG LEWISOHN

A man came to a Polish magnate and asked him: "What do you think of the Jews?" The answer was: "Swine, Christ-killers, usurers, not to be trusted." "But what do you think of Isaac?" "A man after my own heart. An honorable man. A kind man. He saved me from bankruptcy." "And what do you think of Berl?" "I have known Berl all my life. He's one of the best." "And of Shmuel?" "Shmuel is a saint as everyone knows."

The same man went to a rich and pious Jew and asked him: "What do you think of the Jews?" The pious man answered: "A kingdom of priests and a holy nation, the elect of the Eternal, blessed be his name." "And what do you think of Isaac?" "That thief? That scoundrel? May his bones be broken. He looks at you and you are robbed!" "And of Berl?" "A fellow of the same kind, without truth or justice." "And of Shmuel?" "Do you think I am taken in by his piety? A pretentious idiot."

> *You may have your doubts about love,*
> *but you can't doubt hatred.*

ONLY A CIVIL QUESTION

Once Benny Leonard, famous lightweight champion of the world, was on his way to a bout in Chicago in the company of his manager, Billy Gibson. As dusk was approaching, the door of their Pullman car opened and a huge, muscular-looking fellow came in. Looking belligerently to right and left, he called out in a gruff voice, "Is there a Jew in this car?"

Benny Leonard turned fiery red with anger. He made an effort to rise from his seat, but his manager pulled him gently back. "Keep your shirt on, Benny," he tried to soothe him. "This guy must be drunk."

And Benny thought the better of it and sank back into his seat, as the man left the car.

A few minutes later the same formidable-looking fellow returned. Again, turning right and left, he asked challengingly, "Is there a Jew in this car?"

Benny Leonard, now livid with rage, could no longer restrain himself. Despite Billy Gibson's efforts to pull him back he leaped forward and took a defiant position toward the huge fellow, saying, "Yes! I'm a Jew! What do you want to make of it?"

The scowl suddenly lifted from the giant's face, giving way to a delighted grin. "Thank God!" he murmured. "Now we have the tenth man for a *minyan* so we can hold our *Minchah* service in the empty car ahead!"

GENIUSES AND OTHER MESHUGGENEH PEOPLE

Geniuses and Originals

He racks his brains
whether a flea has a pupik.

Mediocre minds like to travel along well-paved ideas. Quite naturally, they want their course in life to be smooth, safe, sane, and flat. Originality they shun like the plague; high places give them dizziness in the head and a scary feeling in the knees. Sometimes it is these who carry off the honors and the money bags in the bazaars of literature and the arts. They like nothing better than to get themselves crowned with bay leaves and anointed with bay rum. From the eminence of their success they then look down their noses at a mere genius.

A genius! Huh! It's easy to say "genius"! But it's not so easy to be a genius! Nor, for that matter, is it all mint ice-cream and cookies for the wife of a genius. The wife of an eminent Jewish philosopher once remarked to me, with a sigh that sounded more like a boast, "Ah! it's so hard to be the wife of a genius!" And by that she clearly implied that she was a martyr and that her great husband was a lunatic. Well, Jews have had quite a few such lunatics, may no evil eye fall on them!

Ever since the French Revolution proclaimed the equality of all mankind, Jews have presented the world with a galaxy of talent far beyond their numbers. There is hardly a field of thought and activity that has not been enriched by their contributions. However, this upsurge of greatness also produced its backwash of lunatics, poor unfortunates who merely teetered on the verge of greatness or who aspired to greatness as the supreme ideal. One little shove forward and they'd soar up to the inspired miseries of genius—one little push backward and they'd sink into the ecstatic joys of lunacy.

Certainly, people like the Jews produced a sizable number of such originals, eccentrics and half-baked universal geniuses. If less mediocre and banal standards prevailed in the world, these famished geniuses would have received the recognition they deserved, their rightful reward of thick sirloin steak smothered with onions. By nature they were endowed with considerable gifts but, due to a lack of opportunity to develop their talents and due to the warpings that frustration worked on their egos, they turned quite daft meshuggeh. *But charm-*

ing none the less. They sparkled with bright ideas, although sometimes they merely startled with unsuspected originality. Their devotion to the "higher things in life" was only matched by their holy obstinacy in pursuing them to the chagrin of the small-minded Philistines, the Devil take them!

N.A.

ZOOLOGY

BY YEHOASH [SOLOMON BLOOMGARDEN]

As great as my love is for *Eretz Yisroel* even so great is my aversion to snakes. When Dr. Mosensohn, about five years ago, came on a visit to America, I seized the first opportunity to ask him what the conditions were in Eretz Yisroel as to snakes.

His report was as follows:

"In Eretz Yisroel there are exactly one hundred different species of snakes. Ninety-eight of them are not dangerous. There's nothing to be afraid of as far as they are concerned. The remaining two, however, are really poisonous, only. . . ."

"Only what?"

"Only Ahroni says that no man born of woman has ever seen those two species in Eretz Yisroel."

"And who is Ahroni?"

Ahroni is the zoologist of Eretz Yisroel who discovers all sorts of native animals and birds, and, in addition, discovers for every one of them a Hebrew name, which is an even more difficult task than discovering the animal or bird itself.

Coming to Rehoboth I learn that this self-same Ahroni lives but a stone's throw from our hotel, and I feel it my duty to pay him a call and thank him personally for the two species of poisonous snakes which, as he assures us, are not to be seen in Eretz Yisroel.

I climb the little hill opposite our hotel; I stride through the market-place, where a couple of Arabs are squatting on the ground, offering, for sale to the citizens of Rehoboth, oranges stolen from Rehoboth groves; I pass by the mail-shack and the eucalypti; then cross a wide street scarred by ruts, and stop before a tiny house.

From behind a high fence a big fowl sticks out a long neck at me, and stares at me out of round, glassy eyes. Evidently he has taken a strong dislike to me, for before I have had time to look him over, he struts angrily back to a corner of the enclosure, and refuses to grant me even a glance.

"Shalom!" The voice sounds like a trumpet, and reverberates across the opposite hill and throughout the quiet colony.

I turn and see before me the owner of the voice—a tall young man with a pale, freckled face, a long nose, fiery-red hair and a fiery-red moustache suggesting a cigar-lighter. He is dressed in white, his coat collar buttoned up to his neck, like a member of a sanitary corps or a hospital doctor. He offers me a warm, freckled hand, and casts a glance now at me and now at the queer fowl for whom he has in his other hand a little basket of chopped cactus-leaves.

I marvel at the fact that the cacti are without needles.

"That's my own discovery," he laughs, and his resounding tenor voice rolls off as far as the Mountains of Judea. "Your Luther Burbank of California worked for years and years in the attempt to develop cacti without spines, and to this day he has not fully succeeded. And here I've done the trick in a couple of minutes. All I used was my wife's cleaver."

He speaks now Hebrew, now German, and every other moment is swearing in Arabic. He refuses to pollute his lips with Yiddish. The Yiddishists—may their names and all memory of them be blotted out!

"Wallahi'l-Azim! [by Allah the all-powerful], it is already two days since the creature hasn't taken a bite into his mouth. He runs about for days at a time like one possessed, and lives on fasting. He longs for the dry sands of the desert. It's too green and too beautiful here for him. You just wait and see. He won't touch even this succulent dish." And as he spoke the tall Ahroni opened a tiny door in the enclosure, bent down, cramping himself like a contortionist, and crept inside with the little basket of cacti in his hands. The ostrich looked at him through its cold, glassy eyes, and did not display the slightest appetite. He did display, however, a great desire to kick his owner in the stomach. Ahroni, it seems, was well acquainted with his ward's tricks, and beat a hasty retreat through the little door.

He tells me that for years he had pondered upon the plan of raising ostriches in Rehoboth, and of importing for that purpose a pair, not from Africa, but from the Syrian desert. So he went off and after great efforts and trouble procured what he wished. The transportation of the ostriches from the desert to Rehoboth was a task of stupendous proportions. For the specimen that I see here they first built a cage of thick stakes, but with his powerful legs he broke them to splinters and made a dash for freedom.

The door of the house is wide open and leads us into an obscure corridor, which serves also as the kitchen. From here we proceed to one of the two rooms which the father of Hebrew zoology occupies. This room serves the three-fold purpose of dining-room, study or library, and—museum. All of this refers only to daily uses, for by night the room is transformed into a bedchamber for part of the specialist's family.

The walls are hung with frames into which are pinned hundreds of specimens representing every species of colored butterfly—every winged denizen of Eretz Yisroel that Ahroni had caught for years.

On the mantle-piece, on the window-sills, and on the bookshelves stood jars containing various species of preserved snakes, mice, lizards, and other equally attractive creatures, delightful to the eye of the zoologist. In the corner, underneath the frayed sofa, and wherever there was an inch of space, stood little boxes of eggs, stuffed birds, and every sort of rare creature. Ahroni began to name a few of them rapidly in Latin, German, and Hebrew. There are a good many Hebrew names in the Mishnah, but many more must be invented. This requires a fundamental knowledge of Hebrew, a fine instinct for the spirit of the language, and an intimate acquaintance with the characteristic peculiarities of the specimens. To create a Hebrew terminology is the most difficult part of the task. He is now at work upon a zoological text-book intended specially for the students of Eretz Yisroel. He is already through with the animals and birds. Now he is working upon the fishes.

He tells me about the *Shefifon*—a tiny poisonous reptile which he found upon the roads in the Syrian desert. This Shefifon has a habit of hiding in the sand and waiting for a rider to approach. Then it jumps up and bites the horse's leg. Hence the biblical description: Like a Shefifon on the road.

"The study of the fauna of Eretz Yisroel," he says, in his resonant voice, at the same time waving his arms like a wind-mill, "helps us toward a better understanding of the Bible, and rectifies a great many errors that our forefathers harbored in *Goluth*.

"Take for example, the verse, *Harhivi Korhatekh ka-Nesher*. How was that translated for you? Most likely in the same way that it was for me and all the other children that went to Hebrew school: 'Make large thy baldness as the eagle.' But what will you say if an eagle really does have a fine head of hair? The real truth is that *Nesher* is not an eagle at all, but signifies the same thing as the Arabic word *nisr*, a vulture, a bird that has not a trace of hair upon its head or even upon its neck. What, you doubt it? Wallahi'l-Azim! I can cite thirty proofs. In the first place. . . ."

I begged to be excused. I assured him that I wasn't very exacting. From that day on, *nesher* to me would no longer mean eagle, even if all the kings of the east and the west should maintain the contrary.

He told me of the expedition in which he took part. That was years ago. Abdul Hamid was sultan at the time. With all his diplomatic cunning and bloodthirsty cruelty the sultan was a great lover of natural sciences. So he commissioned Professor Blankenhorn of Berlin to make an expedition through Turkey for the purpose of exploring the flora and fauna of his realm. Professor Blankenhorn invited Ahroni to become a member of the royal expedition. When Ahroni returned from the expedition he was offered the post of curator of the sultan's zoological collection, at a very high salary, but he refused. His place was in Eretz Yisroel, and his labors belonged to the Jewish people. He wanted Hebrew learning and Eretz Yisroel zoologists to play a leading rôle in the world of zoological science. He showed me a pamphlet in which are described several new species just recently discovered. One of them is the "Bubo Bubo Ahroni," officially catalogued as first discovered by the zoologist "Ahroni of Rehoboth."

He smiled with pride, and his fiery moustache waxed even more fiery. He spoke with passionate heat, putting his heart and soul into every word, and his full tenor voice filled the small room, and the desiccated specimens fairly trembled in their frames on the walls.

En passant, I learned that he was a cousin of the world-famous tenor Yadlovker. The resonant voice is in the family.

A tall woman entered, with hair even redder than his. He introduces his wife. I can tell from her speech that she had plunged heart and soul into her husband's labors.

Ahroni looked at her and his eyes glistened with pride and love: "My wife has a better head than I. If she were to study zoology, she'd make a better zoologist than I."

She told me that they were studying English together. They get up at dawn. By day neither of them has any time. He is busy with his birds, and she has the house and the children to look after. She asked me to listen to her English, and I complied, discovering that for the short time they had been studying they have made astonishing progress.

"Without English," she explained to me, "Ahroni can do nothing." He was in London for the purpose of selling egg specimens to Rothschild, and his ignorance of English was a very great drawback. Whereupon they both resolved to learn English. In truth, only he needed to know it, but it's more agreeable when two study together. So both of them are studying it.

I am not an expert in zoology, but I was sufficiently a judge of English to see that she had done better at it than he.

A little fellow of about six appears in the doorway, and squeaks in a shrill voice: "Adon Ahroni, here's a big fly."

Whereupon Ahroni takes the big fly out of the tot's fingers, looks it over from every side, smacks his lips, and shakes his head with intense enthusiasm. Then he strokes the little fellow's hair, and says in his resonant tenor: "Todah (thanks), sonnie; it's truly a fine fly."

The child turns red to the ears, and jumps merrily out into the street to tell his companions what "Adon Ahroni" has said about his fly.

As soon as the child has gone, Ahroni lets the insect fly off through the window: "The children of the district bring me everything they find in the fields. Naturally, in ninety-nine cases out of a hundred they are of no account, but their intentions are good. They want to help me in my work."

Tea is suggested. Whereupon the zoological table must be cleared. First the books, small and large, then heaps of manuscripts, and last but not least, a little box of dried specimens. After the oilcloth had been cleared and cleaned, we sat down around the table. The zoologist and his wife upon the frazzled sofa, and I upon a chair that groaned at my every move.

I asked him whether it ever happened that one of his zoological specimens spoiled through lack of proper accommodations. The freckled face which up to now was aglow with cheerfulness became clouded. The red head bowed down; he looked at the jars and sighed: "It happened, it happened. In order to keep them as they really ought to be kept, a museum is needed. If I only had about four or five thousand francs I'd build a museum."

"What will you be able to do with such a small amount? The construction alone would cost more than that."

His wife intervenes: "Ahroni can't count beyond five thousand francs. His competence in financial matters does not go any farther than that."

I am inquisitive to learn whether any of the Zionist leaders or institutions have ever displayed any interest in his work.

"There was some talk about giving a stipend of a thousand francs per year, but nothing came of it."

He became even gloomier, and it seemed that his voice was not quite so resonant as before: "You have unwittingly touched another, deeper wound. Just listen. I succeeded in obtaining, in the vicinity of Mount Lebanon, a young hart that had been shot. I believe it is the last of its kind, and the only specimen in the world. I have the hide and the skeleton ready to be stuffed. Any museum would be glad to acquire such a rarity. One foreign museum has offered me a very large price. But I'd rather sell the blown eggs of wild birds, and get along as best I could, than let out of Eretz Yisroel the last hart of its kind. I'll keep it for our first zoological museum, and we simply must have such a museum.

"Wallahi'l-Azim! we'll have it. Only it's too bad that none of our leading public men gives himself any concern about the matter. Just imagine"—and in his excitement he sprang up—"a single specimen in the entire world, and in a people of thirteen million there's not a person to buy it for Eretz Yisroel."

His wife, who, in addition to studying English with the zoologist, was compelled to resort to the utmost economy in household affairs—"to split a groat in two"—sat with her hands folded in her lap, listening to her husband as big tears rolled down her cheeks.

In the self-same room where we sat around to tea, deciding that the Jewish people deserved to be hanged, I happened, several weeks later, to be present at one of the most beautiful and joyous scenes that I have ever beheld.

It was a holiday, and the children from the schools of the surrounding colonies had come together with their teachers to inspect "Adon Ahroni's museum." Since the room was very small, and the number of pupils quite large, the pupils were let in ten or fifteen at a time, and as soon as one small group went out, another entered.

In the middle of the room, near the table, stood the red-headed Ahroni, and his face was beaming. Stuffed animals and birds, brought to light from under the sofa and from the boxes that stood in the corner, were heaped upon the table. The children, with eyes aglow and flaming cheeks, pressed around the tall zoologist on all sides, the smaller ones in front, the older ones behind.

"Children! Do you see this bird? He has a very long beak, and lives on the fish that he catches under water. . . ."

Every one of the children had to touch the bird with his own fingers—if not feel it all over, at least touch the tip of the beak or a feather. And Ahroni saw to it that nobody was slighted. All sort of childish questions filled the air. Ahroni answered in his usual, vibrant voice, describing how the birds feed, how they sleep, how they build nests, and how they protect themselves against their enemies. As he spoke he introduced all manner of funny anecdotes and the children nearly burst with laughter. The teachers who had come with the children were infected with the laughter, and so were the insects and the specimens on the walls, and so were the lizards in the jars. . . .

Quite unexpectedly our hotel has received a large number of guests. The Yiddish novelist Sholem Asch and his wife have arrived from Galilee. They intend to stay here for a while.

Together with Asch came a Petrograd millionaire, and old Feinberg, with snow-white hair, the distributor of "Aunt" ICA's alms in Russia.

Asch's room is right opposite mine. Between us lies the long dining-room. So we keep visiting each other.

There's a knock at the door.

"Yavo!"

In comes Asch. I receive him with great ceremony, invite him to sit down upon the only chair at hand, and treat him to *bon-bons,* which are wrapped in papers bearing Herzl's picture.

It is decided that he has been visiting long enough, and that I must repay the call. So Asch goes back to his room, and before he has closed his door behind him, I knock at it.

"Yavo!"

He receives me with great pomp, and offers me white tartelettes. And thus passes an entire bright day.

We often go strolling through the avenue of mimosa and eucalyptus trees, and from that point we take a long walk as far as Khawaja Musa's orchard. The whole landscape is spread about us in a single sheet of sunshine, and the road over which we pass is thickly planted on both sides with wild flowers of every color.

We speak of everything under the sun, and above all, of Yiddish literature. And the bright sun around us draws forth from us hidden hopes and plans that would never have the courage to reveal themselves amidst ordinary surroundings. All dreams here become endowed with the strength of Samson.

We have a complete plan for issuing all the Yiddish classics in the best style, and in a uniform edition, which will aid to spread the knowledge of Yiddish literature and will be the pride and joy of all friends of the Yiddish tongue.

Money? Maecenases will be found to further the plan. Moreover, the publishers will lose nothing by the job. The edition will prove a huge success, and the books will sell like hot cakes.

In addition to the plan for an edition of the Yiddish classics, which is intended for the Goluth, we have a more romantic plan for Eretz Yisroel.

We will purchase near Rehoboth a large tract of land and found a colony to consist solely of the elite: writers, authors, poets, great composers, painters, sculptors.

Already we can see just how this colony and its beautiful villas will appear. Every house will be a dream in brick and mortar. Before each house, a garden of the most beautiful flowers and plants. The streets will be broad, bordered on each side with grass plots. Everything will be a joy to the eye and an aesthetic delight to poet and artist. We begin to make a list of those whom we shall invite to the colony. There will be no lack of applicants. There will be too many, in fact. What great Jewish artist will not be eager to build himself a villa in our *colonie d'élite?* Mischa Elman, Zimbalist, Schnitzler—not to mention the nationalistic Yiddish writers.

When we broached our plan to the colonist G., his imagination beheld even brighter visions than ours. A wonderul plan. Not far from the colony was just the tract of land we wanted. It belonged to a former colonist who was at that time in New York. He would write him at once. He thought that he would get the land at a very reasonable price. So the land problem is settled.

There is in Rehoboth a young, undersized, blond agriculturist of about thirty. His father is a Russian Jew who settled in Belgium and became there a wealthy diamond merchant. The son studied agriculture and went off to Brazil, where he occupied a professorship in an agricultural school. He came thence to this place, to act as overseer of the large orange grove that his father and several other Belgian Jews had bought in Rehoboth. He makes the acquaintance of both Asch and myself, and invites us to visit him.

He is still a bachelor, but lives in a beautiful house with all the European comforts possible in Rehoboth. He shows us his books, his pictures, and antiques. We are in no hurry with our admiration, however. We wait until he offers us his choice liqueurs, and only then do we praise his fine taste with a truly easy conscience.

At last—

He extracts from a drawer an elegantly bound volume, and begins to read me his French verses. He is an excellent declaimer. The

French nasal sounds impart a solemn tone to his reading. I see that he is highly exalted by his recitation. My eyes seek Asch's in quest of aid. Why only me? And I notice that Asch has finished his Benedictine, and sneaked into the next room, leaving me to my fate.

Nor is this the only time that I was thus abandoned. Once, as we were walking along through the colony, a young workman approached us, dressed in Bedouin garments, and before we knew anything at all, he drew forth from his bosom—a poem. He is a *shomer* in a vineyard. He lives "close to nature," and is on the most intimate terms with starry nights. And he wants expert opinion upon his work.

Asch swears that he is no expert, so the fellow turns to me. I can't offer the same excuse. I want to be original. So I tell him to come some other time.

Now Asch was only visiting Rehoboth, and soon left. So that I had the Yiddishist Bedouin on my hands for a long time after.

The story of the hart that could find no Jewish purchaser had never left my mind since the day that Ahroni first told it to me. When the millionaire from Petrograd arrived at our hotel, it occurred to me that it would be an excellent idea to interest him in that animal. Perhaps he would be moved.

They tell me in Rehoboth that he is worth not a kopeck less than fifteen million rubles. And perhaps more. In Tel-Aviv they say that it isn't quite fifteen, but it's at least six. So I say to myself that he certainly has three millions, and since the rare hart specimen may be bought for a mere four or five hundred rubles, he surely will not say a word, but open his purse at once, saying: "Such a mere trifle!"

So, together with Asch, I took him to Ahroni's. The zoologist showed him bugs, bees, flies, mice, and birds. We looked on in continuous ecstasy. In the meantime, through a skilful cross-examination, I draw out from Ahroni the whole history of his zoological activities and also of the support that he doesn't get, together with the account of the difficulties under which he must pursue his labors and—the story of the hart. Let the millionaire know.

Asch gets excited, and heaps fire and brimstone upon the ingratitude of the Jewish people. And I keep vociferating that it is a blot on our conscience, looking at the millionaire out of a corner of my eye.

Listening to our talk, Madame Ahroni recalls their pitiful plight, and all at once bursts into bitter tears.

Long life to Madame Ahroni. Her tears could not have come more opportunely. This will help.

The millionaire doesn't say a word. But I know that he has been deeply stirred. His eyes, methinks, are somewhat moist. The rare hart is already ours. And unless I am greatly mistaken, Ahroni will have a house of his own and a yearly stipend.

But we do not desist. There is still a jar containing a tiny serpent. Let him see that, too. Let him see Ahroni's greatness, and give with a lavish hand. The millionaire looked at the serpent, and his hand rose.

My heart leaped. His hand was going to his pocket.

How much? A thousand, perhaps, with a promise to give more later.

His hand rises, and rises, and comes to a pause opposite his— mouth.

The millionaire's face expands in a broad yawn, and he says: "It's late. Time to go to sleep."

There are some clever people
who may be compared to
the small fashionable shops:
all their merchandise is displayed
in the show window.—Berthold Auerbach

Clever people are like fragrant roses;
when you smell one rose it's delightful,
but smelling a whole bouquet
you may get quite a headache.—Moritz G. Saphir

WISE PEOPLE

BY BENJACOB

Think not that those are purely sages
*   Whose beard and paunch are large of size,*
Or else the goats through all the ages
*   Must, too, be classed among the wise.*

There are some people who show off with their understanding in the same way that wealthy parvenus show off with their money.—Ludwig Börne

MENDEL MARANTZ—GENIUS

BY DAVID FREEDMAN

ZELDE'S REVOLT

"What is a landlord? A bore! He asks you one question all the time—Rent! What is rent? A fine you pay for being poor. What is poverty? Dirt—on the surface. What is riches? More dirt—under the surface. Everybody wants money. Money! What is money? A disease we like to catch but not to spread. . . . Just wait, Zelde! The time will come! I'll be a landlord on Riverside Drive! We'll have our own home——"

"In the cemetery!" Zelde said bitterly.

"Not so fast," Mendel replied, sipping his tea. "Cheer up, Zelde! What is pessimism? A match. It burns the fingers. What is hope? A candle. It lights the way. . . . You never can tell yet! What is life? A see-saw! To-day you're poor and to-morrow——"

"You starve!" Zelde muttered as she rubbed a shirt vigorously against the washboard.

With a sudden impulse she slapped the shirt into the tub, dried her hands on the apron and resting her fists on her hips, turned to Mendel.

"Why shouldn't I be mad?" she began, replying to a previous question. "Here I stand like a fool scrubbing my life away, from morning till night time, working like a horse, cooking, washing, sewing, cleaning, and everything. And for what? For this I eloped with you from a rich father? Did you marry me—or hire me?"

"I stole you. Now I got to pay the penalty. What is love? A conquest. What is marriage? An inquest! Don't worry, your father was no fool. He made believe he didn't see us run away. We felt romantic— and he got off cheap! What is romance? Soap-bubbles. They look nice, but taste rotten."

"Never mind! Mister Mendel Marantz, I know you too good. You talk a lot to make me forget what I was saying. But this whole business must come to a finish right here and there!

"You talked into yourself you're a great man so you don't want to work and you don't want to listen. Sarah sweats in the factory. Hymie peddles papers. Nathan works by the telegrams. And what do you do? You sit like a king and drink tea and make jokes—and nothing! I betcha you're waiting Jakie, Lena, and Sammy should grow up so you'll send them to work for you too!"

Mendel shrugged his shoulders.

"What's a woman's tongue? A little dog's tail. It wags too much!"

"I know what I talk. You hate work like poison. You like better to smoke a cigaret and close your eyes and invent schemes how to get rich quick. But you'll get crazy quicker!"

"Zelde, you're a old woman. You don't understand. All I need is one drop of luck and that drop will sweeten our whole ocean of troubles. If only one of my inventions succeeds, none of us will have to work. Then Sarah will have dowry. What is dowry? Every man's price. And we'll move out of the fish market. What is success? Fifth Avenue. What is failure? Fifth floor. . . .

"Some day, you'll see. I'll be the President of the Refillable Can Company and save the world millions in tin. Just wait!"

"And who'll buy bread in the meantime? Mendel, remember what I tell you. Knock out this craziness from your head. Forget about this Can Business!"

Mendel's dignity was roused.

"Crazy! That's what you all are! You and all your relatives think I got water on the brain!" He pointed with conviction to his brow. "But up here is the refillable can. Zelde, you see it? It's in the brain, the whole scheme. Up here is full with ideas, plans, and machinery. Thinking, scheming, planning all the time. It don't let me sleep. It don't let me eat. It don't let me work! And I should forget it—ah?

"You're all jealous because God was good to me. He gave your brother, Bernard, real estate; your cousin Joe He gave a shoe factory; your sister Dora, a rich husband. But God gave me *brains* and that none of you got!"

Mendel paced the floor excitedly.

Zelde stood silent and bit her lip. For years she had heard the same flow of rhetoric, the same boast of intellect and the same trust in luck. The net result was always an evasion of work and the responsibility shifted back to her and the children.

Mendel Marantz had brains all right. Otherwise, how could he have existed so long without working?

He always confused her with clever phrases and blurred the issue by creating fictitious ones. And he always succeeded in infecting her with his dreams, until she let him dream on while she did the work. It was that way when they had the candy stand which her brother

Gershon bought for them; it was that way when they kept a vegetable store which sister Dora financed and later reduced to a pushcart; and it was that way now when they had nothing.

By trade a mechanic, by inclination an inventor, and by nature a dreamer, Mendel abhorred the sordid commonplaces of labor and dreaded the yoke of routine. He had been everything from an insurance agent to a night watchman in rapid succession, and had invented at least a hundred different devices for the betterment of civilization while changing jobs. None of these inventions had as yet received proper recognition, least of all from Zelde. But that could not discourage him to such a point as to drive him to work.

He really believed in his powers. That was the tragedy of it. All geniuses have an unalterable faith in their greatness. But so have most cranks. And Zelde was not sure as to which of the two species Mendel belonged.

She was sure of one thing—that the family was hovering perilously near the brink. A single feather added to its burdens and it would topple over. Mendel might take it lightly, but she knew better. She had seen families in the neighborhood crumble to ruin overnight. She had known many who, like Mendel, started as harmless dreamers, hopeful idlers and ended—God forbid—as gamblers, drunkards, and worse.

"How was it with Reznick? Every day he had a chance to make millions while his wife got sick working in the shop. She died working, and the children went to a orphan asylum and he still wanted to make millions. So he made a corner on the coffee market and he lost everything what everybody else had and the only way they could stop him from signing checks with Rockefeller's name was to send him to Bellevue.

"Or Dittenfass? Wasn't he the picture of Mendel? Didn't he hate work like poison and didn't he pay for it? He thought he was smarter from the rest. Didn't his wife used to told him, 'Dittenfass, look out!' But he laughed only. He looked out for himself only. And one day she threw in his eyes vitriol! That's what she threw in his eyes and then he couldn't look any more!

"You can't be too smart. Didn't Karneol try? And it's two years she's waitin' already with swollen eyes he should come back. But he's got to serve three more.

"The best smartness is to do a day's work. If you wait it shall happen miracles—it happens! But the wrong way!

"Maybe you can invent something to make you work," she offered as a possible solution. "Somebody else with your brains could make a fortune. Why don't you make at least a living?"

"Brains make ideas; fools can make money. That's why your relatives are rich. What is business? Blindman's bluff. They shut your eyes and open your pockets!"

"Again you mix me up," she said warily, sensing this new attempt to befuddle the issue. "What's the result from all this? You joke and we starve. It's lucky Sarah works. If not, we would all be thrown out in the street already."

At this moment Sarah entered. She was pale and tired from the climb of stairs. She dropped her hat languidly on the couch and sank into a chair.

Zelde was too surprised to speak. It was only one-thirty. She never expected Sarah before six. An ominous thought flitted through her mind. She looked anxiously at her daughter whose gaze shifted to the floor.

An oppressive silence gathered over them. Then Sarah tried to mumble something. But Zelde understood without hearing. Her heart had told her:

"It's slack! Everybody laid off. Sarah, too!"

What she had dreaded most had happened. The family of Marantz was now over the brink. Zelde stood crushed by the thought of the morrow. Sarah sat staring vacantly, her chin against her clenched hand. Mendel stopped smoking to appear less conspicuous.

Four female eyes detected him, however, and scorched him with their gaze.

The handwriting on the wall was unnecessarily large.

Mendel Marantz knew that his crisis was at hand.

Zelde spoke.

"That settles it. Either tomorrow you go to work or go altogether! Yessir! You, I mean, Mister!"

Mendel had faced crises before. Some he had overcome with a jest, others with a promise, still others with a pretense at work until the novelty wore off. But there was a grimness in Zelde's manner this time that looked fatal. Nothing but a permanent job and lifelong drudgery could save him now. But that would also destroy him.

Tying him down to a position was like hitching a lion to a cart. His mind could not pull in harness. It was too restive and spirited. He would never repeat an act without discovering how much easier it could be done by machinery and immediately he set himself to invent the necessary machine. That was why he could not be a tailor. After he once threaded a needle, he started to devise a simple instrument for doing it, and in the meantime, lost his job. And that happened in every case.

His head was so full of ideas that he often had to stand still to keep his balance. His mind sapped all of his powers and left him powerless for work. In order to work, he would have to stop thinking. He might just as well stop living. Idleness was as essential a part of his make-up as industry was of Zelde's.

"I wasn't made for work," he said with finality. "I mean—for just plain work. Some people work with their feet, others with their hands. I work with my head. You don't expect I shall sit like Simon the shoemaker every day and hit nails till I get consumption. One—two—three, I invent a machinery which hits nails, cuts leather, fits heels, makes patches and I sit down and laugh on the world. I can't work like others just as others can't work like me!"

"You can make me believe night is day and black is white, but it won't help you. It's a new rule in this house from today on—those who work, eat; those who don't, don't. If you think you can invent food, go ahead. So long I live my children is not going to starve. From today on I'm the father from this family. If you don't want to work— I will!"

Mendel was skeptical.

"What is a woman?" he thought. "A lot of thunder, but a little rain."

Still, the shower was more drenching than he supposed.

"Tomorrow morning I go back to be a dressmaker by fancy dresses. Sarah, you come with me. I learn you a real trade."

Then she turned to Mendel with a sneer.

"You thought I play around in the house, didn't you? All right! Now you stay home and play like I did. You want to eat? Cook yourself. You think in the house it's easy? You'll find out different. Send the children to school, go up on the roof to hang clothes, run down with the garbage five floors, buy groceries, wash underwear, mend stockings, press shirts, scrub floors—go on! Have a good time, and I'll pay the bills!"

Mendel admitted that Zelde had worn for some time the family trousers, but he believed that he still wore the belt. However, her inexorable decision disillusioned him. He admitted being caught slightly off his guard. He had never suspected that a type of work existed so near him into which he might be forced out of sheer necessity. Not that he intended to do it! Still——

"What is a woman?" he reconsidered. "Lightning. It's nice and bright till it hits you!"

MENDEL MARANTZ—HOUSEWIFE

It was the next morning that Mendel discovered perpetual motion. The children had taken possession of the house. He dodged flying pillows, tripped over upset furniture, slipped on greasy garbage from an overturned can, found salt in his coffee and something sharper on his seat. He kept constantly moving to avoid falling objects and fell into others. He had planned to have nothing to do with the house, but the house was having a great deal to do with him.

The youngsters seemed to be under the impression that with Zelde all law and order had passed away. Mendel found it hard work to change their minds. It was monotonous to spank Lena, then Jakie, then Sammy. Then over again. It would be better to send them off to school. But they had to be dressed and fed and washed for that!

He was tempted to snatch his hat and coat and leave the house. But what would he do in the streets?

He hesitated, gritted his teeth and set to work by scrubbing Jakie's face till it resembled a carrot.

"What's a wife?" he muttered, and Lena started at the question. "A telescope! She makes you see stars!" And some soap got into his eye.

"Sammy, don't you never marry," he exclaimed with a profound look of warning at the frightened little boy. "What is marriage? First a ring on the finger and later—on the neck. Lena, stop pulling Jakie's hair. She's like her mother. Don't do that Sammy. A tablecloth ain't a handkerchief! Ai! Little children, little troubles; big children, big troubles. What is children? Life insurance. Some day they pay you back—when you're dead. But you like them anyhow. Such is life! You know it's tough, but you try it once, anyhow. . . .

"After all, what is life? A journey. What is death? the goal. What is man? A passenger. What is woman? Freight!

"Jakie, you bad boy! Don't cry, Lena. He didn't mean it. Here's an apple. Go to school. Sammy, get off the bannister! Look out, children! It's a step missing down there! Who's crying? Jakie, give her back the apple! Did you ever hear such excitements? My goodness!"

Mendel, perspired, exhausted, sank into a chair.

"I'm working after all," he noted with surprise. "If this lasts, I don't."

But the trials of Mendel Marantz had only begun. The sensation of womanhood did not thrill his bosom and the charms of house-keeping failed to allure him. A home like a warehouse on moving day tumbled about him. The beds were upset, the table and floor were littered with breakfast leavings, the cupboard was bare, the dishes were piled in the sink, the dust had gathered already as if cleaning were a lost art, and the general atmosphere was one of dejection, confusion, chaos. The magic touch of the housewife revealed itself by its absence.

Zelde had now proved to him conclusively that her presence and service were essential to his comfort. As if he had ever questioned the fact. Why did she go to all this trouble to drive home a point?

"Zelde, a glass tea," he used to say and the tea stood steaming hot before him. "Zelde, it's a draught. Shut up the window," and presently the draught was gone.

"Zelde!" he would call, leaning back in his chair, but why torture himself with things that were no more.

That night when Zelde arrived, masculine and businesslike, through with work and ready for supper, a strange sight greeted her eyes.

The house was in hopeless disorder. The cat was on the table and Jakie was under it, while Lena kept him there with her foot. Sammy's eye had been darkened by a flying saucer which Hymie let go in a moment of abandon. Everything was where it should not be. The kitchen furniture had been moved into the dining room and the featherbeds were in the washtub.

Mendel was nowhere within the range of Zelde's call.

"Where is papa?" she asked sharply, after calming the youngsters with her two convincing hands. "Everything is upside down. I betcha he didn't do a thing all day. My goodness, that man will make me crazy!"

A crashing sound as if dishes in hasty descent, issued from the next room.

Zelde and her retinue rushed to the scene of disaster. With one foot in the sink and the other on the washtub, Mendel Marantz was poised on high, searching through the closet. Dishes, pans, bottles and rags lay scattered in ruined fragments beneath him.

Zelde blazed.

"*Gozlen!*" she almost shrieked. "What do you want up there?"

Mendel steadied himself. His heart having missed a beat, he waited a moment, and then answered quietly, "Iodine."

"What for iodine, what for?" She was still furious, but also a little anxious.

"A small scratch," he explained without moving. "My finger got caught—under the meat chopper."

"Oi! You clumsy! And what's all the rags and the water on the floor?"

"To put by my side and my leg. I—slipped and—the gas range fell on me. My ankle turned around. The soup was good and hot. Maybe you got something for burns?"

Zelde was a little less furious and a little more anxious.

"Then what are you climbing on the walls for? Go in bed. Go—you look broken in pieces!"

She sighed heavily and shook her head.

"After all, he's only a man," she soliloquized. "What can you expect? He don't know if he's alive!"

She continued to scold, but nursed him tenderly.

"How is it? You're an inventor, and you don't know how to light the gas without blowing up the house? A man who can't help nobody else can't help himself!"

After a pause she said, "Maybe I should stay home? Ah?"

"Maybe," he murmured weakly.

Zelde vacillated.

"So what'll be if I stay home?" she prodded.

"It'll be better."

"That I know, but what'll be with you?"

"I'll get well."

"And—?" She expected him not only to recover, but to reform.

"And if I get well, I'll feel good. What is health? A garden. What is sickness? A grave. What is a good wife? A gardener. What is a bad wife? A grave-digger!"

"He's as bad as ever," she thought.

She finally resolved, "It's not such a terrible! He won't die from it and we can't live from it. He'll learn a lesson and I'll earn a living."

And the experiment continued.

It was very hard on Mendel. It was harder on Sarah and hardest on Zelde. But time subdued Mendel's protests and improved his work.

Zelde was surprised at his altered attitude of gradual submission. It almost alarmed her. She had never really intended this radical change to last. She had expected Mendel to rebel more and more violently as time went on and finally to make a break for his freedom and exclaim, "I'm sick and tired of this slavery. I'm going to work!"

Instead, he was getting actually to like it. By degrees, Zelde found less to do in the house after her return from the shop. True, his work was crude and slovenly to her practiced eye. She never would have cleaned dishes as he did, with a whisk-broom, or swept dirt under the table, or boiled soup in a coffee pot, or wiped the floor with a perfectly good skirt.

But withal, Mendel was doing things, and as his domestic craftsmanship improved, Zelde grew more disappointed and depressed. She felt that he was planning to displace her permanently. She pictured him bending over the wash-tub as she used to do; or arranging the dishes in the closet, which was once her favorite diversion; or scouring the pots and pans as only she knew how, and a genuine feeling of envy and longing seized her.

"Thief!" she was tempted to cry. "Go out from my kitchen! Give me back my apron and let alone my housework!"

For she had become nothing more than a boarder in that home, to be tolerated merely because she earned the rent. She saw the children only at suppertime and they looked curiously at her as if they hardly recognized her.

At table, all eyes were turned to "Pa."

"Papa, Sammy took my spoon!"

"Take his," Mendel decreed.

"Pa, I want some more meat!"

"Take mine."

"Pop, Lena stole my bread!"

"Take hers."

"Pa-ah! The thoup ith too hot. I tan't eat it!" Jakie complained, and turned a bruised tongue to his father.

"Take some water from the sink," was Mendel's motherly advice.

Zelde felt like a stranger. They did not seem to know that she was present. She tried to interfere.

"Don't put water in soup, Jakie! Better blow on it."

But the little boy slipped down from the chair without noticing her, wriggled out from under the table, and soon returned, gaily carrying a cup of sink water.

Her maternal instinct rebelled.

"No!" she said warningly, as Jakie tilted the cup over the plate of bean-soup.

But the child, with his eyes fixed on Mendel, poured the contents bravely.

Zelde slapped his hand and the cup fell with a clatter. It was not a hard blow, but an impulsive one. It created a strained and awkward silence. Jakie burst into tears. He ran to Mendel and buried his little face in daddy's lap. A strange woman had hit him!

Something snapped in Zelde. Her appetite was gone. She rose and went into the bedroom and shut the door behind her.

She did not want them to hear her sobs.

It had all turned out so different!

Instead of driving Mendel to work, she had driven herself into exile. Mendel the housewife, was now further from getting a man's job than Mendel the idler, had ever been. Zelde felt she had made a grave mistake. Rather should she have permitted him to idle and mope —he would have tired of it eventually—than that he should be wrongly occupied and contented.

If only she could undo what she had done, she'd be satisfied.

"After all, a house to manage is for a woman," she began, bent upon re-establishing the old order. "A man should do housework? It can make him crazy yet!"

"I believe you," Mendel conceded.

"It don't look like housework should agree with you," she observed.

"Looks is deceiving."

There was a pause. A good deal of understanding passed between them.

"Mendel, hard work will kill you yet," she insisted.

"So will idleness—in the long run. What is death? An appointment. You got to keep it sometime."

"But you don't look good."

"I don't feel bad."

Zelde became a little dizzy. Did he mean to say that he would stick to housework? She tried to tempt him.

"Wouldn't you like, like you used to, to have nothing to do and sit and cross your legs and without you should move, somebody should bring you hot tea?"

Mendel blew rings of smoke at the ceiling.

Zelde continued, scarcely breathing.

"And wouldn't you like to lie on the couch with your hands together behind your head and look on the sky from the window and dream what a great inventor you are?"

An impressive silence followed. On Mendel's face were fleeting traces of an inner struggle.

"And—I'll clean the house," she added softly to clear any doubts that he might still have.

Mendel shook his head.

"It'll be too hard for you," he protested gallantly.

"It's not such a terrible!"

"I haven't the heart to let you," he complained feebly.

"You'll get over it."

His tone became firmer.

"No! Housework is not for a woman. Like the Masora says, 'Be good to your wife and give your children to eat.' That means a man should clean the house and cook for his children! What is a wife? A soldier. Her place is on the field. What is a husband? A general. His place is at home!"

Zelde was chagrined.

"So this is the future what you aimed for?" she chided. "To be a washerwoman and a porter! Pooh! You ought to be ashamed to look on my face! Think what people say! They don't know which is what! If I am the husband or if you are the wife or how!"

Mendel carefully rolled a new cigaret. There was a plaintive note in her anger. He could afford to be defiant.

"Didn't you make me to stay home and work? So! I'm working! What is work? Pleasure!—If you know how!"

And he struck a match.

Zelde sat down to avoid falling down.

"Work is pleasure," echoed through her mind like an explosion. Maybe solitary confinement at home every day had gone to his head. Or maybe—maybe—! She slowly repeated to herself his sally, "What is work? Pleasure!" and "What is pleasure?" she wondered. The shock of the answer almost made her scream.

So that was it! She had suspected something, but *that* would never have occurred to her in a million years. Those floor brushes that she found the other day under the bed, and the mop and the tin pail. They did not belong to the house. To whom *did* they belong? She had certainly seen them somewhere before. Now she knew! At the janitor's!

"No wonder he likes to stay home," she muttered to herself. "I should have known, it's a bad sign if Mendel likes work all of a sudden!"

Her suspicions were still hypothetical, but fragments of evidence were fast falling in to shape an ominous and accusing picture.

One day, upon her return from work, Zelde found Mendel sitting near the window, restfully smoking a cigaret. His legs were crossed under his apron and his arms were folded over his lap. He gazed wistfully out upon the city.

Zelde looked about her in astonishment. The house was tidy, the kitchen spick and span, the wash dried and ironed, the floor freshly scrubbed. A model housewife would have envied the immaculate perfection of the work.

Zelde gasped. So early in the day and already through with all his work! And what work!

"Sarah, I wonder who did it," she finally said to her daughter when she had somewhat regained her composure.

Her groping suspicions now became a startling conviction. Evidence fairly shrieked at her from every corner.

"Only a woman could do this," she thought, overcome by the shock of the revelation.

"Who do you think?" Sarah asked innocently.

"Did you see the way she looks at me?" Zelde exclaimed with mounting fury. "No wonder she laughs in my face. No wonder she tells all the neighbors, 'Such a fool! She works and he plays!' No wonder!"

"What are you talking about?" inquired Sarah, bewildered.

"Never mind! Your father knows what I mean! *She* did it! Rifke! The janitor's wife! I know her all right. She made eyes to Mister Mendel Marantz lots of times! She's older from me by four years but she paints up like a sign and makes her hair buster brown and thinks the men die for her. Ask your father. He knows!"

Mendel sat dumbfounded. His eyes opened like mouths.

"Don't make believe you're innocent. I know you men too good." Zelde broke out violently, "I slave like a dog and that dirty old—" tears of rage stifled her. But with a swift change of tone she added, her finger shaking under Mendel's nose, "Mr. Marantz, remember, you'll be sorry for this!" And she walked out of the room.

Mendel was sorry for her. He turned a puzzled face to Sarah. "When the house was upside down, she said I made her crazy. Now, when it's fixed up she tries to make me crazy! What's a wife? An epidemic. If it don't break out here, it breaks out there."

The next day Zelde fidgeted at her work. She was prompted to fling it aside, rush home, and catch them together—Mendel and Rifke —and pull out the old vixen's hair and scratch out her eyes. But she bided her time. Mendel was no doubt expecting a surprise attack and perhaps had warned his paramour to stay away.

Zelde decided to be wily. She would make believe that she had forgotten and forgiven. But how could she!

That night on the landing of the fourth floor she met Rifke coming down from the fifth. There were only two tenants on the fifth floor—Mrs. Peril Tzvack, a widow who hated Rifke and would never let her into her house—and Mendel Marantz. From which of the two was Rifke coming?

As Zelde entered her home, the same neatness, the same cleanliness and smartness stung her sight. In fact she herself could not have done better. To be honest—not even as good. The house was a mirror of spotlessness. It was so obviously the accomplishment of the wicked woman she had met on the stairs, that Zelde spent a tortured and sleepless night.

She went to work the next morning with a splitting headache and mists swam before her eyes as she tried to sew. Weird thoughts revolved in her mind. If it were only a question of Mendel, she would not hesitate a moment to leave him forever. But the children! A daughter of marriageable age and the tiny ones. What would people say? And even Mendel. True, there was no excuse—absolutely none—for his abominable treachery. She would never forgive him! Still, Rifke, that superannuated flirt, was the kind of woman that could turn any man's head! With that double chin of hers, and the shaved neck and a dimple like a funnel in her cheek! That's what the men liked!

After all, Mendel was a helpless male, all alone in a house. He probably did not know the first thing about housekeeping and would have starved or been buried in dirt if he had not appealed to somebody to help him. And Rifke was just the type to take advantage of a defenseless man in such a predicament. She doubtless opened her eyes at him like two coal scuttles, and pursed her lips—she had a way of doing it which gave the women of the neighborhood heart-failure. And Mendel must have been grateful and kind to her for her assistance and she must have mistaken his attitude for something else. She always misunderstood kindness from men.

So that's how Mendel managed to clean the house so well! And that's why work was pleasure to him! Judging by the amount and quality of the work Rifke was doing for him, their affection for each other must have developed to an alarming degree.

Zelde visualized the hateful scenes of faithlessness in which Mendel probably danced fawningly about Rifke, the fifty-three-year-old "vamp" who cleaned dishes and washed clothes for him as a reward. She must have nudged him with her elbow while she boiled the wash and said invitingly, "Mendel, dear, why are you blind to beauty?"

And Mendel, edging closer, must have answered, "What is

beauty? Wine! The older it gets, the rarer it is!" Then pressing his cheek against hers, he undoubtedly added with tenderness, "You're so fat! It's a pleasure to hold you around! What is a man? Dynamite. What is a woman? A burning match. What is passion? The explosion!"

"Stop it! Your whiskers tickle me," she probably replied with a coquettish laugh and slapped him playfully over the hands with a rinsed shirt.

But she was only jesting, and was perhaps ecstatic with joy when Mendel courageously kissed her on the cheek despite her protests and exclaimed, "What is a kiss? A smack for which you turn the other cheek!" And she probably turned it.

Then Rifke amorously rested her head on his chest and looked up with those devilish eyes of hers, and linking her plump arms about his neck, she whispered, "Love me, Mendel, love me! I am yours!"

And Mendel, planting his feet more solidly to bear her weight, and carried away by the flames of desire, must have gripped her in his passionate embrace and murmured in a throaty voice, "What is love? A broom. It sweeps you away!"

"What's the matter with you, Zelde?" cried Marcus the tailor, biting the thread from a seam. "You stitched the skirt to a sleeve and you're sewing up the neck of the waist! You look white like a ghost!"

Zelde drew herself up, as out of a lethargy.

"Eh! W—where am I? Oh!"

And her face sank into her palms.

Instantly, there was a tumult in the shop.

A startled group of frightened men and women gathered about her.

But Zelde regained her self-control without aid, and pale and faint though she was, she smiled weakly to reassure them all.

"It's nothing. A dizziness. I'm better," she said. But Sarah insisted upon taking her home at once.

"That's right," Marcus advised. "Go home and take a hot tea with lemon. It'll sweat you out."

He added in an undertone to his neighbor, "It's a shame! Such a fine woman! She's got a husband who's a nix."

Zelde refused to have Sarah accompany her home.

"We can't afford you shall lose a half day," she argued. But the real reason was that she did not wish her daughter to behold her father's infamy.

At eleven o'clock Zelde left. As she neared the house her breath became short and rapid. She stumbled several times going up the stairs. She stopped at the door.

Was it voices or was it her imagination?

No. Yes. It was. A man's voice, then a woman's laughter, then some—oh! She could stand it no longer. She broke wildly into the room and dislodged a bulky person who had been leaning against the door. Zelde stood electrified.

It was Rifke. And she was laughing in her face! And there was Mendel. And the janitor, too—Rifke's husband. And two men! With stove-pipe hats and cut-aways and spats! Detectives no doubt! Brought by the janitor to catch his wife and arrest Mendel! Oh, heavens! And there was Morton, Mendel's nephew, a lawyer!

"Oi, a lawyer in the case!" she moaned to herself. "Then everything is lost!"

Zelde was ready to drop, but Mendel took her by the hand and she heard him say, "This is my wife. It's all her fault. She drove me to it."

"We want you to come with us now," one of the strangers said to Mendel.

"What's the matter here, anyhow?" Zelde exclaimed at last.

"I got to go with these people," Mendel replied. "But you can ask—Rifke," he added significantly. "She knows all about it."

Mendel, his nephew, and the two gentlemen departed before Zelde had time to protest. She turned with burning eyes to Rifke—the hussy!

"I wish they could take my husband where they take yours," Rifke began by way of explanation. "You don't know what kind of a husband you got. It's gonna be in all the papers. He did something. Those men that was here watched him and when they seen it, they jumped up like crazy."

"What did he do?" Zelde asked in great alarm. "I betcha you made him to do it."

"I? He says, you made him. I only brought up the people. They knock by me in the door. They say, 'Do Mendel Marantz live here? Where is it?' So I bring them up."

"What for did you bring them up, what for? A blind one could see it's detectives!" Zelde muttered angrily.

"How shall I know it, who they are? When they came in your husband turned white like milk. 'Are you the man which done it?' they ask him and he says shivering, 'Yes'."

Zelde wrung her hands.

"What for did he say 'Yes' what for?"

"Because it's true," Rifke explained.

"What's true?"

"That he done it."

"What did he done what? You'll make me crazy yet. Why don't you tell me?"

"But I told you already!"

"When did you told me, when? You're talkin' and talkin' and it don't come out nothing! What happened here? What did they want here? What's the matter here altogether, anyway?"

"It's a whole lot the matter—with you!" Rifke exclaimed impatiently. "Come over here and look and maybe it'll open your eyes!"

She led the dazed Zelde into the kitchen.

"You see it?" Rifke asked triumphantly, pointing out a mass of wrinkled canvas in the middle of the room.

"What shall I see?" Zelde answered skeptically. "Rags I see!"

"But under the rags!" Rifke insisted. She lifted the canvas. Zelde stood completely bewildered. Her eyes opened wide, then her face reddened. A feeling of indignation welled up in her.

"You can't make a fool from me!" she began at last with rising momentum. "What do you show me, what? An ash-can on wheels! What's that got to do with you and my husband? Don't think I don't know. You show me this, I should forget *that!*"

Rifke began to perspire. She mopped her face with her apron as she struggled to keep calm.

"You don't know what I'm talkin' about and I don't know what you're talkin' about. It's mixed up, everything! Where do you see a' ash-can? This ain't a' ash-can! It looks maybe, like it. But it's ain't. All my friends should have such ash-cans! It's a wonder in the world!"

Zelde's head was reeling.

"So what is it, I'm asking you?" she gasped helplessly.

"It's a whole business!" Rifke replied. "We seen it, my husband Shmeril and me and the people which was here. Your husband showed us. He winds up the can like a phonograph and it begins to play. The dishes go in dirty and they come out clean like after a bath. You see it? On these straps the dishes take a ride. They go in from the back and come out on the front. When it's finished the dishes, your husband opens the box—I thought a man will jump out from it—but it's only wheels and straps and wires and pipes inside! Did you ever!

"Then he pulls off the feet and the box sits down on the floor and he takes out the straps from the back door and puts in such a board with bumps and brushes and he turns the handle and the box rides around like a automobile and washes up the floor till it shines! I tell you the people was standing and looking I thought their eyes would fall out!

"Then your husband stands up the box and puts back the feet and takes out the bumpy board and sticks in a whole machinery with pipes and wheels and winds up the machine and pumps in fresh water and throws in all the old clothes and you hear inside such a noises, and then the clothes come out like frankfurters, clean and washed and ready to hang! Such a business! You don't have to work no more! It works itself! I wouldn't mind to have such a box by me!"

Zelde, dumb with amazement, gazed at the mute, ugly monster before her. She recognized the wheels from the old baby carriage, the legs were from her kitchen chair, the handle from the stove. And now she remembered the can, the brushes, and the mops that Rifke had probably discarded and that Mendel had used in the creation of this freak.

So this was the rival she had been jealous of, the usurper of her rights!

"It makes in five minutes what I do a whole day," Rifke rambled along. "They call it such a fancy name—Combination Housecleaner. It cleans everything. The strangers is from a company which goes to make millions cans like this.

"You're gonna be rich, Mrs. Marantz!

"Who would think from housecleaning you would get rich! Here I'm cleaning houses for twenty-nine years and I never thought from such a scheme! You gotta have luck, I tell you!"

Zelde felt peculiarly humbled. That night she could hardly face Mendel.

"And I thought all the time it was Rifke! Oi, you must think I'm such a fool!"

"Forget it. If not for you I never would have did what I done. You made me to do it."

"I didn't, Mendel."

She added in a caressing tone.

"Your laziness did it, Mendel. You invented that machine because you were too lazy to work."

"What's a wife? An X-Ray. She knows you through and through!"

NEIGHBORLY PREOCCUPATIONS

Once there was a tradesman who was very much concerned with what his neighbors thought about his business. If he did good business, when the Sabbath came around he had his wife light very small candles. However, if business was very bad, he instructed his wife to light the largest possible candles. He explained this strange procedure in the following way:

"When business is good, I feel good. But I'd like my neighbors to feel good too. So I have my wife light small candles. When my neighbors see them they think I'm doing bad business and thus they get comfort from it because they themselves do so badly. On the other hand, when business is bad I get depressed. To cheer myself up I have the largest candles lit to brighten the gloom. And when my neighbors see how well I'm doing because I can afford such big candles, they begin to feel bad. Then I feel bad and they feel bad and so we're quits!"

SUPERLATIVES IN YIDDISH

BY SHOLOM ALEICHEM

strong	stronger	a tree
clever	cleverer	a *mamzer*
strong	stronger	an iron
stingy	stingier	a pig
gentle	gentler	a charlatan
fat	fatter	a *kugel*
scrawny	scrawnier	a dog
broad	broader	a barrel
black	blacker	a tomcat
yellow	yellower	wax
rich	richer	stuffed
good	better	without a gall
bad	worse	a Haman
beautiful	more beautiful	a piece of gold
ugly	uglier	ugly as death
soft	softer	butter
wet	wetter	to wring out
dry	drier	pepper
hot	hotter	a bathhouse
hungry	hungrier	haven't had a thing in my mouth all day.

thirsty	thirstier	fell with my face to the ground.
pale	paler	a handsomer one they bury.
naked	nakeder	just as his mother bore him.
innocent	more innocent	just go and milk him!
foolish	more foolish	just go and salt him into the pickles!
		just go and marinate him in cabbage!
possible	more possible	what do you mean "not possible"?
certain	more certain	what a question!
right	more right	of course!
much	more	p-s-s-sh

DE PROFUNDIS

BY PETER ALTENBERG

Most people have no idea what profound is. They go down to the very depths in order to look for it, while all along they could have found it on the surface. But in order to find it on the surface they would have to be quite deep themselves.

THE PHILOSOPHER

BY SHEM-TOB PALQUERA (THIRTEENTH CENTURY)

There once lived a thoughtful man who sought solitude in order to probe into the problems of creation and being and to determine the purpose of all life. These thoughts preoccupied him all the time.

One day he was walking as usual by the bank of the river, absorbed in contemplation. Suddenly, he lifted his eyes and saw a man standing near by. The man had dug a small hole on the bank and was pouring water from a jug into it.

Surprised, the philosopher asked the stranger, "What are you doing?"

"I am going to empty the river and pour all the water from it into this hole," the man answered.

"This is utter madness!" exclaimed the philosopher. "It's an impossible task!"

"Sillier and even more impossible are the questions you're trying to solve!" retorted the man.

Having spoken thus the stranger disappeared.

UNCLE JULIUS AND THE BMT

BY ETHEL ROSENBERG

I know what you're thinking. You're thinking I made up Uncle Julius, that there is no such person . . . listen, why should we argue? Believe me, don't believe me, he's still my uncle. That little old man of eighty, with the fresh-scrubbed look on his shining face, the delicate pink cheeks, the bright brown eyes, the mouth that quirks over the too-even, too-white dentist-bought teeth, that bald head with the white fuzz over the ears—isn't that a regular story-book uncle? The kind you see in the movies? All right. Can I help it? That's my Uncle Julius. Wait . . . let me tell you about my Uncle Julius and the BMT.

Do him something. When my Uncle Julius travels, he likes to be comfortable. He treats the subway like it was a railroad train, and he is a Pullman passenger. Mind you, for the IRT he has absolutely no use.

"That's also a train?" Uncle Julius asks scornfully. "Does a man have any private life his neighbors push from both sides and hang over you yet? And where does such a train go, tell me?" Uncle Julius clinches it. "So I'll tell you where. To the Bronx with the hills a man needs an iron heart to walk up and down."

No, it has to be the BMT, where the seats are arranged for Uncle Julius' convenience. The first thing he does when he walks in, he takes off his jacket, and he hangs it on the window. Of course he dusts the wall with a piece of Kleenex. You think new suits grow on trees? When the jacket is arranged just so, he leans over, unlaces his high-top shoes, removes them, drops them under his seat. Then he wriggles his toes around in his socks. What do people say? Listen, on the BMT you could hold an Elks' convention and nobody would be surprised. Now Uncle Julius is comfortable, he goes to sleep. How he sleeps!

So time passes, all is quiet, or fairly quiet, until Uncle Julius' station suddenly comes into view. Then you should hear the tumult, the commotion, the shouting. Uncle Julius awakes with a cry, looks about him wildly, and runs for the door.

"Mister! Mister!" the passengers yell. "You forgot your coat. *Hey mister!* You forgot your shoes."

This is a time for such trivialities? Uncle Julius is too busy fighting with the door. The door pushes, Uncle Julius pushes back. The door pushes harder, Uncle Julius gets mad. In the excitement his glasses break. Don't ask me how. Even if he isn't wearing them, they break. Finally he is helped out on to the platform, still fighting, and the door slides shut triumphantly.

"Hey, mister," the passengers yell. "Here's your jacket. Here's your shoes," and they throw the stuff out the window, and wave goodby to him. Uncle Julius sits down on the bench on the platform and puts on his shoes.

Then does he come home? A lot you know about my Uncle Julius. Off he goes to the BMT offices. What's the matter? He isn't a citizen? A taxpayer? So let the BMT give him new glasses. Nice people, the BMT, they give him new glasses. Once. Twice. Three times. How long can the BMT give Uncle Julius new glasses?

"To everything there is a limit," the BMT tells my Uncle Julius. "Please be good enough not to bother us any more." They think they are through with Uncle Julius. And in a way, they're right. They are through giving him glasses. The next item is umbrellas.

"Give me the umbrella," Uncle Julius says to my Aunt Frieda. "It's raining outside."

"As long as it isn't raining in the house," Aunt Frieda shrugs. "No umbrella."

Uncle Julius looks at Aunt Frieda.

"In a man's own house," he says, "when a man asks for an umbrella he shouldn't get wet it's raining pouring rain outside, so first is an argument. Frieda, the umbrella!"

"You'll lose it on the train," Aunt Frieda says stubbornly.

"So I'll lose it," says Uncle Julius. "What's the matter? You maybe don't trust the BMT?"

What can Aunt Frieda do? She gives him the umbrella.

"Why is it," Aunt Frieda asks, "the people throw you your shoes, they throw you your jacket, but the umbrella they don't throw? Why is that, tell me?"

"And if I told you," Uncle Julius sings, "would you know?"

Everything is peaceful until Uncle Julius comes home.

"Have you got the umbrella?" Aunt Frieda yells from the kitchen.

"A question," Uncle Julius answers, hurt. Aunt Frieda is suspicious. She comes out and looks.

"*Aha!*" she says righteously. "Just like I thought. This isn't your umbrella."

"It isn't?" Uncle Julius tries to sound surprised. Then he adds happily, "You never saw such an umbrella. Like magic. You press this button," he presses, "and it flies right away open."

It does and almost knocks Aunt Frieda off her feet.

"America," Uncle Julius says, shaking his head back and forth, "America."

"America, America," Aunt Frieda snaps. "So where did you pick up *this* bargain, tell me?"

Uncle Julius chides her gently.

"Where? Where do you think?"

"Julius! Again with the BMT?"

"What's the matter?" Uncle Julius says. "I'm not a citizen, maybe? I'm not a taxpayer?"

"Look at my taxpayer," Aunt Frieda says scornfully. "You are also a taxpayer? In America every *kapsn* is a taxpayer."

Uncle Julius knows women. He knows Aunt Frieda better. He ignores her.

"Such fine people," he muses. "They know me by heart already."

"A big surprise," Aunt Frieda says. "They know him already. Only every day you're there. That poor BMT," and then adds practically, "So far this is the best umbrella you got from them."

Uncle Julius sighs. "It will be a shame to lose this umbrella, but at least other people will also have a use of it."

"So arrange one time you shouldn't lose it," Aunt Frieda says.

Uncle Julius shakes his head. "Have they got a collection there," he marvels. He half-closes his eyes and studies the fireplace. Aunt Frieda watches him narrowly.

"Well, my philosopher," she says finally, "what's on the mantel you see that I don't see?"

"Have they got a collection from all kinds things," Uncle Julius says dreamily.

"Julius! Look at me!" Aunt Frieda says. "I want only one thing. You should leave the BMT alone."

This is a wish the BMT echoes, and they make it very plain to my Uncle Julius. But my Uncle Julius doesn't take offense. He keeps going back. He likes the BMT, and when my Uncle Julius likes you, do him something, he likes you to pieces.

QUITE SANE

Jacobson, the gents' furnishing store keeper, had a mental breakdown and was committed to an institution. A short while later, his neighbor Kalman, the druggist, went to see him.

"How's Jacobson?" asked the druggist's wife when he returned.

"Not so good—he's really sick!" sighed Kalman, distressed by his neighbor's misfortune.

"What does he say?"

"Say? He jabbered away all the time and I couldn't make head or tail of it."

"How did you talk to him?"

"I tried to get him into a rational frame of mind, talked of down-to-earth things with which he and I were both familiar. I tried to tell him, for instance, that he owed me a hundred dollars."

"Did he recall the debt?" asked Mrs. Kalman.

"That crazy he isn't yet!" replied Kalman grimly.

Art with Tea and Lemon

*What's the most important thing
a writer's got to have?
A small appetite.*

SHYLOCK IN CZERNOWITZ

BY KARL EMIL FRANZOS
TRANSLATED FROM THE GERMAN BY NATHAN AUSUBEL

It was sometime towards the end of winter that Yossel Grün, the *gabbai,* sent for me and engaged me to take his son Shmul to the wonder-*rebbe* in Sadagora.

This Shmul was about my age, that is at the time he was in his twentieth year, but so pale, weak, and sickly that he looked like a boy of twelve. Because Yossel was a pious man he had married him off that same autumn, but to a girl who was two years older than he and who looked as plump and red as a Maschansker apple. However, when six months had passed and there appeared neither sign nor hope of a grandchild, the old fellow became impatient and decided that only the great *Chassidic* rebbe in Sadagora could bring matters to right.

While he was telling me that, I took a good look at Shmul. I thought to myself: "There the old boy is right; without a miracle from the wonder-rebbe, this weak child couldn't possibly become a father." But aloud I assured Yossel that I would carry out any task he requested of me, that I would look after Shmul and take him to the rebbe and make him talk to him of his trouble, because by himself the bashful lad might possibly not be able to state his request.

And so we started on our journey. On the evening of the second day we arrived in Sadagora and stopped at an inn. We found there several Jews who immediately cottoned up to us in a confidential manner and asked us what business brought us to Sadagora. This they asked not so much out of curiosity and even less out of good nature. It seemed that everybody in this wretched nest was taking his living off the rebbe, and for that reason they all served as his voluntary or even paid assistants. On arrival all strangers were closely questioned as to their names, their calling, financial status, and the nature of the request they planned to make of the rebbe. The very next day, when they were received by the rebbe, he was in the position of playing the easy role of an all-knowing one.

"For my part you can all swell up with boils!" I thought, and then aloud launched into a lamentation over the unheard-of fate that had befallen Shmul. I told them that he had been married a little more than three years but that every ten months his wife gave birth to triplets. It was always the same—triplets! In short, in three and a half years he had become the father of twelve children, and by all appearances another set of triplets was already on the way. What a misfortune!

At first the people did not believe it. Then I started to give corroborating details just as if I were the mother: I mentioned all the children's birthdays and their names and I imitated each of their voices. At this even the most crafty of the pious rogues began to believe me and nodded gravely as I talked and tried to console my Shmul. Poor fellow! He was pacing in a disturbed manner up and down and kept silent. But when they said to him, "The rebbe can do everything! Wait and see—he'll lock up your wife's womb for good," he began weeping loudly.

"God protect me against that!" he sobbed. "My father and my father-in-law will beat me so that not a bone will remain whole in my body." And then he started to tell them what his misfortune really was.

At first they cursed me, but when they laid off they began to wonder about my gift for inventing stories. One exclaimed, "On my word of honor, I could have sworn that I myself had seen in the flesh the children he described."

"*Nu*," said I, "my name isn't 'The Poyatz'[1] for nothing!"

"What! Are you the wagoner from Barnow!" they cried. "Are you Rosele's 'Poyatz'? We've heard a lot about you and now you've got to tell us more."

So I related to them my stories, and everybody laughed so heartily that the tears ran down their cheeks. It was on that very night that I heard for the first time the word which for me became the most important, the only word, in my whole life.

Do you want to know what that word was?

Theater!

It was uttered by a man in Sadagora, one they called *meshumed,* apostate, because he was said to have read many German books. "God!" he cried. "What a pity that this fellow should remain a wagoner!"

I laughed. "For my part I'd rather be a prince or a wonder-rebbe!"

"I know something you could be that you'd find even more satisfactory," he answered. "And that is a comedian."

"What's that?" I asked.

"What! You don't know what a comedian is? That's what they call people who play the part of fools in the theater and who make you laugh."

"What's a theater?" I asked.

"It's hard to imagine how backward these Poles are!" he exclaimed in amazement. "Let me explain. Men and women get together in a company, they hire a hall, make up their faces, put on comical-looking clothes and piece together a sort of story, just the kind you cooked up for us before—everything is a lie, not one syllable of truth in it, but so long as you listen to it you believe that it's true and you either laugh or cry. The other people, though, pay down money so that they may look and listen to them."

"And what does the comedian do in the daytime?" I asked.

[1] *In Yiddish—"a clown," derived from the Italian word* bajazzo.

"Nothing! He smokes cigars and is a grand gentleman because he earns enough in the evening."

"That I don't believe," I said.

"Ha, ha, ha!" laughed the Jews of Sadagora. "Listen to him—he doesn't believe! If you like, go to Czernowitz—it's less than a mile away. There you'll find a theater."

"That's what I'm going to do," I replied.

I must say, though, that at the moment I didn't take the matter too seriously. But when I was alone with Shmul in our room at the inn I found I couldn't fall asleep. The thought about the theater was tormenting me. It was just the sort of existence I had always dreamed about: to travel about, to observe people, to learn about their foolishnesses, and then to portray them before audiences. And when it occurred to me that from such pleasure one could live prosperously, I got hot and cold all over. I tossed restlessly about all night long. First towards morning did I manage to fall asleep.

Later we went to the rebbe, and without much talk we agreed short and sweet that he, the rebbe, was to receive from us thirty gulden and in return Shmul was to receive his blessings. Sure enough, at first he demanded fifty gulden but I threatened: "In that case we'll go to the rebbe in Nadworna. He'll gladly take twenty, although his blessings are for twins!" When the rebbe heard such plain speech he quickly agreed to my offer.

As we left Sadagora I turned my wagon to the left in the direction of Czernowitz.

Shmul noticed nothing until we had crossed the Pruth Bridge and entered the Wassergasse, which lies in the suburbs. Then he started to yell that he had no business in the unholy city in which Jews talked High German and ate pig's flesh.

"If that's the way you feel about it," I said calmly, "then get off my wagon and hire yourself another."

Naturally, this only made him hang on to me the more, and we ascended the hill into the city.

In a clearing on the street I saw a tent standing. Before it stood a man dressed in a tight garment made of yellow canvas, so that from a distance he looked naked. He blew on a trumpet and yelled:

"Come in—come on in!"

And the crowd that gathered round him laughed.

"Is that one a comedian?" I asked not a little worried, for I noticed a starved look in his face.

"Yes," a boy answered me.

"Is this the theater?"

"Oh no!" he laughed. "The theater is at the Hotel Moldavia. Here they dance on a rope . . . there are three monkeys inside, too!"

"God be praised!" I thought and asked for the directions to the hotel. Opposite the hotel, before a small Jewish inn, I drew up my wagon and ran across right away.

"The theater is on the first floor," I was told, "but it won't be open until six o'clock."

"Can you please show me some comedians?" I asked the waiter, who looked like a Jew to me, but he was so comically dressed in a black duster jacket with two tails behind.

"What for?" he asked me.

I didn't feel like explaining and repeated my request, but he kept on asking, "What for?"

Losing my patience I blurted out, "Because I want to become a comedian!"

The fellow shook with laughter and, taking hold of my *payyes,* he said, "If you want the Herr Direktor to see you you'd better curl these a little prettier."

At this juncture in stalked a long "Deitch" in modern dress and turned to mount the stairs.

"Herr Direktor!" the waiter called after him. "Here's a new member for your company." Then he proceeded to tell him about my ambition.

The "Deitch" looked me over. He had a terrifying face, pale, frightfully emaciated and smoothly shaved so that his complexion appeared to be half yellow and half blue. His nose was immense and his eyes were piercing. And to all that his face twitched.

When he asked me, "Is that true?" I didn't get frightened, but answered calmly, "Yes," and I told him everything.

The waiter laughed all the time like one possessed, but the Herr Direktor remained grave and finally said to me, "Come along!"

He led me into a room on the first floor. There sat a fat woman rubbing white make-up into her face.

"Eulalia!" said he to her, "I would like you to listen."

And to me he said, "Show us what made you earn the name of 'Poyatz.' "

I mustered all my courage and began to let loose on them my comic antics and wisecracks, one after another. The gentleman looked at the lady, the lady at the gentleman. Unlike others who listened to my carryings on they didn't laugh, but I saw that they were pleased.

"Enough!" said the gentleman at last and started talking with the lady. But it was in High German, and on top of that they spoke very fast so I understood very little what they said.

Finally the gentleman asked me, "What do you think, lad—have you got any talent?"

At that time I didn't understand what he was talking about. I thought he was perhaps asking me whether I had a *tallis*.

"No!" I answered, "but when I get married my bride will have to make me a present of one."

They listened to me bewildered, then they burst out laughing. "I meant," the gentleman explained, "whether you think that you are cut out to be a comedian?"

"Naturally," I answered. "Who—me? Believe me, sir, there has never been anybody who has been cut out for a comedian better than I."

"We'll find out soon enough," he smirked. "Here's a ticket for tonight's performance. After the show meet me in the hotel dining room."

I asked the Herr Direktor for another ticket for my Shmul and, thanking him nicely, I ran like a crazy fellow down the stairs, and then to my inn.

I found Shmul drenched in tears; the poor child was scared to death finding himself alone in the strange city. When I told him that he was to come with me that evening to the theater he wept still more. That was a wicked pleasure, a sin, he said, and he was not going with me. He wanted us to return home that very moment.

"Very well," said I, "you can remain at home if you like. But to hitch our horses right away—not in a million years!"

How can I describe my state of mind? It was as if someone had made me a gift of a thousand gulden, or as if I had drunk too much wine.

So I paced up and down alone before the Hotel Moldavia until it grew dark. My heart beat as if it was ready to burst.

At last they let me into the hall; I was the first to enter. I wanted to take a seat right in the front row but I was made to sit on a bench somewhere in the middle. As soon as they lit the candles I saw how the hall was arranged. But it hardly surprised me. It was almost like in our synagogue: downstairs were the benches for the menfolk, upstairs were two galleries for the womenfolk. Before me hung a large curtain just like in *shul* before the Ark of the Torah, but on it, instead of the Hebrew word for East, *Mizrach,* being embroidered, there were painted on it naked babies climbing one on top of the other.

Later on, when the audience began to arrive, I noticed that after all there was a very great difference between the theater and the synagogue. First of all, all the people consisted of "fine Germans." Second of all, the men went·up to the galleries where the women sat and the women came down to sit with the men. Then suddenly they began to play music in front of the curtain. It was quite lively, just like a dance. But I was in no dancing mood. I was glad, of course, but at the same time I felt frightfully anxious.

At last the curtain rolled up. Amazing! It looked as if it was moving by itself. You couldn't see anyone lifting it.

"Ah, a street!" I exclaimed so loudly that the people around me turned to look at me and laughed. It looked to me like a real street with real houses, a tower, and a bridge.

Suddenly three men came out, all dressed in black, with painted faces and large false whiskers.

They started talking. I only understood that much, that they were good friends and that the conversation was about business. One of the three was certainly the most eminent for he wore a fur coat and the others danced around him. Anton was his name, the same as my friend's, the coachman to the district police officer. This Anton fellow kept clicking his tongue all the time and wagging his head just as if he were very sad.

Then there appeared several other friends, among them a young man with a blond beard who wanted to borrow money from Anton. This brought out the reason why Anton was so sad: he himself had no money and had to borrow some.

Everybody now went out and the city all of a sudden began to wobble and then slid upwards. Now I saw that everything was merely painted on canvas. Instead of the city there appeared quite a lovely room in which were two beautiful girls talking to each other.

Naturally, about what do girls talk? They talked about getting married. But not a single fellow pleased the older one, everyone she made fun of. That one was too gay and the other was too sad and this one was too clever and still another was too stupid. She talked exactly like *Panna* Valeria, the daughter of the steward of Kopeczynce. "Look out there," I thought, "or you'll have the same end as she and remain an old maid. Of course, you're beautiful, but beauty, you know, doesn't last forever." And right in the middle of their talk what should they do but run outside! The room vanished, and again the city.

The blond one then appeared with an old Jew. I said to myself right away, "Now he's going to ask the Jew to lend him some money."

It was exactly that—he wanted three thousand ducats and wouldn't take one ducat less. And this Anton—he should stand surety for him!

"Rotten fish!" I said to myself. "He, too, 's got no money! If the old Jew weren't a donkey he'd make the proper inquiries concerning this Anton." But then and there Anton himself entered and he, too, started talking into the Jew. Shylock, he called him, because, you know how it is—a Christian cannot get a Jewish name correctly. Very likely the old Jew's name was Shyeh.

But Shyeh refused. "Where's your security?" he asked. "On what grounds should I lend you three thousand ducats?" And then he reproached Anton because he had spat at him before and treated him badly all along.

"God Almighty!" I said to myself. "There's no doubt but this fellow Anton is a Pole! Poles behave like that. But when they need money they come crawling to us and flatter us."

In short, the people talked forwards and backwards and sidewards. I didn't understand everything they said, because not even Shyeh spoke like an honorable Jew, but in a High German which he sang through his nose, and wobbling his head all the time.

I looked at him and couldn't understand why he looked so familiar to me. Suddenly I recognized him. It was the same "Deitch" that I had spoken with that afternoon, but now his face was all smeared up and he was dressed up.

"God in Heaven!" I cried out in my amazement. "It's the Herr Direktor!"

Everybody turned around to look at me and laughed.

"What's there to laugh about?" I asked. "I'm sure it's the Herr Direktor!"

"Pst! Pst!" everybody tried to shush me.

I kept quiet and listened to what Shyeh had further to say.

He was ready to hand over the three thousand ducats, but should Anton fail to pay the money back, then he was to have the right to cut a pound of flesh off him.

"Rotten fish!" I thought again. "What'll Shyeh get out of the pound of flesh? I have no stomach for such businesses. With them one only causes *rishus* to Jews! And then again, the district police officer would never allow that, because he himself is a Christian!"

But Shyeh ran out to fetch the money, and as soon as he disappeared the curtain with the naked babies fell down again and the music began to play.

I figured that it hadn't ended yet so I remained seated. The people around me stared at me, whispered and laughed, but that bothered me very little. An old gentleman sitting next to me asked me, "Is this the first time you are in a theater?"

"How else?" I asked. "Do you think one can visit the theater every day in Barnow?"

"Ah, so you're from Barnow!"

"Yes, my name is Sender, and I work for Simcha the coachman, perhaps you've heard of him?"

"I haven't had the honor," he answered.

"The honor!" I exclaimed. "Everybody knows Simcha, and believe me there's no honor to it."

But just then the curtain began to slide up again.

Again a part of the city. A young lad came along dressed like a fool. He made faces, cracked jokes with everybody, even with his old blind father, and that, believe me, I didn't like a bit. He said that he was Shyeh's servant and heaped curses on him—such a good-for-nothing! Jewish bread he eats well enough and then curses him who gives it to him! But if you think that surprised me you're wrong. Take, for example, Yanko, our Dr. Schlesinger's coachman—he does the same thing exactly!

Then along came Shyeh's daughter, quite a beautiful girl, too, but so corrupt, believe me—God be praised!—no Jewish girl in Barnow was quite as rotten. Imagine! With the servants she makes sport of her own father, but to his face, as soon as Shyeh appears she acts obedient and submissive.

But what do you think she does as soon as he leaves? She dresses up as a boy and robs him of his treasure, and when her Christian lover arrives she runs away with him.

Insult and shame! I was so upset I could have torn them to pieces! When Esther, our rich Moses Freudenthal's daughter, eloped with a hussar, at least she didn't insult her old father and left his money alone.

The people in the theater clapped their hands and shouted, "Very good!" and "Bravo!" But I yelled, "She's no good! She deserves a good beating!" And when the people around me heard this, they laughed loudly.

Once more the city scene began to wobble and again the room with the two jolly girls turned up. This suddenly brought me to and I realized that all I saw and heard was nothing but make-believe.

The girls laughed some more—there were several gentlemen with them this time, among them one with a swarthy complexion—and the talk was about a little casket. And then some more talk about the little casket. I wasn't listening too closely—what did their little casket concern me! I kept on thinking how the story of Shyeh and his daughter would end, and whether she'd return home repentant just like Esther Freudenthal, to die before her father's threshold.

But it turned out quite differently.

First there strolled in two laughing gentlemen and told how Shyeh was running half crazy all over town. Then he himself turned up, pale and haggard, but those rascals only made themselves merry over him. They told him that Anton's business affairs were in a bad way and that he wouldn't be able to repay him the loan. In that case, they asked, would Shyeh really take his pound of flesh?

"Yes," the old man said, and he started talking about Jews and Christians, and how bitterly we are persecuted by the Christians. That struck deep into my marrow and into my innermost heart. Until that moment I hadn't thought any too deeply about us and the Poles and thought that that's the way it had to be. But now my eyes were opened to the bloody injustice we had to suffer. Ach! How wonderfully the old man spoke, what words, and in what a voice! Then he started crying and then he gnashed his teeth. A dead silence fell over everyone in the theater; tears came into the eyes of many a person.

Another Jew now appeared and told Shyeh first about Anton, then about his daughter, so that Shyeh began to tremble with rage. It looked as if he was as much grieved by the loss of his ducats as by the flight of his daughter.

In the beginning it puzzled me very much. But later on I thought, "Money is money, but a girl that runs away from her father, and robs him on top of that, is certainly no daughter!"

For the third time the room with the girls was brought on the stage. This time the blond fellow was with them. He opened a little casket and they made a regular wedding feast out of it.

"Mazl tov!" I said. "But how does that concern me?"

At last the curtain slid up again. Shyeh and Anton were standing before a judge. I never before had listened so hard as I did then, so that I haven't forgotten it to this day. Also to this day I'm not sure who was right and who was wrong. It's my opinion that both the Jew and the Christian were right and wrong at the same time.

Really a remarkable story!

Shyeh spoke first: "Anton gave me his signature on this note in which he agreed that I am to cut off him a pound of flesh if he doesn't pay up. I now insist on my rights!"

The judge was an old fellow with a paunch, and quite a dumbbell, may it not be said of another! He didn't trust himself to do any talking and so he sent for an old lawyer. But there also came a young lawyer with a thin high-pitched voice, and when I looked close at him, I saw that it was a woman! Were my eyes fooling me? It was the taller one of the two jolly girls in the room!

She began: "Shyeh is right, but I think he should show mercy."

But Shyeh didn't want to lose his money, to be aggravated and mistreated, and then to show mercy to those that did it to him! That was a little too much!

"Right's on his side!" I thought. But right then and there the blond one, Anton's friend, offered to pay Shyeh the three thousand ducats. Then he doubled the sum, and ended by tripling it. Still Shyeh insisted on his pound of flesh and would take no other payment.

That I didn't like at all! After all, wasn't he getting his money back, even three times as much, so what good would he get out of Anton's death? They all pleaded with him: a human being shouldn't be so unforgiving. I smelled something not so good in this. First of all, it was quite detestable on Shyeh's part, and then again what sort of conduct was it for a Jew standing in a Christian courtroom! Unfortunately, we Jews in Poland know what that means!

"Right!" the girl lawyer admitted finally. "Shyeh is entitled to his pound of flesh, but should he spill one drop of blood while he cuts it out of Anton, then his whole fortune should be declared forfeit."

Now that's what I call a head—a head of iron!

I was very curious to find out what Shyeh was going to do now. I imagined him saying, "Very well, do what you like with my fortune but I insist on my rights." It seemed to me that that was the fitting thing for him to say, since he was such a hardhearted fellow. So what do you think he does? He says, "Now I am ready to take triple the amount I loaned Anton!"

But they wouldn't even give him the three thousand! And at this point began the unjust conduct of the Christians, and it didn't even seem to come to an end. Listen to what the girl-lawyer said: "Because you plotted against the life of a Christian, therefore you yourself should die!"

Plotted against a Christian life! Why then did Anton sign the note? Why did the Court admit the legality of such a note in the first place? Now suddenly they got a bright idea!

Shyeh twisted and squirmed but it didn't help him any. It ended this way: they gave him his life on condition that he turned Christian and gave half of his fortune to Anton.

Really, a very convenient arrangement! Borrow three thousand ducats, don't pay it back, and for this great effort be rewarded perhaps with twenty times the amount!

And what about Shyeh?

Shyeh consented and turned meshumed!

I didn't trust my own eyes and ears any more. I jumped up and clenched my fists.

"What an injustice!" I shouted. "I can't look on any more!"

To my luck the curtain came down just then and everybody got up to leave, otherwise it would perhaps have gone very badly for me. I dashed down the stairs before everyone else and started pacing up and down before the hotel.

I felt I was getting feverish; my teeth started chattering. That excited I had never been before.

"Good God!" I said to myself, "what wouldn't I give to be able to play the role of Shyeh!" But in those days I behaved quite differently than I do now—it was all or nothing!

Only Shyeh struck my fancy. I wouldn't be that Anton for anything! Even less, the blond one! Had I to play their parts I'd do them differently than those "Germans." Anton, for instance, had the same expression on his face all the time, when he stood in danger of his life as well as when he was saved from that danger. Or take the blond fellow, always jolly, even when his friend was in danger!

"Bad clowns—both of them!" I thought. "And I'm going to tell that to the Herr Direktor, too!"

I then made my way to the hotel dining room.

It was quite crowded. At last I caught sight of him at a large table among many ladies and gentlemen, the fat one sitting next to him. He must have already told them all about me because as soon as I came up to him he said, "Look—here he is! The youngest son of the Muses!"

I was very much astonished.

"I beg your pardon," said I, "but my mother has an only son, and her name is Rosel and not Muses; she runs the customs house in Barnow."

Everybody laughed. Then the Herr Direktor asked me, "Well, how did you like the performance?"

"Good and bad," I answered. "There's one thing, though, I'd like you to tell me, and that right away: are you or are you not a Jew-hater?"

"Why?" he asked joking.

"Because I don't know you so well. If you're really a Jew-hater, then what made you speak so beautifully about the injustice done to us Jews by the Poles? And if you aren't a Jew-hater, why did you behave the way you did in the end, first so hardhearted and then so cowardly? Do you know what people are going to say? That all Jews are like that!"

"My dear fellow," he answered, "that's the way the poet wrote it!"

"Who?" I asked, not understanding.

"You know, the man who thought up everything and wrote down the words."

"Don't you make up the play out of your own head?" I asked him very much surprised. "That's what I and all other Jews do with our *Purim* plays!"

"No," said he, and went on to explain it to me.

"Very good," said I, "but surely you must be acquainted with the poet! What I want to know is whether he's a friend of the Jews or isn't he?"

Everybody roared with laughter, but not the Herr Direktor.

"He's been dead three hundred years," said he seriously, "but I can answer your question well enough. He was a noble, great man, therefore he could recognize the injustice done to the Jews. But in his day Jews were everywhere hated as much as they are hated in your Poland today. Therefore, he tried to please his audiences and ended the play in such a way that the Jew was despised and jeered at."

"In that case, why don't you improve the ending?"

"God forbid!" said the Herr Direktor. "I know someday you'll understand what a sin that would be. But do tell me, how did you like the play?"

"Parts I liked and parts I didn't," I replied, and then went on to talk about Shyeh, about Anton, and about that other fellow.

At first they all laughed at me, and everybody else in the dining room got up to gawk and listen to me. But after a while they decided, "He's not so stupid!" and looked at me and wondered.

Finally the Herr Direktor said to me, "Come to see me tomorrow morning at nine!"

I returned to the inn and found Shmul asleep. I lay down but couldn't shut an eye all night long. At last, when morning came I arose, harnessed the horses, and got into my wagon to call on the Herr Direktor.

I found him over his coffee, dressed in a large red dressing gown. With him was the fat one, her head full of paper curls.

"Listen here!" said he to me, "you don't know it, but I myself am a Jew! Of course, I come from another country, from Prussia. But that isn't the reason why I'll accept you gladly into my company. I'll do so only because you most likely have a great talent for acting. Whether you actually have talent for the stage or not I've no way of knowing as yet. As you are now, no one could tell for sure. But as far as I can judge now, you have a first-rate gift for it, even more than I, more than anyone in my company. If you were older now or were comfortably fixed in life, I probably wouldn't be telling you all this. But since you are a wagoner's apprentice, what have you to lose? That's why, provided you are firm in your mind about becoming an actor, I'd like to act as your adviser and helper."

His kind words brought tears to my eyes.

"Thank you a thousand times!" I wanted to say to him, but I couldn't utter the words. Finally I managed to blurt out, "I'm coming the day after tomorrow and I'm coming to stay!"

"No!" he cried, "the time isn't ripe yet for you to enter our merry but insecure existence! For God's sake, no! Remain where you are for the next two years and learn German—that's most important, to read, write, and speak German. Do you have any chance of learning it in Barnow?"

"If it's got to be, I'll find somebody!" I replied.

"Very good," said the Herr Direktor. "I come here every winter and stay from October until March. But for a period of two years I don't want to see you. If you'd like to write to me I'll be glad to hear from you. My name is Nadler, Adolf Nadler. And now, God be with you!"

"And with you, too, kind gentleman," I murmured as tears came to my eyes. "You'll hear from me!"

And I left him. I returned to the inn, bundled my Shmul into the wagon, and returned with him to Barnow.

> *They praise the dramatist*
> *when he draws tears from his audience,*
> *however, the same talent is exhibited*
> *by the smallest onion.—Heinrich Heine*

THE REAL CUSTOMERS
TOLD BY A PROPRIETOR OF A LITERARY CAFÉ

BY DER LEBEDIGER (CHAIM GUTMAN)
TRANSLATED FROM THE YIDDISH BY NATHAN AUSUBEL

Do you want to know something: if you're ever fated to go into the café business, if it is written in the stars that you should be a restaurateur, in that case may God preserve you from falling into the hands of those writing fellows! May a good Providence protect and save you from the clutches of the Hebraists, the Yiddish *intelligentsia,* and the Yiddish poets!

Were you to judge only by the looks of things you'd think I was being drenched under a shower of gold, that I was on the way of becoming a bit of a Rockefeller!

What else could one think? The café is always crowded, always packed tight with customers like a Brownsville streetcar during rush hours. People literally sit one on top of the other and pressed against each other. The place is foul with smoke all the time, like a tavern in the old country. Some even carry on fiery debates standing up. In one word: it is so crowded there's not even an empty place to stick a needle into.

But all that is of no great matter compared to my other troubles. To tell you the truth, I'm hardly doing any business. Customers I have plenty, but I make very little on them. That is, they patronize me all right, but not with orders, only with "hours." Have you any idea what sort of business that is? You'll soon hear. When I tell you that they patronize me with "hours" I don't mean it as a joke. That's a fact! That's what ninety-nine out a hundred of my customers do.

One favors me with two hours a day, another with three, and a third with four, all depending on the customer. Why, I even have customers who patronize me twenty-four hours a day!

Ai, you'll ask, and what about eating? Yeh, I want to tell you *takkeh* about eating!

This is the way it works out: some eat at home, others who are boarders eat at their landladies on account, but in my place most of the customers eat nothing, or at least next to nothing. Every once in a while someone orders a glass of coffee and then waits for a "philan-thropist" to drop in and pay for it. A lot of my customers will take the glass of coffee only when someone is standing treat. But the greatest number sit around reading the papers, smoking "yenem's"[1] cigarettes, discussing everything under the sun, and gushing jokes like a fountain.

As to what I told you about their eating elsewhere, one of my oldest customers is a young Yiddish poet. He patronizes me on an average of ten hours a day, and this is his usual routine: He comes into my café quite early, sits around until lunchtime, and then suddenly he calls over the waiter. "Say waiter!" he orders, "see that no one sits down in my chair! I am just going over to my landlady for a glass of coffee and I'll be right back!" And all this he says with the careless air of a man who signs at least two or three hundred checks every day. And he repeats this order for the second time toward evening before leaving for his landlady's to get his dinner.

Don't laugh! You haven't heard anything yet!

There's another poet, and he comes here only for one purpose— to telephone his lady friend. But since he never happens to have a nickel on him, he asks me to lend him one—that is, one every day.

One writer comes in only in order to fill his pockets with toothpicks. He says that such refined and elegant toothpicks he can get in my café are not to be found anywhere else. Another writer does all his reading and corrects his manuscripts here, and a third comes in regularly to pick up his mail because he has no permanent address.

But hold on a moment, you haven't heard anything yet! There's a certain fellow who comes in regularly; I don't know what he does for a living, but he hangs around the Yiddish newspapers. He's always carrying a pack of papers under his arm and from that, so it seems, he makes a living.

Well, this fellow comes into my café every single day. To eat, you'd expect surely. Hell, no! He comes in to faint! Now don't think I'm joking. I mean just what I say: he comes in to do just that—to faint! That's his habit. And don't make the mistake of thinking that he is a customer of mine! God forbid! When it has to do with eating he eats in another restaurant, where they serve a fifteen-cent table d'hôte lunch, but when it has to do with fainting he comes down to my place.

The first day he fainted there was such excitement in my restaurant you'd think it was after an earthquake. My wife and I were simply numb with fright. You can easily understand the way we felt. When

---

[1]*There are two kinds of cigarettes: your own and* yenem's. *Yenem's is the Yiddish for "the other fellow's."* ED.

a person faints inside a restaurant, do you think it's good for the restaurant's reputation? What can the customers think? That the poor fellow faints because the food was rotten and gave him acute indigestion. What else? Although I personally know from experience that poets don't faint from eating, they only faint to eat!

When we brought him to at last, I asked him, "Mr. Foigelson, what in God's name did you eat here that it should have made you faint?"

"To tell you the truth," he mumbled, "I didn't eat anything here."

So my wife and I opened up on him, but real good:

"Gevalt! Murderer! When it comes to eating you eat elsewhere but when it has to do with fainting you faint here! What do you think this place is anyway—a fainting parlor? A drugstore? A synagogue on a fast day? Where's your sense of fairness?"

So Foigelson aswered, "That's something I can't help! I've got to faint in your café because my crowd's here, and besides it's more comfortable!"

By this time we've already gotten used to him. His fainting makes as much of an impression on us as if a chair were to keel over. If the fellow wants to faint, let him faint! That's his pleasure! In fact, it has become quite an attraction. Everybody knows already that almost every day Mr. Foigelson comes into my café to faint and that we've got to shove ammonia drops under his nose and pour water on him.

What can I do? That's the sort of business it is!

Ai! So you'll surely ask me: how do I make a living? So I'm going to throw the question right back at you: how do I make a living?

Well, let me answer you: all in all it's a rotten sort of life. Believe me, I've plenty of *tzoress,* but I manage to poke through somehow. It sometimes happens that a stranger passes by and drops in for a regular dinner. And sometimes it's even a *goy!* You may not believe it after what I've told you, but it does happen sometimes. And the fact that I'm alive is proof of it!

THE NEO-HEBREW POET

BY ISRAEL ZANGWILL

He came through the open street door, knocked perfunctorily at the door of the room, opened it and then kissed the *Mezuzah* outside the door. Then he advanced, snatched the *Rebbitzin's* hand away from the handle of the coffee-pot and kissed it with equal devotion. He then seized upon Hannah's hand and pressed his grimy lips to that, murmuring in German:

"Thou lookest so charming this morning, like the roses of Carmel." Next he bent down and pressed his lips to the Reb's coat-tail. Finally he said: "Good morning, sir," to Levi, who replied very affably, "Good morning, Mr. Pinchas." "Peace be unto you, Pinchas," said the Reb. "I did not see you in *Shool* this morning, though it was the New Moon."

"No, I went to the Great Shool," said Pinchas in German. "If you do not see me at your place you may be sure I'm somewhere else. Any one who has lived so long as I in the Land of Israel cannot bear to pray without a quorum. In the Holy Land I used to learn for an hour in the *Shool* every morning before the service began. But I am not here to talk about myself. I come to ask you to do me the honor to accept a copy of my new volume of poems: *Metatoron's Flames.* Is it not a beautiful title? When Enoch was taken up to heaven while yet alive, he was converted to flames of fire and became Metatoron, the great spirit of the *Cabalah.* So am I rapt up into the heaven of lyrical poetry and I become all fire and flame and light."

The poet was a slim, dark little man, with long, matted black hair. His face was hatchet-shaped and not unlike an Aztec's. The eyes were informed by an eager brilliance. He had a heap of little paper-covered books in one hand and an extinct cigar in the other. He placed the books upon the breakfast table.

"At last," he said. "See, I have got it printed—the great work which this ignorant English Judaism has left to moulder while it pays its stupid reverends thousands a year for wearing white ties."

"And who paid for it now, Mr. Pinchas?" said the Rebbitzin.

"Who? Wh-o-o?" stammered Melchitsedek. "Who but myself?"

"But you say you are blood-poor."

"True as the Law of Moses! But I have written articles for the jargon[1] papers. They jump at me—there is not a man on the staff of them all who has the pen of a ready writer. I can't get any money out of them, my dear Rebbitzin, else I shouldn't be without breakfast this morning, but the proprietor of the largest of them is also a printer, and he has printed my little book in return. But I don't think I shall fill my stomach with the sales. Oh! the Holy One, blessed be He, bless you, Rebbitzin, of course I'll take a cup of coffee; I don't know any

[1]*Yiddish.*

one else who makes coffee with such a sweet savor; it would do for a spice offering when the Almighty restores us our Temple. You are a happy mortal, Rabbi. You will permit that I seat myself at the table?"

Without awaiting permission he pushed a chair between Levi and Hannah and sat down; then he got up again and washed his hands and helped himself to a spare egg.

"Here is your copy, Reb Shemuel," he went on after an interval. "You see it is dedicated generally:

To the Pillars of English Judaism.

They are a set of donkey-heads, but one must give them a chance of rising to higher things. It is true that not one of them understands Hebrew, not even the Chief Rabbi, to whom courtesy made me send a copy. Perhaps he will be able to read my poems with a dictionary; he certainly can't write Hebrew with out two grammatical blunders to every word. No, no, don't defend him, Reb Shemuel, because you're under him. He ought to be under you—only he expresses his ignorance in English and the fools think to talk nonsense in good English is to be qualified for the Rabbinate."

The remark touched the Rabbi in a tender place. It was the one worry of his life, the consciousness that persons in high quarters disapproved of him as a force impeding the anglicization of the ghetto. He knew his shortcomings, but could never quite comprehend the importance of becoming English. He had a latent feeling that Judaism had flourished before England was invented, and so the poet's remark was secretly pleasing to him.

"You know very well," went on Pinchas, "that I and you are the only two persons in London who can write correct Holy Language."

"No, no," said the Rabbi, deprecatingly.

"Yes, yes," said Pinchas, emphatically. "You can write quite as well as I. But just cast your eye now on the especial dedication which I have written to you in my own autograph. 'To the light of his generation, the great Gaon, whose excellency reaches to the ends of the earth, from whose lips all the people of the Lord seek knowledge, the never-failing well, the mighty eagle soars to heaven on the wings of understanding, to Rav Shemuel, may whose light never be dimmed, and in whose day may the Redeemer come unto Zion.' There, take it, honor me by taking it. It is the homage of the man of genius to the man of learning, the humble offering of the one Hebrew scholar in England to the other."

"Thank you," said the old Rabbi, much moved. "It is too handsome of you, and I shall read it at once and treasure it amongst my dearest books, for you know well that I consider that you have the truest poetic gift of any son of Israel since Jehuda Halevi."

"I have! I know it! I feel it! It burns me. The sorrow of our race keeps me awake at night—the national hopes tingle like electricity through me—I bedew my couch with tears in the darkness"—Pinchas paused to take another slice of bread and butter. "It is then that my poems are born. The words burst into music in my head and I sing like Isaiah the restoration of our land, and become the poet patriot of my people. But these English! They care only to make money and to stuff it down the throats of gorging reverends. My scholarship, my poetry, my divine dreams—what are these to a besotted, brutal congregation of Men-of-the-Earth? I sent Buckledorf, the rich banker, a copy of my little book, with a special dedication written in my own autograph in German, so that he might understand it. And what did he send me? A beggarly five shillings! Five shillings to the one poet in whom the heavenly fire lives! How can the heavenly fire live on five shillings? I had almost a mind to send it back. And then there was Gideon, the member of Parliament. I made one of the poems an acrostic on his name, so that he might be handed down to posterity. There, that's the one. No, the one on the page you were just looking at. Yes, that's it, beginning:

> 'Great leader of our Israel's host,
> I sing thy high heroic deeds,
> Divinely gifted learned man.'

"I wrote his dedication in English, for he understands neither Hebrew nor German, the miserable, purse-proud, vanity-eaten Man-of-the-Earth."

"Why, didn't he give you anything at all?" said the Reb.

"Worse! He sent me back the book. But I'll be revenged on him. I'll take the acrostic out of the next edition and let him rot in oblivion. I have been all over the world to every great city where Jews congregate. In Russia, in Turkey, in Germany, in Roumania, in Greece, in Morocco, in Palestine. Everywhere the greatest rabbis have leaped like harts on the mountains with joy at my coming. They have fed and clothed me like a prince. I have preached at the synagogues, and everywhere people have said it was like the Wilna Gaon come again. From the neighboring villages for miles and miles the pious have come to be blessed by me. Look at my testimonials from all the greatest saints and savants. But in England—in England alone—what is my welcome? Do they say: 'Welcome, Melchitsedek Pinchas, welcome as the bridegroom to the bride when the long day is done and the feast is o'er; welcome to you, with the torch of your genius, with the burden of your learning that is rich with the whole wealth of Hebrew literature in all ages and countries. Here we have no great and wise men. Our Chief Rabbi is an idiot. Come thou and be our Chief Rabbi?' Do they say this? No! They greet me with scorn, coldness, slander. As for the Rev. Elkan Benjamin, who makes such a fuss of himself because he sends a wealthy congregation to sleep with his sermons, I'll expose him as sure as there's a Guardian of Israel. I'll let the world know about his four mistresses."

"Nonsense! Guard yourself against the evil tongue," said the Reb. "How do you know he has?"

"It's the Law of Moses," said the little poet. "True as I stand here. You ask Jacob Hermann. It was he who told me about it. Jacob Hermann said to me one day: 'That Benjamin has a mistress for every fringe of his four-corners.' And how many is that, eh? I do not know why he should be allowed to slander me and I not be allowed to tell the truth about him. One day I will shoot him. You know he said that when I first came to London I joined the *Meshumadim* in Palestine Place."

"Well, he had at least some foundation for that," said Reb Shemuel.

"Foundation! Do you call that foundation—because I lived there for a week, hunting out their customs and their ways of ensnaring the souls of our brethren, so that I might write about them one day? Have I not already told you not a morsel of their food passed my lips and that the money which I had to take so as not to excite suspicion I distributed in charity among the poor Jews? Why not? From pigs we take bristles."

"Still, you must remember that if you had not been such a saint and such a great poet, I might myself have believed that you sold your soul for money to escape starvation. I know how these devils set their baits for the helpless immigrant, offering bread in return for a lip-conversion. They are grown so cunning now—they print their hellish appeals in Hebrew, knowing we reverence the Holy Tongue."

"Yes, the ordinary Man-of-the-Earth believes everything that's in Hebrew. That was the mistake of the Apostles—to write in Greek. But then they, too, were such Men-of-the-Earth."

"I wonder who writes such good Hebrew for the missionaries," said Reb Shemuel.

"I wonder," gurgled Pinchas, deep in his coffee.

"But, father," asked Hannah, "don't you believe any Jew ever really believes in Christianity?"

"How is it possible?" answered Reb Shemuel. "A Jew who has the Law from Sinai, the Law that will never be changed, to whom God has given a sensible religion and common-sense, how can such a person believe in the farrago of nonsense that makes up the worship of the Christians! No Jew has ever apostatized except to fill his purse or his stomach or to avoid persecution. 'Getting grace' they call it in English; but with poor Jews it is always grace after meals. Look at the Crypto-Jews, the Marranos, who for centuries lived a double life, outwardly Christians, but handing down secretly from generation to generation the faith, the traditions, the observances of Judaism."

"Yes, no Jew was ever fool enough to turn Christian unless he was a clever man," said the poet paradoxically. "Have you not, my sweet, innocent young lady, heard the story of the two Jews in Burgos Cathedral?"

"No, what is it?" said Levi, eagerly.

"Well, pass my cup up to your highly superior mother who is waiting to fill it with coffee. Your eminent father knows the story—I can see by the twinkle in his learned eye."

"Yes, that story has a beard," said the Reb.

"Two Spanish Jews," said the poet, addressing himself deferentially to Levi, "who had got grace were waiting to be baptized at Burgos Cathedral. There was a great throng of Catholics and a special Cardinal was coming to conduct the ceremony, for their conversion was a great triumph. But the Cardinal was late and the Jews fumed and fretted at the delay. The shadows of evening were falling on vault and transept. At last one turned to the other and said, 'Knowest thou what, Moses? If the Holy Father does not arrive soon, we shall be too late to say *mincha*.'"

Levi laughed heartily; the reference to the Jewish afternoon prayer went home to him.

"That story sums up in a nutshell the whole history of the great movement for the conversion of the Jews. We dip ourselves in baptismal water and wipe ourselves with a *Talith*. We are not a race to be lured out of the fixed feelings of countless centuries by the empty spirituality of a religion in which, as I soon found out when I lived among the soul-dealers, its very professors no longer believe. We are too fond of solid things," said the poet, upon whom a good breakfast was beginning to produce a soothing materialistic effect. "Do you know that anecdote about the two Jews in the Transvaal?" Pinchas went on. "That's a real *Chine*."

"I don't think I know that *Maaseh*," said Reb Shemuel.

"Oh, the two Jews had made a *trek* and were travelling onwards exploring unknown country. One night they were sitting by their camp-fire playing cards when suddenly one threw up his cards, tore his hair and beat his breast in terrible agony. 'What's the matter?' cried the other. 'Woe, woe,' said the first. 'To-day was the Day of Atonement! and we have eaten and gone on as usual.' 'Oh, don't take on so,' said his friend. 'After all, Heaven will take into consideration that we lost count of the Jewish calendar and didn't mean to be so wicked. And we can make up for it by fasting to-morrow.'

" 'Oh, no! Not for me,' said the first. 'To-day was the Day of Atonement.' "

All laughed, the Reb appreciating most keenly the sly dig at his race. He had a kindly sense of human frailty. Jews are very fond of telling stories against themselves—for their sense of humor is too strong not to be aware of their own foibles—but they tell them with closed doors, and resent them from the outside. They chastise themselves because they love themselves, as members of the same family insult one another. The secret is, that insiders understand the limitations of the criticism, which outsiders are apt to take in bulk. No race in the world possesses a richer anecdotal lore than the Jews—such pawky, even blasphemous humor, not understandable of the heathen, and to a suspicious mind Pinchas's overflowing cornucopia of such would have suggested a prior period of Continental wandering from town to town, like the *Minnesingers* of the middle ages, repaying the hospitality of his Jewish entertainers with a budget of good stories and gossip from the scenes of his pilgrimages.

"Do you know the story?" he went on, encouraged by Simcha's smiling face, "of the old Reb and the *Havdolah*? His wife left town for a few days and when she returned the Reb took out a bottle of wine, poured some into the consecration cup and began to recite the blessing. 'What art thou doing?' demanded his wife in amaze. 'I am making Havdolah,' replied the Reb. 'But it is not the conclusion of a festival to-night,' she said. 'Oh, yes, it is,' he answered. 'My festival's over. You've come back.' "

The Reb laughed so much over this story that Simcha's brow grew as the solid Egyptian darkness, and Pinchas perceived he had made a mistake.

"But listen to the end," he said with a creditable impromptu.

"The wife said—'No, you're mistaken. Your festival's only beginning. You get no supper. It's the commencement of the Day of Atonement.' "

Simcha's brow cleared and the Reb laughed heartily.

"But I don't see the point, father," said Levi.

"Point! Listen, my son. First of all he was to have a Day of Atonement, beginning with no supper, for his sin of rudeness to his faithful wife. Secondly, dost thou not know that with us the Day of Atonement is called a festival, because we rejoice at the Creator's goodness in giving us the privilege of fasting? That's it, Pinchas, isn't it?"

"Yes, that's the point of the story, and I think the Rebbitzin had the best of it, eh?"

"Rebbitzins always have the last word," said the Reb. "But did I tell you the story of the woman who asked me a question the other day? She brought me a fowl in the morning and said that in cutting open the gizzard she had found a rusty pin which the fowl must have swallowed. She wanted to know whether the fowl might be eaten. It was a very difficult point, for how could you tell whether the pin had in any way contributed to the fowl's death? I searched the *Shass* and a heap of *Shaaloth- u-Tshuvos*. I went and consulted the *Maggid* and Sugarman the *Shadchan* and Mr. Karlkammer, and at last we decided that the fowl was *trifa* and could not be eaten. So the same evening I sent for the woman, and when I told her of our decision she burst into tears and wrung her hands. 'Do not grieve so,' I said, taking compassion upon her, 'I will buy thee another fowl.' But she wept on, uncomforted. 'O woe! woe!' she cried. 'We ate it all up yesterday.' "

Pinchas was convulsed with laughter. Recovering himself, he lit his half-smoked cigar without asking leave.

"I thought it would turn out differently," he said. "Like that story of the peacock. A man had one presented to him, and as this is such rare diet he went to the Reb to ask if it was kosher. The rabbi said 'no' and confiscated the peacock. Later on the man heard that the rabbi had given a banquet at which his peacock was the crowning dish. He went to his rabbi and reproached him. 'I may eat it,' replied the rabbi, 'because my father considers it permitted and we may always go by what some eminent Son of the Law decides. But you unfortunately came to *me* for an opinion, and the permissibility of peacock is a point on which I have always disagreed with my father.' "

Hannah seemed to find peculiar enjoyment in the story.

"Anyhow," concluded Pinchas, "you have a more pious flock than the rabbi of my native place, who, one day, announced to his congregation that he was going to resign. Startled, they sent to him a delegate, who asked, in the name of the congregation, why he was leaving them. 'Because,' answered the rabbi, 'this is the first question any one has ever asked me!' "

"Tell Mr. Pinchas your repartee about the donkey," said Hannah, smiling.

"Oh, no, it's not worth while," said the Reb.

"Thou art always so backward with thine own," cried the Reb-bitzin warmly. "Last Purim an impudent of face sent my husband a donkey made of sugar. My husband had a rabbi baked in gingerbread and sent it in exchange to the donor, with the inscription 'A rabbi sends a rabbi.' "

Reb Shemuel laughed heartily, hearing this afresh at the lips of his wife. But Pinchas was bent double like a convulsive note of interrogation.

The clock on the mantelshelf began to strike nine. Levi jumped to his feet.

"I shall be late for school!" he cried, making for the door.

"Stop! stop!" shouted his father. "Thou hast not yet said grace."

"Oh, yes, I have, father. While you were all telling stories I was *benshing* quietly to myself."

"Is Saul also among the prophets, is Levi also among the storytellers?" murmured Pinchas to himself. Aloud he said: "The child speaks truth; I saw his lips moving."

Levi gave the poet a grateful look, snatched up his satchel and ran off to No. 1 Royal Street. Pinchas followed him soon, inwardly upbraiding Reb Shemuel for meanness. He had only as yet had his breakfast for his book. Perhaps it was Simcha's presence that was to blame. She was the Reb's right hand and he did not care to let her know what his left was doing.

When a man falls into his anecdotage
it is a sign for him to retire.—Benjamin Disraeli

If a Jew can't become a shoemaker
he dreams of becoming a writer.

THE SOUL THAT MICE NIBBLED UP

BY LEON KOBRIN

TRANSLATED FROM THE YIDDISH BY NATHAN AUSUBEL

Whenever I think about the tragic types I've known I invariably recall my former neighbor, Solomon Kovarsky. For several months we lived in adjoining flats in a tenement house on Norfolk Street. A bit of a Hebraist intellectual in the old country, here in New York he worked as a presser on children's coats in a sweatshop.

He was a frequent visitor to my house. He liked coming to see me, he said, in order to "sharpen his mind." At the same time, he also managed to "sharpen" my nerves until I was ready to scream.

Some time between eight and nine in the evening we'd hear a knock on the door.

"Aha!" exclaimed my wife, startled. "It must be the mind-sharpener!"

In he'd walk, looking thin and gawky, his face emaciated and pale and overgrown with a black jungle of a beard. Turning on us his dark dreamy eyes he'd say:

"Good evening."

"Good evening."

He didn't wait to be asked to sit down. Then followed an interminable session of "sharpening" the mind so that my poor wife went to hide herself in the next room. I began to hear a drilling and a hammering in my brain as though I were in a blacksmith shop.

First he'd talk about the most recent debates in the Russian Duma. Then he'd go over to the subject of international politics, where, understandably enough, he said, he felt as comfortable as a fish in water. In his opinion the only real statesmen in the world were Jews: Moses, King Solomon, "Israel" Beaconsfield, and Doctor Herzl. The Gentiles! bah! Whom did they have? They had only one great statesman—Bismarck. But how could he compare to a *Yiddisher kupp,* to an "Israel" Beaconsfield, for instance? Feh! Bismarck was only a *cheder yingel* compared to *our* "Israel" Beaconsfield! He'd pronounce the word "Israel" with such esteem and love as though he were talking of a blood brother.

Having clarified for me all aspects of international politics, he went over to the subject of socialism. He doesn't think much of that either. True, *takkeh* it was a good thing, a just thing, but who was going to wait until they'd get through taking away all the money from the capitalists? Not he! He readily admitted that it was unjust that he, Solomon Kovarsky, who was a bit of a Hebrew scholar, who could write so well and because of that his efforts should have been exclusively devoted to writing books, it was indeed shameful that he should be forced by mean necessity to press children's coats in the sweatshop of that ignoramus, Mr. Kasnebes. But, what could one do about it? When in Rome you must do as the Romans, no? You can't go and fight the whole world!

But don't think Mr. Kovarsky was through yet. He hadn't touched yet on the subject of subjects, I mean literature.

He considers himself a very close relation of literature—heaven forbid, not of the "servant girl," Yiddish literature, but of the "princess" herself, Hebrew literature. On the occasion of the fire in the bathhouse in Tribuchovka, the little village in Russia where he was born, he composed a stirring elegy. He wrote it in Hebrew and in very lofty terms, almost in the language of the Prophet Ezekiel. This elegy, which had been published years before in a modern Hebrew journal, he guarded under lock and key in his dresser drawer together with his marriage license. It was dearer to him than any treasure, even as precious to him as his youngest child, Dvoshinka. He cherished it so, he told me, because it reminded him of those days when he was still daydreaming of becoming a great man in Israel. He always produced it as proof, black on white, with which to silence every shallow skeptic who might think that he, Solomon Kovarsky, was just a mere nobody who was born to be a presser of children's clothes.

At the drop of a hat, he'll produce for you his masterpiece. Even if you are a "goy,"—that is, a Jew who doesn't understand any Hebrew—it won't prove any determent to him. Kovarsky is never too lazy to translate his elegy from the Hebrew into plain Yiddish. And, God forbid, should the elegy translated by the author himself, fail to arouse your enthusiasm, you should know that it is only because the inspired lines have lost their *taam* in translation from the Hebrew of the Prophets into the coarse "servant-girl" language of the Dispersion.

At least twelve times in the course of the several wretched months when we lived next door to each other did he read this elegy to me. Twelve separate times in three months. I had to listen to his moving description how the bathhouse of Tribuchovka went up in flames, how the young women *nebbech* had no place to go to for their purification, and how, on account of that, many marriages were put off.

Each time he read it I listened to him patiently, for I saw how deeply moved he was. His eyes shone with inspiration, his pallid cheeks grew flushed, and his voice trembled from sweet excitement. Who could have the heart to say "no" when he wished to read his article over and over again? I realized that it gave him the greatest pleasure. But, seeing how it was depressing me, my wife was afraid that it might even affect my sanity, so she persuaded me to look for another flat.

We moved into rooms on the next block and I grew a little calmer. True, Kovarsky still came to see us, but very rarely. First of all, he worked until seven and sometimes even until nine o'clock at night, and is it nice to go calling so late, particularly on strangers? When we were next-door neighbors he didn't have to stand on ceremony. If he saw a light under the door, he wouldn't hesitate and knock. And then again it wasn't so easy for him to come to see me now, because his wife Basia wouldn't let him. Not that she was so deeply in love with him or that she looked forward so eagerly for his homecoming, but she needed him for many necessary chores: to fetch a pail of coal from the coalman, to take little Dvoshinka off her hands for a while, to subdue Soshinka, who kept her mouth open all day long and yowled, to undress Berele, who didn't give her a minute's rest, and put him to bed.

Often, when he lived next door he'd show up with his entire brood, with Dvoshinka in his arms and with Soshinka and Berele holding onto his coattails. But ever since we moved he rarely came himself and never brought the children.

But, when he did come sometimes it was an occasion to remember, an occasion for *Shema Yisroel!*—for *Hear O Israel!*

He'd swoop down on us like a starving man who hadn't eaten for days and who all of a sudden saw before his eyes a table spread with all kinds of good things, with fish, meat, potatoes, *chremzlech, knishes,* and many other tasty dishes. And he'd get confused and didn't know where to begin. In the same way, Kovarsky didn't know what to talk about first. He leaped from one subject to another, mashed everything into a stew, and in this way "sharpened" his own mind while he bored into mine like a drill, with his interminable "Israel" Beaconsfield, Bismarck, socialism, Tribuchovka, the modern literary movement in Hebrew, the lamented fire in his village, his elegy, and the postponed marriages.

I finally reached a point in his monologue when I thought my head was going to split wide open!

One evening, I sat absorbed at my desk. I started suddenly at a knock on my door.

"Come in," I called.

It was Kovarsky. But, *tatteniu,* how he looked! His dark jungle of a beard was disheveled, a fright to see. He looked pale and confused, his eyes full of fear and anguish, his clothes in disorder. He came in with outstretched, appealing hands and I saw that they were trembling.

"What on earth has happened to you, Mr. Kovarsky?" I asked him, not a little frightened.

"A misfortune!" he stammered. And he stretched out his hands to me even more appealingly. "A misfortune, just see what they have done!"

I looked at his shaking hands and saw he was holding in his palms a little heap of crumpled, yellow bits of newspaper. I stared and did not know what it was all about.

"What's that?" I asked in bewilderment.

"Do you recall my elegy?" he asked hoarsely, looking piteously at me.

I was now even more bewildered.

"But I read it for you so many times! I'm sure you must remember it. After all, you yourself are a writer!"

"But what has happened, Mr. Kovarsky?"

It suddenly occurred to me that the poor fellow might be out of his mind.

"A misfortune has happened to me," he stammered. "Just look!"

And again he showed me the little heap of crumpled bits of paper that he held cupped in his hand.

"Look what the mice did to my elegy that lay in my dresser drawer! But tell me, please, I beg you—maybe you remember the lines of my elegy?"

At this I almost exploded with laughter and restrained my amusement only with the greatest difficulty.

"No, I'm very sorry I don't remember," I muttered.

"What am I going to do then?" he asked me with a despairing groan. Noticing that I was smiling, he spoke in a grief-stricken voice.

"Yes, I'm sure that to you it looks like only a trifle, but to me it is a memento of that glorious time, the time when . . . *oy vay!* . . . eaten up . . . the soul of my youth eaten up!"

And he heaved a deep sigh.

"But how can it be that you yourself don't remember the text of your elegy?" I asked him.

"Not a word, not a syllable," he muttered despairingly.

He then fell silent, was lost in thought for a while. Finally, he came to as if he had just started up from sleep:

"I know what I'm going to do—I'll go to Yampolsky. I must

have read the elegy to him at least twenty times. He's interested in modern Hebrew literature himself. I'm sure he must remember! *A-a-ch!*"

And with this groan he left me.

EITHER OR—

Sammy Goldstein had left Kansas City to become an actor in New York. By dint of perseverance and going hungry for several years he finally got a part in a play. When the show went on tour it eventually reached Kansas City, his home town.

The opening night was a gala occasion for the Goldstein family. They bought orchestra tickets for themselves and for all their relatives and friends. They sat on pins and needles waiting for the curtain to rise.

At last the play began. The first act passed. No Sammy.

Good God! Where was Sammy?

The second act passed. Still no Sammy!

The curtain rose finally on the third act. No sign of Sammy! Only, towards the end, he appeared dressed up as a soldier, and carrying a rifle. He marched stiffly back and forth, without saying a word.

Mr. Goldstein's heart now filled with bitterness at such humiliating treatment for his son. And, when he saw that the final curtain was about to fall, he lost all control of himself and shouted to his son on the stage:

"Sammy, do something, for God's sake! If they don't let you talk —at least *shoot!*"

THE PHILANTHROPIST

A traveling *chazan* once entered a synagogue on the Sabbath and asked the president of the congregation to let him sing the service. The president, who had never heard him sing, was delighted and invited him to do so.

The chazan placed himself before the Holy Ark and began to sing. He had no voice and he bellowed in an unearthly way. The congregation began to murmur. The president then sent the *gabbai* to ask him to stop singing, because the congregation found it intolerable.

"But I like to sing this way," said the chazan, offended.

"It's no use, my friend, we're not going to pay you."

"What can I do," sighed the chazan. "It's too late to do anything about it. In that case I'm giving my singing as a contribution to the synagogue treasury."

"What do you mean 'give'?" retorted the gabbai, getting angry. "How can a man give what he hasn't got?"

> *You don't have to be big*
> *to be great.—Sholom Aleichem*

MRS. RIVKIN GRAPPLES WITH THE DRAMA

BY ETHEL ROSENBERG

"Frieda," Mrs. Rivkin says, "you're doing something tonight?"

Mrs. Pasternak eyes her sister-in-law suspiciously. "Tonight I'm doing like every night. What's the matter you're asking me?"

Mrs. Rivkin shrugs. "I don't know what the lodge wants from my life." She thrusts two tickets under Mrs. Pasternak's nose. "I could swear this is Fanny Markowitz's work. She knows I never go to those benefits."

"Oh, benefit tickets," Mrs. Pasternak says wisely. "So what is it for tonight, Menasha Skulnick maybe? There is an actor for you." She shakes her head back and forth slowly. *"Ai,* that Menasha Skulnick!"

"What Menasha Skulnick," Mrs. Rivkin scoffs. "You think Fanny Markowitz knows who is who and what is what?" Mrs. Rivkin begins to read the mimeographed sheet which came with the tickets. The notice starts off with a gay greeting to the dear sister, reminds her that at the last Ladies' Aid Society meeting the sisters decided to raise money for a worthy cause ("Does it hurt to enjoy yourself a little while you are raising the money?" one of the sisters had asked. A question! This one made a motion; that one said, "Why not?"; the third one said, "I nominate Sister Goldberg to be on the entertainment committee" . . . already the wheels begin to turn . . .), the dear sister is urged to back up this drive one hundred per cent, enclosed are two tickets for a benefit performance of *A Mother's Heart,* more tickets available through Sister Goldberg, signed Fanny Markowitz, President.

"A Mother's Heart," Mrs. Rivkin says. "Maybe you would like to go with Julius?"

Mrs. Pasternak nods her refusal.

"Julius doesn't need so much excitement. Tonight I want he should rest." Mrs. Pasternak hasn't quite forgiven her husband for last night's escapade with Don Ameche. "Why can't you go with Hannah? You'll enjoy it."

"You saw this show already?" Mrs. Rivkin is very disappointed.

"Last year yet. Is that a story." The series of sighs Mrs. Pasternak sends forth from her inner depths conjures up for her sister-in-law an immediately clear and concise picture of what she may expect to see. "Take my advice, Yetta, go and see it. *Ai,* a mamma's heart, it has to be made from iron to stand from the children."

"From iron," Mrs. Rivkin agrees.

"Small children small troubles, big children big troubles," Mrs. Pasternak says—a philosophic gem which captures Mrs. Rivkin's wholehearted approval.

"You're telling me?" she says.

"Take Hannah with you." Mrs. Pasternak reverts to the benefit. "She'll enjoy it."

Mrs. Rivkin is by no means persuaded, however.

"Aaaah," she says, "I'm not so burned to go. What do I have to waste my time. . . ."

"Waste your time? You'll waste your time to go to see such a fine acting?" Mrs. Pasternak is shocked.

"So it means I have to get all dressed up, and *shlepp* myself on the subway, and come home so late. . . . What do I need it?"

"No is no. I wouldn't talk you into it."

If Mrs. Pasternak will not persuade Mrs. Rivkin to go, Hannah will.

"Why don't you go, Ma?" Hannah asks at the supper table that night.

"Sure. Why not?" her mother scoffs.

"Would it be so terrible if you would go out and enjoy yourself once in a while?"

"You think my money grows on trees?" This is a flimsy excuse, as both Mrs. Rivkin and Hannah are fully aware. The truth of the matter is that Mrs. Rivkin is loath to go simply because Mrs. Markowitz is behind this idea of the benefit. Mrs. Rivkin is feuding with the Lodge president, and if Fanny Markowitz says yea, Mrs. Rivkin will certainly say she should live so long. Still and all, Mrs. Rivkin knows her duty as well as the next one. A donation is a donation. She'll pay for the tickets, but she is positively not going, you hear?

"You can talk from today till tomorrow," Mrs. Rivkin tells Hannah.

"O.K. No is no. I'm not going to argue with you. But how will it look, all the other ladies in the Lodge are going, only Mrs. Rivkin stays home?"

Mrs. Rivkin is suddenly inspired.

"It's a shame to waste the tickets," she agrees. "So why don't you call up Howie, and you and Howie go?"

"To see anything called *A Mother's Heart*? Are you kidding, Ma? No, *thank* you."

"What's the matter?" Mrs. Rivkin's feelings are on the verge of being sorely wounded. Hannah averts the crisis hastily.

"Anyway, Howie is working overtime tonight. Listen, Ma, you could wear your new black dress that you bought for Mollie's wedding. Why should it lay in the closet when you have such a good chance to wear it? At least you could show that Mrs. Markowitz your clothes are just as fancy as hers. . . ."

This is a good point. Believe me, Mrs. Rivkin any time has as nice a dress to wear as that stuck-up Mrs. Markowitz, with her Persian-lamb coat and her silver-fox cape. Just because she's the president. . . .

"Thursday night I should go?" Mrs. Rivkin sniffs, but she is weakening. Hannah is quick to catch the drift.

"Believe me, Ma," she says earnestly, "Eddie Cantor won't fall apart if you miss his program one time. You can wear my silver pin on your coat. Here. Take my new scarf, too."

So off Mrs. Rivkin goes with the other "girls" in her new black dress and sporting Hannah's pin and scarf. Off she goes to Second Avenue, and what a world is then opened to Mrs. Rivkin. What a rich satisfaction to cry, to laugh, to live for a couple of hours! When she comes home, eyes shining, voice raised (even more than usual) in excitement, Hannah knows the stage bug has bitten her mother and she is lost. How lost even Hannah doesn't realize in the beginning. I'm telling you, it is like a fever. At first Mrs. Rivkin goes every two weeks, then once a week, then twice a week. Finally she is there every evening. She even begins to have her suppers out . . . in the theaters. She packs some chicken, sometimes a little leftover gefüllte fish from Friday, a piece of honey cake . . . all that is missing is the tea. She arrives early at the theater. Usually she is the first one there. Now Mrs. Rivkin is not one to loiter in the lobby. Why should she stand on her feet when with God's help she will see her friends inside later? The first thing she does is settle herself comfortably. This involves getting her coat wrapped just so over the back of her seat, her scarf into her coat pocket, her gloves into her purse. Then she opens her paper bag and peers in thoughtfully. This is not because Mrs. Rivkin is ignorant of the bag's contents; it is simply a time for careful decision. Is she in an apple mood? No. This she will save for a *nash* while the action on the stage is more or less routine. A good time to eat the apple, and suck out the juice with gusto, is while the chorus is singing and dancing.

For a time Mrs. Rivkin develops a yearning for salami on rye, the bread should have plenty of mustard. As she sits munching her sandwiches peacefully, a napkin spread on her lap to save her "good" dress, she seems unaware of the aroma spreading its maddening fragrance throughout the theater. But after the manager speaks to her tactfully six or seven times, she goes back to chicken on *chalah,* with some small half-sour pickles on the side. Sometimes Mrs. Rivkin finishes off with an orange, or a piece of sponge cake, but mostly she sticks to her honey *lekuch mit nis.* The leftover peelings and cores she returns carefully to the paper bag. This she will throw into the trash basket on her way to the subway. As you can see, Mrs. Rivkin does not hold with the school of thought advocating chocolate bars.

As the theater fills up, she looks around, taking full measure of all comers. Sometimes she greets a friend, or one of the "sisters" from the Lodge. She doesn't leave her seat; she calls her greeting across the theater. Mrs. Rivkin, you understand, is a cordial woman but hardly a retiring one.

"Ma, shush," Hannah says on the few occasions she goes to the theater with her mother. "They can hear you all over the place."

"Don't shushka me," Mrs. Rivkin says impatiently. "Yoo-hoo, Jacobs. How is your mister?"

"How is my mister?" Jacobs yells back, rocking back and forth a little. "Like always."

"Well, God will help," Mrs. Rivkin comforts her, in full voice.

"Ma, *please,*" Hannah begs.

"I'll talk to you later, Rivkin," Jacobs shouts. "Now is time for the curtain going up."

The lights dim; the electric spark of creation leaps from stage to audience; contact is made; the magic of theater begins. But wait! People are coming down the aisle, looking for their seats. They talk, in whispers, it's true, but still they talk. They get into their seats; they stand up to take off their coats. I'm telling you, it's such a commotion they make Mrs. Rivkin can't contain herself.

"Shah!" she shouts, turning her head to glare angrily in the direction of these noisy late-comers. The word "shah" is like the word "fire"; nothing spreads more quickly.

"Shah!" Others in the theater take up the cry energetically. There is such a tumult of "shahs," and "shushes" from people shushing the shahers, the actors are outnumbered. Finally, with one last sibilant shah from Mrs. Rivkin, the theater is quiet and the actors continue.

But how long do you imagine this quiet lasts? With Mrs. Rivkin completely lost in the action on stage? Is it possible you still don't know Mrs. Rivkin?

"Ruchele," the stage mother sobs, "I beg you to consider what you are doing."

Ruchele replies defiantly, upstage. "I don't care. I'm young, I want to live."

You hear? She's young. She wants to live. *Ai*, Ruchele. This is only Act One. You don't know yet what is going to happen to you. But Mrs. Rivkin knows. She has seen this play four times already, three times in benefit performances. She cannot bear to think of it. In agony she cries out a warning.

"Ruchele," Mrs. Rivkin calls from her seat. "Listen to the Mamma. She knows what she is talking."

Instantly the "shahs" ricochet from the walls. Mrs. Rivkin subsides—temporarily—until the villain appears. He is after Ruchele, you understand, and he'll get her too, the no-good loafer, but why doesn't he tell Ruchele he is already married, so she won't bring disgrace to her father and mother in their old years? So all right. So if he won't tell Ruchele, there is someone else who will.

"Don't listen to him," Mrs. Rivkin cries in anguish. "He is already a father from children."

"I come to listen to you *oder* the actors on the stage?" The man in front of Mrs. Rivkin turns around to ask this acidly.

"Look at him," Mrs. Rivkin says in honest surprise. "Remarks from the balcony all of a sudden."

They are both sitting in the orchestra, but this is how Mrs. Rivkin's logical mind works. Well, a few more words are hurled back and forth, the shahers and shushers leap into action; peace is finally restored when Mrs. Rivkin is permitted to get in the last word, and the plot ponderously moves on. Ruchele won't listen to her mother. She won't listen to Mrs. Rivkin. She moves off stage to her rendezvous with eventual shame. Now it's time for a little singing, a little laughing . . . listen, there's enough trouble in the world. The comedian comes out. One look at him and Mrs. Rivkin is already gasping for breath.

"Oooh, I'm dying," she says, clutching at her handkerchief to dab weakly at the tears of laughter in her eyes. Mrs. Rivkin's laughter, like her voice, is full and resonant, but to this no one takes exception. Everyone in the audience is busy rolling in the aisles himself. Humor rocks the theater. The audience gives all. The comedian gives all. He is a pathetic-looking figure, with his ill-fitting clothes and his big, sad brown eyes. He is also a philosopher, the man who looks upon sorrow and travail and sums it all up in a sentence.

"*Ai*," he sighs, giving it to the audience straight, "*ma zul gornisht da leben tsa shtarbin.*" ("We should none of us live to see ourselves die.")

Mrs. Rivkin enjoys a joke as much as the next one. More, maybe. Because when a joke is being told, and Mrs. Rivkin happens to know it, she can hardly wait for the punch line. Between you and me—listen, what's true is true—Mrs. Rivkin is by nature a point killer. I'll give you a for instance. Let's say the comic relief is now on the stage, a man and a woman.

"Well, Rifka," the man says, "how's by you?"

"Aaaah," Rifka says, "my head hurts me."

"You don't say," the man replies sympathetically.

"And here," Rifka says, warming up, laying her hand rapidly on various parts of her chest and side, "and here and here. I don't know. I have sticking pains."

"Tsk. Tsk. Tsk," he says.

"And you shouldn't know what it is, I sprained my ankle yesterday." She pauses, timing the punch line. She waits a fraction of a second too long.

"And *epus* she herself doesn't feel so good," Mrs. Rivkin shouts in high good humor.

"And like she says," Rifka waves a hand in Mrs. Rivkin's direction. "I myself *epus* don't feel so good."

There is perhaps black murder in Rifka's heart, but Mrs. Rivkin really can't help herself. She knows all the lines. What's more, she enjoys them. What Mrs. Rivkin enjoys, she shares.

The manager of the theater tries to explain to Mrs. Rivkin that while the company appreciates her enthusiasm, still and all, enough is plenty. He knows Mrs. Rivkin very well, by this time. Didn't she talk him into giving her special rates because she is a regular customer?

"Mrs. Rivkin," he says after one show, "be so good and come into my office for a minute."

"It's a pleasure, Mr. Schwartz." Mrs. Rivkin bustles in and makes herself comfortable.

"Mrs. Rivkin," he says.

"Excuse me, Mr. Schwartz. I first now see how you decorated over your office. Very nice. You should use it in good health."

"Thank you. Very nice of you. Mrs. Rivkin," he tries again.

"Altogether the tee-ater is very nice decorated," Mrs. Rivkin congratulates him.

"Thank you," Mr. Schwartz says. "What I wanted to say is. . . ."

"For my money," Mrs. Rivkin continues, "not I should make you feel good, this is the nicest tee-ater in the whole Avenue."

"Mrs. Rivkin," the manager says helplessly.

"Also," she pursues, "the finest actors and actorkahs."

Mr. Schwartz bows his head in defeat.

"A very noisy bunch people tonight," Mrs. Rivkin says disapprovingly. "But you are not responsible." She smiles benevolently at him. "There are all kinds people in this world," she tells him. Mr. Schwartz seizes his opportunity.

"Not I should say anything, Mrs. Rivkin, but you weren't so quiet yourself tonight."

"Me?" Mrs. Rivkin stares incredulously. "What are you talking, Mr. Schwartz? I didn't open my mouth once." Mrs. Rivkin is not assuming this attitude. She honestly believes what she is saying.

At this moment a small, excitable man drifts into the office.

"Schwartz," he says angrily, "if I lay my hands on that woman . . . aha!" he says when he catches sight of Mrs. Rivkin. "So!"

"This is Mrs. Rivkin," Schwartz intervenes hastily. "Mrs. Rivkin, I want you should meet Hershel Cohen, our director."

"So, Mrs. Rivkin," Cohen says. "You are the one who insults the orchestra leader."

"Me?" Mrs. Rivkin protests. "How do I insult him?"

"How does she insult him? You hear?" Cohen tears at his hair. "You told him, or not, you don't like how he is leading the orchestra."

"He is also by you an orchestra leader?" Mrs. Rivkin's scorn is unrestrained. "For your information," she tells him, "I know him from the old country yet. He plucked chickens a nickel a chicken, and by you he is an orchestra leader."

Cohen and Schwartz look at each other, raise their eyebrows, shrug their shoulders.

"What has this to do?" Schwartz asks weakly.

"So go tell him," Mrs. Rivkin addresses the air elaborately, "what this has to do."

"Hear me out, Mrs. Rivkin," Cohen says briskly. "I want you should stop making fun from my actors."

"I make fun from the actors?" Mrs. Rivkin says angrily. "Shame on you! The actors and actorkahs from me get the greatest respect."

"Characters," the director rushes on furiously, "we got plenty, and more in the audience than on the stage, if you'll excuse my expression."

"That's a way for a man to talk?" Mrs. Rivkin appeals indignantly to Mr. Schwartz.

"Mrs. Rivkin," Mr. Schwartz interprets Mr. Cohen's speech in a more soothing manner, "the actors if they are all the time interrupted get excited."

Mrs. Rivkin rises majestically.

"I see a person can't open their mouths any more without insults. No," she says to Mr. Schwartz as he attempts to assuage her ruffled feelings, "you don't have to put your finger in my mouth. I know where I'm not wanted."

The two men look at each other. They see that Mrs. Rivkin's feelings are badly injured, and they are extremely uncomfortable.

"Listen, Mrs. Rivkin," Cohen says awkwardly, "maybe in the excitement I express myself not like to a lady. But after all, feelings of my actors must also be considered, or not?"

"They are artistes, you understand," Mr. Schwartz says. "You enjoy them. We want everybody also to enjoy them. But to two people the audience can't listen. So it must be to the actors. From this they make a living, if you know what I mean."

Mrs. Rivkin lays her hand dramatically on her chest.

"From now on," she says, "I wouldn't open my mouth in this tee-ater. A building doesn't have to fall on me."

She sweeps out of the office, incensed.

Cohen shakes his head.

"Go fight City Hall," he says.

"Benefit night," Schwartz says, shaking his head sadly. "Everything happens on benefit nights."

A SURE WAY TO GET ANOTHER READER

Two Yiddish poets, bitter rivals, met in the Café Royale on Second Avenue after not meeting for years. Over a glass of tea with lemon the two began to boast about the progress they had made in their careers.

"You have no idea how many people read my poetry now!" bragged one. "My readers have doubled!"

"*Mazl tov, mazl tov!*" cried the other poet, enthusiastically pumping his hand. "I had no idea you got married!"

SCHLEMIHLOV'S WORKS

BY Z. LIBIN
TRANSLATED FROM THE YIDDISH BY NATHAN AUSUBEL

Schlemihlov is a Jewish poet. He's on the staff of a Yiddish daily newspaper to which he has contributed for about fifteen years. How many poems he has written during these years no one knows. He himself doesn't know. Should someone ask him: "How many poems do you think you've written since you began writing?" Schlemihlov would furrow his brow thoughtfully: "A whole lot . . . a big pile . . . so many I can't count them . . . who knows, maybe five, maybe six hundred . . . who can remember?"

And who really could remember? Or who would take the trouble to count? No one puts too much store by poems that are printed in a daily newspaper. One reads the paper and then throws it away. A moment later it's a dead thing. You throw it into the trash basket. Together with yesterday, yesterday's newspaper disappears, and with it the poet's work.

It could even be that the wretched poet had poured his soul into every verse, had felt that with every line he had spread out on paper a part of his life, his hopes, his dreams and aspirations. Just the same, the newspaper with the poem finds its way into the trash basket and it is as if it had never been written.

Every day for fifteen years Schlemihlov had written a poem and yet there wasn't a tangible sign of one of them. Schlemihlov himself would clip the poems from the newspaper; he collected them. But you know how it is with the life of a Yiddish poet in New York. He lives all cramped up in a tiny flat—enough to suffocate! Where was there room for all of Schlemihlov's poems? Once even, after Schlemihlov had already collected about a hundred poems, his wife became angry because he littered the house with his "silly rhymes" and one fine day she threw them all into the garbage can where the little loafers on the street found them and built a bonfire with them. And so Schlemihlov's poetical works went up in smoke.

On another occasion, after Schlemihlov had managed to collect about fifty clippings, he decided to move his family to another flat. So the expressman left the bundle of clippings lying on the pavement where it mysteriously disappeared.

More than once Schlemihlov started all over again to clip his poems out of the newspaper. Bad luck to him, he had many children, and they were always ailing. After one got through with diphtheria, another began with scarlet fever. Naturally, each time they'd start cleaning up, the Board of Health would carry off the bedding and clothes to disinfect them. As for the verses, the health authorities didn't think much of them. Schlemihlov had to throw them all into the burning stove with his own hands.

At last Schlemihlov saw that it was a waste of effort trying to preserve his poems. He had to agree with his wife when she upbraided him: "What's the use of saving your *shmattes*? You're flooding the whole house with your trash! And after all your trouble in clipping them you've got to burn them yet! Isn't that *meshuggeh, nu*?"

Schlemihlov stopped clipping his poems. He wrote them, carried them to the editor, got his pennies of "soul money," and did what every good reader did—glanced at them in haste when they appeared and then threw them straight into the trash basket.

But a time came, a good and precious time, when suddenly someone recalled that there was in the world a certain eminent Yiddish poet who's name, so it seems, was Schlemihlov, and that this eminent poet Schlemihlov had been writing already for fifteen years. It also became clear that the newspaper for which Schlemihlov wrote had tens of thousands of readers and that these same readers greatly enjoyed Schlemihlov's poems. A publisher of Yiddish books suddenly awoke to this fact. "He has the head of a prime minister, so help me!" thought Schlemihlov.

And this is the way the book publisher figured:

"*Gevalt!* Father in Heaven! There are in New York (may no evil eye fall on them) quite a number of Jewish publishers. They keep on issuing prayer books for the weekdays, and prayer books for the holidays, penitential prayer books, devotional works, fancy psalm books, illustrated *haggadahs* for Passover, *mezuzahs*, exciting love stories, dream books, and *mazl* books—and they make good money from them, too! So the question is, why not publish a volume of the great Schlemihlov's poems? They'll surely sell like potato *latkes!*"

On the day that Schlemihlov found out about it he burst into the house overflowing with enthusiasm, his face radiant with happiness.

There was more than an overtone of revenge in his voice when he said "to his dear life's companion":

"Nu, Rosa, so you kicked around my poems, ha?"

"What do you mean?" asked Rosa, not understanding.

"I mean what I said: you kicked around my poems."

"What are you talking about?"

"You kicked them around, threw them around, burned them up!"

Rosa looked bewildered at her husband.

"You shouldn't have done that!" Schlemihlov rebuked her sternly.

"Shouldn't have done it?" mumbled Rosa. "Shouldn't have done it? What then, I should pickle them? Messed up, dirtied the whole house! What did you need them for, anyway? Take them along with you into the grave? Paste them on your tombstone?"

"It's real merchandise, you *narrelleh!*" replied Schlemihlov proudly.

"What is merchandise—your poetic shmattes that I threw out?"

"You see, you threw them out! If I had them now they'd be salable merchandise."

"What are you talking about, anyway?" asked Rosa, perplexed.

"Someone wants to print my poems in a book," the poet finally let the cat out of the bag, looking at his wife closely in order to see what impression this piece of news made on her.

Schlemihlov had expected that what he'd tell her would amaze her, would explode on her consciousness like a bombshell. Nevertheless, Rosa remained quite indifferent. Yawning, she said to him:

"A what? A book? What do you mean, a book?"

"A book, like all other books."

"Nu, what's that got to do with you?" asked Rosa in a matter-of-fact voice.

"It's going to be a book of my poems," the poet finally explained.

"For what purpose?"

"What a question! Of course, so that people should read them."

"But they've already been read!"

"So they'll read them again."

"I should worry—let it be a book or not a book. Whatever you do, don't bring it home."

"But I'll get good money for it."

Rosa, who was on the point of walking into the kitchen, stopped short when he said this. Full of curiosity she asked:

"What? Money?"

"Yes, I'll get a nice few dollars from my poems."

Rosa understood her husband only too well. She knew what a pipe dreamer and wishful thinker he was. Therefore she didn't take what he was telling her too seriously. Still in all, she found it necessary to ask:

"You mean to say you're going to get money?"

"Yes, Rosa."

"For what?"

"For my poems, of course!"

"You mean poems you're going to write?"

"No, poems I've already written, those poems that you kicked around and burned and threw out. *Oy!* If I only had them now I'd be able to earn a nice few dollars without any effort on my part!"

"You, Schlemihlov, believe anything you're told. You're a ready-made fool for everybody."

"But it's true, Rosa, it's true," interrupted the poet. "I'll get money for them."

"What sort of a fairy tale are you trying to tell me?" exploded Rosa. "What toothache, headache, heartache, and bellyache you always have to get before you earn a dollar out of your writings, so now you're going to tell me that you've found a *goilem* who's ready to pay you a second time for your precious merchandise, ha?"

Schlemihlov finally succeeded in convincing his wife. Rosa now felt angry with herself for having disposed of her husband's clippings so disrespectfully. The important question now was: where was one to get Schlemihlov's poems? There wasn't a single one in sight, as if they had never been!

Schlemihlov began to make inquiries. He was aghast when he found out that his own newspaper office kept no back copies. He looked here, he looked there, but not a sign of a poem anywhere. Everywhere he was told: where is there the *meshuggener* who's going to collect Yiddish newspaper clippings?

Schlemihlov tore his hair with exasperation. "Fifteen years a poet! For fifteen years I wrote a poem every day, and where did they all disappear, just like a stone thrown into the water!"

Rosa felt guilty, tried to excuse herself.

"Nu, what is one to do? You live in a crowded flat and you've a lot of children, and each one of them keeps on ailing; one has diphtheria, and another has scarlet fever, and a third has measles!"

"It's bad, very bad," muttered Schlemihlov, with a sigh. "I guess it can't be helped."

Just the same, the poet continued to make inquiries, possibly there'd be somebody who might have saved his poems. He felt exactly like an unfortunate father who has lost track of his children, yet never surrenders the sweet hope of finding them some day.

And sure enough, one fine day Schlemihlov heard the following astonishing story:

Somewhere in Yonkers, so to speak behind the Dark Mountains, there lived a Jewish rags peddler. He was a great eccentric. One of his more endearing insanities was to collect newspaper clippings of the works of Yiddish writers. About this rags peddler there were some odd stories told. For instance, it was said that he had put aside two rooms in his flat for storing his Yiddish newspaper clippings. Both rooms were filled from floor to ceiling with them. Only in such a town as Yonkers, people said, where rent costs "a mere nothing," could anybody afford such a luxury.

Schlemihlov grasped at this piece of information like a drowning man at a straw. One fine morning, he made an expedition to Yonkers in order to have a talk with the rags peddler. Unfortunately, he didn't find the peddler at home, only his wife.

"He'll come soon," she told him.

"Does your husband have a collection of old Yiddish newspapers?" asked Schlemihlov.

"Two rooms full!" the woman answered with bitterness. "He's busy every evening with that sort of thing. He clips and cuts and sorts—the Devil only knows what for! You know my husband is a rags peddler, and whenever he can lay his hands on a bundle of old Yiddish newspapers he brings it home, messes up the house so that I could scream. He clips and cuts, clips and cuts—two whole rooms full of them!"

Schlemihlov was very anxious to take a peek at what was in the two rooms. The peddler's wife obliged him.

When the poet saw the piles of Yiddish newspaper clippings his heart began to beat with excitement. He had never seen so many clippings in his life. Besides the piles that were neatly arranged on the shelves, the clippings filled many boxes and barrels.

"I wish I knew in which barrel my glory lies buried," wondered Schlemihlov.

And as he stood wondering, the peddler arrived. Schlemihlov's heart began to pound.

Out of politeness the poet first spoke about other matters, but finally he turned the conversation to the business on which he had come.

"And Schlemihlov's poems you have?" asked the poet with beating heart.

"What a question: 'Do I have?' Of course I have! I have everything!"

"Do you have many of Schlemihlov's poems?"

"A whole lot of them."

Schlemihlov grew cold with excitement.

"Won't you please make sure?" he begged the peddler.

"Why certainly. It's in a separate barrel."

Several minutes later Schlemihlov was looking down on a heap of his own writings. The unfortunate father had at last discovered his long lost children, and what a moving scene that meeting was!

Schlemihlov almost flung himself at "his" barrel, as if it contained a great treasure. There they were—his poems! Yes, there in the barrel, in the city of Yonkers, in the home of a rags peddler lay the works of his brain and heart!

For fifteen long years he had written for Jews, for fifteen years he had dug out "pieces of heart" with his pen, written with the blood of his veins, poured out in verses his consecrated soul . . . tears, travail of creation, beautiful phantasies, dreams, thoughts, imagery . . . yes, for fifteen whole years! His entire youth lay entombed there, there in the barrel!

And Schlemihlov's pale face flushed with excitement, and tears began to tremble in his eyes.

"Mister, make it snappy! I've no time to bother with you," the peddler prodded the poet as he stood with bowed head before his creations.

"Ha! What did you say?" asked Schlemihlov with a start.

"Come! I've no time," said the peddler, shooing the poet out of the room.

"Listen here, mister," asked Schlemihlov. "Why do you need all that?"

"What all that?"

"All those newspapers."

"That's my business," answered the peddler coldly.

"Why don't you ask who I am," asked Schlemihlov.

"What's it my business who you are?"

"I'm Schlemihlov," the poet introduced himself modestly.

"Schlemihlov?" echoed the peddler, indifferently. "Let it be Schlemihlov! *Sholom aleichem,* mister."

"*Aleichem sholom,*" answered the poet.

And throwing no more than a glance at Schlemihlov, the peddler continued in the same cold manner.

"Nu, nu, mister! Come on! Let the barrel alone! Come, I've got no time!"

"Listen just one minute," pleaded Schlemihlov. "I'd like very much to have my poems."

The peddler looked at the poet with incredulity. "What do you mean *your* poems? At this moment they happen to be *my* poems."

And with that he carefully closed the door on the clippings.

Schlemihlov felt as if he had been drenched with cold water. He felt enraged but he knew he was helpless.

"What on earth do you need my poems for?" he asked.

"It's not your *bubba's* worries!" the peddler snapped back rudely. And addressing himself to his wife, he ordered:

"Shayneh, you can serve dinner now."

"Sit down, mister," curtly said the peddler's wife, pointing to a chair. And she busied herself setting the table.

Schlemihlov sat down feeling wretched.

Completely ignoring the poet, as if he were not there at all, the peddler ate his dinner and chatted with his wife about various business matters.

Unworldly as Schlemihlov was, nonetheless he grasped quite clearly that the peddler meant business and that he, Schlemihlov, would have to buy his own verses from him in cold cash.

"How much would it be, mister, if I were to buy from you the clippings of my poems?"

"The whole barrel?" asked the peddler coming to the point with businesslike dispatch. There was a suggestion in his voice that a king's ransom lay in that barrel.

Schlemihlov understood perfectly well what the peddler was after.

"Who needs the whole barrel?" he asked sharply. "Do you think I am meshuggeh?"

"How many clippings then?"

"Oh, no more than fifty, sixty," answered the poet casually.

Schlemihlov knew that his publisher did not intend to include more than that number in the volume.

"There was a man here a year ago," said the peddler with suggestive emphasis. "He bought from me thirty clippings of his novel. Believe me, he paid me good money."

Schlemihlov clearly understood the hint. He, too, was expected to pay "good money" for his clippings, and his heart grew heavy with anxiety. In the last few minutes a change had come over him. The pressure of circumstances had driven the poet out of him and in his place blossomed out a canny businessman. And Schlemihlov began to speak now like a businessman.

"Why should I pay you good money for pieces of old junky paper?"

"You see some people do," retorted the peddler impatiently.

"You seem to think that just because you found one fool you're going to find other fools."

"Did I send for you, mister?" snapped the peddler. "Anybody who wants to buy my merchandise has got to pay."

"Do you call old verses 'merchandise'?" jeered Schlemihlov.

"Sure it's merchandise! A poem is a very fine thing. I myself read them once in a while."

Hearing the rag peddler's defense of poetry, Schlemihlov almost beamed with pleasure. But the businessman in him quickly suppressed his natural feelings.

"Don't be foolish," the poet ridiculed him. "What person these days wants to look at a poem? You can find some lunatic interested perhaps in a Yiddish novel but where is the meshuggener for Yiddish poetry? Maybe you're going to say I'm that meshuggener? Nu, is it unnatural that I, who wrote these poems, should want to own copies of them? You can believe me when I say that they won't be any kind of a bargain for another customer."

"Since it's no merchandise to you, let me alone, mister," replied the peddler coldbloodedly.

But Schlemihlov the businessman held on doggedly to the works of Schlemihlov the poet.

"Sell me fifty! How much do you want for fifty?"

"I'll sell them to you if you'll make it worth my while," answered the peddler craftily.

"Show me the goods once more," asked Schlemihlov.

The peddler again unlocked the door where he kept his newspaper collection and the poet followed him to the barrel where his clippings were stored.

When Schlemihlov saw his poems again he could hardly conceal his enthusiasm.

"Look! There are my poems!" he almost shouted. With trembling hands he began to pull the clippings out of the barrel.

"Don't be in such a hurry, mister!" the peddler rebuked him. "Not with the hands, mister, not with the hands!"

"Why not?" asked Schlemihlov with annoyance. "Certainly I have a right to choose my own poems?"

"No, you haven't," replied the peddler. "If it has to do with choosing, I'll do the choosing."

"You have the *chutzpah* to tell me that you're going to do the choosing of *my* poems?" snorted Schlemihlov, boiling over. "What do you mean, *you'll* choose? What do you understand about my poetry?"

"Sh-h-h! Don't get so excited, mister. If you don't want to buy you can go. Who's stopping you?"

"But have a heart—at least let me look at them!" begged Schlemihlov.

But the peddler remained unmoved.

"You don't know what's inside the barrel," he replied shortly. "Everything has been put away in order. Just let me handle it and everything'll be all right."

The peddler pulled out of the barrel a bundle of neatly folded clippings which he spread out on the table. Putting on his spectacles, he began to examine the clippings. One seemed to draw his special attention; he read it through and said:

"Oy, what a fine poem! Fine, ai, fine! Worth its weight in gold."

"What is it?" asked Schlemihlov, feeling highly flattered.

"It's called *My Childhood Years*," answered the peddler. "Do you want it?"

"All right," said Schlemihlov. "I'll take it."

The peddler handed the poet his poem. Schlemihlov began to read it. His eyes sparkled and his face became flushed with pleasure.

"You see, mister, I'm quite a judge of poetry," said the rags peddler, triumphantly. "Do I have to tell you? It's one fine piece of merchandise! It's worth good money to anybody."

Hearing the words "good money" again, Schlemihlov was startled out of his poetic revery and in one instant he was again transformed into the businessman. By a convenient lapse of memory he now forgot that he had had anything to do with his own poems. He was being offered merchandise at which he was now looking with the cool eyes of a tradesman who didn't want to be cheated and was anxious to get his money's worth. Once more scanning his poem with an exaggerated air of judiciousness, he finally passed sentence on it.

"This is a shmatte! A rag, not a poem!"

"Oh, go on," guffawed the peddler. "What are you talking about? Why, it's a precious stone, every word begs to be kissed!"

"It's not worth an empty eggshell," countered Schlemihlov scornfully.

The peddler took another poem out of the bundle and went on to examine it.

"What is that?" asked Schlemihlov.

"A wonderful piece of goods, I'm telling you, it's absolutely priceless."

"I mean what is its title?" asked Schlemihlov.

"It's called *My First Love*," replied the peddler, handing the poem to its author.

Schlemihlov read it with turned up nose, then threw it aside.

"What's the matter—it's not good enough for you?" asked the peddler.

"Pfui—it's just mud!" answered Schlemihlov.

"On the contrary, every word is a pearl!" heatedly argued the peddler.

"What do you know about poetry?" said Schlemihlov with a superior air. "I'm telling you it's a tasteless thing, a lifeless wooden thing! Who should know better, you or I?"

The poet and the rags peddler debated the merits of Schlemihlov's poetical works so long and furiously that the peddler finally lost all patience. He suddenly grabbed up the clippings and flung them back into the barrel.

"I don't like such smart customers as you!" he raged.

And with equal heat Schlemihlov retorted, "For my money I want merchandise, not shmattes!"

Distraught and offended, he left the peddler's house.

Several weeks later, after thinking over the matter carefully, Schlemihlov came to the following conclusions: First, that he wanted very badly to have his book of poems published, and secondly, that without the barrel of clippings in Yonkers he couldn't accomplish it. So he put on his "deaf cap" and made the trip to Yonkers for the second time. But it was too late! The poet found that the peddler had moved, and he could find no one who knew where. Worse yet, by this time the man who had offered to publish the poems had lost interest in the project and had practically forgotten all about the poet.

And so Schlemihlov's poetic works *nebbech* were not fated to see the light of day!

AN EPITAPH

BY BENJACOB

> *Here lies Nachshon, a man of great renown,*
> *Who won much glory in his native town:*

'Twas hunger that killed him, and they let him die—
They give him statues now, and gaze, and sigh—
While Nachshon lived, he badly wanted bread,
Now he is gone, he gets a stone *instead.*

NO ENEMY OF HIS

BY DER LEBEDIGER (CHAIM GUTMAN)
TRANSLATED FROM THE YIDDISH BY NATHAN AUSUBEL

I don't know how others feel about the literary critic Seligman, but I assure you that I'm no enemy of his. True enough, he ripped into my book, and in what an ugly manner too! Believe me, for no reason at all! But after all, a man has a right to his own opinion! *Nu,* so he doesn't have a good opinion of me as a writer! Just the same, let me tell you, were I to hear that Seligman broke his neck—believe me it wouldn't upset me a bit!

Now understand me, I'm no enemy of his! I know that a critic is entitled to his own opinions. Nu, so he doesn't consider me talented! Must I be talented in everybody's judgment? And still enough, were I, for instance, to be walking on the street, and were I to see Seligman walking ahead of me and a car came speeding along right behind *him* and it looked as if he was in danger of being run over—do you think for a moment that I'd shout a warning to him?

Please don't misunderstand me—I'm not that man's enemy! But I couldn't feel any pity for him if I were to see him in trouble. Did he have any pity on me when he lashed into my book in such a disgusting way? You know how it was: I made up my mind I was going to publish a book. I needn't tell you what heartache a Yiddish writer has to go through before he sees his book in print! And here comes along a man (so to speak—*a man!*) and with the greatest of ease he plunges his knife into me: "What a waste of paper!" he issues sentence on my book. Do you get that? I could understand it perfectly if the fellow went ahead and wrote an unfavorable critique, pointing out all the flaws and shortcomings in my work: here it's contradictory, there it's overwritten, here it's poorly conceived, there it's badly written. That I could understand very well. It would be proof that the man was only being critical and exercised his rightful function as critic. But to go ahead and assassinate a writer in cold blood—that's an unpardonable outrage!

As I said before—I'm no enemy of Seligman's. Well, so he doesn't think much of me! But let me tell you, if I, for instance, were to be taking a stroll on the Williamsburg Bridge, and he too, and if I suddenly saw him try to jump into the East River, I wouldn't make a single move to hold him back. Of course, I concede that a literary critic also belongs to the human species, but so help me if I'd try to keep him from jumping! Do you want to drown, go ahead and drown! Who is stopping you? And to be perfectly candid, who the devil needs critics, especially a cutthroat like Seligman?

I don't have to tell you again that I'm no enemy of his. Still in all, if I were to be passing by his house late at night and I were to see flames shooting out of his windows, I wouldn't be in any hurry to ring the fire-alarm box. Neither would I rush into his house to wake him. Let him burn, with pleasure! Maybe I'd save his wife and children. Poor things! Are they to blame for having such a *paskudnik* for husband and father? But Seligman I'd let burn! When such a golden opportunity arises and he's on fire—let him burn!

Now I certainly am no enemy of his! Everybody knows that a critic has to have his own mind and he can even have a bad opinion of a writer, but forgive him—why should I forgive him? Of course it's not nice to wish bad luck even to a critic. I wish Seligman no harm; let him live on until he's a hundred and twenty and dear God, may it be without a head and legs and hands! And also let me tell you, were I to meet that fellow face to face somewhere in a deserted spot, he and I and nobody else, I know I wouldn't be responsible for what I'd do to him. I don't know whether I'd kill him outright, but I certainly wouldn't let him out of my hands with all his limbs whole!

You can see for yourself that I'm no enemy of his! Don't I know that literary criticism is a trade, a trade let us say, exactly like being a butcher. Of a butcher it is expected to chop up bones, saw through a side of meat, tear out veins, and rip out guts, why shouldn't a critic do the same? Just the same, if I were to learn that he was struck down by lightning, that paskudnik, I'd even recite the blessing over lightning! And to be perfectly frank with you, I think I'd even get pleasure out of it. Nu! so what? So there'd be one damn butcher less in the literary slaughterhouse!

But you've got to understand that at bottom I'm really no enemy of his!

What's the one good thing that all people, without exception, have?
A good opinion about themselves.

Contributors

AGNON, S. J. (CZACZKES), 1880– :
Novelist. Born in Galicia, Austria,
settled in Palestine. Writes in
Hebrew.

AL-CHARIZI, YEHUDAH, c. 1200 A.D.:
Poet. Born in Spain. Wrote in
Hebrew.

ALTENBERG, PETER, 1859–1919: Humorist and wit. Born in Vienna,
Austria. Wrote in German.

AN-SKY, S. (S. Z. RAPPOPORT), 1863–
1920: Folklorist, poet, and dramatist. Born in Russia. Wrote in Yiddish and Russian.

ASCH, SHOLEM, 1880– : Novelist,
dramatist, and short-story writer.
Born in Poland; now in the U.S.A.
Writes in Yiddish.

BABEL, ISAAK, 1894– : Novelist and
short-story writer. Born in Russia.
Writes in Russian.

BAR-HEBRAEUS, 1226–1286: Physician
and humorous anthologist. Converted Jew, rose to be Maphrian
of the East, or head of the Jacobite Church. Born in Syria. Wrote
in Arabic.

BENJACOB, ISAAC, 1801–1863: Poet
and epigrammatist. Born in Lithuania. Wrote in Hebrew.

BERGELSON, DOVID, 1884– : Novelist, short-story writer, and dramatist. Born in Russia. Writes in
Yiddish.

BIALIK, CHAIM NACHMAN, 1873–1934:
Foremost Hebrew poet. Born
in Russia, settled in Palestine.
Wrote in Hebrew, and also in
Yiddish during his early period.

BLOCH, JEAN-RICHARD, 1884–1947:
Novelist, short-story writer, dramatist, and critic. Born in France.
Wrote in French.

BÖRNE, LUDWIG (LÖB BARUCH), 1786–
1837: Literary critic and political
writer. Born in Germany. Wrote
in German.

BRANDES, GEORG (COHEN), 1842–1927:
Literary critic, essayist and biographer. Born in Denmark. Wrote
in Danish.

DER LEBEDIGER (CHAIM GUTMAN),
1887– : Humorous writer.
Born in Russia, emigrated to
the U.S.A. Writes in Yiddish.

DER TUNKELER (JOSEPH TUNKEL),
1881–1950: Humorous writer.
Born in Poland, emigrated to the
U.S.A. Wrote in Yiddish.

DICK, ISAAC MEIER, 1807–1903: Humorous short-story writer and
wit. Born in Lithuania. Wrote in
Yiddish.

FEUCHTWANGER, LION, 1884– :
Novelist, dramatist, and short-story writer. Born in Germany.
Writes in German.

FINEMAN, IRVING, 1893– : Novelist
and scenario writer. Born in
U.S.A. Writes in English.

FRANZOS, KARL EMIL, 1848–1904: Novelist, critic, and short-story writer.
Born in the Ukraine, emigrated
to Galicia, Austria. Wrote in German.

FREEDMAN, DAVID, 1898–1936: Humorist and gag writer. Born in Rumania, emigrated to the U.S.A.
Wrote in English.

FRUG, S., 1860–1916: Poet. Born in
Russia. Wrote in Yiddish, Hebrew, and Russian.

GOLD, MICHAEL, 1894– : Novelist,
playwright, and literary critic.
Born in U.S.A. Writes in English.

GOLDING, LOUIS, 1895– : Novelist,
short-story writer, and poet. Born
in England. Writes in English.

GROPPER, JACOB, 1890– : Poet.
Born in Bukovina, Austria. Writes
in Yiddish.

HALEVI, YEHUDAH, 1085–1140: Poet and philosopher. Born in Toledo, Spain. Wrote in Hebrew and Arabic.

HATVANY-DEUTSCH, BARON LAJOS, 1880– : Novelist, dramatist, and journalist. Born in Hungary. Writes in Hungarian.

HEIJERMANS, HERMANN, 1864–1924: Dramatist and novelist. Born in Holland. Wrote in Dutch.

HEINE, HEINRICH, 1797–1856: Lyric poet, prose satirist, and novelist. Born in Germany, died in exile in France. Wrote in German.

IBN EZRA, ABRAHAM, 1092–1167: Poet and religious scholar. Born in Toledo, Spain. Wrote in Hebrew and Arabic.

KATZ, LEO, 1892– : Novelist, short-story writer, and journalist. Born in Bukovina, Austria, settled in Vienna. Writes in German and Yiddish.

KERSH, GERALD, 1909– : Novelist and short-story writer. Born in England. Writes in English.

KOBER, ARTHUR, 1900– : Humorist and playwright. Born in Galicia, Austria, emigrated to U.S.A. Writes in English.

KOBRIN, LEON, 1872–1946: Novelist, playwright, and short-story writer. Born in Russia, emigrated to the U.S.A. Wrote in Yiddish.

KOVNER, B. (JACOB ADLER), 1877– : Humorous writer. Born in Galicia, Austria, emigrated to the U.S.A. Writes in Yiddish.

KRAUS, KARL, 1874–1936: Poet, dramatist, critic, and journalist. Born in Prague, settled in Vienna. Wrote in German.

LEVENSON, SAMMY, 1911– : Humorous writer and performer. Born in the U.S.A. Writes in English.

LEWISOHN, LUDWIG, 1883– : Novelist, critic, anthologist, translator, and teacher. Born in Berlin, Germany, emigrated to the U.S.A. Writes in English.

LIBIN, Z., 1872– : Short-story writer and playwright. Born in Russia, emigrated to the U.S.A. Writes in Yiddish.

MAIMON, SOLOMON, 1753–1800: Philosopher. Born in Lithuania, emigrated to Germany. Wrote in German.

MANDELKERN, SOLOMON, 1846–1902: Poet and Bible scholar. Born in Russia. Wrote in Hebrew, also in Yiddish, Russian, and German.

MENDELE MOICHER SFORIM (SHOLEM JACOB ABRAMOWITSCH), 1836–1917: Referred to as "The Grandfather" of modern Yiddish literature. Novelist, short-story writer, and satirist. Born in Russia. Wrote in Yiddish, also in Hebrew.

MOLNAR, FERENC (NEUMANN), 1878– : Playwright. Born in Hungary. Writes in Hungarian and German.

NADIR, MOISHE (ISAAC REISS), 1885–1943: Wit, satirist, poet, playwright, and critic. Born in Galicia, Austria, emigrated to the U.S.A. Wrote in Yiddish.

NORDAU, MAX (SUEDFELD), 1849–1923: Critic, historian, dramatist, philosopher, and Zionist leader. Born in Hungary, emigrated to Germany and France. Wrote in French and German.

OGUS, AARON D., 1865–1943: Humorous short-story writer. Born in Russia, emigrated to the U.S.A. Wrote in Yiddish.

ORNITZ, SAMUEL, 1890– : Novelist and scenario writer. Born in U.S.A. Writes in English.

PALQUERA, SHEM-TOB, 1225–1290: Poet and philosopher. Born in Spain. Wrote in Hebrew.

PARKER, DOROTHY (ROTHSCHILD), 1893– : Poet, wit, and short-story writer. Born in U.S.A. Writes in English.

PERELMAN, S. J., 1904– : Humorous writer. Born in U.S.A. Writes in English.

PERETZ, I. L., 1852–1915. Short-story writer, poet, dramatist, critic, and essayist. Born in Poland. Wrote in Yiddish. Together with Mendele Moicher Sforim and Sholom Aleichem he forms the great triumvirate in modern Yiddish literature.

PREACHER OF DUBNO, THE (RABBI JACOB KRANTZ, "DER DUBNER MAGGID"), 1740–1804: Celebrated itinerant preacher. Born in Lithuania. Wrote in Hebrew.

REISEN, ABRAHAM, 1876– : Poet and short-story writer. Born in Russia, emigrated to the U.S.A. Writes in Yiddish.

ROSENBERG, ETHEL, 1915– : Writer of humorous fiction. Born in the U.S.A. Writes in English.

SAPHIR, MORITZ G., 1795–1858. Wit and humorist. Born in Hungary, lived in Germany and in Vienna. Wrote in German.

SCHNEOUR, ZALMAN, 1887– : Novelist, poet, and short-story writer. Born in Russia, lived in Germany, now in the U.S.A. Writes in Hebrew and Yiddish.

SCHORR, ZYGMUNT: Humorous writer. Born in Galicia, Poland. Contemporary. Writes in Yiddish.

SHOLOM ALEICHEM (SHOLEM RABINOWITSCH), 1859–1916: Foremost humorist and satirist in modern Yiddish literature. Wrote novels, plays, short stories, monologues, sketches, et cetera. Born in Russia, died in New York.

SPEKTOR, MORDCHE, 1858–1925: Novelist and short-story writer. Born in Russia; emigrated to the U.S.A. Wrote in Yiddish.

STEINBERG, ELIEZER, 1880–1932: Poet. Born in Russia, emigrated to Brazil. Wrote in Yiddish.

STEINBERG, JACOB, 1886–1947: Poet. Born in Russia. Wrote in Hebrew, also in Yiddish.

STEINBERG, YEHUDAH, 1863–1908: Novelist and short-story writer. Born in Russia. Wrote in Hebrew and Yiddish.

SUHL, YURI, 1908– : Novelist in English and poet in Yiddish. Born in Galicia, Austria, emigrated to the U.S.A.

TASHRAK (ISRAEL ZEVIN), 1872–1926: Humorous short stories and Talmudic anthologies. Born in Russia, settled in the U.S.A. Wrote in Yiddish.

TIEMPO, CÉSAR (ISRAEL ZEITLIN), 1906– : Poet and playwright. Born in Buenos Aires, Argentina. Writes in Spanish.

UNTERMEYER, LOUIS, 1885– : Poet, critic, anthologist, and lecturer. Born in the U.S.A. Writes in English.

VULFARTS, M.: Humorous writer. Born in Latvia. Contemporary. Writes in Yiddish.

WENDROFF, Z. (ZALMAN WENDROWSKY), 1879– : Humorous short-story writer. Born in Russia. Writes in Yiddish.

WERFEL, FRANZ, 1890–1945: Poet, novelist, and dramatist. Born in Prague. Wrote in German.

WOLFE, HUMBERT, 1885–1940: Poet and translator. Born in England. Wrote in English.

YEHOASH (SOLOMON BLOOMGARDEN), 1871–1927: Poet, short-story writer, lexicographer, and Bible translator. Born in Russia, emigrated to the U.S.A. Wrote in Yiddish.

ZANGWILL, ISRAEL, 1864–1926: Novelist, short-story writer, playwright, and essayist; a noted Jewish leader. Born in London. Wrote in English.

Glossary

ach: an exclamation of surprise, dismay, or disapproval.

ach and *vay:* alas and alack, woe be to it!

Adar: the twelfth month of the Jewish year.

Adenom: a Dutch-Yiddish corruption of *Adonai,* my Lord; i.e., my God!

Adoishem: an indirect reference to the Deity, since any direct mention of God's name is forbidden to orthodox Jews.

a guten Shabbes: a good Sabbath—the salutation at parting during the Sabbath.

aleph: the first letter in the Hebrew-Yiddish alphabet.

ayeleh: the unhatched egg inside a chicken.

baal-tefilah: the precentor, the leader of prayer.

baba. See *bubba.*

baba stories (*bubba mysehs*): grandmother tales; i.e., fairy tales, inventions.

balabusteh: a mistress of a household, a competent housewife.

bar-mitzvah: the confirmation ceremony for Jewish boys when they reach thirteen.

bar-mitzvah becher: a small wine-cup, usually of silver or brass, presented to a *bar-mitzvah* boy for use during his recitation of the *Kiddush,* the benediction, on the Sabbath and on holy days.

batinka: dear little father. (Ukrainian).

batlen (pl. *batlonim*): an unworldly Talmudic student with no gift for practical everyday life. In every east European ghetto there were to be found such misfits, made so by poverty, constant religious study, and a lack of opportunity.

belek: the white meat of a chicken; a dish made with *belek.*

benshing: an anglicization of the Yiddish word *benshen,* to say grace after meals.

bet: a letter in the Hebrew alphabet; in Yiddish it is pronounced *bays.*

Bima: the platform in the synagogue where the *chazan* sings the service and the rabbi delivers his sermon.

blintze: a roll of thin dough containing a filling of cheese or *kasha* (groats).

boychik: a little boy. By adding the Yiddish-Russian "chik" to "boy" a brand-new word was added to English in the United States.

brazhek: a Russian intoxicating drink made from fermented grain.

briss (*brith*): the circumcision ceremony which takes place on the eighth day after the birth of a Jewish boy.

bubba (*bube, baba*): grandmother.

bulke: a roll.

Cabala (*Cabalah*): "the hidden wisdom"; a body of mystical knowledge that, beginning with the thirteenth century in Spain, stood in opposition to the rationalism of the *Talmud.*

challeh (*cholleh, chalah*): white bread specially baked for eating on the Sabbath and on holy days.

chasseneh: wedding.

Chassid (pl. *Chassidim,* adj. *Chassidic*): a member of a Cabalistic mystical sect centered around wonder-working rabbis as mediators between God and man. This sect was founded in the Ukraine by Rabbi Israel Baal-Shem, or "Master of the Name"; i.e., a wonder worker, during the middle of the eighteenth century.

chazan (pl. *chazanim* or *chazonim*): a cantor.

cheder (*chayder, chedar*): old-style orthodox Hebrew school.

cheder-yingel: a boy who studies in a *cheder.*

chine: playful humor, humorous anecdote.

chochem: a sage.

chochma: wisdom.

cholent. See *schalet.*

chremzlech (*chremzlach*): the plural for *chremzl,* a pancake made of *matzo*-meal, which is eaten during the week of Passover.

chupeh: the marriage canopy under which bride and groom stand during the wedding ceremony.

chutzpah: impudence, unmitigated nerve.

chutzpanik: an impudent fellow.

coff (*koph*): the letter in the Hebrew-Yiddish alphabet resembling the letter *k* phonetically.

daled: a letter in the Hebrew-Yiddish alphabet.

Deitsch: a German, but also refers to a Jew dressed, not in the traditional clothes of the east European ghetto, but in modern Western attire. This was regarded among the ghetto orthodox of former days as a form of heresy, and even as a steppingstone to apostasy.

draydlach (*draydlech*): the plural of *draydl.* From the German *drehen,* "to turn" or spin. These are small metal or wooden tops, having four sides, and are spun around with two fingers. Jewish children traditionally play with them during *Hanukkah,* the Festival of Lights.

drosha: sermon, speech.

dybbuk: a soul condemned to wander for a time in this world because of its sins. To escape the perpetual torments inflicted upon it by evil spirits, the *dybbuk* seeks refuge in the body of some pious man or woman over whom the demons have no power. The *dybbuk* is a Cabalistic-Chassidic conception.

ech: a groan, a disparaging exclamation.

Elul: the sixth lunar month in the Jewish calendar.

epis (*epus*): something, a reference to something vague.

Eretz Yisroel (*Eretz Yisrael*): the Land of Israel.

essrig (*esrog, ethrog,* pl. *essrogim*): a large, sweet-smelling citrus fruit of the lemon family used together with the *lulav,* made of palm, myrtle, and willow branches, in the synagogue procession during *Sukkoth,* the Feast of Tabernacles.

et: a minimizing gesture, a negative exclamation.

feh: an exclamation of disgust or disapproval.

feldsherr (also *feldsher*): a practical medical practitioner in east European countries but having neither the training nor status of a qualified physician.

flaishegeh leffel: dietary correct spoons used for meat soups, et cetera.

fressen: to gorge, to gourmandize.

fressing: gourmandizing; by adding the English suffix *ing* to the Yiddish word *fress,* we have a new English word in the vocabulary of American Jews.

gabbai: a treasurer or warden of a synagogue.

Galuth (*Goless, Goluth*): the Jewish Dispersion, the Exile.

ganef (or *ganev*): a thief.

gaon: a genius, a title of honor given to great Talmudic scholars. It was the title given to Rabbi Elijah of Vilna (the *Vilner Gaon*), the celebrated eighteenth-century Talmudist.

gefillt helsel (*gefüllt hälsel*): stuffed chicken-neck skin.

gelt: money.

Gemara (or *Gemarrah, Gamorrah*): the Aramaic name for the *Talmud.*

gesheft: business.

gevalt: outcry of alarm, fear; exclamation of exasperation and amazement.

gimmel: letter in the Hebrew-Yiddish alphabet.

goilem (*golem*): a numbskull—"a clay goilem," a stupid clod.

goy (pl. *goyim*, adj. *goyisher*): a Gentile.

goyeh: a Gentile woman.

gozlen: a murderer, a violent criminal.

grager (or *gragar*, *greger*): a traditional Jewish toy that makes a disagreeable grating noise, used by Jewish children in the synagogue during the reading of the *Megillah*, the Book of Esther, upon each mention of the name of Haman the Wicked.

gribbenes (or *grivvenes*, *greeven*): small crisp pieces left from rendered poultry fat, eaten as a delicacy or combined with *kasha* groats or rice.

groschen: small German silver coins whose old value was about two cents.

gut yom-tov: good Holy Day!

gymnasia (or *gymnasium*): the Russian secondary school.

Habdalah (*Havdolah*): the benedictions and prayers recited at the conclusion of the Sabbath over a cup of wine, the smelling of spices, and the kindling of a light.

Haggadah (or *Hagadah*): the book containing the Passover home service of the *Seder*. It consists in large part of the narrative of the Jewish exodus from ancient Egypt led by Moses.

haida: Russian cry used frequently by drivers, meaning: let's go, here we go.

halevai (or *alevai*): exclamation implying better for me if I hadn't done that; a regretful retrospection of something past.

Hanukkah: described variously as The Festival of Lights, The Feast of Dedication, and The Feast of the Maccabees. It is celebrated for eight days from the twenty-fifth day of *Kislev* (in December). It was instituted by Judas Maccabeus and the Elders of Israel in 165 B.C. to commemorate the rout of the invading forces of Antiochus Epiphanes and the purification of the Temple sanctuary.

Hanukkah lamp: an eight-branched lamp, usually of brass, with an extra branch serving as *shammes*, or monitor. On each of the eight successive days of *Hanukkah* an additional candle is lit together with one in the monitor.

Hasid. See *Chassid*.

hazan or *hazzan*. See *chazan*.

hock-flaish: chopped meat, meat balls.

Holy Ark: also called The Ark of the Law, is a chest or closet in a synagogue placed against the wall facing Jerusalem, and containing the Holy Scrolls of the Torah.

homentaschen (also *hamantashen*, s. *homentasch*): triangular pockets of dough filled with poppyseeds or prunes, eaten during *Purim*, the Festival of Lots.

hopak: a vigorous Russian folk dance.

hruba: the back wall of a Russian kitchen oven; by pressing against it one keeps warm on cold winter days. It also has a narrow platform which is used for sleeping.

intelligentsia: the Russian word for the intellectual class.

Kabala. See *Cabala*.

kabtzen (*kapsn*): a pauper.

Kaddish: the mourner's prayer recited in the synagogue during services thrice daily for eleven months by the immediate male relatives of the deceased, who must be more than thirteen years of age. Also means a son who recites the *Kaddish* for a parent.

kaleh: bride.

kapote: derived from the old French word *capote*, or coat. It is a long coat of medieval origin which Jews continued wearing in the east European ghettos centuries after it had gone out of fashion among Christians.

kasha: groats.

kashe: a question.

kest: the ancient ghetto practice whereby the young bride's parents supported, in their own home, their daughter and son-in-law for a specified period of time after their marriage.

Kiddush: the blessing of sanctification recited by the male members of an orthodox household over wine in a brass or silver cup during the Sabbath and on holy days before meals.

kinderlach: an endearing variant of *kinder,* children.

kishkeh: stuffed beef casing; also called "stuffed derma."

kittel: the white coatlike shroud every pious Jew has prepared against the day of his death. He also wears it in synagogue on *Yom Kippur,* the Day of Atonement.

klezmer (pl. *klezmorim*): a Jewish folk musician, usually one playing at weddings in a band consisting in the main of several string and wood-wind instruments.

knaydlach (or *kneidlach,* s. *kneidel* or *knaydl*): balls of boiled *matzo* meal cooked in chicken soup, sometimes separately.

knishes (s. *knish*): potato or *kasha* dumpling, fried or baked.

koogle: see *kugel.*

kopeck (or *kopek*): a small Russian copper coin; there are 100 kopecks in a ruble.

kosher: food that is permitted to be eaten, and prepared, according to the Jewish dietary laws.

kotchkeh: duck.

koved: honor.

kreple (pl. *kreplach*): a small pocket of dough filled with chopped meat; it is usually boiled and eaten with chicken soup.

krima tarterum: cream of tartar.

kuf: letter in the Hebrew-Yiddish alphabet.

kugel: noodle or bread suet pudding, sometimes cooked with raisins.

kvass: a popular fermented drink of Russia.

kvassnik: a maker or seller of *kvass.*

lamdan: a scholar.

landsman (pl. *landsleit*): a man from the same town in the old country.

lange mem: a letter in the Hebrew-Yiddish alphabet used at the end of a word in writing.

latke (pl. *latkes*): pancake.

lattes: patches.

latutnik: a cobbler, a layer of patches.

léb: affectionately added on as a suffix to the name of some person; i.e., "Hashe-léb," meaning Hashe-my-life, or, Hashe-dear.

le' chayiml: "to life!" the traditional Jewish toast.

lekech: honeycake, usually with nuts in it.

lekuch mit nis: lekech with nuts.

lemeshkes: fools, lambs to be shorn.

ligner: a liar.

Litvak: Lithuanian.

lokshen: noodles.

luftmensch: "an air-man," an individual with no fixed trade, business, or income, who is forced by circumstance to improvise a living.

lukshon (*lokshen*) *kugel:* a *kugel* made of noodles.

lulav (*lulev*): a palm branch dressed with myrtle and willow used together with the *essrig* (see above) in a religious rite during *Sukkoth,* the Feast of Tabernacles.

lutchnik: the kindling compartment in the old Russian oven.

Ma'arib (also *Ma'ariv*): the evening prayer service.

maaseh (also *myseh*): a story, an anecdote.

machorka: a cheap smoking material used in Russia instead of tobacco.

maggid: a preacher.

mama-léb: mama-my-life!

mamele (*mameniu*): little mama, dear little mama. Also an exclamation. Often used in addressing a baby or child.

mamzer: a bastard; a clever fellow.

mandlen: almonds. Soup *mandlen* are pelletlike pieces of baked dough.

matzo (pl. *matzos, matzoth*): unleavened bread, thin flat biscuits, exclusively eaten during the Passover Festival to recall the Jewish exodus from the Land of Bondage, Egypt.

mazl: luck.

mazl-tov: good luck. The salutation for happy occasions such as weddings.

melamed (pl. *melamedim*): Hebrew teacher in a *cheder.*

menorah: the traditional Jewish seven-branched candlestick.

meshuggaas: insanity.

meshuggeh: insane.

meshuggeneh: adjective of the above. Also, an insane woman.

meshuggener: an insane man.

meshumed (pl. *meshumadim*): an apostate from Judaism.

metzieh: a bargain.

mezuzah: a small rectangular piece of parchment inscribed with the passages Deut. VI, 4–9 and XI, 13–21. The parchment is rolled up and inserted in a wooden or metal case and nailed in a slanting position to the right-hand doorpost of every orthodox Jewish residence as a talisman against evil.

mikveh: indoor Jewish ritual bath or pool.

milchiger: one who has eaten dairy foods exclusively for the period prescribed by Jewish dietary regulation. Sometimes the word is used as an adjective.

milchigs: dairy foods.

millionchik: a millionaire.

minyan: a quorum of ten Jews required for public worship.

Mishna (*Mishnayos*): a compilation of oral laws and Rabbinic teachings, edited by Judah ha-Nasi in the early third century A.D., which forms the text of the *Talmud.*

mizinke: the youngest child.

moujik (or *muzhik*): a Russian peasant.

m'shpucha (or *mishpocha*): family.

Mussaf (or *Musaf*): a part of the Sabbath and Holy Day prayer service in the synagogue.

na: an exclamation—"here you are!" "Take it!" or, "There you have it!"

naches: pleasure, happiness.

narrelleh: little fool.

nash: to take something for one's sweet tooth.

nasher: one who has a sweet tooth.

nebbech: a Yiddish exclamatory word used as an expression of pity.

nee: Dutch for "no."

nogid: a rich man.

nu: well? so what?

nudnik: a bore.

och: Dutch equivalent for "ach."

oder: or.

oi, a shkandal (*oy, a skandal!*): Oh, what a scandal!

olim besholim: a Dutch-Hebrew corruption of *olov hasholom,* peace be upon him!

oy: the Yiddish exclamation to denote pain, astonishment, or rapture.

pakrishkes: hot pot covers laid on to ease pain.

Pan (*Pani*): Polish for *Mr.*

pani-bratzi: Polish for pals, intimates.

Panna: Polish for *Miss.*

Parnass: president of the congregation.

parnosseh: a livelihood.

paskudneh: ugly, revolting.

paskudnik: an ugly, revolting, disgusting fellow.

patchkeh: to mess with, to make a mess.

payyes: the side curls worn by the ultra-orthodox Jews.

pekeleh (pl. *pekelech, pekelach*): a bundle, a little package.

perutah: a small coin.

Pesach: the Festival of Passover, commemorating the Jews' liberation from the Egyptian bondage.

Polisher Shool (*Poilisher Shool*): the Polish Synagogue.

poretz: a Christian landowner, a nobleman.

pshol von!: Russian for "get out of here!" (addressed to a dog).

psiakrew: Polish curse word.

pupik: a belly button.

pupiklach: a dish of chicken gizzards.

Purim: Festival of Lots, celebrating the deliverance of the Jews from Haman's plot to exterminate them, as recounted in the *Book of Esther.*

Rashi: Rabbi Solomon ben Isaac, the most celebrated of all Bible exegetists and commentarians. He lived in Troyes, in Champagne, 1040–1105. His name has remained a venerated household word since.

Reb: mister.

rebbe: rabbi.

rebbetzin (rebbitzin): the wife of a rabbi.

rebbie: a rabbi, as well as a *melamed,* a teacher of Hebrew in a *cheder.*

retech: turnip.

rishus: harm, evil; refers especially to anti-Semitic acts.

Rosh Hashanah: the Jewish New Year, the most solemn day next to *Yom Kippur,* the Day of Atonement.

ruble (rouble): silver coin of Russia; in Czarist times it had the exchange value of fifty-one cents.

schacher-macher: a business manipulator, a finagler.

schalet (shalet, scholet): potted meat and vegetables cooked on Friday and simmered overnight for the Sabbath noonday meal.

schlemihl: a clumsy bungler, an inept person, butter-fingered.

schlimazl: a consistently luckless fellow, a ne'er-do-well.

schmaltz: rendered animal fat.

schnorrer: a beggar who shows wit, brass, and resourcefulness in getting money from others as though it were his right.

Seder: the Passover religious home service recounting the Jewish liberation from Egyptian bondage in the days of the Pharaohs.

sedrah (or sidrah): a section of the Pentateuch, the Five Books of Moses, prescribed for weekly reading on the Sabbath in the synagogue, or for study by children in religious school.

selig: blessed; used in recalling a beloved deceased—"mama *selig.*"

sha (shah): a peremptory hissing sound, a request for silence.

shaaloth u tshuvoth: religious questions and their rabbinical answers.

Shabbes: the Jewish Sabbath.

Shabbesdigen: adjective of *Shabbes.*

Shabuoth (Shevuos, Shevuoth, Shabuat): the Festival of Weeks, or Pentecost. It originally was a harvest festival.

shadchan (pl. shadchonim): a marriage broker, a matrimonial agent.

shalach-monehs: the gift of cakes, sweets, fruit, and wine customary for sending during the Feast of Purim.

shammes (pl. shammosim): a synagogue sexton.

Shass: the six divisions of the *Talmud.*

Shechinah (Shekhinah): God's radiance or presence; a neo-Platonic idea.

sheitel: a wig; before the wedding the ultra-orthodox bride has her hair cut off and she wears a *sheitel* ever after.

shihi-pihi: a colloquialism—"a mere nothing."

shiva: the seven days of mourning following death in the family.

shlattenshammes: a communal busybody, a tale carrier, a mere messenger.

shlepp: to pull, to drag.

shmatte (pl. shmattes): a rag.

shmelke: a pal, intimate.

shmendrik: a fool, a simpleton.

shmiggege: same as *shmendrik.*

shofar: ram's horn blown during the synagogue services on *Rosh Hashanah* and *Yom Kippur.*

sholom aleichem: Yiddish salutation with a handclasp on meeting—"peace be to you." The person greeted responds in reverse—*aleichem sholom,* "to you be peace."

shomer: a watchman; specifically refers to the armed Israeli watchman in the agricultural settlements.

shool (also shul, shule, shoole): synagogue.

shtik goy: idiomatic expression for one inclined to heretical views, or to ignorance of Jewish religious values.

shtrymel (shtreimel): a traditional hat of medieval origin worn by East

European pious Jews; it is trimmed with fox tails and is usually worn on the Sabbath.

shtus: a joke, nonsense.

Shulchan Aruch (Shulchan Aruk): a sixteenth-century compilation by the Cabalist, Rabbi Joseph Caro of Safed; it is a codification of Jewish law and serves as a handbook for ritual conduct among the pious.

siderl (derived from *siddur*): Hebrew book of daily prayer.

Simchas Torah: "Rejoicing over the Torah," a festival which celebrates the completion of the reading of the Torah, i.e., the Five Books of Moses. It takes place on the last day of *Sukkoth,* the Feast of Tabernacles.

soifer (also *sopher, sofer*): a Jewish scribe or copyist; one who writes out with a goose quill, in the traditional manner, the Scrolls of the Torah.

sukkah: a special "tabernacle," with a roof of green boughs and the interior decorated with hollowed-out melons and fruits, in which the family dines during the Feast of Tabernacles.

Sukkos (Sukkoth): the Feast of Tabernacles, a survival of the ancient festival on which Jews were required to go on a pilgrimage to Jerusalem.

taam: taste, charm.

takkeh: an emphatic—"really!"

tallis (tallith): prayer shawl.

Talmud: the Corpus Juris of the Jews. It is a compilation of religious, ethical, civil, and legal decisions and teachings interpreting Scripture. It was completed about A.D. 500.

Talmud-Torah: a modern Hebrew school.

tante: aunt.

tatte (tattele, tatinka, tatteniu): papa.

tatte-mame: papa-mama, parents.

tayglach: holiday candied cake.

tchizshik: a finch.

tefillin (tfillin): phylacteries.

Tisha b'Ab (Tishabov): ninth day of the Jewish month of *Ab,* set aside by Jewish tradition for fasting and mourning over the destruction of the Temple and Jerusalem by the Romans in A.D. 70.

toonked: dunked.

tov-tov: good-good.

tréfa (tréfeneh or *trifa):* food forbidden by Jewish dietary laws, or improperly prepared.

trefniak: one who eats *tréfa* food.

tsibbeleh: onion.

tsimmes: dessert, most often stewed prunes, sweetened carrots, and noodles.

tyereh: dear, dear one.

uriman (urimeleit, pl.): a poor man, a beggar.

Ve' Adar: the thirteenth month of the Jewish embolistic year.

yachne: a slattern, a coarse, loud-mouthed type of woman.

yarmulka (yamulke, yarmulke): skullcap.

yeshiva (yeshiba): Talmudic college.

yeshiva bocher (pl. *yeshiva bocherim):* a student in a Talmudic college.

Yiddisher kupp: a Jewish head, Jewish brains.

yingele: little boy.

Yom Kippur: the Day of Atonement.

yom-tov: holiday, holy day.

zaydeh (zadeh): grandpa.

zhukel: insect.